Did Not
Make
THE LIST

Yvette Scott, 18

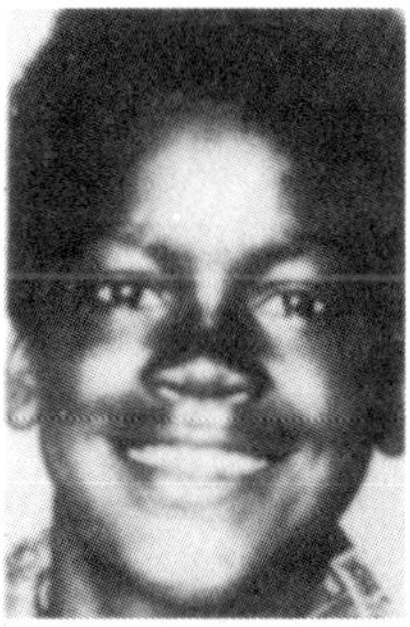

Edward Hope Smith, 14

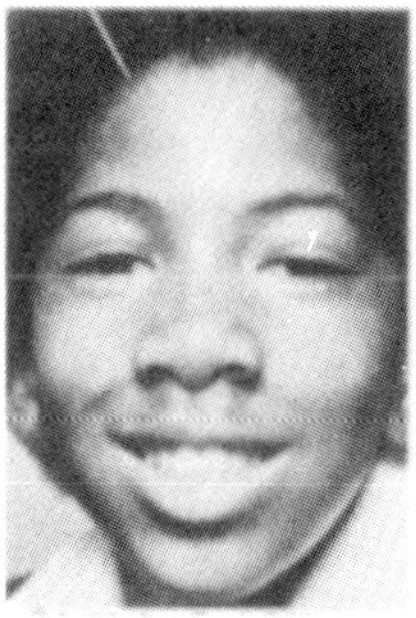

Alfred Evans, 14

Did Not
Make
THE LIST

Gayle Neeley, 25

Did Not
Make
THE LIST

Ernestine Burkett, 24

Milton Harvey, 14

Did Not
Make
THE LIST

Sandy Winford, 25

Did Not
Make
THE LIST

Catherine Taylor, 25

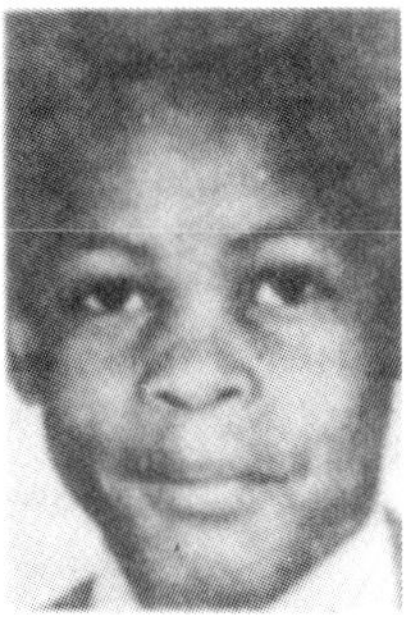

Yusuf Bell, 9

Did Not
Make
THE LIST

Ronald Robinson, 20

Did Not
Make
THE LIST

Charles Landers, 26

Jefferey Mathis, 10

Angel Lenair, 12

Did Not
Make
THE LIST

Billy Eugene Hill, 19

Eric Middlebrooks, 14

Did Not
Make
THE LIST

Larry Watkins, 25

Did Not
Make
THE LIST

Bernard Burch, 26

Christopher Richardson, 11

Did Not
Make
THE LIST

Bonnie Crawford, 26

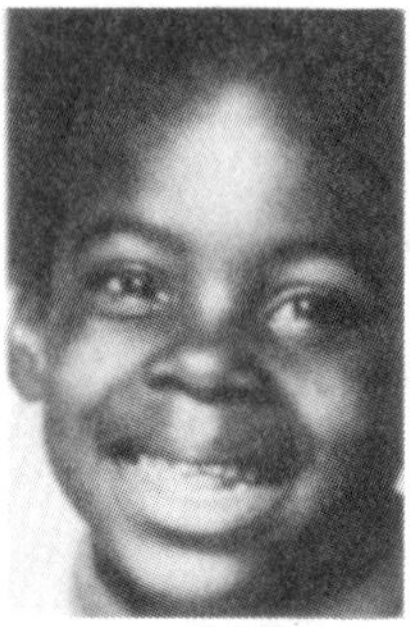

LaTonya Wilson, 7

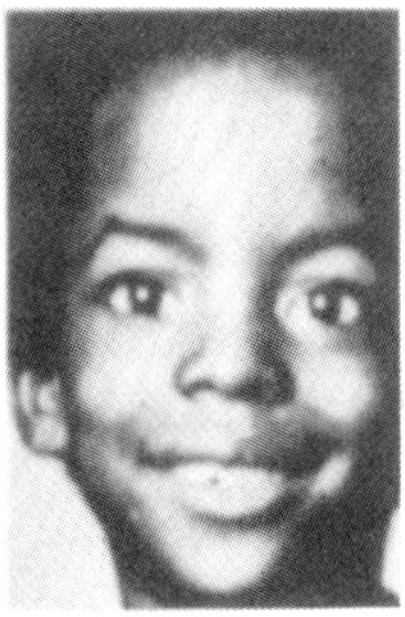

Aaron Wyche, 10

Did Not
Make
THE LIST

James Owens, 21

Did Not
Make
THE LIST

Kathy York, 25

Anthony Carter, 9

Did Not
Make
THE LIST

Vernelle Tye, 21

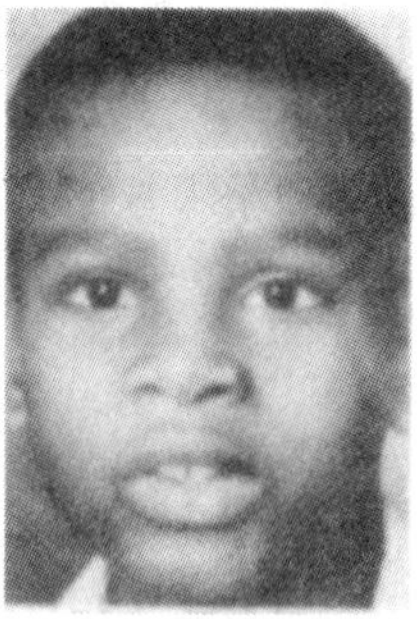

Earl Terrell, 11

Did Not
Make
THE LIST

Cynthia Montgomery, 14

Did Not
Make
THE LIST

Angela Bacon, 16

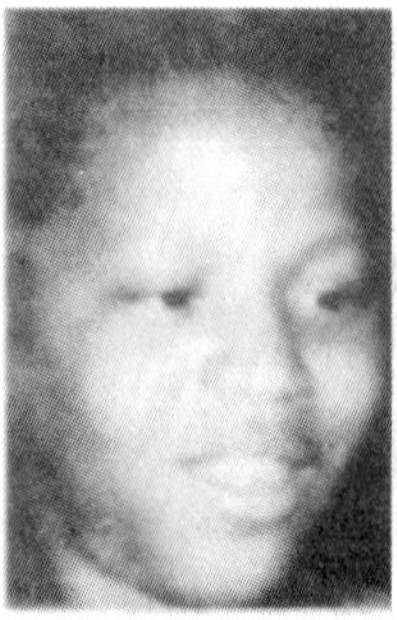

Clifford Jones, 13

Did Not
Make
THE LIST

Joseph Lee, 17

Did Not
Make
THE LIST

Beverly Harvey, 18

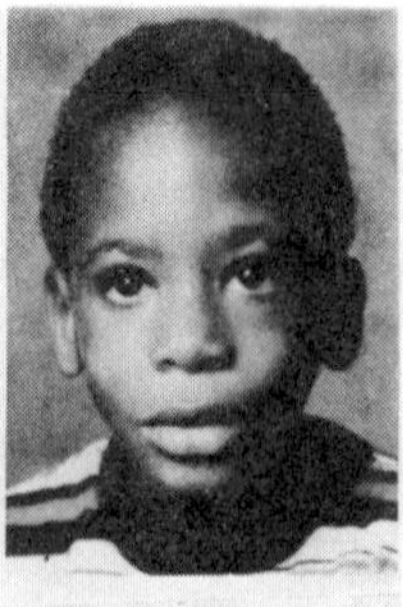

Darron Glass, 10
(still missing)

THE LIST

By Chet Dettlinger
with Jeff Prugh

Illustrated with Photographs

PHILMAY ENTERPRISES, INC.
ATLANTA

ISBN 0-942894-04-9

First Edition
1 2 3 4 5 6 7 8 9 10

This book is dedicated to my wife . . .

Mary Dettlinger

Jeff asked me, "Who are you going to dedicate the book to?" Whom else could I dedicate it to? A lot of wives put their husbands through school. Most expect a fancy return, too. Mary supported me through the writing of this book in every way imaginable, including putting bread on the table. I know what her motive was. It was to let me write, which fulfilled a lifelong ambition. She did it to make me happy. I couldn't appreciate it more. There are a lot of people to whom I owe a lot. I couldn't write enough books to dedicate one to each of them. But, I just might try. Thanks to Mary.

. . . and to Jeff's brother,

Vince Prugh

. . . who listened—and cared—when few others did.

Contents

"I Asked Him What He Does"

SHERLOCK HOLMES: *"...I'm a consulting detective, if you can understand what that is. Here in London we have lots of government detectives and lots of private ones. When these fellows are at fault, they come to me, and I manage to put them on the right scent. They lay all the evidence before me, and I am generally able, by the help of my knowledge of the history of crime, to set them straight. There is a strong family resemblance about misdeeds, and if you have all the details of a thousand at your finger ends, it is odd if you can't unravel the thousand and first."*

DR. JOHN WATSON: *"But do you mean to say...that without leaving your room you can unravel some knot which other men can make nothing of, although they have seen every detail for themselves?"*

SHERLOCK HOLMES: *"Quite so. I have a kind of intuition that way. Now and again a case turns up which is a little more complex. Then I have to bustle about and see things with my own eyes. You see I have a lot of special knowledge which I apply to the problem, and which facilitates matters wonderfully..."*

—From: "A Study in Scarlet"
By Sir Arthur Conan Doyle

Eula Montgomery opened the door a crack. She peered anxiously at the stranger on her doorstep one rainy night in Atlanta's predominantly black Dixie Hills section.

I held up my business card identifying myself as a *Los Angeles Times* correspondent. I asked if I could talk with her about her daughter, Cynthia, who had been murdered.

It was the winter of 1981. I had received a tip that the investigation by the Atlanta Metropolitan Task Force on Missing and Murdered Children was in shambles. I had no idea how badly the police were stubbing their toes. They were overlooking murder cases that sat right under their noses. I wouldn't have known to pay any attention to Cynthia Montgomery's case if it hadn't been for a bearded, bespectacled fellow named Chet Dettlinger.

All I knew about him was that he was one of several Atlanta ex-cops who were investigating the cases on their own, and that he even had predicted reliably where some kids would disappear and where others would turn up dead.

Chet Dettlinger returned my call one weekend in February of 1981, when Atlanta overdosed on "They Found Another Body" headlines, as well as newscasts that began: "It's 11 o'clock, and there's a curfew in Atlanta. Do you know where your children are?" We agreed to meet for breakfast.

Now Chet Dettlinger analyzed the cases for me on a homemade map of a portion of metropolitan Atlanta. He had sketched in only a handful of streets, but he had listed the names of many victims.

I'm forever enamored of maps, if only because they represent something solid in our lives. They give us a sense of stability and order—everlasting reference points in an ever-changing world.

Unfurling his map across the table, Chet Dettlinger showed that many victims were geographically connected and knew each other. His map made sense of the cases. It provided a basis for understanding this American nightmare—an understanding that was lacking everywhere else I had looked during the investigation.

In a lower corner of his map, I noticed a legend which matched victims' names with numbers spotted around the streets. Many of these names were unfamiliar to me, including: "MONTGOMERY."

"Who are these people?" I asked.

"They're murdered people, too."

"Children?"

"Children and adults."

Their names fell on me like a ton of bricks. Suddenly I realized that Atlanta's problem was worse than what our public officials were telling us.

"But what about the Task Force list?" I asked.

"Screw the list!" Chet Dettlinger said. "It's arbitrary. It has no parameters. Nobody knows how big our problem is. Nobody knows when it began, and we may never know if it ends. But you can write this down: Before we're through dealing with it, they'll be counting adults, too."

"You're the first person," Eula Montgomery said, "who's ever come out here to ask me about this."

Where were the police? Well, she said they hadn't come to her with questions. So, after waiting for more than two months after Cynthia died, she went to them.

Now another two months had elapsed, and Eula Montgomery said she had not heard again from the police since she visited them. Hadn't she been asked about the young man who lived one block away and was questioned as a "material witness"—and then released? No, she said, she hadn't heard anything about Cynthia's case.

Eula Montgomery has since taken her family elsewhere, still far removed from the public stage, where mothers of other murdered Atlanta children (and adults) had criss-crossed the United States in a plethora of talk shows, rallies, news conferences and fund-raisers—the money going to victims' families.

Which victims' families? Not Cynthia Montgomery's, or those of the other unfamiliar names on Dettlinger's map. Cynthia Montgomery's mother never asked for money. But she wasn't eligible for any, either. Nor was reward money available if Cynthia's murder were somehow solved, even though then-Mayor Maynard Jackson ballyhooed $500,000 for the solution of the children's murders.

Actually, the reward would be available for the solution of the murders of ex-convicts who were 21 and older. But it wouldn't apply in Cynthia Montgomery's case, even though she was only two weeks beyond her 14th birthday when she was strangled by a person, or persons, unknown.

Why no reward? The culprit is The List. If a victim's case wasn't put on The List of murders assigned to the Task Force, it was as if that victim hadn't existed. It wasn't unusual to hear news reports like the one that stated: "Fourteen-year-old Cynthia Montgomery of Atlanta was found murdered today. She is *not* one of Atlanta's missing or murdered children."

Not to the news media and public officials, perhaps—but to Eula Montgomery?

Chet Dettlinger was right about the adults. Four weeks after our meeting, the first of five adult victims was added to The List. But earlier victims—both children and adults—still would be ignored. One victim at first was left off The List with explanations like "at 16, he's too old."

Something else Dettlinger told me had borne out. He had said that there were more unsolved cases of murdered females who never made anybody's list during this time period than unsolved cases of males on The List. Although two females were on The List as it was originally drafted, they never were seriously considered by officials as part of the cases. It took several demands by City Councilwoman Mary Davis, then chairperson of the council's Public Safety Committee, before Lee P. Brown, Atlanta's public safety commissioner, finally produced a roster of unsolved murders, which showed Dettlinger's contention to be true.

While we talked over coffee and maps, I asked Dettlinger what he does. Back then, he taught criminal justice and directed a regional police training academy at a junior college in Rome, Georgia, 80 miles away. But it was soon apparent that what Dettlinger does differs from what he is. He prefers to talk about what he *isn't*. He eschewed labels like "private eye" and "investigator" and "detective."

"Why do we have to have labels?" he asked. He conceded, however, that "analyst" is about as close as anything to a description of what he is. Essentially, Dettlinger is an educator, thinker, writer, philosopher and iconoclastic cop. He likes to think about thinking.

Chet Dettlinger is 48, and has a wife, four children and one grandchild. He's an ex-street cop, a gregarious man of keen intelligence and wit, a Southerner who thinks fast and is quick on the drawl. "Mom said I was vaccinated with Victrola needle, and she was right," he says.

He once was honored by the National Conference of Christians and Jews for his police work among minorities, back in the days when Jim Crow sat in legislatures, in jury boxes and on courtroom benches across the South.

He helped establish educational and training standards tied to salary incentives for Kentucky's police, as chief of police planning for the Kentucky Crime Commission. He was a consultant to the United States Justice Department and a finalist for the job of chief of police in Seattle.

He came to Atlanta as the assistant to the chief of police and, in an organizational change, his title became assistant to the public safety commissioner. His voluntary investigation of Atlanta's murders led to a paradox: he was called in as a *suspect* by the Task Force, then was asked by the FBI to brief friends of the Special Agent in Charge—educators from California—as a paid *expert.*

While the police looked for a killer, Chet Dettlinger drove Atlanta's streets, finding connections among the victims. He scoured the death scenes, rapped on doors of housing projects and interviewed grieving families, armed only with an engaging informality, an unquenchable curiosity and a boundless arsenal of questions that nobody else asked.

"The police are trying to catch a killer— I'm trying to stop the killings, and there's a big difference," he was fond of saying.

He took some Task Force officers through a panorama of the cases that was new to them. He briefed reporters, editors and entire news departments. He was asked to brief investigators of the second largest metropolitan Atlanta police department, the DeKalb County police. He found one child *alive* in one day—after the authorities couldn't find the child in 30. He would interview convicted killer Wayne Williams, and be invited to sit at the defense table during Williams' trial in 1982 for the murders of two adults.

Along the way, Chet Dettlinger would ask me to participate in writing this book, a labor of three years which often found our roles upside down—he pounding the typewriter, and I pounding the streets.

This is not a ghosted, but, rather, a co-authored book. What follows is a look at three American institutions—the police, the courts and the press—in the setting of what the authors believe is one of the most reported, but least told, stories of our time.

—Jeff Prugh
Roswell, Georgia
October 22, 1983

The Dream

The rented white Ford van nearly misses the exit. Suddenly it leans hard, almost capsizing, as it clings to the cloverleaf off-ramp from Interstate 85 onto the Palmetto Parkway.

"Damn, man! Watch that shit!" the passenger scolds the driver. "Hey, we got thousands of dollars in computerized sounds back here, and you drivin' like an asshole!"

If the passenger happens to be Wayne Williams, he's a pudgy, bespectacled child of the Electronic Generation. At home, he keeps both ears plugged into a police scanner. On the streets, one eye peers through a TV-camera lens at fires, wrecks, shootings or any other late-night calamity he videotapes after flashing his media card and being waved through the roadblocks.

His other eye gazes for stars. It scans the housing projects in the hope that maybe, just maybe, there are fledgling Michael Jacksons or Diana Rosses or Dionne Warwicks or Lou Rawlses out there, waiting to be discovered. Maybe someday Wayne Williams will nurse them and rehearse them, and they'll all make beautiful music together, humming all the way to the bank.

Wayne Williams is a Pied Piper in headphones. A would-be Leader of the Band. He's turned on by ambition. He's tuned in to tape players, turntables and treble clefs. His dreams carry him irresistibly to a bright-lights Tomorrowland, where life is no longer an audition, home is the top of the Top 40 charts and the streets are paved in gold and platinum.

Climb into the time capsule now. Buckle your seat belts. And fly back into the 1970s, on a sentimental journey to Georgia. Like everybody else, you'll have to change planes in Atlanta.

Atlanta. Capital of Georgia. Umbilical cord of the Confederacy. Cradle of the civil rights movement. Heartbeat of the American South.

And when you reach Atlanta, you meet unfamiliar faces in familiar places. They are a blur at first, a montage of "Me Decade" America. But when you zoom in for a closeup, their lives are entangled in common threads. They interweave through an urban tapestry of shopping malls and car washes, disco dancing and *Star Wars* games, fast food and loud music and life in the fast lane. Destination: the American Dream.

It is June of 1977, and Wayne Bertram Williams, broadcasting prodigy, is riding north from Columbus, Georgia, to the studios of radio station WRAZ on Highway 166—to an office building he shares with Zone 4 of the Atlanta police department.

Here is a 19-year-old black kid who won't be confined to anybody's ghetto. Before he was 16, he put a homemade radio station on the air. He played records that had Dixie Hills rocking.

If you lived in the red-brick housing project there, a few blocks from Wayne's house, you moved your feet and shook your booty to the big beat. On the Starting Line of Life, you already had to line up many yards behind other blacks who were born lucky enough—like Andrew Young and Maynard Jackson, the present and previous Atlanta mayors—to go to college someday at Morehouse or Howard or maybe even Harvard.

You clamored for escape from streets of shattered glass and broken dreams. You hustled quarters by carrying sacks of groceries. Or you made bigger, easier money by dealing in dope, sex or "hot" merchandise like stereos, cameras and guns—at the sleazy hangouts on Auburn and Stewart avenues, or the hideaways of Grant and Piedmont and South Bend parks.

You also indulged in escapism in the Fantasyworld outside. You could only imagine the roar of the crowds downtown at the Omni Sports Arena, when the Hawks win on a shot at the buzzer, or when a Jackson Five concert brings down the house. You wondered what it must be like, losing yourself in the swirling lights and Saturday night fever that engulf the black-is-beautiful people in the glittery clubs along Campbellton Road.

Wayne Williams' picture already had been in *Jet* magazine. He had posed at his radio station with a smiling Benjamin Hooks, who then was the first black commissioner on the Federal Communications Commission and now is executive director of the National Association for the Advancement of Colored People (NAACP).

If that incident didn't set Wayne apart, then a meeting with another visitor did. His name: Andrew Young, who had installed Wayne, a seventh grader, as student council president at Anderson Park School. Two years later, Young would campaign for Congress over Wayne's air waves by granting Wayne an interview. Then Andrew Young would go home and tell his wife, Jean: "This is one of the brightest kids I've ever met."

Patrick Rogers is 13. He's big and tough for his age. You just don't mess with Pat Man. He lives across town from Wayne Williams in the Thomasville Heights housing project, which really is no different than the South Bronx or South Chicago or Watts, except that it's surrounded by a lot more trees.

Pat Man is Bruce Lee in an Afro hairstyle. A devotee of karate. As he kicks and chops his way down Atlanta's meanest streets, imaginary villains fly through the air. They fall in crumpled, lifeless heaps—in gutters among the broken beer bottles and rusty muffler clamps.

Patrick would switch from mayhem to beebop, snapping his fingers as he boogies on down the street in hesitating rhythm. If Patrick couldn't fight his way out, he would sing his way out. And if he couldn't sing his way out, he would survive on the streets. Pat Man rode out front with the big dudes, in the summer of 1977.

Back then, Pat Man's uncle, Willie Paul Rice, was 36 and doing time in a Georgia prison on a drug rap. It's easy to visualize Pat Man puffing on a "roach," a tiny chunk of leftover pot, with a hairpin clamped on it, passed delicately to him by his buddies in the front seat of Richard Hill's car. Pat Man is proud of his older friends like Richard, who, at 22, is a maintenance man at the Thomasville Heights apartments and has a precocious 9-year-old brother named Timothy Hill.

Now you can see Patrick taking a final deep drag, kissing the thumb and forefinger of each hand. He clamps the "roach" in the hairpin. Then, like an Olympic relay runner, he makes sure that the paper-wrapped gold is safely in the hands of the next man before he leaps from the car and slams the door with a flourish.

There he goes, dashing across the basketball court that lay between the road and trash dumpster. He's heading home—to the back door of the apartment where Patrick's mother, Annie Grace Rogers, raises eight kids and raises hell when they don't behave.

On the dead run, Patrick no longer is felling the bad guys or trilling a soul song to screams of adoring females or a member of the gang. Now he pivots and breaks for the basket with the timing of Dr. J. He intercepts the pass and, cutting a graceful backward arc through the air, he flips the ball up, up, up—underhanded—as the clock runs down. Three...two...one...zero! Swish! The ball goes through! Pat Man is MVP of the NBA.

Not far away, 7-year-old Aaron Wyche stands half in awe and half in consternation as Pat Man disappears into the doorway, the slamming screen barely missing Pat Man's ass.

Aaron can't shoot the ball 10 feet off the ground yet. He's convinced he never will. So he mostly dribbles the ball. But, every third stumble, he aims at the basket and then—oof!—he pushes the ball upward with all the strength he can muster. Every effort is an "air ball". He knows that nobody does it better than his neighbor, Pat Man.

To Aaron Wyche, Pat Man is a cross between God and Muhammad Ali.

Go back 20 more years, to a simpler America. The year is 1957. You're in Muhammad Ali's hometown, Louisville.

Look over there, on Main Street. See that boyish, rookie cop on the beat? He's only 21, a few years older than Wayne Williams and Patrick Rogers would be in 1977.

The cop is yours truly.

As a kid, I loved policing and policemen. My daddy was a cop. I learned to spell "P-O-L-I-C-E" before "cat". Ten other cops lived in our neighborhood. I played with policemen's sons and fell in and out of puppy love with their daughters. On my block, asking "What are dirty pennies made of?" and answering "Dirty coppers!" would get you punched out in a hurry.

I hadn't even finished recruit school when my idealism was challenged. Twenty-five years later, with some of the highest quality experience possible, I would remain unshakably idealistic about what policing *could be.* But my opinion of what it *is* has nosedived.

My first few nights on the streets in 1957 etched lasting impressions. I rode with cops who loafed, drank and slept on the job. My starting salary was $3,720 a year, paid monthly. The chief of police was limited by the state constitution to $7,200. So perhaps I shouldn't have been surprised when I discovered that many cops looked the other way and wrote phony reports, often in exchange for graft, payoffs, bribes and stolen or confiscated merchandise.

My first partner had a cherubic face, but devilish ways. On our first night on foot patrol together, a sergeant told us that a robbery had occurred about 20 miles away and that the state police were chasing the robbers west toward Louisville on U.S. 42. He instructed us to go to 4th and Main Street, which also was U.S. 42 and the first through street on the Dixie side of the Ohio River.

We were supposed to stand by, at that intersection, in case the chase got that far.

"What do we do?" I asked my partner as the sergeant drove away.

"First of all," he said, "we walk re-e-e-e-al slow-w-w-w. Next, we don't worry about it, anyway, because they ain't never gonna get this far. But, if they do, we look for a concrete wall to hide behind. It's that simple."

Now I heard a siren wailing. Seconds later, I saw the flickering sweep of the red flashers atop a gray Kentucky State Police car. Then came the throaty engines of the chase car and the getaway car. They approached at hellfire speed. Suddenly, two blocks away, the getaway car slammed wildly into the side of a car emerging from the bridge, which spans the river between Louisville and Jeffersonville, Indiana.

The robbers hastily squirmed out of the wreckage. They scampered away and disappeared into the maze of railroad trestles that border the river. All of a sudden, gunfire crackled.

"Let's go," my partner said. He turned and began walking rapidly, in the *opposite* direction, away from the scene.

I hesitated, but soon followed in disgust. My only instructions had been to "do whatever your partner tells you to do."

A while later, we came upon an accident at 6th and Walnut. My partner told the persons involved that he would call someone to take the report. He headed for a telephone. The Louisville police department, and many others, didn't own portable radios then.

"Can't *we* take the report?" I asked him.

"Sure, we can," he said, "if you're willing to hang around the station house after we get off and fuck with all that paperwork."

The December night was bone-chilling. We adjourned into a warm building to ferret out the information. My partner called me aside and handed me a $10 bill.

"When you make out the report," he whispered, "put the *passenger* in the blue Buick down as the *driver*."

"What?"

"Well, the guy in the Buick's got a little problem. He ain't got no driver's license. He's in the right and the insurance company's gonna pay off, anyway. And...there's 10 bucks apiece in it for us."

I had walked away from the river incident, but I figured our chances of getting in trouble were too good this time. "You keep both 10s," I said, "and I'll make out the report the way I see it."

My partner looked at me as if I were crazy. Shaking his head, he returned to the licenseless driver and explained that I was a "new guy, wet behind the ears," and that I would learn, but this just wasn't the driver's lucky day. He gave the man back one of the two 10s. After all, my partner had done *his* part.

That officer's daddy had been a cop, too. I wondered how he could do what he just did. Now, I realize that he'd just given me an accelerated crash course because, knowing that my daddy was a cop, he assumed I already knew "how it is."

Even so, it would be years before I would realize that one problem with policing wasn't a few rotten apples, but rather a rotten barrel that we keep throwing good apples into. Within weeks, even the best apples in police work are usually soggy and acceptably wormy.

My idealism about the press, too, was battered, scarred and all but left for dead on Louisville's streets. Early one morning, my partner—this time a likeable fellow named George Martin—and I heard the dispatcher announce that five men had escaped from the Jefferson County Jail.

As we turned the corner onto Gray Street, near the General Hospital, I saw a man in an ill-fitting suit at the door of a chopped and channeled 1934 Ford. He was way too old for that car.

"Stop, George!" I yelled.

"Huh?" he said drowsily.

"Turn around!"

Instead, George drove around the block. When we returned, the car was there, but the man was gone.

A woman watched us from the second-story window of the four-plex on the corner.

"Do you know whose car this is?" I hollered up at her.

"That's my son's car," she replied. "Why? Something wrong?"

"How old is your son, ma'am?"

"He's 20. Hey, what's wrong?"

The man we saw was much older than 20. We sped away, in guesswork pursuit. We drove in concentric circles, expanding each circle by one block each time we turned. In another four blocks, we saw the man. He didn't try to run. When we stopped alongside him, he raised his hands.

Hours later, a reporter from the *Louisville Times* interviewed me about details of the capture. That evening, the *Times* front-paged the story, which said, in essence, "Police Nab Escapee When Woman Hails Them". The woman was quoted as saying something akin to "Stop that man! He's trying to steal my car!..."

I couldn't believe my eyes. As I read on, I saw no similarity between what had happened and what I was reading. It was my first brush with inaccuracy by the press. It wasn't to be my last.

My police car rolled to a stop at the intersection of Preston Highway and Eastern Parkway.

Looming prominently nearby is Pee Wee Reese Lanes, a bowling alley named for its owner, the former Brooklyn Dodger shortstop and teammate of the late Jackie Robinson. I once had dated Pee Wee's niece, who later became a Louisville police officer after I left the department.

As I rode alone that day, a motor bike suddenly raced across my bow. It wasn't a true motorcycle, but a Whizzer (a motorized version of the Schwinn bicycle that was popular in the 1940s). But this was 1958, and the rickety bike had seen better days. It carried no lights and no license plate, just two young black kids.

I quickly hung a left and flipped on the red flasher. The biker pulled to the curb. He had no driver's license. The bike had no windshield and no fenders—and appeared unsafe at any speed. The kids could have gotten hurt.

I called for a wrecker to haul in the bike. Next, I took the passenger, the younger of the two, to his home. The older one stayed in the back seat of my car for a trip to police headquarters. He sat docilely, gazing out the windows. He was a big kid, about 16— the same age as Patrick (Pat Man) Rogers would be many years later when I would first hear of Patrick.

Unlike Pat Man, who relied on karate, this kid looked as if he could take you out with one old-fashioned fist punch. I'm glad he didn't try with me.

By radio, I contacted Louisville police officer Joe Martin and asked him to meet me at headquarters. There, I took the teen-ager to the snack bar across from the booking clerk and awaited Joe's arrival.

Soon Joe Martin ambled through the door. "Whatcha got, Little Ches?" he asked, using a nickname that distinguished me from my father, "Big Ches," who also was a Louisville police officer.

"Well, Joe," I said, "I've got a friend of yours here, and I thought maybe I could turn him over to you—and you could get him straightened out."

Joe Martin looked for the first time at the strapping youngster. "Good God!" he said, his face reddening a bit beneath his white burr haircut.

Joe recognized him instantly as an amateur boxer he managed during off-duty hours—Cassius Clay.

Two years later, Joe would train Cassius for a trip to Rome, where Cassius would win the gold medal in the 1960 Olympic Games light-heavyweight division. Soon thereafter, Cassius Clay's face would become one of the most recognizable throughout the world.

On the trip to police headquarters, I had driven Cassius down a street that would change names—as Cassius himself would—after he would become heavyweight champion of the world. Walnut Street then, it's Muhammad Ali Way now.

The teen-ager on the back of the bike had been Rudy Clay, Cassius' younger brother and not a bad puncher, either. He would become Cassius' sparring partner.

From a physical-danger standpoint, that may have been my lucky day. They both were nice, gentlemanly kids, and I guess I scared them about as much as they could scare me now.

Twenty-three years later, Muhammad Ali would come to Atlanta and pledge just under $400,000 in reward money to try to uncover the killer or killers of Atlanta's youths.

The time capsule circles over Atlanta. You have a window-seat panorama of the 1970s, then the 1980s.

You see the Atlanta that worships the late Martin Luther King Jr., who preached on Auburn Avenue, marched on Washington and told the world, "I have a dream that one day on the red hills of Georgia, the sons of former slaves and the sons of former slave owners will be able to sit down together at the table of brotherhood. . ."

You see the Atlanta of Jimmy Carter, who sits in the Governor's Mansion on West Paces Ferry Road, then runs for President, admits he has "lusted" in his heart and tells campaign-trail crowds, "I will never lie to you."

You see the Atlanta I fell in love with, when I arrived with my wife and four children in 1973, after my long tenure as a Louisville street cop and police planner, then as Acting Deputy Director of the Kentucky Crime Commission.

As I sat in a plane that circled Atlanta in a holding pattern, waiting to land at bustling Hartsfield Airport, I couldn't help but notice a mysterious skyscraper rising into the darkness and twinkling with strobe lights. Later, I would learn that it's the 836-foot-tall smokestack of Georgia Power's Plant McDonough generating facility, hard by the Chattahoochee River, northwest of downtown Atlanta. The smokestack towered over a river bridge which, eight years later, would become a focal point during the height of Atlanta's murders—and in my life.

Atlanta was incomparably beautiful, a shining city in a forest of pines, live oaks, dogwoods and magnolias. Modern, but aged. Large, but small. A city slicker and a country cousin, all in one. She pretended to be an international city when all she had that was international was one of the world's busiest airports. But Atlanta was the major leagues. There were the Braves, the Falcons, the Hawks, the Flames, a champion soccer team and a vibrant promise of a new life in the Sunbelt. Here was a city that reached for its tomorrows and clung to its yesterdays. "Uptown Down South," someone would call her.

I had admired, too, the prize-winning columns of the late Ralph McGill, who had written in the *Atlanta Constitution* that segregation should be kicked off the buses and that blacks no longer should be banished to the back seats. I figured that a city with Ralph McGill's courage, dignity and sense of moral outrage couldn't be all bad.

I wasn't ready for the black-white politics of Atlanta, whose population would change during the 1970s from 51% black to 66% black. When Atlanta elected Vice Mayor Maynard H. Jackson as the first black mayor of a major Southern city in 1973, the color of city government rapidly changed, too.

Jackson, an eloquent, 300-pound lawyer, skillfully spoke the language of the civil rights movement. But Jackson never had gone to jail, as Martin Luther King Jr. did during the bombings of Birmingham, or got his nose bloodied, as John Lewis (now an Atlanta City Councilman) did during the siege of Selma.

At City Hall in Atlanta, Jackson quickly threw his considerable weight around. Heads rolled. Arms got twisted. Verbal sparks spewed all over town. Charges of "reverse discrimination" were hurled by whites when Jackson insisted that blacks get a piece of the action—in constructing the new airport, or running City Hall and the police department.

It all portended some of Atlanta's most cataclysmic years. But then, Atlanta probably was destined for tumult, even back in 1837, when she began as just an obscure stop on a railroad. That's when an engineer named Stephen H. Long pounded a wooden stake into the red Georgia clay and christened the community "Terminus."

From there, the city-to-be would undergo two name changes—to "Marthasville" in 1843, after the daughter of Georgia's governor, and then to "Atlanta" in 1845, as a feminine derivative from the Western & Atlantic railroad line.

Railroading, in fact, would keep the economic lifeblood of Atlanta (then pop. 10,000) pumping. It also cast her in a starring role during the Civil War. Nobody knew Atlanta's strategic importance better than General William Tecumseh Sherman and his Union Army troops. They put torches to Atlanta, reduced her to ashes and shut off the Confederate Army's supply lines in 1864. The surrender at Appomattox was inevitable. So were the last gasps of the Confederate States of America.

But while Sherman set fire to Atlanta, he ignited her soul. Out of all that wartime rubble (the city treasury contained only \$1.64—in Confederate money) came a burst of civic energy and pride that produced Coca-Cola, Georgia Tech and Margaret Mitchell's "*Gone With the Wind*"—benchmarks of enterprise, technology and literature that are known around the world.

Atlanta, however, didn't always put on a pretty face. In 1913, a 13-year-old girl was found murdered in the basement of a pencil factory. Leo Frank, a supervisor at the factory, was tried, convicted and sentenced to hang amid cries of "Kill the Jew!" But, doubting a janitor's testimony, Governor John Slaton commuted the sentence to life imprisonment. (Slaton's grand nephew, Fulton County District Attorney Lewis Slaton, would publicly express reservations about the guilt of murder suspect Wayne Williams in 1981, but then would successfully prosecute him in 1982, likening him, during final arguments, to Hitler, Idi Amin and Attila the Hun.)

An angry lynch mob hanged Leo Frank from an oak tree near Marietta, northwest of Atlanta, in 1915. But, unexpectedly, an eyewitness surfaced in 1982. Alonzo Mann, 83, said he had been a frightened 14-year-old boy who saw the janitor carry the girl's unconscious body to the basement of the pencil factory. He said he had stayed silent all these years, for fear of his life. He said he was guilt-ridden, heartsick and wanted to lay "that burden down."

Groups including the Anti-Defamation League of B'nai B'rith endeavored in 1983 to clear Leo Frank's name, only for the Georgia Board of Pardons and Paroles to deny Frank a pardon. But Leo Frank's defenders fight on relentlessly. They call the case "the worst episode of anti-Semitism in the United States, and continues to be a blot on Georgia's criminal-justice system."

As recently as the 1950s, Atlanta and Birmingham grappled for the title of economic and cultural "capital" of the Southeast. They had almost identical populations of about 350,000. They also shared something else in common—a dislike for each other.

Atlanta and its leaders, notably Mayor William B. Hartsfield, pushed for economic expansion in the 1950s—and grudgingly tolerated social change in the 1960s. Governor-to-be Lester Maddox did nothing, however, to enhance Atlanta's national image as the city "too busy to hate" when he brandished a pick-ax handle at blacks who tried to integrate his fried-chicken restaurant.

Still, Atlanta had a white moderate in Herbert Jenkins for its chief of police. He began hiring blacks as officers before anyone had to prod him by agitation or protest.

By contrast, Birmingham was symbolized by "stand patism" economically and by Eugene (Bull) Connor, the city's police commissioner, on the front lines against desegregation. It was Connor who brought worldwide attention to Birmingham in 1963 by unleashing police dogs and fire hoses against demonstrating blacks. Ultimately, Alabama's largest city had to be dragged, kicking and screaming, into the late 20th Century.

By the mid-1970s, Atlanta would pride itself as the undisputed hub of the so-called "New South," a city of robust growth, prosperity, racial moderation and biracial political stability. It was building a new airport and a rapid-rail system that would be the envy of other cities. It would put up gleaming hotels and cultivate a thriving convention trade, third only behind New York and Chicago. A mostly white district sent a black man to Congress. He was Andrew Young, a New Orleans dentist's son, who became a rural preacher, then marched in lockstep with Martin Luther King Jr. in the 1960s and stumped the nation for black votes on behalf of Jimmy Carter in the 1970s.

By 1980, Atlanta would be home base for nationally known black politicians such as Georgia state Senator Julian Bond and for powerful black businessmen such as insurance mogul Jesse Hill and contractor Herman Russell. The city also would boast of an unusually large black middle and upper class, owing partly to Atlanta's nationally respected black colleges such as Morehouse, Spelman and Morris Brown.

But the scathing realities of contemporary urban America would take a toll on Atlanta. Twice in the 1970s, Atlanta was the nation's "Murder Capital," and in the winter of 1977, the city was gripped by the "Lover's Lane" killings, in which three young blacks were shot to death and three others were seriously wounded. One suspect was a police officer.

At the same time, whites would move inexorably to the suburbs. Businesses would stake out new turf beyond the city's nothern perimeter. Whites *and* blacks (including Julian Bond and baseball slugger Hank Aaron) enrolled their children in private schools. Atlanta's public schools, which were integrated in 1961, would become 92% black by the 1980s. A dwindling tax base would exert severe strains on city services already strained by thousands of workday commuters, tourists and conventioneers who swarm into downtown Atlanta.

What's more, class distinctions would become increasingly stark. First-time visitors to Atlanta from other major cities would be awe-struck by her magnificent homes and opulent, skylighted shopping malls, where the parking lots seem to overflow with expensive BMWs, Mercedes-Benzes and Cadillac Eldorados. These same outsiders need not look very far to find some of America's most squalid public housing, a vivid reminder that 27.5% of Atlantans have incomes at or below the poverty level. Only Newark, with 32.8%, has a higher proportion of poor people among major U.S. cities.

Today, Atlanta (pop. 425,000) is increasingly black, the centerpiece of a 17-county metropolitan area (pop. 2 million) that was—and is—predominantly white. There is talk of expanding Atlanta's boundaries to the Interstate 285 highway that encircles the metropolitan area. But it's only talk. For now, too many white suburbanites abhor the thought of their properties being annexed, in effect, by predominantly black Atlanta. And too many blacks inside Atlanta's city limits don't want their political muscle diluted.

Atlanta's politics have been controlled by blacks for 10 years; its money has been controlled by whites forever, although blacks now ride a high tide of minority-participation laws that give them bigger slices of the economic pie. In many instances, the tables are turned now, two decades after the "COLORED" and "WHITE" signs came down. Today, a black can succeed in business in Atlanta *because* of his or her skin color, not in *spite* of it.

But politics in Atlanta are always black *and* white, regardless of what anybody tries to tell you. Compromises are not always hammered out along

Democratic and Republican Party lines. In fact, you can't tell all the players and their teams *with* a scorecard, except at primary election time. Deals in Atlanta's smoke-filled rooms are often struck with an eye on skin color.

Attorney Mary Welcome would tell me, for example, that when a Fulton County Superior Court judgeship was open, a young black man wanted the job. He had become a municipal judge by way of the political experience he got as an assistant prosecutor for Lewis Slaton, who is white and has been Fulton County's District Attorney since 1965.

Slaton declined to endorse the young black man, who had worked for him for 11 years. Someone else got the judgeship. But two years later, when the position came up for full-term election, a compromise was reached between two factions:

—The black power structure of Fulton County, notably County Commissioners A. Reginald Eaves, the former Atlanta Public Safety Commissioner, and Michael Lomax, the County Commission chairman, who, like Eaves, had become a protege of then-Mayor Jackson.

—The lily-white Republican power brokers on Atlanta's affluent north side. The deal gave predominantly white North Fulton County a white at-large commission seat in exchange for Republican support for Clarence Cooper, now 41, to the bench of Superior Court. There, Cooper would preside over the trial of Wayne Williams in the murders of two black Atlanta men.

The classes of white Atlanta span the northside mansions of Buckhead and the high society of the Piedmont Driving Club (whose whites-only policy angered activists in 1976, when one member, Griffin Bell, was tapped by Jimmy Carter to be U.S. Attorney General) to the ramshackle bungalows of Cabbagetown, a downtown community that lies in the shadow of an erstwhile cotton mill.

Cabbagetown has been home for teen-age boys (who along with some black male contemporaries) had been photographed in the nude and having sex with men in a child-homosexual molestation ring run by three white men now serving prison terms. Two Cabbagetown boys pleaded guilty, at ages 16 and 17, in the slaying of an attorney they allegedly had tried to pick up at a bar frequented by homosexuals. They are serving life sentences.

Scratch the surface of black Atlanta, and you will find a true story that is *not* stereotypically Southern, *not* one of paternalistic whites oppressing hat-in-hand blacks.

This, instead, is a story of *class* more than race, of *classism* more than racism.

It is set in the large, black Atlanta middle and upper class of Andrew Young and Maynard Jackson, who got head starts and went to good schools. Unlike others who had to, they didn't have to hustle grocery sacks or nickel bags or easy sex.

It is set in the black Atlanta of Reginald Eaves and his successors as Public Safety Commissioner, Lee Brown and George Napper, who got post-graduate degrees, learned the political ropes better than they knew the streets, and rode coattails to the top.

It is the black Atlanta of Arthur Langford Jr., who said, "I have a dream..." in a play he wrote about Martin Luther King Jr., then ran for City Council in a battered, string-driven car. When his companion, Fred Williams, told him, "Man, you're a Councilman now! You can't drive this thing anymore," the new car that Langford obtained ran over the Dream and turned it to dust.

It is the black Atlanta of Langford's one-time attorney, City Council President Marvin Arrington, the target of a 1983 roast that poked fun at Arrington's dispute with Mayor Andrew Young over the city's proposed water-rate increase (which is opposed by many Atlantans who are poor).

Young on Arrington: "I'm working on how to get the water rate down on that swimming pool of his."

Arrington: "When I get through filling up my swimming pool, I'm going to go over and sit in Andy's Jacuzzi."

The black Atlanta of Young and Jackson, of Eaves, Brown, Napper, Langford and Arrington is galaxies removed from the black Atlanta underclass they are supposed to serve—out there in the hardscrabble world of Dixie Hills and Thomasville Heights and East Lake Meadows.

It is the black Atlanta of kids named Earl Terrell and Lubie (Chuck) Geter, who would cruise for the Dream with a middle-aged white pornographer who chased the Dream, too, before going to prison.

It is the black Atlanta of Cynthia Montgomery, a teen-age child of the ghetto who would seek the Dream by becoming a woman of the streets.

It is the black Atlanta of Pat Man Rogers, who with his buddy, Junior Harper, would write and sing *"Running Girl"* and *"Lonely Without You"* and *"I Feel Your Love in the Sunshine."* Then they would win second place in a talent show and touch the Dream, at long last—out there beyond the dumpsters, the dopers and the chunks of glass in the streets.

Atlanta is a paradox, a place where tradition cohabits with transition. It is antebellum homes and contemporary condos, office towers and office parks. It's a city that's born again and porn again. It's preachers and teachers, hookers and hustlers. It's the town of Benjamin E. Mays, esteemed black educator, and Mike Thevis, convicted white pornographer.

Atlanta also is where political brokers woo new minorities. Having built his black power base, Maynard Jackson courted the gay vote, just as Andrew Young would do after him. In Atlanta, as in New York and San Francisco, the closet door swings open, and homosexuals step out, by the thousands. The door would open at a dilapidated house on Gray Street, where Timothy Hill, the kid brother of Pat Man's buddy, Richard Hill, would spend the night with men who are openly gay.

But, unlike San Francisco, Atlanta is where no public official or candidate for public office—black or white—has yet dared to step out of the closet.

The scene: Downtown Atlanta. A Friday night in 1973. The sidewalks throb with shoppers and strollers, suburbanites and city folks.

Underground Atlanta is jumping. The Varsity Drive-in is jammed. The Fox Theater is filled. In clubs and pubs, in bistros and discos, downtown is uptown and the fun never sets.

Look closely at the faces in the crowd. That stranger you see is a refugee from the police beats of Louisville—yours truly.

Now I'm a newcomer to Atlanta, and I'm window shopping with my wife, Mary. As we walk along Peachtree Street, I'm ambivalent. I sense that Atlanta is teetering.

"This town," I tell Mary, "is right on the edge. It's about to soar...or sink."

Would this be The Dream?

Or...

The Nightmare

In Memoriam

THE LIST

1. Edward Hope Smith, 14	July, 1979
2. Alfred Evans, 14	July, 1979
3. Milton Harvey, 14	September, 1979
4. Yusuf Bell, 9	October, 1979
5. Jefferey Mathis, 10	March, 1980
6. Angel Lenair, 12	March, 1980
7. Eric Middlebrooks, 14	May, 1980
8. Christopher Richardson, 11	June, 1980
9. LaTonya Wilson, 7	June, 1980
10. Aaron Wyche, 10	June, 1980
11. Anthony Carter, 9	July, 1980
12. Earl Terrell, 11	July, 1980
13. Clifford Jones, 13	August, 1980
14. Darron Glass, 10 (still missing)	September, 1980
15. Charles Stephens, 12	October, 1980
16. Aaron Jackson, 9	October, 1980
17. Patrick Rogers, 16	November, 1980
18. Lubie Geter, 14	January, 1981
19. Terry Pue, 15	January, 1981
20. Patrick Baltazar, 11	February, 1981
21. Curtis Walker, 13	February, 1981
22. Joseph Bell, 15	March, 1981
23. Timothy Hill, 13	March, 1981
24. Eddie Duncan, 21	March, 1981
25. Larry Rogers, 20	March, 1981
*26. Michael McIntosh, 23	April, 1981
27. Jimmy Ray Payne, 21	April, 1981
28. William Barrett, 17	May, 1981
29. Nathaniel Cater, 27	May, 1981

*—John Porter, 28, April, 1981 (added by prosecution)

Note: Victims are listed by the month in which they disappeared.

In Memoriam

NOT ON THE LIST

1979

1. Yvette Scott, 18, stabbed
2. Gayle Neeley, 25, stabbed
3. Ernestine Burkett, 24, strangled
4. Sandy Winford (male), 25, shot
5. Catherine Taylor, 20, shot
6. Ronald Robinson, 20, shot
7. Charles Landers, 26, shot
8. Billy Eugene Hill, 19, shot
9. Larry Watkins, 25, shot
10. Bernard Burch, 26, shot
11. Bonnie Crawford, 26, shot
12. James Owens, 21, stabbed
13. Kathy York, 25, strangled
14. Vernelle Tye, 21, strangled
15. Unidentified male, shot
16. Unidentified male, shot
17. Unidentified female, unknown

1980

18. Cynthia Montgomery, 14, strangled
19. Angela Bacon, 16, blow to head
20. Joseph Lee, 17, shot
21. Beverly Harvey, 18, stabbed
22. Johnny Johnson, 27, shot
23. Clyde Hamilton, 25, shot
24. Melvin Spencer, 24, bludgeoned
25. Terry Jones, 23, shot
26. Edward Scales, 26, stabbed
27. Eldred Cheves, 23, shot
28. Mary Ector, 25, strangled

1981

29. Faye Yearby, 22, stabbed
30. Bronzelle Pettaway, 21, shot
31. Terrell Black, 24, shot
32. Effie Hall, 24, shot
33. Jo Carron Lane, 24, shot
34. Candy Lane, 26, shot
35. Yvonne Miller, 27, shot
36. Danny White, 26, shot
37. Carolyn Trammel, 23, stabbed
38. Anita Baynes, 24, shot

1981

Since the arrest of Wayne Williams

39. Clarence Davis, 16, shot
40. Stanley Murray, 21, shot
    (uncle of List victim Curtis Walker)
41. Unidentified girl, strangled
42. Unidentified male, unknown
43. Unidentified male, shot
44. Kenneth Johnson, 17, shot
45. Roderick Williams, 23, shot
46. Unidentified female, unknown
47. Unidentified male, unknown

1982

48. Female, 26, shot
49. Female, 22, strangled
50. Female, 28, stabbed
51. Female, 26, stabbed
52. Male, 27, shot
53. Male, 27, shot
54. Male, 26, shot
55. Male, 26, stabbed
56. Female, 25, shot
57. Male, 23, shot
58. Male, 19, shot
59. Female, 19, shot
60. Male, 28, shot

1983

61. Male, 25, unknown
62. Lucretia Bell, 13, strangled
63. Unidentified male, unknown

Note: The foregoing list of victims who did not make The List does not purport to be complete, inasmuch as record-keeping by law-enforcement agencies is too often inaccurate and incomplete.

Sources: FBI Uniform Crime Report; police departments of Atlanta, East Point, Alpharetta, and Fulton and DeKalb counties; Fulton County Medical Examiner.

"We are leaving no stone unturned."

—**Maynard H. Jackson**
Mayor of Atlanta
February 20, 1981

1

The Way It Is, Was and Will Be

In July of 1979, the city of Atlanta was engaged in the universal and perpetual task of trying to make its police operation work. There were no labor problems. Although there was litigation, there was no widespread "blue flu." There were no "job actions" beyond the standard malaise.

No one was "cooping," a Big Apple term for carrying a pillow and alarm clock to the job. Still, the knack of sleeping—but never missing a single call on the police radio—was no less refined in Atlanta than in every other American police department. Generally, things were pretty much normal with the Atlanta police—the way they always are.

Administrators searched for the "minor adjustments" to fine-tune the agency so that it could, at long last, accomplish what it is supposed to accomplish—whatever that is.

"If only there were more men and more money," they lamented. But there weren't enough men or money—and there never had been and never will be. It's just as well. We already waste enough money on the myth that policing is a viable solution to many, let alone all, of our crime problems.

Policing cannot be fixed because its theories of "crime" prevention are fallacious and its practices are bankrupt.

There is no single problem called "crime." Instead, there are many crime problems—an as yet uncounted number. Therefore, policing—a singular solution—is not capable of affecting most crime problems, even if it were functioning perfectly. Yet those engaged in policing think it is, and we blindly trust it.

The so-called remedy of "more men and more money" could serve only to solve some of policing's problems, but none of the problems that policing is supposed to solve.

Since 1970, a lot of money has been spent on improving police-community relations. Actually, this had been identified by the President's Commission on Criminal Justice as a problem in the 1960s. But nobody threw money at the problem until the 1970s—when the problem wasn't as severe. In the 1980s, it has become common practice to rate a police department's "effectiveness" by how few of the citizens it is supposed to serve complain of "police brutality"—not by how many citizens applaud the department for what it's supposed to do: protect lives and property.

Every attempt to make the police system work, no matter where or when, simply leads to new labels disguising the same old barren practices. The best result attainable is that police become increasingly efficient at doing the same old ineffective things.

Policing has proved to be an indispensable service that saves lives, responds to emergencies and provides 'round-the-clock social services. But, it only *pretends* to prevent crimes. The illusion cast by screaming sirens, squealing tires and cops in two-handed pistol stances while crying "Freeze!" serves to delude nobody more than the police themselves. Thus, the drug busts are always "the biggest ever," and the murders the "worst ever seen."

The truth and the shame is that the police are virtually all we have to defend us against criminal attacks—and these illusions of police potency are unfair to the police, who never quite measure up, and potentially fatal to the rest of us.

Another reason the police system cannot be fixed is that so many of its undertakings are invalid. Many criminal acts are simply not subject to prevention or detection by police patrol or "good ol' hard-nosed detective work." Andy Griffith, the mythical sheriff of *Mayberry,* a re-run TV show which should be required viewing for any police officer who begins to take his crime-control efforts seriously, said during one episode that in spite of all the scientific advances in police work, no one had come up with anything better than "sittin', waitin', and watchin'!" Unfortunately, he was right.

Policemen and policewomen themselves are often victims, even perpetrators, of crimes. A case in point occurred in 1983 when the Atlanta police major in charge of what they call "crime prevention" attempted to murder his wife and then committed suicide. Also in 1983, an off-duty Atlanta policewoman was arrested and charged with shoplifting, and an Atlanta policeman pleaded guilty to two counts of misdemeanor extortion, having been accused of twice demanding and accepting $20 bribes from a prostitute for not arresting her on charges of prostitution.

These aren't the only examples of transgressions by police in Atlanta or any other U.S. city. We've seen police officers charged with burglary, rape, sodomy and other offenses. In 1983, two ex-Chicago cops were charged with skimming money from a Las Vegas casino. And in recent years, dozens of Georgia law-enforcement officers, including chiefs of police, and sheriffs, have been charged with trafficking in drugs.

Therefore, it is invalid to assume that police presence will enforce laws, let alone prevent an attack on someone else's person or property. Police presence might prevent such an attack, but so might a sudden rainstorm or a random passerby.

If you look down from the revolving blue, bubble-roofed Polaris restaurant atop the Hyatt Regency Hotel in Atlanta, you might see a police car passing by on Peachtree Street. It must give some a secure feeling to know that the policeman inside the car is patrolling to prevent "crime."

But it is that very car that some police administrators say keeps the officer from accomplishing his purpose. Let's try something "new," they say. Take the officer out of the car and put him closer to the public. Let them "pound the beat." How quickly they forget. The reason police were taken off foot patrol and put into cars in the first place was that foot patrol didn't work, either.

You can see the cop on Peachtree well from your perch atop the Regency, but the cop can't see you. And, either you or the cop would need X-ray vision to see someone's room getting ripped off on the 69th floor of the hotel across the street, or to see the bookkeeper doctoring the books and pocketing the company's cash in a 20th-floor office of the building next door.

And what if someone were being murdered in the room just below you? What effect would that officer patrolling the street have on any of these criminal acts? Absolutely none! It wouldn't make any difference if he were walking, flying, riding a horse or standing motionless. Patrol, the primary thrust of police efforts in the prevention of crimes, is helpless against most criminal acts, even those right under its nose—or, as in our example, above its head.

For police patrol to work even in those cases where it would be feasible, conditions must be perfect. The police would have to be at the right place at the right time; their efforts would have to succeed, and the criminals' counter efforts would have to fail.

The problem is, no system to allocate police resources can work because the times and places available for one criminal to act are, for all intents and purposes, infinite. Now multiply infinity by the number of potential criminals, and you will see why policing wouldn't work even with a near-infinite number of resources.

Police preventive patrol is designed around a theory that two elements must be present before a "crime" can be committed: (1) opportunity and (2) desire. O.W. Wilson, a widely recognized chronicler—and practitioner—of American police administration, wrote that conspicuous police patrol would eliminate both of these elements.

Wilson was wrong! First, he overlooked at least one other element that must be present for someone to commit a crime successfully. That is the *means*. The opportunity and desire for men to go to the moon long existed, but no one landed on the moon until someone came up with the means.

Second, I've never seen anyone demonstrate any way—short of chemicals or surgery—to alter anyone's desires. How do you learn to want *not* to want something? Actions might be altered; desires, no.

Third, the assumption that conspicuous patrols diminish the would-be criminal's opportunity is bunk. If anything, conspicuous patrols (even in unmarked police cars—which always look like unmarked police cars) announce when the opportunity to commit crimes is greatest because they are also "conspicuous by their absence." Criminals who have the means and the desire, and who might be deterred by police presence, simply wait for the "conspicuous patrol" to leave, then go on about their business. Others might steal the police car.

To illustrate that police patrol does little to prevent certain crimes, let's look at the Atlanta murders. More victims lived on, were found dead on and disappeared from Memorial Drive than any other single street in Atlanta. Significantly, the police are forced to be on Memorial Drive more often than any other street in the Atlanta area.

The gas pumps where the Atlanta police cars are serviced, as well as the repair facilities, are on Memorial Drive. So is the central headquarters of the Atlanta metropolitan area's second largest police force, the DeKalb County police. This means that most Atlanta and DeKalb police cars are on Memorial Drive at least six times a day. People on many American streets won't see a single police car even once a month. And, if it is too inconvenient for the police, some streets will never see a police car unless one is summoned. On that same Memorial Drive is a State Police post and at least two other Atlanta police facilities, as well as the Georgia State Capitol, with its attendant police presence.

On the 11 other streets closely involved with the "Atlanta murders," there are three other State Patrol facilities and various other Atlanta police facilities, including those dealing with "crime prevention" and the Police Athletic League (PAL), as well as a storage lot for vehicles towed by the police.

A police officer lived next door to 10-year-old Jefferey Mathis, who made The List of Atlanta's "missing and murdered." Another officer lived across the street from the man who would be accused of killing most of the victims on The List, Wayne Williams. That officer once had had Williams assist him by calling headquarters for help in quelling a disturbance.

Ted Bundy, who ranks up there with the most notorious of the mass and serial killers and abusers of women, worked for a rape-prevention program. A recent accused dismemberer in Britain is a former London bobby. Need I say more?

The best the police have ever done is to *displace* crimes. They move them from place to place, from time to time and consequently even from would-be victim to victim. But the end result is always abject failure when it comes to prevention, reduction or eradication of crime problems.

If there is a bright spot in police activities relating to crimes, it's apprehension, which the police too aften confuse with prevention. If you have to apprehend someone, then prevention has, in most instances, already failed.

The problem with counting on apprehension to prevent or control future crimes is that no one knows what to do with the apprehended. Primarily, we warehouse them. When the warehouse gets full, we turn them loose to ply their trade. The premature return of criminals to the streets is an oft-heard and valid complaint of the police.

But even in this area, the police do not do as well as they would have you believe. Their record of apprehensions is greatly inflated by the standard practice of "clearing" cases "by arrest." "Cleared by arrest" means that the "suspect" was not tried and convicted. The suspect might not even have been charged with the crime.

Such is the case in the Atlanta murders, wherein Wayne Williams was arrested, charged, tried and convicted of two murders. But police statistically cleared 22 additional cases. Therefore, they show a clearance rate of 85.8% in the "Atlanta murders," although they made arrests in only 6.9%.

Even with the aid of this kind of statistical wizardry, police clearance rates for major crimes (defined as "Part I" by the FBI Uniform Crime Report) usually average out to between 15 and 20%.

In my experience, only two immutable factors have affected crime rates. These are evolution and demographics. The popularity of the automobile had a profound effect on horse-theft, just as computers will eventually affect robbery. But this is little solace. Just look at the auto-theft rates, and save yourself the pain of trying to imagine what criminals ultimately will do to—and with—computers.

If you want to cloak yourself with instant expertise, preach the demographics of crimes. The age group that is responsible for most of the violent crimes is shrinking in size as a portion of the entire population. The population bulge from the World War II "baby boom" has worked through to middle age. Therefore, the rates of violent crime will fall. And they will continue to fall until the demographics change—no matter what the police do or don't do.

As violent-crime rates fall, a lot of so-called experts will be heaped with praise they don't deserve. Which, in a sense, is all a part of the process of averaging out, since a lot of these same "experts" were criticized when violent-crime rates were going up.

In spite of the plausible-sounding, albeit hackneyed, answers given when asked why "crime" is up—or down—police "experts" really haven't the slightest idea. When asked "why crime is up," they reply, "Crime is up because reporting is better"—or "Crime is up because the courts are tying our hands." You've heard these answers and others like them.

Now that violent-crime rates are going to drop, some naive reporter will ask: "Why is crime down?" I'll bet that not one of these "experts" will say that it is because reporting got worse or the courts untied our hands. Instead, it will be because of the creation of the horse patrol, or the abolition of the horse patrol—whichever they might have just done—or for an equally inane reason.

I recall that an Attorney General of the United States once explained a sudden increase in crime rates by blaming the severely cold winter. I wanted to ask if I could leave my doors unlocked when Atlanta swelters in summer heat. If cold causes crimes, it should follow that heat stops them. This may indicate why the federal system is no better off than the state and local *gendarmes*.

Some of these same "experts" such as George Napper, Atlanta's current public safety commissioner, have said that "poverty causes crime." Have you ever heard of an impoverished Mafioso? Poverty may cause some crimes, sometimes; but even with property crimes, the motivation fluctuates with the moment. Try greed, reward and enjoyment, for a few.

Moreover, in asking "Why?" the media and the "experts" are asking the wrong question. If they could find out, which they cannot, it could only serve to satisfy someone's curiosity. Trying to control crimes by finding out why they happen is like designing a contraceptive on why people have sex. Even if you find out, they'd still be doing it. A better question is "How?"

Take, for instance, the police use of M.O. (*modus operandi*) files. They search them fruitlessly, trying to guess *who* committed a crime. But if they were to study them to find out *how* crimes are committed, they might discover new ways to prevent them.

In March of 1981, Steven Judy was executed in the Indiana State Prison, having been convicted of four murders. One was by strangulation; three by drowning. Half the victims were males. One was an adult; three were children. So much for M.O.

But officials who perpetuate M.O. and other myths merely demonstrate that there is no "body of knowledge" on which to base their so-called profession. The ignorance stems from their predecessors, who trained them in the myths—and now they pass on the misdirection to their successors. They even offer Ph.D.s in alchemies such as "criminology" or "criminal justice." This is why we are served not just by a police force, but a police farce.

Like a football running back who was described as "slow, but easy to tackle," the Atlanta police agency has been inefficient, but it has severe problems, too! Its woes are compounded by a rather recent change in the direction of the flow of racial bigotry from white suppressing black to black suppressing white. "A rose is a rose," a pundit said, and racism is racism, whether expressed in trigger words like "boy" or bureaucratese like "affirmative action." Both portend that someone is about to get the shaft. The Atlanta police were drowning in the lava of a black-white political eruption in 1979.

Atlanta's police suffered from years of poor management. Primarily, it outgrew its small-town organization, which worked only as long as the chief who had grown with it was around. When he retired, it went to hell.

Through the 1960s, Atlanta's police department was tantamount to a kingdom. It was overseen by a benevolent king, Herbert Jenkins. He enjoyed a good reputation and even better national "PR," mostly because of his handling of black-white street confrontations of the 1960s. In 1970, I had invited Chief Jenkins to Kentucky, along with then-soon-to-be FBI Director Clarence Kelley, as keynote speakers for the Kentucky Chiefs of Police Task Force—a group that I chaired.

Herbert Jenkins' successor, John Inman, always looked clean scrubbed. His hair stayed freshly cut, and he dressed impeccably, though not particularly chic. Although my long hairstyle must have irked Inman, he never said so. Toward the end of my stay with the Atlanta police, I noticed that his hair was lapping over the tops of his ears and, although it was silver, it made him look younger.

What Inman inherited was more a hodgepodge of feuding feudal lords. Inman never succeeded in wedding the competing factions, as few police administrators do. If the factions weren't black and white, they would be Democrat and Republican, Masons and Knights of Columbus, or simply "ins" and "outs."

John Inman's rise to power had been accelerated by his relationship with Howard Massell, whose brother, Sam, was elected mayor in 1969. But soon after Howard helped John ascend to the throne, their association soured. This resulted in a broad rift between Inman and Mayor Massell.

Atlanta was an "Impact City," which is another bureaucratic buzzword for how to squander the taxpayers' money.

For whatever reason, Washington was unhappy with progress in Atlanta. Eventually, Mayor Massell entered into an agreement with the Law Enforcement Assistance Administration. LEAA would threaten to pull the $19 million grant, but would refrain from doing so if the mayor would hire a "professional" police administrator (as if there were any such thing). Both sides of the agreement seemed to fit Massell's purposes well. He saw an opportunity to deal with John Inman.

In 1973, I learned that the position of Assistant to the Atlanta Chief of Police was open. I leaped at the opportunity. There were those who warned me away. There have been many times that I wish I had listened.

But, as luck would have it, I became that new Atlanta police administrator. From the standpoint of my police career, it was all bad luck. Unwittingly, I had buried my law-enforcement future in the jungle of the Atlanta police department and the city's zebra politics.

I came from an agency that ran fast, accomplished a lot and wanted to accomplish more. My first mistake was not realizing that I had not transferred that environment along with my family and personal belongings. The Atlanta police agency moved sluggishly and had been dragged about as far toward the

20th Century as it would be with the carrot of federal bucks. My years at APD were spent on a most important facet of my education — learning how *not* to do things.

Before I arrived, the political climate in Atlanta had heated from tepid to torrid. The specter of Maynard Jackson, a black, being elected mayor filled the political horizon. Jackson was soon to be reckoned with in police politics.

The challenge posed by Maynard Jackson relegated the Inman-Massell quarrel to a back burner. Massell wanted to stay on as mayor, and Inman wanted almost anybody but Jackson to be mayor. They became strange bedfellows, the kind politics is said to make often.

My arrival in Atlanta was rather inauspicious. WSB radio did proclaim me "Newsmaker of the Week." A sergeant met me and turned over the keys to a new police car. I was shown my office, which was hardly big enough to turn around in. Foolishly, I started the job as if I were fishing with dynamite in a goldfish bowl.

Meanwhile, John Inman had not endeared himself to the black-power structure. His extensive use of decoy and stakeout tactics, combined with a general hard-line attitude, resulted in a high incidence of shootings by police. The fact that most people shot were black served to support the contentions of both extremes. Blacks saw the high numbers as proof of white-racist attitudes on the part of the police department. The police viewed the same set of facts as proof that blacks committed most of the violent crimes that these tactics were designed to combat.

It also was Inman's habit to establish new positions, even entire new units, without bothering about budgetary niceties. He staffed his new units with persons taken from other units without abolishing their old positions. A continuous game of musical assignments followed as each commander struggled to fill vacancies in his unit.

The results of this organizational chicanery was a police agency with more than 2,000 positions and fewer than 1,750 budgeted bodies, to say nothing of the continuing hole caused by turnover. Of these almost 1,750, at least 200 were underbudgeted as a result of Inman's penchant for promoting people into supervisory positions for which no funds had been allocated.

It would have taken the Wizard of Oz to stretch the people available to fill the positions—provided that he could have found out how many people there were at any given time, let alone where they were presently assigned or even what their rank was. Such information was unconscionably not at your fingertips in the Atlanta police department.

Since no commanders in the APD approached the level of mathematical wizardry, but were repeatedly forced to try their hand at it, the upshot was constant turmoil, ruffled feelings, frustration and abysmal morale on the part of everybody except the most "in" of the "ins."

One of the most interesting Atlanta police units was the "library detail." Its officers didn't, as I'd first thought, chase book crooks. Rather, they looked through a two-way mirror in the library men's room in search of homosexuals. Imagine what they said of their jobs when neighbors asked, "What do you do?"

It was easy for Inman to reward by promotion. Since the money didn't exist to pay the new supervisor and everyone knew it, it didn't cost the city anything.

He or she became an "acting sergeant," or an "acting" whatever, and went about procuring and displaying the outward trappings of the new responsibilities. To be paid accordingly, one had to work up that list until reaching a high-enough slot to be among the few authorized in the budget for that rank.

It sometimes got ridiculous. For instance, W. W. Holley was a lieutenant, an acting captain and an acting major—all at the same time. Holley and everybody else who held an "acting" rank were counted on each roster that listed their names. Thus, when you asked how many "thises" or "thats" there were in the Atlanta police department, things never added up correctly. It was a CPA's nightmare.

How many police did Atlanta have at any given moment? Probably only Gertrude Paisley knew. She had been Herbert Jenkins' secretary and was a holdover in the John Inman regime. There was little choice but to keep her on the job. She was the only person in the whole building who knew the king's system.

Whenever the people in Planning and Research needed a count of police officers in one configuration or another, they had to count noses throughout the entire department, rather than having access to an automatically updated manning chart. This happened at least twice a month.

On the glass wall beside her desk, Gertrude Paisley had taped a sheet of letter-size paper. She neatly divided it with a horizontal pencil line. When an officer left the department, she put a mark above the line (using a slash through four marks for every fifth). When someone was hired, she put a mark below the line.

This was the personnel system in the police department of the "World's Next Great City."

Maynard Jackson had recruited his one-time Morehouse College classmate, A. Reginald Eaves, from Boston to work in his 1973 mayoral campaign. Eaves quickly sensed that police were the No. 1 issue. "Everywhere we went," he said, "the first question people had was, 'What are you going to do about the police?'" Everywhere Eaves went, he spoke to a black-only constituency.

For an Atlanta election, the whopping 68.8% turnout by black voters was the largest ever—by either blacks or whites. Jackson got 95% of those black votes and 17.5% of the white votes—to win with 59.2% overall. At 35, he became the first black mayor of a major Southern city since Reconstruction. I was glad then that Maynard Jackson won.

My personal feelings about Jackson had nothing to do with Inman. But, Jackson moved quickly and decisively by firing John Inman as chief of police. He announced the appointment of Clinton Chafin, a competent, white career police officer, as Inman's replacement. Inman, however, wasn't ready to be replaced. He thought he had the law on his side.

Inman refused to vacate his office, both the title and the physical space. Chafin commandeered my office, which was next door to Inman's. These two offices formed sort of an inner sanctum, separated from the rest of the "chief's office" by a floor-to-ceiling glass partition. Although the glass door in the partition was seldom closed, Gertrude Paisley formed a barrier superior to any hardware.

I had gone to Louisville for the Kentucky Derby. Returning, I found I was the man without a chair. Suddenly, into the office marched a squad of heavily armed police. The officers carried automatic weapons at port arms, with bandoliers of live ammunition slung over their shoulders.

John Inman strode from his office, shouting that he was chief of police. He spoke so excitedly that he chewed his words. But John Inman hadn't been interrupted while eating. Instead, he was locked in his office, impatiently awaiting the arrival of the armed officers.

Inman ordered the storm troopers to remove Clinton Chafin from the "premises," a word which—like "edifice" and "perpetrator"—is a favorite in the Atlanta police argot. You came to expect at least one "premises" per paragraph per report.

Now the offices of the chief of police in Atlanta looked for all the world like a scene from a banana-republic revolution. Bloodshed was not the remotest of possibilities.

Clinton Chafin emerged and proclaimed that he, not Inman, was chief of police. He ordered the armed men to leave. I made a mental note that if there were an election, I'd vote for Chafin. His order for the armed men to leave was the only thing in the shouting match that had made sense so far.

The officers became confused. One long-time supervisor began to cry. Some of the leaders of the armed men filtered into Inman's office. Others plus the entire rank-and-file shuffled away in disarray. Among those entering Inman's office was Major Julian Spence, commander of the SWAT (Special Weapons and Tactics) unit that had paraded its asininity into the outer office only minutes before.

For my part, I telephoned a friend and told him to "send a message to Garcia." Did Atlanta have zero, one, or two chiefs of police? Not knowing who, if anyone, I was assistant to at the moment, and thoroughly disgusted with the entire circus, I went home.

After John Inman's unsuccessful counter-*coup d'etat*, Mayor Jackson went to Fulton County Superior Court, seeking injunctive relief. The mayor was granted an injunction forbidding Inman from interfering with Clinton Chafin in the performance of Chafin's duties as Atlanta's chief of police.

But it was tough to "one-up" John Inman, a gutsy street fighter. Using the private exit from his office to avoid service of a subpoena, he hustled to DeKalb County Superior Court. There, Inman secured an injunction against Mayor Jackson and Clinton Chafin, preventing them from interfering with Inman's performance as chief of police. (Part of Atlanta lies in Fulton County and the rest in DeKalb County.)

Soon after the armed confrontation, Clinton Chafin faded into the background. Inman eventually won the court battle. The law, indeed, was on John Inman's side, but the war wasn't over, as far as Mayor Jackson was concerned.

The mayor's solution was to change labels again. He created a "Department of Public Safety." In this organizational configuration, the police, fire and Civil Defense departments would cease to exist. They would become bureaus reporting to the "Public Safety Commissioner." The title of "chief of police" was to be abolished, and John Inman would be named "Director of Police Services," a title without a job to go with it. A national search for a public safety commissioner began.

As the selection ground inexorably closer, John Inman tried an interesting "end run." He decided to make a mass promotion. It would put him in a "no-lose" position. If the promotions stuck (although Inman privately admitted that he didn't think they would), he could command a lot of new loyalty from below, regardless of who was appointed above him as public safety commissioner. Also, with these promotions, there'd be no room for the new man to promote anybody for years. If the promotions didn't stick, he would still command some loyalty out of appreciation. And, the new man would be disdained by those he demoted.

In the end, Jackson appointed A. Reginald Eaves, then 39, a former prison director in Boston, to the newly created job of Atlanta public safety commissioner. This appointment of the mayor's ex-college chum triggered outcries of indignation and cronyism. I thought the complaints were sour grapes. For many white cops, it wouldn't be easy to take orders from a black. Which is undoubtedly why many left the Atlanta Police Bureau like movie goers scurrying for the exits when somebody yells "Fire!"

Eaves told me—in one of the few personal conversations I ever had with him—that he had once been run out of town by a white cop and that he'd never forgotten it. He vowed that he'd be sure that white cops remembered it, too.

White cops felt that their power was being usurped. Black cops felt that they had for too long been excluded from that power. Both were right, and both were wrong—and never the twain shall meet.

Now I worked for A. Reginald Eaves, a contemporary. "Call me

Commissioner Eaves," he once scolded me when I tried to be friendly and addressed him as "Reggie" like his black peers at City Hall did. Amused at his stern gesture, I thought of myself as "too black for John Inman and too white for Reginald Eaves."

I know that Eaves had no grasp of my capabilities. With John Inman, it had been more a question of his not wanting to be bothered with my ideas when his mind was occupied with more basic problems of survival. I'm sure that Eaves viewed me as an "Inman man"—and a white one, at that.

John Inman was uncharacteristically silent. We all wondered why. At least, I still wonder why. He didn't complain even when Eaves reassigned him from the central headquarters building to a loft-type office in the City Auditorium, several blocks away from where the important decisions were being made.

Inman hung in there for years, drawing his salary and not rocking the boat. Finally, Mayor Jackson ordered that Inman be given something to do. Inman threatened to refuse orders and to go back to court. Instead, he quietly and uncharacteristically retired.

All during Atlanta's murders, I never heard John Inman make a public utterance. It wouldn't surprise me if no one was asking. If nobody was, somebody should have been. In light of Inman's disdain for Mayor Jackson's administration, anything Inman might have said for the record probably would have been interesting and newsworthy.

Eaves' main accomplishment while in office was no small one. He managed to defuse the issue of police brutality that had smouldered for several years in Atlanta's black communities.

Meanwhile, other firestorms swirled around Eaves' office. When a nephew of Eaves was discovered to have been awarded a CETA (Comprehensive Employment/Training Act) job, it stirred charges of nepotism and aroused considerable anger.

A Boston City Councilman also charged Eaves with taking some furnishings from the house that the local government had provided him in Boston. Eaves insisted that he had paid for the furniture.

A. Reginald Eaves didn't keep a low profile. He rode in snazzy cars and surrounded himself with bodyguards and beautiful women. When he came on the scene, he usually was late and with entourage. Reggie Eaves didn't merely make an entrance; he *swept* in. To accusations that his car was loaded with expensive options that cost more than the $3,900 that the city normally allotted for its commissioners' vehicles, Eaves shot back, "I'm giving too much time and effort to this city to try to prove that I'm the good nigger. If I can't ride in a little bit of comfort, to hell with it."

At the same time, Atlanta's bus drivers generally were better paid than its police officers. The drivers had a strong union and were up to their billfolds in federal grant money.

Meanwhile, Eaves fired Atlanta's FOP (Fraternal Order of Police) president, accusing him of lying. I knew that if this kind of action were applied across the board, Atlanta's police bureau would be a lonely place to work—if indeed there was *anybody* left.

One of Eaves' first acts as public safety commissioner was to abolish all "acting" ranks. On the surface, it seemed to be a sound move because there was no budget for the positions, anyway. In truth, however, the purpose and result was to knock down the seniority claims of numerous white male officers, as well as a handful of blacks and women, to promotions. Some had waited for years, having been promised higher pay somewhere down the road. Eaves' action instigated rounds of litigation over hiring and promotions, which led to court-ordered job freezes—all to the benefit of no one.

While John Inman had steadfastly fought the installation of any promotional system for fear it might detract from his flexibility, Reginald Eaves insisted that one be established. Federal "affirmative-action" regulations gave Eaves the tools to form a legally discriminatory system which would favor blacks and serve Eaves' desires very well.

Reginald Eaves kept refining the system until it produced the exact results he wanted. But, in 1978, Eaves was forced from office in the wake of a promotional-exam cheating scandal when some black officers, notably Bill Taylor, blew the whistle on Eaves and other black officers involved.

Eaves was charged with ordering that answers to a 1975 promotional exam be given to 19 black officers to insure their advancement. Bill Taylor, who prepared the exam, had stated that Eaves once told him: "Well, I want these people to score high enough so that I will have no problems promoting them, but you get with Sgt. [Thomas N.] Walton and you work that out. I don't want to know anything about it."

The cheating scandal drove a wedge between Eaves and Mayor Jackson—and it would stand as an epitaph to politics in the Jackson Administration.

Into this storm came Lee P. Brown, Ph.D., or "Doctor Brown," as some Atlanta politicians called him. Brown, 40, was an even-tempered, articulate police administrator from Portland, Oregon, by way of San Jose, California. Like Eaves, Brown was part of a fast-emerging black elite and had limited street experience. But Brown didn't follow Eaves' flamboyant style. He didn't parade in the streets during vice raids, or luxuriate in the trappings of power.

Lee Brown's arrival in Atlanta was another that I personally welcomed at the time. Through Atlanta's murders, I empathized with him because I understood the job of public safety commissioner.

Brown had to rely on the experience of those around him because he lacked that experience himself. Unfortunately, too many of those around him lacked experience, too. Reginald Eaves had seen to that. The result was that Lee Brown never would seem to grasp the "Atlanta murders." He would misunderstand, or be misled, about what happened. And he would remain confused throughout the ordeal, as evidenced by his confused and incorrect testimony for the state in the trial of Wayne Williams.

Much of the gloss of Atlanta's Camelot image had gone by 1979, the year after Lee Brown arrived. Reports of violent crimes (mostly black on black) were changing perceptions of downtown Atlanta for the worse. Underground Atlanta, a once-popular fun zone with gas lanterns and cobblestone streets, was on the verge of shutting down even before construction of a MARTA (Metropolitan Atlanta Rapid Transit Authority) subway line would apply the *coup de grace.*

At 5 p.m. on weekdays, downtown Atlanta now joins a parade of other American cities and becomes a virtual ghost town, with white office workers streaming for the perceived safety of the suburbs. Five years earlier, in 1974, Atlanta's downtown had brimmed with shoppers and visitors until the wee hours.

Atlanta also got unwanted national headlines in 1979 as "Murder Capital, U.S.A." with 231 homicides—the nation's highest per-capita rate. But, if you understand the fallacies in the FBI's Uniform Crime Reporting system, such figures wouldn't deter you from taking a stroll downtown. This homicide comparison, like so many police statistics, is meaningless. On the basis of population density alone, these figures are skewed.

People laughed when comedian Pat Paulsen, in his satirical presidential campaign, promised to cut street crime in half by "building twice as many streets." But annexation had lessened many a city's crime problems and drawn no laughter.

A headline in the *Atlanta Constitution* of July 20, 1983, reads: "Young [Mayor Andrew Young]: Stop talking crime, promote city." In the article, the mayor is quoted as saying that Atlanta's "crime" image "is something that's generated in the fears of people who haven't been downtown and don't really know what's going on in Atlanta."

This is what Mayor Young said for local consumption.

But later, speaking about the Atlanta murders for network news, he sang a somewhat different song:

"Maybe we shouldn't get over it. We should never get over the death of Martin Luther King or Dallas, the assassination of—of . . . [Young's voice quivered ever so slightly] John Kennedy. Maybe we shouldn't get over it, but we'll find a way to go on in spite of it . . ."

What has been going on in downtown Atlanta?

Well, Atlanta's "too busy to hate" image nationally was hurt by the fact that at least two of those "Murder Capital" homicides in 1979 occurred in front of eyewitnesses on busy *downtown* streets. One victim was Dr. Marc Tetalman, 35, a white Ohio State University nuclear-medicine specialist, who was in Atlanta for a convention.

But Marc Tetalman's death never would appear on a list (still another list) of unsolved killings that the Atlanta City Council's Public Safety Committee would request—and receive—from Lee Brown in the summer of 1981. Amazingly, Brown had accepted the list and passed it on, despite this glaring omission. Tetalman's murder remains unsolved, although some police officers think his killer himself was killed in a drug shootout.

During that fateful summer of 1979, Georgia's governor ordered state troopers into Atlanta's streets to help the embattled Atlanta police. A tire dealer, J.K. Ramey, put up a controversial billboard: "WARNING...You are now in the City of Atlanta, where the police are underequipped, undermanned and underpaid. Proceed at your own risk."

Soon after the Georgia State Patrol officers were removed from the city, Patricia Barry walked north on Peachtree Street with another young woman. It was October 13, 1979, a bright Indian-summer day—and Patricia's 26th birthday. Suddenly a black man emerged, brandishing an automatic pistol he'd purchased in an Atlanta pawnshop. According to police, the man fired the handgun, killing Patricia, and then shot and killed himself. Police said Patricia apparently didn't know the gunman, who had just been released from a New Jersey prison psychiatric hospital.

That this human time bomb went off in Atlanta, rather than New Jersey, New York or anywhere else, is an accident of fate and shows how our criminal-justice system simply displaced another crime. Public officials like Andrew Young would prefer that we stop talking about these problems. But that won't make them go away. What we must do is stop singling out certain cities as better or worse when it comes to problems of crime. They're all about the same—rotten!

Patricia Barry was a white secretary who had worked in the law offices of former Georgia Governor Carl Sanders, one of Atlanta's most powerful movers and shakers. Sanders, outraged by the killing, called a news conference and sniped at Mayor Jackson's administration. He demanded "less jawbone and more backbone" in law enforcement.

Among those experienced Atlanta police officers who bailed out was Clinton Chafin, who became chief of police for Fulton County. In fact, the entire Fulton County police department had defected from the Atlanta police force. Before the Fulton County police department was formed in 1974 (which, not coincidentally, corresponded with the arrival of A. Reginald Eaves), the unincorporated areas of Fulton County were policed under contract by a contingent of the Atlanta police department.

When Fulton County's police became an independent department, Atlanta's police force shrank from about 1,750 persons to about 1,350. But more important, the ratio of black to white officers soared in Atlanta because most of Fulton County's officers were whites who left the Atlanta police.

Another refugee from Atlanta's force was W.K. (Jack) Perry, who was as able a homicide investigator as could be found anywhere. During the last days of July of 1979, Perry, a long-time commander of the Atlanta police homicide squad, took an early retirement. He also took a parting shot at Atlanta's political administration. He complained that "too many murders, not enough investigators and the wrong set of priorities weren't going to let things get any better."

Jack Perry had turned in his resignation to Mike Edwards, who then was deputy director in charge of criminal investigations. Mike was a confidant of Atlanta's first black chief of police, George Napper, another Ph.D. in criminology (the title of chief of police was re-established after Inman retired and Napper took over). Mike Edwards and George Napper shared an interest in the academic side of criminal justice, but Mike offered something that Napper didn't have—practical experience.

Back in 1979, Mike Edwards was on the spot. He was the glue that tried to hold together a rare mosaic—Atlanta's *nouveau*-powerful black police administration and her street-scarred white cops, who for years had toiled in the trenches of reality.

It was a combustible mixture—something America hadn't seen in a major city in more than 200 years. But here it was in Atlanta—on the last week in July, 1979.

Billboard shouts Atlantans' complaints about their police in the summer of 1979. Meanwhile, children's bodies were being found. But police would deny that a problem existed until almost one year later. By then, at least 17 children had been murdered. (George Clark/Atlanta Constitution)

2

Police Science Applied

Did you ever notice how the Good Guys seemingly always win on those shoot-'em-up TV shows like *Starsky and Hutch, Today's FBI* and *Quincy*?

On television, you see America's criminal-justice game played the way its players hope you'll think it's played. But if you followed Atlanta's multiple-murder story—and the events which led to the conviction of Wayne Williams for two of those murders—you saw how the game is actually played: Badly!

Any resemblance between police work on TV dramas and in the real world is purely coincidental. The Atlanta killings became one of the least told and understood stories of my lifetime, contrary to the belief of the late best-selling author, Thomas (Tommy) Thompson, who wrote that these cases had been "steamrollered" by the news media.

TV cops may solve one or two armed robberies per hour. Quick mathematics indicate that police officers in the United States solve an armed robbery on the average of once every four years. *Hawaii Five-O* always relies on the computer and the lab. In 1972, the Midwest Research Institute conducted a study of laboratory usage by Kentucky police and discovered that a Kentucky police officer sent evidence of any kind to any lab anywhere on the average of once every 50 years.

The Atlanta story, for one, became a tragedy of errors, to wit:

—A Fulton County prosecutor convinced a judge to drop charges in the August, 1980, murder of a 16-year-old girl, alleging that the Atlanta police had, among other things, lost the case file and the evidence, which had been stapled to the file. When asked by a reporter how such a mistake could happen, the prosecutor shrugged and said, "Keystone Cops."

(Then-Atlanta Public Safety Commissioner Lee Brown denied in 1981 that the file had been lost.)

—Investigators, in removing skeletal remains from the scene where two victims had been found in January of 1981, didn't notice other remains, including teeth, at the scene. This angered Fulton County medical examiners, who publicly criticized the investigators and threatened to prosecute them for disturbing the crime scene. Today, the mother of one of those two victims doubts that the victim is her child. She believes that the medical examiner has incorrectly identified the remains as those of her 11-year-old son.

—The death of 21-year-old Jimmy Ray Payne—one of two charged to Wayne Williams in July of 1981—had *not* been ruled a murder when Williams was indicted for murdering him. When a reporter asked about it, the medical examiner changed the cause of death on the death certificate from "undetermined" to "homicide." The reporter said the examiner told her that he had "checked the wrong box" on the death certificate. He would later tell that same story under oath in the Wayne Williams trial. But how can one check the wrong box on a form that doesn't have a box to check? The word "undetermined" had been typewritten onto the death certificate.

—Other victims' mothers have valid reasons to believe that the wrong bodies were buried in their children's graves. One mother said that authorities told her in October of 1980 that a body that had been buried as a "John Doe" two months earlier was actually that of her teen-age son. The medical examiner also would repeat this statement under oath, but an *Atlanta Constitution* reporter had told me in October of 1980 that she had been told by the medical examiner that "the body is still in the morgue."

—Nearly three months after a 16-year-old boy was found dead and was buried, Atlanta police went to the boy's home to try to arrest him!

—At the height of the murders, Atlanta detectives swarmed over the apartment of a young black woman. They looked for clues as to who might have murdered her. At the same time, they had another missing-child case: the woman's baby was missing. Police broadcast their famous "APBs" (all-points bulletins), but there was no trace of the child for 48 hours . . .

Until . . .

Until the baby's grandmother reopened the apartment for the first time since the police had left. She found the infant's body under the pillow of a couch in the room next to the mother's murder scene. The baby had been smothered to death and had been there all along. Police explained that the adjoining room "wasn't part of the crime scene" to be searched.

As Atlanta's mystery deepened, I learned that it was far worse—in numbers—than our public officials were telling us. More victims were *not* (but should have been) part of the official investigation and body count—or, were *not* on "The List"—than were on it.

The List, which consisted only of cases assigned to a special police Task Force that had been formed amid community pressure in July of 1980, ended

DECEDENT'S NAME: JIMMY RAY PAYNE | SEX: Male | DATE OF DEATH: April 27,1981

RACE: Black | ORIGIN OF DECEDENT: American | DATE OF BIRTH: Sept. 1,1959 | AGE: 21 | COUNTY OF DEATH: Fulton

CITY, TOWN or LOCATION OF DEATH: Atlanta | HOSPITAL OR OTHER INSTITUTION NAME: Grady Memorial Hospital | DOA

STATE OF BIRTH: Alabama | CITIZEN OF WHAT COUNTRY: USA | MARRIED, NEVER MARRIED, WIDOWED, DIVORCED: Never Married | SPOUSE: None | WAS DECEDENT EVER IN U.S. ARMED FORCES: No

SOCIAL SECURITY NUMBER: Unknown | USUAL OCCUPATION: None | KIND OF INDUSTRY OR BUSINESS: None

RESIDENCE—STATE: Ga. | COUNTY: Dekalb | CITY, TOWN or LOCATION: Decatur | STREET AND NUMBER: 1840 Hillsdale Dr. | INSIDE CITY LIMITS: Yes

FATHER'S NAME: John Henry Payne | MOTHER'S MAIDEN NAME: Ruby Nell Jones

INFORMANT'S NAME: Ruby Nell Jones | MAILING ADDRESS: 1840 Hillsdale Dr.,Decatur,Ga. | RELATIONSHIP: Mother

BURIAL, CREMATION, REMOVAL: Burial | DISPOSITION DATE: May 2,1981 | CEMETERY OR CREMATORY NAME: Kennedy Memorial | LOCATION: Ellenwood, Dekalb, Ga.

FUNERAL SERVICE LICENSEE: Raleigh Rucker | ESTAB. LICENSE NO.: 719 | NAME AND ADDRESS OF FACILITY: Raleigh Rucker Funeral Home, 341 Candler Rd. S.E., Atlanta, Ga.

EMBALMER: [signature] | EMBALMER LICENSE NO.: 1993

PART I. IMMEDIATE CAUSE: ASPHYXIA

Due to, or as a consequence of: UNDETERMINED MECHANISM

PART II. OTHER SIGNIFICANT CONDITIONS | AUTOPSY: Yes | IF YES, WERE FINDINGS CONSIDERED IN DETERMINING CAUSE OF DEATH: Yes

WAS OPERATION PERFORMED | DATE OF OPERATION | CONDITIONS FOR WHICH OPERATION WAS PERFORMED

ACCIDENT, SUICIDE, HOMICIDE, UNDETERMINED: Undetermined | DATE OF INJURY: Unknown | DESCRIBE HOW INJURY OCCURRED: Unknown | HOUR OF INJURY: Unknown

PLACE OF INJURY: Unknown | LOCATION: FOUND Chattahoochee River between 285 & Buckhead Atlanta, Ga. Fulton

DATE SIGNED: June 16,1981 | HOUR OF DEATH: Unknown | PRONOUNCED DEAD AT 7:00 P.M.

NAME AND TITLE OF CERTIFIER: SALEH A. ZAKI,M.D.,MEDICAL EXAMINER | ADDRESS OF CERTIFIER: 50 Coca Cola Place,S.E. Atlanta, Ga 30303

CERTIFICATE OF DEATH/STATE OF GEORGIA

DECEDENT'S NAME: JIMMY RAY PAYNE | SEX: Male | DATE OF DEATH: April 27,1 Found

RACE: Black | ORIGIN OF DECEDENT: American | DATE OF BIRTH: Sept. 1,1959 | AGE: 21 | COUNTY OF DEATH: Fulton

CITY, TOWN or LOCATION OF DEATH: Atlanta | HOSPITAL OR OTHER INSTITUTION NAME: Grady Memorial Hospital | DOA

STATE OF BIRTH: Alabama | CITIZEN OF WHAT COUNTRY: USA | MARRIED, NEVER MARRIED, WIDOWED, DIVORCED: Never Married | SPOUSE: None | WAS DECEDENT EVER IN U.S. ARMED FORCES: No

SOCIAL SECURITY NUMBER: Unknown | USUAL OCCUPATION: None | KIND OF INDUSTRY OR BUSINESS: None

RESIDENCE—STATE: Georgia | COUNTY: Dekalb | CITY, TOWN or LOCATION: Decatur | STREET AND NUMBER: 1840 Hillsdale Dr. | INSIDE CITY LIMITS: Yes

FATHER'S NAME: John Henry Payne | MOTHER'S MAIDEN NAME: Ruby Nell Jones

INFORMANT'S NAME: Ruby Nell Jones | MAILING ADDRESS: 1840 Hillsdale Dr., Decatur, Ga. | RELATIONSHIP: Mother

BURIAL, CREMATION, REMOVAL: Burial | DISPOSITION DATE: May 2,1981 | CEMETERY OR CREMATORY NAME: Kennedy Memorial | LOCATION: Ellenwood, Dekalb, Ga.

FUNERAL SERVICE LICENSEE: Raleigh Rucker | ESTAB. LICENSE NO.: 719 | NAME AND ADDRESS OF FACILITY: Raleigh Rucker Funeral Home, 341 Candler Rd. S.E., Atlanta, Ga.

EMBALMER: [signature] | EMBALMER LICENSE NO.: 1993

PART I. IMMEDIATE CAUSE: ASPHYXIA

Due to, or as a consequence of: UNDETERMINED MECHANISM

PART II. OTHER SIGNIFICANT CONDITIONS | AUTOPSY: Yes | IF YES, WERE FINDINGS CONSIDERED IN DETERMINING CAUSE OF DEATH: Yes

WAS OPERATION PERFORMED | DATE OF OPERATION | CONDITIONS FOR WHICH OPERATION WAS PERFORMED

ACCIDENT, SUICIDE, HOMICIDE, UNDETERMINED: Homicide | DATE OF INJURY: Unknown | DESCRIBE HOW INJURY OCCURRED: Unknown | HOUR OF INJURY: Unknown

PLACE OF INJURY: Unknown | LOCATION: Found Chattahoochee River, 285 & Buckhead Atlanta, Ga. Fulton

Saleh A. Zaki M.D.

DATE SIGNED: August 6, 1981 | HOUR OF DEATH: Unknown | PRONOUNCED DEAD ON April 27,1981 AT 7:00 P.M.

NAME AND TITLE OF CERTIFIER: Saleh A. Zaki,M.D.,Medical Examiner | ADDRESS OF CERTIFIER: 50 Coca Cola Place,S.E. Atlanta,Ga. 30303

First, the medical examiner ruled Jimmy Ray Payne's cause of death as "undetermined" (see left circle, top illustration), but Wayne Williams was indicted for Payne's "murder." Then a reporter who had been alerted by Chet Detlinger to look for non-homicidal causes of death asked the medical examiner about the discrepancy. The medical examiner changed the death certificate to show "homicide" (left circle, bottom illustration).

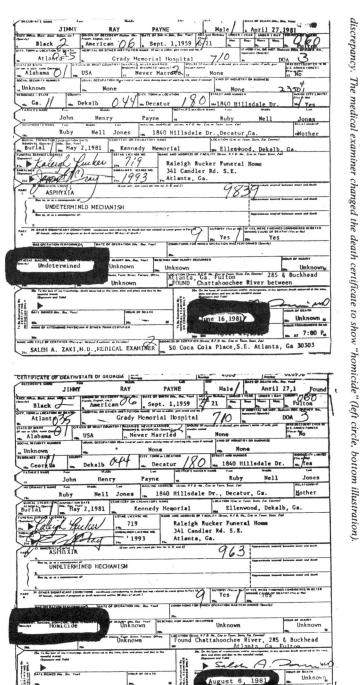

with 28 slain victims, plus 10-year-old Darron Glass (missing since September of 1980). The prosecution added a 29th murder case at the trial of Wayne Williams—that of 28-year-old John Porter. But that excludes at least *63 more* unsolved Atlanta-area killings of blacks who fit the arbitrary age, sex, race and cause-of-death parameters that the authorities used for The List.

Meanwhile, after Wayne Williams was jailed in June of 1981, the authorities simply stopped counting and adding names to The List. The Atlanta police-FBI Uniform Crime Report tabulations show seven unsolved killings of blacks—ages 15 to 25—in Atlanta's city limits from July through December of 1981 while Williams was in jail.

The FBI report also shows an additional 15 black victims (ages 13 to 28) of unsolved killings in Atlanta for all of 1982 and the first quarter of 1983. The youngest victim, a 13-year-old girl named Lucretia Bell, was found in her bedroom in March of 1983, a victim of "asphyxiation by strangulation." The story never made the local papers.

As recently as August of 1983, the Atlanta newspapers downplayed the discovery of skeletal remains of a male, about 600 feet off Cascade Road in southwest Atlanta, not far from where the remains identified as those of 10-year-old Jefferey Mathis were found in the winter of 1981. Also, in August of 1983, the body of a male was pulled from the Chattahoochee River (the same waterway that yielded six victims in 1980 and 1981). The victim was presumed to have drowned—a cause of death that the medical examiner had said under oath in 1982 that he could not rule out in the death of 21-year-old Jimmy Ray Payne.

Remember, these additional killings in the FBI report are recorded within the city limits of Atlanta. Slightly more than half the victims on The List were found outside Atlanta's boundaries.

Even so, the body counts by Atlanta's police—even in this day of push-button computers—remain so confusing that many people give up trying to straighten them out. It's all enough to make one cry out, "Can't anybody count?"

Today, nobody knows for sure whether Atlanta's killings are the work of a multiple murderer, or more than one killer, or a combination. One reason nobody knows is that we may never know whether victims not on The List had fibers on them to match those of victims on The List. Is the Georgia crime lab looking for fibers from these additional victims to match those fibers from Williams' house and cars? Later, we would get an opportunity to ask that question of Larry Peterson, the state crime lab's fiber analyst.

Wayne Williams was convicted on February 27, 1982, of two murders on The List. Then 22 more murders were blamed on him ("cleared by arrest" is the standard term used by police, who do it all the time) without benefit of a trial. These 22 additional slayings include a 13-year-old boy's strangulation, in which the police had five eyewitnesses point to a black male suspect. But police made no arrest in the case.

It's important to keep in mind, too, that all those cases which were not put on The List—an alarming number, to be sure—don't come close to adding up to all unsolved murders in the Atlanta area. They merely fit the fluid parameters of The List—parameters that the authorities themselves established and changed with no logic.

Using these police parameters, then, it's impossible to say whether Atlanta's murders stopped—that is, unless you first ask, "*Which* murders?" The truth is, unsolved murders of young blacks—or whites, for that matter—never stop. The problem is, few of us give a damn unless they're hyped by the press.

When I discovered that many victims both on and off The List lived near—and knew—each other, it was clear that these killings were *not* random, no matter how much our public officials tried to tell us otherwise. I made this discovery as early as November of 1980, when Patrick (Pat Man) Rogers disappeared.

Our first priority, I suggested to anyone who would listen, should be to know everything possible about the *victims,* rather than just look for *suspects.*

My sidekick, Mike Edwards, and I were rebuffed at every turn. The victimology was essentially ignored. Lee Brown and others leading the investigation insisted that the cases were not connected—personally, geographically, or any other way.

Yet even as these officials intensified police patrols and poured more manpower, computers, millions of taxpayers' dollars and other resources into the investigation—and even as the City Council imposed curfews—Atlanta's killings did not stop. Rather, the frequency of the killings escalated.

During the height of the killings, I found a 15-year-old boy *alive* in Florida, in one day, after the authorities had searched in vain for him for 30 days.

For all these voluntary efforts at citizenship, I suffered perhaps the ultimate humility: I was called in by the Atlanta police as a *suspect* in the killings in April of 1981, one month before Wayne Williams was stopped and questioned the first time, and then released. But much of my ego was salvaged three months later, in July: I accepted the FBI's invitation to brief two out-of-state educators on the cases as a paid *expert*!

What happened with the system in Atlanta is not unique. You're likely to find it doing a pratfall in Any Town, U.S.A., whether it's New York, Chicago, Los Angeles, Pocatello or Sheboygan.

Instead of being literate, clever, thorough, scientific, relentless and righteous, our criminal-justice system is illogical, inept, corrupt, mired in superstition and myth, reliant on luck and far more dedicated to covering up its mistakes and shortcomings than protecting our freedom.

We pat the system on the back when it stumbles onto a suspect who may have murdered 30 or more persons. We fail to see the truth that the system failed when the first victim was slain. How many murders are too many?

Atlanta's police leaders could have had Wayne Williams as a suspect as early as November of 1980, more than half a year before he was arrested. But they didn't because they stubbornly refused to look closely at the disappearance of 16-year-old Patrick (Pat Man) Rogers that same month, November of 1980.

These same police officials ultimately were rewarded in 1982, not long after the ink on the "Wayne Williams Guilty" headlines had dried: Public Safety Commissioner Lee Brown departed to take a $75,000-a-year job as Houston's chief of police; Chief of Police George Napper (who, interestingly, had been taken *off* the murder investigations) was appointed public safety commissioner by Atlanta's new mayor, Andrew Young, who also promoted Task Force commander Morris Redding to chief of police.

All but forgotten was the fact that at least 13 black children and adults had turned up dead—and were added to The List—between November of 1980 (when Patrick Rogers vanished from the Thomasville Heights neighborhood) and May of 1981 (when Wayne Williams was stopped near a Chattahoochee River bridge). If Williams is guilty, they need not have died!

Patrick Rogers disappeared after telling a friend's mother that he had found a music promoter who was going to help him and Junior Harper, the friend, make it big in the music business. This could be the show-business break they'd been dreaming about.

That promoter's telephone number was on handbills that had been circulated in the fall of 1980 in Thomasville Heights, according to witnesses interviewed by newsmen and the FBI many months later. The promoter's name: Wayne Williams.

In any event, nobody in authority apparently knew about Wayne Williams in November of 1980 because nobody on the Task Force was asking about Pat Man or his dead little neighbor and companion, 10-year-old Aaron Wyche. Both victims had not been put on The List.

What emerges, then, is a story of three American institutions—the police, the courts and the press. What the police and the press did *not* do during the height of the slayings—the questions they did *not* ask and the professional responsibility they neglected—severely narrowed the world's perception of what really happened in Atlanta. The court system performed no better.

It remains a story of lingering misconceptions, fed by manipulation of the media. Even today, Wayne Williams is almost universally perceived as the convicted Atlanta "*child* killer," even though he was found guilty of killing two *adults*—Nathaniel Cater, 27, and Jimmy Ray Payne, 21, both convicted felons. These hardly are children, by my definition.

More important, and contrary to popular belief, Atlanta's murders did *not* stop with the arrest of Wayne Williams in June of 1981. The police stopped counting, and the press stopped reporting. Few have noted that the last child killing on The List occurred sometime in March of 1981 (the disappearance date was March 13, 1981). This was a full three months *before* Wayne Williams went to jail.

Who else went to jail during that time? Who left town, died, or was otherwise incapacitated? There were other multiple-murder suspects convicted in Atlanta during 1981. James Walraven, a 31-year-old white former tennis instructor, was accused of three so-called "bathtub murders" of young white women. He was tried for one and convicted; then his conviction was overturned by the Georgia Supreme Court because of a trial error by the judge. Walraven was retried and found guilty in September of 1983.

In addition, a male suspect admitted killing three young women, all of whom had been found dead in locations near those where victims who were on The List had been found. None of these young women made The List.

As it was, most journalists were—and still are—mesmerized by The List of 28 murder victims, even though it should have been plain that these deaths were being arbitrarily assigned to the Task Force investigation without any valid parameters. As a consequence, nearly everybody was blinded to the myriad other unsolved-murder victims who never made anybody's list.

Thus, we were observing the folly of hordes of reporters from Atlanta and around the world, reduced to waiting for the police to tell them who was, in effect, "officially" and "unofficially" murdered.

One of those adults who didn't make The List was a 21-year-old black male who was shot and killed in July of 1981, the month *after* Wayne Williams was jailed. The cause of death was the same as that of victim No. 1 on The List. But it was too late for his case to make The List because, after all, Wayne Williams was no longer on the streets. The victim couldn't possibly be connected to any of those on The List, right?

Wrong! Lo and behold, the victim was a 21-year-old uncle of (and shared an apartment with) a 13-year-old boy found slain before Williams' arrest and who made The List. Nobody knew about the 21-year-old because nobody was asking.

If the Atlanta story was an American tragedy, it also played in a theater of the absurd. It was a traveling road show by some victims' mothers, who raised tens of thousands of dollars while raising the eyebrows of skeptics who still wonder where all the money went. It was big-city power politics by a mayor who urgently appealed for—and got—$4.2 million for Atlanta from the Reagan Administration. It was a news media merry-go-round of death scenes, green ribbons, psychics, red-beret-clad Guardian Angels from New York's subways, a $250,000 Frank Sinatra-Sammy Davis Jr. benefit concert (proceeds going to the investigation), a self-proclaimed preacher accused of fraudulently soliciting funds in a clown suit, and an oil company donating $58,000 worth of "Save Our Children" trash-bin posters inscribed: "Chevron cares!"

America has never seen anything like it. In Chicago, nobody was forewarned of any multiple murders until the bodies of at least 28 of John Wayne Gacy's 33 or more male victims—all young and white—were found beneath Gacy's house. In Houston, the "Candy Man" slayings of 27 boys and young men—and the unearthing of their bodies—did not come to light until after a teen-age boy told police he had shot and killed their murderer after a quarrel.

Atlanta's nightmare, by contrast, unfolded body by body on the front pages in 1980 as a mystery. But there seemed to be no mystery whatsoever, behind the scenes, about the killing of one teen-age boy. Atlanta police, documents show, had a suspect and five eyewitnesses in the strangulation of 13-year-old Clifford Jones, a black male visitor from Cleveland, who disappeared on August 20, 1980; was found the next morning, and made The List.

One eyewitness told police that the suspect, a black male, molested Jones sexually, then strangled him with a yellow rope and said, "He's dead." (Jones was one of the few victims on The List who was strangled with a rope.) The suspect then washed the body with a rag and soap, and then clothed it, the eyewitness said.

Two other eyewitnesses said they saw someone deposit a large item wrapped in plastic beside a trash dumpster near a laundromat, and then make a telephone call. The police (who later said they responded after receiving an anonymous telephone call) arrived to find a body wrapped in plastic. It later was identified as the body of Clifford Jones.

Oddly, the police never arrested the suspect, or anybody else, in Clifford Jones' death, citing what they called insufficient evidence. The suspect was *not* Wayne Williams.

Yet today, Clifford Jones' case is officially closed, and his death is charged to, of all people, Wayne Williams! It is one of those 22 additional slayings formally charged to Williams without a trial.

As bodies turned up week after week in 1980 and 1981, mostly in wooded areas and open lots (and only a handful in or near rivers), the terror crescendoed. As Atlanta's mayor and City Council imposed curfews and ordered citywide door-to-door canvassing for tips or clues, children all over the city were reported having nightmares, wetting beds and sleeping fitfully (sometimes with lights on). Most of this anguish could have been averted, if only these same officials had acknowledged that there were personal and geographic links among the victims and that the pattern was emerging on or near only 12 major connecting streets—not citywide.

Again and again, the masses were reminded in the media that Atlanta's police, the FBI and other agencies were absolutely baffled about these cases, but were leaving "no stone unturned." They were told that there were no clues, motives or suspects for nearly two years—and God only knows how long before that. Police investigators kept their lips sealed like steel traps—except when some information apparently was leaked selectively to the news media, which often attributed the leaks to "sources close to the investigation."

Money became an issue in Atlanta. While some victims' mothers, con men and fast-buck artists raised thousands of dollars, then-Mayor Jackson sat at a table covered with stacks of money announced as a $100,000 reward fund. On television spots, the mayor appealed for Atlantans to come forward with tips. He vowed that the reward would "shake the trees." As it was, the leaves didn't even rustle. Not one acorn fell.

At the same time, Jackson took the unusual step of persuading Washington to help finance a local murder investigation. The city was running out of money to pay overtime and other mounting investigative costs, the mayor said early in 1981. (In fact, the city had sufficient funds to subsidize the investigation until June 1, 1981, a city finance official said in the spring of 1981.)

Perhaps a hint of the investigative bungling that was to come surfaced when Atlanta's probe began in the summer of 1980. It started with an illiterate document that was undated, unaddressed, unsigned and inaccurate. It had been culled, in part, from information that was abysmally flawed.

It is commonly believed that the police are aware of names of all murder victims within their purview. Not so. When a reporter asked Public Safety Commissioner Lee Brown about investigations into the slayings of two teen-age Atlanta girls, their names meant nothing to him and he seemed unfamiliar with the cases. "You'll have to refresh me on that," he said.

Not only did the police not know the names of the victims, they could not compile a list that made sense. The common perception is that the mere touch of buttons on a whiz-bang computer will result in—*voila!*—printouts of murder victims in every imaginable configuration. Not so.

In 1981, for example, researchers for the *Los Angeles Times* learned that some U.S. cities keep poor statistics, if they keep any at all. In New York, the police department had not kept up-to-date records for four years because of "staff cutbacks." And when homicides were recorded, they weren't broken down by race or age. In Boston, statistics didn't indicate the victims' ages. In Los Angeles city and county, no racial figures or age breakdowns of unsolved murders were available.

The original document for Atlanta's investigation listed five murdered and three missing children. Hindsight tells us that there were at least 17 murdered children when the Task Force was organized in July of 1980. And common sense tells us that there were at least 50 times as many missing children in Metropolitan Atlanta during that same month.

The name of every traffic violator can be obtained in seconds. Missing cars are in computer banks. Missing children were not even considered in earnest until early 1983. What priorities!

Even the investigation's working premise as to when Atlanta's murders began—July 25, 1979—is arbitrary. Someone evidently asked for a report on missing and murdered children over the previous year. The report, which was written in late July of 1980, begins: "Over the past 12 months . . ." Any novice statistician would have selected a period such as a fiscal year for which comparison data might be available. Not our scientific police system.

To say that Atlanta's investigation was sloppy is putting it charitably. Leads were not pursued. Claimed eyewitness accounts of murders were dismissed out of hand. Discretion was upside down, with police *recruits*—not experienced officers—deciding what information should be passed on to investigators.

In at least two cases, eyewitnesses who knew the victims said they saw the victims get into vehicles with "two males." Yet when the cases were closed in the wake of Wayne Williams' conviction, Lee Brown told reporters that there is "absolutely no evidence" that more than one person was involved.

If anything bogged down the investigation (and blocked the public's understanding of Atlanta's murders), it was The List. When Lee Brown compiled a list of "missing and murdered children," he put some victims on it—and left others off—at his whim. Certainly it was Brown's prerogative to assign any cases he saw fit to the Task Force for investigation, but to do so arbitrarily, without valid parameters, created a distorted picture of Atlanta's crisis. The only constant parameter of The List was race. But that ignored the fact that white kids and adults, too, are murdered in Atlanta.

As the death toll climbed, other parameters used by the police were in flux. Brown insisted that the cases on The List were not connected. But he often explained why a certain victim was not placed on The List by saying that the victim's case was "not connected" to the cases on The List (which he also said were not connected to each other). What logic!

And when the parameters did change, no effort was made to reconsider cases which already had been scrapped, but now would fit.

Faye Yearby, for example, was found dead in January of 1981, tied to a tree and her hands bound. But she never made The List because:

—She was, at 22, too old (however, when the authorities stopped adding names to The List after Williams' arrest in June of 1981, the oldest victim on The List was 27).

—Yearby was a female (but so were 7-year-old LaTonya Wilson and 12-year-old Angel Lenair, who had been slain and were on The List when Yearby was found).

Yearby was stabbed (but so were Anthony Carter, Eric Middlebrooks, William Barrett and John Porter). Carter and Middlebrooks were on The List when Yearby died. Barrett, 17, was added later. Porter, 28, was added during the Wayne Williams trial.

In fairness to the news media, some reporters turned up information that the police didn't. A few also persistently challenged the validity of The List. Mostly, however, reporters allowed themselves to be led, misled and spoon-fed information that police and public officials don't understand to this day.

And sometimes the information was made public without qualification, even if it happened to be wrong.

As Atlanta's tragedy intensified, the work of local forensic scientists seemed right out of an episode on *M*A*S*H,* rather than *Quincy*. Medical examiners made questionable identifications of victims despite protests by mothers who swore that the remains identified as those of their children were, in fact, not their children.

The cause of death for many victims was unknown. The word "unknown" was later dropped in favor of "probable asphyxia" when it became clear that no one could be convicted of a murder that medical examiners could not say had happened. If "asphyxia" means that one stops breathing, does "probable asphyxia" mean that one "probably stopped breathing"? And don't we all die when we stop breathing?

The List, along with impeding the investigation, controlled hundreds of thousands of dollars pouring into Atlanta. Only the 28 murders that eventually wound up on The List would apply to the reward money, which had grown to $500,000 with a pledge by former heavyweight champion Muhammad Ali. Which meant that anyone who might solve, say, Cynthia Montgomery's or Faye Yearby's murder would not be eligible for even a penny. All because they never made The List.

For those victims who did make The List, it also meant that their families were eligible to participate in the huge sums of money donated by caring people all over the world. The upshot was that families of adults who were convicted felons who made The List (Jimmy Ray Payne, 21; Nathaniel Cater, 27, and Michael McIntosh, 23) could share in contributions that had been raised for "children."

The families of other murdered children in Atlanta still scrimp to rear five or six siblings in roach-infested apartments without help from anyone. These families' children are not "officially" murdered—just dead at the hands of an unknown killer or killers.

3

Almost Nobody Noticed

On July 28, 1979, a woman walked along Niskey Lake Road in southwest Atlanta. Her eyes scanned the road shoulder and the kudzu-clad slope that dropped sharply from the roadside to form a wooded ravine. She looked for redeemable bottles, cans and anything else of value. What she found was astounding, and it confounded the combined forces of the FBI, the Georgia Bureau of Investigation and a multitude of local police agencies.

First, the woman saw a human leg. Vines had caught it at the ankle and prevented the body from slipping down the embankment. It was the body of a teen-age boy.

And so begins this story that is told unlike those of most other multiple-murder cases, which focus almost exclusively on who is—or is presumed to be—the killer or killers. This is a story in which hordes of *victims*—and their inter-personal relationships—will upstage the handful of suspects the police turn up.

Mike Edwards had worked for me as a major in charge of Planning and Research during my stint with the Atlanta police. Our association had a rocky beginning. I liked Mike, but I doubt that the feeling was mutual back then.

Eventually, my working relationship with Mike Edwards grew into a friendship. It solidified when Mike left his promising career with the Atlanta police to take a public stand against what he viewed as corruption in the police agency.

But little did he know in July of 1979, as he reviewed his investigators' gruesome findings of murders on Niskey Lake Road, that he and I would walk down that same road one year later—two ex-cops trying to convince our erstwhile compatriots that they had a problem they apparently didn't want to see.

Mike told me that investigators found the body of a young black male who had been shot with a .22-caliber weapon. The body was dressed entirely in black. After the body was removed, death's acrid smell lingered. Less than a football field away, they found the body of another young victim, also dressed in black. There was no obvious cause of death for the second body.

A missing-persons report had been filed on a 14-year-old boy, Edward Hope Smith—"Teddy" to his friends. Smith lived within walking distance of Niskey Lake Road.

Another boy was missing at that time. Alfred Evans, 14, was from another part of town. His brand of basketball was more advanced than that of Patrick (Pat Man) Rogers. When Alfred played, it wasn't as easy to win—or steal—the championship because there were referees in striped shirts and a scorekeeper at the East Lake Meadows Community Center. And the cheering crowds were not entirely imaginary.

Another star of the East Lake Meadows neighborhood was "Billy Star," the alias or "street name" for William Barrett. He tried out for the East Lake Meadows team, but didn't make it. By age 17, he joined another team, the Georgia DOR (Department of Offender Rehabilitation). "Billy Star" was a youthful offender, convicted of a felony and incarcerated at a Georgia youthful offender facility. Although he didn't make the roster with Alfred at East Lake Meadows, he would join Alfred on The List of Atlanta's missing and murdered.

Like "Pat Man," Alfred Evans went to martial-arts movies. Now it was July 25, 1979, and Alfred asked for—and received—permission to go uptown to see one of those Kung-Fu episodes. As Alfred bounded out the front door, a neighbor drove slowly from the curb.

"How 'bout a lift to the bus, man!" Alfred yelled at the driver. As the neighbor now recalls, Alfred took a short ride with him to the corner of East Lake Boulevard and Glenwood Road, there to wait for the arrival of the white MARTA bus with its wrap-around stripes of orange, yellow and blue.

Sometime later, Alfred must have run across an old school chum, Edward Hope (Teddy) Smith, who lived next door to a teen-age friend named Lee Gooch. Gooch had another friend, Patrick (Pat Man) Rogers. One night in Underground Atlanta, Pat Man bought Lee Gooch a beer. Then Pat Man doffed the 10-gallon hat which belonged to his mama, Annie Rogers, and plunked it down atop Lee's closely cropped, springy hair. "My man!" Pat Man said affectionately.

The late show ended, and Alfred's mother, Lois Evans, began to pace nervously. It's easy to imagine her wondering, "Oh that boy, that damned boy—he'll be the death of me yet. Where the hell is he?"

Lois Evans wrung her hands and slept in fits and starts that Friday night.

And when the sun came up, her son still was not home. Anxiously, she telephoned the DeKalb County police. She finally reached someone who told her that she lived in a part of DeKalb County that is policed by the Atlanta police. Lois Evans says she was told: "You'll have to notify Atlanta."

The advice was easier given than followed. Atlanta's Missing Persons Section was closed on weekends and wouldn't open again until 9 o'clock Monday morning.

July, 1979

The medical examiners working with dental records quickly identified one of the Niskey Lake Road victims as Edward Hope Smith, 14.

But, the second body was a puzzler. The clothing was similar to that worn by Alfred Evans when he was reported missing, although there was a belt that Lois Evans would later say was *not* Alfred's. The approximate age, height and weight were right for Alfred Evans, but according to police reports, "The dental charts of Alfred Evans were compared with the second body found at Niskey Lake [sic], but there were *no similarities* [emphasis added]."

Detective Mickey Lloyd had interviewed a lot of witnesses. The story he pieced together put Alfred Evans and Edward Hope Smith together at a pot party on County Line Road, not far from Niskey Lake Road.

Several persons claimed to be eyewitnesses. One said that Evans had shot Smith and, in a fit of rage, one of Smith's friends had strangled Evans—only to be killed himself by a fourth person. The fourth person was *not* Wayne Williams.

For some time after the incident, Detective Lloyd—at least once, in company with Atlanta reporter Paul Crawley of WXIA-TV (Channel 11)—searched the Niskey Lake Road area for a third body. Meanwhile, the second body lay in the morgue unidentified.

As far as the police were concerned, the incident went down as a pair of drug-related killings. However, officially, the police were looking at only *one* murder. Since the cause of death was unknown for the second body, it wasn't necessary to put it in the FBI Uniform Crime Report as a homicide. Statistically, the second body fell through the cracks of the system. It didn't exist.

September, 1979

Fourteen-year-old Milton Harvey left home one morning to pay a bill at a Citizens & Southern Bank. He made the payment and apparently headed back home. The bicycle he had been riding was found on a dirt road between the bank and the giant, white drive-in movie screen which, for a long time, had been a landmark in Milton's neighborhood.

Sandy Creek Road was more sand than creek. A dusty dirt trail, it had a street sign, but little else to recommend it as a thoroughfare. It runs along the northern edge of Charlie Brown Airport (named for a local former politician). It's strictly a dirt-on-dirt pathway.

No one apparently saw who parked the bicycle on Sandy Creek Road. Or, no one cares to tell. The nearest house is beyond a curve and across a ridge. The area is so sparsely traveled that chickens and dogs laze on the road together in leisurely coexistence.

Had Milton Harvey left the bicycle there to reclaim later, thinking it was more secure in solitude than along a nearby busy highway? Had it been dumped there by a killer, or by someone who stole it and left Milton Harvey to walk into the clutches of a monster? Did Milton Harvey leave the bike willingly or not?

Milton Harvey hadn't gone to school that September day, although he was supposed to. He told his mama he was ashamed of his shoes. He wouldn't worry about school again—or his shoes.

October, 1979

Slightly more than one month later, I read in the *Atlanta Constitution* that a 9-year-old boy was missing after going to the store on an errand. It was October 22, 1979. His name was Yusuf Bell.

I was reading the paper in my office, barely two blocks from Yusuf's house. "I've already read this—it's old news," I thought. But, I was wrong.

As the days shortened and the nights got crisper, Thanksgiving Day was not far off. About three weeks after Yusuf Bell had disappeared, the decomposed body of 14-year-old Milton Harvey was found on a desolate stretch of Redwine Road in the Atlanta suburb of East Point, not far from Atlanta's new airport, but a long way from the bicycle.

The part of Redwine Road which yielded the remains serves as an impromptu dumping ground. Milton Harvey's body was found among piles of rubbish, decaying furniture and shells of erstwhile brand-name appliances which dotted the area. Rotting clothes and garbage were everywhere. In the middle of this squalor is a gorgeous lake. The sanitation department blunted the obvious contrast in vistas by setting an ugly, olive-drab dumpster on the shore.

The cause of death in Milton Harvey's case is still unknown. Like the second body at Niskey Lake Road, Milton was originally left off The List of missing and murdered children, when it would be prepared eight months after the discovery of his remains.

One reason Milton Harvey had been left off The List was because the original Task Force documents were prepared by the Atlanta police. Since the place where he was found was a few feet beyond the Atlanta boundary line in East Point, Atlanta police were not concerned with his case.

There still was no official recognition of the second boy in black found dead along Niskey Lake Road, even though there was no jurisdictional problem. But if Milton Harvey was to be counted on The List with his cause of death "unknown," why would the second boy in black on Niskey Lake Road *not* be counted? Was it because the authorities weren't sure who he was? This is another example of the illogic that afflicted those in charge of these investigations.

The home where Yusuf Bell lived on Rawson Street has since been replaced by the MARTA right-of-way.

Today, this point is marked by the tracks of swift-moving silver trains, rather than those of a little boy whom *Rolling Stone* portrayed as a genius anxious to build computers. Whether Yusuf's dreams matched those which were attributed to him in his eulogy, no one will ever know. But then, no one ever does, right? Chances are, his dreams would have changed a hundred times in the normal course of growing up. But things would not take a normal course for Yusuf Bell.

Yusuf's displaced mother, Camille Bell, moved into an apartment of the McDaniel-Glenn project in the Mechanicsville area of Atlanta, where she could look out the door and see Rawson Street. Within months, she was evicted. The Atlanta Housing Authority denies that it evicted her. It contends, instead, that a normal attempt was made to collect the rent.

Mayor Jackson was appalled. Camille Bell was grabbing national headlines and television time as the unfortunate mother of a child whose disappearance the Atlanta police department could not solve. It wasn't the most politic time to throw her out on the street, and Jackson castigated the AHA director for this action. When the vacant apartment was inspected, it was "two feet deep in garbage," according to an internal memo. I wondered if this had been Yusuf's way of life, or whether the garbage had been a special greeting prepared for the evicting authority. Or was it vandalism?

On the fateful day, Yusuf was playing at a neighbor's home. She offered him some change to run an errand. He quickly accepted. He padded his way to a grocery store on McDaniel Street at Georgia Avenue. He bought the can of snuff she wanted, but never made the delivery.

If Yusuf Bell disappeared on McDaniel Street, as the police report said, then he was within two streets of Cap'n Peg's, a fast-food restaurant that would be heard from repeatedly in these cases. Surely, Yusuf had been within a couple of blocks of Cap'n Peg's when he bought the snuff, but I picked a spot about three blocks away for the point of Yusuf's disappearance.

There, a chain-link fence separates a playground from the pavement of

Fulton Street in the 300 block. A connected row of dumpy, red-brick apartments ends where the fence begins. Head-high bushes 20 or so feet apart stand like sentries until you reach the opening that funnels kids in and out of the playground.

It would be almost one year later—in September of 1980—a month before the anniversary of Yusuf Bell's disappearance that Camille Bell and Willie Mae Mathis were passengers in my 10-year-old Cadillac convertible. As we drove down Fulton Street, Camille called out for me to stop.

"See that bush over there?" she said, pointing. "It was right there, by that bush, that the lady who lives in that house [she pointed in another direction] says she saw Yusuf get into a blue car with John [Camille's estranged husband] on the day he disappeared." Camille continued, "The lady knew me, she knew Yusuf and she knew John. The only thing is, she drinks a lot."

On November 8, 1979, one day short of two weeks after 14-year-old Milton Harvey was found, a man forced his way into the abandoned E.P. Johnson Elementary School at Fulton and Martin streets. It was 9:30 a.m. He found Yusuf Bell's decomposed body stuffed into a maintenance trap, a hole in the concrete floor to provide access to pipes. "I had to take a piss" was the explanation accepted for 39-year-old John Henry Tye's venture into the boarded-up and chain-locked school. Tye was a school custodian.

The police surmised that Yusuf Bell had been carried in because the floors were dirty and the bottoms of his bare feet were clean. A woman says she saw Yusuf earlier on the day he disappeared. She said he was wearing brown cutoff trousers. "He and they were filthy," she said. Adhering to the butt of Yusuf's cutoffs was a small piece of masking tape. Sticking to the masking tape were fibers. One was a green rug fiber. They were sent to the crime lab for analysis.

If Yusuf's feet now were clean—and he had been walking the streets barefoot—did someone bathe him? An eyewitness would tell police later that this is exactly what happened to another victim.

It was this story of "bathing" victims that gave birth to some occult theories about the murders. There are, of course, other explanations.

Camille Bell's estranged husband, John, had not shown up for Yusuf's funeral. That perplexed Camille. She would have been even more perplexed had she known that John and a lady friend had been interviewed by the police about Yusuf's disappearance. During the questioning, John insisted that Yusuf would be found unharmed, but the lady friend said she had experienced a psychic vision of Yusuf's body being buried under concrete.

Soon Camille learned that John's absence from the funeral was legitimate. From that point on, she became upset with people who hinted that John's activities were suspect. But, the only hint that I had of any problem with John came from Camille herself, although the police were interested in him.

All that Camille ever saw of Yusuf after his disappearance were those brown cutoffs. She didn't view his body. Identification was made by a friend of the family—interestingly, *another* custodial employee of a school system.

The medical examiner's report said Yusuf had been strangled. It was a ligature strangulation (something had been drawn tightly around his neck). But there was no mention of the fibers (beyond those adhering to the masking tape) which later would be used by the state to connect the death of Yusuf Bell to Wayne Williams. The fibers also would link Yusuf to another victim who witnesses said was bathed and who also suffered a ligature strangulation.

In both of these cases, there were suspects *other* than Wayne Williams. But an arrest would have invalidated the fiber evidence unless there was more than one killer acting in concert. Two or more killers would have voided the prosecution's theories unless they both lived in Williams' house. Neither of these suspects did.

Camille Bell watched the investigation of her son's death first with patience, then with disappointment and finally with anger. If the police were doing anything, it wasn't enough to satisfy her.

Five months had elapsed since the two bodies had been found along Niskey Lake Road. The police were looking at two, perhaps three, perhaps four murders, depending upon how one classifies the victims. One was shot. One was strangled. Those were unquestionably murders. Two died from unknown causes, and one of these two was yet to be identified. The police weren't anxious for new homicide cases to investigate. They'd had their fill. They saw no connections among the four cases. In fact, they saw no problem.

The week of March 9 through 15, 1980, in Atlanta's history should be bordered in black. Back on Page 19-B of the *Atlanta Journal-Constitution* on Sunday, March 16, was an obscure report that the body of the *third* young girl found murdered that week had been discovered. Almost everyone overlooked the significance of that report.

On March 4, 1980, Angel Lenair arrived home from school. She went to her closet and changed into her jeans and matching jacket. About 4 p.m., she went outside again. If anyone ever saw her alive again, he or she isn't talking about it.

Angel's mother, Venus Taylor, then 32, had brought her to Atlanta only two months earlier, in January of 1980, from Chicago, where Venus had been in trouble with the law over controlled substances (narcotics). The tiny apartment she furnished since moving to Atlanta was tasteful. She supported herself and Angel on the money she made as a cocktail waitress at the Mahogany Club on Campbellton Road (Georgia 166). But when the club lost its license, she lost her job.

Venus Taylor worried about the relationships that Angel may have been cultivating. Their home was very close to an Army base at Fort McPherson, and Angel was a 12-year-old who was beginning to act more woman than child. Venus Taylor worried even more one day when an older man who lived in an apartment across the street expressed an interest in Angel.

On March 10, about 4 p.m.—nearly six days to the minute after Angel had disappeared—the body of a young girl was found. Her hands were tied behind her and fastened to a tree. A pair of women's panties (not hers) were stuffed down her throat. Wound taut around her neck was an electrical cord.

Venus Taylor saw the commotion in the wooded lot across Campbellton Road and ran to the scene—just as they shut the ambulance doors.

"That's my Angel!" she cried. "Let me see my baby!"

A homicide officer shunted her away. "We don't know *who* it is, lady," he said. The ambulance sped away.

Venus Taylor's intuition was confirmed at the morgue. The body was identified as that of Angel Lenair. There at least were some leads in Angel's case. Two men had been questioned. One had a sex-offense record. Another flunked a lie-detector test and returned for the time being, at least, to his home in Chicago.

Was Angel sexually assaulted? The autopsy stirred controversy on this point. "Assaulted" is the key word. It's certainly a word that is often misunderstood and has led many would-be investigators down many a blind alley.

The autopsy did show there were hymen tabs. In other words, the hymen had been broken. It did not, however, indicate that this was related to the murder. There were abrasions in the genital area, but they could have been caused by something as simple and innocent as lifting her off the ground by the waistband of her jeans.

With many sexual crimes, the evidence of sexual activity is perforce left not with the victim but with the perpetrator. Furthermore, in many of these Atlanta cases, we are dealing with skeletal remains. Therefore, when the medical examiner says there is no evidence of sexual assault, it does not by any stretch of the imagination mean that no sexual activity took place. Thus, sex as a motive cannot be ruled out, period.

Venus Taylor pushed past the attendants at the morgue to view her daughter's body. She said Angel resembled an "old woman."

She also publicly agreed with activist Dick Gregory's hallucination that the entire case was a plot by the Atlanta-based U.S. Center for Disease Control (CDC) to obtain a certain chemical for the manufacture of interferon, a drug used to treat cancer and herpes. The story went that the chemical could only be obtained from the penises of black children and only during a very short period after death.

The interferon rumor probably originated with a form designed and circulated by CDC at the request of the Task Force. It was an effort to use the highly touted resources of the CDC, which traces commonalities in the spread of disease. So, why not the commonalities in the spread of murder? It was probably one of the smartest things done during the investigation, but I don't know how well it was done.

The two other girls who were mentioned in that *Journal-Constitution* story on March 16, 1980, never made anybody's list. I'm convinced that Angel did make The List because her mother was active with the mothers' committee. This was one of the few things Angel had in common with 7-year-old LaTonya Wilson, the only other female who would make The List. The mothers of both victims were members of the Committee to Stop Children's Murders when The List was originally drawn up. No other female murder victim's mother was, and no other female made The List.

On March 11, 1980, another black child spent his last day ever at home. Ten-year-old Jefferey Mathis left home, heading for the Star Service Station about two blocks away. He left to buy a pack of cigarettes for his mother.

"I know it was about 7:30," Jefferey's mother, Willie Mae Mathis, said. "*Three's a Crowd* was on TV when I asked Jefferey to go out. He walked back into the bedroom. I heard the door slam, and I never seen him again."

A blue car headed west on Gordon Street from the traffic signal beside Anderson's Produce Stand. Jefferey and one of the Anderson boys had been feuding. They had clashed on March 10 and again on March 11. "It was over him giving candy to my girlfriend," the Anderson boy told me.

When the car reached the intersection of East Ontario Avenue one block away, it made a question-mark-shaped turn. The car then headed the wrong way, north on East Ontario. It stopped beside a silver fireplug, and Jefferey climbed into the back seat. "I don't think he was forced in," one of Jefferey's classmates reported. She said she had watched the incident from the "wash house" (laundromat) on the southeast corner. The car wasn't more than 40 feet away. "It was 7:30," she said. "I was watchin' the time to get the wash out of the machine."

Jefferey Lamar Mathis' laughing face never was seen again peeking through the doorways of the shops along Gordon Street. Until now, that had been a daily occurrence. There always was the chance that someone would want an errand run, but from now on, Jefferey wouldn't be there to run it.

By now, a few Atlantans began to take notice that something was amiss with Atlanta's children. Camille Bell's protestations grew louder. She was articulate and lived in the ghetto, which made her good copy for reporters. She came across so eloquently on TV that she constantly made waves and ruffled the establishment's feathers. She was joined by a man who wore a preacher's collar. He called himself the Reverend Earl Carroll.

Eric Middlebrooks was 14. He lived at 345 Howell Street with a foster mother, Evelyn Miller. Eric's biological mother didn't come from her North Carolina home for Eric's funeral; perhaps she couldn't afford to. When Eric died, there was no such thing as The List to get on—and to furnish money for such things.

About 10:30 on the night of May 18, 1980, Eric walked into the house. He took a phone call (could it have been from his killer?), and went to obtain a hammer "to fix his bike," according to a police report. After Eric walked back out the door, no one reported seeing him alive again.

The next morning, just before 7 o'clock, Eric was found bludgeoned to death with a blunt instrument. The bicycle lay a few feet away. Both tires were flat. Some pocket change lay nearby, but there was no hammer. Under his white T-shirt were superficial, V-shaped wounds. Caught in a rip in his tennis shoes was a clump of red fibers. A crime-scene technician sealed the shoes in an evidence bag. One year later, fibers would be on many people's minds.

Eric's body was found in the rear of 247 Flat Shoals Road. It wasn't immediately obvious—unless you were looking at a map, as I was—that 247 Flat Shoals was almost right at the intersection of Moreland Avenue and Memorial Drive, two major thoroughfares. It was another of Atlanta's every-which-way intersections that had given birth to such neighborhood labels as "Five Points" and "Little Five Points." Atlanta must have a street laid out on the tracks of every rebel who ran from General Sherman. Unfortunately for the visitor, six streets may come together at one point, and each might be named "Peachtree" something or other. In Atlanta, the Peachtree streets outnumber the peach trees.

A pile of rumpled fenders and auto hoods between the double overhead doors of a gray, cinder-block garage in an alley marked the spot where Eric Middlebrooks apparently drew his last breath. Stare too long at the spot and two Dobermans are only a chain-link fence away from having a part of your ass. "Where were the Dobermans on May 18, 1980?" I wondered.

Next to the gray garage is a multi-story building covered in multi-colored glass. Faces—some pretty, some pained, some longing—look out of the sealed windows. Some beckon to any male who happens by. The sign on the corner of what was once a Mark Inn motel (another child victim would be found inside a Mark Inn) throws a cold shower on all but the most ardent machismo. It reads "State of Georgia, Department of Offender Rehabilitation." A sober mind wonders if any of the women interned there had been sent up for murder. The building has since been reverted to a hotel of a different chain.

As you look from the murder scene to the end of the alley which dead ends into the fence of the Interstate 20 right-of-way, you could see the Kentucky Fried Chicken sign on the corner of Faith Street and Moreland Avenue.

Howell Street, where Eric Middlebrooks lived, spent a part of each sunny day in the shadow of that sign. The house is separated from the death scene by a 100-foot-wide strip of concrete that runs from Florence, South Carolina, to Odessa, Texas.

Eric Middlebrooks had an older half-brother, Kerry. Even though they were not particularly close, the mystery of Eric's death was at least partly responsible for Kerry's decision to join the Atlanta police force in December of 1980.

In the summer of 1981, a little more than a year after Eric died, Kerry Middlebrooks stopped a Chrysler that had weaved from curb-to-curb in the sultry predawn hours along Piedmont Road.

"What do you say, brother?" the driver greeted him.

"You're not my brother," Kerry answered.

"Of course I am."

"Oh, no, you're not. My brother is dead."

The man became argumentative and belligerent. Kerry Middlebrooks arrested Leon Hall, 34, a disciple of the late Martin Luther King Jr. and a long-time activist in the civil rights movement. Two days later, Hall was fired from his job as community and consumer affairs director in Mayor Jackson's office. Hall's primary assignment during the previous year had been to coordinate assistance, much of it financial, for families of Atlanta's murdered and missing children. It was ironic that one member of one of those families, doing his job, cost Hall his. Hall soon went to work in the 1981 mayoral campaign of a candidate backed by Jackson—Andrew Young.

Some of us long had wondered what was going on in Leon Hall's office at City Hall, inasmuch as Willie Mae Mathis said she was scolded for selecting a white funeral director instead of a "brother". Willie Mae insisted on using the white-owned mortuary because the funeral it offered was much less expensive, although City Hall was picking up the tab from the donations.

Interestingly, too, an Atlanta police detective assigned to the Task Force also owned a mortuary that handled the funerals of victims of some the murders being investigated by the Task Force. Did the news media know it? Yes. Then why wasn't such a bizarre twist to the Atlanta story reported?

Kerry Middlebrooks says he has a pretty good idea about who killed his brother (it apparently isn't Wayne Williams, whose name, he said, meant nothing to him before Williams' arrest). Eric Middlebrooks' slaying is one of those cases "cleared" by the arrest of Wayne Williams, even though Williams was never officially charged, indicted or tried for it. I was surprised to learn that Kerry had never heard about Eric leaving home with a hammer. I got the information about the hammer from a police report. One wonders what information is shared with the cop on the beat. Would other cops with a personal interest less than that of Kerry Middlebrooks know even less?

Of course they knew less—and they complained openly on television about it.

With the death of Eric Middlebrooks, questions sprang up everywhere. Was his killing in any way related to the death of Yusuf Bell? "No," the police said. Again, the police paused to worship the false god, "M.O." Eric was 14; Yusuf was 9. Eric was bludgeoned, and Yusuf was strangled. And on it went.

The authorities harped on the differences in the cases which later they would say were clearly part of a "pattern" that implicates Wayne Williams.

The Atlanta police now counted three unsolved murders of young black boys (those we knew about), with a fourth in East Point and a fifth (the second body at Niskey Lake Road) in limbo. But all of these discoveries of bodies had taken place miles apart, and there was no recognizable pattern, except that all were black males and two were 14 years old.

What made Eric Middlebrooks' case so intriguing was that he was said to have been a witness in a robbery case—and there were, as a result, certain suspects who would have benefited from his death. Other police sources deny that there was to be any testimony. What is clear is that the suspects in the robbery were interrogated by police as suspects in Eric's murder.

Throughout the first year of the investigation, the police insisted that the Middlebrooks case was not connected to the others. They said, as they too often do, "We know who killed Middlebrooks. We just can't prove it." That's for sure! One interesting sidelight of this syndrome is that police automatically rule out their "killer" in one case as a suspect in the others.

It took a while, but The List finally recognized Christopher Phillipe Richardson, who disappeared on June 9, 1980. Originally, he had been ignored for jurisdictional reasons. He lived on and disappeared from Conway Drive at Memorial Drive, slightly more than one mile east of the Atlanta city limits.

Christopher lived in as pleasant a community as any of the victims. The neighborhood is nice, but nondescript. Even though you've been there a few times, you still have to look for the street sign to make sure you're in the right place. His middle-class home was the product of his grandparents' labors.

Yet his life was not routine. His mother had been consistent, if unfortunate, in her selection of mates. Both Christopher's father and his stepfather were in penitentiaries.

At 11, Christopher probably didn't understand his prognosis. It wasn't necessary, anyway. There was no future for Christopher Richardson.

He was on his way to the community swimming pool, wearing walking shorts. His mother, Sirlena Cobb, told me, "He didn't have any regular swimming trunks." Yet months later, the police would show Sirlena a pair of swimming trunks. "The police insisted they were his," she said, "but like the teeth pictures they showed us, Mama and I both said they weren't Christopher's." Christopher Richardson's death would be attributed to Wayne

Williams by fibers on a pair of swimming trunks that his mother said were not his.

But, back in June of 1980, the disappearance of Christopher Richardson was of no special concern to the Atlanta police. Like Milton Harvey, he was somebody else's problem—this time a problem for the DeKalb County police.

June, 1980

LaTonya Wilson went to sleep in only her white panties and a slip.

She should have been dreaming beautifully anxious dreams. Tomorrow would be her birthday. A birthday is momentous in the life of anyone. For a girl about to turn 7, it's really special.

Yet for LaTonya, there would be very little of tomorrow. At 2 a.m. on June 22, 1980, a scarcely believable incident occurred, according to a neighbor who said she witnessed it. She said a black man removed a window pane from the casement window of Apartment 7 at 2261 Verbena Street, in a housing project in Dixie Hills on Atlanta's west side.

It could have happened that way, Gail Epstein of the *Atlanta Constitution* assured me, although she had difficulty swallowing the story. "I felt the putty around the removed glass," she said. "It was fresh. A maintenance man had replaced it only the day before."

The actions of this maintenance man—at least the person who investigator Don Laken (nicknamed the "Dog Man" because he used tracking dogs) thought was the maintenance man—were to form another part of the occult theory which occupied the minds of many who wanted to solve this horrendous string of murders.

Theories about this individual would take on a stronger ring of truth long after Wayne Williams was convicted. The man confessed to a bizarre murder. Lynn Whatley, Wayne Williams' attorney on appeal, who interviewed this man in his jail cell, swears that pictures of "all the victims" were found in the man's room when he was arrested for the more recent murder. Maybe the "Dog Man" was right!

The black man outside LaTonya Wilson's apartment, according to the neighbor's account, carried the unbroken window pane to a nearby dumpster (that's where police found it) and deposited it carefully among the other refuse of congested urban poverty. Returning to the window, he reached through, turned the lock and opened the entire sash.

If, as the neighbor said, the kidnapper climbed through that window, he stepped squarely onto a bed where two other Wilson children were asleep. Neither woke up. Once inside, he stole LaTonya from her bed, carrying her past the door of her parents' room. He walked out the back door, leaving it ajar. Outside, he is said to have paused in the parking lot to speak with another black male, all the while holding the limp figure of LaTonya Wilson under his right arm.

I wonder if 26-year-old Nathaniel Cater was home that night—in the apartment upstairs above the violated window of Apartment 7—and if his future was being plotted in the parking lot below. I also wondered if Cater might have been in the parking lot below—talking to a second man—and that what he saw and/or heard had sealed his fate and formed the connection between his death and LaTonya's—a link that police and prosecutors deny could exist.

Fifty yards away, in another apartment in the same project, another Atlanta girl should have been dreaming sweet dreams. Cynthia Montgomery, 13, had just been accepted into a summer camp which promised not only fun, but money.

The police said Aaron Wyche had fallen from a railroad trestle.

A safe distance away—miles, in fact—a medical examiner perused the police report. "Damned fool kid," he could have thought. It was easy to imagine this 10-year-old kid taking a shortcut home across a railroad trestle at 2 o'clock in the morning. Maybe he heard a mournful whistle of a fast-approaching train in the distance. Maybe so, but it's a fact that no one bothered to find out if a train was due on that trestle anywhere near the time that Aaron supposedly fell.

Then, too, maybe he simply strayed too close to the edge and teetered for a moment, trying to catch his balance like a tightrope walker, before he lost the battle and fell.

In any event, it must have been an accident. It would be rare for a 10-year-old to commit suicide and rarer still for one to do so by jumping off a railroad trestle. (However, in the next year, Atlanta would have two such deaths of teen-agers which would be ruled exactly that—suicide—even though they didn't jump. They simply sat and waited for a train, according to police.)

"Accidental death," the DeKalb County medical examiner, Dr. Joseph Burton, ruled in the Aaron Wyche case. The cause of death was officially ruled positional asphyxia. Aaron supposedly landed in such a way that his head was turned so that he could not breathe. Certainly he had been alive on the way down, since his fingers still clutched leaves from the tree he would have had to have fallen through. This is the story that was told.

A railroad worker had found him lying there, fully clad in a red-and-black striped shirt, blue cutoff trousers and high-topped tennis shoes.

July, 1980

Anthony Carter was 9, the second youngest on The List. He lived on West

End Avenue near the East Ontario Avenue home of 10-year-old Jefferey Mathis. Close by, within one block, lived other young blacks whose names would soon make headlines—Joseph (Jo-Jo) Bell and Timothy Hill. Both were Anthony Carter's neighbors.

For someone at such a tender age, Anthony Carter kept late hours. He was last seen playing with a friend about 1:30 a.m. on July 6, 1980—only one block from home at 979 Cunningham Place.

Anthony had been stabbed in the front and back. A police report said his body was discovered about 8:15 p.m. on July 7. The people who work less than 50 yards from where the body was found say it was more like 5:30 p.m. on the previous day, July 6.

Anthony Carter died over the Fourth of July weekend. The business did not open until the second shift on Monday, July 6. That's when the body was discovered, the employees said. Something is very wrong with the timing and/or the police reports in the Anthony Carter case.

From the advanced state of decomposition, it is difficult to believe the body had been there for fewer than two days, let alone one. Yet it's also hard to accept that the body would have lain in front of an open business without being discovered sooner. Some investigators speculated that the body had been transferred to the site where it was found, perhaps long after Anthony was killed.

A heart-rending story in the paper one Sunday in June of 1980 told of a woman whose daughter had run away from home almost a year earlier. At least, she knew her missing child was alive on Christmas of 1979. She got a call from the child then, but hadn't heard from her since. The woman had lost her job, expended her savings and lost everything she owned in a vain search for her daughter.

She had concluded that the police don't do much about missing children. It certainly isn't a top-priority item with them. The private detectives she had hired at great personal expense had been of no help.

I knew the woman was right. If ever a problem cried out for a solution, it was that of the missing child.

A few days earlier, I visited the director of the Georgia Crime Commission, Jim Higdon. At his office, I ran into Mike Edwards, who said he had opened his own private investigating business with Bill Taylor, one of the ex-Atlanta cops who had pulled the rug from under A. Reginald Eaves in the cheating scandal. Mike gave me his card, and we made promises to call each other.

Back home, I stood in the driveway, dripping wet from washing my car. I constantly thought of the woman who didn't know where her daughter was. I turned off the hose and went inside to give Mike the call I had promised him.

I told Mike that missing children constituted a problem that was ripe for quality people to investigate. I reminded him that LEAA was phasing out and that some of the best criminal-justice people in America would be out of work. They couldn't get back into the existing system, but they'd be anxious to keep their fingers in a business they knew and liked.

I figured that would provide the nucleus of a nationwide system of quality people. That they were scattered across the nation would eliminate one of the costliest problems for the searching parents—travel. Other ideas danced in my head, but Mike interrupted.

"You know, Chet," he said, "we've got a hell of a problem right now in Atlanta with missing kids. Have you been reading about all the kids who have disappeared and some of them are turning up dead?"

We talked a while longer and decided to meet at a restaurant later in the week.

I invited a friend, Dick Arena, to join us. Dick was formerly an organized-crime analyst with the Kentucky State Police and he had worked for me at the Kentucky Crime Commission. He had many talents. Dick, Mike, Bill Taylor and I met over coffee in a Denny's in northeast Atlanta. We looked at a lot of ideas and finally settled on two alternate courses of action.

The first, which I thought would be fruitless, was to volunteer our services to the Atlanta police. The second was to contact the mothers and volunteer our services directly to them.

Lee Brown, the public safety commissioner, and George Napper, the chief of police, had no love for Mike Edwards. Although he was a former confidant and ally, Mike had fallen into disfavor and had become a constant thorn in their official sides.

Mike had attempted to resign as deputy director over an issue of professional conscience, but in doing so, he had made public too many of the Atlanta Police Bureau's internal problems to suit the chief and the public safety commissioner.

Brown refused the resignation and fired Edwards. Edwards withdrew the resignation and sued Brown. A judge would rule in 1981 that Edwards had been fired unfairly, without a hearing, and ordered Brown to pay Edwards $15,000 from his own funds. A lien was slapped on Brown's holdings when Brown decided to leave town and work elsewhere. But city officials put up a bond for the amount that was owed to Edwards.

A higher court ruled in Brown's favor in 1983, but the flak still whizzes overhead like tracer bullets in the night.

In 1980, Mike wrote to Chief Napper. Napper shunted him to Morris Redding, who had succeeded Mike as head of investigations. I told Mike that I wouldn't waste my time on such a meeting because I knew what the result would be.

Dick Arena and Mike went to see Morris Redding at police headquarters. They discussed with him the problem of Atlanta's missing and murdered children. Redding, they said, told them that it was simply a "political problem" and not to worry about it. This angered Dick, who heats up under the collar seldom but rapidly. He told Redding that if the murders and disappearances kept up, he would know he had a real political problem when the ABC, CBS and NBC cameras arrived. How prophetic Dick's remark was.

Mike returned with the word that I already anticipated. Atlanta didn't want our help. We placed a call to Camille Bell, but couldn't reach her.

Ten-year-old Jefferey Mathis still was missing, four months after he left to get cigarettes for his mother in March of 1980. When we weighed all the priorities, Jefferey's case seemed a good one to start with. We contacted his mother, Willie Mae Mathis, and offered our services—at no charge—to help locate her son. Mrs. Mathis agreed, and we were officially in the case.

Assured that Mrs. Mathis wanted our help—and knowing the Atlanta police didn't—we decided to go public. Dick Arena arranged a press conference, at which Mike was to read a short, prepared statement. Because Mike was embroiled in the controversy with Lee Brown, we let Mike call the news conference, figuring that somebody would show up.

Our news conference held a surprise for me. Mike had invited his long-time associate, Jack Perry, to join us at the microphones. I didn't know Jack all that well at that time. My first reaction was very negative. I knew that Jack was running for sheriff of Rockdale County, a bedroom suburb southeast of Atlanta. I was afraid that he was using our platform only for political purposes. As a result, I stayed quiet. Two strikes were enough. Mike could be written off as sour grapes and Jack Perry as an opportunist. I thought the issue was too important to risk striking out in our first appearance.

Mayor Jackson would later accuse Jack Perry of having escaped from bad-conduct charges on a technicality. He would also say that Perry preferred the "racist policies" of John Inman. The mayor made those statements on Cable News Network. Perry sued Mayor Jackson. Now everyone seemed to be suing everyone else (everyone but me, that is). If Jack Perry is a racist, he never showed it in my presence. I do know that Jack Perry has been damned good to me. I've grown to like him as much as I've always appreciated his skills as a homicide investigator.

The day after our press conference, Camille Bell and a few other victims' mothers met with the Public Safety Committee of the Atlanta City Council. Shortly thereafter, Lee Brown announced the formation of a "Task Force" to look into the problem of missing and murdered children. The Task Force then consisted only of five persons. Brown said he had contemplated the idea for some time and that it was in no way a reaction to pressure from mothers or any other group. "Your ass," I muttered to myself.

As Mike Edwards, Jack Perry, the others and I began to circulate in the areas of the cases, the press followed us. Invariably, Mike and Jack criticized the Atlanta police. Then a reporter would ask us a basic question about the murders, and we didn't know the answer.

"Sour grapes—it's all coming across like sour grapes, Mike," I told him. "It's embarrassing me."

I decided then and there that after my daughter's wedding in August of 1980, I would learn these cases and know them better than anyone else in the world—or I would get out. Never mind that I was flat broke and not earning one penny.

Morris Redding, who had expressed his understanding of the cases to Mike and Dick as a "political problem," soon would be assigned to head up the investigations. Guys wearing badges on their chests and braid on their caps would draw hundreds of thousands of dollars to solve a problem they would make worse.

4

Fire, Brimstone and Platitudes

July, 1980

Willie Mae Mathis contracted with us to help her find her 10-year-old son, Jefferey—a service for which we would charge no fee. The first request we received from Mrs. Mathis was to check on the Reverend Earl Carroll.

She didn't trust Carroll, who, by the way, may not be a Carroll, an Earl or a reverend. To be sure, the pastor of the Wheat Street Baptist Church later would state that Carroll was not the assistant pastor of his church, as Carroll had claimed.

The man who lives with that name—and wore a turned-around white collar—already had been charged once in a flim-flam operation. He was involved in the violation of tape-recording copyrights.

If Mrs. Mathis suspected that everyone was a threat to her, it wouldn't be surprising. She lost her husband, Jefferey's father, to a blast from a robber's gun. Jefferey had disappeared while on an errand that shouldn't have taken him more than two blocks from the safety of his own home. After Jefferey's disappearance, a relative had come to Atlanta to spend a comforting visit with Willie Mae, only for the relative's own son to drown in an Atlanta swimming pool.

Now someone driving a blue car had made advances to Willie Mae's daughter, Valerie. Could it be the same blue car that witnesses said swallowed Jefferey? Valerie Mathis, who already was a mother, though still a teen-ager, had been approached while walking on the sidewalk a few feet from her home, less than a block from where Jefferey had disappeared in March of 1980.

Mrs. Mathis thought the Reverend Carroll drove a blue car. Three years later, in 1983, Willie Mae Mathis would be a telephone guest on a Chicago radio program that I was interviewed on. On that show, she would say that Wayne Williams was the driver of that blue car.

Mrs. Mathis had not liked Carroll's involvement in her son's case to this point. On April 29, 1980, she called Detective Roz Richardson of the Atlanta police Missing Persons unit. As Richardson reported, "Some friends of hers said that a man, dressed in a clown's suit, had been collecting money in several shopping centers in the area. He carried a sign saying that the money was being collected to use as a reward in helping located [sic] the person or persons responsible for the disappearance of Jefferey Mathis..."

On May 5, 1980, Jefferey's mother called the police again. The police report reads, in part: "...she had received a call from a Rev. Carroll [who] had gotten her name from a flier [sic]. He informed Mrs. Mathis that he was working with Camile [sic] Bell and Mrs. Lanier [sic] [actually Venus Taylor, mother of 12-year-old Angel Lenair] trying to get them together to raise reward money. Mrs. Mathis stated that she became suspicious of Reverend Carroll when he began talking about having clowns in shopping centers collecting money..."

In June, Willie Mae met with Carroll, Camille Bell and Venus Taylor at Paschal's Hotel restaurant, which during the 1960s was where the late Martin Luther King Jr. and his top aides plotted strategy for the civil rights movement. There, the four of them founded the Committee to Stop Children's Murders. Apparently Willie Mae's business relationship with Carroll did nothing to enhance her trust of him.

Willie Mae had left a message on the answering machine at Mike's office, asking for Dick Arena, our primary contact with Mrs. Mathis, to call her. It was July 24, 1980.

Dick returned the call. The Committee to Stop Children's Murders was sponsoring a meeting that night at the Wheat Street Baptist Church. The Reverend Earl Carroll was on the program, and Mrs. Mathis wanted us to be there.

The Wheat Street Baptist Church is one of those misnomer churches. It actually sits at Auburn Avenue and Yonge Street in downtown Atlanta. In some less affluent day, its parishioners may have met on Wheat Street, but not anymore.

We arrived early. Our objective was to check out every car that arrived for the meeting. We were particularly interested in Carroll's car and in giving Valerie a chance to eyeball him and say "yay" or "nay" about him being the man who had accosted her.

Before we went inside, we had established to Valerie's satisfaction that neither Carroll nor his car was involved in her harassment. Also, none of the cars there matched the description of the one that had picked up Jefferey.

A carpeted stairway led from the sidewalk to the second-floor sanctuary. The landing was more like a large room, and there I noticed Sergeant H.L. Bolton, head of the newly formed Atlanta special police Task Force. The bulge and hitch in the right side of his summer suit coat revealed to the educated eye a pistol that the coat was worn to conceal. Mike gave Bolton some information that he had held for him. Mike also provided him a list of license numbers we had observed outside the church. Bolton gave the numbers to one of his men to copy. I wondered why they didn't already have them.

As I entered the church, I was reminded of a day during the 1960s when, as a police patrolman, I had been dispatched to a west Louisville church where an open-housing protest meeting was in progress. I doffed my hat, only to be ordered to put it back on by a commanding officer. He couldn't stand to see a policeman out of uniform, but he didn't seem to mind passing the hat himself at various bookie joints and to bootleggers on the 1st of each month.

The sanctuary is clean and quiet and sufficiently holy. In keeping with the tradition of Christianity, it also is sufficiently uncomfortable. I always thought the Buddhists had the right idea. They made it soothing to go to church. The pews at the Wheat Street Baptist Church were beautifully varnished and hard as Gibraltar.

I settled into the last row on that sweltering July night in 1980. The printed program which the well-scrubbed little girl had handed me at the door lay in my lap. I hadn't looked at it yet.

Off to my left was the choir loft, which concealed a pipe organ that throbbed with prelude music. Children in choir robes lined the railing, their smiles almost too wide for their faces. I closed my eyes, almost hoping that the ghost of Martin Luther King Jr. would begin preaching again of his dream. For years, the church had been a gathering place for many of King's followers, even though he had been co-pastor of the Ebenezer Baptist Church, not far away on Auburn Avenue.

The Reverend William Holmes Borders, pastor of the Wheat Street Baptist Church, led the dignitaries to seats behind the podium. They sat facing the audience.

The choir struggled through still another chorus of *"Jesus Loves Me."* What the singing lacked in quality was made up by enthusiasm. Borders smiled, thanked the choir and asked for an encore. I winced. Everyone smiled—choir mothers proudly and everyone else painfully. A smile was the kindest form of laughter.

A polished, articulate black man with a Ph.D. in psychology reminded me from the pulpit that I was my brother's keeper. He concluded with emphasis on the last syllable (as in "es-tab-lish-*ment*") that this tragedy was the result of man's mistreat-*ment* of his fellow man. Thus, he said, the sober were driven to drink and the innocent to kill.

"Bull-shit," I thought, glancing around to make sure I hadn't thought it aloud. His words reminded me of the "crime"-prevention commercial in which we are urged not to leave our keys in our cars so as not to make a "good" boy go bad by tempting him to steal.

The man gave us a 20-minute synopsis of all the sociological buzz words he had learned—and not an original thought. The talk had been about 19 minutes and 59 seconds too long. Those who never heard of Durkheim and anomie didn't understand; those who had were not impressed.

The choir revved up again. My ears begged my mind for diversion. I picked up the program and began to study it. The program consisted of three white pages stapled together in the upper lefthand corner. Across the top, letters about one-quarter of an inch high read "The Conference on Children's Safety." In the center of the page was a large bold "80." It left the impression that it was the first of what would be an annual affair, but it was the first and last. Across the bottom, it read: "Dr. William Holmes Borders, Conference Chairman. Camille Bell, Chair*person*."

Inside the front cover was a bigger-than-life cheeseburger, complete with sesame-seed bun, mayo, lettuce, tomato, onion, ketchup and pickle—all I could discern from the black-and-white reproduction. The bottom half of the page was dedicated to a coupon with which I could buy one "Whopper" and get another free at the Burger King on Cascade Avenue.

It was steamy hot. Borders summoned an usher to the front of each aisle. "Jesus Christ, they're going to pass the plate," the newsman sitting to my right moaned. He began to dig into his pockets, hoping for enough change to look credible without breaking out a dollar bill. Reality made me immune. I didn't have enough money to buy gas to look for a murderer, let alone pay for hot air.

The program called for Venus Taylor to be the next speaker. But if she was, I must have been too engossed in the hamburger to notice. When I looked up, Camille Bell stood at the pulpit, addressing the audience. I had missed the introduction of the other "mothers," who, according to the program, included one father whose surname differed puzzingly from that of his victim son. (Later, I would wish that I had paid closer attention to those introductions. It might have dismissed the problem of who 10-year-old Willie Sherman was.)

I guess I was engrossed in the father and son because their surnames were different. Or maybe it was simply because he was the only father listed. But my eyes stuck on the line that read: "Jessie Griffin, Father...Aaron Wyche, age 10, accidental death."

Who was Aaron Wyche? And what was the name of a kid who died in an *accident* doing on a list of murdered and missing children? I drew a circle around Aaron's name, which was sixth on a list of eight. I folded the program and laid it on the pew beside me.

Camille Bell, whose 9-year-old son, Yusuf, had been found slain the previous November, was giving child-safety tips. They were nothing I hadn't heard before—even 40 years ago. I remembered sitting in the basement cafeteria of Louisville's Holy Cross School. The building still stands as a reminder of the outmigration of white blue-collar families who were basically

Catholic, while the west end of Louisville was increasingly settled by blacks who were not Catholic. The landscape of western Louisville is dotted by boarded-up symbols of this social change.

Back then, we were being shown a scratchy, 16-mm. one-reeler. The sound had all the quality of a hand-held tape recorder with a dying battery. On the screen was a sinister-looking "dirty old man." The turned-up collar of his trenchcoat ran to the brim of his bent fedora, leaving only his leering eyes to strike fear into our baby hearts. His left hand held some lollipops. His right hand was poised to seize the throat of a wide-eyed little girl who was enticed by the candy.

The voice of the narrator on the soundtrack blended into that of Camille Bell as my mind returned to the present. "I used to tell my children," she was saying, "'Don't get in a car with a stranger.' Now I tell them, 'Don't get in a car or truck with *anyone.*'"

Now that was a twist. It was too calmly said to be paranoia and too emphatic to be just a dash of added caution. Camille Bell didn't believe that Yusuf had gotten into a car with a stranger. She hadn't yet told me someone had reported seeing Yusuf climb into a car with "John."

Still another discordant offering from the choir made me squirm. I considered escape. Funny how free people often become tied to their seats by social pressure. But Earl Carroll was next on the program and he, after all, was my main reason for being there.

Borders now entreated us to join with the choir. The sound got louder, but more bearable. The rhythm picked up with the clapping of hands. This was more like it. My foot began to tap.

Like a cheerleader, Borders urged the crowd on to louder repetitions of "Hallelujah!" and "Praise the Lord" and "Amen!" Sergeant Carter never did a better job when he stood nose-to-nose with Gomer Pyle, shouting, "I can't hear yew!"

Earl Carroll was on the program officially to introduce the guest of honor, Atlanta Chief of Police George Napper. Carroll prayed some, even imparted a little fire and brimstone on us. It seemed more than a tad hypocritical. Here was a man who recently had changed from clown suit to clerical robes in his approach to solving the children's murders. It was sort of like a prisoner laying down his dog-eared copy of *Penthouse* and picking up his uncracked Gideon Bible before walking down the hall to a meeting with the parole board.

Napper was not believable. He started with a platitude. He ended with a platitude and in between he filled in with platitudes. His rhetroic was a vacuum. The spectators had come to the conference hoping to find a way to make their children safe. I knew better. Here was Napper quoting the Bible, again and again. If the Bible would make Atlanta's children safe, they never would have been unsafe. We needed—and the occasion demanded—something useful from the chief of police. Only a few of us in the audience knew in advance that neither Napper nor any other chief of police had any idea of what to do about the situation. I wondered if Napper knew that.

Finally, a wiry, black man in the audience could stand it no more. He leaped to his feet and shouted, "George Napper, quit tellin' all these lies! These people came here to hear something about what you're gonna do about these killin's and you keep tellin' all these lies!"

Feet shuffled. Voices murmurred. Pandemonium erupted. The man stomped out, announcing that he had a petition that the people could sign and he would wait on the landing. He set up a card table and a chair, along with a ream of paper, which made a statement about the spontaneity of his interruption. He was a politician—presumably honest. I never will forget him using the few minutes of "equal time" he got from the local TV stations during a recent Atlanta election to challenge the veracity and honesty of his opponents. He was probably right, but he lost. But then, honesty is only a prerequisite for election in grade-school civics books. When are we going to stop lying to our kids?

Now, another black man rose, demanding an answer to what seemed a pointless question. Reasoning with him was like asking the name of a member of the Communist Workers Party and getting 27 pages of vintage Mao Tse-tung in return and still not learning the party member's name. Borders finally tricked the man into relinquishing the floor. "The sly old fox—he's handled hecklers before," I thought.

Next, a young man who identified himself as a police officer stood and asked, "Where are all the fathers?" He then complained about black communities being matriarchal and how fathers had abdicated their social responsibility. I thought the officer was right, and his eloquence was welcome, but his words were directed at the wrong people—those who felt responsible enough to attend.

Napper stood there mute. He wasn't used to a captive audience going wild. The arguments heated up. They shot from floor to speaker, across the aisles and across the backs of pews. Napper was the focus, but he might as well have been in Alaska. No one listened because everyone talked. A too-cute, anchor-type woman television reporter rushed down the aisle, towing a burdened cameraman by a microphone cord.

"Blessed are the peacemakers," I remembered. But, "discretion is the better part of valor," I remembered better. I walked out of the church and into the corridor to chat with the politician and two plainclothes cops, all of whom were enjoying Napper's predicament.

Little did I suspect that before the year ended, the Reverend Earl Carroll would sue the man he had introduced, Chief of Police George Napper, contending that the Atlanta police were harassing him. Nor did I know that a note signed "Rev. E. C." (could it be Earl Carroll?) would turn up significantly in the flight of a suspect to New England for his own safety.

I glanced back inside the door to the sanctuary. Had it been a different day, a different time, and had the crowd been predominantly white, not black, it would have looked for all the world like the Spencer Tracy version of the Scopes Monkey Trial. Fat women fanned furiously with those hand-held fans that look like Ping Pong paddles. Everyone had an opinion, but everyone also took sides.

No one, including, unfortunately, the Atlanta chief of police, was willing to admit there might be another explanation, that neither evolution nor creation was guaranteed to be right. No one was seeing the killings for what they were. They were *not* random kidnappings, and no amount of warnings or prayers was going to change the outcome at all. Attempts such as this meeting to make our children safe would only add to the paranoia of a city that didn't understand what was happening—and to our children's fear.

5

Psychic-ed Out

On the morning of July 30, 1980, Homer Williams, father of Wayne Williams, took the family's 1979 Ford LTD to the service department of Hub Ford in the Buckhead section of Atlanta. The sleek, red car looked much better than it ran. Because the dealer would have to keep the car for at least a week, Homer rented a Ford compact and returned home.

Later that same day, Earl Lee Terrell left his home at 1930 Brown's Mill Road. With some neighborhood friends, he headed for the South Bend Park swimming pool, across from the Lakewood Fairgrounds, a few miles south of downtown Atlanta, on Georgia 166.

At the pool, Earl enjoyed an 11-year-old boy's prankish fantasies. He ran around the pool, hauling the bottoms of little girls' swimming suits to their ankles. The sight of young children in the nude was not acceptable at the public pool, but it was a fetish with John David Wilcoxen, a white man who lived across the street from South Bend Park. A lifeguard evicted young Earl Terrell from the pool. John David Wilcoxen would emerge in headlines months later.

Earl Terrell sat for awhile on one of the park benches that ring the circular pool. Then—he disappeared. A woman said she saw him after 3:30 p.m. "He was," she said, "standin' on the corner near Jonesboro Road, cryin'."

We would learn that after Earl left the pool area, he stopped at a nearby house, looking for a boy who lived there but wasn't home.

Earl wasn't supposed to leave home that day. Beverly Belt, Earl's mother, said he was on restriction for bad behavior. But Earl's grandma had said it was all right for him to go swimming. When Earl didn't come home, his relatives scoured the neighborhood, looking for him. They were about to call the police when they received a strange telephone call on a next-door neighbor's phone.

On the line, they said, was a man who "sounded like" a middle-aged white man with a Southern drawl. Vickie Terrell (we wondered if Terrell really was her surname), Earl's aunt, listened to the caller, whom she quoted as saying, "I've got Earl. Don't call the police." The caller, Vickie Terrell said, wanted to talk to Vickie's sister (Beverly Belt? The police report does not clarify this point).

Between five and 10 minutes after the first telephone call, the phone rang again. The same male voice said, "I've got Earl. He's in Alabama. It will cost you $200 to get him back. I will call back on Friday."

Vickie Terrell went next door to tell her sister, Beverly Belt, about the caller. But Beverly, who had just returned from work at 10 p.m., dismissed the call. She thought Earl would be with friends. Beverly had many good friends in the neighborhood. In fact, she said, "all the neighbors" were her friends. She might have been surprised to see what some of them told authorities about the tenor of her children's life and how they behaved. A white family in the neighborhood offered to provide the $200 demanded by the caller.

Beverly Belt would later publicly criticize the Atlanta police for releasing information about the telephone calls. She said she believed the man would have called back Friday, as he said he would, if the earlier calls hadn't been widely reported.

Earl Terrell's father was not James Belt. Nor was it Willie Terrell, who fathered Beverly's four other children and gave Earl his surname. Rather, it was Bennie Yarn. Neighbors said that Bennie Yarn was trying to get custody of Earl.

A wiretap was placed on the neighbor's phone in anticipation of a Friday call from the man who said he was holding Earl Terrell. He didn't call back, but the tap netted one black man who was questioned by police but later released.

Meanwhile, investigators working the Earl Terrell case would stumble onto a child-pornography ring. Part of it operated on the fringes of South Bend Park, where Earl Terrell had gone swimming on the day he disappeared. One of three men who would be arrested in the pornography case—then convicted and sent to the penitentiary in 1981—was John David Wilcoxen, who lived on Compton Street. From his front door, you can almost look into the South Bend Park gymnasium.

The police confiscated a boxload of pictures—"2,000 to 4,000," one police report says. All the pictures, they insisted, were of white (not black) boys. "There is no connection with *the* murders," the authorities told the public, even though they had evidence that there might be a connection.

A 15-year-old witness told the authorities: "I know that [the boy—name omitted] has been to Dave Wilcoxen's house on several occasions. I know that [the boy] has passed off Earl Terrell as being his little brother . . . I have not seen it but I know that [the boy] and Earl Lee Terrell have probably been in Dave Wilcoxen's house on several occasions. I am very familiar with Earl Lee Terrell and [the boy]."

The man who had actually been caught with the pictures had rented a room at the Alamo Plaza motel. The Alamo, with its Spanish-style facade, sits on the edge of Stewart Avenue's porn and nudie strip, a block from where 14-year-old Lubie (Chuck) Geter would disappear.

The man with the pictures was identified in police reports. His home was on Glenwood Road near the East Lake Meadows housing project's bus stop, where a neighbor had taken 14-year-old Alfred Evans. The man had also lived at 1st Avenue and Memorial Drive for 10 years. This is the intersection where a 17-year-old named Kenny Brown says he heard a screaming boy murdered by gunshot. This area would become a focal point in the disappearance of 10-year-old Darron Glass and the murders of William Barrett and Angela Bacon.

The man told police he had spent three years in a California mental hospital. The reason, he said, was "child molestation." He also told police he had been arrested in New Orleans for the same offense. He explained that he obtained the photographs of the nude children from a closet at John David Wilcoxen's house.

Meanwhile, police had checked out the 15-year-old witness' story. They located and talked with the boy, whose name has been omitted in the account of that witness' claims. "I'm good friends with Earl Terrell—I call him Peanut," he told them, according to a police report. "Earl and I used to pose as brothers to everybody . . . I am also familiar with John David Wilcoxen, Lionel St. Louis and Frank Hardy. All three of these men have administered sexual acts with me. I have been with Frank Hardy at least three to four times in his little *blue* [emphasis added] car, and each time . . . he administered sexual acts with me and he paid me approximtely $5.00. I've had sex with St. Louis . . ."

The police report continued: "I've been in Dave Wilcoxen's house approximately 20 times or better where he administered sexual acts with me. He also *took my pictures* [emphasis added—the witness is a black youngster] and he paid me $5 for the act."

An Atlanta police recruit assigned to the Task Force would also dispute the authorities' whites-only story when the pornography ring surfaced publicly. He says he helped carry the pictures the police had confiscated at the Alamo Plaza into the Task Force offices and that there were pictures of black boys. The pictures, the recruit said, were kept in Task Force commander Morris Redding's office. "Later, when we carried the pictures out of the office," the ex-recruit added, "all the pictures of black boys were gone."

Of course, many of these claims are just that—claims. But the same can be said for any witness' testimony. But in the case of testimony, a jury gets to decide. The ex-recruit, Kenneth Lawson, would in 1982 testify for the defense at the Wayne Williams trial. But at that trial, there would be no mention of

Wilcoxen, St. Louis, Hardy or the man with the photographs.

The boy who said he had been in John David Wilcoxen's house also told police: "I know that Earl Lee Terrell has been in Dave Wilcoxen's house at least 20 times. I also remember seeing Earl Lee Terrell over here on several occasions when I was not with him at Wilcoxen's house.

"I remember that [two other males] and me are the ones that took Earl over to Dave Wilcoxen's house on several occasions. I remember sometimes . . . Dave Wilcoxen would take us to a lake or wooded area where he would get our cookies [administer oral sex].

"I am familiar with a boy named *Chuck Geter* [another victim, also known as Lubie Geter—emphasis added]. I remember seeing Chuck Geter ride with David Wilcoxen on the back of his [Wilcoxen's] motorcycle on at least two occasions. I remember Geter making comments to me and Earl [Earl Lee Terrell] on several occasions about us going to Dave Wilcoxen's house. Each time he made these comments to us, we always told Geter that he was doing the same thing we were doing to get the money. This would make Geter mad and he would walk away and leave us . . .

"I know that Earl had oral sex done to him by Dave Wilcoxen, because that was the purpose of us going to Dave's house. Dave would also pay me money each time that I brought a new person over to his house for sex."

These kinds of activities should have come as no surprise to Atlanta investigators. When the killings intensified later in 1980, these investigators were advised by a Kentucky friend of mine, John Rabun, to join forces with social workers and not rule out child sex-for-hire as a factor in the murders. Some children earn as much as $200 a night, Rabun said, for providing sexual favors to adults.

Rabun, as manager of the Louisville-Jefferson County Criminal Justice Commission's Exploited Child Unit, visited Atlanta at my suggestion, but not until after the Atlanta police refused to hear him out. We then contacted the Justice Department, which invited Rabun to meet with the authorities at a closed-door meeting arranged by the department's Community Relations Service. Even so, when Rabun suggested that some or all of Atlanta's slain children may also be victims of "sexploitation," he said Atlanta's authorities showed little interest.

"If the same set of murders occurred in Louisville, my working assumption would be to pursue that angle [child sex] until we could prove otherwise," Rabun said, noting that many youngsters who run away from home are vulnerable to physical advances by adults. "You've got kids who may be rebelling against their own families. Then you've got the same kids who are suddenly shown love and adoration by strangers outside their families. What else can a 12 or 14-year-old do the first night out and be an instant success—and make a lot of money?

"The trouble is, the kid's pimp or procurer gets most of that money, and then they eventually may fight over it . . . You have a situation that is made-to-order for tragedy."

Meanwhile, few took those phone calls to Earl Terrell's neighbor's house very seriously, but I always thought they provided an interesting twist to the cases. With a voice saying Earl was in Alabama and demanding a ransom, the calls seemed to clear the path for the legal entry of the FBI into the case under the Lindbergh law, which pertains to interstate kidnapping.

Had the calls not come before the police were notified, and had the caller asked for more money, it might have been difficult to convince some of us that the calls were not a ruse for exactly that purpose—getting the FBI into the case (legally—in reality, it was already there).

In a few months, Atlanta Mayor Maynard Jackson and the FBI would be locked in an imbroglio with political and constitutional overtones. The mayor was demanding assistance from the FBI. The FBI countered that it had no legal basis for entering the cases.

Actually, the FBI had already quietly entered the cases months earlier. I wondered whether the only result of Mayor Jackson's demands was to tear off the FBI's cover. Back in June of 1980, a police department spokesman had reported that the FBI had, indeed, entered the case of 7-year-old LaTonya Wilson, in the event that she may have been kidnapped and taken across state lines.

But all that seemed to have been forgotten by the mayor, who by late 1980 was politically appealing for FBI help that already had arrived. It seemed that the FBI was on solid legal footing to enter the Terrell case. With Georgia's own Jimmy Carter sitting in the White House, it's hard to believe that any loophole—particularly one as big as the ransom phone call—would not have been exploited.

But it took the Reagan Administration to order the Justice Department directly into the murder cases (as opposed to kidnapping—kidnapping across state lines is a federal offense, while murder is not)—a decision that stands on shaky constitutional ground at best.

Earl Terrell's mother clung tenaciously to the hope that Earl was alive even as the summer of 1980 turned to autumn, then winter. She believed that he was out there, somewhere, and if he could only get to Jonesboro Road, he could find his way home. If the other woman who said she saw him sobbing on a street corner near Jonesboro Road was right, then Beverly Belt was wrong. Maybe they were both wrong. Earl Lee Terrell was dead.

So now we had a Task Force. How was the investigation going?

By August of 1980, leads in the murder cases were concealed like an aging movie star's wrinkles. You knew they were there, but you couldn't find them by just looking. Those that had already surfaced had long since begun to grow cold because of lack of followup.

Police continued to treat each case like a missing-persons case until a body turned up. Since missing-persons investigations have never enjoyed a high priority in police operations, the non-results were predictable. From the outset, these investigations should have been handled with the same urgency as homicides. But even as long as eight months after Earl Terrell disappeared, victims were still not being assigned the priority of a Task Force investigation until after their remains were found—even though they might have been reported missing months before. And some victims' cases were ignored for additional months, even after these same victims had been found dead.

If you report someone missing to the police, you have this mental picture of people jumping up and scurrying off to look for him. Such is not the case. It is business as usual. As in the Jefferey Mathis case, the radio-broadcast "lookout" is perfunctory. It isn't the kind of message that most police officers bother to write down—or, for that matter, even to listen to. There would be no written record kept at the communications center—at least none that would survive one shift change. In three hours, when the new shift came on duty, the message itself would be as unaccounted for as the person it mentioned. Contrary to public perceptions, notifying the police and in turn having them notify their brother officers by radio *does not* cause the message to be entered immediately into the department's information system. It could be days before that happens or, at the very least, not until after a formal report is taken.

Remember when Jefferey Mathis disappeared in early 1980? Atlanta's ordeal already had gone on for at least eight months. But, when 14-year-old Lubie (Chuck) Geter would be missing in January of 1981—10 months after Jefferey's disappearance—Geter's case would receive virtually the same apathetic treatment as Jefferey's.

Nobody would immediately notify the Task Force, even though this was supposed to be standard operating procedure by the winter of 1981. The Task Force, a special unit created to investigate the disappearances and murders of "children," had existed for almost six months when Lubie Geter disappeared.

Despite Public Safety Commissioner Lee Brown's and Mayor Jackson's statements that "no stone is being left unturned," when Lubie Geter was reported missing, the information was not sent to the Task Force for more than 36 hours. No large-scale search or investigation of the crime scene (where he was last seen) began until two days after the police were originally notified.

Captain Johnny Sparks, who was in charge of Crimes Against Persons (which included missing persons), would be reprimanded in the winter of 1981 for his handling of the Lubie Geter case. But the reprimand came only after apparent attempts to make scapegoats of two women officers who were under Sparks' command and who would be transferred. One of those officers,

Sergeant T.A. Sturgis, had been the *only* Atlanta police officer to express a concern, in writing, about the unusual number of children being murdered. She did so even before Camille Bell marched on City Hall.

For his purported role in the Lubie Geter fiasco, Captain Sparks would be stripped of most of his command. But, oddly, the one responsibility which was left to him was the command of the Missing Persons unit—even after having been accused of messing up, of all things, a missing-persons case! That in itself is a statement by the Atlanta Police Bureau of where missing-persons cases rank among other crimes against persons.

It was the "business as usual" approach to missing children—even with so many turning up dead—that Mike Edwards and Jack Perry constantly complained about in the media. I made it a point never once to criticize the police publicly for the duration of the investigations. I figured it could only hurt.

To anyone, it might be inconceivable that missing children would remain the bureaucratic stepchild of the Atlanta Police Bureau as late as January of 1981—especially with millions around the world following the cases in newspapers and magazines and on radio and television.

August, 1980

During late 1980, news-media pressure on the police mounted every day. With nothing concrete to go on, everybody seemed willing to chase anybody's wild goose. It all blazed an inevitable trail into what I called the "psychic phase" of the investigation.

At this juncture, no one in Atlanta was experienced with psychic involvement in criminal investigations. We knew that psychics' work had been futile in Columbus, Georgia, where the so-called "Columbus Strangler" killed seven elderly white women between September, 1977, and April, 1978. The Columbus cases remain unsolved. They merely *stopped*, seemingly as spontaneously as they started (not when somebody went to jail).

But psychics weren't supposed to be always right. You didn't need to look very far to find plenty of instances where their work had been highly praised. My colleague, Mike Edwards, was prone to follow psychics' leads. But as soon as I heard the word "psychic," my "crap detector" started sounding off like the alarm on Jack Benny's imaginary vault.

Already, Mike had been on several fruitless treks, armed only with a seer's clues and the naive encouragement of yet another "believer." So far Mike hadn't interested me in any of these odysseys based on messages from the astral plain. I didn't think that anybody's dream was worth the first chigger bite.

Still, a phone call from Mike intrigued me. He'd been in touch with a famous psychic who had written a book about her experiences in helping police solve "impossible" murder cases. To be sure, the accomplishments she listed in her book—and which she recounted on the Phil Donahue television show—sounded impressive.

Mary Hylbak, the "Mid-day" coordinator for the Atlanta all-news radio station, WGST, had contacted the psychic, Dorothy Allison, a 55-year-old New Jersey author, after her talk-show appearance. Mary sought a general interview on Dorothy Allison's experiences, but the conversation soon turned to the Atlanta murders. Dorothy Allison was intrigued—and immediately said so. Her comments about stopping the madman who was killing "my little darlings" were sweeter than saccharin.

Mary Hylbak put Dorothy Allison directly in touch with Mike Edwards. Mike taped his telephone conversations with Allison. She had given him various clues, which she preferred to call "nouns," to say nothing of clauses, phrases and even a few sentences she threw in.

Armed with these clues, Mike had singled out an area he thought should be searched. He persuaded me to go along. Before we left, Mike dubbed the tape and sent a copy to Atlanta Police Sergeant H.L. Bolton, the Task Force's initial commander.

We climbed into Mike's blue Dodge van and headed for places unknown to me. Now in early August of 1980, my knowledge of Atlanta's geography was superficial at best. But I was soon to take a crash course.

South Bend Park stretched alongside a creek which fed into the South River. At the other side of the park, a few feet from the green-gabled shelter house, a dirt road turned off Lakewood Avenue. I slid down from the bucket seat, missing the van step, which was just a little too far to reach. The heavy chain which blocked our progress along the dirt road was not locked. I lifted it from the hook on a leaning iron pole.

Now we drove the winding, narrow swath in the woods, easing into and out of a succession of potholes and ruts. I wondered if the Chrysler Corporation had outfitted Mike's van with square tires.

As we jounced along, Mike began briefing me on what I was supposed to look for:

—Red, blue or purplish flowers.

—The smell of burned plastic.

—The number "315"

—And, of course, a body.

Enroute, Mike explained to me how he had selected the site we would search. He said it had to do with looking in a certain direction, toward a clear lake or "Crystal Lake," and proceeding five miles south, as the crow flies. I almost expected him to tell me he had to offer a sacrifice and chant an incantation. The logic still eludes me, perhaps because there isn't any.

It was an interesting afternoon. There was a variety of red, blue and purplish flowers. Most adorned the kudzu vines which, during the summer, are in full bloom from North Carolina to Alabama. There was a smell of burned plastic, or a reasonable facsimile. At least, the odor was more pungent than those from my Vantage 100 cigarettes.

At one point, I emerged from the woods into a chest-high thicket of grass. To the north of that grassy patch was the swimming pool where Earl Lee Terrell had been last seen alive a few weeks earlier.

Civilization resumed about 10 feet from the roadway. A 28-foot-wide path yielded exactly what one might expect from modern man in his natural setting: soda-pop and beer cans, whiskey and wine bottles, empty white paper bags which once wrapped hamburgers and french fries, plus other artifacts, including pink panties.

Only a few discarded bicycle parts held any promise. There was no "315" and, to my simultaneous joy and despair, no body. My first supernatural scavenger hunt added up to plenty of nothing.

We hooked up the gate chain again and headed north. All we had to show for our afternoon in the woods was a rusting 20-inch bicycle wheel, and a toy racing number plate inscribed "98."

Returning to Mike's office, we passed other locations that Mike somehow related to Dorothy Allison's clues. The magic in them seemed to be that they were as generic and endemic to wherever you are as air, grass, water and trees. The venture ended with Mike asking me if I would go out with him again the next day. "Sure," I answered. I actually enjoyed the search, although I hated to admit it.

The next day, we were joined by Dick Arena. Along with his police experience, Dick had manned a Cold War listening post on the Turkish-Russian border. He excelled at analyzing the slightest bits of information.

We headed west—beyond where we had searched the day before—to the Lakewood Fairgrounds. The old exposition center, with its Spanish-style architecture, had enjoyed a rebirth as a locale for the filming of two Burt Reynolds movies, *"Smokey and the Bandit,"* Parts I and II.

It was the Lakewood Fairgrounds where one Atlanta public official—then-City Councilman Arthur Langford Jr., chairman of the Council's Public Safety Committee, which monitors the police and fire departments—had troubles with a federal grand jury over alleged activities involving the 1978 Southeastern Fair.

At about that same time, another Atlanta public official—Deputy Police Chief Eldrin Bell—was implicated in an investigation into whether police were being paid off to protect gambling at the fair. But no one was arrested for gambling, and Bell was not formally charged. He was cleared by the office of Fulton County District Attorney Lewis Slaton, who would prosecute Wayne Williams.

It was not the first time that Eldrin Bell's activities had been questioned. Bell, who once was Mayor Jackson's bodyguard, had steadily climbed the police ranks, stalked by controversy at almost every rung.

In 1975, an Atlanta police car assigned to Bell was set afire in the driveway of a woman friend whom Bell was visiting. In 1979, police investigated Bell about his alleged relationship with an Atlanta nightclub owner who also was being probed about his reputed ties with organized crime. The investigative unit's commander, Major Bill Clark, resigned from the police force after charging that Police Chief George Napper had tipped Bell in advance about the investigation. Napper was cleared by a City Attorney's investigation, which also was unable to prove the charges against Bell.

By 1981, Eldrin Bell would be called a "cat with nine lives"—his career hanging perilously by a thread, only for him to land on both feet. That same year, Bell would be accused of misusing his authority and receiving a $3,000 fee as "security consultant" in authorizing the use of Atlanta police cars in the filming of another Burt Reynolds movie, "*Sharkey's Machine.*" Bell reportedly returned the money after Chief Napper refused to let him continue working with the film's production company. Whereupon Bell filed a lawsuit charging that Napper forced him to quit as a security coordinator at the Omni Sports Arena—another moonlighting job.

Meanwhile, when we arrived at the Lakewood Fairgrounds, the place swarmed with Atlanta police. We drove unchallenged into the middle of the official search. No one in our car would have permitted us to do it—if the shoe had been on the other foot.

We stopped near the outside rail of the old race-car track that now dominated the fairgrounds landscape after Smokey and his Bandits blew up the gigantic old roller-coaster. A police helicopter hovered low over the lake that occupied the infield of the oval dirt track. Halfway around the track, two police officers bounced stiffly along on their matching chestnut mounts.

Mike and I decided that nothing was to be gained by sharing the search with the Atlanta police. Dick Arena, however, opted to stay with the official undertaking. One Atlanta police officer decided that our adventures might be less boring. He abandoned his post without a how-do-you-do to a supervisor and joined Mike and me as we set off for greener pastures to search.

We headed for a place the officer thought was called "Lake Christy." This interested Mike because it sounded like Dorothy Allison's "Crystal Lake." I hadn't yet seen *"Friday the 13th,"* or I would have jumped all over that "Crystal Lake" business (in the movie, teen-age counselors at a summer camp were all killed in and around "Crystal Lake"). "Lake Christy" turned out to be Lake Charolette (sic), or so the yellow letters on the brown, saw-tooth-rimmed sign announced.

If Dorothy Allison had missed on what was past, we were about to miss on what was yet to come. Our search was three months premature. Nine-year-old Aaron Jackson's body would be found one block from the entrance to Lake Charolette, beneath a South River bridge, just off Forest Park Road in November of 1980.

Later, yet another psychic would claim credit for predicting the location of the Aaron Jackson murder scene. Atlanta police entered this psychic's prediction in their files, and later Judge Clarence Cooper would select it as a piece of information that tended to be exculpatory to Wayne Williams. I wonder why the judge overlooked the other thousands of psychic predictions that would have tended to be exculpatory to Wayne Williams.

A strange twist to the story of Atlanta's murdered "youths" would focus on the 1981 murder of an attorney whose body would be left at Lake Charolette by two "youngsters" after an alleged homosexual tryst. There "could not be" a connection to the other murders, however, since "Wayne Williams was in jail," and obviously, the murders had "*stopped*," right?

Everywhere we stopped, my companions would say it "looks like the place" that Allison described. The reason was the omni-present kudzu blooms. To me, it was like a visit to an archeological dig. It was a weird, almost eerie place.

There were abandoned houses and even a cracked, decaying swimming pool that now more closely resembled a sunken, exotic weed garden. Here and there was an occupied dwelling. Each reflected a bygone opulence.

Like cattle skulls in a desert, the rusting carcasses of 1960s-model automobiles rested on their sides, tops and axles. Chickens, ducks, mean-assed-looking dogs and even a pig prowled the open spaces. Twenty yards on either side of every lived-in house, it was jungle again.

Lake Charolette itself was big and potentially beautiful, with some care. I wondered how one of nature's gifts could fall into misuse within five miles of the asphalt and concrete of downtown Atlanta. But there it stood, with not even a stray fisherman in sight.

Off the roadway you couldn't see a space where a body might not be hidden. A visible pair of tire tracks passed through an opening in a fence bearing a rusting sign: "BEWARE OF DOGS." The sign also listed a telephone number which included the digits "3," "1" and "5."

"315" had been a Dorothy Allison clue. She had mentioned in the small print that the numbers might be transposed or even out of sequence. As far as I was concerned, she needed a new set of blades for her crystal-ball wipers.

The tire tracks went on up the hill through 2-foot-high grass and ended at a building that looked like an abandoned airplane hangar.

"Chet, why don't you walk up and check that out?" Mike suggested.

"Bull-shit," I replied. "I can read. The sign says, 'Beware of Dogs.'"

"Aw, hell," Mike shot back, "That's obviously an old sign left over from when that building was occupied."

"OK," I said, "then *you* walk up and investigate."

We compromised by driving up the hill. It's a good thing we did. Within 50 yards of the building, we were surrounded by feverishly yelping, angrily barking, scroungy-looking, snarling mongrels. I was afraid they might eat the car.

The Atlanta policeman with us hollered a greeting to a young black man who leaned against the front of the building, on the two rear legs of his ladder-backed wooden chair.

"Shut-up!" the man screamed—once. Immediately, it was quiet. Not another growl or whimper was heard from what looked like at least 150 dogs. Beside the pack of dogs that had met us on the hill, there were more—many more—chained inside the building.

The policeman flashed his badge and motioned for the black man to approach the car.

"What the hell is this?" I asked as the man drew closer. We had discovered the kennels of "Bad Dogs, Incorporated," a security-dog training kennel.

The road circled the lake and, on the way back to the entrance, we saw a fire-gutted building. It would have been easy to overlook. Only a stone fireplace and chimney poked out of the rubble, which was blanketed with strangling kudzu vines. I was about to be introduced to another Dorothy Allison clue. Mike remembered that she had said something about a body lying in a place that "resembled a cave." The fireplace would qualify as cave-like, Mike decided.

I stepped gingerly through the charred debris. In a way, walking on kudzu is like walking on an ice-covered pond. You're never sure when you'll be introduced to what is just below. Our search turned up the usual assortment of panties, shoes, socks, cans, bottles, oil-soaked rags and used spark plugs. There even were some kids' clothes that *might* have been bloodstained. We left it up to the officer to decide whether to leave the scene as it was and notify whomever he cared to.

I hadn't seen anything that I hadn't seen before and wouldn't see a hundred times again. I would remember this trip again a few months later when the *Atlanta Consitution* reported on one of the United Youth Adult Conference's organized volunteer searches: that the searchers had found clothing "similar to—but not the same as" that worn by 14-year-old victim Lubie Geter. I remembered that I had passed up several trailer-truck loads of that kind of evidence during our psychic searches.

As we returned to the Lakewood Fairgrounds, Mike pointed out various places that seemed to jibe with other Dorothy Allison "nouns." No matter where we went, we found something that made her predictions seem on the verge of coming true. I might not solve these cases, but I was determined to find out how the "professional psychics" operated. My unbridled cynicism about psychic visions returned in one swoop.

I asked Mike for a list of the clues Allison had given him. He removed a dog-eared piece of paper from his shirt pocket. I read the scribbled clues:

1. Reynolds. (That's why she picked Lakewood Fairgrounds, I thought, because Burt *Reynolds* had made his movies there. Not so, I soon found out.)
2. Claire. (It could be "clear," as in the clear water of Crystal Lake, a footnote explained.)

3. Ice—"Why do I see ice?" (Mike noted that Dorothy Allison had repeated this question three or four times.)

4. A hospital.

5. A monastery or something that resembled one.

6. A meeting hall.

7. A policeman had died nearby. (It could have been a natural death, Mike had noted.)

8. A body could be in something that looks like a cave.

9. A bar.

10. "315."

11. "48."

12. Red, blue, or purplish flowers.

13. The smell of burning plastic.

14. A bell (as in Southern Bell; it could be a telephone).

"What did she ask you, or what did you tell her," I asked Mike, "before she gave you these clues?"

"She only asked one question," Mike replied. "She asked me where the last kid disappeared from. I told her, and she started giving me the clues."

A metro-Atlanta atlas lay open on my lap. It was opened to the area we were searching. The car lurched to a stop. Mike looked around. Then he said: "I remember a retired officer who lived in this area and died of a heart attack a few years ago."

"Aw, come on, Mike," I pleaded. I was up to my nose in gullibility. I looked out the window and my eyes fell upon a street sign: "Polar Rock Road"! I remembered the Allison clue: "Why do I see ice?" Now I gazed at the atlas and found Polar Rock Road. There it was! Right close to "Reynolds" Road, which ran into the fairgrounds near the South Bend Park swimming pool, just south of "Claire" Street.

I started laughing. "Why do I see ice?" I kept repeating to myself. The mystique of a psychic giving clues from hundreds of miles away evaporated quickly. Hell, I could do it for any place from Anywhere, U.S.A. If Dorothy Allison could do it for Atlanta from Nutley, New Jersey, I could also do it for Hoboken, or Philadelphia, or Anchorage from Atlanta, Georgia.

In a minute, we were back at the Lakewood Fairgrounds, "Hey, Dick, come here a minute," I called. "I want to show you how to become a psychic." Dick puts some stock in astrology, *et cetera.* I don't.

The cover of my atlas contained a backdrop of red, blue and purplish flowers. The first major object to the east of the fairgrounds, which appears on the map, is the Southview Hospital. Its Red Cross marking stood out against the yellow-and-green background of the map. Immediately north of the fairgrounds is a seminary (well, at least it's similar to a monastery).

Mike hunched over the open door of the car, his elbows resting on the roof. "Dick," I said, "you can do it with maps. Remember, Mike gave the location where the last kid disappeared. And, here are the clues on the map within a mile of where the kid disappeared."

Some psychics are good investigators, and for those whose information is going to be useful—except for an occasional random stab in the dark that seems to come true—fact, knowledge and logic, not an ultranatural force, act as a crystal ball. The chances are 50-50 that the body will be found close to the point of disappearance. Find out where that point is, and look it up on a map. Then give clues that can be found close by on the map. You've got a 50-50 chance of being right. Soon people familiar with the half you're right about will swear by you and recommend you to others, while the other half won't complain because you never claimed to be 100% correct. But remember that 50% is about 30% better than the police do. But, the police work at it.

"That's all well and good," Mike rejoined, "but how do you explain the number '48' and the number '315?'"

My eyes moved to the bottom of the page in the atlas. I hadn't noticed it before, but it read: "Joins Map 48."

It took a while longer to figure out the "315," but sometime later we found it printed lightly in the background, as part of a postal zip-code information furnished on the map. The entire area around South Bend Park is in postal zone 30*315*!

Dick Arena and I went back to Mike's office to listen more closely to the Dorothy Allison tapes. At one point in the recording, Mike told her, "I was a cop for 20 years." She interrupted him pointedly and said at the top of her voice, almost shouting, "Clemente! Clemente! Could there be Clemente here?"

Dick played back that part of the tape again and again.

"Chet, that's a code," he said. If there were someone else in the room, saying things out loud would give that other person a chance to look things up. In my opinion, "Clemente" is a code that tells something to the other person in the room.

I forgot about this incident for awhile, but it would come back and hit me like a 2-by-4 across the nose.

Dorothy Allison was coming to Atlanta. The media hype bordered on the outrageous. It was like the talk about Santa Claus in the weeks before Christmas. But you were relatively sure that these seemingly intelligent adults in the news media didn't really believe in the physical presence of Santa Claus.

Allison's paperback book was conspicuously displayed at a Peachtree Center newsstand. She said she wouldn't leave "until the killer was behind bars." Of course, the Japanese had said in 1941 that they would fight for a thousand years. And the special police Task Force in Columbus, Georgia, said it would continue the effort until the murderer of those elderly women was brought to justice. Of course, the Japanese surrendered unconditionally four years later—and the Task Force in Columbus gave up a lot quicker than that.

Well, Dorothy Allison didn't fare any better when reporters asked her about the killer or killers. She said she was "following him" in her mind. She said she could "see his every move." "I have mental control over him," she said. Then, on Atlanta television, she challenged the killer to "come and try to strangle me."

Chief George Napper had painted himself into a corner on this psychic business. Napper found out that Allison was talking directly to Mike Edwards. On the outside chance that she possessed any psychic powers, Napper wanted to be absolutely certain that she gave her information only to the police.

Napper called Mary Hylbak at WGST and demanded Dorothy Allison's unlisted telephone number. According to Mike, Allison informed him that she had been told by Napper that any future dealings in Atlanta were to be with the "official" police investigation.

Dorothy Allison maintained a surreptitious contact with us. In fact, she called and gave us the name of a suspect that her "investigation" had developed. Since no more than four people, including the chief of police, were supposed to know that name, Mike couldn't help using the information as a little surprise for Napper. When I turned over my information to Detectives Mike Shannon and John Woods, Mike gave them the name of the suspect without telling the name's significance. He asked them to mention the name to Napper, which, according to the two officers, they did. The discovery of the "leak" caused quite a flap in the chief's office, which delighted Mike to no end.

In the media, Dorothy Allison became a creation of the Atlanta police—a Frankenstein they didn't want. The headlines proclaimed that she was on her way to solving the Atlanta murder cases as a guest of the Atlanta Police Bureau.

When she arrived in Atlanta, she stayed at a luxurious hotel and drank expensive wine, for which the city picked up the tab. Allison's performance didn't match her claims or those of the two men who traveled with her—ostensibly police officers from Pennsylvania and Louisiana, respectively. The media hype quickly turned to media gripe. And just as quickly, Dorothy Allison left town.

If the Dorothy Allison flap wasn't the obituary for George Napper's Atlanta police career, it was his epitaph with the Task Force. He remained chief of police, but Lee Brown removed him from any role in the children's cases (other than visiting parents' homes to tell them their children were found dead).

Thus, Atlanta's murder cases took on another unique twist. The chief of police was not to be involved in trying to solve the greatest murder mystery ever to confront the very department he commanded. George Napper, at 41, soon would apply for the job of police chief in Berkeley, California, next door to his childhood hometown of Oakland, only to have the deal fall through soon after his application was announced. He would later be promoted to the job of public safety commissioner by Atlanta's newly elected mayor, Andrew Young.

I had put the Dorothy Allison farce on the back burner. Then one afternoon, months later, I was working in my office at home. An old *Rockford File* rerun, starring James Garner, appeared on television.

The story was about a psychic who met a private investigator (Rockford), who once was a police officer. Through Rockford, the psychic gained credence with the official police agency, which, in turn, gave the psychic a public aura of authenticity.

As events in the screenplay unraveled, the psychic promoted his book on a national TV talk show and told about how he helped the police solve important cases.

"Now where have I heard *this* before?" I mused.

Rockford's psychic's name was *Clemente*!

6

Geography of Murder

August, 1980

For more than a month during the summer of 1980, I had pored over the information in photo-copied police reports—those Mike Edwards had been able to obtain through midnight requisitions.

The information was terribly inaccurate. One police-prepared chart said Eric Middlebrooks was last seen on May 18, 1980, but his body was found on May 10, 1980. Nine-year-old Anthony Carter, the chart said, was stabbed to death, but he was still missing. Atlanta Public Safety Commissioner Lee Brown had accepted a report containing these kinds of inconsistencies and allowed it to be released uncorrected.

If this part of the police information was wrong, then all of it was suspect. No part of a murder investigation can be allowed to be sloppy. I turned to the geographic data. At least, it would be verifiable. There would be three points: (1) where the victims lived, (2) where they disappeared and (3) where bodies were found (if found).

Plotting these points on a map, I would discover a geographic pattern—that the Atlanta murders unfolded on or near 12 major streets that link up in the configuration of a misshapen boot. By the time I got around to drawing the map in late August of 1980, Christopher Richardson, 11, and Milton Harvey, 14, had been added to The List. So had Earl Terrell, 11. Terrell and Richardson still were missing.

It is ironic that these three children (three of the four who would be added to The List in August), though they had disappeared months apart, would come together from three far corners of my 12-street route—and be found dead within yards of each other at the fourth corner. These pieces of the puzzle fit perfectly and told me I was right.

CHET'S MAP

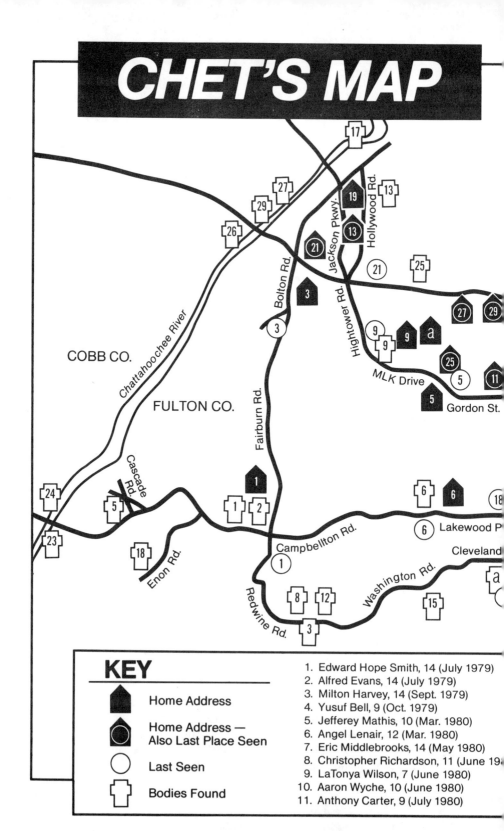

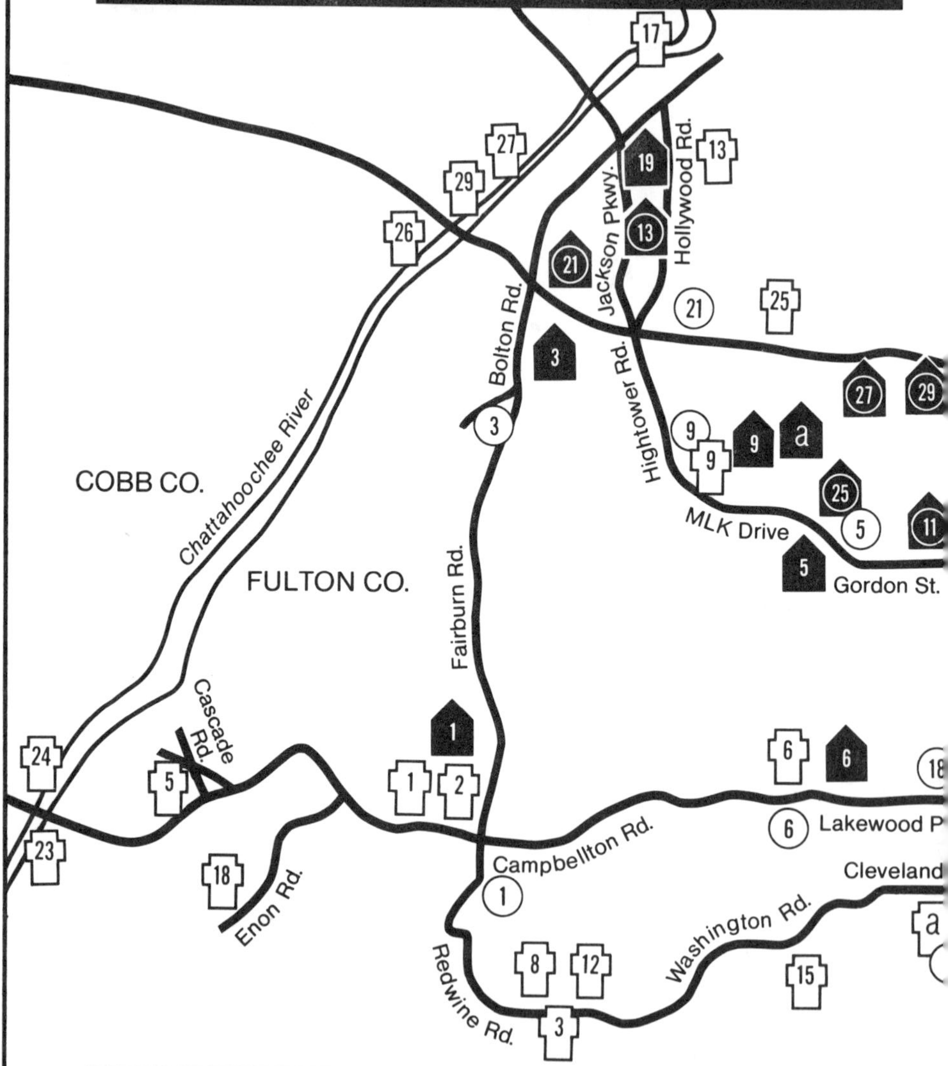

KEY

Home Address

Home Address — Also Last Place Seen

Last Seen

Bodies Found

1. Edward Hope Smith, 14 (July 1979)
2. Alfred Evans, 14 (July 1979)
3. Milton Harvey, 14 (Sept. 1979)
4. Yusuf Bell, 9 (Oct. 1979)
5. Jefferey Mathis, 10 (Mar. 1980)
6. Angel Lenair, 12 (Mar. 1980)
7. Eric Middlebrooks, 14 (May 1980)
8. Christopher Richardson, 11 (June 19
9. LaTonya Wilson, 7 (June 1980)
10. Aaron Wyche, 10 (June 1980)
11. Anthony Carter, 9 (July 1980)

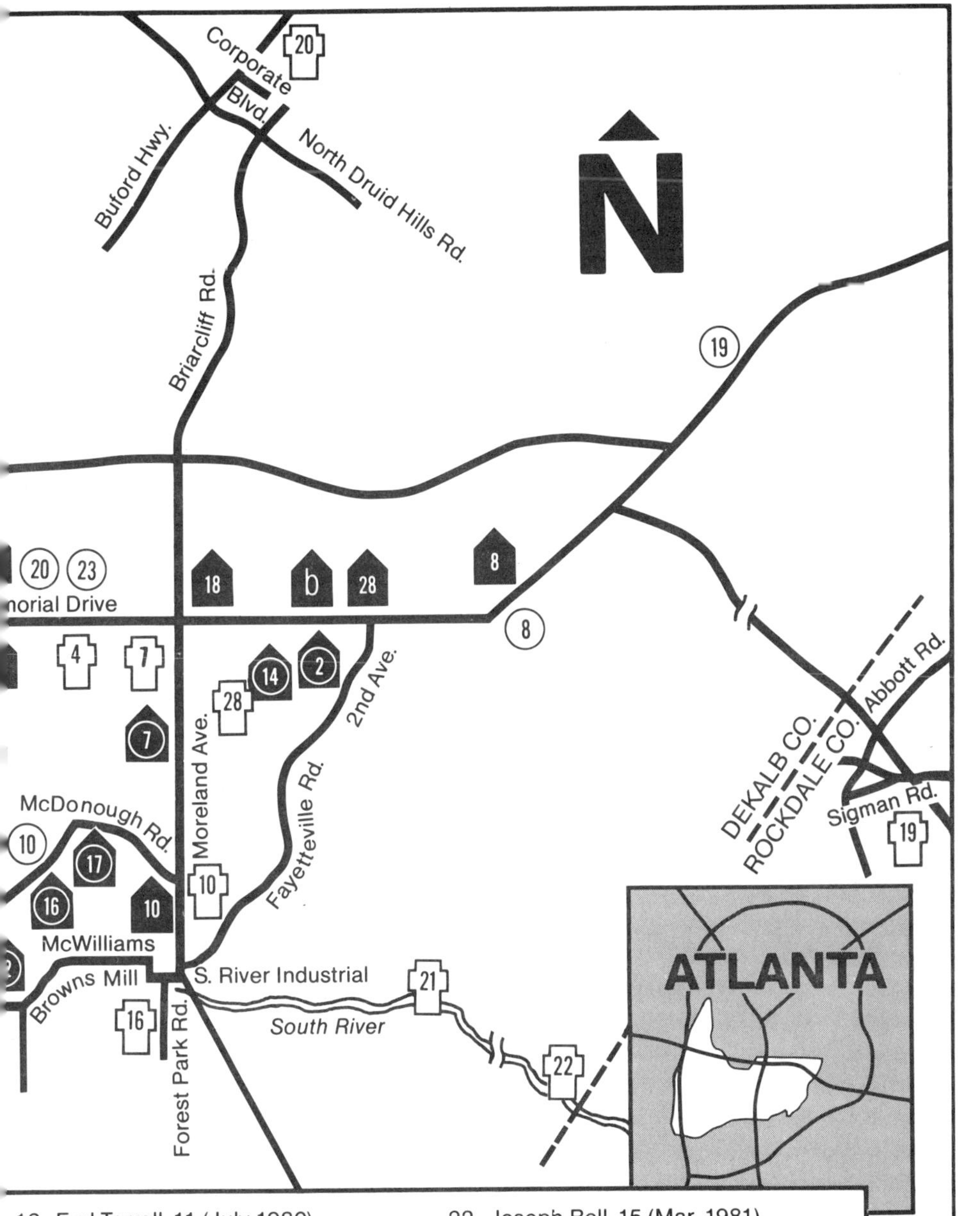

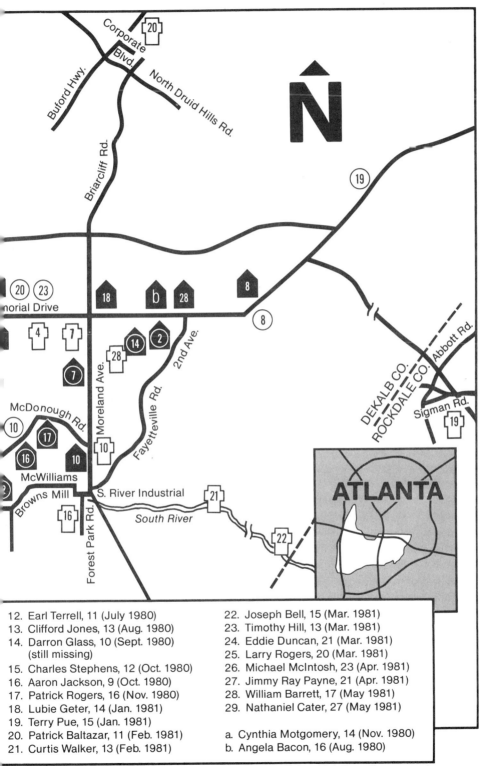

12. Earl Terrell, 11 (July 1980)
13. Clifford Jones, 13 (Aug. 1980)
14. Darron Glass, 10 (Sept. 1980) (still missing)
15. Charles Stephens, 12 (Oct. 1980)
16. Aaron Jackson, 9 (Oct. 1980)
17. Patrick Rogers, 16 (Nov. 1980)
18. Lubie Geter, 14 (Jan. 1981)
19. Terry Pue, 15 (Jan. 1981)
20. Patrick Baltazar, 11 (Feb. 1981)
21. Curtis Walker, 13 (Feb. 1981)
22. Joseph Bell, 15 (Mar. 1981)
23. Timothy Hill, 13 (Mar. 1981)
24. Eddie Duncan, 21 (Mar. 1981)
25. Larry Rogers, 20 (Mar. 1981)
26. Michael McIntosh, 23 (Apr. 1981)
27. Jimmy Ray Payne, 21 (Apr. 1981)
28. William Barrett, 17 (May 1981)
29. Nathaniel Cater, 27 (May 1981)

a. Cynthia Motgomery, 14 (Nov. 1980)
b. Angela Bacon, 16 (Aug. 1980)

Note: Victims are listed by the month in which they disappeared.

At first, all I could see was Interstate 20 and Interstate 285. This wasn't surprising since these two roads dominate the map in the area where the killer(s) seemed to be working. But soon, I saw that the points were more than close to I-20; they were *on* Memorial Drive.

The *Atlanta Journal* of Thursday, August 21, 1980, brought dreary news of yet another victim, 13-year-old Clifford Jones, who was found strangled. Like 12-year-old Angel Lenair, Jones had just recently come to Atlanta from a Northern city—this time Cleveland.

I plotted the three points for Clifford Jones, and—Eureka!—I saw the pattern emerge more clearly than ever. The map I was drawing now hinted at the uncanny predictability it would demonstrate throughout the remainder of Atlanta's crisis.

By November of 1980, the map enabled me to predict correctly where some victims would disappear and where other bodies would be found. During the time I made these predictions to the police and members of the press—and saw them materialize—Lee Brown held news conferences to deny that *any* pattern existed.

In the newspaper reports of the death of Clifford Jones, Atlanta's new homicide commander, B.L. Neikirk, said, "The finding of the body north of I-20 destroys the pattern [Brown was denying any pattern] of six bodies found south of I-20."

I couldn't believe it. The pertinent points in the Clifford Jones case established a geographic pattern—not destroyed it. Neikirk spoke of six bodies, but there were already nine. He was obviously ignoring those outside Atlanta police jurisdiction, as if there were no multi-jurisdictional Task Force. Even at that, Neikirk was wrong. The six bodies in his jurisdiction had not all been found south of I-20. In any event, police must learn that no logical geographic pattern can be established unless imaginary jurisdictional lines are ignored.

Neikirk's officers apparently were sticking pins in a map. The pins were too thick. Eric Middlebrooks had turned up dead *north* of I-20, but so close that a pinhead might cover up enough area to make the scene look like it was south of I-20. But, wouldn't you expect the homicide commander to know where a body was found?

Neikirk wasn't seeing what I was seeing because he was plotting only one point per victim—where the bodies were being found. Atlanta's tragedy was a missing-persons case, too. But police traditionally don't give a damn about missing persons.

My three-point base gave me 32 points to look at for the 12 cases I was considering—three for each of the eight dead victims (I was not yet looking at Aaron Wyche) and two for each of the four who were still missing. Neikirk, ignoring two-out-of-three points for each murder victim and all of the points for the missing persons, was looking at *six*, all told.

With more than five times as many points to study (which were available to both of us), is it any wonder that I saw a pattern that the police didn't—and that they never caught up to what I was trying to tell them? They still don't understand it.

Mike Edwards agreed to meet me at an International House of Pancakes near the Northlake Mall. When I showed him the 32 points and major thoroughfares that connected them, he was excited: "By God, Chet, it *is* a pattern!"

We talked for a moment about the Task Force's preoccupation with Interstate 20. Mike made several interesting observations. First, he said that if the police were looking for a kidnapper searching for random victims, they weren't too likely to find him looking for prey on a limited-access highway. A random kidnapper *would* be working the surface streets. Secondly, he pointed out that while a location might be extremely close to an expressway, it might be necessary to drive miles to get to it because of the location of the on-off ramps.

Roy Innis, director (or pretender to the throne) of the Congress of Racial Equality (CORE), depending on whose version you listened to, came to Atlanta in 1981 and called a news conference on the steps of City Hall. Waving an envelope over his head, he proclaimed that he had a picture of the "Atlanta killer" inside.

Soon the news media would report Innis' claims with a minimum of qualification—and then would be kept busy checking out reports of damage and unpaid bills at various Atlanta hotels where the Innis entourage stayed.

Billboards would go up all around Atlanta, showing black and white "Atlantans" pulling "together" in an imaginary tug-of-war with an unseen opponent. The same theme permeated Atlanta's TV screens. We were constantly urged and reminded to pass on information to the police.

Meanwhile, Roy Innis had no difficulty obtaining an audience with top officials, including Lee Brown and Special Agent-in-Charge John Glover of the FBI's Atlanta field office, who went to see Innis.

But billboards and TV spots be damned, John and Mary Q. Public couldn't even get the time of day from the Task Force. Some members of the public held what they considered evidence until it molded; but, too often, the cops never showed up.

So when Brown and Glover went to Innis, the average Atlantan couldn't help but think that Innis had something of real value. Not so, Brown and Glover said later.

I met with Innis and Shirley McGill, the woman upon whom his story was based. In Miami, the media had committed a *faux pas* by releasing the photograph and long criminal record of the *wrong* Shirley McGill. I was told by a member of Innis' group that McGill had contacted a disc jockey at Atlanta radio station WAOK-AM and told him of dating the "Atlanta killer." He switched her call to the station's newsman, Ron Sailor. Sailor, in turn, referred her to Innis.

Sailor would soon leave WAOK for WSB-TV (Channel 2) to provide black experience on the news staff covering the murders. Meanwhile, across the hall at WSB radio sat a reporter who happened to be one of the most knowledgeable about the murder cases. She also happened to be black. But, she was forced to use her own time to pursue the case. Her name: Kaleeka Rogers.

I had been asked to meet with McGill and Innis by Sondra O'Neal, a Ph.D. from Emory University. When she phoned, she mentioned things that only I should have known. These were incidents which had happened to me but which were as yet unpublished. Where did she get the information? I wasn't concerned that Dr. O'Neal knew these things, but rather that the security of manuscripts I had left with a friend, Dr. Fred Crawford, also of Emory University, might have been compromised.

The meeting was held in a private apartment on Memorial Drive, a location in the heart of the murder incidents. But Innis and his group were looking at places far removed such as Athens, Georgia, and a farm in Cobb County near Cobb County police headquarters.

Shirley McGill's version of the killer changed from a Miami drug dealer to an Atlanta cab driver by the time I got to talk with her. Nothing else that she said she saw is supported by any evidence yet uncovered in the Atlanta murders.

But McGill's story was used as the basis for a report in *Us* magazine (March 30, 1982). Writer Micki Siegel wrote, "Everyone knows that 28 children and young men were abducted and killed over a two-year period." Wrong! First, no one knows how long the Atlanta tragedy has been going on. Next, there may have been many more than 28 victims—there may even have been less. Again, no one knows. By the time Siegel wrote her article, the prosecution in the Wayne Williams trial had added the name of a 29th murder victim. But conversely, it then linked Wayne Williams with 23 victims. Rather than "everyone knows...," the truth is, no one knows.

There is evidence to suggest abduction in only four of the cases. And in only one, the case of LaTonya Wilson, does that evidence go beyond a single telephone call.

Us also reported that the body of a woman had been found in the Chattahoochee River. Not so. Not during these investigations, at any rate. The body of a woman was found in a lake very close to Niskey Lake while Siegel was in town to write her story.

She wrote that "many... women were slain in ways similar to... the *children* [emphasis added, adults make up 20% of The List]." Except for grinding, crushing, cremation or dissolution, it would be difficult to rule out any cause of death as not being similar to those of victims on The List. With 10-year-old Darron Glass still missing, it may be impossible to rule out any. In spite of what *Facts on File*, a source of the "facts" in many journalistic stories, says, it is not a fact that 19 of "the" victims died an asphyxial death. Many died from unknown causes which medical examiners began calling "probable asphyxia" as more and more unknowns made their diagnoses look like a roll of the dice. In addition to unknown and the non-malady, probable asphyxia, there were stabbings, a shooting, bludgeonings, strangulations of various types, suffocations and even combinations of the above.

John Feegel (a Fulton County assistant medical examiner) did not testify, as *Us* reported, that 12-year-old Charles Stephens "had been killed either by a plastic bag placed over his head or stuffed down his throat." Had he said it, though, it would have been akin to saying he was either shot or hit over the head by a gun. Shirley McGill said she saw a child killed by forcing a plastic bag down his throat, but plastic bags were just one of the theories—guesses, if you will—tossed out by the medical examiners for how victims "might have died."

I went to the Cobb County location, where McGill claimed to have witnessed "sacrificial murders," to meet with the Innis group. But I saw no bodies, no blood, no bones, no altars, no crosses—no proof whatsoever that Shirley McGill saw what *Us* said she saw.

Later that night, Dr. O'Neal would call to tell me that a couple of young "toughs" on motorcycles had given the Innis group dirty looks and that a black car had almost run them off the road on the way back to Atlanta.

On March 30, 1983, a teach-in was held at Morris Brown College in Atlanta. When I arrived, Dr. Sondra O'Neal was speaking. By now, the incident of the swerving car had grown into a life-threatening attack. Camille Bell, too, spoke from that podium, demonstrating a militance not hinted to in her utterances before more conservative audiences. She warned her "brothers and sisters" to prepare for the day when "they" come to put "us" into "concentration camps." Incredible!

Micki Siegel wrote of "retarded" victims. The idea of retarded victims had its genesis in the struggle of authorities to explain something they didn't understand. They found themselves adding adults to The List of murdered "children." At the trial of Wayne Williams, no evidence would be introduced as to the IQ of any victim on The List. Most likely, none was ever sought.

The *Us* article is right when it says no one can "dismiss the idea of a cult." What the article does not say is that no one can prove the idea, either. When you don't know, you also can't rule out the CIA, the KGB, Satan, the KKK, the Center for Disease Control (as activist Dick Gregory suggested), the NAACP, the will of God, the police, the UN, or an alien from outer space, all of which I have heard accused with equally non-compelling "voodoo" proof.

The article speaks of a strange map and ceremonial candles being found, but neglects to mention that the map led to a "black Hebrew" temple and that the ceremonial candles were found during Hanukka observances.

I followed that map to the temple and was puzzled by a crudely lettered sign, one of many nailed to a tree at the edge of the temple property. "Welcome," it says. "Keep out!"

To me, the most important information gleaned from my meetings with the CORE representatives had nothing to do with cults, or, for that matter, with Shirley McGill. It came from Al Starkes, Innis' Atlanta lieutenant. Starkes talked about what he had heard, rather than what he dreamed or surmised or conjured or found in the magic of numbers or the planets.

He said that Clifford Jones had last been seen entering a "washhouse" (laundromat) that was widely known for homosexual gatherings.

Later, I verified Starkes' account in secret police files, which as yet have not been released to the press or public. The Clifford Jones murder provides probably the strongest reasons to doubt the validity of the evidence on which Wayne Williams was convicted.

Mike Edwards and I decided to take to the streets and see if the lines I had drawn on paper translated into a real pattern on the pavement. We started on the eastern end of Memorial Drive, where Christopher Richardson had lived and disappeared.

As we drove west on Memorial Drive, we passed the house where teen-ager Angela (Gypsy) Bacon stayed, although we didn't have any reason to take notice at the time. Just a bit farther down the street lived a 10-year-old boy named Darron Glass. In two more short blocks, we passed the East Lake Meadows housing project, where Alfred Evans had lived and was last seen (according to initial reports).

A few more blocks farther west, we reached Moreland Avenue. If we had turned left, we would have been able to drive straight to the place where 10-year-old Aaron Wyche had died in the so-called "accidental" fall. Instead, we drove on to the next alley, which is where 14-year-old Eric Middlebrooks had been found beside a bicycle. Across the expressway, with nothing else in between, was the house where Eric lived and was last seen alive.

Soon we resumed our westward journey. Just before we reached Atlanta-Fulton County Stadium and the State Capitol, we could see to our left the E.P. Johnson Elementary School, where 9-year-old Yusuf Bell's body had been found.

In front of us and overhead were the garish, yellow-primed girders of the MARTA rail line construction. Beneath those I-beams once stood the house on Rawson Street where Yusuf Bell had lived.

Memorial Drive ends in a peculiar intersection that resembles the peace symbol of the 1960s, without the circle around it. We made a slight left curve. The sun stayed in our eyes, but the name of the street had changed to

Whitehall. The next traffic signal was one block from where Yusuf Bell had disappeared, according to his mother, Camille Bell.

In two more blocks, we took a short detour to the dumpster where 9-year-old Anthony Carter had been found stabbed to death. Only two weeks before, Angela Bacon had been murdered across the street from the Carter death scene. But, she had not made The List, and it would be months before I would understand her case.

Just beyond these two scenes was the grocery store where Yusuf Bell went on the errand to buy the snuff. And beyond that store was the fast-food stand, Cap'n Peg's. On the corner directly across from where Angela Bacon died was a liquor store that would play an interesting role in these cases.

As we continued westward across Atlanta, the street changed names again—to Gordon Street. The spire of the West Hunter Street Baptist Church, another misnomer institution, loomed in front of us. The church, pastored by Ralph David Abernathy, housed the headquarters of two organizations which would also figure prominently in the cases. One was the United Youth Adult Conference (UYAC), a social-service agency headed by then-City Councilman Arthur Langford Jr., and the other was the Challenge School for Boys, then directed by Brandon Southern.

One day I would stand in front of that church and comment to Peter Arnett (Pulitzer Prize-winner for his reporting on Vietnam) that this was a strange place in the murder cases—a place where victims would come out one door, searchers out of another and suspects out of both.

Next door is an Atlanta tourist attraction—the home where the late Joel Chandler Harris wrote his famous *"Uncle Remus"* stories about Br'er Rabbit, Br'er Fox and other characters. Some were made into Walt Disney movies and all were translated into 27 languages for the enjoyment of children throughout the world. What a stark contrast between someone who would use this neighborhood to bring pleasure to children and another who would defile the memory of him. Children who once came here to laugh and have fun now stayed away in cold-blooded fear.

Within the next five blocks, we passed the home of Anthony Carter, who had been found stabbed by a dumpster, and the homes of two future victims.

In a moment, we were staring at the silver fireplug where Jefferey Mathis disappeared. He lived down an adjoining street, only one block away.

In eight-tenths of a mile, Gordon Street merges with—and becomes—Martin Luther King Jr. Drive. We stopped for the traffic signal, and I saw the West Lake MARTA station on my right. I could not then know the scene that would unfold before me months later at this point—where my map had taken me the first time it was used.

Now we approached the intersection of MLK and Hightower Road. For the first time on our tour, Mike *had* to flick on the turn signal. We turned right and off to our right, one block away, was the home of 7-year-old LaTonya

Wilson, who allegedly had been kidnapped by the man climbing through the window.

Of course, at that time, we knew nothing about Nathaniel Cater, who lived in that apartment building, too; or, of Cater's and Wilson's next-door neighbor, Amp Wiley, or of Wiley's neighbor across the street, Cynthia Montgomery.

But more important, what we didn't know at that moment was the fact that LaTonya Wilson's yet-to-be-discovered body was only 50 feet away, atop the steep hill that blocked our view to the east.

Along MLK, we had passed the law offices of Lynn Whatley in a building shared with Zone 1 of the Atlanta Police Bureau. Whatley was the family attorney for a retired couple who lived around the corner on Penelope Road. Their names: Homer and Faye Williams. They had one son whom they doted on. His name: Wayne.

Whatley also would represent Lapas Favors, one of two brothers who would be accused—along with their 21-year-old cousin, Anthony (Amp) Wiley—in the particularly brutal slaying of Jean Buice, 34, in broad daylight in a suburban park. (The Favors initially plea-bargained for a reduced sentence and testified against Wiley, saying they merely watched Wiley kill the woman. After Wiley was convicted, they changed their pleas to "not guilty," only to change them back to "guilty" again, the very next day.)

Amp Wiley was out of jail on bond at the time of the Buice murder. He had been accused of raping a young girl who lived next door to him. It wouldn't escape my notice that three of his other next-door neighbors were murdered. Two, Nathaniel Cater and LaTonya Wilson, would make The List. A third, Cynthia Montgomery, 14, would not.

And these would not be the only victims with connections to Amp Wiley. Wayne Williams would not only be convicted of killing Wiley's next-door neighbor, Nathaniel Cater, but also 21-year-old Jimmy Ray Payne. Payne and Wiley had at one time dated the same woman.

Authorities now insist that there can be no connection between the deaths of Nathaniel Cater and his 7-year-old downstairs neighbor, LaTonya Wilson. But what if Nate Cater was one of two black men a witness says she saw standing between Cater's and Wiley's houses—one of whom she said had LaTonya under his right arm?

We proceeded north on Hightower Road to check out the locations in the death of Clifford Jones, who had been seen entering the laundromat. I did some quick arithmetic and, not counting 16-year-old Angela Bacon, who wasn't on The List, we had gone by 17 of the known points without *having* to make a turn (though we had made several for convenience sake).

Meanwhile, after crossing U.S. 278, we passed the Bowen Homes housing project, where a young boy named Curtis Walker shared an apartment with his mother and his youthful uncle, Stanley Murray. The apartment was located on the same street as a day-care center that was destined to change the political face of the Atlanta murders.

Hightower breaks into two streets. You can proceed north by Jackson Parkway or by Hollywood Road. We chose Hollywood Road because it passed closer to the points where Clifford Jones lived, disappeared and was found dead.

Once on Hollywood Road, we passed the cemetery where Clifford, according to his mother, Eunice Jones, was too afraid to walk past alone. Immediately across from the cemetery was the apartment that housed 15-year-old Terry Lorenzo Pue and his family.

A short distance later, we drove into the small shopping center at Perry Boulevard and Hollywood Road. Shortly before 2 a.m. on August 21, 1980, the Atlanta police had received an anonymous telephone call. The voice said that the body of a black boy was lying beside a dumpster in this shopping center. The body was that of Clifford Jones.

At that shopping center, we passed a beer joint. Typically, on a hot August night, people milled around outside. The beer joint was no more than 20 feet from the dumpster. From there, the area opened into a playground flanked by small cottages that overlooked the playground and the rear entrances of stores in the shopping center.

"Somebody had to see something," I told Mike.

Someone *had* seen something and told the police about it. I never understood how this part of the story escaped publication. (The Atlanta newspapers had been asked to withhold four stories. This was not one of them.) Al Starkes of CORE knew at least a part of the story, so somebody obviously was talking. But the Atlanta police continued to tell the world there were absolutely no leads in the murders. That contention went unchallenged in the media.

Just before Hollywood Road ended at Bolton Road, we turned left and in a jiffy we were sitting in front of the Starvin' Marvin store at Bolton Road and Jackson Parkway. This was the northwest corner of the route and one of four locations where Mike Edwards and I would suggest the establishment of police stakeouts.

Six-tenths of a mile north on Jackson Parkway, with no intersections in between, is the Jackson Parkway bridge, which carries Jackson Parkway to the county line, where it changes names to South Cobb Drive and continues north into Cobb County. The county line at this point is the Chattahoochee River.

As Bolton Road dips south, it merges with Fairburn Road. Soon, along the Bolton-Fairburn corridor of the route, we were passing the intersection of Nash Road, where Milton Harvey lived, just north of U.S. 278.

Just a block west of this corridor is the parallel-running Kimberly Road. Off Kimberly Road is the entrance to the housing project which contains 4191 Cape Street, where 14-year-old Edward Hope Smith (one of the two victims at Niskey Lake Road) lived next door to another teen-ager named Lee Manuel Gooch.

When you turn from the lovely, tree-draped tranquility of Kimberly Road, you drive into the forlorn streets of Edward Hope (Teddy) Smith's neighborhood. There, you wince over the probability of a flat tire. You know that a steel-belted radial is a prohibitive underdog to the shards of glass or nail-laden flotsom strewn all over the project.

The project is brick, stone and concrete, with yards consisting only of dirt polished by millions of footsteps. It's the kind of a place where a lawnmower salesman would go broke. Here, you don't mow the lawn, you sweep it, if you do anything. Most people don't. Trash dumpsters are as much a visible part of the neighborhood as fireplugs and sewer caps. Paper of every description, bologna rinds and last week's empty cans form a *Hansel-and-Gretel* path between the dumpsters and almost every door.

Property abuse and neglect have established permanent residence in this neighborhood. Shingles hang askew. Wood-framed screen doors, some minus screens, define angles with the openings they are supposed to seal.

To be sure, it's not the picture of Atlanta that civic boosters peddle to the rest of the nation in their $1-million ad campaign—a successor to the city's innovative "Forward Atlanta" promotion that wooed business during the 1960s. But don't feel smug. If your town promotes itself, it lies by omission, too. They all do.

Atlanta ranks 29th nationally in population (425,000), but fifth in the United States in public housing, which was introduced to this country in Atlanta during the Franklin D. Roosevelt Administration. Atlanta has 15,300 units of public housing crammed with 51,000 residents, or almost 12% of its population.

A drive through this project where Edward Hope Smith and Lee Gooch cavorted could qualify as an Olympic event. You slalom past a three-tired Buick, a dying Lincoln and a Cadillac whose fading luster is covered by years of grime, only to find your path blocked by a car-to-sidewalk conversation. The participants are either oblivious or immune to your right to use the public way. You honk your horn, and if you're lucky, you only get cussed out—for being right.

Absolutely nobody—despite official protestations to the contrary—is policing these mean streets effectively. In a sense, anarchy is never more than a trigger-word away. It's an incident waiting to happen. If you're not a native, you're frightened; and if you're not frightened, you're ignorant. For the average American, it's an uneasy visit to a foreign country.

If Edward Hope Smith or Lee Gooch were runaways, who could blame them? Anyone in his right mind would run away from all of this if he could. Responsibility hasn't caught up with freedom as a priority in this neighborhood.

Soon we were at the intersection of Campbellton Road (Georgia 166) in southwest Atlanta. To the left, along Campbellton Road, was the home of 12-year-old Angel Lenair. She had disappeared and been found dead just across the street from her home. Her mother had screamed after the ambulance, just as the girl's remains were taken away.

Farther to the east along Georgia 166 are the Lakewood Fairgrounds and South Bend Park, where John David Wilcoxen, convicted of child molestation, lived. It was also at South Bend Park where 11-year-old Earl Lee Terrell had disappeared from the swimming pool.

Of course, events that would surround persons named Faye Yearby and Charles Stephens had not happened yet. But they would—right there at the fairgrounds, at the east end of Georgia 166.

We made a right turn and, in two blocks, were driving along Niskey Lake Road. Less than 30 seconds north of Georgia 166, we reached the scene where Edward Hope Smith and the other boy (unidentified), both dressed in black, had been found slain.

Weeks later, Mike would tell producers of ABC News' *20/20* program about the death scene on Niskey Lake Road. In his colloquial fashion, Mike had said "on Niskey Lake," leaving off the word "Road."

ABC took Mike literally. In October of 1980, a segment of *20/20* about the murders would erroneously show file footage of skin divers pulling a body from a lake. The network intimated that this was the scene at "Niskey Lake." But the closest the water flows to the 1700 block of Niskey Lake Road is in the pipes beneath the ground that extend to the city reservoir.

In the midst of morbidity, there is seldom an opportunity to laugh. But I laughed my ass off at ABC and hoped that its Iranian-hostage coverage, which I had devoured for months, hadn't been equally screwed up. At least, I wasn't laughing at one of those tastelessly crude jokes about Atlanta's murders that you occasionally heard if you are white, but only *over*heard if you are black.

We headed south again and, within a block, we passed the skating rink where Edward Hope Smith was officially reported last seen. But others said that they had seen him and Alfred Evans together at a pot party on County Line Road, which is within walking distance of both Smith's home and the death scene on Niskey Lake Road.

We drove on for several more miles, the longest stretch yet without encountering a location pertinent to the murders. Finally, we came to where Redwine Road slides into Fairburn Road. Driving south, as we were, it was a left-hand turn; but coming north, the streets blend as smoothly as coffee and cream.

We didn't know it then, but the map had taken us again within 50 feet of the remains of still two more victims. Since both had been missing for longer than a month at the time, it is reasonable to assume they were already there. The remains of Christopher Richardson, who was last seen headed for a swimming pool, and Earl Terrell, who was last seen just after being ejected from one, lay in the woods close together near a cluster of large boulders.

Astounded by what the map had put together for us, Mike and I called it a day. In retrospect, the most astounding thing about the day was that we had driven by the locations where *seven more* victims—all then alive—lived, would disappear from and would be found dead. Only five of those seven would make The List.

What's more, we had driven within a block of the house of Wayne Williams, who would be accused of killing them. All of these revelations came from a map that spelled out a geographic pattern that officials still deny exists. When asked later about the map, Public Safety Commissioner Lee Brown would say, "Anybody can draw a map." Deputy Police Chief Eldrin Bell would ask, "What good is it?"

On our way home, we talked again about 10-year-old Aaron Wyche, who the authorities had said died in an accidental fall from a "railroad trestle."

If I was right, there should be a route connection between Redwine Road on the southwest, where we had ended our day's journey, and the point on Moreland Avenue on the southeast, where Aaron Wyche had been found dead. There also should be a connection from Wyche's body to the points for other victims to the north.

Our problem was, neither Mike nor I could find the railroad trestle to nail down that point.

Mike was teaching a class at DeKalb Community College. As luck would have it, one of his students was the DeKalb County policeman who responded to the original call about the body of Aaron Wyche. The officer described the scene for us in great detail. He said it was located precisely at Moreland Avenue and Constitution Road.

Why in the hell did Aaron get on that trestle? His family said he was afraid of heights! He wouldn't even climb over a fence, they said.

Aaron Wyche's mother, Linda Wyche, lived at 1065 Henry Thomas Drive, in the Thomasville Heights housing project. The house was less than a mile north of the location where Aaron's body had been found at 3 a.m. on June 24, 1980. Witnesses said they had seen Aaron in a blue-and-white car with two black males at Tanner's Grocery Store on McDonough Boulevard at about 4:30 the previous afternoon. The description of the car matched that of two suspect cars in the disappearance of 10-year-old Jefferey Mathis—even down to the Bondo (fiberglass patch) on a fender of one.

Tanner's Grocery stands in the shadow of the dreaded "Big A"—the federal penitentiary, which has housed some of the nation's most incorrigible criminals, including Al Capone. The murder rate inside the "Big A" once approached that of the city of Atlanta. Today, it houses scores of *Marielistas* from the 1980 Cuban boatlift. Some of their companions on the outside have boosted Miami's violent-crime rates off the charts.

The grocery is about a half-mile west of the apartment of Aaron's mother. Police told me they later learned that Aaron was last seen alive in the

Moreland Avenue Shopping Center, which is about one mile *north* of the apartment.

The police could be right, but I didn't think so then and I still don't. I'm convinced that some investigators confused the cases of Aaron Wyche and Aaron Jackson, his 9-year-old friend and neighbor who was to turn up dead in November of 1980. Both were found beneath bridges which were less than a mile apart. Aaron Jackson *had* been seen at the Moreland Avenue Shopping Center. Were the police checking on the wrong Aaron?

Mike and I returned to the intersection of Moreland and Constitution to find the damned railroad trestle. Lo and behold, we soon found that there was *no* railroad trestle for Aaron Wyche to fall off of! Instead, he had been found at the base of a highway bridge which passes over two railroad tracks. The bridge is six lanes wide. It blends so well into the surrounding terrain that were it not for the guard rails, which are almost as high as Aaron Wyche was tall, most people wouldn't notice that they were on a bridge when passing over it. The bridge has sidewalks and is perfectly safe to walk across. There is no way Aaron Wyche could have fallen off that bridge. Jumped or been thrown, maybe; but fall off, no way.

Aaron Wyche had died in June of 1980. In January of 1981, I would brief more than 50 DeKalb County police officers at the request of Dick Hand, their commander. The detectives who investigated the Aaron Wyche case insisted to me that Aaron had been on his way home from the Moreland Avenue Shopping Center when he fell off the "trestle."

But, Aaron's mother lived north of the bridge between the shopping center and the bridge.

By itself, the discrepancy in the Aaron Wyche case was tragic only for his family. But in the overall panoply of Atlanta's murders, it was catastrophic. It meant that the police were dealing with an accident, not a murder. Consequently, there was nothing to investigate. It means that Aaron Wyche was not plugged into the authorities' thinking about the cases.

The discrepancy kept the Wyche case off The List for more than seven months. Accordingly, not recognizing the Wyche case caused authorities to ignore the Patrick Rogers case for more than three months. During that time, the details that could have been learned by officials weren't just ignored; rather, they were overtly excluded. They wouldn't listen when I insisted to both Brown and Hand that the Wyche case was a murder and not an accident.

Reporter Gail Epstein had begged and cajoled me to come to the offices of the *Atlanta Constitution* and brief the other *Constitution* reporters and editors who were being assigned to the cases, as the newspaper beefed up its coverage. I talked for seven hours about the cases, beyond midnight and without dinner (but with ample refills of coffee). I had given the newspaper a copy of my map, which it had hung on the wall and kept updated—to my surprise. Later, the newspaper would print my map as its own. "Staff" map, the caption read. Bullshit! It was my map, down to the error I had made when first drawing Fairburn Road.

"Aaron Wyche didn't fall off any railroad trestle," I told Gail's editor.

"But the medical examiner says . . .," the editor insisted.

Five or six appeals to reason later, I turned emphatic. "I don't give a damn what the medical examiner says," I sniped at her. "Aaron Wyche didn't fall off any railroad trestle."

I explained that when the medical examiner looked through a microscope (as if they did), comparing white corpuscles with red ones, I would demur. I didn't know a red corpuscle from a cherry Popsicle. But when it came to his value judgment that Wyche had fallen from a railroad trestle that wasn't there and my judgment that he didn't, mine was better—despite the discrepancies in our titles, incomes and public visibility.

These cases had taught me that medical examiners seldom make medical findings. They guess a lot and conjecture even more. They are as apt to be wrong as anyone else. But they are believed and their opinions are accepted because they carry the Godlike title of "Doctor," even though some are not even that.

The medical examiner had relied upon leaves clutched in Aaron's hand to determine that he had fallen through the trees. But the tree he would have fallen through was more like a bush. Aaron could easily have grasped the lower limbs of the tree from a position on the ground.

The *Constitution* had packaged glossy photographs of the victims on The List, as well as reprints of articles for out-of-town journalists who swarmed into Atlanta and asked to be "filled in" on the story. The college where I was teaching wanted a set of the photos. I called Gail Epstein and asked her for one set. The newspaper sent the pictures and a bill for $75. I telephoned Gail, who assured me that the $75 billing was correct. I told her what the *Constitution* could do with the bill and the pictures. Pointing out that they could owe me for oodles of time and gas, to say nothing of a "staff" map, I got a set free of charge, but our relationship went downhill from there.

What happened in the Aaron Wyche case? A medical examiner perceived the word "trestle" to mean what it is supposed to mean—a span without railings and with open spaces between the railroad ties. As a result, he ruled a murder an accident.

When someone says, "Oh, but that's just semantics," it makes me furious. It's semantics, all right, but not *just* semantics. Just as numbers are the symbols of mathematics, words are the symbols of logic. Plug in the wrong symbol, and you get the wrong answer—except by accident. A police officer who didn't know what a railroad trestle was became the Achille's heel of a murder investigation that cost more than $9 million. It's just semantics?

In 1977, I had worked for a company that had offices on Stewart Avenue at Cleveland Avenue, about two miles from South Bend Park. That company also had offices on Moreland Avenue, just south of the Constitution Road bridge. A shortcut between the two offices was used by motorists who knew the area well. The shortcut takes you almost to the front door of Earl Terrell's house—and then to within a few feet of the Aaron Wyche death scene.

The rest of the ride from the beginning of the shortcut back across town to Redwine Road, where Harvey's body had been found, consisted of Cleveland Avenue, Main Street (East Point), Washington Road, Camp Creek Parkway and Desert Road. These streets all formed a single thoroughfare which would be heard from again. I drew in the streets on the map, connecting Harvey's body on the far southwest with Wyche's, all the way across town on the southeast.

It remained only to decide whether to connect the Wyche point with the cases on the northeast by using a road to the northeast that went back to East Lake Meadows, or by going straight north on Moreland Avenue to the Middlebrooks points at Memorial Drive.

The locations where Aaron Wyche lived and disappeared would have told me. But I didn't then know what they were. But an incident in November would lock down the last leg of the route. It would be due north on Moreland Avenue.

The "railroad trestle" from which Aaron Wyche, 10, was said by authorities to have fallen "accidentally" to his death is actually a highway bridge, which children walk safely across every day. When Chet Dettlinger found no "railroad trestle" exists at the scene, he pleaded with authorities to reclassify Wyche's death a murder. Not until seven months later did they reopen the case and add it to The List. (John White/Chicago Sun-Times)

7

"Gypsy" and "Cinderella"

August, 1980

Walter Mitchell was 16, black, frail and slightly retarded. He wore a tiny jewel in one pierced ear lobe. In some ways, he fit the profile of other Atlantans who had been slain and of still others who would turn up dead.

One afternoon in August of 1980, he strolled along Auburn Avenue in downtown Atlanta. "Sweet Auburn," they called it back in the 1960s, when civil rights protests simmered there, but never exploded like they did in many other U.S. cities.

On this street, Martin Luther King Jr. shared the pulpit with his father—and his hopes with parishioners—at the red-brick Ebenezer Baptist Church. His tomb lies next door. His birthplace is a church manse, a block away.

Years ago, "Sweet Auburn" was the mainstream of economic, cultural and social life for Atlanta's blacks. "Sweet Auburn" was where you lined up outside the Royal Peacock Club ("Atlanta's Club Beautiful") on Friday, Saturday and Sunday nights, and then crammed inside to see the stars of rhythm 'n' blues, the kings and queens of the big beat.

The Peacock was "where it's at" in the 1950s and early 1960s, where stars like Jackie Wilson, Fats Domino, Ray Charles, James Brown, Hank Ballard and the Midnighters, LaVern Baker, Little Esther, the Dells, Little Richard, the Coasters and Dizzy Gillespie sang and danced and blew up a storm way past the wee hours, even until the sun came up.

Today, "Sweet Auburn" has gone sour. The Peacock no longer struts its stuff. Hookers strut theirs. Fifteen-year-old girls who are made up and dressed to the nines so they look 18 to 25 are hustling in the seedy bars and nightspots between Fort Street and Piedmont Avenue. Or they're trying to flag down potential customers who drive by in cars.

It was along this block of Auburn Avenue that Walter Mitchell recognized a familiar face. She was black and sinewy, with a close-cropped Afro hairstyle.

"Don't I know you?" he asked.

She looked at him vacantly.

"Don't I know you?" he asked again. "What's your name?"

"Gypsy," she replied.

Now the memories flooded back. "Gypsy" was Angela Bacon, also 16. She and Walter had attended school together in Atlanta a few years earlier. Then they lost touch. Kids go through a million changes between adolescence and their late teens. But now, Gypsy and Walter remembered the yesterdays. Their reunion became a friendship that would be measured only in a pocketful of tomorrows.

Gypsy was aptly nicknamed. She had run away from home. Her father had hanged himself years ago. Her mother had died only three months earlier, on Mother's Day. Gypsy had lived in a foster home in suburban Clayton County, south of Atlanta. When she came to dislike foster-childhood, she moved into her grandmother's house on Memorial Drive in Atlanta, across from East Lake Park. On a tree in the front yard was a small sign: "Rooms for Rent—Men."

But Angela stayed there only two nights in late August of 1980, according to her grandmother, Isabel Porter. "I saw her go into the front yard after supper, about 7:30," Mrs. Porter recalled. "I never saw her again."

On Auburn Avenue, several miles west of her grandmother's house, Angela was "trying to be" a prostitute, another relative recalled, adding that Angela was somewhat retarded.

There, Angela met Cynthia Montgomery, who then was 13 and nicknamed "Cinderella." When Angela was reunited with Walter Mitchell, both were on probation from juvenile court—she as a runaway, he as a burglar who, according to a prosecutor, had unsuccessfully tried to implicate two other youths who were, like Walter, said to be homosexuals.

Walter told Angela that she could stay with him—at his grandmother's house—on a quiet street across Interstate 75-85 (the stretch through Atlanta in which both these major arteries use the same right-of-way is known as the "connector") from Atlanta-Fulton County Stadium. She moved in on Thursday evening, August 21.

It would have been about the same time that a boy named Kenny Brown said he witnessed a murder almost across the street from Angela's grandmother's house, back across town on Memorial Drive. Meanwhile, Walter's grandmother and other relatives welcomed Gypsy as "family."

For the next 48 hours, Gypsy and Walter rekindled old times. They saw an R-rated double feature, *"Game of Death"* and *"Return of the Dragon,"* starring karate-idol Bruce Lee, at a downtown moviehouse. On Atlanta's southwest side after dark, the two youngsters wandered in and out of clubs.

During the pre-dawn hours on Sunday, August 24, 1980, the day I started work on my map, Gypsy and Walter were en route home. As they walked eastward together on the righthand side of Georgia Avenue, a few feet east of Stewart Avenue, a black man in a dented and scuffed-up station wagon drove up and stopped alongside them.

"Hey, boy! Come here!" the man yelled. "I want to talk to you."

Walter Mitchell said he saw a pair of handcuffs dangling from the rear-view mirror. He wondered if the man was a plainclothes cop. He walked behind the car to the driver's window and observed a butcher knife stuck through the sun visor.

As Walter remembers it, the station wagon was light green or pale blue, with light-blue interior, wood side panels and luggage rack on top. The driver, he said, appeared to be about 60, with "little bitty" eyes and a black beard flecked with gray. He wore a green shirt and blue work pants, Walter said, and his breath smelled of strong drink.

"Do you two want a ride home?" the driver asked.

"No, sir," Walter replied. "We don't ride with strangers."

"Do you know Larry?" the man asked.

"No."

"Do you know James?"

"No."

"Do you know Ray?"

"No."

As I heard Walter repeat this dialogue, my mind automatically asked about Atlanta murder victims: "*Larry* Rogers? Jimmy [*James*] Payne? Jimmy *Ray* Payne?"

Then, Walter said, the man turned toward Gypsy, who stood beside the vehicle on the passenger side.

"Come over here young lady," the man beckoned, opening the door. "You have a seat right here."

Gypsy obliged and sat on the front passenger seat, with the door open, her feet still on the pavement.

Suddenly without warning, the vehicle leaped forward, with Gypsy screaming, "Help! Let me out!" And almost as suddenly, the vehicle stopped. Its jerk-like stop hurled Gypsy onto the street.

Then, Walter remembered, the man instantly backed up the station wagon. And just like that, Walter said, the man deliberately drove the vehicle forward again—right over Gypsy—and sped east on Georgia Avenue.

Angela (Gypsy) Bacon was dead. Walter Mitchell was an eyewitness to a frighteningly brutal murder. The impact, he said, knocked Angela airborne before her body fell, bleeding from severely lacerated flesh, onto the 500 block of Georgia Avenue.

Again, the geography was significant. It was less than half a block from where 9-year-old Anthony Carter had been found one month earlier. A 37-year-old woman named Catherine Lois Clark had been found murdered at almost exactly the same spot two months before. It was two blocks west of Cap'n Peg's, a Georgia Avenue seafood stand that was a hangout for several youths who would be slain. Cap'n Peg's would surface again and again.

Walter Mitchell said he never saw the station wagon's license number. Fearing that the driver soon would return to look for him, Walter ran across the street to a liquor store, where another murder victim-to-be was a regular customer.

True to Walter's fears, the station wagon returned to the scene, as Walter crouched in hiding at the liquor store. He watched the vehicle move slowly past Angela's body and then disappear again, east on Georgia Avenue.

Walter said he ran back onto the street and hailed a cab. The cabbie called his dispatcher on the radio to request an ambulance and the police. Then he parked his taxi at an angle so it would detour traffic around the body.

"The man said, 'Be cool,'" Walter said of the cabbie, "but he didn't wait for the police to come. I guess he thought they might blame *him*."

Within minutes, Walter said, an ambulance arrived from Grady Memorial Hospital, and an attendant injected a tranquilizing drug into Walter's left arm. "They had to calm me down," Walter said.

Then police cars arrived. Two officers, Walter said, took him to headquarters for questioning and then drove him home. It was past 3 a.m. "I was too scared to go to sleep," Walter said. "Every time I shut my eyes, I saw that station wagon."

The next day, he said, two Atlanta police officers visited him at home and took him to give him a polygraph examination. "They said they'd heard that I pushed her in front of the car," Walter said. "I told them the truth."

From there, he said, the officers took him around the neighborhood in search of the station wagon. In an hour or so, they came upon a light-colored station wagon parked near an apartment. A black man stood nearby.

"They asked me if that was the right man and the right station wagon," Walter said. "I told them, 'It might be, but I'm not sure.' So they locked up the man, anyway. He looked tall and slim. The man I saw that night was short and stout. All I could say was, 'It *might* be him.'"

Her nickname on the streets was "Cinderella," but her life was not the stuff of fairy godmothers and glass slippers. It was one of pumpkins, mice and scullery maids.

Cynthia Montgomery had a round face and sparkling eyes that radiated the curiosity of a child. She also had the streetwisdom—and figure—of a young woman.

Tucked away in her mother's purse is a color snapshot of Cynthia. She is standing against a backdrop of lush Atlanta greenery, wearing a simple, V-necked, white dress, with hands on hips, in a fashion model's pose. When the picture was taken, Cynthia was only 12.

Cynthia was born out of wedlock on Halloween Day, 1966, in Alabama — one of eight children of Eula Montgomery, a resolute, quiet-spoken woman who seemingly has endured two lifetimes of heartaches and cannot work full-time because she is a diabetic.

One son was in jail in 1980. The other children, including Cynthia, shared a wretched three-bedroom flat in Dixie Hills in west Atlanta with their mother, a stepfather, a cousin and dozens of roaches.

They lived in the shadow of what once was a broadcast tower that had served a radio station operated by young Wayne Williams, who lived five blocks away. Dixie Hills also was where 7-year-old LaTonya Wilson, whom Cynthia knew, allegedly had been kidnapped from her bedroom in June of 1980. LaTonya's upstairs neighbor was Nathaniel Cater, then 26.

It's a lifestyle that cries out for anyone to try to escape. One who did was Cynthia Montgomery. But not too far, and not for too long.

When Cynthia went to sign up for a 1980 summer camp that was co-sponsored by the National Football League Players Association and the AFL-CIO, her mother made sure that Cynthia took along her birth certificate. The camp was restricted to 14-to-16-year-olds. Cynthia was 13.

The camp's director was Mel Pender, an erstwhile Olympic Games star sprinter, whose favorite expression is said to be "I'm good!" and who would be quick to anger when a reporter would ask him probing questions about the camp. Either the camp officials didn't bother to demand to see Cynthia's birth certificate, or Cynthia avoided showing it to them. Or, if they did see it, the birthdate meant nothing to them. They apparently took Cynthia's word. One camp roster listed Cynthia as 15.

So, in July of 1980, Cynthia rode on a bus with other youngsters to the campsite at West Georgia College in Carrollton, a town of about 17,000.

West Georgia College, which sits about 40 miles southwest of Atlanta, by way of Georgia 166, appears sequestered in idyllic simplicity. Its psychology department is nationally acclaimed and attracts many students from out of state. Its football team, resurrected for the first time since the 1950s, won the NCAA Division I (small college) football championship in 1982. But the college is not immune to incidents that are more typical of Atlanta's urban mainstream. You may hear Carrollton residents whisper about a campus drug bust, or rumors of an educator accused of hypnotizing some students and then engaging in sex with them.

To many of the campers, the college's laid-back setting offers fresh air and an escape from the bricks and concrete and garbage stench of Atlanta's housing projects back home. All told, about 450 youngsters attended three 11-day sessions in 1980. Each session consisted of 150 campers, predominantly black and poor. Many campers had signed up through federally funded Comprehensive Employment/Training Act (CETA) programs in their inner-city neighborhoods.

Unlike most camps, where kids come away only with T-shirts and possibly a poison-ivy rash or a few bee stings, the NFLPA's campers in Carrollton were paid stipends from CETA funds. One camp organizer explained that the youngsters were attending a "vocational-exploration" camp, in which they operated their own mock bank, post office, radio station, newspaper, photography studio and general store.

"Believe me, these kids were there to *work,*" Anita Lee, the camp assistant director, said. "They didn't go there just to lie out in the sunshine all day. We taught them about the world of work, and how to write a check and manage money. And they are under constant supervision. The staff got the kids up at 6:30 in the morning and stayed with them until lights went out at 10:30 at night."

In a tragic coincidence, Anita Lee was told one night at the camp that her 17-year-old brother, Joseph Lee, a non-camper and a college-bound student, had been slain in an alleged holdup at a Tenneco service station near his home. The station is in suburban East Point (southwest of Atlanta), close to where the body of 14-year-old Milton Harvey had been found, where the bodies of two youngsters on The List would be found, and where an adult was killed in a drug scheme that apparently had gone bad.

Joseph Lee was shot to death in July of 1980, the same month that the Task Force was organized. His slaying is unsolved. Joseph Lee, who was 10 years younger than one of the men Wayne Williams would be accused of killing, never made The List.

As for the camp stipends, it is not clear why some youngsters were paid more than others. CETA officials in Atlanta gave conflicting explantations. The per-session amounts ranged from $55 to $272.80 for each child, they said. And not everybody could agree on how many hours per day the children actually worked for the money.

When Eula Montgomery visited the campsite one Sunday with a busload of other parents, she didn't have to ask Cynthia if she liked camp. Cynthia's beaming face said it all for her. Cynthia introduced her mother to her camp counselor, Pam Stone, then a basketball player at Valdosta (Georgia) State College; to some of the present and past professional athletes who conducted sports clinics, and to other campers. The camp's roster of sports figures included Alfred Jenkins and Dewey McClain of the Atlanta Falcons; Charlie Criss, formerly of the Atlanta Hawks, and Tony Jeter, a University of Nebraska football star in the 1960s and now a retired NFL player. Also listed among the camp's instructors was former U.S. Olympic sprinter Wyomia Tyus.

Cynthia's counselor remembered that Cynthia particularly enjoyed a class in photography. It was taught by a young man named Tony Riddle, who lived in Atlanta on West End Avenue, only four doors away from 9-year-old List victim Anthony Carter. But a girl camper who had befriended Cynthia remembered that Cynthia "didn't like" the class and was "trying to get out" so she could join her in a radio class.

Another camper who is of interest to us attended a radio class at that same camp. He also was a neighbor of Tony Riddle. Fifteen-year-old Joseph (Jo-Jo) Bell would be slain in 1981 and would make The List. Until then, he would live on Lawton Street, a block from West End Avenue.

When the camp session ended, Cynthia returned home with a notice entitling her to receive money for having attended. Cynthia's stipend was $272.80, according to CETA's account records. Her mother recalls that Cynthia received "around $230" (after taxes). They picked up the check together, she said, at a neighborhood center and were instructed to cash it at the downtown branch of an Atlanta bank.

Exactly why they couldn't simply cash the check closer to home, or at any bank, is not clear. But that hardly mattered to Cynthia and her mother. When they arrived at the downtown bank, they were directed to a woman cashier, as were throngs of other campers and their parents. Mel Pender, the camp director, was at the bank, directing the youngsters like a traffic cop—to the cashier.

To Cynthia Montgomery, a child of poverty, any windfall of at least $200 must have seemed like a small fortune. Perhaps it was a Cinderella-like dream. Her mother was surprised that Cynthia had received any money at all, let alone such a substantial amount.

The money didn't last long. Cynthia went to a beauty salon and got a $50 hairstyle. She and her mother spent the rest of the money on new school clothes for Cynthia. But they also bought a special gift for Cinderella—a $39 pair of designer boots.

As Eula Montgomery looks back on it all now, Cynthia's life soon swerved into a dead end. Eula suspects now that Cynthia's tailspin "began at the camp."

In August of 1980, Cynthia disappeared from home. Eula's blood ran cold. All summer, she had seen Camille Bell and several other grieving parents of murdered Atlanta children, complaining on TV that the police paid little, if any, attention to the killings. She reported Cynthia's disappearance to the police. The case was assigned to the Missing Persons unit.

Meanwhile, unbeknownst to Eula and the police, Cynthia showed up at the Salvation Army Girls' Lodge downtown, near 10th and Peachtree streets. It's a shelter for runaway girls, not just from Atlanta, but from all over the nation. During the summer of 1980, the shelter reposed in one of Atlanta's most notorious pockets of prostitution. For years, pimps loitered outside, vigorously recruiting the runaway girls with promises of big money and lavish clothing.

Not surprisingly, the Salvation Army decided to move the shelter out of downtown—to a small frame house on Howell Mill Road in northwest Atlanta. "Things had gotten so bad," Salvation Army Captain John Jordan said, "that we had to walk the girls to the bus—just to keep the pimps away from them."

Where were the police? How were they checking the lodge? Certainly the Missing Persons unit has a system to check lodges for runaways to see if there are any "missing persons" there. Perhaps an undercover cop could play pimp and share in the success the criminals have in finding whom they want there. After all, missing and murdered children were Atlanta's No. 1 priority at that time, according to all public pronouncements. "No stone is being left unturned," they said—except, perhaps, for checking lodges designed for missing children. Where were the police? Well, a man who lived at the Techwood Homes housing project, a few blocks away from the lodge, remembers sitting in a coffee shop one night at 10th and Peachtree. He said he watched one pimp stuff money into an envelope.

Then, the man said, the pimp strode across Peachtree Street to a vacant lot and handed the envelope to an occupant of what appeared to be an unmarked police car. I've seen the same thing happen in broad daylight with uniformed police in fully marked cars. Such an incident is *not* the exception that proves the rule.

This, then, was the home away from home that greeted Cynthia Montgomery. On the Salvation Army Girls' Lodge application form, she wrote that she needed "time to rest." She also wrote the telephone number of her aunt—not her mother. A supervisor later recalled that Cynthia had told her that she had been living with friends and that they were trying to raise money to bail out Cynthia's 21-year-old boyfriend from the DeKalb County Jail.

While Cynthia was in the shelter's office, a man from the United Way special services agency arrived to photograph a Nigerian woman who worked in the office. He said he needed a runaway girl to pose in the picture. Cynthia reluctantly consented. Sitting atop the desk, Cynthia grinned and held a telephone receiver to one ear, as if she were calling home. She wore a T-shirt inscribed: "National Football League Players Association."

Cynthia stayed only briefly at the shelter—from August 9 to 12, 1980. Then, she was gone again—a runaway from a runaway shelter. "She was just a baby," the supervisor recalled. "She giggled a lot and never really was very serious. All she needed was some counseling and direction. She could do something with herself, if she only had the chance."

Nobody knows whether Cynthia and her friends bailed her boyfriend out of jail. We're not even sure of his name.

The next time anybody heard from Cynthia, the telephone rang at Eula Montgomery's apartment. The woman caller identified herself as a worker at a cafe a few miles away. She told Eula that Cynthia had been arguing with a man who had escorted Cynthia and two other girls into the cafe. The man demanded that Cynthia leave with them, but Cynthia refused, the woman said.

How did the woman know it was Cynthia? She explained that Cynthia had gone into the ladies' room, then emerged and slipped her a handwritten note with her name and her mother's telephone number on it. Soon a frightened Cynthia left the cafe with the man and the other girls, the woman said. They drove away. The woman telephoned Eula, and Eula telephoned the police.

Within minutes, an Atlanta police car arrived at Eula's residence in Dixie Hills. She hastily climbed into the vehicle, which then sped away from the project. But, along the way, the driver unexpectedly detoured to a MARTA rail station, Eula recalled. He explained that he had to dispatch another officer who was riding in the car. Translated, it means that he was giving another policeman a ride to the rail station and completed that trip before going in pursuit of the "missing girl" who had left a note for "help." Eula was incensed. They arrived at the cafe too late. She and the officer asked questions. The only obvious answer was that Cynthia was gone again.

The next time anybody saw Cynthia was several days later, near the Wheat Street Garden Apartments, less than two blocks from the Wheat Street Baptist Church. There, only a month earlier, the pastor, William Holmes Borders, had co-chaired the "Conference on Children's Safety" with Camille Bell. Now, Cynthia stood there crying and terrified. But, no one came to help her. It seems that talk about concern for children's safety is easier to find than the concern itself.

Soon the Reverend Borders and his Wheat Street Baptist Church would have troubles of their own concerning apartments in the neighborhood. The City of Atlanta was acting against Borders and his church because of substandard conditions in the apartments, which were rented to the poor and owned by the church. The residents eventually were forced to evacuate the apartments.

Two people who lived at the apartments were concerned about the girl-child who was crying on the corner. They were Cynthia's aunt and cousin. The cousin asked Cynthia, "Honey, what's wrong?"

The cousin told us that Cynthia had been washing clothes in a laundromat that afternoon when a man accosted her with what she said looked like a .38-caliber handgun. The man was described as "about 32 or 33...sort of well-dressed," wearing a cowboy hat and blue jeans. He drove a black Pinto, and his name she knew only as "Priest." She said that he and Cynthia apparently had been quarreling. He was believed to be Cynthia's pimp.

Cynthia's aunt telephoned Eula Montgomery across town. Eula promptly rode the bus to the Wheat Street Garden Apartments and took Cynthia back home to Dixie Hills.

But home for Cynthia now was the streets. And I wondered about the efficacy of the counseling Cynthia had received at the NFL Players Association camp and the Salvation Army hostelry. The counseling had accomplished its goal. Cynthia now knew that there was a better life, which was all well and good.

But in two weeks, the camp was closed, and the well-to-do athletes went their affluent ways. Now it was left for guys with names like "Priest," "Big Red" and "Smitty" to show Cynthia a way—the deadly way—to achieve that better life. Cynthia wasn't equipped to perform the athletic feats that had led only a few from the despair of the ghetto. But her body could make her money in other ways. And if that better life was out there, why not go for it?

At night, Eula Montgomery locked the apartment door so that it could not be opened from the inside or the outside. And Eula kept the only key. But Cynthia escaped a second time, apparently squirming out a window in the second-story flat while the family slept. Again, Eula notified the police. She also said she contacted the family's Fulton County social worker in hopes of obtaining special counseling for Cynthia.

But it seemed that the only special attention Cynthia got was from the "johns" along Auburn Avenue. Cynthia Montgomery was 13, going on 30. She would work the streets in expensive fall clothes. Her cousin said Cynthia got herself a new pimp, who looked "about 40 or 41" and wore maxi-coats. He also drove a late-model, red-and-white Cadillac, the cousin said, and Cynthia had said "the dude treated her real nice." His name, the cousin said, was "Smitty."

8

Earwitness to Murder

August, 1980

Kenny Brown tossed fitfully in his bed one night during Atlanta's most scorching summer on record. Finally, at 4 a.m., he headed for his cousins' apartment in the East Lake Meadows public housing project, where an electric fan might make sleep come easier. Quietly leaving the house he shared with his wheelchair-bound grandfather, two brothers and two sisters, he walked south along 1st Avenue on Atlanta's mostly black east side ("Atlanta-in-DeKalb") toward Memorial Drive.

Suddenly a child screamed: "Ma-ma! Ma-ma!"

Kenny Brown froze. The cries came from inside a car that had stopped ahead of him—along Memorial Drive—with its lights on and motor running.

Brown, 17, black and poor, was a high school dropout. He knew the streets, but didn't know how to read their names. His heart pounding, he crouched behind a clump of bushes and small trees alongside the curb.

Forty yards away, the car stood illuminated by a streetlight (do streetlights really prevent crimes?). Brown remembers fuzzily that the vehicle was either a Chevy Nova or an Oldsmobile Cutlass, either powder blue or pale green.

I saw problems with his description of the car. Usually, young boys are as accurate witnesses about vehicles as can be found. But a Nova and a Cutlass are as different as a Nova and a Ford.

In any event, Kenny Brown originally had told a friend, Dreenna Andreu, that the car was a green Nova. He recalled clearly that the car was elevated in the rear, with the number "350" affixed to the left front fender. I wondered how he read that number from behind a bush, 40 yards away. But I knew that anyone familiar with cars would realize that if anything were on that part of a Nova's front fender, it would be the number "350."

Now, as the child wailed on, Brown saw a black man emerge from the car and run around the front to the passenger side. It was impossible to see the man's face distinctly enough to identify him, but he remembers that the man wore a green shirt, dark trousers, a silver bracelet that glistened under the streetlight and a black flat cap with its front snapped to the top of its bill. Kenny Brown gave further details that I didn't think he could have seen from where he saw them.

I would ask DeKalb County Public Safety Director Dick Hand to have his officers talk with Brown. Hand did. They agreed with me that Kenny Brown had seen all or part of what he said he had seen, but that he didn't see it from where he said he did.

The man, Brown said, hurriedly opened the passenger door and pulled what appeared to be a black boy—maybe 10, or 11, or 12—from the car. The boy put up stubborn resistance and clasped tightly to the door post. But the man's strength prevailed, loosening the boy's grasp. Seconds later, Brown saw the man drag the boy through a narrow clearing in the woods across Memorial Drive.

In an instant, they disappeared into the darkness—down a pathway that had been worn by so many others who used it as a shortcut to visit their friends and families at the East Lake Meadows project, which loomed faintly in the background.

All of a sudden there was a gunshot. It came from the woods where the man had vanished with the screaming boy in tow. But now there were no screams, just silence.

Moments later, the man re-emerged through the same pathway opening. But now the boy was limp, his body draped across the man's forearms. The man struggled to insert a key into the deck lid and opened it. Then he rolled the lifeless body into the trunk.

Now the man slammed the deck lid shut. He climbed behind the wheel and drove off. Kenny Brown emerged from his hiding place and ran toward Memorial Drive, trying to see the car's license tag number. As the car sped into the darkness, Brown could see only that the tag was white—the same color as Georgia's and, unfortunately, that of every neighboring state and many other states, as well.

Kenny Brown stood at the streetcorner and watched the car turn south from Memorial Drive to 2nd Avenue and disappear. He would tell this part of the story to his friend, Dreenna Andreu.

Months later, Dreenna would be watching television when WSB-TV's Wes Sarginson would interview me across a cluttered table at Katz's deli on Cheshire Bridge Road. My map lay crumpled across plates and bowls, displacing coffee cups and utensils. I pointed to a spot on the map and told Sarginson that the route turned south from Memorial Drive to 2nd Avenue.

At that time, I had never heard of Kenny Brown or his story. But Dreenna would be watching the WSB-TV (Channel 2) news that night, and the coincidence of Kenny's comments and mine about 2nd Avenue south from Memorial Drive were too much for her to ignore. The next morning, Dreenna called me.

Had the man who sped away in the car seen Kenny Brown? If so, would he come back looking to kill him, too? The thought struck Brown and so did terror. He forgot the heat and bolted back to his grandfather's house. When he burst through the front door, he was nearly out of breath. He excitedly related the news to his brothers and sisters, then entered the darkened room where his grandfather lay awake.

There, Kenny Brown told him the horror story he had seen and heard.

"Kenny, you keep your mouth shut about this," his grandfather warned sternly. "Don't get involved—you hear what I'm saying?"

Kenny Brown nodded.

"You keep walkin' these streets at night," his grandfather went on, "and somebody's gonna get you—if you ain't careful."

By mid-September of 1980, we were ready to open our "tour of death" to the public. Dick Arena made most of the arrangements, and I obtained a church meeting room on Memorial Drive as a gathering point.

The pastor was shocked when I told him that he preached in the geographic heart of the Atlanta murders. That was supposed to be happening to other people in other parts of town, he had thought. Which indicates just how poorly the geography of these murders was understood from media reports and police warnings to the public.

Together with a psychic, Dick had invited a woman who belonged to the same astrology club as he and his wife. This woman had "run" all of the murdered children's birthdates—those on The List. She came up with virtually the same information as had all the other astrologers I'd heard from (and there were plenty). Which wasn't too surprising. They all use just about the same charts and books. One thing they all kept telling me was that the killer walked with a limp. Wayne Williams has no problems with his legs.

I was to supply transportation to the meeting for Willie Mae Mathis and Camille Bell, two of The List victims' mothers. Mike had invited Dixie Foster, an ex-Atlanta cop-turned polygrapher. Joining our traveling party were Bill Taylor, Mike's business partner; Dale Kirkland, a GBI (Georgia Bureau of Investigation) agent who was also a member of the Task Force, and Jeff Scott, a freelance writer who was preparing an article on the murders for *Atlanta Weekly,* the Sunday magazine of the *Atlanta Journal-Constitution.* Jeff was the 11th member of the group, which included Dick, Mike and me.

Mike and the astrologer each brought their vans. We would use both and communicate by CB radio. Before we left the church, we gathered for a brief meeting. For the first time, I contended that there were either 13 victims, rather than the 12 now on The List—or, the still unidentified second body dressed in black along Niskey Lake Road had to be that of 14-year-old Alfred Evans.

I wanted to get the body count straightened out so the investigation could proceed on the right foot. I knew the base data was poor, but I didn't yet know how poor. And I didn't know what a mental block The List would become for anyone who tried to understand, investigate or write about these cases. No one, including GBI Agent Dale Kirkland, reacted to what I thought was a very important disclosure.

That September afternoon in 1980 was the first time I had been introduced to Camille Bell, even though I had seen her before on television and in person. As Willie Mae and I pulled up in front of Camille's Fulton Street project apartment, Camille scurried along the street toward us on her return from a quick shopping trip. She didn't bother to go into her house. Instead, she placed a small white sack on the floor of my car and climbed in. I still have the two pairs of children's socks that Camille had purchased that day. Now, whenever I see her, those socks have come to be an "in" joke—she accusing me of depriving her kids of them.

Jeff Scott telephoned me many months later. Beside confirming that Camille had told him the same story she had told me about the blue car and who was in it, Jeff told me two other things. One was that he'd written what he said was a hard-hitting story based on the route—which he thought held a lot of validity—only for his editor to demand a rewritten version focusing on the victims' mothers.

Jeff Scott also said he had a tape recording of an interview with Dr. Joseph Burton, the DeKalb County medical examiner. On the tape, Jeff said, Burton contended that there was no possibility of murder in the case of 10-year-old Aaron Wyche, and that it was strictly an accidental death. Jeff had asked Burton about it because I kept insisting to him—and to anyone who would listen—that murder was a distinct probability in the Wyche case. If correct, Jeff's tape would be very interesting to me.

Why? Between the grand tour and Jeff Scott's call, I had some bizarre, behind-the-scenes dealings with the medical examiners. They didn't know that questions being asked by some news persons were originating with me. Some of the questions asked by Gail Epstein of the *Atlanta Constitution* had to do with the identification and cause of death for Alfred Evans. But others also asked by Epstein of Joseph Burton were about the possibility of murder in the Aaron Wyche case. Epstein told me, "He said he never did rule out murder in the Wyche case." This obviously differed from what Jeff Scott said his tape revealed.

Camille Bell thinks fast on her feet. Her prominent, "drop-temple" eyeglasses had helped make her a familiar face. She appeared countless times on television—and would appear again and again. Her eloquence made "good copy" for journalists who would arrive in Atlanta from far-away places and seek her out.

En route to our meeting at the church on Memorial Drive, Camille and I exchanged ideas. Her world views were much more in accord with mine than were her views of the Atlanta murders. But back then, Camille wasn't talking of preparing for the day when the "white power structure" would force blacks into concentration camps. At least, not to me she wasn't.

Later, I was to wonder which views she really held. What she told me and said in the media was diametrically opposed to what she told at least one group of blacks I heard her address. Many members of the Communist Workers Party sat in the audience that night. I assumed that Camille, although she once belonged to the volatile Student Non-violent Coordinating Committee (SNCC), was more opportunistic than sincere.

On the murders specifically, Camille listened to too many psychics and rumor mongers to suit my understanding. But she wasn't alone. The families of the children were highly susceptible to rumor. Many journalists interviewing the parents for "firsthand" information got only warmed-over rumors.

Mike Edwards' blue Dodge van led the way, with Dick Arena riding shotgun, and Bill Taylor in the not-very-well-home-rigged rear seat. The rest of us followed in the astrologer's vastly more comfortable nine-passenger van.

As we passed by the East Lake Meadows project, I pointed out that all the children had lived—and disappeared—and their remains had been found—on or near the streets we would travel on. Dale Kirkland gave no indication of anything unusual as we drove through the East Lake Meadows area. His was a non-reaction that I would find highly interesting before the week was over.

By the time we reached the abandoned E.P. Johnson Elementary School, where Camille Bell's son, Yusuf, had been found dead in November of 1979, I wondered what her reaction might be. But I needn't have worried, for Camille and the psychic had struck up a strong rapport. Their conversation ran to pentagrams and other beasties of the occult.

As we alighted from the vans, Camille and the psychic walked away together toward the school building (which has since been razed) to study the form of a cross that was cast in the concrete lintel above the front door. One thing I learned about pentagrams and other "ominous" signs is that if you want to see one badly enough, you can find one everywhere you look. I almost went blind, looking for them in places where some said they were plain as the nose on your face.

I stood across the street from the school, on ground where a row of houses had long since been torn down and replaced by weeds, broken bottles, used syringes, and what-have-you. Each of us tried to avoid a drunk who sauntered up to tell us about all the "bad shit" that "went down" on this corner. "Why," he said. "you could even get your car stolt [sic] if you weren't careful!"

Camille Bell had lost far more than a car on this corner. As I stared at the deserted, red-brick schoolhouse, I thought of the coincidences surrounding the men who found and identified the body of Yusuf Bell. Both were school maintenance men, and neither could be found at the addresses given in police and medical examiner reports.

Yusuf Bell's body was decomposed, but not as severely as one could expect for the 27 days that he had been missing. This, plus the possibility that both the body and the boy's clothing may have been washed since the time he was last reported alive, raised the possibility that Yusuf had survived for some time after he disappeared—at least a few days.

Decomposition can be deceiving. It must be particularly tricky for one Fulton County medical examiner, who said that the presence of isoprophyl alcohol and acetone in one of the bodies could not be explained by decomposition. Telephone calls to two medical examiners who deal with many murders—one in New York, the other in Florida—elicited a somewhat different opinion. Isoprophyl alcohol and acetone, they said, could indeed be a product of decomposition. One of the two medical examiners refused to be quoted, but he was critical of the fact that Georgia is one of the last states to permit non-M.D.s to perform autopsies.

Having been instrumental in establishing a medical-examiner system in Kentucky while I worked for the Kentucky Crime Commission in 1973, I was well aware of the folly of using non-medical, "medical" examiners. What I didn't know then, however, was how futile those with "M.D." behind their names could also be.

But I had wanted to establish a meaningful medical-examiner system for years. As a rookie cop, I watched a non-medical, elected coroner use a yellow pencil to probe for a bullet in the head of a shooting victim. The coroner then nonchalantly tucked the pencil back in his pocket. Next, he called the victim's relatives aside and—before making a ruling—asked about the status of the victim's insurance!

The coroner later ruled the death a suicide, even though the evidence at the scene showed that the victim had been forcibly restrained; that she had been shot with a pistol purchased that afternoon by her husband, who was fresh out of the Kentucky State Penitentiary at Eddyville, and that the entry wound was high on the back of her head. All of which shows that—in criminal cases—Georgia has no corner on illogical medical determinations.

Moreover, it all is yet another example that so many findings by medical examiners are based on flimsy guesswork, not on precise science. I'm sure that medical examiners are well aware of their own fallibility. In their own way, they try to point it out while not sullying the mystique that keeps doctors wealthy. It is the press and the public who assume that these "findings" are *more* than value judgments and pure guesses.

John Feegel, a doctor-lawyer-writer, performed autopsies as a Fulton County associate medical examiner during the height of Atlanta's murders. Feegel would testify during the Wayne Williams trial in 1982 that he had no intention of writing a book about the killings. I knew his testimony was questionable because I had received a rejection slip on a manuscript, based on the murders, from a publisher who wrote that he already was considering a manuscript on the subject by Feegel.

While I served on Williams' defense team, I pointed this out to chief defense counsel Al Binder, who asked Feegel about it in court. Under oath, Feegel said that he was not writing a book on the subject and, in fact, "would not." In 1983, a book by Feegel was published—a novel about young black boys dying in a Southern city.

We have documented other cases from Georgia, Florida and Alabama, where victims whose cause of death has been ruled accidental were found—when exhumed for second autopsies—to have bullets in their bodies. There has been ample publicity about the machinations of the Los Angeles County coroner's office.

We reboarded the two vans and went off to finish the tour. Dale Kirkland, the GBI agent, remained quiet. For that matter, so did most everyone else, except Camille and her psychic companion. They conjured and conjured and conjured.

After we arrived at Redwine Road, where 14-year-old Milton Harvey had been found dead, Mike decided to take a detour that was unfamiliar to me. He was searching still another area, enticed by psychic Dorothy Allison's so-called clues. On the way, our resident psychic—not Allison—proceeded to tell us what the killers look like. One wore a Ban-Lon shirt, she said, and he flew in only occasionally to Atlanta's Hartsfield International Airport. Camille agreed with these descriptions. They were, she said, the same killers she'd been "seeing" in her dreams.

Suddenly an ear-rending screem filled our van. "Oh, my God! My, God, there he is now!" the psychic cried.

"Where? Where?" Camille Bell shrieked.

"There, right there! The killer! Don't let him get me!"

Camille and the psychic dived onto the floor of the van. The driver didn't know whether to keep going, stop, or bail out. I, for one, was astonished at what was happening.

"Get the license number!" someone shouted.

Some guy was innocently depositing something into the trunk of his car. Our van lurched backward so we could get the license number. The poor fellow might have thought the Martians had landed. Anyone would be startled by this vanload of strangers gawking and pointing at close range, with strange cries and screams coming from inside their van.

This kind of "sighting"—and these kinds of license numbers to check—were devouring too much of the Task Force's time and energy. For this kind of craziness, Mayor Jackson soon would ask for federal money to pay "overtime" costs of the Task Force. And Uncle Sam would pick up the tab.

Watching the psychic and Camille roll frightfully on the floor of the van ended my interest in our trip. It also reinforced even more my opinion about the value of psychics in an investigation. I had other valid questions, too, about psychics.

It was Friday, September 19, 1980—one day after our safari. The news was out: another Atlanta child was missing. Nothing to worry about, the Atlanta police assured. Ten-year-old Darron Glass was "just a runaway." He'd been missing from home since the previous Sunday, September 14.

Why had they waited five days to make this disappearance public? The public's impression was that dead children lay all over town—and now there had been no public-alarm broadcast for this child for five days! So what if Darron Glass did run away! So had Cynthia (Cinderella) Montgomery and others who would turn up dead.

Mike telphoned me to see if I had heard about Darron Glass' disappearance. I told him I had, but I didn't have any particulars.

"Are you sitting down?" he asked. "You're not ready for this. Do you know where this kid lived and disappeared from?"

He waited for an answer.

"No, Mike, I sure as hell don't."

"Well, he lived at 2289 *Memorial Drive.*" Mike stretched out the words for emphasis.

"God damn! Isn't that right next to East Lake Meadows?"

"You're damned straight it is. And do you know what, Chet? We drove right by there the other day—one day *after* he disappeared."

"I wonder if Dale Kirkland [of the Task Force] knew he was missing then."

"I don't know, but he damned well should have," Mike replied. "I'm sure as hell going to call him and ask him."

Mike called back to inform me that he had not been able to reach Kirkland. He added that the police were regarding the disappearance lightly because of Glass' runaway status. "I told them," Mike went on, "that if that kid disappeared on Memorial Drive, they'd better get off their asses and go find him—that he was *gone*!"

Because of what we had seen, Mike and I realized that the geography had become a parameter in and of itself. Not recognizing the geography was one of the gravest errors—from a prevention standpoint—made by officials in their handling of these cases. If they couldn't see all the geographic relationships, they should at least have been able to grasp the Memorial Drive connections.

In any event, as early as October of 1980, our map and tours prompted

Mike and me to recommend police stakeouts in four locations. These would be the points where the route changed directions—the corners of the map, so to speak. If I was right, they had to be crucial points in the case. They turned out to be exactly that:

1. Redwine Road—Two more bodies would be found here in January of 1981.

2. Moreland Avenue and South River Industrial Boulevard—Another victim would be found dead, one intersection west of here in November of 1980.

3. 2nd Avenue and Memorial Drive—Another victim who lived here would be found dead in May of 1981.

4. Jackson Parkway and Bolton Road—Long afterward, for reasons of their own, not becuase of our suggestion, police would establish a stakeout at a bridge six-tenths of a mile north of where we recommended in September of 1980. Police would say that at least two victims' bodies were deposited in the Chattahoochee River there in April and May of 1981. On May 22, 1981, the day before the stakeout was to be called off, this stakeout team would stop Wayne Williams after a splash was heard.

I didn't think that anyone was out there prowling this large perimeter, randomly picking up people and killing them. These likely were streets that the killer(s) traveled regularly, whether going from home to work, work to play, play to home, or whatever.

If, say, the same car were seen with any frequency at all four of these points where we had urged stakeouts, we would have an excellent suspect. The one point where a car would be seen most often would be the one closest to the suspect's home. That's because the place we go most often, no matter where else we have been, is home. (Wayne Williams would be stopped at the recommended point closest to his home, Jackson Parkway just north of Bolton Road.)

For weeks after our "tour of death," we mostly ran down leads in the neighborhood where still-missing 10-year-old Jefferey Mathis lived before he went on his errand to buy cigarettes. We also checked out inconsistencies in the police reports.

Mike Edwards, Jack Perry, Dick Arena, Bill Taylor and I canvassed the area between the Star Service Station and Jefferey Mathis' school. Soon we were followed by a camera crew from WSB-TV (Channel 2). I felt more than a little pretentious.

Jack Perry went to the fruit stand to talk with the boy that Jefferey had fought with before he disappeared. The boy was most cooperative, but the boy's daddy—who was called to the fruit stand by another relative—slammed the door in Jack's face.

Dick Arena meandered around and found, to no one's surprise, that the neighborhood brimmed with people who played the "bug," the numbers. He came away wondering if any of the kids had used their tennis shoes for more than one kind of running. Running numbers is one of the most profitable forms of running. Rum-running had run in Jefferey Mathis' family. Willie Mae, Jefferey's mother, has a police record for selling illegal whiskey.

I talked to the woman who lived in the house by the fireplug where Jefferey was last seen. When I arrived, her children played unattended on the front porch. My knock, not my mere presence among her youngsters, brought the woman to the front door.

I asked her if she had seen *anything* unusual on the day Jefferey disappeared. She said, "No." In fact, although she had heard something about a little boy disappearing, she had no idea that it had occurred in front of her house.

"The police haven't been here to ask you about it yet?" I asked.

"No," she said. "Ain't been nobody by here to ask me nothing."

You'd have thought that by now, the police would have been out in the neighborhood, talking to parents about their children's safety, especially with the offices of a police "crime-prevention" unit so close by. But in more than six months, the police had not even come by to look for witnesses in the Jefferey Mathis case.

At least, they hadn't come by to ask the woman who lived closer than anyone else to the point where Jefferey disappeared.

Mike Edwards found the little girls who said they saw Jefferey get into the blue car. We showed them a copy of the *Auto Trader,* a classified-ad magazine that contains hundreds of pictures of different kinds of cars for sale. But the girls were unable to single out any car that looked like the one they saw Jefferey get into. Which meant that they probably wouldn't recognize it if they saw it.

One day, shortly after Jefferey Mathis disappeared, some of his classmates complained to their teacher that two black men had tried to lure them into a car parked near the schoolyard. The youngsters said the car was blue and white. They also recited the license number. The principal gave police the information, along with another youngster's observation that the car had been abandoned on a nearby street.

The police follow-up report said they had looked for the car and couldn't find it. End of police search—and, apparently, end of police interest. That occurred in March of 1980.

I first saw that police report in early August of 1980. Mike called a friend at police headquarters and succeeded in getting the car's registration—basic, like kindergarten, police procedure. We had the owner's name and address and the vehicle identification number (VIN). It was a 1972 Buick.

Mike telephoned the registered owner, pretending to check on a large number of traffic citations which had not been paid on the car. The voice at the other end quickly volunteered the information that he had sold the car in February of 1980. He then told us to whom he sold it.

Mike recognized the buyer's name as that of a man who not only dealt in cars, but in cigarettes without brand names and in coke you can't use to make highballs.

The car buyer's story was that he had resold the car immediately. He gave us the name and address of the new owner. We wondered if he were a regular customer. Mike, Dick and I left the office and went to the address we had for the Buick's latest buyer. The house sat on a corner. The street that ran beside the house was the street where the youngster had told his principal that he saw the two men abandon the car.

In front of the house sat a blue-and-white 1972 Buick. It fit the description of the car in the disappearance of 10-year-old Aaron Wyche to a "T," down to the broken taillight and the Bondoed damage on the rear. But the car didn't have the correct tag number as given by the children and the Georgia Motor Vehicle Division. Georgia hadn't changed metal license plates since 1976, and in Georgia, the tag stays with the car.

Dick Arena hopped out and, shading his eyes from the sun, read the "VIN" from the plate on the dashboard. It *was* the right car. We drove off after noticing a lot of gaily-striped athletic socks hanging on the clothesline in back of the house.

First, we checked on the license number that was now on the car. Sure enough, the new tag number was registered to the Buick—but this time to the people who lived at the address where the car was parked.

April 1, two weeks after the children at Jefferey Mathis' school said they saw the two men, was the deadline for buying a new decal to revalidate the 1976 metal tag for 1980. For some reason, someone had gotten an entire new tag for this car. This would be perfectly legal and easy to do, but it would be unusual unless the old plate was badly damaged, disfigured, or faded. But the old plate had been legible enough for the schoolchildren to read the number.

Bill Taylor knew some people who lived in this neighborhood. They told him that no young men or grown boys lived in the house where the 1972 Buick belonged. Had it been winter, we might not have wondered so much about it. Whose sweatsocks were hanging on the clothesline?

Mike Edwards returned to the home of the little girls who had seen Jefferey Mathis get into the car. Mike got their mother's permission for them to go with him to look at the Buick we had found earlier. They said it was *not* the car that they had seen Jefferey get into.

We gave our information on the 1972 Buick to the Task Force, just as we had with all other information we had gathered. This time we put special emphasis on the similarities between the Buick and the one Aaron Wyche had been seen getting into at Tanner's Grocery Store on McDonough Boulevard. I knew that lead would not be checked out because Aaron Wyche was not on The List—he wasn't even considered murdered. His case was closed. But it would be reopened long after the lead on the Buick had gone stone cold.

The mystery of the 1972 Buick grew even deeper. We would learn that on the night Jefferey Mathis had disappeared six months earlier, his brothers went looking for him at the home of the people who owned the Buick. What were these connections among Jefferey Mathis, the house and the Buick? We never got a satisfactory answer from the Mathises.

If the Task Force developed anything on the house or the Buick, I would be surprised. Unless such information tended to show the guilt of Wayne Williams, it was supposed to have been included in the "Brady" materials (Brady materials are those documents known to the prosecution which tend to be exculpatory to the accused). I would read the Brady file in the Jefferey Mathis case, and it showed no suspects developed from the Buick. Was the Brady material complete? If not, on appeal of a court decision, it could be a reversible error!

Kenny Brown didn't stay quiet very long. A week or so after he'd "earwitnessed" what he said was the murder of a small boy along Memorial Drive, Brown noticed a group of black youths emerging from a neighbor's yard.

Tall, thick foliage obscured most of the white, Southern-style plantation house that had survived the onslaught of urban sprawl. In grander years, these lands were rich in cotton. The ramshackle house of Kenny Brown's grandfather backed up to the plantation house, which was for sale and had been unoccupied for weeks. All the owner's possessions had not been removed.

Could the youths be burglars? Brown thought so. He telephoned the owner, Dreenna Andreu, a young white fashion designer who had befriended him and other black youngsters in the neighborhood. One of those youngsters often played at Dreenna's house and ate fruit from the trees in her backyard. He was 10-year-old Darron Glass, who still is one of Atlanta's missing children.

Dreenna Andreu is a feisty, free-spirited woman who recently had moved away, far across town. She still kindled friendships from her old neighborhood, but she also bore scars from her years there. She spoke of the ever-present dope-pushing in the streets, day and night—unabated by any official action.

Did anybody really expect that the pushers would walk up to one of the conspiciously marked partrol cars which occasionally drove by—to "prevent crime"—and offer to sell the officer a nickel bag? Of course not. But apparently that is what the police system was waiting for as it continued its regular "crime-fighting" patrols of the neighborhood.

In June of 1979, a black man had regularly followed Dreenna home from her job at the Lakewood Fairgrounds, the scene of Charles Stephens' and Earl

Lee Terrell's disappearances and where Faye Yearby had been found murdered, at Pickfair Avenue and Pickfair Way.

The same man also had been following a woman associate of Dreenna from near the Fairgrounds to her home in Douglas County, by way of Georgia 166 across that part of the Chattahoochee River where two bodies would be found. When Dreenna told me this, only Earl Lee Terrell had disappeared, so she could not have known of the geographic connections to the other murder cases.

At Dreenna's home, the man made a forced entry and attacked her. He bloodied her face and left her badly beaten. She would tell me that when she telephoned the Atlanta police, they seemed to take forever to respond. But when they did, they took an interest in her case, greater than they take in most. They arranged for a police officer to be stationed in her home. But on the second night the officer was in her home, Dreenna said, "He tried to put the make on me. That's when my problems with the Atlanta police department began."

When Dreenna returned to her old home after receiving Kenny Brown's call, she called police. Her home and garage had been broken into. An Atlanta police officer came right away and started asking questions. When the woman officer questioned Brown, Dreenna recalled, the officer was contentious and skeptical about what she had seen that afternoon.

"Well, ma'am," Kenny Brown told the officer, "there's a lot of other things I've seen around here. But I've been told not to get involved—and not say anything about them.'"

Dreenna's eyes widened. "Kenny," she said "what *else* have you seen?"

Brown then recounted his story about the shooting of the boy on Memorial Drive. Dreenna said the officer wondered aloud if the boy could have been the same victim whose body had been found inside a dumpster a few days earlier on Hollywood Road. However, that victim—13-year-old Clifford Jones—had been strangled, not shot, on August 20 or 21, 1980. And his body was beside—not inside—a dumpster.

Now we knew that at least one Atlanta beat cop knew less than was reported in the newspaper about the Clifford Jones case. Her training had not served to enhance her recall of the incident beyond what one would expect from a "civilian" (a derogatory term used by police for the rest of us).

Could the victim have been 11-year-old Earl Lee Terrell, who had vanished nearly two months earlier and still was officially missing? The time lapse argues strongly against it.

Could it be Kenny Brown's neighbor, 10-year-old Darron Glass? Not if the time frame reported by Kenny Brown is correct. But Brown wasn't sure of the date, and Darron Glass disappeared from that same area on Memorial Drive within two weeks of the dates given by Brown. Darron had not yet disappeared, albeit he would soon vanish, from almost that exact point on Memorial Drive.

Who, then, was it? We may never know. Ten of John Wayne Gacy's victims in Chicago have yet to be identified. In this case, we don't even have a body.

The Atlanta police seemed genuinely interested, at first. They made an appointment with Dreenna and Brown to return a few days later with a sketch artist. They asked that Kenny Brown, in the meantime, try to recall as many details as possible. He did recall numerous descriptive details, and Dreenna wrote them all down and saved them for the police. But the police never returned. Dreenna said she made countless telephone calls to the police, but never talked again to anyone who was interested in Kenny Brown's story.

If Brown were telling the truth, Atlanta had at least one more murdered child who had not been identified and had not been put on anybody's list. The Kenny Brown story would show up in the "Brady" files, but in the case of victim Edward Hope Smith (a friend of Brown's neighbor, victim Alfred Evans). The problem is, Smith was found dead a full year before Kenny Brown says he saw the incident. Even so, Smith, too, had been shot. The multimillion-dollar computer operation of the Task Force at least got that much right.

9

The Nitty Gritty

September, 1980

The police still reported sightings of 10-year-old Darron Glass, two weeks after he disappeared. Mike Edwards had been working on the Glass case. He managed to explain a lot of those reported sightings by discovering that another child—also named Darron Glass—lived in the same neighborhood as his namesake.

The insistence by authorities that Glass was "only" a runaway finally became overkill when the *Atlanta Constitution* front-paged a story that Darron Glass "may be alive." His family supposedly was receiving phone calls from him. We ran down that story and found a minor flaw: It may well have been Darron calling, but if it was, you couldn't be sure because whoever kept telephoning the home of Fannie Smith (Darron's foster mother) kept hanging up without saying anything.

Mike kiddingly pointed out that Darron must be calling him, too. "Every day when I check my phone answering machine," Mike said, "there's a couple of yards of tape run off by somebody who calls and never says anything." We all agreed that this was too common an occurrence to leap to those front-page conclusions that Darron Glass was calling home.

Mike told me that the investigation had revealed that Alfred Evans and Edward Hope Smith, also 14, knew each other before they were found slain near each other. Additionally, Mike said the investigators on the case agreed with me that the second body was, in fact, that of Alfred Evans. Later, I wouldn't be so sure.

"The problem," Mike said, "is that the mother refuses to identify the body."

"Seems to me," I said, "we've got a bigger problem that that."

"What's that?"

"The dental charts, Mike. The police report says that there are no similarities between Evans' charts and the teeth in the second body at Niskey Lake."

Mike slowly stirred his coffee and looked up, puzzled.

Mayor Maynard Jackson was saying that the police investigation had received "high marks" from police officials all over the country.

Lee Brown had arranged with the Police Foundation (a branch of the Ford Foundation) to bring to Atlanta six of the most recognized detectives in the United States. The purpose of their visit was to have them evaluate the investigation. The press had the public thinking that they were here to help solve the cases. This was not true. Instead, they were to be used as consultants often are by government, to take the heat off the officials.

I telephoned a friend in Washington who was in a position to know first-hand what the "Super Cops," as the press dubbed them, really thought about the Atlanta investigation. He swore me to secrecy, so I can't use his name. He said the report by the visiting detectives was that the Atlanta investigation was one of the most fouled-up they had ever seen. He added that Commissioner Brown had been notified of the investigators' criticisms.

I began painting a verbal scenario for Mike on the Alfred Evans case. "We've got two bodies beside the roadside," I told Mike. "One is quickly identified. The other is more decomposed. The two corpses are taken to the morgue. It's hot. People are busy as hell. They're tired. The two victims are dressed very similarly and have very similar physical characteristics.

"Somebody accidently picks up the dental charts of the already identified body [Edward Hope Smith] and compares them to the mouth of the other body, thinking he has the charts of a missing kid [Evans]. There are no similarities. *Voila!* No identification. What do you think?"

"It sure as hell could have happened that way, Chet."

"How can we find out?"

"Well, let me call Dale Kirkland and see if he can check it out for us."

That was fine with me, although I wasn't sure that Kirkland was too eager to help us. If he were, he would have been more open with us about missing 10-year-old Darron Glass. I thought he might even urge the Task Force to look closely at my map and the geographic connections among so many victims. After all, I had taken Kirkland past Glass' home and the place where Glass disappeared *before* the boy's disappearance was made public.

We went back to Mike's office, where Mike phoned Kirkland. I listened as Mike repeated my scenario about the possible mixup of the dental charts.

When their conversation ended, I shook my head.

"I don't expect too much from that, Mike," I said.

"We'll just have to wait and see," he said.

On October 9, 1980, another Atlanta black child was missing. Twelve-year-old Charles Stephens had not been seen since late that evening. But, shortly before 7:30 the next morning, the body of a young black boy was found lying on a grassy hill at the entrance to the Longview Trailer Park in East Point, a suburb on Atlanta's southwest boundary.

Mayor Jackson announced and decried the death of Charles Stephens in remarks that night at the NAACP Freedom Awards dinner in Atlanta.

By my count, Charles Stephens was the 23rd victim. Or was he the 24th? The identification of the second boy in black was still up in the air.

The news media, awaiting the police assessment of the case, wondered if Charles Stephens would become Atlanta's 14th murdered or missing child. It was like buying a new car and waiting for the dealer to tell you what kind it was and whether he would let you keep it. One thing was for sure: you were going to pay for that car. Another was for sure: Charles Stephens was a murdered Atlanta child, whether they put him on The List or not.

As the information on Charles Stephens filtered in, I couldn't believe my eyes and ears. I rushed to the map, checking the locations that the radio account was giving me. I compared them with my own pattern, not expecting to find any relationships with the other points on the map.

My expectations were wrong. Charles Stephens lived and disappeared at 1707 Pryor Circle. If I didn't have the map in front of me, I would have joined too many other Atlantans, including the Task Force, in not realizing that Stephens' address was alongside the Lakewood Fairgrounds, where Earl Terrell had disappeared 71 days earlier.

But where was the Longview Trailer Park? I learned that it was a block south of the intersection of Norman Berry Drive and Cleveland Avenue. This was exactly on the route—drawn more than a month earlier—which connected the Redwine Road scene on the southwest with the Aaron Wyche case on the southeast.

Within the week, two more youngsters—Darron Glass and Charles Stephens—now were added to The List.

I would learn that a neighbor named Jerome Clark had seen Charles Stephens playing on a skateboard near the dumpster in front of Clark's residence on Pryor Circle (where Stephens had lived, too). It was the evening of October 9, 1980. Jerome Clark said he saw a man emerge from between Buildings 1701 and 1714, on Pryor Circle. Clark spoke to the man, but the man didn't respond.

Charles Stephens was no stranger to trouble in the Pryor Circle neighborhood. About six or seven months before his death, some neighbors accused him of killing their dog. They further accused Charles of stealing their television set. The police were called and allegedly found the TV "in or about Charles' residence," according to a police report.

The security guard on Pryor Circle said these same neighbors moved away, right after they registered their complaints about Charles. The guard added that it wasn't unusual to see Charles Stephens out late at night. Sometimes, the guard said, he saw Stephens at the Zayre department store in the Lakewood Shopping Center (the same location where 14-year-old Lubie [Chuck] Geter would disappear) on Georgia 166.

Jerome Clark said it was about 8:30 or 8:45 p.m. when he saw Charles Stephens on the skateboard. He told Charles: "Get your butt in the house." He added that Charles didn't reply, but instead looked up the hillside and made a kind of a "Tarzan" yell.

Clark would later tell the FBI that on the Sunday (October 12, 1980) after Stephens' body was found, he saw a black man walking in the neighborhood. It was, Clark said, the same man he had seen between Buildings 1701 and 1714 on October 9, the night Stephens disappeared.

Another man tried to offer information to the police about Charles Stephens. The man had gone to a corner grocery and asked the clerk to call the police. He waited there for an hour and left. The police never came. The store clerk then called the FBI and provided as much information as he could remember.

An FBI agent went to the laboratory to see if any new evidence had been developed from the findings of Charles Stephens' body. Eureka! The lab had a positive match on a fiber from that body! But it wasn't any reason to pop champagne corks yet. A uniformed East Point police officer, first on the scene, had thrown a blanket over the body. The FBI agent explained in his report that the officer had erred, "...thereby contaminating any fiber evidence that may have been available to aid us in our investigation..." The Keystone Cops had struck again.

It would be important to remember at the Wayne Williams trial that an FBI agent, viewing the evidence at the lab, had said that it was contaminated. Unfortunately, like so many other things, the jurors would not realize the full import of that statement, if they were aware of it at all.

Even so, Charles Stephens would become one of those victims who the police would say was killed by Wayne Williams. Stephens' case also would be among those cleared by Commissioner Lee Brown without benefit of a trial. The reason? Fiber matches!

Stephens' body had numerous fibers, but two particularly interested me. The FBI fiber expert would say that one of those fibers "*could*" have come from the trunk of a red 1979 Ford LTD owned by Homer Williams, Wayne's father. Could they? The FBI "expert" also said other fibers could have come from a throw rug in the back of a white 1970 Chevrolet station wagon driven by Wayne Williams when he would be first stopped by police shortly before 3 a.m. on May 22, 1981. They *could* have come from these cars, I suppose. But I don't think they did.

Fibers from a red 1979 Ford LTD? Well, a 15-year-old boy told police that he knew Charles Stephens. The boy said, according to the police report, "Charles had a male friend whom he met every day for two consecutive weeks, except for Saturdays and Sundays."

Could this be the man Jerome Clark had told the FBI he saw between the two houses on Pryor Circle while Stephens was riding the skateboard on the street?

The 15-year-old boy further told police that Charles Stephens would meet the man about 4 o'clock each afternoon—about a block from Stephens' house. On one occasion, the youngster accompanied Charles and the man on a ride. Returning to where the man had picked them up, Charles and the 15-year-old boy got out of the car and, the man said, "Charles, you remember what you got to do tomorrow?" Charles told him "yes." This occurred on September 24, 1980, about two weeks before Charles would disappear.

The boy also told police he sometimes followed Charles to his daily meetings with the suspect. Then he'd watch Charles get into the man's car, and they would drive off. The car in which the boy rode with Charles and the man was a brown two-door.

But the boy described another car to police that he said Charles and the man had ridden in. "It was," the boy said, "a Ford LTD, red in color with a red interior." The boy added that the car had wire-chrome wheels.

Wayne Williams did not fit the description of the suspect given by the boy. Williams had driven a car that fit the description of the red Ford LTD, but Williams' car didn't have wire wheels. "This car was a bad ride," the boy said.

Wayne Williams no longer had the red Ford when Charles Stephens got the fibers from a similar car. But someone else whom Charles Stephens rode with did have a red Ford. Even so, no jury would hear this testimony.

The young boy went to tell police that he and Charles Stephens smoked a "joint" after they returned from their ride with the suspect. Prodded by his mother, the boy began talking of Charles Stephens "selling reefer" He said he'd seen Charles with a stack of small yellow envelopes wrapped with a rubber band. The boy said he had watched Charles sell marijuana to people on the street. Charles' customers included several grownups and children in the neighborhood, the boy said.

After interviewing the boy, the reporting officer and GBI Agent Dale Kirkland went to Charles Stephens' residence. There, they looked for two shirts that Charles bought on the day of his disappearance. They found them in a bag in his closet. On the closet shelf, the officers also found half a marijuana cigarette.

Still another suspect in the Charles Stephens case surfaced immediately. Later, in December of 1981, I would tell Mary Welcome and Al Binder, defense attorneys for Wayne Williams, about this suspect. Whereupon Mary Welcome would blurt out, "You don't mean it. I know that guy. He's my client. Hell, we've got to find him. He owes me a bunch of money." Now we were getting down to the nitty-gritty.

The day after Charles Stephens turned up dead, a witness gave a statement at Task Force headquarters. He first was asked to pick the suspect he was talking about from a photo lineup. He did so easily. At least, we know that he knew whom he was talking about. The date was October 11, 1980.

The witness went on to tell a fascinating story, as recounted in a police report: "On Thursday [October 9, the night Charles Stephens disappeared], I and a subject named [he furnished the suspect's name and nickname] conducted a drug transaction of approximately an ounce and a half of cocaine [at] Interstate 285 [and] Camp Creek Parkway at a Tenneco Station, in suburban East Point. [This location is near the place on Redwine Road where one victim had been found and two more would be discovered months later.]

"I met [the suspect] at approximately 10:30 p.m. on Thursday [October 9]...When I got in the car, I observed a small body being wrapped up in a green sheet located in the back seat of [the suspect's] car. [His] car is a brown Lincoln with tan or light brown interior."

The witness went on to explain how the suspect obtained cars from a dealership on Campbellton Road (Georgia 166)—near the home of Angel Lenair—by trading dope for a free ride whenever he needed one. He was partial to *brown* cars, the witness told police. It had been a brown car that Charles Stephens and the 15-year-old boy rode in with Charles' man friend.

The witness continued, as the police report states: "I noticed that the child was not breathing because the material that was wrapped around him was not moving at all. [The suspect] advised me to forget what I saw during the initial conversation of the drug transaction, while I was observing what was located in the back seat...On Friday morning [October 10], I noticed a note on my car, saying [to] call [the suspect]. Urgent! At this time...I asked officers to meet me..."

The man who gave the police this information apparently felt compelled to do so. He was wanted by authorities himself.

The police wanted to talk with him further, so they brought him in for another interview. But first, they informed him that they had a warrant for his arrrest for giving them a false name in their previous interview.

He told them he had known the suspect since September of 1979, when they met in a local jail. He added that he'd been buying cocaine from the man since October of 1979.

Moreover, the witness said that the suspect had asked him about procuring young boys, that he would give him $20 to $30 for a few minutes of (child) sex. The suspect had, on several occasions, propositioned him, the witness said.

From there, the witness repeated his story about what he'd seen on Thursday night, October 9. This time he told police that the body in the car was wrapped in a blanket, not a sheet. The color of the blanket, he said, was pea *green*. He said the body was that of a black youngster, about the age to start high school. He said the blanket was not just thrown over the boy's body, but that he was "wrapped like a mummy."

"As [the suspect] was giving me cocaine out of his glove box," the witness continued, "I asked him—'cause I was concerned about the boy—was he all right?...he looked like he wasn't breathing. [The suspect] answered by saying [the boy] was barbed out. 'Don't worry about him.'"

The police told the witness he must have seen people "barbed out before." The witness replied that he had—and that the boy didn't look "barbed out" to him.

Then the police asked if the boy would have had to struggle to move. The witness answered: "Definitely had to struggle to move, the way his arms were. You could see the impression of his arms down by side of his body...His head, the back of his head and a portion of the left of his face" could be seen outside the wrapping. He added that the body faced the back of the automobile, "laying on his stomach, and his head was kind of tilted toward the back."

The witness said that after he tested the coke, he asked about the boy again. He said the suspect lost his temper. "He told me not to worry about it. He said it was none of my business, and did I want to do this deal or forget it?..."

They only occasionally had met at the Tenneco station near Redwine Road, the witness said. Interestingly, the suspect was said to have a record for armed robbery, and 17-year-old Joseph Lee was murdered in an alleged armed robbery at this same Tenneco station in July of 1980, the month the Task Force was formed. Lee never made The List, and his case was not solved.

The witness went on to describe how he could set up meetings by telephoning the suspect at home. He told police that he had seen the suspect do drugs—usually a mixture of cocaine and heroin. "Speed ball," the witness called it. "He injects it in a syringe."

The police asked if the suspect was doped at the time the body of the boy was seen in the car. "He was definitely doing cocaine," the witness replied.

Why had the witness called the police and risked the chance of being captured himself? He told police that he first had tried to borrow enough money to get out of town.

"Why do you want to leave town?" a GBI agent asked.

"Because, I am scared for my life," he replied. The note left by the cocaine dealer on his car had shaken him up "real good," the witness said.

The dealer had never actually threatened him before, the witness said, but "he'd talked about his mean person." He added that the suspect himself had packed pistols before (.22-caliber, I wondered).

The police asked if the suspect had ever talked about picking up children—and, if so, where?

"Yes, he's mentioned it to me," the witness replied. "I have heard him say he's gone out to Grant Park...He said some boys hustle their body [sic]."

"Did he ever say he'd had sex with the kids?" the policeman asked.

"Yes, what you would take as having sex with a boy," the witness told him. He explained that the suspect was a "hawk, a chicken hawk"—an older male who craves sex with young boys.

The police had a polygraph test administered to the witness. He passed. They then booked him on the warrant and as a material witness. Their next step was to find the suspect's common-law wife. They did—in another local jail. They asked for—and received—her permission to search the apartment she shared with the suspect.

But before the police went to that apartment, they looked for a woman friend of the witness. They found her at her home, on a street that runs off East Lake Road, at East Lake Meadows and Memorial Drive. After talking with her attorney, the woman agreed to talk with the police. She said she had dated the witness three times, but hadn't seen him since September.

When asked if she had ever met the witness' wife, she said she had met her at the Dial Inn motel on Shallowford Road in northeast Atlanta. The motel is only a few blocks from my home.

The suspect's apartment sat on the corner of Georgia 166 and Interstate 285, behind a shopping center. I was obviously interested in these geographic coordinates.

In their investigation of the suspect, the police turned up a connection between the suspect and their long-time informant. It seems the informant had been an accomplice of the suspect in past crimes. Officers who worked with the informant regularly said the informant's credibility had been excellent. Police brought the informant in for questioning.

The informant said the suspect was "capable of anything." He stated that "it would not be unheard-of for the suspect to haul a body to a location for disposal." Moreover, the informant confirmed that the suspect had homosexual tendencies (I would have called them bisexual, based on his common-law wife arrangement). The informant gave the police names of the suspect's homosexual partners, whom the informant knew.

The suspect often furnished young boys for these men and, in turn, got drugs, the informant told police. The informant went on to say that, for the most part, these men have "kids working for them in illegal activities. At one point, about six months ago, [he] had kids stealing drugs for him." The suspect, he said, had a police badge and police identification.

"The informant confirmed," the police report went on to say, "the suspect worked the lower south side and Campbellton Road [Georgia 166] to Decatur [the East Lake Meadows neighborhood]. The informant, when asked, told us that the homosexual associates already mentioned lived in boarding homes located off Bankhead Highway [U.S. 278] and Jackson Parkway [where the bridge incident involving Wayne Williams would occur]. He stated that he has been to this location and described the apartment as being furnished well...When asked about the carpet, he stated it was *green* [emphasis added]."

The police noted that everything this informant said agreed with what the original witness had told them. The details also confirmed that this suspect was meeting all the geographic parameters which my map had set for a valid suspect. While I read the foregoing police report—months after the conviction of Wayne Williams—my skin crawled.

How I wished the jurors could have heard the statements of these witnesses. How I wished they had the background in these cases to have understood them. Suppose, I thought, the police had charged the suspect and had forgotten the fibers (which they would have gladly done if they had anything else) and the jurors had heard this testimony. They would have convicted someone else for these murders.

It would have been possible for the jury to have heard some of this testimony, since Charles Stephens' case was one of the 10 "pattern" cases introduced at the trial of Wayne Williams for the murders of Jimmy Ray Payne and Nathaniel Cater. But these witnesses were not asked to testify.

The police report continued: "The informant states the suspect now has small children working for him in the 'stop and cop operation' [street corner-to-car drug sales] all over town. He does not know about this operation being conducted in East Lake Meadows."

The agents who wrote the report said they then went to Task Force headquarters, where they briefed the GBI's Robbie Hamrick, one of the top two Task Force officials, on their findings. It interested me to know that officers John Woods and Mike Shannon of the Task Force took my map and other information to then-Atlanta Police Chief George Napper in early November of 1980, after I'd taken them on the route. The information about the dealer-suspect was coming in at the same time. Those who read both the report and my information could not help but see implications in these cases leap off the pages at them. Yet the Task Force never put the two together—something I would remember after a long talk I would have with the Task Force's Robbie Hamrick months later.

All this would happen even after the informant said, "The suspect almost always utilizes I-285 to Camp Creek Parkway to Washington Road to Main Street [in] East Point and then to Cleveland to Brown's Mill."

These were the precise streets on the southern leg of my map.

The medical examiner guessed—he called it a finding—that Charles Stephens was "apparently suffocated with Unk [unknown] object at an unknown time on an unknown date." This is quoted from Charles Stephens' death certificate. Would you want to go to prison on *that* kind of testimony?

Among the fibers found on Charles Stephens were numerous white animal hairs tipped in black. The police and prosecution would say they came from Wayne Williams' dog—a claim they themselves would finally admit was extremely weak. Also found were two *Caucasian* head hairs, which no one mentioned then or later at the trial.

Inside the boxer shorts—found 950 feet from the scene—were two Negroid pubic hairs—not Stephens' and not Wayne Williams', according to the state crime lab. The crime lab's report in the Stephens case made another statement about fibers that would interest me later. It noted "one partially melted yellow synthetic fiber consistent with a carpet fiber." But the state later would claim that the fiber came from a toilet-seat cover.

The autopsy report in the Charles Stephens case reads: "The penis is circumcised. There are no wounds seen on the penis or the scrotum. Two testes are palpable in the scrotum." Thus, the autopsy and others I read conflict drastically with widespread rumors that some of the victims were castrated or otherwise sexually mutilated.

October 8 was a day that would change earwitness-to-murder Kenny Brown's life forever.

He left his house for an appointment at noon with a man at a nearby job center. But the man was not there. Retracing his route along Boulevard Drive, he went toward his aunt's house.

Along the way, he said, he was confronted across the street from the Sammye E. Coan Middle School by several teen-age boys he knew. The one who did the talking, Brown said, was 13-year-old Tracy Jordan, whom he had been in a fight with earlier.

"He told me he'd been suspended from school," Kenny Brown said, "and he asked me how he could keep his mama from finding out. I told him to wait by his mailbox. 'When the letter from the principal comes, just tear it up.'"

Brown said Tracy then went toward home, and Tracy's friends left in another direction.

Back at his aunt's house, Kenny Brown heard the clatter of police helicopters overhead, but paid scant attention. Late in the afternoon, he returned to his grandfather's house. There, he said, someone told him, "Kenny, the police were here looking for you."

"I thought they wanted to ask me some more questions," Brown said, referring to the small boy's slaying he had reported along Memorial Drive in August. "So I sat out by the curb and waited for about a half hour. They never came back, so I went inside."

In the evening, there was a knock on the door. Two Atlanta police officers stood outside.

"Kenny Brown?" one asked.

"Yeah."

"You're under arrest."

As Kenny Brown recalls, they ordered him to lie on the ground. When he sprawled on his back, he said, they told him to lie on his front while they frisked him. One officer kicked him across his head, he said.

Brown was taken downtown to Atlanta police headquarters. He was charged with kidnapping and aggravated sodomy. The alleged victim was Tracy Jordan. The rape allegedly had occurred before noon in a wooded area across a quiet street from a row of small houses, about a block from the Coan schoolyard.

At the police station, Kenny Brown said, officers accused him of killing some of Atlanta's black children and then tried to get him to confess. One officer, he said, struck him across his chest and slammed him against a wall. He said he had been advised by his lawyer, a public defender, not to answer any questions. He recalled that one child they accused him of killing was Brown's neighbor, 10-year-old Darron Glass, who now had been missing for about three weeks.

In the case of *State of Georgia vs. Kenneth Bernard Brown,* a plea of not guilty was entered by a public defender on Kenny Brown's behalf. Brown did not take the witness stand.

But Tracy Jordan and a white arresting officer, R.A. Brown, a member of the Task Force, told Judge E.T. Brock a markedly different version of the story that Kenny Brown had related about the alleged events of October 8.

They also told somewhat conflicting stories: Tracy testified that he was on his way *to* school and late for class when the incident allegedly occurred. Officer Brown testified that Tracy had been suspended *from* school (which matches what Kenny Brown said).

In his testimony, Tracy Jordan said under oath that Kenny Brown asked him if he wanted to help him sell "some reefer," or marijuana, and that Tracy said "no."

Then, he said, Kenny Brown held a gun and a knife against him and dragged him "about 50 yards" into "some woods over there by the park." No one asked how Kenny Brown, with only two hands, managed to do it.

Under questioning by Atlanta City Solicitor Mary J. Stewart, Tracy testified that Kenny Brown said, "Pull down your pants."

"Okay," Stewart said. "Did you do that?"

"No," Tracy said.

"What happened then?"

"He pulled them down."

"Did he pull down your outer pants?"

"Yes."

"And, then, what did he do?"

"He pulled off one of my shoes and pulled off the other one."

"And, then, what happened?"

"And, then, he took out his penis or something."

"Um-hmm."
"Then he got me."

10

The Pierced Ear

October, 1980

Thirteen-year-old Cynthia Montgomery stood at the corner of Auburn Avenue and Fort Street in downtown Atlanta, looking for a prospect—and some action. It was 1:15 a.m. on October 5, 1980. She saw a man driving slowly by and she whistled. When the motorist stopped, she walked to the car and asked, "What's happenin'?"

"I'm just ridin' around," the man said.

"You wanta date?"

"Yeah, maybe."

"You got $20 and $5 for a room?"

"No."

"How 'bout $20 then?"

"Yep. What do I get for $20?"

"A half and half."

Instead of the $20, Cynthia got a free ride to the "Green Bar Hotel" (jail). The motorist was a cop. He arrested Cynthia and charged her with prostitution and solicitation for sodomy.

However, she told the police her name was "Cynthia Smith" and that she was 18. The police had found one of Atlanta's missing children and didn't know it. Authorities bought her story. She was taken to the Fulton County Jail, an adult facility, where she was booked as Cynthia Smith.

The Atlanta police Missing Persons unit, meanwhile, had turned up no trace of Cynthia Montgomery. At night in Dixie Hills, Eula Montgomery lay awake with worry, losing hope and wondering if she had lost Cynthia forever.

But, a week or so later, the telephone rang. It was Eula's son, calling from the Fulton County Jail, where he was an inmate. "I saw Cynthia here!" he exclaimed. Eula telephoned the police to tell them that the missing person they were looking for had been put in their jail by one of their police.

The futility of the police system of searching for missing persons is again demonstrated. First, the police don't find a missing infant under a pillow at a murder scene. Then the system doesn't look for, let alone find, a missing girl at a home for missing girls. Now it couldn't find a missing person in its own jail.

Eighteen months after Wayne Williams was convicted, a 2-year-old girl disappeared in Atlanta. Several hundred Atlanta police waged a massive search within hours. The *Atlanta Constitution* would use the incident as an example of how the murdered-and-missing experience had improved the Atlanta police.

Improved them at what? Once again, they had shown a marked increase in efficiency at doing the same old ineffective things. Nothing the Atlanta police did helped locate that little girl. She wandered into the arms of a kind lady, as so many stray tots do.

On the morning of October 13, 1980, the first chilly day of autumn, Eula Montgomery and Detective Carolyn O'Neal of the Atlanta police Missing Persons unit proceeded toward the jail. They would obtain Cynthia's release and take her to a juvenile detention facility, next door to Atlanta-Fulton County Stadium.

They hadn't traveled very far when an emergency call suddenly filled the police radio frequency. A horrible explosion in a furnace boiler had ripped apart the nearby Bowen Homes day-care center, near Bankhead Highway (U.S. 278). The blast killed four small black children and a black teacher. It also ignited shockwaves of suspicion.

Was it foul play? After all, weren't eight other black children dead and four others missing—at least officially? Mayor Jackson, who was whisked to the scene almost immediately, spoke through an electric bullhorn and tried to reassure a hostile throng that the explosion was an "accident." His words were drowned out by hoots and jeers.

Bowen Homes became an emotional powder keg. Detective O'Neal told Eula Montgomery that they had better stop at Bowen Homes en route to the jail. While O'Neal joined other officers at the scene, Eula stood by for what must have seemed like an eternity. Cynthia's case would have to wait, as well it could. Hours later, Eula and Detective O'Neal finally drove to the Fulton County Jail.

The detective questioned Cynthia about "Gypsy," 16-year-old Angela Bacon, the victim of the hit-and-run killer.

"She asked Cynthia if she knew her," Eula Montgomery recalled, "and Cynthia said, 'Yes.' Then she asked Cynthia if she knew any of Angela's friends, but Cynthia seemed afraid to talk about it. Then Detective O'Neal said to her, 'If you run away again, you will be next.'"

Cynthia was ordered by a juvenile-court judge to stand trial on November 25. She was released to the custody of her mother, but Cynthia's homecoming was short-lived. Early the following Sunday morning, October 19, while the rest of the family was asleep, Cynthia again escaped from the second-floor window.

Cynthia Montgomery walked Atlanta's mean streets, where life can be cruel, but money is often easy. She was a three-time runaway from Apartment 10 at 31 Shirley Place, N.W.

On the phone, Mike Edwards' voice oozed excitement. "Chet," he said, "guess what I heard on the grapevine?"

"What's that?"

"I heard they identified the second body at Niskey Lake. It was Alfred Evans! How about that?"

"You're kidding!" I said elatedly.

"Trouble is," Mike went on, "I can't get anybody who is anybody to confirm it for me."

"What the hell is the big secret?" I wondered aloud.

"Damned if I know."

"Mike, do you think they're covering their ass?"

"What do you think?"

Mike laughed a gutteral, knowing laugh.

A week or two earlier, I had sat in Mike's office when he got a call from Gail Epstein of the *Atlanta Constitution.* Mike juggled her questions for a few minutes, then said, "Wait a minute! Dettlinger's here. He knows. Let me let you talk to him."

Mike handed me the telephone. It was the first time I had talked to Gail, but we would be comparing notes almost every day for the next four months. Her questions were hurried and demanding. She wanted to know how many kids were dead.

"You're asking *me*?" I said, trying to slow her down. "Well, that depends."

"Come on," she said. "What do you mean, *depends*?"

At last, I sensed an opportunity to tell the whole story about The List and the confusion over the body counts. How wrong I was. I started explaining, but she interrupted.

"Look," she said, "I'm on deadline. I've got editors looking over my shoulder. I just want a simple answer to a simple question. How many kids are dead?"

My first reaction was anger. My second was wonder. My third was silence. I didn't answer. Instead, I held the receiver high over my head and hollered for Mike. "Here, you take this," I said. "I can't talk to her."

A few days later, I cooled off and telephoned Gail at the *Atlanta Constitution.*

"Hey, Gail, this is Chet Dettlinger. Remember me?"

"Hi," she replied in a friendly voice.

I invited her to take the tour of death with me. She jumped at the chance. We set a date and time.

"Gail," I went on, "what I called you about was Alfred Evans." I explained the scenario about the confusion over the identifications and the fact that we had called Dale Kirkland of the Task Force. And now we were hearing rumors that I was right. At least, these rumors pointed to the second body along Niskey Lake Road having been identified as Alfred Evans.

The next morning, Gail had a front-page, byline story. She had slashed through the red tape and gone right to the Fulton County medical examiner. He confirmed that the second body had been positively identified a week or so before. He said it was Alfred Evans!

But, for me, Gail's story raised more questions than it answered. The identification, Gail's story explained, had been made from dental charts. The story highly praised Atlanta Police Detective Roz Richardson for her fine work in finally finding the "misfiled dental charts of Alfred Evans."

The story went on to say that Evans had been strangled.

"Hold it! Just a damned minute!" I yelled while reading the story. "How can they say that?"

When the body still was unidentified, the cause of death was said to be "unknown," not strangulation.

"How the hell did they make the dental-chart identifications?"

"What did they do, exhume the body? It's been 15 months since that body was found!"

The story in the *Constitution* explained that it had taken so long to make the identification because Alfred Evans' mother would not identify the body. The medical examiner was sorry, he said, "to have to prove it to them [the parents]."

I wasn't buying this story. They just happened to make an identification because of so-called brilliant police work—on the very week I had informed the Task Force that I thought the dental charts had been screwed up.

I was back on the phone to Gail Epstein: "Why not go back to the medical examiner and ask him some more questions?"

"What questions?" she asked, now trying to slow me down.

I spelled out the questions for her:

—How could they say the identification had been made from dental charts that had just been located, when they had said just after the body was found in 1979 that Alfred Evans' dental charts had been checked against the mouth of the victim and that there were *no* similarities?

—Was I right? What dental charts did they use 15 months earlier, back in July of 1979—when the body was found?

—What did they compare the "recently-found" dental charts against? Surely the body found along Niskey Lake Road had been buried long ago. Were they comparing a chart with another chart?

—What new evidence had they uncovered that allowed them to fix the cause of death as strangulation, when 15 months ago—with the body lying in front of them—they said the cause of death was *unknown*?

Gail called back that evening. "First of all," she said "the body is still in the morgue."

"What? That's incredible!" I said.

"The M.E.," Gail continued, "says it's not possible that they compared Evans' dental charts before, because they had never been requested before." Now, how could this be reconciled with the police report, which also said the charts were "routinely obtained"? I *hope* they are routinely obtained.

"Wow! Do you know what that means, Gail?"

These were the possibilities: The medical examiners erred back in 1979 and didn't compare the teeth of the unknown body with the dental charts of a missing boy—even though that missing boy fit the description of the unknown in so many *other* ways. Or, somebody's not telling the truth.

"Somebody has got to be covering their ass, Gail," I said. But she didn't see it that way.

Why was the cause of death now changed from "unknown" in 1979 to "strangled" in 1980? Gail explained that the medical examiner told her that he was under pressure from the Task Force to supply a cause of death.

"Since they had ruled out gunshot, stabbing, poisoning and so on," Gail continued, "he said it was *probably* asphyxiation, *probably* strangulation."

"Holy God, Gail!" I said. "What a story!"

Gail didn't think so, but I certainly did. Here was the medical examiner saying that he had changed the cause of death to reflect a murder—under pressure from the Task Force—and it wasn't a story. What *is* a story? From that October day in 1980 on, there never was another "unknown" cause of death in these cases—but there were to be many more "probable asphyxias." But official police releases would return to the "unknown" label for Alfred Evans.

After Gail hung up, I telephoned Ken Englade of the *Florida Times Union,* Jacksonville's morning newspaper, at the Georgia State Capitol, where he covered the Georgia legislative session. He had worked with me on other stories. I asked Ken if he would go across the street from the capitol and get a copy of the death certificate in the Alfred Evans case. I couldn't wait to see what had been listed as the official cause of death.

Ken Englade called back to say no one could give him a copy of the death certificate. "They said they don't have to prepare a death certificate on a body," he said "if it's found more than a year after the death."

"Ken, they're either putting you on or putting you off," I said. "This body was found back in 1979, less than three days after Alfred Evans disappeared.

It took them 15 months to *identify* it, not to find it."

We never were able to obtain a copy of that death certificate. None was furnished to Wayne Williams' defense. But along the way, several other things kept Alfred Evans' identification alive as perhaps one of the most potentially explosive aspects of these cases.

To recap the strange chain of events in the case of 14-year-old Alfred Evans:

A body is found in 1979, and the cause of death is ruled "unknown." Then, 15 months later in 1980, it is reported as "strangulation." Then, after an inquiry by an Atlanta newspaper reporter, it is changed to "probable asphyxia —probable strangulation." Then another newspaper's reporter attempts unsuccessfully to get a copy of the death certificate—and just as quickly, official police press releases begin once again to carry the cause of death as "unknown." What is going on here?

In February of 1981, I would tell the story of Alfred Evans to David Page, an investigative reporter for Gannett News. He was working for Gannett's Atlanta station, WXIA-TV (Channel 11). David looked over the medical examiner's files and told me that he'd found a note stuck in the Alfred Evans file. The note, he said, asked the question that I had raised: "Please check to see if the dental charts in case number . . . [the Edward Hope Smith case] could have mistakenly been used in case number . . . [the Alfred Evans case]."

No date appeared on the note. But, the note's chronological placement in the file corresponded exactly with the time when I had raised the question with the Task Force's Dale Kirkland, who said he would check. The next entry in the file after the note was a notation that the body had been identified as that of Alfred Evans.

There would be more startling questions raised later in the Alfred Evans identification, but, meanwhile, we still couldn't get answers to the ones we already asked.

A body is found, and the identification is not completed. It cannot be a missing person named Alfred Evans because those dental charts have "routinely" been obtained and there are "no similarities." Fifteen months later, in October of 1980, an inquiry is made to see if perhaps the wrong dental charts have been used.

Almost immediately, an identification is made that the body is, in fact, Alfred Evans—who officials had said earlier it could *not* be. A newspaper reporter says the identification was possible because the body was still in the morgue in October of 1980.

But, later, Alfred's mother, Lois Evans, would say that the medical examiner notified her in October of 1980 that her son had been buried in August of 1980 as a "John Doe." Ergo, no identification had been made prior to burial. The muddle over the identification of Alfred Evans would become even more tangled. What in the hell *is* going on here?

In May of 1981, William Barrett, a 17-year-old black male better known by his street name of "Billy Star," would become one of those Atlanta victims

who were strangled. At least, that's what the medical examiner would say. Barrett also would have stab wounds that were inflicted "after death," according to the medical examiner.

Reporter Paul Crawley of Channel 11 would call me about William Barrett. Paul was convinced that the connections among the victims were important. He had established many on his own. "Where should we start with Barrett?" he asked.

"Well, Paul, since Barrett lived near 2nd Avenue and Memorial Drive," I said, "he probably knew some people in East Lake Meadows. Let's visit Alfred Evans' mother and see if there are any connections between Barrett and her son."

Lois Evans answered our knock from the kitchen. "Come in," she said. Hers is a kind of breezy hospitality that I couldn't get used to, particularly under the circumstances then in Atlanta. But among the principals in these cases, it was much more the rule than the exception.

Two of Lois Evans' grown daughters joined in our conversation in the living room. I asked Mrs. Evans if it were possible that Alfred might have known William Barrett, or "Billy Star," as the kids called him. She said she wasn't sure, but she thought that Barrett had played basketball at the recreation center where Alfred played on the neighborhood team. Then one of Alfred's sisters said that Barrett did play ball at the "rec center," and "so did Darron Glass [still missing] hang around there."

I asked Alfred's sister if she knew "Gypsy" (slain 16-year-old Angela Bacon), who had lived across Memorial Drive from East Lake Park. She said she knew a "Gypsy," but wasn't sure if she was Angela Bacon.

"I knowed Jo-Jo Bell's mother, though," she volunteered. "She and I was in prison together." Doris Bell, the mother of 15-year-old Joseph (Jo-Jo) Bell (who had been found dead just the month before), had served time for the killing of Jo-Jo's father.

Lois Evans testified that her daughter had "done time" with Jo-Jo's mother, whom she called by her first name, Doris. She also said that Alfred's cousin had dated another victim, 16-year-old Patrick (Pat Man) Rogers. Next, she told us that the uncle of yet another victim (13-year-old Curtis Walker) at one time had been a maintenance man at the East Lake Meadows project where the Evanses lived.

Lois Evans' interesting repository of connections among many victims seems inexhaustable. They included connections that we looked at previously, but now she was adding many more to our collection.

Paul Crawley asked Mrs. Evans if she had given this information to the police.

"No," she replied. "They ain't never asked me. I haven't heard from them in over nine months now."

Paul and I looked at each other, shaking our heads. Lois Evans' reply was an all-too-familiar refrain. The title of this book could have been "*They Didn't Ask.*"

I asked Mrs. Evans if she'd mind talking with me about the identification of her son's body. I didn't want to add to anyone's grief. I explained to her, for the first time, my role in that identification.

She talked openly. First, she would explain, however, that she had reported Alfred missing "right away" in July of 1979—not on August 8, 1979, as the police said.

"You know," she said, "I never did get a chance to look at that body straight on." She spoke as if "that body" and her son were not related. "They only let me look through a window," she said, "and then I could only get a side view... I went back two or three times, and I never got a good look."

The realities of the Alfred Evans case are stark and horrible. What they had at the morgue, for more than a year, was a badly decomposed body. Looking at a body that had been lying in the summer sun and exposed to animals and insects can't be anybody's favorite occupation. For anyone who never has been subjected to such an ordeal, my advice is: "Don't!"

So, back in July of 1979, authorities had a severely decomposed body—and a mother, Lois Evans, who went to see if she could identify it as that of her missing son.

Then, as we talked in her front room in 1981, Lois Evans would turn my mind upside down, by recalling her visit to the morgue back in 1979.

"I asked the man," she said, "'Do that body have a pierced left earring?'" The man, she said, told her it didn't.

"I asked him again, 'Does that body have a pierced ear?'"

Again, the man answered that there was no pierced ear and no evidence that there ever had been one.

"Then that body ain't my boy," she said she told him. "My boy's got a pierced ear." Whereupon the body was *ruled out* in 1979 as that of her son, Lois Evans told us.

What does that mean? What did we have now? There were several possibilities. While all were intriguing, none was palpable or acceptable.

—Is Alfred Evans buried in Edward Hope Smith's grave? Is this what the dental-chart mixup led to? And is such a blunder being covered up?

—Is the Fulton County medical examiner wrong about the body at the morgue not having a pierced ear?

—Is the mother, Lois Evans, wrong about her own son's ear being pierced?

—Is Alfred Evans still missing, four years later? And was this the mysterious "third" body that police continued to search for (after the two others had been removed) and who lay there unidentified without a pierced ear?

—Is there an entirely different child buried in one of the two graves?

—What is the truth about the dental charts?

—Who do you think is right about the pierced ear?

Lois Evans dropped yet another bombshell on the quickly tattering image of forensic pathology. She testified that she had taken her son's dental bridge to the medical examiner and that the bridge didn't fit the body at the morgue.

The medical examiner would admit under oath that, try as they might, they couldn't make Alfred Evans' dental bridge fit in the mouth of the body in question. He said he didn't think that was unusual.

Both Lois Evans and the medical examiner would testify that Alfred Evans had been buried in August of 1980—13 months after his death and, more interestingly, two months *before* they magically found the dental charts to identify him with!

How could they match those dental charts with a body that already was in the ground?

11

The Pea in the Shell Game

October, 1980

Jeff Scott had rewritten his *Atlanta Weekly* story to focus on the mothers to suit his editor. Thus, readers wouldn't see what this reporter chose to report, but rather what his editor wanted the masses to read. Undoubtedly, the editor thought it was what they wanted to read. Later, I would learn that another publication, *Atlanta* magazine, had turned down a story critical of the authorities because it was "too hot to handle." The magazine turned down excerpts from this book, too.

Although I disagreed with them often and couldn't understand their high rate of inaccuracies concerning the Atlanta murders, I could have no personal complaint with the Atlanta newspapers. They would give my information ample coverage, if inadequate understanding.

Amazingly, despite the gaps, holes and blind spots in reporting on the murders, both major Atlanta newspapers entered their coverage of the story in the Pulitzer Prize competition in 1981 (the *Constitution* still was in the running after 115 entries in the "General Local Reporting" category were narrowed to 20).

Neither paper won the Pulitzer, but Edward Sears, managing editor of both the *Constitution* and *Journal* (and who was a Pulitzer juror that year), defends his papers' reporting on the story. Recalling his remarks to the 1983 Associated Press Managing Editors convention, Sears told the *Atlanta Business Chronicle:* "I had to stand up in front of all the newspapers in the country and tell them why we did a better job on the story than they did and make them like it."

But not everybody who worked for the Atlanta newspapers during the height of the killings agrees with Sears. One former top editor contends that neither paper assigned its best available editors and reporters to the story. "Never," he said, "has a major newspaper covered such an important story so poorly."

Gail Epstein of the *Atlanta Constitution* had taken the tour of death and seemed politely underwhelmed. Steve Oney of the *Constitution* told me that he, too, had to change the thrust of an *Atlanta Weekly* article because his editor thought he had given too much credence to my "theories." Oney went on to win a Nieman Fellowship at Harvard for his writing prowess. Steve Dougherty, also of the *Constitution,* wrote a long and sympathetic article about my work, only for an editor who didn't understand the geographic nuances to attach a comment that detracted from the credibility of my work. That comment was wrong.

I had much better luck with the radio and TV people—notably Cable News Network and National Public Radio—and the non-local publications and news services such as the *Los Angeles Times,* Gannett newspapers (including the *Cincinnati Enquirer* and the *Ft. Myers,* Florida, *News-Press*), *Paris Match* and the *Florida Times-Union.* Perhaps the trees weren't blocking their view of the forest.

The major national television networks were something else again. I never heard from NBC, but a copy of my map showed up on one of its reports. I took a CBS crew on the tour of death—and paid for my car's gasoline—but not one word from me, or input based on my information, appeared on a special in the wake of the Wayne Williams trial. The network's lack of understanding of the story was reflected when Dan Rather, after reciting names and ages of all 28 murder victims on The List (including five adults), signed off by saying, "Twenty-eight *children* are dead."

I briefed one ABC producer for 12 hours, only for him to be sent to El Salvador on a breaking story. Even so, he worked long and hard with correspondent Bob Sirkin, whose reports challenged the validity of The List. I briefed another ABC producer for most of one evening. Finally, he would look at ABC's Atlanta Bureau Chief and ask: "Do you think we can get all of this in—in four minutes?"

Perhaps the one reporter who grasped the cases quickest was David Page of Gannett's WXIA-TV (Channel 11). Unfortunately, he was taken off the murder cases and put to work on a documentary about the dangers of asbestos—a special being prepared for the May (1981) ratings "sweeps."

Two award-winning investigative reporters of the *Atlanta Constitution* seldom reported on the Atlanta murders—perhaps Atlanta's biggest story since the civil rights movement, if not the Civil War. Of all the handsome and pretty faces who sat behind the "anchor" desks on television, the only ones I ever saw working in the trenches were Wes Sarginson of WSB-TV (Channel 2) and Roz Abrams of WXIA-TV.

Given these experiences, I learned not to expect too much by way of understanding from the news media. They didn't have the time—and seemingly not the latitude—to gain a thorough comprehension of the cases. News directors wanted something snappy for the 6 o'clock package—and that doesn't lend itself to the plodding pace often dictated by complicated logic problems.

As for the print media, the editor is a hard sell—two steps removed from reality. He or she somehow manages to keep the publisher out of prison, the owners out of the poor house and the reporters in a snit. Unfortunately, in doing so, the editor too often molds public perceptions, not public understanding.

Now Hyde Post, an *Atlanta Journal* reporter, asked about the route. I agreed to meet with him at Mike Edwards' request. Post stared briefly at the arrangement of streets that linked up to represent the final journey of 22 young victims. The count on The List then stood at 14 murdered and missing.

Hyde Post was even less enthusiastic about the geography on paper than Gail Epstein had been while seeing the real thing. It's not that Gail wasn't interested. She just wasn't as interested as I thought she should be. Hyde Post wasn't interested at all.

"Do you have any date and time data?" he asked.

"Yeah, I've got it," I replied, "but it isn't worth a damn."

I explained to him that the obvious discrepancies in the chronological data had forced me to look at the geography for something with validity.

I dug out the information that Hyde Post asked for and laid it on the desk in front of him.

"Hey, look at this," Hyde remarked. He had, he thought, "discovered" a pattern of disappearances that he said approximated one every 3½ weeks. Now it was *my* turn *not* to be impressed. I pointed out to him that it was only *one day* between the disappearances of 7-year-old LaTonya Wilson and 10-year-old Aaron Wyche.

But Post insisted that Aaron Wyche had nothing to do with it. Officials had not put him on The List. It was immediately apparent that The List was going to shape Hyde Post's thinking and thus that of some of his readers. Never mind that The List wasn't correct; it was official.

I tried to update Hyde Post on the fate of Aaron Wyche and the faulty report that Wyche fell off a "railroad trestle." But it seemed to matter little to Post. He wasn't particularly interested in my theories. But this wasn't a theory; it simply was a little-known fact—one obscured by the "official" version of Wyche's death as an accident.

I tried to point out a few facts which countered Post's theory about children vanishing every 3½ weeks.

"What about the two kids who died about the same time in July of 1979 and were found together on Niskey Lake Road?" I asked.

Post wasn't interested in the second body along Niskey Lake Road. It was not on The List. It would be only four days before the boy-in-black along

Niskey Lake Road would take his rightful place on The List. In fact, Evans already was "officially" changed from missing to dead on The List, but it was kept a secret until I tipped Gail Epstein.

I also pointed out that The List showed 134 days—not 3½ weeks—between the disappearances of 9-year-old Yusuf Bell in 1979 and 12-year-old Angel Lenair in 1980.

"Sure, but those are earlier cases," Post said. "The pattern," he explained, began with the disappearance of Eric Middlebrooks on May 18, 1980.

"What about the time lapse between LaTonya Wilson and Christopher Richardson?" I asked. Both had disappeared since Middlebrooks—LaTonya *13 days* after Christopher.

"She's a girl," Post explained, referring to LaTonya. "This pattern applies to the boys."

So Hyde Post's 3½-week cycle began with Eric Middlebrooks and included only boys who were on The List of cases that Atlanta's public safety commissioner maintained were not connected. I stared at the ceiling in dismay. "Don't let the facts get in the way of a good story," I wanted to say, but didn't.

The next morning, Sunday, October 12, 1980, the front page of the *Atlanta Journal-Constitution* read: "Pattern Discovered in Child Slayings Here." The byline was shared by Hyde Post and Peter Scott.

> "The timing of the disappearances was sporadic at first, but for the past six months black boys have been vanishing with almost clockwork precision—one every 3½ weeks. . . ."

My meeting with Hyde Post—which I thought might add to his knowledge about the cases—had only served to further cloud the public's understanding. I read on in disbelief, disgust and a hint of despair of ever straightening out this mess.

> "Investigators said they are aware of the pattern [Ah, the official imprimatur!], but have come to no conclusions about its significance. A GBI agent said the Task Force is examining the time angle, 'but we haven't done any in-depth investigation.'"

Two items in the foregoing paragraph caught my eye. First, if the Task Force was aware of a pattern that didn't exist, it was a victim of The List of victims it was helping to compile—and the investigation was in trouble. Second, if, after 90 days from its inception, the Task Force hadn't looked closely at the date-and-time data, the investigation was in deeper trouble.

> "An examination of the dates shows that there were never less than 21 days separating the disappearances of young black males and never more than 27 days."

The only exception, the article went on, was "not a boy, but a girl." The exceptions would appear later, when I won my battles to get Aaron Wyche and Patrick (Pat Man) Rogers on The List. There were no Woodwards or Bernsteins in Atlanta looking for the exceptions. It was hard to *give* a good story away.

In reality, the time span in days between disappearances of victims on The List was 5, 41, 47, 134, 7, 38, 22, 13, 3, 13, 24, 21, 25, 25, 22, 10, 54, 18, 16, 13, 11, 11, 7 and 10. For boys only from Middlebrooks on, it was 22, 14, 13, 24, 21, 25, 25, 22, 10, 54, 18, 16, 13, 11, 11, 7 and 10. Michael McIntosh, Jimmy Ray Payne, William Barrett and Nathaniel Cater are not included (they are the last four victims on The List) because the dates of McIntosh's and Cater's disappearances are uncertain.

"M&Ms," some reporters tastelessly called them, perhaps too flippantly. I'm convinced that had there not been possible racial overtones, the "M&Ms" would have taken their place alongside "Zodiac," "The Boston Strangler" and "The Hillside Strangler."

In some ways, I wish the press had found a catchy label. "Missing and murdered children" was too deeply ingrained to change, even long after it no longer fit. The label itself took the story beyond too many people's understanding.

Meanwhile, against a backdrop of the shooting of National Urban League president Vernon Jordon in Ft. Wayne, Indiana, and the horrible slayings of black men in Buffalo—where hearts were actually cut out of chests—and the then-unexplained slayings of blacks in Salt Lake City, Atlanta's troubles in 1980 spawned rumors and speculation of a national conspiracy of genocide against blacks.

When four small black children—all 3 years old—and a black teacher died in the boiler explosion, it ruffled Atlanta's normally calm emotional exterior. Mayor Jackson realized that the doubters who hooted and shouted him down were the very voters who had sent him to City Hall seven years earlier. Now Jackson was exposed, at long last, to the political volatility of the child-murder cases. Until then, he had been shielded from them so successfully by Lee Brown.

I trembled when I discovered that Bowen Homes lay on the route that I had drawn two months earlier, in August of 1980. Did anyone else realize it? Did anyone else care about the route? Even if the location were purely coincidental, I wasn't eager to point it out to anyone. Now was not the time to pour fuel on the fire. I wouldn't mention it later when a boy who lived on the same street as the day-care center in Bowen Homes disappeared.

Technicians from the state crime lab arrived at the blast scene, only to be ordered away by Atlanta police. Instead of allowing an on-site inspection, the police opted to transport the evidence away later by truck. Why? The technicians complained, but I never heard an acceptable explanation, except that it was "police business." The police didn't owe me an explanation. Or, did they? Whom do the police work for?

John Lewis, president of the Atlanta cab drivers' association and an active politician, told me that he was appointed to a committee to calm public alarm over the Bowen Homes boiler explosion. He said that in that role, he had approached Lee Brown and asked for an opportunity to reconstruct the blasted boiler.

Brown, he said, told him that the reconstruction was already underway. According to Lewis, Brown promised that the committee would be given an opportunity to study it. When no call came from Brown, Lewis returned to the public safety commissioner's office, only to be told that the reconstruction had already been finished and disassembled.

The explosion at Bowen Homes nagged at me. For one thing, the geographic parameters fit so neatly. I didn't want to think that a relationship existed between the explosion and the other child killings, but certainly there *could* be.

Could be. Could be. Could be. The words haunted me like Count Dracula. Whenever anybody had asked me about the killer or killers by saying, "Could it be . . .?" I replied, "The answer to 'Could it be?' is always 'yes' when you don't know." Now *I* was asking the same question of myself. I couldn't ignore my own advice.

The explosion ignited a few days of finger-pointing. Thereafter the issue was left for the civil courts and the insurance companies to settle. As a society, we tolerated it. Not until 1983 were victims' families awarded an out-of-court settlement for an undisclosed sum.

If Bowen Homes' tragedy was not related to the children's murders, its political fallout was. Within hours of the blast, Atlanta's officialdom began to paint itself into a corner. Atlanta now was a self-accused city of terror.

The political cosmetics were rubbed on quickly, all over Atlanta.

First came the curfew. It was ludicrous from the outset. Because it applied only to juveniles under 15, it affected only 20% of metropolitan Atlanta's population. In accord with the jurisdictional (city of Atlanta only) and age limitations of the curfew law, it could have affected only seven (or 25%) of the 28 murders that would make up The List. Obviously, it didn't affect any.

Yet Atlanta's public officials declared the curfew a huge success. I don't know what it might have succeeded at; but, by any measure, it was no success in dealing with the murders. That should come as no surprise, since there was no possibility that it could succeed in the first place. Thirteen murders and one disappearance recorded on The List had occurred during the 15 months before the curfew went into effect; 15 murders were added to The List in only seven months *after* the curfew went into effect.

The curfew would have failed under any circumstances, but consider how ill-conceived it was: First, it was in force only at night. But most victims on The List disappeared during the daytime. Second, a curfew could only be applicable if the selection of victims were random. That's not what happened in Atlanta.

It was obvious as early as September of 1980 that the victims likely knew their killer. But back then, officials weren't even ready to admit that the killings were connected. It would be a strange experience for me to sit at the Wayne Williams trial and hear the prosecution say that the murders were all connected (all except six, which later would become five) and that Wayne Williams had known the victims before their deaths.

But in the days of the "successful" curfew, Mayor Jackson was saying that the killer had turned to older victims because the youngsters were under tight control. On its face, Jackson's statement seemed plausible, but it had no validity.

It seemed logical (but wasn't), for instance, in February of 1981 when some officials and some members of the news media would attribute the finding of the *"first"* body in DeKalb County to the then-recent scolding of the Task Force by Dick Hand (DeKalb public safety director). Certainly it seemed plausible—that is, if you went by The List as it stood then and omitted Aaron Wyche, whose body had been found by the railroad tracks beneath the highway bridge in DeKalb County eight months earlier.

Yet, in a few weeks, when Aaron Wyche's case would be added to The List, most of the media and officialdom continued to say "the killer is following the publicity." They would now tell us that Douglas County Sheriff Earl Lee's comments about the investigation had caused the killer to leave a body in Douglas County "like he had left one in DeKalb County for Dick Hand."

What hogwash. The body found in Douglas County had been deposited in the Chattahoochee River. But another body found at almost the same place in the river was a Fulton County case because it was closer to the Fulton County side of the river when pulled out.

Ignorance about valid cause-and-effect relationships was almost the rule in the Atlanta murder cases. And it afflicts many of the day-to-day pronouncements of police officials—certainly not limited to their observations about murder. For example, the *Atlanta Constitution* published without qualification the comments of a "police investigator" who said that the finding of 20-year-old Larry Rogers' body relatively close to Rogers' home indicated that the aggressive patrols of the Atlanta police had forced the "killer" to stop transporting victims over long distances.

Had the police investigator and the *Constitution* forgotten that Eric Middlebrooks, Angel Lenair and Yusuf Bell had been found much closer to their homes than Larry Rogers was to his? Middlebrooks and Lenair turned up dead within one intersection of home—all of this even *before* Atlanta first began its "aggressive" patrols.

The police investigator's plausible statement was not logical because it ignored the facts: All victims *found* in the same geographic corridor as Larry Rogers were close to their homes. All victims who had been reported *missing* from that corridor, except for 10-year-old Jefferey Mathis, had also been found close to their homes.

Those who were transported over long distances were, for the most part, taken outside the city of Atlanta. And one could only assume—not know—that anyone was being transported dead. The only evidence of this occurred in the case of 12-year-old Charles Stephens—evidence which the police choose to ignore—and in the case of Larry Rogers himself. A witness would testify at Wayne Williams' trial that she saw Wayne Williams transporting a slumped-over Larry Rogers (sitting upright in the front seat of a vehicle in broad daylight), obviously not deterred by the possibility of aggressive patrol.

If a victim was alive, and particularly if he or she didn't mind being transported (which is much more likely the case), then no amount of patrol—aggressive or timid—would have prevented the transportation.

Another problem with Atlanta's investigation was its inability—despite the highly publicized use of computers—to assimilate information that didn't surface in a neat, chronological sequence. Compounding this problem was the random chronology for assignment to The List. Victims were not assigned in the same order that they became victims. And, until the very last of the Task Force's days in 1982, it only considered victims who were on The List. This, after all, was what The List was—a roster of cases assigned to the Task Force for investigation.

Thus, The List seriously impeded the investigation. It controlled what information was allowed to reach the investigators, and it dramatically affected the conclusions drawn from the information.

There would be no way to know that three victims knew each other if only one was on The List and being considered. This was the case with Aaron Wyche, Patrick Rogers and Aaron Jackson. Information from the other cases was not available to assist the investigators in the Jackson case. Rogers was a Cobb County case; Wyche was a DeKalb County case, and Jackson was an Atlanta case. Their files were not sent to the interjurisdictional Task Force because—you guessed it—these victims weren't put on The List.

When Mayor Jackson ordered door-to-door canvassing in October of 1980 for clues and tips, it was yet another political ember from the Bowen Homes explosion. It was the continuation of a rush job of political action. It was do-something-even-if-it's-wrong time. It was the normal three-pronged political attack on a non-political problem: (1) throw words, (2) look busy and (3) throw money.

None of the above is germane, but all might suffice until the problem accidentally is solved or solves itself. The sad part is that the sponsors of such cosmetics sincerely believe that they will work. It's yet another example of doing more of an ineffective thing because you don't know what else to do.

But the canvassing effort only served to dilute the available manpower. The quantity of manpower is not nearly as important as the *quality*. But since police efficiency is measured in response (meaning arrival)—not results—their job is finished once the officer arrives at the scene. The outcome will vary by the circumstances and the individual responding. All too often, people accept this police impotence with the sympathetic rationalization that "the police came, but there really wasn't anything they could do." It's when the police don't come that people really get hot.

The door-to-door quest for clues and information was misdirected and self-defeating. While police manpower was spread out supposedly over all of Atlanta, the problem continued to be confined to the same narrow corridor that I had outlined in August of 1980. No meaningful information was developed by the canvass.

Meanwhile, people complained that they got little response to their efforts to volunteer information. On those occasions when an officer did show up to talk to them about it, they seldom, if ever, heard about it again. The additional manpower could have been better utilized to process the information that the Task Force was not adequately following up.

The canvassing by police officers and firefighters would, the mayor said, cover every home in Atlanta. I asked one interested Atlantan if the canvass had reached his home. It happened that he lived within a mile of five of the victims, four of whom made The List. "They never knocked on my door," Wayne Williams said.

Then came the sweetening of the reward money. In a spider web of murder cases like Atlanta's, few people realize how complicated it can be to offer—and claim—reward money.

Some bounty hunters think they may get rich in a hurry. On the other hand, some public officials apparently believe that you need only to write a check someday to the person who solves the murders.

But it's not that simple.

Originally, rewards of $1,000 were posted in each case. Since there were then 14 cases on The List, that would mean a reward fund of at least $14,000, right? Careful, now. Later, it was announced that *the* reward had been "raised" to $10,000. Unless that meant that the fund now totaled $140,000 (which it certainly did not at that time), including $10,000 for each case, the "raising" of the total reward to $10,000 actually would mean a *reduction* of $4,000.

Immediately after the Bowen Homes tragedy, a flurry of activity swirled

Preparing to throw $100,000 at the problem, Mayor Maynard Jackson waits to announce a reward that will "shake the trees." But no reward was ever paid. What happened to this—and millions more dollars—earmarked to solve Atlanta's "children's" murders? Standing guard are Mike Shannon (left) and John Woods, soon to join the Task Force and be briefed on the cases by Chet Dettlinger during a bogus-taxi ride. (George Clark / Atlanta Constitution)

around the reward fund. Mayor Jackson announced that the figure was being raised again—this time to $50,000. Then, in the next breath, he hastened politically to add that in a short time, a week or two, the fund would be boosted to $100,000.

Who in his right mind would try to collect the $50,000? Why not wait and come forward after the reward becomes $100,000? This statement by the mayor was both self-serving and self-defeating.

At the time of the mayor's announcement, a furious hard-sell job was in progress, particularly aimed at the Fortune 500 companies. The fund-raising tactics learned from the civil rights movement had not been forgotten. The endorsement of City Hall, with its accompanying business to throw around, made these tactics even more successful. Extortion or greed can shake the earth; but together, they can move mountains.

On October 22, 1980, the reward fund was increased to $100,000. "This will shake the trees," Mayor Jackson promised. Months later, the reward offer would be fattened to $500,000.

When pledges and donations for the reward fund topped $100,000 and approached $150,000, Mayor Jackson decided that $100,000 was enough. I wondered what his determination was based on. The other $50,000, he said, would be used for "other purposes." My heart begged to ask him, "What is half as important?"

Whatever the mayor thought it was, half again as much money as was available for the reward fund now was available to do something else. And presumably, every dollar that came in thereafter would be available, too. How much would that be?

As comedian Richard Pryor might put it, "All of this fund-raisin' must have got good to 'em." After all, it wasn't long before an unresolvable tangle of fund-raising drives was going full blast. They raised a total estimated at more than $5 million! And whatever happened to the *reward* money that Earl Carroll had collected while wearing clown suits as early as March of 1980?

In 1981, former heavyweight boxing champion Muhammad Ali would pledge to raise the reward fund from $100,000 to $500,000. Maynard Eaton, a reporter for WXIA-TV (Channel 11), told me that he was present when Ali made the original offer. Eaton said that Ali wanted to boost the fund to $1 million, but after a hurried call to a financial adviser, Ali revised the offer down to a commitment of just under $400,000.

While Ali's offer was magnanimous, the probability of one penny ever being paid as a reward was very slim. Ali's pledge was a feather in Mayor Jackson's cap, but it caused him problems, too. They were problems that the mayor's political savvy had taught him to ignore away. If you are mayor of Atlanta, how do you turn down Muhammad Ali under any circumstances? If you are a black politician, it becomes even harder. And when the money offer is for kids—most of whom are hero-worshippers of Ali—a refusal becomes impossible. Why any talk about refusing the money? Why? In fairness to Ali, that's why.

Remember that the mayor had already assured Atlantans that a $100,000 reward was *enough*. It would have been easy for the mayor to justify accepting Ali's $400,000 pledge by saying circumstances had changed. But hadn't the mayor already collected another $50,000 he had earmarked for "other purposes"? If circumstances had changed, why not also exhume the extra $50,000?

Was it fair to Muhammad Ali for the city of Atlanta to bank the earlier $50,000, instead of letting him reduce his commitment to $350,000? That still would have kept the reward fund at $500,000, which was, after all, what Ali and the city officials had agreed on. Was it fair to reward-fund contributors to have the $50,000 politically shunted off without their permission? But who could complain? How would you know what part of the $50,000 contribution was yours?

No rewards were paid. Whatever happened to that money?

As if that weren't enough, had those in charge of the reward fund ever thought about how the money might be paid out? My bet was that they hadn't.

I would express my doubts in 1981 to Jeff Prugh of the *Los Angeles Times*. When Jeff would try to find out from Commissioner Brown's staff just exactly how the reward would be paid, someone promised him a copy of the procedural guidelines. Jeff's research assistant, Elizabeth Siceloff, would go to Brown's office to pick it up. She waited and waited and waited.

Finally, Brown's staff produced a photocopy of a document stating that the reward money applied only to specific murder cases. They were listed on the reverse side—as I had guessed, only the cases on The List. But, lo and behold, The List on the reverse side was seven months and 13 dead children (official count) out of date. The document went on to say that Commissioner Brown would decide how the reward would be paid.

When Lee Brown would hold his next press conference, Paul Crawley of WXIA-TV would be waiting for him. Following my line of reasoning, Paul would ask why the reward did not apply to other dead children's cases—those whose murders also were unsolved, but had not been added to The List.

Paul Crawley would ask specifically about two slain teen-age Atlanta girls. Brown wouldn't be ready with a logical answer. "Those two cases," he would tell Paul, "are not on The List because they are not connected."

"Does that mean, then, Commissioner," Paul counter-punched, "that you are now saying that the other cases on The List are connected?"

"I didn't say that," Brown would say testily, and walk away.

The very next day, the city would issue a news release stating that the reward money would be disbursed in the same manner that had long been established. The reward would be divided by the number of cases on The List—and that sum would apply to each case for information leading to the arrest and conviction of the perpetrator.

Someone obviously was not telling the whole truth. The information given to Prugh a short time earlier shows that the procedure had *not* "long been established." The method of distribution had been hastily put together after the questions became embarrassing.

Mayor Jackson's next move in October of 1980 was to call for a moratorium on Halloween trick-or-treating. According to Hyde Post's time-lapse theory, the Halloween weekend would claim the next victim.

In neighborhoods outside Atlanta's city limits, Halloween was unimpeded, and the curfew didn't exist. There, costumed little goblins huddled closer together than usual. An eerie reality settled over this scariest of all scary nights. Parents or older brothers or sisters stood tighter guard than usual, perhaps hoping that someone was guarding them. A real killer was on the loose. They felt as if danger could lurk behind every tree and bush. In Atlanta, it was truly an ungodly Eve of All Saints.

On Saturday, November 1, 1980, a depressingly familiar scene filled TV screens. Police cars lined a road that most had been on before. The lonely stretch of road held the entrances to Lake Charolette (sic), a trucking company and a police tow-in lot.

Like crepe paper at a high school prom, yellow crime-scene marker tape twisted and stretched through the area. The tape blocked the access to the South River bridge on Forest Park Road, one block south of South River Industrial Boulevard, one of the 12 connected streets on my map.

Inside Atlanta's city limits, where the curfew was in effect, where patrols had been beefed up in anticipation of reporter Hyde Post's 3½-week cycle, where the mayor had called for cancellation of the celebration of Halloween, where police cars were seen regularly (next to, of all things, the police tow-in lot), another Atlanta black child had been found dead.

Aaron Jackson Sr. returned home from a roofing job in suburban Stone Mountain. His 9-year-old son wasn't home. But that was not unusual. Maybe he was over at Ms. Williams' house. She is a woman who had befriended young Aaron, took him to movies and let him stay the night.

Aaron Jackson Jr. lived at 818 Norwood Drive. He had been a friend and neighbor of 10-year-old Aaron Wyche, now dead. The Atlanta police didn't consider this connection. They didn't ask the question. Why should they? Aaron Wyche had not been called to their attention. After all, he was just a kid who had fallen off a railroad trestle back in June of 1980, in the "far-away" land of DeKalb County, inches from the city of Atlanta.

Nor would the DeKalb County police seek to find out if young Aaron Jackson knew a child who was their responsibility—Aaron Wyche. And why should they? What possible connection could the death of a child in Atlanta have to that of an "accident" victim in DeKalb County?

DeKalb officers might know about Aaron Jackson. Television rushed to his death scene in force. But Atlanta officers would not have had any such opportunity to know about Aaron Wyche. Unfortunately, nobody had sent a TV crew to the "railroad trestle" when Aaron Wyche's body was found that early morning back on June 24, 1980.

Today, too, the TV crews don't fight for position at the locations where some children are found murdered. The media wasn't—and isn't—covering all murders of children. It was The List that was the story.

Five months later in 1980, when Aaron Jackson died, more people knew he had died than had ever known of him while he lived. Had Aaron Wyche been put on The List, the world would have been notified of his death, too. But Aaron Wyche wasn't on The List—not yet, anyway.

Police investigators said that Aaron Jackson had been last seen at the Moreland Avenue Shopping Center. Aaron's body was fully clothed: blue jeans, a white shirt with a brown design and black tennis shoes. He was found on the bank of the South River at the southeastern corner of the Forest Park Road bridge.

Police and some private investigators knew that Aaron Jackson lived in the vicinity of the Thomasville Heights apartments at McDonough and Moreland. They also knew that his body was found under a bridge. They knew that he had last been seen at the Moreland Avenue Shopping Center. The trouble is, most of them didn't know there were two Aarons who fit all of these parameters.

How could they know? Only one, Aaron Jackson, had made The List. As a consequence, there was constant confusion over where "Aaron" lived, where "Aaron" was last seen alive and where "Aaron" had been found dead. Ask three officials, and you might get three different composites of the two Aarons' final journeys.

Aaron Jackson Sr. had become concerned when young Aaron didn't come home. The elder Jackson strode next door to his sister's house to ask her advice. Inside her tiny living room, a television set shouted information about the unidentified black child who had been found dead under the bridge. Aaron Sr. knew that bridge was close by. Like other parents, he was concerned about the child killer. He had discussed the danger with his son many times.

Anxiously, he called the police. They asked him if they could bring some pictures by for him to look at. The picture on top of the stack showed a boy's foot sticking out from underneath a shroud. They needn't have gone any further. Aaron Jackson Sr. recognized the black tennis shoe. Aaron Jackson Jr. was dead.

Some people said that Aaron Jackson was "laid out," and word circulated about a "gentle" killer. No killer is gentle! *Life* magazine would report that a rock "pillowed" his head. But it wasn't reported that the same rock broke the skin. The rock might have been enough to kill him, had he not been dead already.

Mike Edwards and I went back to the scene immediately after the police said it had been thoroughly searched. We found enough material to stock a grade-school paper drive. This was in stark contrast to other scenes stripped entirely of evidence by DeKalb County evidence technicians. Someone said Aaron Jackson may have been suffocated. Officially, he was one of those who died of "probable asphyxia." If it was suffocation, I hope it wasn't with the pillow case that Mike and I found lying under the bridge—in plain sight.

Had Hyde Post been right about his 3½-week lapse between each case? He was sure that his prediction had been borne out. I couldn't argue—especially now. But what good did these predictions do? Hyde Post predicted when—and I predicted where—but Aaron Jackson is still dead.

Included in the "Brady" files (which were supposedly selected by Judge Clarence Cooper, who presided over the Wayne Williams trial) is a copy of a report from a psychic. Three witnesses verified that the psychic had picked the exact location for the finding of Jackson's body.

Brady material is supposed to be "evidence" which tends to disprove the guilt of an accused. Did the inclusion of this information in the "Brady" mean that the judge and the police believed that the conjuring of a psychic was "evidence"? If so, there should have been bushel baskets full of psychic information in the Brady files—it seemed that no two psychics ever saw the same thing.

In fact, the police said they were so certain that Hyde Post was right that they had "beefed up" their patrols, based on his pattern. But these patrols had done no more good than the normal saturation of Memorial Drive with police cars. Aaron Jackson died in spite of these increased efforts. More of the same old ineffective things, I thought.

All of this tells us that police-manpower allocations have little or no effect in the prevention of murder. Police officers have known that for years. So why put so much stock in beefing up patrols?

When Aaron Jackson's body turned up, I wanted to scream, "It doesn't work, Goddammit! It doesn't work!" It still makes me want to cry.

Sometimes the FBI didn't fare much better with the Task Force than the average citizen when trying to get information. As one FBI agent reported:

"November 1st and 2nd were regular off days and were taken by both myself and Special Agent Smith. On Sunday evening, November 2nd, we both learned that still yet another body [Aaron Jackson] had been found . . . We called the Task Force office in an effort to try and find out something about that and no one seemed to be able to tell us anything at that time."

Soon another predictable murder would happen. It would be one that should have buried the Hyde Post 3½-week-cycle theory forever, but it didn't. The police would be told two days in advance—within one mile—where the next murder case would occur.

But when the murder would happen, the Task Force would ignore it. It would ignore the case from November of 1980 until the end of February of 1981—too long in an investigation in which Atlantans were told that "no stone is unturned."

Climbing through kudzu, authorities remove the body of Aaron Jackson, 9, from the edge of the South River on November 1, 1980. The body of Aaron's friend, Patrick Rogers, 16, would surface in the Chattahoochee River one month later. But Lee Brown would testify erroneously at Wayne Williams' trial that the first river victim was not found until March of 1981. (George Clark / Atlanta Constitution)

12

Nonprofit

Arthur Langford Jr. had a dream. As an Atlanta teen-ager in the 1960s, he dreamed that someday he would become a force in the city's struggle for social justice, if not its politicians' lust for power.

He had been student-body vice president at Price High School. At Morris Brown College, he would write a play entitled *"The Life of a King,"* and he would star as Martin Luther King Jr. himself. If you sat there and shut your eyes and listened to Langford's shrill voice mimmick King's, you'd almost swear that King had come back from the dead.

At 22, Langford became "Reverend" Arthur Langford Jr., an associate pastor of the Free-for-All Baptist Church, by decree of the head pastor. Langford also organized the United Youth Adult Conference (UYAC), a nonprofit, social-service agency which one day would bask in favorable publicity by organizing searches during the height of Atlanta's murders—and by finding the remains of 7-year-old LaTonya Wilson on the group's very first search.

The chairman of UYAC's board would be John Cox, a confidant of Langford and Maynard Jackson. Cox exudes an amiable, soft-spoken manner that belies his reputation as a forceful, behind-the-scenes mover and shaker in Atlanta's black community. Some blacks call him the city's "Black Godfather."

In 1973, Arthur Langford Jr. opted for still another world—politics. He ran for an Atlanta City Council seat from the 9th District, where he lived less than a mile south of Bankhead Highway (U.S. 278) in northwest Atlanta. He campaigned on virtually no money—and in a rickety old car in which he had to tug on a string to operate the accelerator.

To everybody's surprise, Langford swept into office without a runoff—and with a fraction more than 50% of the vote. At 23, he became the youngest person ever elected to a municipal office in Atlanta.

At a post-election party, he met a labor organizer named Fred Williams, who would become a close associate. In 1971, Williams had quit his job in New Jersey and moved to Atlanta, drawn by the idealism of the civil rights movement.

Langford also forged ties with the Reverend Hosea Williams (no relation to Fred Williams), a rotund, bewhiskered Democratic state legislator who is no stranger to controversy. He marched and went to jail with Martin Luther King Jr. in the 1960s, then was jailed again in the 1980s as a result of charges that he left the scene of an auto accident.

"You," Hosea Williams told Arthur Langford Jr. in 1973, "are the only one in town who can be the only thing politically he wants to be . . . If you want to be the mayor, you can be the mayor. You have to do one thing. That's stay honest with the people . . . Be honest and stick with the people, and all hell cannot stop you."

In 1974, City Councilman Arthur Langford Jr. drove a new car, flexed his political muscles and made his voice heard downtown. "We've got to do something about saving the children of this city," he said. He proposed that the city give $200,000 to a youth program at the Butler Street YMCA, where he had been youth-services director. He also tried to organize a group called the Soul Patrol, hoping to use federal grant money to train youths to monitor suspicious activities in neighborhoods. The name "Soul Patrol" left little doubt about which Atlanta youngsters he wanted to organize.

In 1975, Langford called a news conference and warned that federal budget cuts in youth programs might lead to disturbances among Atlanta's jobless and idle teen-agers during the summer. He announced a citywide rally with the call letters "S.O.S" (for "Save Our Summer"). "Unless monies are made available to continue our summer programs in Atlanta," Langford said, "we're going to be in for a long, long, hot summer."

Although it would not be a "long, long, hot summer," enough public money flowed to Atlanta to keep a city program called "Super Summer" afloat. Some of the money went to UYAC, Langford's agency, which now had added Fred Williams to its board of directors.

Of UYAC's share of these public funds, $1,500 was to be paid to a woman whose job title with UYAC was designated as "coordinator." She was to be paid in bi-weekly installments of $300 between June and August of 1975, according to a document Fred Williams has saved.

The woman did no work in the "Super Summer" program, but she was paid, anyway, Fred Williams said.

Summertime. And the money was easy. Fred Williams said that he and the woman kept $1,000 of her $1,500 stipend and, by prearrangement, kicked back the remaining $500 to a public official.

Fred Williams now wonders how much money was being paid to others for no work—before and after the woman left the payroll. UYAC would participate in subsequent summer programs for youngsters, including the federally funded $5 million "Safe Summer '81" in response to the murders.

Atlanta's officials would hail "Safe Summer '81" as a success. But was it really a safe summer in 1981? Well, tell it to the families of three teen-age girls and a teen-age boy who would be found dead in Atlanta and its metropolitan area during that summer. These children did not make The List because no one was keeping a list anymore. What's more, by keeping other kids safe, would "Safe Summer '81" make some politicians rich?

In late 1980 and early 1981, Arthur Langford Jr. would lead hundreds of volunteers in UYAC's weekly "Operation Search" for bodies and clues in Atlanta's murders.

Those searches would bring UYAC thousands of dollars in private donations—from groups as diverse as the Southern Bell telephone company ($150), radio station WAOK ($2,500), Citizens Trust Bank ($100), Local 218 Laundry-Dry Cleaning Workers Union ($1,000), Cisco's nightclub ($300) and the Atlanta Mason Choir ($25), among others. My eyes widened when I saw a $100 contribution reported from "Gemini Agency, Inc." Could this "Gemini" be associated with Wayne Williams' Gemini group?

All told, UYAC reported receiving corporate grants and public contributions (between October 1, 1980, and February 26, 1981) totaling $8,328. The agency reported that expenses for items such as "search supplies," "consumables and postage," "telephone," "travel (gas and oil)," "fund-raising expenses," "professional fees," "food," "maintenance," "children's entertainment" and "miscellaneous" totaled $7,838. That gave UYAC a net of $490 for the five-month period.

This report, however, did not include a subsequent sum of $15,000 received by UYAC in the spring of 1981 from the Heublein Foundation, which is affiliated with the corporation that owns Kentucky Fried Chicken, a donor of food for the searches.

UYAC's "Operation Search" received what the agency called "in-kind services and resources" from at least 30 groups. They included Kentucky Fried Chicken, McDonald's, Coca-Cola, Dobbs-Paschal catering service, the Hyatt Regency and Marriott hotels, MARTA and the Atlanta Board of Education.

Fred Williams is a chunky, round-faced man who left behind a life of hard knocks in his native New Jersey. There, he was a heavyweight boxer, served time in prison and drove trucks.

In Atlanta, he possessed a keen sense of the city's soul and its political rhythms, having worked as Langford's chief lieutenant at City Hall and at UYAC. At a private party, Williams once inadvertently walked in on two Atlanta public officials who, he says, were participating in a homosexual act.

In 1978, Arthur Langford Jr. was riding high. *Ebony* magazine picked him as one of America's 50 top young black leaders. He also was chairman of the Atlanta City Council's Public Safety Committee, which oversees the police and fire departments.

At the same time, Langford and Fred Williams operated UYAC in a spirit of entrepreneurship. In one endeavor called "Project Rehab," UYAC was designated to receive federal grant money from the Department of Housing and Urban Development (HUD) to revitalize some of Atlanta's substandard homes for senior citizens and other persons on low or fixed incomes.

But, in 1979, "Project Rehab" came under fire. Television station WAGA (Channel 5) reported that UYAC had received as much as $200,000 in federal funds for the project, with help from the City Council (of which Langford then was a member), only for some Atlantans to complain that no work had been done on their substandard houses as promised. WAGA's investigative reporter, Richard Belcher, asked hard questions. He got evasive answers.

Now Langford's life went from high tide to riptide. On January 18, 1979, Langford was indicted by a federal grand jury on charges of extortion, lying to grand jurors and suborning perjury. The indictment charged Langford with using his position as the City Council's Public Safety Committee chairman to extort money from Donald Pavel, promoter of the 1978 Southeastern Fair at the Lakewood Fairgrounds, near Georgia 166.

Langford and Pavel had reached an "understanding," according to the indictment, that Langford would make sure that Pavel would have "no problems" in obtaining city fire and sanitation services at the fair. The indictment also stated that Langford agreed to try to get Eldrin Bell, an Atlanta deputy police chief, to reduce fees for providing security at the fair.

(Bell had been implicated, but cleared, in late 1978 in yet another controversy surrounding the fair—an investigation into whether police were being paid off to protect gambling at the event.)

This indictment added that Langford agreed to try to waive the city's $350-a-day licensing fee that was charged to Pavel during the fair.

As for the perjury charge, the indictment accused Langford of lying to the grand jury in 1978 when he denied receiving money from the fair—for himself or UYAC. According to documents in U.S. District Court in Atlanta, Langford was questioned before the grand jury as follows:

Q.	"You've received no compensation or money in any form directly or indirectly related to the Southeastern Fair?"
LANGFORD:	"Not at all."
Q.	"Has anyone on your behalf?"
LANGFORD:	"No, not at all."

Q.	"You have no agreements for such?"
LANGFORD:	"No, not at all. My main interest for being at the Southeastern Fair—we were there last year—was getting jobs for young people. I was not out at the Fair as a council person. I was out at the Fair as president of the United Youth Adult Conference."

As for the charge of suborning perjury, the indictment stated that Langford attempted to urge Fred Williams to "testify falsely that there was no way that payments of a specific sum of money could be correlated to the work performed by a specific person."

For his part, Fred Williams had been the self-professed "bag man" at the fair. He said he had delivered $3,000 in cash from Pavel (who now is deceased) to Langford.

But then, Williams said, he was tipped by acquaintances that he might be "set up" to be caught with the money. "I'd been carrying the money for five days and giving it to him," Fred Williams says. "I had no proof it wasn't wrong. The public would believe him [Langford], a City Councilman, before it would believe me."

Fred Williams said he then told Langford he wanted no part of anything to do with the fair. Then he discreetly arranged to tell his story to FBI agents, who in turn equipped Williams with a "body bug" so he could secretly record subsequent meetings with Langford.

At one of those meetings, on September 29, 1978, Langford told Fred Williams that he would arrange for two lawyers—Marvin Arrington (also an Atlanta City Councilman and now the council's president) and Tony Axam—to represent Williams and Langford's brother, Michael (another UYAC official), before their forthcoming grand jury appearances.

Tony Axam, who in 1981 would briefly join Mary Welcome as a defense attorney for Wayne Williams, would become a law partner of David Franklin, an influential adviser to both Maynard Jackson and Andrew Young.

(Franklin's wife, Shirley, is Atlanta's chief administrative officer in the regime of Mayor Andrew Young; Axam's wife, Clara, is commissioner of the city's Department of Administrative Services.)

The federal government transcribed part of Fred Williams' secretly recorded tape, which formed the basis for its charges against Langford of suborning perjury. Portions of the tape appear in the court record as follows:

LANGFORD:	"What they do bring you a subpoena?"
FRED WILLIAMS	"Yeah."
LANGFORD:	"Oh. Yeah. They call you as witness. They ain't got on yours for what. Mine had an explanation to it, why I was comin'."
FRED WILLIAMS:	"So what I . . ."
LANGFORD:	"Ask you . . ."

FRED WILLIAMS: "So what if . . ."

LANGFORD: "And Mike about, uh . . . *See at first we're gonna try and talk to Tony 'fore y'all go—and Marvin—so they can tell y'all—you know—what you should say!* But, um, um, you're is just witnesses. They goin'—they'll pay y'all for comin'. I know! It probably, uh, you and Michael signing for all that money."

There was a time when Arthur Langford Jr.'s lawyer—City Council president Marvin Arrington—had agreed also to represent Fred Williams and Langford's brother, Michael, before their grand-jury appearances in advance of Arthur Langford's indictment and trial.

It didn't cost Fred Williams and Michael Langford very much for legal advice. And, in this instance, attorney-client confidentiality was unusally inexpensive, too.

"Ge'me a quarter, and you ge'me a quarter!" Arrington is quoted in the court record as telling Fred Williams and Michael Langford, apparently unaware (as were Arthur and Michael Langford, who also were in Arrington's office) that Williams was secretly recording the conversation for the government.

"Got a retainer from each of you!" Arrington went on. "The next thing I hear, I'm giving out legal advice free . . . I'm your lawyer, and anything we discuss is confidential!"

How times would change.

When Arthur Langford Jr. challenged Arrington, the incumbent, for an at-large City Council seat in 1981, Langford was defeated resoundingly by Arrington.

(The authors twice made appointments with Langford to interview him for this book. But Langford did not keep either scheduled appointment.)

"Councilman Indicted as Extortionist," one Atlanta headline read on January 18, 1979.

At 29, Arthur Langford Jr. had hit rock bottom. He was only the third city public official in Atlanta's history to be indicted while in office. If convicted on all three counts, Langford would receive up to 30 years in prison and/or be fined up to $25,000.

Reaction to Langford's indictment was swift and strong. One by one, his friends surged to his defense. They included people in high places—then-Mayor Maynard Jackson, Fulton County Commissioner A. Reginald Eaves, attorney Mary Welcome, Georgia state legislator Hosea Williams, Southern Christian Leadership Conference president Joseph Lowery and City Councilman James Howard.

At a church rally organized by Hosea Williams, a standing-room-only crowd of 750 sang hymns, passed the collection plate (raising $4,040 for Langford's legal defense) and heard Lowery, the church pastor, shout from the pulpit: "I'm tired of the powers-that-be, conspiratorially or non-conspiratorially . . . destroying and weakening black leadership!"

Arthur Langford later stood before the crowd and said: "I want to say to you tonight, I am an innocent man . . . I've got a God who promised me a long time ago He'd never leave me alone . . . You would never know the experience I've been through, and Lord knows I needed this tonight."

Another speaker, Corine Brown, who headed the 9th District Youth Council, called Langford's indictment "a lynching, 1979 style." She told the crowd: "When I saw on television they had my councilman, I cried like a baby."

Corine Brown later would play hostess to talent shows featuring young black musicians at the Oasis Ballroom on Bankhead Highway, in Langford's district. One of the disc jockeys, she said, was Wayne Williams.

Barely a week after the indictment, Arthur Langford Jr. and his followers called a news conference to say that UYAC's offices had been burglarized weeks earlier—between January 5 and 8, 1979. They reported that UYAC's financial records, checkbooks and membership rolls and typewriters had been stolen. Hosea Williams and his ex-SCLC sidekick, Tyrone Brooks, charged that the FBI may have burglarized the offices.

Why did Langford's group wait so long to go public with its report of the burglary, when it was said to have occurred weeks earlier—*before* Langford's indictment? Some Atlantans wondered if the burglary had been faked—to destroy financial records that the government sought.

At his UYAC offices, meanwhile, Langford noticed that a staff member was conspicuously missing: Fred Williams. Langford fired Fred Williams as director of the federally funded "Project Rehab." Reason: Williams had not reported for work since January 15, the day that the government hustled him and his family out of town in the witness-protection program.

At the trial of Arthur Langford Jr. in May of 1979, the federal government's key witness was Fred Williams. The trial, however, was declared a mistrial by the judge when a juror was overheard to comment about former federal Budget Director Bert Lance, a defendant in a trial on charges of banking irregularities which was in progress, also in Atlanta. The juror was reported to have said: "All politicians are crooks."

Langford was retried one month later, again with Fred Williams testifying for the government. This time a jury found Langford "not guilty" of all three charges—extortion, perjury and suborning perjury. Reports circulated that one juror held out against conviction, saying she couldn't believe that a preacher could do such a thing.

Amid shouts of jubilation by Langford's supporters, Langford thanked God, hugged his wife and went back to work at UYAC and City Hall.

It remained for Langford to resurface in the headlines in 1980 and 1981 while leading the volunteer searches during the height of Atlanta's murders.

He also would run in 1981 for the City Council again—this time for an at-large seat, not for the seat from his district.

But this time, as mentioned, Langford would lose to the incumbent, who paradoxically had been his lawyer at the 1979 trial—City Council president Marvin Arrington.

During the campaign, Arrington demonstrated that they don't play softball in Atlanta politics. He publicly charged that Arthur Langford Jr. had lived off the "public trough."

When 12-year-old Charles Stephens' body was found in October of 1980, no one was more surprised than I that he, too, had lived on, disappeared from and turned up dead on streets that I had selected as a pattern two months before.

As additional disappearances and deaths occurred, I expected to use the new information to define the pattern more clearly. Yet there had been two more cases added to The List (Stephens and missing 10-year-old Darron Glass) since the map was drawn, and both had fit the geographic pattern to a "T." No refinements were yet necessary.

But I was taken aback when 9-year-old Aaron Jackson fell victim to a phantom killer and was found just off a little-known street called South River Industrial Boulevard. A visitor to Atlanta might stumble onto Memorial Drive or Georgia 166, two mainstreams of the route in Atlanta's murders. By contrast, you have to *know* where South River Industrial Boulevard is. You go there on purpose. This finding strongly suggested that the route was not a collection of geographic coincidences and that the killer was no newcomer to Atlanta.

On November 8, 1980, one week after Aaron Jackson was found dead, I had an appointment with Gail Epstein and Ken Willis, reporters for the *Atlanta Constitution.* I took them to the Constitution Road bridge, where 10-year-old Aaron Wyche was found dead alongside railroad tracks below.

The proximity of the deaths of the two Aarons, Jackson and Wyche—and the fact that they were neighbors—suggested that they knew each other. By taking the two reporters to the Aaron Wyche death scene, by showing them the relationships and by demonstrating that there was no "railroad trestle," I might rekindle interest and support in reopening the Wyche case.

The little white Pinto with "Atlanta Journal-Atlanta Constitution—Covers Dixie Like the Dew" stenciled on its sides scooted past the truck terminals and hard-drink hangouts that dotted Moreland Avenue.

As we approached the bridge over the railroad tracks at Constitution Road, I leaned against the back of the front seat and asked the driver, Ken Willis: "Do you feel safe right now? Aren't you afraid we'll fall off?"

"What?" Willis replied, a look of bafflement on his face.

"I just thought you might feel uneasy on this dangerous railroad trestle?" I teased.

"What railroad trestle?" Willis asked.

"That's what I've been asking for five months now," I countered.

We made a U-turn at a break in the raised traffic island and headed back north across the bridge. I pointed to a road just beyond the end of the span and suggested that we park there.

The street was actually the entrance to a truck depot which sat in a valley, flush with the railroad tracks. We left the car there and walked back toward the bridge. The sidewalk along Moreland Avenue continues across the bridge. The first 20 or so feet of terrain that can be seen from the bridge form a gently sloping, grassy hill. At almost the bottom of that slope are a few small trees and bushes, including a tree that resembles a mimosa. About four feet from ground level, you could still see where a limb—no more than ¾-inch in diameter—was snapped from the tree. The limb itself lay a few feet away.

The sidewalks on the bridge are littered with drink cans, bottles, paper, bits of cloth and myriad nuts, bolts, broken braces and pipes—offal from the thousands of automobiles, trucks and vans which pass this point each day.

From the mid-point of the bridge on the east side, you can look down and follow parallel train tracks for miles. But from that point, the bridge is so wide that six lanes, two sidewalks, a traffic island and a railing prevent you from seeing where the tracks go westward.

The area around the twin polished rails of steel below was freshly oiled and tarred. A blotch of tar had been found on the bridge railing above. The investigators in the Aaron Wyche case thought that the tar had gotten on the railing when Wyche stepped on it with his shoes. How?

Besides, the top railing on the bridge is cylindrical—not the kind of object you try to stand on. And the top railing is cantilevered.

By leaning out over the bridge railing and leaving my feet, I tried to demonstrate that it would be virtually impossible for a child smaller than 5 feet tall to fall off the bridge accidentally. Jump? Yes. Fall? No. Suicide? Maybe. Accident? No way! Murder? Probably. If the two reporters were impressed, they didn't say so.

I had burned a lot of midnight oil preparing for my meeting with the two reporters—and for a meeting with two Task Force officers that same evening—on November 8, 1980.

My map was unfurled across the twin bed which doubles as a couch in my office-den at home. There wasn't anything on that map that I had created. It represented *no* theories. The families, the victims and the killer or killers had created the facts that the map represented. I had merely arranged these facts in a way I understood. I was dealing only with what I *knew* as fact—not what I or anyone else *thought.*

That map, that sheet of unfolded paper, was radiating those facts simultaneously and continuously. It was saying things about the relationships among those facts that I couldn't yet comprehend—some I wasn't even seeing yet. I knew how Dr. Frankenstein would have felt. I had put all these pieces together, breathed life into them by my travels and created a monster that I could never fully understand. The map taunted me.

Had I claimed to be a psychic, I might have been asked to be on the Johnny Carson show. But I wasn't a psychic and I didn't claim to be. What I was espousing was simple logic—a logic that had been indisputably more accurate than the thoughts of Dorothy Allison, the so-called seer from Nutley, New Jersey, or any other psychic.

The city of Atlanta had picked up Dorothy Allison's hotel and wine tabs. This same city would later impose upon me to pay my own transportation costs to its offices so that I might be questioned in these cases as a suspect.

At home, I found myself talking aloud to the map, commanding it to yield its information. "Come on—tell me what you know!" I screamed. After hours of false starts that led nowhere, I became intrigued by another of the map's geographic patterns.

Was it significant? Maybe. Was it real? Of course. It was there. Every victim who lived in the corridor along Memorial Drive through Martin Luther King Jr. Drive across the middle of my map—from victim Eric Middlebrooks on the east to victim LaTonya Wilson on the west—had been found close to home and close to where they disappeared. The one exception was Jefferey Mathis.

From Eric Middlebrooks on the east, all victims had been transported clockwise toward Redwine Road (and in two cases, all the way to Redwine Road, the southwesternmost point on the route). From LaTonya Wilson on the west, all victims had been transported counterclockwise toward Redwine Road (one all the way to Redwine Road).

This reaffirmed what I thought earlier might be true. The route seemed to be a compilation of streets that a killer or killers traveled regularly in the due course of their lives and business.

What else was it telling me now? Well, beside the directional patterns and the indications that the victims—at least those in various clusters—more than likely knew each other, the map was saying that to date there probably had not been any "copy-cat" killings.

The chances were remote enough that a "copy-cat" killer selected a victim from a street where other victims had disappeared. They were remote enough that this same victim would have lived on the same streets where other victims had lived. But the chances of a "copy-cat" killer selecting a disposal location which was also on one of those streets was almost nil. Now consider the possibility of that victim knowing at least one other victim on The List, and you have to doubt that any of the killings was random, or done by "copy cats."

On October 18, 1980, the Saturday after the Bowen Homes boiler explosion, the first volunteer search was mounted. About 300 persons turned out. The police had selected a section near Dixie Hills as the area to be searched. Why? Probably because it is where 7-year-old LaTonya Wilson had been reported kidnapped from her bedroom in June.

The police considered LaTonya's disappearance to be the least likely case on The List (which they said was composed of non-connected cases) to be connected to the other cases on The List. Thus, less interference had to be brooked from a situation—in this case, a volunteer search—which they regarded as a nuisance to their investigation.

I laughed a few weeks later when the search leaders expressed the same concerns about other police advice. A quarrel erupted between the searchers and the police. Eldrin Bell, who had risen to a deputy chief of the Atlanta police department under Maynard Jackson and had close ties with Arthur Langford Jr., the leader of the searchers, was appointed liaison.

Eldrin Bell's first move in November of 1980 was to direct the searchers to the area where 9-year-old Aaron Jackson had been found—beneath a bridge along the South River. It was an area, Bell said, that had not been thoroughly searched. Bell's remark was curious. He should know! It was the Atlanta police's responsibility to see that it *had been* thoroughly searched. A non-police person would assume that this responsibility had long ago been carried out—back when Aaron Jackson's body was found.

Earlier, the facade was ripped off the criminal-justice system: a group of the searchers, more loosely organized than the Boy Scouts, had found a child's body within one-half mile of her home in only *two* hours—after the authorities had searched in vain for four months! Inside a fence with a locked gate, one searcher found the remains of the small black child. A tuft of hair lay nearby, clamped in a muddied blue barrette.

LaTonya Wilson's skeleton was found at the end of Verbena Street. It was very close to her home at 2261 Verbena Street, Apartment 7.

Now, for the first time, the volunteer searchers organized by Arthur Langford Jr. and UYAC realized that in many of these cases, only bones would be found. It wasn't the common perception of finding a child's remains. Most people expect the dead to resemble the embalmed and artistically recreated corpses at wakes.

Moreover, the volunteers' ranks swelled from 300 to more than 3,000 the following Saturday. At the same time, a frustrated public soured on the pontifications of city officials, who continued to insist that "no stone is being left unturned" by the police.

Now, thanks to the yellow crime-scene ribbons, I could see—from the street—the place where her body lay. Had I been paid to look for her (as the authorities were), I would be embarrassed. But I feel worse—a sense of shame. I flagellate myself for not finding LaTonya Wilson, for being imperfect. But then, I rationalize by telling myself, "Thank God, you didn't! They would have arrested you for her murder." (The clothes hanging in my closet no doubt are dotted with fibers from Wayne Williams' home, which I have visited many times while preparing for the trial and trying to gain a better understanding of the cases.)

Months before that inaugural search in October of 1980, the route on my map would have told the authorities where LaTonya Wilson might be found. But they weren't interested.

I detected another simple fact in the clarity of locations which the map projected. The murder cases had, for six months, moved inexorably eastward along the southern perimeter of the route.

Newsweek must have run across a newspaper clipping that I don't remember. In March of 1981, the magazine would report: "Chet Dettlinger, a private investigator, drew a map and thought he saw a clockwise pattern to the murders."

The editors—or, for that matter, the writers of the *Newsweek* article—never bothered to ask me what I thought I saw. I didn't like it. It made me feel unclean. There were too many touts during these cases willing to throw 100 dart ideas at the wall, hoping one would stick and everybody would forget the other 99. I didn't want to be among them.

I wrote to *Newsweek,* trying to explain that to say I *thought* I saw a clockwise pattern was a small, out-of-context and misunderstood part of the Atlanta story. Furthermore, it was like saying that cartographers *think* they see North America in the Western Hemisphere. "What's there is there," I told *Newsweek.* The magazine didn't respond to my letter.

Based on what the map was telling me, I had predicted to reporters Gail Epstein and Ken Willis on November 8, 1980, what I would repeat that evening to officers Mike Shannon and John Woods of the Atlanta Police Bureau.

Shannon and Woods were part of the Task Force. They had said they were impressed with what I had shown and told them in our first meeting. They asked to meet with me again.

The three of us had an idea: I would take them around the route, and they would try to reconstruct the paths the murderer (or murderers) might have taken in specific instances.

That evening, a maroon-and-white taxi cab arrived at my house. "Riverside Cab" was painted on each front fender. A complete rate schedule was stenciled on each front door.

Mike Shannon drove, and John Woods rode shotgun. Both wore streetclothes. Shannon is a small, raw-boned man with glasses. Woods has a full face, half-wreathed by a medium Afro. Although it hadn't yet dawned on me, they had appeared together in newspaper photos—as the uniformed Atlanta police officers standing behind Mayor Jackson and the tabletop piled with reward money.

I climbed into the back seat. Shannon's face radiated intensity and fascination with his assignment. He leaned across the front seat and pulled down the flag on the meter. "Where to?" he deadpanned.

We headed for Atlanta's eastern perimeter—Interstate 285 and Memorial Drive—an intersection where we would begin (the umpteenth time for me) the tour of death. We drove right in front of the DeKalb County police headquarters. We planned to drive the route in a clockwise fashion, a departure from my normal itinerary. When we reached 2nd Avenue in Decatur, we turned south toward Moreland Avenue and Constitution Road, instead of proceeding west toward downtown Atlanta.

2nd Avenue took us to Bouldercrest Road, which blended with Key Road. In moments, we passed by the Atlanta city prison farm and the Atlanta police department's pistol range. Thus, the route had taken us to two more streets where the police had every reason to travel regularly.

Key Road intersects Moreland Avenue just north of the Constitution Road bridge, the death scene in 10-year-old Aaron Wyche's case. We parked the make-believe taxi on the same street where I had parked earlier that same day with Gail Epstein and Ken Willis, the *Constitution* reporters. I walked onto the bridge again.

I waited until both officers had fully realized that there was no railroad trestle. Then I made the same prediction I had made to the two *Constitution* reporters.

"Look," I said, "if the geographic patterns that I see developing continue to hold true, then the next incident should happen to the north or east of this point on one of these streets." North, I explained, would be Moreland Avenue toward Memorial Drive. East would be back along Key Road, Bouldercrest and 2nd Avenue, to the East Lake Meadows housing project.

"You really think so?" Shannon asked.

"The map says so," I replied. "It's been unbeatable up to now."

Shannon was intrigued. We abandoned our clockwise approach and decided to check out the northward possibilities. Our curiosity was roused by the very thought that we were crystal-ball gazing.

We drove very slowly. Behind the high brick wall that stretches for about a mile—from just north of the Constitution Road bridge to just south of McDonough Boulevard—stood the house of 9-year-old victim Aaron Jackson. I pointed out the approximate location to the two officers.

Soon we passed the brick-and-concrete apartments of the Thomasville Heights project, where Aaron Wyche's mother lived. Thomasville Heights, which backs up to the Georgia State Police Academy, was a bit cleaner, but no less congested, than any other project I visited during these murders.

We approached the Moreland Avenue Shopping Center on our right. Aaron Jackson had been last seen alive here. Interestingly, the shopping center included a Georgia State Patrol driver's license examining station. It was yet another reminder that police presence obviously had not been a deterrent in these murder cases. Which isn't very comforting when you realize that the first line of defense for our life and freedom is based upon this mythical premise.

We returned to the vicinity of Memorial Drive. Officers Shannon and Woods decided to enact a "let's pretend" scenario. We swerved left on one residential street to another. Then came a hard right and one-half block to Howell Street, where 14-year-old Eric Middlebrooks had lived (at 345 Howell Street). Then we took a frontage road to Moreland Avenue. We glided through a stop-sign intersection in second gear, as only cops can do comfortably. We turned left across Interstate 20, past Tippens Appliance and Furniture showroom, left through the parking lot, and left again in the alley.

Just like that, we had covered the entire Eric Middlebrooks route—from where he lived to where he was found dead, beside his bicycle. Time elapsed? Less than 90 seconds.

"How's that?" Woods asked.

"Not bad for beginners," I replied. "Something tells me you guys have been in a hurry on these streets before."

I laughed. They laughed. It was a laugh we could share. We all had been there before. On different roads and in different times, perhaps, but on similar missions.

Back on Memorial Drive, we headed west for the Atlanta-Fulton County Stadium and downtown. After Memorial Drive changed names to Whitehall, we turned left onto McDaniel Street. That took us one block to the apparent location where 9-year-old Yusuf Bell had disappeared in October of 1979. Now, on our left, was what remained of Rawson Street, where Yusuf had lived.

Mike Shannon seemed determined to set a land-speed record. Navigating these streets, he said, was fun to him. In less than three minutes, we covered the Yusuf Bell route, which normally took me 10 minutes. But then, I usually stayed on the pavement and within the speed limit.

We eased around the back of the abandoned E.P. Johnson Elementary School, where Yusuf's body had been found in November of 1979. Two figures lurked in the schoolyard, darkened by shadows from the L-shaped, brick building. When Shannon steered the Plymouth taxi cab onto the schoolgrounds, the two intruders fled. One fell, but came up running, seemingly without missing a stride.

We sped through the neighborhood, street to street to alley and back to street again. Suddenly the two intruders appeared again, observing our taxi cab from a safe distance.

"Got a nickel bag?" officer Woods shouted to them.

"No, man, we ain't got nothin'," one replied.

We rolled closer to them. But when we reached a certain point, they ran away again, as if we had pushed a button that marked the spot where we invaded their space.

"Not dealing," Shannon commented dryly.

"Nope, only using," Woods remarked. "They don't want no company."

Now it was dark. The curfew was in effect. The kids we confronted now were too young to be out. "Killer'd have to be a 'lympic champion to catch them two," Woods observed.

We drove back up Fulton Street. Something had caught Shannon's eye on a side road when we went by the first time. There, parked on a deserted stretch of roadway, along a fenced construction-storage lot, was a late-model Mercedes-Benz 450SL coupe. A bearded white man slouched in the seat behind the wheel. A slim black man minced up to the Mercedes and stuck his head in one window.

The headlights of our pseudo-taxi flashed onto the rear of the Mercedes. The black guy made like the pretty girl in a magic show. Poof! He disappeared.

"Drug deal," I commented.

"Nothin' that sophisticated," Shannon said, disagreeing. "Just a little hanky-panky, man to man, you know."

"You wanta see drugs?" Woods asked. "Hell, Shannon, take him up to McDaniel-Glenn [housing project]."

First, Shannon checked the license tag on the Mercedes. It was registered to an M.D. "Still sounds like a drug deal to me," I wanted to say, but didn't.

We turned onto Glenn Street, near the residence of Camille Bell, mother of slain Yusuf Bell. Dope pushers lined the curb like crows on a phone line. We sat in front of the residence where a 23-year-old fellow named Michael McIntosh lived. Across the street was Cap'n Peg's, the fast-food stand. Fifteen-year-old Joseph (Jo-Jo) Bell might have been working there that night. But who the hell cared? Neither McIntosh nor Bell was important to these cases. Not yet.

In retrospect, I wonder, too, if 16-year-old Patrick (Pat Man) Rogers was disco-dancing the night away at the McDaniel-Glenn community center, as he often did. Indeed, many teen-agers and young adults who would surface in these cases might have been there. At least seven who frequented the area were alive on that November night in 1980, but they would turn up dead within the next six months.

When young Pat Man partied at McDaniel-Glenn, he always bought heaping quantities of hot dogs. Dapper in his cowboy hat, Pat Man always purchased the hot dogs on credit. "His credit was good," one of the regulars there told me. "Man, he taught karate!"

And don't forget Cap'n Peg's.

We headed west to the Gordon Street confluence with Martin Luther King Jr. Drive, at least two miles from Dixie Hills. On the way, I explained to Woods and Shannon about the proximity of 7-year-old LaTonya Wilson's kidnapping to where her body was found.

I felt odd, telling two officers on the "missing and murdered children's Task Force" about the murders. But they had sought *me* out, shortly after they were assigned to the Task Force. "The Task Force won't tell us anything," they said.

When we reached Gordon and MLK, we stopped for the red traffic light. Gordon Street bent to the left and merged into MLK. The intersecting thoroughfare was Anderson Street. On the northeast corner of Anderson and MLK was the West Lake MARTA station. It was the same place where Mike Edwards and I had paused on our first trip, back in September of 1980.

Looking at my map, Shannon said, "If you want to drive to where the [LaTonya] Wilson kid lived and was found, you wouldn't go down MLK like you've got it drawn. Let me show you something."

We turned right onto Anderson and crossed the MARTA tracks. Then we hung a left on the first available street. Now we were parallel to MLK as I had it drawn, but we were one block to the north. We were traveling on Penelope Road.

Penelope Road turns into Verbena Street. Before I could say, "Where the hell are we?" we were in front of LaTonya Wilson's apartment. I couldn't know it then, but that short ride on Penelope Road (our third side route of the night) was one of the most prophetic of my life.

Here's why: in a few short blocks, we had passed the home of 14-year-old Cynthia Montgomery (who had run away three times and still was missing, but whose name would surface in news reports that very week), the home of 26-year-old Nathaniel Cater (whose body would be found in the Chattahoochee River the following May) and the home of 22-year-old Wayne Williams, who in June of 1981 would be arrested for the murder of Cater and then would be indicted also for killing 21-year-old Jimmy Ray Payne, another of Pat Man's buddies.

Shannon and Woods soon would be pulled off the cases. Would we have put it all together? I doubt it. But we were tantalizingly close without even trying.

Without a doubt, we were on to something. There's no question that if those two Atlanta police officers and I had been allowed to work together a while longer, we would have made a significant breakthrough. After all, we had followed the route of my map past the front door of the man who would be arrested and charged with two killings, months of man-hours (and many killings) later.

We returned to the route, retracing our path along Penelope Road, past Wayne Williams' house. Before we reached Hightower Road, the officers received a call advising them to contact their office. We stopped at the corner of Hightower and U.S. 278 to use the telephone. The boiler explosion had occurred here a month before. And 13-year-old Curtis Walker would disappear from this intersection three months later.

The telephone call produced a message to call Mike Edwards. A woman who said she witnessed a suspect at the scene of 9-year-old Aaron Jackson's death about the time he was killed one week earlier had telephoned Mike Edwards. She had contacted the Task Force six days earlier, she said, and had gotten no response. Regardless of what Atlanta's city fathers wanted Americans to believe, this was the rule, not the exception.

Before our November night's journey ended, Mike Shannon, John Woods and I would pass within six-tenths of a mile of the bridge that Wayne Williams would cross before he would be stopped for questioning in May of 1981. We also would drive again within 50 feet of where the bodies of 11-year-old Christopher Richardson and 11-year-old Earl Terrell—both still missing—would be discovered, to say nothing of the locations that would prove fatal to at least 17 more people.

Did somebody say, "Anybody can draw a map"?

13

The "Pat Man" Connections

November, 1980

Barely two days after I had traveled twice in one day to the highway bridge at Moreland Avenue and Constitution Road, 16-year-old Patrick (Pat Man) Rogers—karate buff and singer—disappeared from Thomasville Heights, his family's home in southeast Atlanta.

Just as the map had led me to predict two days earlier, Pat Man's disappearance on November 10, 1980, during the height of Atlanta's murders occurred one mile north of the bridge where 10-year-old Aaron Wyche had been found and where I had made the prediction. Thomasville Heights also was only one-quarter mile from where slain 9-year-old Aaron Jackson had lived. I was flabbergasted.

Reporter Gail Epstein was unmoved. "The police say he's a runaway," she assured me about Pat Man.

"Where have I heard that before?" I asked her.

"Well, this time they've got a good reason," Gail said. "He's running from a burglary warrant."

"I don't give a damn what they say," I countered.

I didn't know what police officers Shannon or Woods thought, if anything. One officer would tell me that when they gave Chief of Police George Napper the wealth of information from my map—which I had put together for them—Napper wanted to promote them on the spot. Then I was told that when it was found out that they had obtained the information from me, Shannon and Woods were taken off the murder cases and reassigned from the Task Force to a lesser role. Shannon would tell me later they were told to "check the housing projects on our beat for suspicious persons."

I telephoned Kaleeka Rogers (no relation to Patrick) of WSB radio. If Gail Epstein and the police weren't interested in the probable connections among Pat Man, Aaron Wyche and Aaron Jackson, maybe Kaleeka would be. She seemed selfless in her determination to see Atlanta's horror ended.

I told Kaleeka that I thought Aaron Wyche and Aaron Jackson had to know each other, simply because of the proximity of where they lived. And now, there was Pat Man, who had lived so close to Aaron Wyche, and they had to know each other, too.

Kaleeka went to see Annie Rogers, Pat Man's mother, at Thomasville Heights. Mrs. Rogers verified that Pat Man had, indeed, known both Aaron Wyche and Aaron Jackson. She walked to the back door and pointed to another apartment across the courtyard, only 25 yards away. She was pointing out where Aaron Wyche had lived with his mother, Linda.

Annie Rogers became interested that November day in 1980 in finding out just exactly whom her son did know. Over the ensuing months, she strung together for us the Pat Man connections.

If Pat Man's case were added to The List, the authorities would have an opportunity to recognize that there was considerably less randomness in these killings than they were imagining and saying publicly.

Had the authorities understood the Pat Man connections, many lives could have been saved. In addition, millions of dollars could have been saved, not squandered in attempts to keep children safe from a so-called kidnapper who wasn't there.

The toll in frightened and paranoid children in metropolitan Atlanta is no doubt decades away from being thoroughly assessed. I still vividly remember the polio epidemics and quarantines of my childhood. Compared to the hyperbolic hype imparted to the children of Atlanta during the height of these slayings, polio was about as worrisome as a hangnail. The hype in Atlanta came from ill-informed and/or misunderstanding adults. Some even came from adults with vested interests. But it wasn't a killer who was frightening the children; it was the ill-conceived solutions to the problem.

Some black leaders stirred up hatred against a presumed "white racist killer or killers" and came out sounding just like the bigoted, prejudiced people they got on their soap boxes to condemn. The Reverend Jesse Jackson opined that the killings were racially motivated, no matter what race the "killer" might turn out to be.

"Black people don't kill their children," insisted the Reverend Joseph Lowery, president of the Southern Christian Leadership Conference. Other than Oriental or American Indian, that left very few colors for the as-yet-unidentified killer to be.

Some whites proclaimed that a white city administration and white police leadership would have quickly solved the cases. This ignores the fact that virtually half the cases on The List did happen in jurisdictions with white administrations and white police leadership.

The closest thing to a racial consensus was built around the premise that had the victims been white, more would have been done. Tell it to the white families of the white victims of the "Columbus Strangler" or of the "Snowman" in Birmingham, Michigan.

The Communist Workers' Party trumpeted, "There never has been a black mass murderer." Never mind that these were not "mass," but rather serial or multiple murders. Had they forgotten Uganda's ruler, Idi Amin?

It was this kind of misdirection that would begin a multimillion-dollar "Safe Summer '81" program, three months *after* the last non-adult was put on The List and two weeks after authorities arrested the accused "child" killer (Wayne Williams has been accused, but never convicted, of killing any children).

Then the same politicians who had dubbed the curfew a success proclaimed "Safe Summer '81" a resounding success. They cited the fact that no more children were added to The List—a list that nobody had been keeping since before the summer-recreation program began.

In June of 1980, Aaron Wyche had turned up dead on Moreland Avenue. He was a friend of Pat Man.

In November of 1980, Aaron Jackson had been found dead one block from Moreland Avenue. He was a friend of Pat Man, whose siblings said that Patrick "liked" Jackson's sister.

Since Aaron Wyche's death was immediately ruled an accident, his killer could breathe easily. No one was being sought as a suspect in a murder that had not officially happened.

But when Aaron Jackson's death was quickly called a murder (there were no significant differences between their deaths, except five months, five bodies and five blocks), Pat Man no longer always put on his tough-guy exterior. He fearfully told Annie Rogers, "Mama, he's getting closer." Nine days later, on November 10, Pat Man vanished.

The mystery of 14-year-old Cynthia (Cinderella) Montgomery's whereabouts deepened. Eula Montgomery's small black-and-white TV set had crackled with more tragic news: Aaron Jackson found dead on November 1...Patrick (Pat Man) Rogers disappears on November 10. According to the reports, Aaron is—but Patrick isn't—"one of Atlanta's missing or murdered children."

Saturday morning, November 15, dawned rainy and dreary in Atlanta. At a Mark Inn motel on Cleveland Avenue, a stretch of the route a few miles south of downtown Atlanta, a woman named Sara Davis opened the door of Room 311. There, the nude body of a young black female lay strangled.

The police were called. When officers arrived at the scene, they prepared a routine report. It identified the victim as "Cynthia Smith" and her birthday as

"10-31-61," which would have made her 19.

A vehicle from Meadows Funeral Home (which, incidentally, was operated by a mortician who was at the same time an Atlanta police officer assigned to the Task Force) transported the body to Grady Memorial Hospital. There, the victim was pronounced dead. The body then was taken to the Fulton County morgue.

Eula Montgomery had been at the Fulton County Jail all day, visiting her son. She did not return home to Dixie Hills until evening. When she arrived, her children broke the devastating news: the police had come to the apartment during the day to tell them that the body found inside Room 311 was that of Cynthia Montgomery. Barely two weeks after her 14th birthday, we knew that Cinderella would not live happily ever after.

When Cynthia Montgomery was found dead, her prostitution trial was only 10 days hence. Did someone fear that Cynthia would say too much in open court? The news of her slaying surged through the grapevine around Auburn Avenue. A relative of hit-and-run victim 16-year-old Angela (Gypsy) Bacon recalls that a man driving a taxi had been showing off pictures of a girl he called "Cinderella." The pictures, she said, were of Cynthia Montgomery.

Officers Mike Shannon and John Woods of the Task Force had told me that in November of 1980, they heard that an eyewitness had said he had seen Cynthia being forced into a car downtown at Central City Park.

Meanwhile, on Saturday night, November 15, Eula Montgomery paid a tearful visit to the Fulton County morgue to identify the body. As she gazed into the viewing room, she saw two articles of clothing that she never knew Cynthia had owned. One was a red dress, the other a luxurious fur coat.

But Eula also noticed two belongings that were hauntingly familiar. They were purchased just before Cynthia turned into Cinderella.

Propped up, near the body, were Cynthia's $39 pair of designer boots.

Someone had reported seeing a man sprinting away from the Mark Inn on the night of November 14 or the morning of November 15. Could it have been Cynthia's first pimp? Could he have been jealous of her second pimp? Or had Cynthia now fallen out with her second pimp? Was it a sadistic "john" or someone else altogether?

The Atlanta police said they know who killed Cynthia. They just can't prove it. Uh-huh. I've heard that one again and again since my police career began 27 years ago. It wasn't even the first time I'd heard it in Atlanta's cases. The police even said privately that Cynthia's death could not be connected to the others since they "knew who killed her." Since they apparently didn't know who killed the others, had they ever wondered if the person who killed Cynthia might have killed the others, too? That so-called "killer" was, by the way, later exonerated.

Eula Montgomery waited in vain, she said, for the police to come back and ask her questions. She waited through Christmas and she waited for New Year's Day. Neither would be a happy occasion in Dixie Hills—and the police *never* came.

LaTonya Wilson and Cynthia Montgomery, acquaintances who lived less than 200 yards from each other, were dead. LaTonya had made The List; Cynthia had not. Cynthia joined Pat Man, Aaron Wyche, Angela Bacon and others as Atlanta children who were murdered, but were "*not* one of Atlanta's missing or murdered children." Pat Man and Aaron Wyche eventually would be "elevated" to The List, but the others would not.

Cynthia also may have known LaTonya's upstairs neighbor, Nathaniel Cater, who, at 27, would die in 1981. We know she was a friend of slain Angela (Gypsy) Bacon, who did not make The List, and that she had attended summer camp with 15-year-old Jo-Jo Bell, who did. We knew, too, that she had known Christopher Richardson.

We were told that Cynthia was not put on The List because she was a prostitute—and prostitutes "are treated as adults." Yet real adults—not 14-year-old perceived adults—would soon make The List. Would the authorities reconsider Cynthia? No. They just couldn't plug those non-chronologically found facts into their thinking. Tragic!

For me, the late fall of 1980 was miserably frustrating. Pat Man Rogers still was missing. On Pearl Harbor Day, December 7, 1980, the body of a black male was found floating in the Chattahoochee River northwest of Atlanta—in the jurisdiction of the Cobb County police.

At first, the body was not identified. Initial reports stated that the body was that of an adult. Even without an identification, authorities were quoted as saying the body had "no connection" with the child cases. The story didn't make the front pages.

For three more weeks, those who had nothing to go on, except the media stories which followed the "official line," believed that an older man had drowned in the Chattahoochee. In fact, by the time three weeks had elapsed, many had forgotten that anyone's body had been found in the Chattahoochee.

But then, on December 21, Cobb County authorities said that the "adult" found in the Chattahoochee River was, in fact, 16-year-old Pat Man Rogers. The officials didn't expect it to be Pat Man, so apparently no early attempt was made to eliminate the possibility of the corpse being that of Patrick Rogers. Atlanta's officials constantly reminded the public that the "missing or murdered *children's* cases" remained their first priority. Therefore, an adult body could wait—and so could Pat Man. He wasn't on The List! That he had lived near—and knew—other victims was ignored or elicited no concern.

First, Pat Man's case had not been put on The List because he was a "runaway." Now he was found murdered and he still didn't qualify. Why not? Authorities said that Pat Man was too old. The List, at that time, embraced victims aged 7 to 15. Pat Man was 16. Of the 13 victims who would be added to The List after Patrick Rogers' death, more than half, or seven, would be older than Patrick.

Geographically, the authorities said the Patrick Rogers case didn't fit because Pat Man's body was found in the Chattahoochee River, where no other body had yet been found. For my route, it was an anomaly and occasioned the first adjustment I had made in the route since its creation four months earlier. I added the Chattahoochee River on my map. The authorities ignored it.

The fact that Pat Man's home—and place where he disappeared—were on my route was enough for me. The police investigation, as illustrated earlier, wasn't even considering locations other than where the body was found. Of the 13 victims added to The List after Patrick Rogers' death, almost half, or six, were found in the Chattahoochee River.

Patrick Rogers, the authorities said, was a "runaway." So what! They had said the same about other victims before—and they would say it again. Cynthia Montgomery was a runaway when she died. Others would be, too. And Darron Glass ran away so well that he still would be unaccounted for, three years later.

I always thought that runaways were "missing children." But then, I always thought that a murdered child was a "murdered child." Not so, if you follow the nonsensical media reports in Atlanta. We were again told that 16-year-old Patrick Rogers, who had been missing for three days short of one month and found murdered, "is *not* one of Atlanta's murdered or missing children."

I wondered: What was Patrick Rogers running *from*? One thing was certain: If, as the police thought, and Gail Epstein accepted, Pat Man was running from a burglary warrant, he was running from one that hadn't been issued yet. Pat Man disappeared on November 10, 1980. The warrant that police said he was fleeing wasn't issued until *two days later,* on November 12. Of the five other victims found in the Chattahoochee River after Pat Man died, at least four had police records, and at least three had been charged with burglary.

Did Pat Man know too much? And could Pat Man have been running from a *killer*? Two children—Aaron Wyche and Aaron Jackson—who were considerably younger and smaller than Pat Man, but who both had been "friends" of Pat Man, had been slain. Now Pat Man disappeared.

Could it be similar to the John Wayne Gacy killings of young boys and men in Chicago, where the tentacles of the killer reached out to some victims through a third party? Certainly the timing of Pat Man's disappearance, coming so closely on the heels of Aaron Jackson's murder, indicated that a Gacy-style situation was possible, and shouldn't be ruled out. By February of 1981, I would be pretty certain that it couldn't be ruled out.

Moreover, the finding of Patrick Rogers' body in the Chattahoochee River on the northwest side of town might point directly at the top of any such pyramid of murder. Perhaps the person at the top operated near the Chattahoochee River. Maybe the person—or persons, for that matter—had assistance in killing and/or disposing of other victims.

Of course, this is one of those damnable "could-it-be" theories. But it would clear up many of the mysteries in these cases. And it makes more sense than the *potpourri* of choices offered as explanations by the prosecution in the Wayne Williams trial. The pyramid theory was not in the grab bag. But then, the state didn't have the map to suggest it.

In any event, the Chattahoochee River would remain an apparent anomaly for me for some time. Pat Man's residence was across town from the river, and the exact spot from which he disappeared is still open to question. The initial report said that Pat Man walked his 7-year-old brother, Isaac, to the bus stop near their home at 7 a.m. on November 10, and never was seen again. This, however, does not appear to be the case.

A neighbor, the mother of Patrick's friend and singing partner, Junior Harper, says that Pat Man visited her house later on November 10, looking for Junior. But Junior wasn't home. She related that Pat Man said it was important that he find Junior because Pat Man finally had located a manager who might help them strike it rich as singers.

Unfortunately, seven months would elapse before this information was gleaned. Nobody was asking. Then, when the right question was finally asked, it was asked by a TV reporter who was checking on a suspect.

During those seven months between Pat Man's death and the arrest of that suspect, 13 more victims would be added to The List and a 14th would be connected at the trial of Wayne Williams. The state would eventually say that Wayne Williams *killed all 14* of those people.

If this information about the music manager had surfaced earlier, it should have led to a suspect as early as November 1980! Certainly the connections would have been easy to find. And they were fresher—more obvious—in November 1980, when Pat Man disappeared, than they would be the following June, when a music manager would be arrested. His name was Wayne Williams.

Sometime in November of 1980, printed flyers began to appear in the Thomasville Heights area. They solicited young musical talent and bore a telephone number—none other than that of Wayne Williams! Junior Harper would say that he knew that Pat Man had a flyer, but he could not say that it was the one with Williams' phone number on it.

Williams says that he became concerned about his contacts with children because of the publicity about the "missing and murdered children." He says he called the Task Force to inform it of his recruitment plans. Its answer, he said, was, "Ahh, don't worry about it."

Wayne Williams told me something else about the distribution of those flyers in Thomasville Heights. He said that he had decided to go there at the suggestion of a woman he had met at yet another Atlanta housing project. That woman was the mother of the young man who gave 14-year-old Alfred Evans a ride from his apartment to the bus stop, from whence Evans disappeared. The woman was president of the East Lake Meadows tenants' association. Where have I heard of that housing project before?

Pat Man had vanished, according to later police data, from the Moreland Avenue Shopping Center, where Aaron Jackson and perhaps Aaron Wyche had, too. After his conviction in 1982, Wayne Williams would tell me in an interview at the Fulton County Jail that he had, indeed, caused circulars to be handed out in the Thomasville Heights area. And he would say it was in November. But he added that it was late November—around Thanksgiving, *after* Pat Man had disappeared. He would tell me that he could prove when the brochures were printed and that it was after November 10, the date Pat Man disappeared. But defense attorney Al Binder would tell me—during the trial and before my interview with Williams—that there had been two printings of the circulars. *One* invoice for typesetting was dated November 24.

Wayne Williams would go on to say that he did not personally distribute the handbills. Instead, he said, he had a young man do it for him and paid him for the work. He would say that he rendezvoused with his employee at the *Moreland Avenue Shopping Center.*

But these weren't the only pieces in the Pat Man connection with Wayne Williams. Long after the trial, in a different interview, Williams would recall for me that he and Pat Man had a mutual friend, a white boy who went to Grady High School with Patrick Rogers. In the interim, I would learn that this boy had spent the night with Pat Man shortly before Pat Man's disappearance. But I was not aware of the boy's connection with Wayne Williams when I got that information.

Pat Man's case obviously was a turning point in the Atlanta murders. But the police missed the turn and went off on a tangent. The Task Force wouldn't investigate Patrick's death because Lee Brown steadfastly refused to add him to The List.

Lee Brown missed the importance of Pat Man's case then—and he still ignored it when he testified at Williams' trial.

After Patrick Rogers turned up dead in December of 1980, no more pre-teen "little boys" were added to The List. The geography changed, too. The streets didn't change, but the killer(s) ranged farther and farther from the heart of the city when disposing of victims. It was necessary only to extend the streets on my map, not add new ones. Even those Chattahoochee and South river findings would occur at bridges carrying one of the streets on the map—or, at a secluded point to which one of those streets represented the main access.

Now, as the geographic pattern began to stretch, the map began showing "holes"—places where no activity had been reported, but should have been occurring if the patterns were correct. In this way, it began to say where victims who had long been sought as "missing" might be found. And *they were.*

Had the authorities recognized the Pat Man connections in November of 1980, when I was pointing them out to the media, the police and to almost anybody who would listen, they could have been ready for these impending changes. But they had not recognized them—and they would not be ready for the changes.

They were completely baffled by the change in early 1981 to older victims—a change signaled by the death of Pat Man. They were fooled by the use of rivers to dispose of victims—another signal sent loud and clear by the Pat Man connections.

One need only to refer to Lee Brown's confused testimony about what he called the change in this pattern—the placing of victims in rivers for the first time. This change, he said at Williams' trial, took place after February 11, 1981. Pat Man, you will recall, had been found in a river on December 7, 1980.

Joseph Burton doubles as the medical examiner for both Cobb and DeKalb counties. He made the determinations in both the Aaron Wyche and the Patrick Rogers cases.

This is a mini-statement about the maxi-problem of jurisdictions. Wyche and Rogers lived almost next door to each other in Fulton County. But Burton examined Wyche's body as part of his official duties in DeKalb County, and he examined Rogers' body as part of his official duties in Cobb County. Burton apparently called in Fulton County medical examiners for consultation.

It was about this time that Fulton County Medical Examiner Robert Stivers was rendering an opinion in the Cynthia Montgomery case. When he announced his opinion, I was both shocked and delighted. Stivers said he thought Cynthia Montgomery, Aaron Wyche and Patrick Rogers should be added to The List because of the "similarities" in the manner of their deaths. Lee Brown refused. It might be viewed both as his prerogative and his responsibility.

For three more months, until late February of 1981, Pat Man's case would lie in limbo. Finally, DeKalb County Public Safety Director Dick Hand reopened the Aaron Wyche case. I sought and secured for Aaron Wyche a place on The List. As soon as Wyche was added, it became obvious to the authorities that Pat Man should be, too.

Gail Epstein telephoned me at my office in Rome, Georgia. "Congratulations," she said.

"For what?" I asked.

"They just put Patrick Rogers' name on The List."

Her call was gracious and appreciated. Now, of the three biggest battles I had fought, I had won two. Few would know that I was the one fighting those battles. I attacked relentlessly, but behind the scenes, by supplying those media people who would listen to me with the right questions to ask.

The battle I lost was for the recognition of Cynthia Montgomery. It was a battle fought for a much different reason than the Wyche and Rogers encounters. In the two boys' cases, it was imperative that they be considered a part of the whole if the murders were ever to be stopped—as opposed to stopping of their own accord, as so often happens.

Cynthia represented the "good fight." Cynthia represented striving for justice, fairness and logic. I felt that the death of any one child was deserving of as much attention as that given any other child, or group of children, who met the same fate. Cynthia's case embodied sexual, racial and class discrimination, carried out by those who say publicly that they abhor those vices the most.

By June of 1981, Pat Man's death could be directly connected to at least 13 of the other victims, seven of whom died after Pat Man did. Shouldn't these potential victims have been identified in advance by the Pat Man connections?

The body of Nathaniel Cater, a convicted felon, would be pulled from the Chattahoochee River on May 24, 1981. Of course, Patrick Rogers had been pulled from the Chattahoochee. Cater was 27. Rogers was 16 (too old, at first, they said, to go on The List).

Not one iota of the Pat Man connections would be testified to at the trial of Wayne Williams. All the jury would ever hear of Pat Man would come in the closing arguments. Had I been Wayne Williams, the testimony I would have feared the most would have been about Pat Man. Along with Cap'n Peg's, this stands as the strongest suggestion that there's a Wayne Williams connection, too.

It was late February of 1981, months after Pat Man had been buried—and shortly after his murder case had finally been added to The List. Two Atlanta police officers knocked on Annie Rogers' door at Thomasville Heights.

"Is Patrick Rogers here?" one asked.

Annie Rogers' hands covered her mouth in shocked disbelief. "No, he ain't here," she said.

"Ma'am, we sure need to find him bad," the other officer said. "We have a warrant for his arrest."

14

A Chief Sees the Light—and Sees Red

Relying mainly on an Atlanta police detective's testimony, a Fulton County grand jury indicted James Charles Gates, a 56-year-old unmarried black laborer with a long police record, on October 31, 1980, for the hit-and-run murder of Angela (Gypsy) Bacon.

It should have been big news in Atlanta—that a man had been arrested and indicted for the murder of an Atlanta child. But it wasn't. Angela wasn't on The List.

So the indictment of Gates was all but relegated to the oblivion of non-history, instead of hailed as the breakthrough it would have been had "Gypsy" been on The List. Again, the hypnotic, "blinder"-like effects of the arbitrary List are profound.

Gates was arrested on November 1, 1980, the same day that the body of 9-year-old Aaron Jackson was found. He was, according to an attorney familiar with the case, sleeping when police arrived at the condemned apartment where he lived.

It was the same apartment building where 28-year-old John Porter slept whenever he had quarreled with his mother. Porter would spend his last night alive in April of 1981, sharing that building with Gates before being found stabbed to death on a vacant lot a short distance away.

"Old Man" Gates, as the Porter family next door called him, had a record dating from 1941. It included convictions for burglary, cruelty toward wife, involuntary manslaughter (reduced from homicide), carrying concealed weapons and selling liquor illegally. In the Angela (Gypsy) Bacon case, he obtained a lawyer and was released on $10,000 bond on November 17, 1980.

Then, just when the case was about to go to trial in January of 1981, the charges against Gates were unexpectedly dropped. Again, there were no headlines. It was the same week that the 52 American hostages had been released in Iran and Ronald Reagan succeeded Jimmy Carter as President. The List of Atlanta murders was momentarily upstaged by stories of yellow ribbons and inaugural festivities.

As for the "unofficial" murder of Angela Bacon, it was tucked away in obscurity. In a ruling that went virtually unnoticed, Fulton County Superior Court Judge Charles A. Wofford dismissed the murder charges against Gates, on the recommendation of Assistant District Attorney Charles Hadaway. The date: January 22, 1981.

Sitting in the courthouse were Angela Bacon's grandmother, Isabel Porter (no kin to John Porter), and aunt, Cleo Pitts. They had eyed Gates as they waited for the trial to begin. When the judge announced his ruling and the prosecutor explained his motion for dismissal, Isabel Porter and Cleo Pitts listened in disbelief. They had come to attend a murder trial, but now our criminal-justice system was again itself on trial. As the two women followed the prosecutor down a corridor, they shouted, "That man killed 'Gypsy'! Why did you let him go?"

The prosecutor tried to explain that there was not enough evidence to present to a trial jury, even if there had been enough to tell a grand jury. The two women didn't buy this story—and still don't.

For that matter, the prosecutor didn't buy Walter Mitchell's eyewitness story, which he said contained too many inconsistencies. He didn't buy the grand-jury testimony of an Atlanta police detective, Sergeant J.A. Walker, either. "The witness [Walter Mitchell] was incredible, and the car could not be connected with the crime," the prosecutor, Charles Hadaway, said. He added that the prosecution had been "misled" by what it regarded as an overzealous detective who wanted desperately to clear the case.

I, too, had trouble with Walter Mitchell's story, which he would tell Jeff Prugh of the *Los Angeles Times*, in March of 1981. Some details differ from what Mitchell had been quoted as saying in the *Atlanta Constitution* in August of 1980, shortly after Angela Bacon was killed.

But then, even the police reports themselves differ. The one on public file, which Jeff obtained, corroborates Mitchell's account that the driver backed up and ran over Angela. But it says nothing about an attempted rape, a blouse, or the suspect trying to hit Mitchell (these details had appeared in the *Constitution* story). So, if neither the eyewitness nor the police can be believed, who can?

What's more, the prosecutor said that the medical examiner told him that Angela Bacon's killing was "probably done with *a blow to the head* and probably not done by a car [emphasis added]." Now you see that Angela could fit neatly on The List. Both Patrick Rogers and Eric Middlebrooks were said by medical examiners to have died from blows to the head. But, what the prosecutor says that the medical examiner told him—and what the medical examiner wrote on the official document—are two different things.

The official cause of death is listed as "assault by auto." Why the discrepancy? Is it ass-covering time again?

It's hard enough to solve a murder when the apparent lone eyewitness cannot be taken at his word. But it is infinitely more difficult when the officials who are trying to solve it cannot be taken at their word. According to the prosecutor, we can't take the word of the police or the medical examiner. But if we can, then we can't take the word of the prosecutor. That puts the citizens in a no-win position.

James Charles Gates' lawyer, meanwhile, had been able to convince the prosecution that Gates' station wagon could not have run over Angela. The lawyer, L. Paul Cobb Jr., was prepared to produce witnesses who would testify that Gates' vehicle was in a repair garage at the time Angela was killed.

In the spring of 1981, I would visit Gates' residence on Capital Avenue and check out the station wagon that was parked outside his door. As I quietly approached the vehicle, I heard a man and woman conversing inside the dilapidated apartment. I noticed that the vehicle had been damaged, as the police reports said. It was the right color and had the wood-grain sides. But the roof appeared never to have had a luggage rack—and the sun visor contained no evidence that a butcher knife had ever been stuck through it, as Walter Mitchell had said.

Would you accept this as proof that it was not Gates' vehicle that killed Angela Bacon? Apparently the prosecutor did ("The car could not be connected with the crime"). That might indicate that this vehicle didn't kill Angela. But, I would learn another lesson in logic when I ran across a witness who told me that Gates had *"two"* light-blue Ford station wagons!

What also hurt the state's case, the prosecutor said, was that some of the evidence—a sample of Angela's skin—and the entire case file had been unaccountably *lost* by the Atlanta police. The evidence, he explained, was in a small envelope, which was stapled to the file.

"Is it unusual," the prosecutor was asked, "for the police to lose evidence here?"

He shook his head. *"Everything,"* he said, "is unusual about this case."

"How did they ever lose the evidence and file?"

The prosecutor shrugged and suppressed a grin.

"Keystone Cops," he said.

Later in the spring of 1981, Jeff would find two witnesses who said they had seen a black man driving a station wagon that matched the description given by Walter Mitchell. They explained that they had observed the man driving the vehicle during the summer of 1980, *before* Angela Bacon died. They said they had heard about the murder over a radio and saw a composite sketch that resembled the driver they had seen. They added that they told an Atlanta police patrolman about it in August of 1980, after learning of Angela's murder. But, they said, they never heard from the police again.

Jeff arranged to take the two witnesses—a father and son—to the Fulton

County District Attorney's office. There, only the son was interviewed by investigators. What made their story so compelling to Jeff was that they had volunteered one shred of information that matched one that Walter Mitchell had shared with him. They, too, said the station wagon's sun visor had a butcher knife stuck through it.

On January 20, 1981, a young black boy told the Atlanta police that somebody tried to kidnap him near the Lakewood Fairgrounds—at the corner of Pickfair Avenue and Pickfair Way. This wasn't the first incident—nor would it be the last—that happened there in connection with Atlanta's murders.

One block north, 12 year-year-old Charles Stephens had lived and disappeared. Three blocks to the east, 11-year-old Earl Lee Terrell disappeared after going swimming at South Bend Park.

In August of 1980, a student at the Challenge School for Boys told the school's director and the Atlanta police that two black men had abducted him in a blue car at the Stewart-Lakewood Shopping Center and taken him to Pickfair Avenue and Pickfair Way.

Back in March of 1980, a witness had said he had seen a man in a blue car with then-missing 10-year-old Jefferey Mathis near that intersection. In the first week of January of 1981, 14-year-old Lubie (Chuck) Geter was last seen at the Stewart-Lakewood Shopping Center.

These two locations—the shopping center and the streets named "Pickfair"—are less than a mile apart. The street that takes you from one to the other goes nowhere else and has no other intersections. So, if police patrol really works, and if the police knew anything about where these crimes were occurring, you would think that almost 1½ years into Atlanta's murders (by official reckoning), the police would be keeping a weather eye on the area around Pickfair Avenue and Pickfair Way, right?

The day after the small boy reported the attempted kidnapping (January 21), someone found the stabbed body of Faye Yearby, a 22-year-old black woman, at the corner of Pickfair Avenue and Pickfair Way. Parked close by was a green car. Yearby had been tied to a tree and her hands bound behind her. The scene was chillingly reminiscent of the finding of 12-year-old Angel Lenair, whose body had been left in an almost identical position, not far away on Georgia 166, almost one year earlier.

So much for fancy police manpower-allocation systems and the like. Perhaps the police were too busy canvassing in other parts of Atlanta to afford manpower to watch this neighborhood.

Mayor Jackson would constantly tell us that police were doing "thousands of things they can't tell us about." Hell, I knew better than that. There weren't 10 things they knew to do. Perhaps the mayor meant they were doing the same 10 things 100 times each and more.

A flurry of police activity centered on the green car, Could it have been the green car that had been sighted in other cases? Police lost interest when they discovered that the car belonged to Faye Yearby. They had been looking for the car of a killer, not a victim. They never added Faye Yearby's death to The List—despite the geographic links and other similarities that should have been hitting investigators between the eyes. They said she was too old for The List, at 22. But she looked even younger. The officials still thought that the killings were random. Did they also think that the killer was checking the ages of his victims to see if they qualified? At 22, Yearby was five years younger than one man Wayne Williams would be convicted of killing—Nathaniel Cater.

I mentally filed away Faye Yearby's killing with other pieces of data that had surfaced in this small area surrounding the Lakewood Fairgrounds. In addition to the reports by the two young boys, the locations in the Terrell, Stephens and Geter cases, the sighting of Mathis and the death of Yearby, there was the nearby house of John Wilcoxen, a pornographer convicted of child molestation. And an abandoned house overlooking the fairgrounds contained Polaroid film backings and discarded boys' undershorts, suggesting that the house had been used for child pornography.

You'd think you would have needed a traffic cop to direct only the police cars that should have been patrolling this area. No such luck—for Faye Yearby. Instead, city recreation crews installed a basketball goal and erected a steel barricade at the intersection of Pickfair Avenue and Pickfair Way to entice kids to this isolated (and dangerous) place.

Late on Thursday night, January 22, 1981, I swerved my wife's red Camaro onto Georgia 400 and headed for the north Georgia mountains. I accompanied Mary to a conference held by her employer. Georgia 400 differs from an interstate highway in name only. It stretches from the money belt of north Atlanta, past the resorts of Lake Lanier and up into the foothills of the Appalachians.

Just before we left, I received a call from Gail Epstein of the *Atlanta Constitution*. She said that yet another black youngster, Terry Lorenzo Pue, 15, was missing from home. Reports of missing black youths were not unusual in Atlanta during these ultra-sensitive weeks. People who earlier might have been disturbed if they hadn't heard from their children in a full day now called the police if a child was 15 minutes late in reporting in.

Pue had last been seen at the MARTA bus stop in front of his northwest Atlanta apartment-home. Terry lived almost exactly half way between the points where 13-year-old Clifford Jones lived and was found strangled at the Hollywood Plaza Shopping Center.

Across Terry Pue's street is a cemetery. It's the same cemetery which

Clifford Jones' mother had said Clifford was afraid to walk past alone, even on the opposite side of the street.

By contrast, Terry Pue was fearless. He had defiantly bragged to friends that he "ain't afraid of no killer." Other kids looked up to him. He was big, tough and fast. His body, in fact, would be the first in Atlanta's killings (at least 23 by now, although Terry Pue was only the 14th put on The List) that police said showed any signs of struggle with his killer. Curiously, autopsy reports did not verify the police version.

When Terry Pue turned up dead, it set off nervous tremors among many streetwise black kids. Terry Pue once lived in the apartment later occupied by another victim, Edward Hope Smith. He knew Smith's buddy and next-door neighbor, Lee Gooch. He knew the kids at East Lake Meadows, where both his sister and a girlfriend lived. He knew Lubie Geter, who more than once visited Terry at the Challenge School. Now many kids on the streets considered: if the killer could get Terry Pue, then he could get them, too.

Gail Epstein knew I would be interested in Terry Pue because she closely followed the geographic connections, keeping a large map I had furnished her on the wall behind her desk. Terry Pue fit!

I slept in Friday morning, January 23, while Mary attended her meeting. About 10:30, she burst into our room during a coffee break to awaken me with bad news: Terry Pue's body had been found on Sigman Road, southeast of Atlanta in Rockdale County, one of the newest bulges in metropolitan Atlanta's outward growth.

I snatched my atlas from my briefcase and located Sigman Road. It was far southeast of anything else that had happened in the cases. It seemed then to be an anomaly. But, like most anomalies, it sooner or later would give way to logic.

Until now, only the finding of Pat Man in the Chattahoochee River, northwest of Atlanta, had not yet been fully explained, at least to my satisfaction. The location where Terry Pue's body was dumped would be very near Interstate 20. This bothered me. In January of 1981, the Atlanta police and the FBI were using Interstate 20 as the basis for their geographic understanding of the cases. I was convinced that they were wrong. If I wasn't right, then nobody had found a handle to these cases yet. U.S. 278, which had always been an integral part of the route, ran all the way to Sigman Road. In fact, just before U.S. 278 reaches Sigman Road, coming from Atlanta, it crosses over onto Interstate 20, and at Sigman Road, Interstate 20 *is* U.S. 278.

On this southeast side of metropolitan Atlanta, U.S. 278 is known as the Covington Highway. Where it exits on Atlanta's northwest side, it is Bankhead Highway. Along the way, it passes by Techwood Homes—in front of Georgia Tech—and crosses Gray Street, a focal point in the cases yet to be uncovered. It also passes by Bowen Homes, where the boiler exploded, and by the house of 14-year-old Milton Harvey, victim No. 3 on The List. Then it leaves Atlanta over the bridge where 23-year-old Michael McIntosh would last be seen.

One week before Terry Pue disappeared, an anonymous caller had telephoned newly elected Sheriff Vic Davis of Rockdale County (ex-Atlanta homicide chief Jack Perry had lost the election to Davis). The caller told the sheriff that a body could be found on Sigman Road in Rockdale County. A massive search was undertaken—and covered by the news media. Nothing was turned up.

The same caller soon was back on the line. "You didn't find that one," he said, "so I'm gonna lay another one right on top of him for you." In a few days, Terry Pue's body was found on Sigman Road, within a mile of where the search had taken place the previous week. The caller had been a white man, according to police. Was there still another body on Sigman Road? There is still one victim missing, on The List.

Long after Wayne Williams would be convicted, someone found a skeleton at Sigman Road and Interstate 20. "No connection [to The List]," police would say. There probably is no connection, but I cannot bring myself ever to take the news media's word for it. What a shame.

The setting outside the Unicoi Lodge where we stayed was rustic. Inside, the rooms were spartan—typical of a low-budget motel, with one large exception: no television sets.

I had returned from breakfast shortly before noon on January 23 when the telephone rang in our room. On the line was Dennis Kauff of Atlanta station WSB-TV (Channel 2). He asked me to come to the studio to be interviewed on the Terry Pue case. "No way I can make it before tomorrow night," I said.

"I'll call you back," Kauff said.

He did call back with an alternative. Soon I was driving down the twisting mountain road—with the tops of 80-foot-tall Georgia pines on my right and the roots of others on my left—headed back to Helen, Georgia. There, I stopped in the heart of town to ask a local cop where a helicopter would land. He directed me to a large field, "up the dirt road, behind the bank," about a half-mile away.

I bounced the red Camaro off the road and into the open field. I figured that the car could easily be seen from the air. Suddenly the clatter of Channel 2's helicopter attracted my attention. It loomed ever larger in the midwinter sky. Finally, it roosted about 50 yards from my car. The rotor was still whirring when anchorman Wes Sarginson ran toward me in a head-protecting crouch. His encumbered cameraman waddled close behind.

I spread my maps on the hood of the car and explained the geographic relationship of Terry Pue to the other victims. I wasn't sure that any of it was making any particular sense and I really wasn't sure that Sarginson cared about the map, anyway. But since authorities weren't talking, my map at least provided three minutes for the 6 o'clock package. Soon the whirlybird faded into the sky from whence it came, and I returned to Unicoi.

Shortly before 6 o'clock that evening, I left my room and went to the communal TV set in the lobby. The door on the room next to mine opened. Out stepped Dick Hand, a larger-than-life fellow who appeared more relaxed than usual in a white turtleneck sweater. Hand is public safety director of DeKalb County. DeKalb is Atlanta's very wealthy young brother. Everything is a little cleaner and newer, and things operate smoother in DeKalb. A part of the city of Atlanta lies in DeKalb County.

Dick Hand was at one time an Assistant U.S. Attorney in Rome, Georgia. He is a cop's cop and commands a lot of respect inside and outside his department. He has been chairman or president of just about every law-enforcement organization in Georgia. Unlike Public Safety Commisioner Lee Brown in Atlanta, Dick Hand retained full control over the police department. There was no intervening position of chief of police. There is now. The DeKalb County police department is the second largest—and by far the most efficient—in metropolitan Atlanta. It is perhaps the most efficient in the Southeastern United States. As police departments go, it is damned good.

Dick Hand, too, had come to the lobby to watch the news. He greeted me as he settled into the chair next to mine. Minutes later, he was startled when my face appeared on the tube.

Suddenly his surprise turned to undivided attention. On television, I was explaining the connections between the murders and Memorial Drive. Much of Memorial Drive is in Dick Hand's jurisdiction. In fact, his modern, multi-storied police headquarters, complete with helipads on top, sits right on Memorial Drive at Interstate 285, east of Atlanta.

When the news ended, Hand asked if I had the maps with me. I told him I did and accepted his invitation to join him in his room. We talked for hours, and he took notes. Dick Hand was about to turn from taking a passive to an active role in the Atlanta murders.

Dick returned from dinner and took up the conversation again. Now we sat on the green-cushioned pew that surrounded the huge open fireplace in the lobby. As the night wore on, his agitation showed clear through. He realized that the Atlanta officials were not keeping him fully informed.

Even though Hand had a full-time representative assigned to the Task Force, he was forced to admit bitterly, "Ninety percent of what you've told me tonight, I didn't know!"

He had not been at all aware of the myriad connections along Memorial Drive. He thought the Atlanta officials were keeping something from him. But I felt that they probably couldn't tell him because they didn't grasp it themselves. You have to go to *every* scene, which is something no Task Force investigator ever did, to realize that disparate addresses on Eastlake Drive, Dahlgren Street, Flat Shoals Road, 2nd Avenue and Rawson Street are all within a few hundred yards of Memorial Drive, one of those 12 important streets on my map. And when you stick pins in a map to represent those addresses, most of them show up along Interstate 20, as well as Memorial Drive. But when you look at the map, it is Interstate 20 that you see right away.

Dick Hand walked to where I was talking with the chief of police of a small Georgia police department. He broke into our conversation as if the man weren't there. Which indicated preoccupation on Hand's part. He is, after all, a gentleman.

"You know, Chet," Hand said, "we have a case where the remains of an unidentified black female child—cause of death unknown—were found back in '79. Oh, it was sometime... sometime before Christmas, anyway. We found her body right off Memorial Drive, near the Columbia Mall."

Long before our conversation took place, Atlanta police were looking into the disappearance and possible murder of a young boy who lived just off Memorial Drive. His name: Alfred Evans.

A witness gave police a statement in which he spoke of a connection between *"Q's"* ("Q" is a nickname for Alfred Evans) disappearance and the death of a little girl whose body had been found recently on Memorial Drive. Atlanta police noted in their report that they couldn't recall any such body of a young girl being found on Memorial Drive in all of 1979. On that basis, they dismissed the man's information out-of-hand.

Did they check? If so, did they ask the DeKalb County police? Alfred (Q) Evans lived in East Lake Meadows, in "Atlanta-in-DeKalb," which is policed by the Atlanta police. A few blocks to the east, just before you get to Columbia Mall, the city limits sign marks where the DeKalb police take over from the Atlanta police.

Had the monster called "jurisdiction" reared its ugly head again and devoured still another police investigation looking for a body and another with a body looking for a name? It is the rule, not the exception.

From the time of my meeting with Dick Hand, the information about the little girl was on copies of my map, which had been furnished to the Task Force and published in the *Atlanta Constitution* and *Journal.*

"I've made up my mind," Dick Hand said resolutely. "When I get back to the office Monday, I'm going to put together a team of investigators. We'll do our own investigating from now on. Would you be able to come by and fill them in on what you know?"

"I'd be happy to," I assured him. He asked me to call him. I promised I would.

Mary and I were on our way back to Atlanta the next night when the news blared over the car radio: Terry Pue had not disappeared from in front of his home. He had been seen later. In fact, he had spent the night in a Krystal hamburger shop. Would this break the geographic pattern? Had Terry Pue become the only murdered child not to have disappeared from a street along my route?

When the route was fashioned in August of 1980, there were 12 children on The List. When No. 13 went down, I was surprised by the coincidence that it followed the pattern I had deduced from the first 12. When No. 14 followed suit, it was more amazing. By the time No. 17 happened and the pattern still held, I began hoping the pattern would break. I felt the pressure. I obviously had a grasp on something, but I wasn't entirely sure where it all might lead.

Terry Pue was victim No. 23 on my list, and I fully expected the pertinent points to be on the route. I would be shocked now if they weren't. I stopped at a mini-market and telephoned the city desk of the *Atlanta Constitution.* Could they tell me the exact location where Terry Pue was last seen at a Krystal?

"Sure, Chet," a familiar voice answered. "Let's see, ummm, it was—ah, yeah, here it is, at the —at the Krystal in the 5000 block of *Memorial Drive.* Need the exact address?"

"Naw," I said, hanging up the phone. "That's close enough."

Amazing, I thought. Terry Pue disappeared from a point on the route at least *10 miles* from his home, which is also on the route.

Back in the car, I scanned my atlas and checked the location of the 5000 block of Memorial Drive.

"Guess what!" I said to Mary. "The kid disappeared from Memorial Drive, just east of U.S. 278. From that point, it would be at least seven miles shorter to take U.S. 278 to Sigman Road than to use Interstate 20. By God, I was right!"

We might never have known that Terry Pue had made it to Memorial Drive had it not been for the fine work of two *Atlanta Journal* reporters, Hyde Post and Jonathan Maye. While researching a "day in the life of" story about Terry Pue, they overheard a waitress comment that "the kid who was murdered" had spent the night at a sister Krystal hamburger stand on Memorial Drive. The reporters gave the information to Rockdale County authorities, and soon police verified that Pue had been there.

Witnesses said that Terry Pue had spent the night at "the Krystal" in the shadow of DeKalb County police headquarters. He dined with money that he swindled from the A&P next door. His scam was simple: he went to the back of the A&P, where empty bottles were piled high. He took some of them around to the front and sold them back to the A&P.

At the Krystal, waitresses asked Pue if he was all right. He told them he was waiting there for his mother to pick him up. The curfew would not have affected Pue because he was outside of Atlanta's city limits, where it was not in effect. And, at 15, Pue was older than the curfew limit of 14, anyway.

At the trial of Wayne Williams, the prosecution again would miss the geography in these cases by ignoring Pue's connection with Memorial Drive. It would eschew the witness at both the Krystal and the A&P in favor of a witness who had known Pue long ago. The witness would testify that he had seen Pue in East Point (where some thought Pue was going), although Pue apparently didn't recognize the witness. At least, Pue hadn't acknowledged the "friend's" greeting.

Terry Pue's daddy pulled a picture from the mug-file lineup. He identified it as the picture of a man who had told him in 1979 that Terry needed talking to—that he "should stop messing around with the sissies around the colleges," or he would be killed.

Is this what would take Terry Pue to within two blocks of DeKalb Community College's central campus on the last day he was to be seen alive?

I would remember the admonition given Terry Pue's father when I would hear that yet another victim was holing up on a college campus during his "disappearance," and again when I would investigate yet another questionably-accidental death on the campus of Georgia Tech.

Now the Stone Mountain police department was receiving anonymous telephone calls. The police thought he sounded like the same man who had been calling the Rockdale authorities. They successfully traced a call. It had come from a man who lived on North Indian Creek Drive—across the college campus from where Terry Pue was last seen alive.

Two weeks later, Dick Hand publicly criticized the Task Force investigation. He announced the beginning of his own investigative effort. It would lead to Aaron Wyche and Patrick Rogers finding their rightful places on The List.

And I thought I went to Unicoi just for the ride.

I already had driven down the sloping driveway that passes between Lee Brown's office in Atlanta and a strip joint called the Body Shoppe. Now I was due at the DeKalb County police department to brief the group that Dick Hand had assembled.

You can *feel* the difference between the levels of efficiency in the DeKalb County police operation and the one in Atlanta. It's there in the snap of the people walking by, in what the military calls *espirit de corps.*

I was surprised at the size of the group that Dick Hand had called together. There appeared to be more than 50 people in the dark-paneled room. They filled the chairs at the long conference table and extra chairs that ringed the front and inside walls of the room. Some even stood along one wall, which was to my right. Dick Hand stood alone, arms akimbo, against the wall to my left.

It was during this briefing that I had an experience with the detective who, I was later told, had been assigned to the Aaron Wyche case. That discussion is covered elsewhere. But I was about to make an interesting discovery about how the Task Force operated.

"Have you ever seen this map before, Vivian?" Dick Hand directed his question to Sergeant Vivian Underwood, his full-time representative on the Task Force.

"I've seen a lot of maps," she replied.

"How about this particular one?"

"I'm not sure about this particular one."

"Vivian," I asked (I had known her from the council that oversaw operations of the regional police academies; I then directed one of the academies, and she was on the council), "how long would it take to drive to all the points depicted on this map?" I knew it would be about 5½ hours—at the speed limit. I wanted to know if she knew.

"I don't know," she replied.

"An hour? Two hours? Three hours? Ten? A week?"

"I don't know," she answered, somewhat testily.

"Anyway," she volunteered to my surprise, "there's only one person on the Task Force who's ever been to *most* of those locations."

"Who's that?"

"Dale Kirkland," she said without hesitation.

I should have known. Dale Kirkland is the Task Force member whom I had taken on the tour in September of 1980. Mike Shannon's and John Woods' stay on the Task Force had been brief, and they were on other assignments. So, contrary to what *Life* magazine would express, there were some things the Task Force couldn't know that I knew.

By January of 1981, Eula Montgomery still had not heard from the police—not one word since they first told her children that her 14-year-old daughter, Cynthia, had been slain. A murder investigation certainly should include some kind of background check on the victim. You'd think they'd at least phone Mrs. Montgomery and ask, "Do you know anyone who might have wanted to harm your daughter?" But the Atlanta police had not even done that much.

At home, Eula Montgomery disconsolately sorted out Cynthia's possessions, which included a small Bible. Cynthia's handwriting was scrawled on some of the unprinted pages at the front. When Eula squinted for a closer look, she noted that Cynthia had written gushingly about an older man she loved—a man named "Smitty."

Cynthia twice now had used the alias Cynthia "Smith." This no doubt was "Smitty." But who was "Smitty"? Eula didn't know. Maybe the police would know. But if they did, they hadn't bothered to ask Eula what she might know about him. She said she had not called the police because she realized "they were busy" with the massively publicized murders—the ones that made The List. She thought they'd get around to Cynthia.

But, meanwhile, maybe Cynthia's Bible would offer a clue about her death.

When Eula Montgomery telephoned the police, her call was switched to the homicide squad, not the Task Force investigating the murders of Atlanta's children. Cynthia, who was 14 by two weeks when she died, didn't for some reason qualify for the preferential treatment of The List.

The call was fielded by Mickey Lloyd, who had been assigned to Cynthia's case and reputedly is one of the Atlanta Police Bureau's most skillful young detectives. It was Lloyd who had searched in 1979 for a third body along Niskey Lake Road.

Eula Montgomery made arrangements to take the Bible to police headquarters. There, while talking with Lloyd, Eula said, they were interrupted by a familiar voice across the room. It was that of Detective Carolyn O'Neal, who told Eula, "I'd like to see you when you're finished here."

A short while later, Eula said, O'Neal asked her one question: "What do you know about Cynthia running around with those gypsies?"

Gypsies? Eula shook her head. She said she knew nothing about gypsies.

Could they be the gypsies on Gordon Street? I remember Dick Arena reporting that he had seen a truck loaded with youngsters. He said they hopped off at various places along Gordon Street to distribute circulars that advertised the fortune-telling services of "the Reverend Mother Dorothy," one of a spate of palm readers who operate on Atlanta's south side. Her residence was 1214 Gordon Street, two blocks west of the West Hunter Street Baptist Church, which was the headquarters for the searchers and the Challenge School for Boys.

Or, could they be the gypsies near Carrollton? Just east of Carrollton, where Cynthia Montgomery had attended summer camp (along with Jo-Jo Bell), was an unpretentious house along Georgia 166, the highway to Atlanta which was a part of the tour of death.

A large, wooden sign by the roadside heralded a palm reader named "Mother Doria," who purportedly is Mother Dorothy's sister. The address in Carrollton was listed in the Yellow Pages as the "McMillen Co.," which repairs and refurbishes furnace boilers. The "McMillen Co." also was listed in the same telephone book's white pages as occupying 1214 Gordon Street—Mother Dorothy's location—in Atlanta.

Boilers! I couldn't help but recall that crisp, tragic October morning in 1980 at Bowen Homes, where those pre-school kids and that teacher died when the furnace boiler blew up.

Or, is it possible that Eula Montgomery didn't hear Detective O'Neal correctly?

Did O'Neal wish to speak to her again about "Gypsy" (the nickname for slain 16-year-old Angela Bacon, Cynthia's friend), rather than "gypsies"? These questions would go unanswered. Detective O'Neal declined to be interviewed.

15

"I Found Lee Gooch"

December, 1980

Atlanta got a holiday respite from the killings in 1980, just as it had at the end of 1979. *Adios*, 3½-week cycle—again! Yet even as Atlantans exchanged gifts and prepared to toast 1981, each day without any tragic incident was foreboding. Would it happen again? Soon? Was this the eye of the hurricane?

Paul Crawley of Channel 11 commented on how strange this news story was. A body would be found, then a flurry of heated activity—then nothing. As someone came up missing, the story oozed out. There was little to report, little more to say than somebody was missing. Oh, there were friends and relatives to interview, but most said the same things. If the new cases were adding anything to the police's store of information, the police weren't talking.

The authorities took advantage of the myths and mystique surrounding the badge. They acted mum, as they always do. The media was convinced that the police just weren't telling them anything about anything. In spite of Mayor Jackson's extolling the long list of things the police were doing that they couldn't tell us about, I suspected that Lee Brown was telling the truth. He didn't know anything to tell the media.

On January 3, 1981, Lubie (Chuck) Geter, a 14-year-old black male, met with his supplier of auto air-fresheners at the National Pride car wash in the 1500 block of Memorial Drive. It was within walking distance of Lubie's home on Dahlgren Street at Memorial Drive.

The car wash was close to Murphy High School, where Lubie was supposed to spend six hours each weekday, but often didn't. It was also near one of his favorite hangouts, Anne's Snack Shop. There, kids' snacks sometimes included the cigarettes they carried in their pockets—the kind without brand names on them.

Lubie and a friend had begun the day with equal quantities of the deodorizers they peddled for cash. But Lubie's sales went slack. The supplier suggested that Lubie try working the Stewart-Lakewood Shopping Center, several miles away.

Lubie's mother said it was the first time Lubie ever had gone there. It wasn't. Lubie was, in fact, a regular around the Stewart-Lakewood Shopping Center, where the man who runs the car wash across the street told me that he had warned Lubie more than once about being out there alone. But, Lubie knew and often frequented the same places as missing 11-year-old Earl Lee Terrell did near the Lakewood Fairgrounds, which you can see from the shopping center parking lot.

Lubie Geter asked his older brother for a ride. His brother obliged. It was better to stay on Lubie's good side, since Lubie was a reliable source for ready cash whenever the older brother needed a loan. "Chuck made over $20 a day, hustlin'," his brother said.

Stewart Avenue is a carnival of car lots. The bright lights arranged in Maypole fashion on several lots projected an illusion of circus tents or merry-go-rounds to airline passengers who strained for night-time views of Atlanta from planes that circled and waited to land at busy Hartsfield International Airport.

The street is replete with flashy neon, street walkers, porno shops and con men. If you can't buy it on Stewart Avenue, it isn't for sale. You can spend a few bucks more than it's worth to watch the topless (and sometimes bottomless) waitresses pretend to be exotic dancers at the Purple Onion. Or you could visit with one of the flimsily clad masseuses at the Harem House.

The Harem House sat next door to an XXX-rated cinema which offered a double feature. The movies always were montages of writhing lust, complete with moans, cries of ecstasy and an interminable succession of closeups. Seen one? You've seen them all.

Behind the Coke machine and other automatic vendors that lined one wall of the Early American whorehouse decor of the cinema lobby was a "bookstore." One could only wonder if the promise of the book jackets was fulfilled by the pages inside. Each book is hermetically sealed in plastic wrap. A sign on a wall reminds you: "If You Open, You Buy!"

Glass cases enclosed a wide selection of plastic devices. Some were battery-powered. Others could be inflated to life size. Nearby was a weird display of horned, knobbed and ribbed flesh-colored devices. The 8-mm. movie racks weren't as full as they once were—testimony to the popularity of the home-video player. To the left of the lobby, bathed in dim purple light, sat a row of individual projection booths. A sliding bolt was available to lock each door from the inside. A sign warned: "Only One Person in a Booth at a Time."

A few blocks away on Stewart Avenue is another, less elaborate emporium of erotica. It all is a carryover from the heyday of Mike Thevis, the Atlanta porno magnate who is serving time in federal prison for racketeering and conspiracy to murder.

The tentacles of Thevis' operation reached my hometown of Louisville, where the porn market was ravaged by firebombs and other "knocks in the night." Thevis was an escapee when the murder along the Chattahoochee River, for which he now serves time, occurred. He walked out of the New Albany, Indiana, Jail after allegedly bribing a guard to allow him a conjugal visit, in privacy. From the second floor of my fifth-generation family home (on the first street south of the Mason-Dixon Line at that point), I had often stared at the double-decker Sherman-Minton bridge which joins Louisville and New Albany.

When you tour Stewart Avenue's sleazy side of Atlanta nightlife, you almost forget that a late-1970s crusade to shut down some of the city's massage parlors was started by then-City Solicitor Mary Welcome. The crusade was carried on by then-Fulton-County Solicitor Hinson McAuliffe (now retired), who is praised by some for "smut fighting," and damned by others for "book burning."

But this is how Stewart Avenue looked when Lubie Geter used to hang out there. Today, there are telltale signs that the sex shops are making a comeback, thus end all such campaigns to legislate the morals of others into conformity with those of the lawgivers. What such laws *do* accomplish is the corruption of elected officials and police, the institutionalization of hypocrisy and the making of rich black marketeers richer.

Two witnesses would say that Wayne Williams once was employed as a guard and counter clerk at two yellow-front bookstores.

These two witnesses said that they had driven Williams from his alleged job to his home on Penelope Road. They would successfully pick Williams from a lineup arranged at the Fulton County Jail. But this was no great feat. Wayne Williams' face had been seen so often in Atlanta publications and on Atlanta television screens that he would be as recognizable in the city as Hank Aaron.

Williams denied these witness' reports, and the prosecution didn't think enough of them to bring them up at Williams' trial. Even so, the prosecution would try to paint him as a regular at another pornhouse—an allegation which was refuted by the owner of that establishment.

The second bookstore on Stewart Avenue, at the corner of the Lakewood Freeway (Georgia 166), provided the setting for an unusual incident reported by a man named Willie Turner. On the night of March 24, 1980, one day short of two weeks after 10-year-old Jefferey Mathis disappeared, Turner went to Atlanta police headquarters and gave this report:

> "On Monday I seen [sic] a white male and the black boy was sitting in the car and I pulled up by them at the redlight then they turned in [sic] adult bookstore on Steward [sic] Ave. Then I called the police and they didn't show up. He was driving a blue noble [sic] . . . [The word "noble" was lined out and "NOVA" was scrawled over it] and the license plate was bent so I couldn't tell what it was.
>
> "Last night, March 23, I saw the same man behind a [sic] old building but the boy wasn't with him. He pulled an army .45 on me and told me not to move while holding the gun on me we [sic] walked to the car and then drove off. Then I called the police and reported it."

But again, the police didn't show up. So Turner went to police headquarters, begging police to take the kind of information they were canvassing all over town for.

I first read this statement in September of 1980. For me, it raised more questions than it answered.

What black boy? Any descriptions? Which adult bookstore on Stewart? There were two. Were the police dispatched? If so, why didn't they show up? Any further description of the car? What old building? Where? Why did he pull a gun? Was he driving the same car the second time?

Handwritten on the bottom of the report was the name "Mathis."

Roy Whang, a private investigator of Chinese ancestry, had offered to help. Dick Arena would decide that he had done all he could do. Mike Edwards would take a full-time job, which would separate our efforts. Jack Perry had always done his thing, and I hadn't seen Bill Taylor since the earliest days.

Jeff Prugh always kids me about my role in so many facets of these cases by asking: "Who *is* that masked man?" But I was seriously beginning to feel like the Lone Ranger. However, there was no Tonto—and Silver was getting barely 8 miles to the gallon. I could use all the help I could get.

Roy Whang leaped at the opportunity to seek out Willie Turner. No phone number for Turner was taken by the police. But there was an address. Whang went to the address, which was very close to slain Yusuf Bell's home in the McDaniel-Glenn area. It turned out to be the home of Willie Turner's father. Willie himself didn't live there. The elder Turner was not cooperative, but Whang managed to extract Willie's address from him.

Willie Turner told Whang that the boy he had seen was 10-year-old Jefferey Mathis, who still was missing after going on the errand to buy cigarettes. "I kept tryin' to tell them [the police] that," he added. "I recognized the boy from a picture in the paper, and that's why I called the police in the first place."

The police non-response didn't surprise me. Earlier, in the Mathis case, I read a police officer's report, in which she wrote that she had gone to a certain address, looking for a boy nicknamed "Rockhead." But when she got there, an unidentified male (she didn't know what "Rockhead" looked like) answered the door and told her that "'Rockhead' is asleep in the bed and can't come to the door." The officer left. End of search for "Rockhead," who subsequently disappeared, we think, to Alabama.

The bookstore that Willie Turner said he told the police about was the one catercornered from the Stewart-Lakewood Shopping Center. Victims Lubie Geter and Charles Stephens had frequented the shopping center. It was, in fact, where Geter was last seen alive. Turner could not remember the exact location of the old building, but he thought it was on Campbellton Road (Georgia 166). The building, he said, formerly had something to do with recordings. The name of the business had started with an "O."

Turner's explanation about the gun made the least plausible part of his story at least acceptable, if not believable. Turner was wearing his security guard uniform, and the man had been up to no good inside the building. Turner did not think that the man recognized him from the previous incident. But Turner recognized the man and the car. Yes, it was the same blue Nova.

The police might have been interested in that blue car. They already had eyewitness reports that Jefferey Mathis had gotten into a blue car. They had found one witness who said that one of the two occupants of that car could have been a white man. Now, they had another witness who said he saw Jefferey Mathis in this blue Nova.

Willie Turner told Roy Whang that in the six months that had elapsed since he gave this statement to police, no one had contacted him to ask him any questions until Whang showed up. Again, in Atlanta's Task Force murder investigations, an all-too-familiar refrain was "No one asked."

I gave these details to Gail Epstein. The *Atlanta Constitution* didn't run a news story, but it later ran an editorial based on them. The editorial decried the fact that there had been no followup on Willie Turner's story in more than six months—and when there was, it was by a private detective. When the editorial attacked this police screwup, I winced because the editorial writer got parts of the story "bass-ackwards."

It would be many months before Mike Edwards would tell me that he thought he had located the building on Campbellton Road that Willie Turner had spoken of. It sat across the street from a two-story brick office structure that used to house a police precinct and the broadcasting operations of Wayne Williams. We didn't know that then.

Williams, of course, is black. The man Willie Turner said he saw was white. It made me recall the answer I had given so often when asked to conjecture on the race of the killer or killers. "It's as likely to be a black *and* a white," I said, "as it is a black *or* a white."

Lubie Geter and his buddy got into an argument. Lubie refused to share his remaining air fresheners. He wanted to make the money himself. Lubie climbed out of the car in front of the Big Star food market in the Stewart-Lakewood Shopping Center. The other two headed back toward the East Lake Meadows housing project.

Keep in mind that the jury at the trial of Wayne Williams never would be told what you're reading now. If the reports of some eyewitnesses who were never called to testify are accurate, Lubie Geter got into and out of several vehicles that day. First, it was a red pickup truck, then a white one and finally a white-and-black Oldsmobile Cutlass. What were the purposes of Lubie's side trips?

During December of 1980 and January of 1981, the FBI had been receiving anonymous telephone calls from someone identifying himself as the killer. These calls had been traced to Stewart Avenue pay phones in the vicinity of the Stewart-Lakewood Shopping Center.

It was about this same time that another boy said two black men in a blue car picked him up across the street from the Stewart-Lakewood Shopping Center. His testimony would change drastically at the Wayne Williams trial. The boy knew Geter and he knew Terry Pue. He was a student at the Challenge School for Boys. We began to call him the "X" kid, to protect his identity. He might have been the only potential victim to escape from the killer(s). He said there were two black men in the car.

Brandon Southern had been director of the Challenge School for Boys from the time it had been situated just around the corner from Jefferey Mathis' house. As a friend of the Mathis family, he had known Jefferey since the boy was 1 year old. Back then, a young boy named Michael McIntosh attended the Challenge School. Brandon Southern would also tell of another young black who visited with Terry Pue and others at the Challenge School. His name: Lee Gooch.

The X kid and another youngster from the Challenge School would attend at least one of The List victims' funerals. On the way home from the funeral, a car pulled alongside them and stopped. The driver made them an offer. It was one they didn't refuse. The man making the offer had played the organ at the funeral.

The two boys went to an apartment in Cobb County, west of Atlanta, near the Six Flags Over Georgia amusement park. There, they met three adults. One of those adults was a transvestite, light-skinned and red-haired. When Lee Gooch would disappear, he would say that a light-skinned black man with red hair was involved in the Atlanta murders. In fact, he said the man was "in my neighborhood."

Officials took a deep interest in the apartment. An albino or an extremely light-skinned black might provide an alternative explanation for the increasingly numerous reports of attempted kidnappings and suspicious appearances with young black boys by a black and a white, who were often said to be with a red-haired woman.

The police made a deal. They didn't make an arrest of the adult who took the boys there. Instead, they subverted him into an informant.

Their interest also heightened when their informant told them that the transvestite had suddenly disappeared. This explains yet another incident: a "transvestite" was found dead of an apparent overdose in Cobb County. Which prompted a mass mobilization of the Task Force and other units working the "children's" cases.

January, 1981

Morris Redding, the Task Force commander, was incensed that word of the disappearance of Lubie Geter had not been sent immediately to the Task Force. But Lee Brown, the public safety commissioner, said publicly that the correct procedures had been followed in the Geter case.

A few days later, however, Brown approved disciplinary actions taken against Atlanta police detectives Carolyn O'Neal and Thetis Sturgis for allegedly mishandling the Geter case.

O'Neal and Sturgis didn't take this attempted scapegoating lying down. Through their attorneys, they passed the buck upward toward Captain Johnny Sparks, who headed the Atlanta police Crimes Against Persons unit. Both detectives were proved correct, but neither was put back to work on the "children's" cases.

Lubie Geter's disappearance was another of those intriguing cases in which a child who lived on one street of my route disappeared from another street on the route, miles from the first, and would be found on another street on the route, many miles from the other two streets. Lubie's house at Dahlgren Street and Memorial Drive was at least 10 miles from where he disappeared at the Stewart-Lakewood Shopping Center, Georgia 166.

Two days after Lubie Geter vanished in January of 1981, another Atlanta youngster was reported missing: 15-year-old Lee Manuel Gooch of 4205 Cape Street in southwest Atlanta.

Nothing to worry about, the Atlanta police said. This was another "runaway." That line was getting threadbare. Actually, there were several things to worry about. First, Gooch fit all the official criteria. Second, he fit the geographic criteria. He lived next door to 14-year-old victim Edward Hope (Teddy) Smith. How close can you get? Third, I knew that Gooch knew several other victims on The List, including 16-year-old Patrick (Pat Man) Rogers.

I put Gooch in the same category with Pat Man. Pat Man, the authorities said, was running from a burglary warrant. Gooch, they said, was fleeing a stolen-car charge. I thought they might be fleeing a *killer*, and I knew that Pat Man had already lost his battle.

Now I was worried for Lee Gooch, and the police were repeating their pattern of mistakes. Wouldn't it be better to put Gooch *on* The List and be wrong?

In the shadow of the skyscrapers of Five Points in downtown Atlanta is the building which houses both the *Atlanta Constitution* and the *Atlanta Journal.* The building dominates Spring Street on its rear side, although its front is just another facade on Marietta Street.

Where northbound Spring Street meets the Omni hotel-shopping-office-sports arena complex, it takes a sweeping curve to the west. You feel that you are going to smash into the newspaper building as you head straight for a beige wall with each paper's masthead emblazoned in large metal letters. Across the street is the Omni Sports Arena, home of the Atlanta Hawks professional basketball team.

South of the newspaper building and east of the Omni is the newspapers' parking lot, where stray pages of newsprint have blown against the chain-link fence.

A thief now stole one of the newspapers' white Pintos. In two quick turns, he was at the Omni. He offered a ride to several kids, including a neighbor whom he saw standing on the corner. The neighbor said the driver was Lee Gooch. He also said he turned down Gooch's offer of a ride home.

Whoever rode with Lee Gooch that night made it home without incident. The stolen car was hidden, where it was available for quick retrieval and future use.

The next night, Lee Gooch ventured out in the stolen car again. This time, unfortunately for Lee, he was a passenger in the back seat. When the police chased down the car on Brown's Mill Road, near the home of still-missing 11-year-old Earl Lee Terrell, Lee Gooch couldn't get out quickly enough to escape. He was locked up on charges of auto theft.

As soon as Lee Gooch was released from custody, with a trial date still pending, he was gone again. A child? Yes, at least chronologically. From Atlanta? Yes. Missing? Yes. One of Atlanta's missing or murdered children? No! Not according to the media reports. His name was not on The List. Lee Gooch, they said, was being seen at the downtown Atlanta bus station.

On that fatal October morning, unheated water hit the super-heated chamber of the boiler at the day-care center. Until that day, the political aspects of the murder cases had been handled as deftly as any ever have been. Atlanta had been plunged into a cauldron of troubled waters, but its mayor so far had averted getting singed.

Few people understand the role of a public safety commissioner or director. Like any other job, it becomes what its occupant makes of it—or at least what his boss will let him make of it. It is unusual for a public safety commissioner to take as active a role in policing as Atlanta's have done. But then, Atlanta in effect has had no chief of police, a eunuched chief of police or a weak chief of police since it adopted the public safety department concept in 1974. That may change now with the elevation of Morris Redding to chief of police.

Organizationally, the position of public safety commissioner exists only for one reason—to insulate the mayor (or chief executive officer, if elected) from the day-to-day political booby traps of operating a service that deals with people's (voters') lives and freedom. When viewed from this perspective, Lee P. Brown did a masterful job.

In January of 1981, a third party arranged a meeting between Brown and me. I told him, "I wouldn't have been able to quietly take the political flak for all the killings like you have." I couldn't understand why Brown was assuming responsibility for all the cases on The List when, by my count, just one more than 50% were city of Atlanta cases.

When the mother of Patrick (Pat Man) Rogers stood in the audience at the taping of the Phil Donahue show and demanded that Brown tell her why her son wasn't on The List, I would have had to say, "You'll have to ask Bob Hightower [the Cobb County public safety director] that question, ma'am. Your son's case is a Cobb County case."

I told Brown that, and then I added, "Commissioner, that boy belongs on The List!"

I also told Brown that the handling of the case of (then-missing) 15-year-old Lee Gooch was a political—and tactical—mistake. Brown had asked for my opinions, so I was giving them to him.

Lee Gooch had been missing for more than three weeks when I met with Brown. Yet news reports repeated the refrain that he "was not one of Atlanta's missing or murdered children."

The police and the *Atlanta Constitution* would insist that he was being seen regularly at the downtown bus terminal. I told the commissioner that I didn't think Gooch was there, but if he was, it looked awfully bad that more than 1,300 Atlanta police couldn't catch him and take him home. After all, Atlanta's "missing and murdered children" were the first priority, weren't they?

I could understand Lee Brown's reluctance to place Gooch's case on The List. But The List meant something different to Brown than it did to the news media and the public. Brown had tried often enough to explain the difference, but his explanation never stuck. I thought it was time for Brown to tailor his use of The List to the public's expectations. He could do so without changing the Task Force operation one iota. Gooch's disappearance offered the perfect opportunity.

If, as Brown thought, Lee Gooch was a runaway and could easily be located, why not put his name on The List and bring him home? It would be the Task Force's first *victory* in 18 months of failures!

From a political standpoint, there were two flaws in leaving runaways off The List. First, it precluded success. If you count only the ones you think you aren't able to win, you won't win many. Second, assigning a runaway to The List would avert the embarrassment of being forced to do so when the "runaway" is found dead, as several were.

But if Lee Brown would put Gooch on The List and then really make it a priority to find Gooch, maybe Brown could bring him back alive. If he didn't think he needed a victory—although I'm sure he did—I could assure him that the people of Atlanta needed one.

Brown listened quietly as I went through the rest of the myriad connections the map had uncovered for me. When I finished, I knew that Brown felt I had wasted his time. I knew I had wasted mine.

I left feeling more frustrated than ever, but with one determination. If Lee Gooch was findable, I, by God, would find him.

Lubie (Chuck) Geter had been missing for six days and Lee Gooch four days when the news media reported a gruesome discovery on Redwine Road on the southwest corner of my map. Two more bodies had been found.

My telephone rang that evening. Someone on the city desk of the *Atlanta Constitution* asked: "What is your guess as to who the bodies are?" The map said one body should be that of 11-year-old Christopher Richardson or 10-year-old Darron Glass, but not both. I was unsure about who the other might be. I told the newsman that it should be Richardson or Glass, perhaps both—but I didn't think so.

The discoveries dominated newscasts on Friday night, January 9, 1981. The following Sunday morning, Ken Englade of the *Florida Times-Union* and I drove to the scene on Redwine Road. To our amazement, there was no security. There was no police car or, for that matter, no other person in sight.

On Saturday morning, January 10, a furor had erupted. Fulton County Medical Examiner Dr. Robert Stivers threatened to file charges against federal, state and local law-enforcement officers for disturbing the skeletal remains found in the woods off Redwine Road. Stivers' statements speak for themselves as to his opinion of how police handled this crime scene:

> "They broke the law yesterday. They disturbed the crime scene without permission of the medical examiner's office . . . We are very angry . . .
> "When he [Sergeant J. E. Hendrix, investigator from the medical examiner's office] arrived, there was an FBI agent and [technicians from] the state crime lab plowing around in the ground and they had completely disturbed the scene."

Newspaper accounts said that 250 uniformed Atlanta policemen, GBI and FBI agents and East Point police had conducted a shoulder-to-shoulder search on Saturday, January 10. But on Sunday, officials from the medical examiner's office returned to the scene. Stivers obviously wasn't happy. He told reporters:

> "Dr. [Saleh] Zaki [assistant Fulton County medical examiner] was at the scene . . and true to my own predictions, they found 11 more teeth and some more bones and a sternum important to the case. So those idiots really did mess us up . . . In one skeleton, we've only got about four teeth in one of those skulls, and who knows if some nut picked up the skull and shook it? We're having a real problem with identification and that could be why."

On Tuesday, January 13, 1981, one set of remains found on Redwine Road was identified as those of Christopher Richardson. It would be the following Saturday before the other remains were assigned to Earl Lee Terrell. Both victims were 11.

Some sources at the *Atlanta Constitution* told me that the medical examiners couldn't make up their minds as to whether the second victim was Terrell or Darron Glass. Logic would dictate, then, that they didn't have the slightest idea who it was. Terrell and Glass didn't look anything alike.

When I heard about the Terrell examination, these same sources at the *Constitution* told me that five pathologists had "voted" on the identification, and the results were "Terrell 3, Glass 2"! Still another phenomenal *positive* identification had been made by medical "science." Soon the *Constitution* would run a feature story telling of the outstanding job done by the local medical examiners in victim identification. It was as if someone unaccountably were trying to *force* a balance in the news coverage.

January's bad news surged on relentlessly. Faye Yearby, 22, turned up dead. So did Terry Pue, 15; and now Richardson and "Terrell." Lee Gooch still was missing when February dawned, and no relief was in sight. Two more bodies would be found on Friday the 13th, and two more children would disappear and die before March.

I heard murmurs among people who should know better that there now was a "pattern" of bodies discovered on Fridays. Although I tried to convince them that finding the bodies was a function of the investigation, not the perpetration, they insisted on trying to make something of this new "pattern." I ranked this theory well behind the then-extinct 3½-week cycle.

February, 1981

Against this backdrop of dreary news, the police took a lackadaisical approach to the disappearance of 15-year-old Lee Gooch. Gail Epstein called me one evening and read her story for the next morning's edition of the *Atlanta Constitution*. She would report that Lee Gooch had been seen at the bus station again.

"Aw, come on, Gail, don't run that bullshit," I whined. I had heard it too many times. After all, 1,350 police officers should be able to find one kid at one bus station and take him home.

"But this is the real thing," Gail protested. "This time it was his older brother who spotted him."

"I don't give a damn if your source is Superman!" I said. "I don't believe it! If I were 20 years old and was talking to my 15-year-old brother who'd been missing from home for weeks and he refused to come home, I'd pick his ass up and carry him home!" Gail went ahead with the story.

I telephoned Kaleeka Rogers of WSB radio. I knew she had a good rapport with Lee Gooch's family. I asked her if she could arrange for me to visit Lee's parents. She set up a meeting with them for Sunday morning, February 8.

Dick Arena and I climbed into my wife's red Camaro and headed across town to meet Kaleeka at the International House of Pancakes on Campbellton Road. After breakfast, the three of us set out on step No. 1 toward finding Lee Gooch.

Geraldine Gooch, Lee's mother, greeted us in the front door of their two-story apartment. My first question to her was aimed at confirming that Lee had known his slain next-door neighbor, 14-year-old Edward Hope (Teddy) Smith, victim No. 1 on The List and one of the two bodies dressed in black and found along Niskey Lake Road back in the summer of 1979.

"Yes, Lee knew Teddy," Geraldine Gooch said. "They were friends."

Then I asked about those published reports that her older son had seen Lee at the bus station. "I don't know why he told all that stuff," Geraldine Gooch began. "He didn't know that. He wasn't even at the bus station that day. He was at work 'cross town. I asked him why he said it, and he said, 'Mama, I don't know.'" So much for the "news" that Lee Gooch was at the bus station.

Eugene Gooch, Lee's father, sauntered in from the street. An uncle of Lee Gooch joined us from upstairs, as did a teen-age friend of Lee from the street. The tiny front room filled up with others who joined our circle around the coffee table.

The teen-age friend turned out to be a neighbor named David Green. It was David who had recounted how Lee Gooch had offered him a ride home from the Omni in the stolen *Atlanta Journal-Constitution* car.

David wouldn't tell us more. But I was convinced he knew more, perhaps a lot more. Dick Arena questioned him hard. We pleaded with him to tell us more—for Lee's safety. David stood, shifting nervously from foot to foot, eyes riveted to the floor, lips sealed and shrugging off any further comment.

The police had said that Lee Gooch had run away on other occasions. "Where did Lee go the other times he ran away?" I asked.

Lee's mother shook her head. "He wasn't a runaway," she said. "He always went to his grandmother's house when he didn't want to be here."

That grandmother's house, it turned out, was across the street from where 9-year-old Yusuf Bell lived before he ran the errand to buy snuff and then turned up dead in November of 1979. So Lee Gooch probably knew Yusuf Bell, too, I thought, and he was no stranger to McDaniel-Glenn and Cap'n Peg's.

I asked if anything unusual had happened since Lee disappeared.

"Like what?" Eugene Gooch asked.

"Well, have you had any unusual phone calls?"

"Not that I remember."

"Has anybody come looking for Lee?"

"Well, the police was here yesterday again, and the newspaper people and the television people have been here. And David here, he's been by about every day. Then there was this man came knockin' on the door one night for Lee. But, er, no, that was 'fore Lee disappeared."

I was intrigued by the stranger in the night. "Tell me about the man," I said.

Eugene Gooch told of a black male in his early 20s. The young man, he said, came to the door and asked for Lee on the night the car was stolen. The man said Lee had his keys. Eugene Gooch woke up Lee and asked him about the keys. Lee came downstairs, rubbing sleep from his eyes, and told the man that David had his keys. The man left, and Eugene Gooch never saw him again.

My God, could he have been *The* Man?

David Green still wouldn't cooperate. The three of us continued to pepper the family with questions about the night caller, but we elicited no further information.

I started to make overtures to leave. Somebody had to question David Green further about the man whose keys he had, but it was obvious that he wasn't going to talk to us. Not today, anyway.

I also was satisfied that Lee Gooch was not hanging around the bus station. The Atlanta Falcons were playing football on television that afternoon and, as was my custom in those pre-NFLPA strike days, I was anxious to return home to watch the game. Then I would figure out how else I would try to find Lee Gooch.

But first, I asked one more basic question: "Have you received any unusual mail?"

My question was answered by another question. "Do you think we ought to show him the slips?" Eugene Gooch asked Geraldine.

"Yeah," she replied, "go on and show him the slips."

Eugene disappeared into another room and returned carrying an envelope. He removed what appeared to be several pink slips of paper, each about 4 by 8 inches. He fumbled with them, trying clumsily to stack them in some order that suited him. Finally, in his frustration, he stuffed them back into the envelope and shoved it at me.

The envelope carried the seal and return address of Leon County in Florida. It was addressed to "Mr. Lee M. Kimball" at the Gooch residence on Cape Street. I pulled the papers from the envelope. My jaw dropped.

I handed them to Dick. He would immediately recognize what they meant.

The envelope contained nine slips of paper, each printed by computers and each representing a separate traffic-violation delinquency (failure to appear in court) for offenses committed in Tallahassee, Florida, on January 14, 1981. Each sheet carried the name of the violator as "Lee M. Kimball, 19, of 4205 Cape Street, Atlanta, Georgia."

"Who is Kimball?" I asked excitedly.

"That's my maiden name," Geraldine Gooch replied.

Well, it was clear that Lee Gooch—or someone using his identifying information—had had a run-in with the law in Tallahassee, nine days after Lee Gooch was reported missing and during the time he was being "seen" at the Atlanta bus station.

Because the age shown was 19, I first thought that it might be a murderer.

"Did you show these to the police when they were here yesterday?" I asked.

"No. They didn't ask."

Dick Arena and I explained the situation to Kaleeka. I asked Mrs. Gooch if I could use her phone to call the FBI. Kaleeka interrupted, saying that she "owed it to George Napper [Atlanta's police chief] to call him."

"That's fine with me," I said, "but I'm still going to call the FBI. It's an interstate situation, anyway."

The receptionist at the FBI field office in Atlanta took a few minutes to locate an agent. When the agent came to the phone, I told him who I was and that we had something that he needed to look at right away. He took the address, and I gave him some time-saving directions. He said he would be "right out."

Kaleeka called Chief Napper. He was at church and would return her call, someone said. He never did.

Meanwhile, in less than 45 minutes, there was a knock on the door. Two youthful white males stood there in sweatshirts, running shoes and blue jeans. They identified themselves as FBI agents "Smith" and "Jones" (honest!).

We turned over the information to the agents, and they carefully recorded it. The agents said they would contact Tallahassee and would call me. Dick, Kaleeka and I left.

The football game had just ended when the phone rang. It was one of the FBI agents. He had good news and bad news. The good news was that they had received a telephoto of the person involved in Tallahassee. It was Lee Manuel Gooch. He had been in the Tallahassee jail since January 14!

The bad news was that the authorities in Florida had released him "yesterday," February 7. Lee Gooch had been involved in a wild chase while driving a Chevrolet that had been reported stolen in Tennessee. I couldn't understand the screwups in Florida. Nor could the FBI agent.

Why was Gooch not taken to court from his cell in the Leon County Jail?

Why was Gooch, who Florida authorities thought was an adult, not forced to make bond before being released? Had they forgotten to charge him with the most serious of the violations he was involved in—the felony of car theft?

Why was a felon released from jail without verifying his identification?

This was our criminal-justice system, creaking along as always—this time in Florida.

By Monday, February 9, Gooch was back in custody in Tallahassee after he had unexpectedly returned to "get my car." He met with reporters in Tallahassee and was quoted as saying, "A man in my neighborhood snatched some kids in December. It's a kidnapping deal. There's a lady in the neighborhood who knows who he is, but she's scared to tell."

It all should have been quite interesting to the Atlanta authorities; but if it was, they betrayed little interest publicly. In fact, a psychology professor at Florida A&M University wrote a letter to a mutual friend. In the letter, the professor said: "Atlanta authorities called the Leon County people and told them not to pay any attention to anything that Lee Gooch has to say."

The professor was contacted because some of her charges had interviewed Gooch. "He's just a runaway," the professor quoted Atlanta officials as saying, "and he should be treated as just that."

This unbelievable level of disinterest in the possible Lee Gooch connections was best expressed by Roger Harris, assistant information officer for the Atlanta Department of Public Safety. "We won't disregard his story," Harris was quoted in one Florida newspaper, "but I don't know if he'll be questioned. I kind of doubt it, though." (None of the Lee Gooch interviews was covered in the Atlanta papers.)

Can you believe that? These were the infamous Atlanta murder cases, in which our public officials had insisted repeatedly that "no stone is being left unturned." And now they doubted if they would question Lee Gooch! And the media would ignore his claims of knowledge about some of the Atlanta murders.

Here was a kid they were going "all out to find"—even though he hadn't made The List. Yet, he spent three weeks in jail in Tallahassee, Florida— and that's not Tallahassee, Switzerland, but the next capital city south of Georgia. But if Atlanta officials hadn't been able to find a missing girl in the Fulton County Jail in Atlanta, how could we expect them to find a missing boy in a Florida jail?

Soon another Atlanta youth was missing. Lee Brown said he hoped that the Atlanta police would have the same good fortune in locating him as they had in finding Lee Gooch.

"Jee-zus Christ!" I screamed, seething. If Lee Brown and the Atlanta police were to have the same good fortune as they did in the Lee Gooch case, it would mean that I would have to go look for the kid.

I found Lee Gooch!

16

The Suspect Was NOT Wayne Williams

February, 1981

On February 5, 1981, the badly decomposed body of 14-year-old Lubie (Chuck) Geter was found in the woods close to Enon Road at Vandiver. The scene was about as far south of Georgia 166 as the 1700 block of Niskey Lake Road is north.

The geographic pattern continued to hold. Just as the discovery of slain 15-year-old Terry Pue had pushed the Memorial Drive corridor farther east of Atlanta, the finding of Lubie Geter simply pushed the Georgia 166 corridor farther to the west. Pat Man's finding in the Chattahoochee River—to the northwest—still seemed to be the only anomaly.

The Fulton County police had observed a car that aroused their suspicions. The driver was James Comento, but the tag was registered to Metro News Productions at 1817 Penelope Road, N.W., in Atlanta. The Fulton County police went to that address one January night in 1981. There, they spoke with a young man named Wayne Williams. He told them that Comento was using the car legitimately. The police seemed satisfied.

Apparently the Fulton County police, who had their first Task Force case with the death of Lubie Geter, didn't give the Task Force the information from their visit to Wayne Williams. If they did, then the Task Force ignored it. This would keep its record intact. Until he was arrested, not one item concerning Wayne Williams, his home, his cars or any other possible connection with the murders could be found in the Task Force's multimillion-dollar computer operation, which is still praised in published reports for its "value in solving the cases." What value?

It wasn't the first time that the names of Comento and Williams had been linked. Nor would it be the last. Homer Williams, Wayne's father, and Jim Comento had visited the home of Willie Mae Mathis, mother of then-missing Jefferey Mathis, in the summer of 1980.

This was shortly after Willie Mae's nephew had drowned in an inner-city swimming pool. Comento was a paramedic; he was trying in vain to get the city of Atlanta to permit him to use a police radio in his vehicle, a privilege theretofore extended to Walter Kaplan, a local jurist who is credited with saving many lives.

Comento thought that Mrs. Mathis' familiarity with the problems surrounding the responses to her nephew's drowning—and her prominence as the mother of one of the "missing children"—might combine to help him win the permit.

Homer Williams' motivation is not so clear. Perhaps the Williamses intended to use the radio, too. It might help in their news-gathering operation. Wayne Williams still occasionally shot video footage, trying to sell it to TV stations.

Months later—after his conviction—I would discuss alibis with Williams again. He would insist that the Fulton County police had him under surveillance from Lubie Geter's disappearance—through the finding of Terry Pue—during most of the first three weeks of 1981. I would ask him how he knew that, and he would tell me that Louis Graham (assistant chief of the Fulton County police department) "told my lawyer that."

I knew that Graham thought Williams was innocent, and still does. But I didn't think Williams' claim held water. Louis Graham's reason for his position on Williams' innocence was not based on an exonerating, full-time surveillance of Wayne Williams. Graham would deny that Williams was ever under surveillance by the Fulton County police, but he did confirm the questioning of Williams about Comento and the car.

A man was walking his dog, looking, he said, for "illegal rabbit traps." Soon the dog came back to him, its mouth containing something suspicious. It led the man to the remains of Lubie (Chuck) Geter.

Geter had been stripped of everything but his undershorts. The rest of his clothes were found one-quarter of a mile away. This led me to think that the murders in many of these cases occurred close to the places where the bodies were found. At least, it would make as much sense as the prosecution's yet-to-be-proved suggestions to the jury that all the victims whose deaths are associated with Wayne Williams were killed in Williams' house.

Wayne Williams would tell me that he could prove that one of the children was not murdered in his house.

"Which one?" I asked.

"Clifford Jones," he replied. He would say that on the night that 13-year-old Clifford Jones was found strangled (Jones had been missing for only 12½ hours) in August of 1980, the Williamses' house was "full of relatives from out of town and they occupied every room."

I would tell Wayne Williams that I thought the state did a superb job of supporting his contention that none of the children—or adults, for that matter—was killed at his house. Reason: despite exhaustive searches, not one actual fiber, fingerprint or anything else from any of the victims had been found in Williams' house. In fact, police and technicians would remove only *sample* fibers—not *suspect* fibers—and the FBI fiber expert would say only that the fibers found on victims *"could have"* come from Williams' home or cars.

In the Clifford Jones case, I didn't need anyone to prove to me that Wayne Williams didn't kill him, let alone in Williams' house. Clifford Jones had disappeared on the afternoon of August 20, 1980, one month after the Task Force had been formed.

Initial reports stated that Clifford was in his neighborhood, looking for discarded aluminum cans when he disappeared. But the police didn't find the bag of cans under the porch of the house where Clifford stayed with relatives until the next day, August 21—hours after he turned up dead. Their "no-stones-unturned" investigation the day before had failed to turn up the cans.

Al Starkes of CORE would tell me that Clifford Jones' siblings had seen Clifford go into the laundromat at the Hollywood Plaza Shopping Center in northwest Atlanta.

There, a black man killed Clifford, according to a 19-year-old boy who told authorities in 1980 that he witnessed the killing. The man, he said, strangled the child with a yellow rope around his neck. Clifford Jones was one of the few victims on The List known to be strangled with a rope.

In the meantime, the witness went on, the man and two other men had fondled the youngster's penis. He said the boy was crying when they removed his clothes. "They messed with the boy's behind, chest and legs," the eyewitness added.

Then, he said, the suspect and another man "got him in the butt... He was hollering real loud, saying he wanted to go home. [The suspect] put a rope around his neck and pulled it. [The suspect] and [the other man] said, 'He's dead.'"

From there, the eyewitness said, the suspect washed the body with soap and a rag, then reclothed it. Clifford Jones, though clothed when found, was missing some of the articles of clothing he had worn when he disappeared.

At least one Atlanta police officer wanted to arrest the suspect. But he was overruled by superiors. They chose not to accept the 19-year-old boy's eyewitness story, explaining that he is retarded.

(However, the fact that a teen-age eyewitness, Walter Mitchell, was said to be retarded didn't stop authorities from arresting James Charles Gates as the suspect in the hit-and-run murder of 16-year-old Angela [Gypsy] Bacon and successfully obtaining an indictment of Gates, based on Mitchell's eyewitness testimony.)

But others who would talk of the strangulation murder of Clifford Jones were not said to be mentally difficient in any way.

One of the men that the boy said had "messed" with the victim confirmed that he was inside the laundromat on August 20, drinking beer. Others were there, too, he said. But then he left, the man said, leaving two other men inside with an "unknown young black male, about 13 or 14."

The man said that they went to the suspect's residence, taking the boy with them. He added that two other neighborhood boys were there—one about 14 or 15, the other about 16. (One boy who lived in the same neighborhood—15-year-old Terry Pue—was yet to become a victim.) The man went on to say that the suspect likes young boys. He also described a hooded robe belonging to the suspect.

The murder suspect himself told investigators that around 4:30 p.m., a little boy came into the laundromat and asked for a job picking up trash and sweeping. He said the boy stayed until about 8:30 p.m.

Still another man would tell of spending a night with the same suspect. He had met the suspect, he said, at the Silver Dollar lounge—across from the downtown Atlanta bus depot—in July of 1980. Together, he said, they went to the suspect's residence and engaged in sex together.

The same man said he met another man at the Silver Dollar lounge in November of 1980. That man, he said, was in his late 20s and named "Nate" (Nathaniel) Cater (another murder victim-to-be), who he said sold "bum" reefer and had sex with men for money. Another of the man's acquaintances was 23-year-old Michael McIntosh (still another victim-to-be), whom he met around the corner from the Silver Dollar—at the Cameo Lounge.

In the muggy darkness after Clifford Jones disappeared, a man who lived in one of the small houses behind the shopping center said he saw a man emerge from the residence of the suspect. The man he saw was carrying a large object, cradled in his arms. The object was wrapped in plastic. The man laid, or rolled, the object on the ground next to a trash dumpster, the witness said, adding that the man wore a loose-fitting hooded robe like the one described as belonging to the suspect.

Two other eyewitnesses confirmed the man's account of someone leaving the plastic-wrapped object by the dumpster. All these eyewitnesses said they know the suspect. One said she wondered why the suspect was carrying trash to this dumpster when, in fact, he passed another.

The suspect then went to a phone booth and made a call, eyewitnesses said. A short time later, in the predawn hours of August 21, the Atlanta police—

responding to an anonymous telephone call—found Clifford Jones' body by the dumpster, wrapped in plastic.

A teen-age girl—speaking of the witness who told police he was at the laundromat drinking beer when the boy came in—described an incident that occurred the morning after the boy's body was found. She said the same witness asked, "Was he wrapped in plastic?"

Whereupon the girl's grandmother asked a logical question: "How would *he* know?"

When the 19-year-old eyewitness was called back for questioning, he told authorities that the boy was originally outside the laundromat, picking up bottles, and that the suspect took him inside and offered him money not to tell anyone of the sexual molestation.

Amazingly, in spite of these vivid details given them by eyewitnesses, the Atlanta police decided privately that there was not enough evidence to charge the suspect with the strangulation of Clifford Jones. They would go on to tell the public, month after month, when Atlanta's killings intensified in late 1980 and early 1981, that they had absolutely no suspects, leads or clues in *any* of the cases when, in fact, they had at least *five eyewitnesses* in the Clifford Jones case—a case that had *made* The List!

To be sure, the evidence provided by these eyewitnesses is stronger than the sum of that which would be presented in the trial of Wayne Williams, whom nobody saw kill anyone.

The suspect in the murder of Clifford Jones was in his late 20s. He would be sentenced on other charges in March of 1981, the month when the last child under 17 would disappear during the height of Atlanta's murders. The charges—one count of aggravated assault with intent to rape, and one count of aggravated sodomy—would be brought by a mother who complained that her young son had received sexual advances from the suspect.

The suspect would serve 10 months in the Fulton County Jail (part of them concurrently with Wayne Williams) and would be released during the Williams trial.

The jury at the trial of Wayne Williams never would hear any of these eyewitnesses' accounts and details surrounding the murder of Clifford Jones back in August of 1980, even though the judge, the prosecutor and the defense attorney were fully aware of this evidence.

All of which points up yet another weakness in America's criminal-justice system. In the murder of Clifford Jones, an administrative decision by the Atlanta police decided that the evidence wasn't strong enough to bring charges against the suspect. This, in turn, prevented a jury from seeing or hearing the evidence. Something is wrong with a system that allows the police, wittingly or unwittingly, to decide what a jury should and shouldn't see or hear.

But discretion is upside down in the criminal-justice system. Judges and prosecutors are supposedly bound by iron-clad "rules" that decree that juries cannot be given "irrelevant" material. But these rules do nothing to prevent jurors from being given incorrect or fallacious material. Often the truth is barred by a technicality, while conjecture is allowed in torrents.

Policemen, on the other hand, make life-and-death and freedom decisions on the spot. A policeman must decide to arrest before any of the fancy rules takes over. So the police decision not to arrest the suspect in the Clifford Jones case inadvertently kept the jury from hearing a more plausible explanation for Jones' death than any that could be told about Wayne Williams. But Williams wasn't charged or tried in the Jones case. It was another of those "cleared by arrest" situations.

The Jones case was not one of the 10 so-called "pattern" cases introduced in Williams' trial for the murders only of Jimmy Ray Payne and Nathaniel Cater. One reason the Jones case was withheld from the trial of Wayne Williams was to keep the jury from hearing about the other suspect. Since the Jones case was not being considered, the other suspect was deemed "irrelevant." Although the defense tried to introduce it, it was not allowed to. Irrelevant? Hell, this may have been the most relevant piece of information that could have been brought into the Williams trial.

After the trial, the Clifford Jones murder was attributed by authorities to Williams, based only on "matching fibers."

It would be the state's contention, as stated by state fiber experts and repeated by FBI fiber experts, that the fibers could have only come from contact with Wayne Williams' environment. I totally disagree. But this is the state's contention.

Therefore, if Wayne Williams is guilty of one of the cases with the fiber links, he must, according to the "proof" submitted by the state, be guilty of *all* the cases with fiber links. Conversely, *if Wayne Williams is not guilty of one of the cases with a fiber link, then he cannot be proved, according to the testimony of the prosecution's own experts, guilty of any.*

This makes it perfectly clear why the state did not want the evidence in the Clifford Jones case introduced to the jury. Since at least five eyewitnesses could have testified that Williams did not kill Jones, what do you think? No jury had opportunity to decide, so you be the judge. Relevant?

There were real eyewitnesses in this case, not the so-called variety who would appear at the Wayne Williams trial and testify that they had seen Williams with one victim or another, hours, days, weeks, even years, before the victim disappeared and died. If true, such testimony would prove that Wayne Williams lied when he said he had not known any of the victims. But it would not even intimate that he had killed any of them.

In the Clifford Jones case, three witnesses place the victim with the suspect for at least four hours of the 12½ he was missing. The suspect himself admits this is true. Another witness says he saw the suspect kill the boy. Still two more say they saw him dispose of the body.

If Wayne Williams killed Clifford Jones, then he not only has the so-called

Gemini split personality that the prosecution would say he has, but he also has the supernatural power to transfigure himself magically into another man's body and to live simultaneously in that body while living in his own body. The suspect in the Clifford Jones case is *not* Wayne Williams.

Meanwhile, the residence where the real suspect in the Clifford Jones case was seen to carry the body from and place it by a dumpster is only a mile from the bridge where the prosecution in the Wayne Williams trial would contend that the bodies of 27-year-old Nathaniel Cater and 21-year-old Jimmy Ray Payne were thrown into the Chattahoochee River. It is very near the laundromat where one of Jones' siblings saw him enter on the day he died.

As soon as I saw this, I said to myself, "A laundromat—hmm, what a perfect place to find any combination of fibers you could imagine!" The prosecution argued that only one environment could produce the same combination of fibers as those found on the victims. This, it said, was the environment of Wayne Williams. But, how about a place where the environments of many people are collected together, where the fibers from one environment are blended with those of others by filters and traps designed for the very purpose of collecting loose fibers? How about a laundromat?

On the day after 14-year-old Lubie (Chuck) Geter was found dead, 11-year-old Patrick Baltazar walked to the restaurant where his daddy worked. He borrowed some money to play the coin-operated video games at the Omni. It was early in the evening of February 6, 1981.

Patrick Baltazar's proposed visit to the Omni—a futuristic, skylighted complex—would lead some authorities to believe that the Omni figured strongly in Atlanta's murders. It even had the prosecution calling witnesses who thought they saw Williams at the Omni—not with any victims or on the days that any victims disappeared, but simply, at the Omni.

The state even brought a witness to show that Lubie Geter had been to the Omni—not with Williams—not on the day that he disappeared—but simply, at the Omni. These appearances are about as rare as grass on a golf course—and about as relevant to these murders, too, I might add.

Actually, the 435 Foundry Street address where Patrick Baltazar lived sits just beyond the end of a tunnel that extends from the rear of the Omni. The Omni and home were virtually the same place to Patrick Baltazar.

When Parick Baltazar didn't show up at home that Friday night, it wasn't unusual. He was known to stay overnight frequently at various places. Too many people, including some police, jump to the mistaken conclusion that the last place a person is reported missing from—or even on the way to—is the actual place of the disappearance.

So we have only the father's information that Patrick was headed for the Omni to suggest that he disappeared from there. On the other hand, the fact that he didn't arrive home suggests that he never arrived at the Omni, either.

Patrick Baltazar was not the most predictable person. He frequently skipped school and then often went to the home of two of his buddies who lived on the corner of 2nd Avenue and Memorial Drive. While he was there, Patrick had been known to smoke a "toke" or two.

Patrick Baltazar, too, probably had gone somewhere other than where he was thought to be going—perhaps miles away. It made sense for Baltazar to be in the Buford Highway area, northeast of Atlanta, where his body was found. It's where he worked part-time in a restaurant.

Patrick's older brother would fill in for his father at work while the elder Baltazar walked the streets of Atlanta in search of Patrick, a pistol strapped at his side.

Patrick's mother and some of his siblings had moved to New Orleans. Patrick himself had not lived long at 435 Foundry Street, and he didn't stay there often. The house actually is on Haynes Street, but it sits on the corner of Foundry Street. Until a few months before his death, Patrick had lived with his family in more pleasant surroundings—an apartment on Cleveland Avenue in south Atlanta. At the time he lived there, 14-year-old Cynthia (Cinderella) Montgomery was murdered in the motel across the street.

Patrick Baltazar was a tough kid, like Terry Pue and Pat Man before him. He died anyway. A subtle change was taking place in the pattern of the Atlanta "children's" murders. The ages of victims being placed on The List were gradually turning older.

At Bethune School in Atlanta, Patrick's fifth-grade teacher would say that Patrick told her he would do anything for money.

"Anything?" she asked.

"Anything," he repeated.

Patrick had been playing cat-and-mouse with people he thought might be each a killer. He once boasted to friends: "I'm gonna catch him myself and get the reward." One day it might have been a case of the "cat" getting too close, closer than Patrick had bargained for; and on another, he must have joined the "cat," not knowing that it was the killer.

On one occasion, Patrick Baltazar was playing in the front yard of an apartment house near his school. He had a friend in that apartment complex, an older fellow who from time-to-time took a minute to "roughhouse" with Patrick on that same lawn. The man was an ex-convict who, at 21, was considerably older than Baltazar. His name was Jimmy Ray Payne.

On the week before Christmas of 1980, Jimmy Ray Payne had been watching TV in the apartment he shared with his mother and sister. The news of the death of another Atlanta youth screamed at him. "Aww, that's my buddy, Pat Man," he told his sister, referring to 16-year-old Patrick Rogers.

The woman who lived in the apartment in front of where Patrick Baltazar was playing said that a man in a white van was watching him play. When the man started to follow Patrick, she said, Patrick ran.

After she saw Wayne Williams' picture on TV, she would say the man was Wayne Williams. Nobody ever would hear her say that in court because nobody would ever ask her to—despite the fact that she had made the identification of Williams on local television. Although Baltazar would be one of the so-called "pattern" cases introduced at the Wayne Williams trial, no one would testify that he ever saw Williams with Baltazar. Such a witness was available, but not subpoenaed. I cannot understand why not. I can see no difference between the quality of her identification than those who were introduced in other cases.

It amazed me that none of these people came forward *before* they saw Wayne Williams become almost a permanent fixture on their TV screens at home. Yes, I know they didn't know it was Wayne Williams before they saw him on TV. But, in many cases, the people said they had known the victim they had seen Williams with. And certainly the victims' pictures also were widely publicized at the time of their disappearances.

So there was no reason for them not to come forward earlier with the important information that they had seen these victims with someone. This is one reason I simply don't believe they saw what they now think they saw, with a few marked exceptions.

On another occasion, Patrick Baltazar and one of his "runnin' buddies" were destroying furniture they had stolen. A man started after them. Baltazar went to a phone and called the Task Force, saying the "killer" tried to get him. Luckily, it hadn't been true this time—I think. The Task Force quickly snatched another defeat from the jaws of victory by neglecting to respond to Baltazar's call for help. There are recordings of his call, but no excuses for not responding.

On Friday, February 13, during one of the coldest weeks of the winter of 1981, a cleanup man came upon a tennis shoe, then an ankle, then a leg. The autopsy said it was a black male, 5-foot-4 and 120 pounds. The identification: Patrick Baltazar.

The police report and flyers the police distributed stated that Patrick Baltazar stood 5 feet tall and weighed 100 pounds—markedly smaller than what appeared in the autopsy report.

The cause of death in Patrick Baltazar's case was ligature strangulation. Found near the scene was a white rope stained with a gummy black substance. Some of the fibers found in the various other cases also had a black substance adhering to them. But there is no indication in any of the laboratory reports if tests were run to see if the substance was the same on the rope and the other fibers. The rope was—in all cases—the closest thing the police ever found to being a possible murder weapon.

A dental assistant on her way to work that Friday morning had seen a green car. She gave DeKalb County police a description. The driver, she said, was a white male, with shaggy blond hair. She added that the car had been parked alongside the point where Baltazar's body would be found in the afternoon. When she saw the car that morning, the parking lot was almost empty.

Patrick Baltazar's body had been found fairly close to my home—in an office park called Corporate Square, in a predominantly white section of DeKalb County.

The touts were out in force again. "The killer was taunting the police," someone said. For example, one story was told that Dick Hand had criticized the Task Force, so the killer left a body in DeKalb County to embarrass Hand. My friend, Mike Edwards, talked with Dick Hand, and they agreed, yes, that was a definite possibility.

I told Mike they needed brain transplants. But among Mike's theories—which were beginning to digress farther from mine—was that the killer definitely was responding to the news coverage. According to Mike, the body of Terry Pue had been left in Rockdale County for Jack Perry. Now Patrick Baltazar was left in DeKalb County to spite Dick Hand.

"Finding of Baltazar's body in Northeast DeKalb an anomaly," the headline on Gail Epstein's story read. "First body found in DeKalb County." "Won't they ever understand?" I thought. Aaron Wyche had been found in DeKalb County seven months earlier, but he had not yet made The List. And I remembered the unidentified little girl who Dick Hand had told me was found at Columbia Mall in DeKalb County in 1979.

The DeKalb County police handled the Baltazar crime scene with their customary efficiency. The DeKalb technicians picked the site clean, removing whole bushes to the crime lab. The DeKalb County medical examiner, Joseph Burton, went to the scene before the body was removed. Back at the morgue, he would remove an unusual brownish-red fiber along with others from Baltazar's body and/or clothing.

Joseph Burton estimated that Patrick Baltazar had been dead for 72 hours, but the time was open to question. It always is, if you have only the medical examiner's guess as the time of death. The body was partially frozen, with a ligature strangulation mark around the neck.

If Patrick Baltazar had been dead for 72 hours, then he had been alive for 72 hours after he was last reported being seen. Chances are, he was in DeKalb County going about his business, just like Terry Pue had been when he, too, disappeared. But the Task Force's thinking was anchored at the Omni in downtown Atlanta.

Reporters and police still hovered around the Patrick Baltazar scene when the unbelievable news of the finding of yet another black child's body blared from their two-way radios. The second victim found on this Friday the 13th would be identified as that of Jefferey Mathis. But, was it really that of still-missing 10-year-old Darron Glass?

On the morning of that same Friday, February 13, 1981, I had called Agent James Procopio at the FBI's Atlanta field office. On the only two previous meetings I had with the FBI, we seemed to be in closer agreement than I was with any of the local police or Task Force people I had talked with.

The first time I had talked with Procopio, I asked him if the FBI might want to pick up some evidence that Dreenna Andreu, the friend of earwitness-to-murder Kenny Brown, had been holding for months. Neither the Atlanta police nor the DeKalb County police seemed interested in looking at the evidence.

"Where do I know your name from?" Procopio asked.

"Well," I paused, "I'm the director of the regional police training academy in Rome, Georgia."

"Oh, yeah, that's where I know you from."

"No, it isn't," I shot back, "I'm the nut with the map, too." By now, the map had been shown many times on television. Procopio invited me to the FBI office to talk with him and another agent about the route. I was delighted.

When you enter the FBI's outer office in Atlanta, you have to talk to a receptionist on an intercom. She and the other employees work behind a glass security partition. She told me it would be a few minutes. I asked her where the public restrooms were.

"Out the door, down the hall and to your left," came the semi-electronic reply.

"I wonder if these will be safe here?" I said, in jest, sitting my briefcase and maps on the counter. I wouldn't think it so funny the following June, when a gunman who lived in south DeKalb County across the street from victim Eric Middlebrooks' policeman half-brother, Kerry Middlebrooks, would capture the FBI headquarters, take hostages and then be shot to death.

But this would be the second embarrassment for the FBI in the Atlanta cases. The first occurred when, in the winter of 1981, an FBI agent assigned to the Task Force was shot at home and left for dead. Later, it was learned that the would-be assassin had been hired by the agent's wife.

After a few minutes, Agent Procopio greeted me. We went inside to a table located in a suite of offices. Each office was connected to another at both ends, except the first and last. Procopio told me to wait. He went to get his partner.

As the three of us talked, we were joined by a third agent who just happened by. He listened attentively. Then still another agent arrived. Then another and another. Soon I was fielding questions from at least seven FBI agents. All seemed genuinely interested. What a contrast with the Task Force and the Atlanta police.

The agents asked how many of the cases I thought were connected. I told them I thought at least 24 *could* be connected. My count was higher than that of The List, but that didn't seem to bother the FBI agents.

"What are the *fewest* that you think could be connected?" someone asked.

I told them that when I eliminated every case I could for *any* reason—for example, the females, simply because they were females; and one male because he was the only stabbing victim on The List at that time, *et cetera*—I could reduce the minimum of connected cases to 18.

"Seventeen!" blurted a youthful appearing agent standing beside me. "What about Jefferey Mathis? How can you justify his connection?"

"It's simple," I responded. "Besides being the right age, color, sex and so on, he lived here." I pointed to the location on the map where Mathis had lived. "He disappeared here," I continued, pointing to a second location (Jefferey Mathis still was officially missing, 11 months after he disappeared while running an errand for his mother.)

"You're jumping too many streams," the agent said, using jargon from the FBI National Academy, where I had spent a week or two myself.

"I'm not jumping any streams." I countered. "I'm simply representing the facts as they are. It's logic."

"What about the logic of the investigation?" the agent asked.

From what he said, I gathered that the FBI's investigation of the Jefferey Mathis case had turned up something I hadn't heard about. I sighed and thought to myself: "I sure as hell hope they've turned up something I haven't heard about." I knew the Task Force had turned up plenty of nothing. If the FBI had nothing, too, then we were in really deep trouble.

The agents were courteous, curious and keenly interested. After our session, one called me aside.

"Keep on going the way you're going," he assured me. "You're on the right track." He confided that he had seen the killings in four different clusters grouped around the four corners of my map. "What you've shown today," he said, "shows me how these four clusters can be connected." I promised to send the agents copies of my map.

Only one week earlier, in February of 1981, I had called the FBI to report where I thought missing 15-year-old Lee Gooch was. Since I was right about Gooch, and since my map didn't seem to be too much at odds with the FBI agents' thinking, I guess they were willing to listen to what I had to say. Months later, the FBI would call on me for a favor.

Now, on Friday morning, February 13, 1981, I had telephoned the FBI again because the map was telling me something new. The geographic patterns said that a body should be just to the north of Georgia 166, but farther west than Enon Road, where Lubie Geter's body had been found a few days earlier.

Agent Procopio told me that a team of agents was searching in that general area. He said he would give them my information by radio. Later that day, an FBI search team found the skeletal remains of a young child on Suber Road—just north of Georgia 166 and a few blocks west of Enon Road, just as the map had predicted.

On the 6 o'clock news, an FBI agent said the agents had gone to the location as a result of a telephone tip. But, on the 11 o'clock news, Atlanta's Special Agent-in-Charge, John Glover, denied that there had been a phone tip. "Just a routine search," he said. But I knew better. I'm the one who had called the FBI.

Everybody knew rather quickly that the first body found on that Friday the 13th was that of Patrick Baltazar. But the skeletal remains found later would take a while to identify, if they ever were. Everything I could see pointed to still-missing 10-year-old Darron Glass.

By now, life had become one news-media inquiry after another. I was on the phone when I wasn't on the phone. My ears got sore, but my voice never gave out. I constantly talked with reporters, always willing to tell them everything I knew, searching and begging for someone who might understand the untold story of the Atlanta murders.

That Saturday, 24 hours after the two victims were found, I took the grand tour for only what seemed like the thousandth time. This time I swapped opinions with two reporters about the identification of the skeleton found on Suber Road the day before. We all concluded it would be Darron Glass.

Soon, however, we were jolted by the voice on the AM car radio. It told us a different story—that the remains were those of 10-year-old Jefferey Mathis.

"No way," I said. "There's no way that is Jefferey. No way."

We had been told that the skull found on Suber Road was that of a child with a pointed head and a receding chin. Darron Glass had both of these features, very prominently. Jefferey Mathis had neither. Moreover, we knew the night before that the medical examiner's investigators had gone to see Fannie Smith, Darron's foster mother. There, some of their findings were verified as matching with Darron Glass.

Most important to me, the scene was described to me as one that I thought would better fit an early-fall crime than one that happened in the early spring. The immediate ground cover over the skeleton was pine cones and pine needles—which one would expect to find if the season immediately after the body was deposited was autumn. If it had been a spring crime scene, one would have expected to find viney-type vegetation growing around the long bones and even through the skull openings. I was told there was none.

Darron Glass had disappeared in late summer, only one week before the start of autumn. Jefferey Mathis, on the other hand, had disappeared only one week before the start of spring. If what I had been told about the crime scene was correct, then the victim was much more likely Darron Glass than Jefferey Mathis.

I thought back, too, to my talk with the FBI agents. They didn't think Mathis was connected to the others. I'd bet they had good reason for saying that. I'm not totally disillusioned about the FBI yet, just non-naive. If they were right, this should not be Jefferey Mathis. There was no question in my mind that this latest case was a part of the real pattern.

This possible mistaken identity of two missing 10-year-olds was reaffirmed by the medical examiner himself. On Friday, February 13, the medical examiner had said that the dental charts of both Darron Glass and Jefferey Mathis had been compared to the remains—and no one could make an identification with them.

Then, on Saturday, February 14, when the medical examiner announced that the remains were those of Jefferey Mathis, he based his decision partially on his ability to *rule out* Darron Glass—not rule in Jefferey Mathis—because of (no kidding) the dental charts. I had seen the fallibility of these medical examiners' dental-chart identifications demonstrated all too well in the Alfred Evans case. I wasn't buying this identification, either. Now, the medical examiner hadn't really identified Jefferey Mathis. Instead, he said he had *eliminated* Darron Glass.

Worse yet, the medical examiner admitted that he didn't really know who the victim he had identified as Jefferey Mathis was when he told the *Atlanta Journal*: "We are as positive as we can be at this point that the remains are those of Jefferey Mathis. However, *if there were another 10-year-old child missing, it would be baffling* [emphasis added]."

The medical examiners demonstrated again that they, too, were caught up in the fallacies of The List. Here they had the skeleton of a young boy. Only two young boys were still missing, according to The List. The medical examiner says he was able to rule out one, so it must be the other, right?

Wrong! First, no one has any idea exactly how many 10-year-old young boys—let alone those who are 8, 9, 11 and other ages that might fit—are missing and available to be discovered dead in the Atlanta area.

I recalled the story that teen-ager Kenny Brown told of the late-summer murder he witnessed on Memorial Drive, virtually across the street from Darron Glass' home. The skeleton could be of that victim, assuming the incident actually took place, or it could be one of many other young victims.

Keep in mind that at least 33 youngsters were missing in Chicago, and nobody was looking for them when bodies were found under and near John Wayne Gacy's house. Children missing from anywhere could theoretically be lying dead somewhere in Atlanta and be completely unheard of, let alone looked for here. After all, the child the authorities now say was Alfred Evans was buried in a grave marked "John Doe."

If, then, it's not Darron Glass or Jefferey Mathis, it could be almost anybody among the 50,000 children authorities say are missing in the United States. I will always doubt that the body of Jefferey Lamar Mathis lies in the grave beneath the marker that bears his name. So, too, will his mother, Willie Mae Mathis. Is it Jefferey Mathis, who after nearly four years, is still missing?

Remains purported to be those of 10-year-old Jefferey Mathis are followed by Jefferey's mother (partially hidden at upper left). Mrs. Mathis now says the coffin does not contain the remains of her son. Is it Darron Glass? Or could it be almost any other 10-year-old who is believed missing? (United Press International)

17

Cap'n Peg's

February, 1981

There was no letup. On February 19, 1981, another Atlanta child was missing. Thirteen-year-old Curtis Walker left home in Bowen Homes at 946 Wilkes Circle, Apartment 497. He headed east on Bankhead Highway (U.S. 278) from the intersection of Hightower Road. If those streets now are familiar, both had been on the route since August of 1980—six months before Curtis Walker disappeared.

Unlike recent other cases of missing children, the Atlanta police took Curtis Walker's disappearance seriously right away. Within only five hours, Curtis' case was assigned to The List.

Was it a political decision? Well, Curtis lived at Bowen Homes, where four children and an adult had been killed in the furnace-boiler explosion—and, on the same day, Mayor Jackson was booed by residents while trying to keep the political volcano from erupting.

Don Laken, the "Dog Man," had come to town in November of 1980. Laken was doing a great deal of detective work while he and his dogs joined in the organized Saturday searches and many impromptu safaris. Our paths had not yet crossed, primarily because he was concentrating on a particular suspect and what he considered the occult connections in the case.

Using his dogs, Laken traced the steps of Curtis Walker to the rear of a school building on Bankhead Highway, where other witnesses said they saw a young boy get into a yellow car.

Throughout these cases, people wondered why "nobody is seeing anything." The killer took on an aura of brilliance. If he wasn't super sharp, how could he get away with it for so long? Well, the competition wasn't that steep. People regularly "get away with it"—and various other "its"—for long periods of time, except on TV shows. Real-life criminals are, for all intents and purposes, "career criminals." Crimes pay well to "criminals."

People were seeing things. They simply weren't seeing what they expected to see or what they were being conditioned to notice. They kept looking for youngsters being forced into a vehicle by an old person. What was happening right under their noses, instead, was victims willingly joining teenagers and other youths. What people were reporting were homosexuals—not necessarily killers—making normal attempts to pick up "dates."

Don Laken also brought his wife to Atlanta from their hometown, Philadelphia. They became closely involved with the mothers' committee. Laken traveled often with Camille Bell, and, based on my experience with Camille, I imagine they enjoyed discussing the occult and supernatural forces they saw at play. He once brought me a map that he put great stock in. The points on his map had been determined, he said, by a psychic who passed her hand over the map and marked wherever she felt a "hot spot."

Don Laken made many interesting discoveries while collecting a lot of information. I wish that I could communicate with him better, but we couldn't bridge the gap between my cynicism and his penchant for mixing fact with conjecture to come to a conclusion. I think he was close to unraveling several of the mysteries that still exist about these cases.

Few would ever know that Curtis Walker had lived far across town at one time, in the Thomasville Heights apartments—a history shared with Pat Man and Aaron Wyche. But Pat Man and Thomasville Heights were to surface again before we learned the fate of Curtis Walker.

On March 2, 1981, Joseph (Jo-Jo) Bell, the 15-year-old son of Alfred Evans' sister's prison mate, disappeared. The police steadfastly refused to put Jo-Jo Bell on The List.

Jo-Jo had come home about 4 p.m. and changed clothes. He scooped up his basketball and headed out the door, saying he was going to work. His boss, Richard Harp, said that Jo-Jo Bell had called earlier. He told Jo-Jo he had no work that day. But Jo-Jo stopped by, anyway, on his way to play basketball.

Jo-Jo worked for a fast-food restaurant on Georgia Avenue, on the edge of the McDaniel-Glenn housing project. Its name was Cap'n Peg's. It sat right down the street from so many of the pertinent locations in these cases. Soon it would be a focal point itself.

It would be at Cap'n Peg's that a man would be arrested with the prison identification card of 21-year-old Jimmy Ray Payne in his pocket—only a few days after Payne's disappearance.

The man said he had found the card at the liquor store on the corner of Georgia and Stewart avenues, close to where 9-year-old Anthony Carter was found stabbed and where 16-year-old Angela (Gypsy) Bacon was killed. This is the same liquor store where 22-year-old Faye Yearby had purchased an occasional bottle of booze.

Across the street from the back door of Cap'n Peg's was the home of another ex-convict—23-year-old Michael McIntosh. A block away from Cap'n Peg's lived 17-year-old Kenneth Johnson, who worked part time at the fast-food restaurant. Also down the street is the grocery store where 9-year-old Yusuf Bell was sent to buy some snuff. In back of Cap'n Peg's is the McDaniel-Glenn community center, where Pat Man danced and where "Billy Star" (William Barrett) would go to pay a bill for his mother on his last day alive.

On the morning after he would be questioned at the FBI field office in Atlanta, Wayne Williams called a press conference. One question he was asked was to explain his associations with younger children. Williams produced a contract which showed that his relationship with children was completely professional. The address listed in the contract for his Gemini singing group was 325 Georgia Avenue—astonishingly, the same address as Cap'n Peg's.

A reporter later sensed a "smoking gun" and called this to Wayne Williams' attention. Williams said the address typed on the contract was a mistake made by his attorney. He showed where he had penciled in the "correct" address, he said, "in my attorney's presence."

Not so, said a representative of the attorney to Paul Crawley and me. The attorney would stand by the address typed on the contract. It was, he said, the address furnished by Wayne Williams. There had been no mistake, as far as the attorney was concerned. He knew nothing of a penciled change.

Jo-Jo Bell's sister said she had seen Wayne Williams in Cap'n Peg's watching her as she danced with Jo-Jo. The manager of Cap'n Peg's at first denied ever having seen Wayne Williams. But as the media attention mounted, he said that Wayne Williams had been a regular customer.

Wayne Williams would tell me that he had never been to Cap'n Peg's. "I don't like fish," he said, wrinkling his face.

"I don't, either, but I've been to Cap'n Peg's several times during this investigation," I reminded him.

I was astonished that, like the "Pat Man connections" and other startling revelations yet to come, not a single mention of any of these Cap'n Peg's connections was made—or asked for—in the Wayne Williams trial, even though Jo-Jo Bell's is one of the 10 "pattern" cases. The prosecution brought witnesses to try to place Wayne Williams with Jo-Jo Bell. But ignoring the Cap'n Peg's connections made it appear that the prosecution had neglected to do its homework.

It was because of data like the Cap'n Peg's connections that Alvin Binder,

Wayne Williams' attorney, told me he would not put me on the stand during the trial and that Binder's successor, Lynn Whatley, said he would not use me on appeal. Rather, they wanted to use my information where it would be exculpatory. Both said that they were afraid that the prosecution would, on cross examination, elicit testimony from me that would be more damaging to Williams than some of the witnesses the state would introduce.

So we're not talking about theory and conjecture here. We're talking about facts that the defense feared, that were never introduced by the state. Why? I can't really say, but I've always felt that the state simply did not understand the relationships among all these victims—and, in particular, how they would be demonstrated with examples like Cap'n Peg's. The state made a feeble attempt to do so with the Omni, but failed.

Richard Harp, the manager of Cap'n Peg's, would report to police that another employee, Jerry Lee, took a phone call on March 3, 1981. It was, he said, Jo-Jo Bell asking for help and moaning, "I'm almost dead." Police were able to run a partial trace on the call, but it yielded an area far too large to be of much benefit. The general area was in northeast Atlanta, not germane to any of the known suspects. Jerry Lee would say that the call came on March 4. He added that Jo-Jo called him by name, "Jerry."

The only other known cases of reported telephone calls from victims were said to be the unspoken calls to the home of missing 10-year-old Darron Glass and a report by Patrick Baltazar's teacher that Patrick had called her on the phone, but said nothing and merely sobbed.

Richard Harp said he had seen at least three attempted kidnappings outside his restaurant and had given the police a license number. Harp added that Jo-Jo Bell had socialized with homosexuals. Indeed, Jo-Jo Bell and his smaller companion, 13-year-old Timothy Hill, did cavort with self-proclaimed homosexuals at a house on Gray Street, a location that would surface frequently in these cases after the disappearance of Jo-Jo Bell. Harp also said that another "regular" at his store—23-year-old Michael McIntosh—hung around with gays.

Jo-Jo Bell often partied at the Dunbar Community Center. Harp said that a man known only to him as "Dorsey" told him that he had seen Bell at Dunbar on the night of March 2, 1981, and that Jo-Jo got into a car with two black males.

A young boy would cause a stir after Wayne Williams' conviction in 1982 by giving a statement to a black female "private-eye" called "P.J." Lemuel. Through former state Representative Mildred Glover, this statement would come to Williams' attorney, Lynn Whatley. In it, the boy said that he had seen someone other than Wayne Williams murder Jo-Jo Bell (whose case would be among 22 closed and attributed to Wayne Williams without a trial). But back when Jo-Jo was still missing, the boy was telling a different story.

Doris Bell, Jo-Jo's mother, said she got a phone call about 7:30 p.m. on March 7, 1981. A female was on the line. "She told me she had Jo-Jo," Doris

Bell said. "At this time, a beep came on my line [she had a "call-holding" phone]. I didn't get a chance to talk to the lady." Ouch, I thought. Doris Bell continued: "She called back in about 10 minutes. She talked to my daughter and my son."

An investigator asked Doris Bell: "Did you contact any law-enforcement officers about this at that time?"

"I called the Task Force right away," she replied.

"Did anyone come out to talk to you from the Task Force?" the investigator continued.

"No."

Doris Bell went on to say that she later told the FBI about the call.

In February of 1981, reporter Paul Crawley had asked me to brief the editorial and management staff where he worked—at WXIA-TV (Channel 11).

When I shared my information with them, news director Ron Becker said he agreed with me that the killings were not random. He pointed out that just two months before, Lee Brown had called him and other Atlanta media executives together to ask their cooperation in dispelling any notion that any cases were connected.

At WXIA-TV, I met David Page, an investigative reporter for the Gannett chain (owner of WXIA-TV). "We need to talk," he said.

"Any time," I replied.

"Later," he said.

About this time, the media demands on my time virtually exploded. Reporters who interviewed me included, among others, Peter Arnett, an Associated Press correspondent who would contact me again when he moved from New York to Atlanta to join Cable News Network. My work was reported in *Life, Newsweek, Black Enterprise, Paris Match* and *TV Guide,* as well as on radio and TV stations and in newspapers across the country. A young woman in the criminal-justice class I was teaching at Floyd Junior College told me her mother had telephoned from Hawaii, saying that she had seen her daughter's teacher quoted in a Honolulu newspaper.

Almost all the reporters I met wanted to take the "grand tour." One was a French reporter, a native Belgian named Jean Pierre Van Grieb. He was accompanied by a former inspector with the Paris police. I spoke French *en peu,* and they spoke English a little. If you understand French, you appreciate the belly laugh that Van Grieb got when the young woman clerk at the Citgo gas station asked him if he had "two pennies."

Paul Crawley, too, wanted to take the tour. He along with Roz Abrams, then a WXIA-TV anchorwoman, and Judy Farmer, who had volunteered to help me in the cases, piled into Paul's open 1965 Mustang convertible.

Paul took me to a place that I hadn't yet visited—the death scene for 11-year-old Patrick Baltazar. Paul had been there, covering the story for his station.

Two days later, Paul Crawley took the tour again. This time he brought his Channel 11 colleague, David Page. As we rode, they grasped the implications of what we were seeing like no one had done before.

We knew that one of Pat Man Rogers' hangouts was a fast-food restaurant on Moreland Avenue, near Interstate 20. As we left the home of slain 14-year-old Eric Middlebrooks, we remembered that Eric had left his home in May of 1980 after taking a telephone call. As we drove the short distance to where Eric's body had been found near his bicycle, we noticed that our route took us right past the outdoor pay phone at Pat Man's hangout. It was probably the same route that Eric would have taken because it not only was the shortest, but the only one without going far out of the way.

Could Pat Man have been connected with Eric Middlebrooks' murder? We wondered. David Page and I looked at each other with an instant professional rapport that I wouldn't find again in these cases until Al Binder came along.

Did we have a John Wayne Gacy-type case, in which third parties were being used to contact victims? Maybe. The map said it could be.

Ron Becker of Channel 11 said he would do anything he could to help with my investigation. I asked if I could use his station's helicopter and pilot.

"You got it," he said. "Just let me know when."

I made arrangements with the audio-visual department of Floyd Junior College to take a cameraman with me. We would videotape the entire route.

The chopper strained against the restraints that anchored us to the roof of the station. Suddenly we vaulted skyward. What a difference a few thousand feet made! The first leg of the flight took us west from the Krystal on Memorial Drive, where 15-year-old Terry Pue had last been seen, far across town to the Charlie Brown airport, where the bicycle ridden by 14-year-old Milton Harvey had been found.

We hovered low over street intersections—actually low enough to read the street signs. We flew sideways above major thoroughfares to obtain good video footage. In more remote areas, we landed to inspect the scenes where bodies had turned up. We flew through the canyons of downtown Atlanta's skyscrapers, where I could see workers in their offices. We flew backward for pictures that panned away from scenes.

Our final location was above the Constitution Road bridge and the death scene of 10-year-old Aaron Wyche, who still was not on The List. As we sat still in mid-air above the bridge, I looked along Moreland Avenue to the north. I could see Pat Man's and Aaron Wyche's apartment houses, Aaron

Jackson's house and the locations near Memorial Drive where Eric Middlebrooks lived, disappeared and was found dead. I could see Moreland Avenue beyond Interstate 20, reaching far into northeast Atlanta.

For three weeks, I had wondered about the headline on Gail Epstein's story, which stated that Patrick Baltazar's death scene was an anomaly. Now it dawned on me that it wasn't an anomaly at all. Three major roads led directly to Corporate Square, the Baltazar death scene in DeKalb County. One was Briarcliff Road. Although I live one block from Briarcliff on Atlanta's northeast side and my wife works three blocks from Moreland on the southeast side, I had not—since Baltazar's death—recalled that Briarcliff was simply an extension of Moreland!

These two streets merely change names at their intersection with U.S. 278. They are, in essence, one street. This meant that victims Aaron Jackson, Aaron Wyche, Patrick (Pat Man) Rogers, Eric Middlebrooks and Patrick Baltazar had at least one geographic point on the same street, with victim Lubie Geter's house only two blocks away.

Patrick Baltazar's case simply had extended the Moreland Avenue corridor to the north. The Baltazar location was no anomaly.

Had it not been for my helicopter's-eye view, I may never have seen the connections among Baltazar and the others. The pieces meshed like the gearwork of a fine clock—that is, all but one piece. Pat Man Rogers had been found far from anyone else—in the Chattahoochee River.

In March of 1981, Jeff Prugh invited me to have dinner at Nino's. There, we met with Lawrence Schiller, who was producing "*The Executioner's Song,*" a made-for-TV treatment of Norman Mailer's partly fictionalized book on the life and misadventures of killer Gary Gilmore, who was executed in Utah by a firing squad in 1977.

Now Schiller was working on a similar proposal for ABC on the Atlanta murders. Soon he would hire Toni Cade Bambara, an Atlanta poet-novelist, to write the screenplay. But the project ultimately was dropped.

Meanwhile, under the aegis of Gerald Rafshoon, CBS was contemplating a similar project (Rafshoon, an advertising executive, had been Jimmy Carter's presidential media adviser). Actress Jane Fonda's company, too, explored a possible motion picture on the Atlanta murders.

At about this same time in 1981, Mayor Maynard Jackson decried attempts to "exploit" the Atlanta murders for profit, while Thomas (Tommy) Thompson, author of "*Blood and Money*" and other best-sellers, expressed surprise when he learned that at least eight books were in progress on the Atlanta story. Thompson wrote in California that such a profusion of written words would cause him to "mourn the loss of trees." After all, he wrote, hadn't the Atlanta story already been "streamrollered" by the news media? Answer:

the media had barely even grazed the story's surface.

At Gladstone's, a media watering hole, David Page and I discussed the cases and the geography. He made me an offer I could have refused, but didn't. I contracted with WXIA-TV to be a consultant on the cases.

It would be the first money I would make while investigating the murders. But the stipend wouldn't come close to recouping the money I had spent on gas and other costs.

Soon David had to leave. As a parting shot, I told him something that I had been thinking about for some time, but hadn't told anyone, except Dick Hand of the DeKalb County police.

"Don't forget the importance of the South River," I told David, "in the geography of these cases."

The next day, March 6, I saw David on the 6 o'clock news. He was reporting the discovery of yet another body—that of Curtis Walker. "This is David Page," he said, "coming to you live from the banks of the *South River.*" That night, he telephoned and asked: "Do you always pull rabbits out of a hat like that?"

The river where Curtis Walker's body was found was close to Mike Edwards' house. The wags were at it again. Did the killer leave this one for Mike Edwards? Not very likely.

Earlier that day, a DeKalb fire truck had ground to a halt on Waldrip Bridge Road next to a South River bridge. A firemen scurried down the riverbank, looking for a turtle—dinner for the firehouse. Instead, he observed the badly decomposed body of a young black male. The medical examiner would write:

> "The body was caught on a limb which jutted out from the stump into the river. The body was folded across the limb—jackknifed around the limb."

While Curtis Walker had been missing, severe rains had swollen the South River. Walker's body could have come from almost anywhere upstream.

"Asphyxia—probable suffocation," the medical examiner said of Curtis Walker. Another Atlantan had stopped breathing. The medical examiner's finding told us no more than that.

Meanwhile, at the South River, officials floated a stretcher downstream. It was covered with a sterile white sheet. They maneuvered the body onto the stretcher (violating the sterility), then folded the sheet around it.

As the orange-and-white EMS (Emergency Medical Service) ambulance left for the morgue, the body accompanied by Medical Examiner Joseph Burton, DeKalb County police and firemen swarmed down the riverbanks to search for clues.

The autopsy in the Curtis Walker case is consistent with others indicating no sexual mutilation. The boy, the medical examiner said, had probably been dead for most of the 15 days he was missing—and most likely was dead when he went into the river.

Thus, without saying so, the autopsy does *not* rule out drowning as a cause of the asphyxia. The autopsy continues: "There is some bruising to indicate that the child was held down, indicating perhaps some resistance on his part."

It's strange how the "perhaps" and other fuzzy words get lost in the translation. Most of the world now perceives Curtis Walker as having struggled with his killer. Nobody knows that except the killer. And apparently, no one knows how Walker died, except the killer. If the medical examiner knew, he wouldn't have said "*probable*" asphyxia.

Also notable in the Curtis Walker case was the laboratory report that "identifiable latent prints have been developed on the evidence submitted." The report asked that these prints be compared with those of any suspects. I had seen references to fingerprints in lab reports on other murders on The List, but I would wait at the trial for someone to say that Wayne Williams' prints matched any of the latent prints that had been developed as evidence. No one did.

The pastor of a church near the Curtis Walker death scene placed an ad in the newspaper for the killer to call him. He received a call from a man who identified an article of clothing that the police had kept a secret.

But the police had informed the pastor about the clothing so that he could confirm the authenticity of any calls he might receive. The man's knowledge of the clothing checked out. But, in the end, he was arrested—not for murder, but for making a false report. If making a false report to a pastor is against the law, many of us are in real trouble.

As in many murder cases, the "crazies" had come out of the woodwork. But it was different in Atlanta. Not very many people were claiming responsibility, as is often the case. In many widely publicized murder cases, "nuts" almost stood in line to confess.

Not so in Atlanta, where it seemed as if more "nuts" were trying to solve the cases than take credit or blame for them. The lengthy time span of the cases—and the constant picture of law enforcement's futility—undoubtedly attracted many people and groups outside the normal criminal-justice system to Atlanta's murders. Those outsiders were equally as futile.

In Atlanta, there was so much public cooperation that no one was prepared to deal with it. The offers of community help and information were handled almost as abysmally as the investigation itself—thus, debunking the oft-heard platitude mouthed by police that public cooperation contributes mightily to "crime" prevention. It certainly didn't prevent any of these crimes.

When people telephoned, they expected to speak with *the* Task Force—not, as I heard so many say, "just the regular police." But a bigger problem was that some got to speak to *no* police.

To solve part of the problem, I suggested that the police departments print armbands inscribed "Task Force" for all their officers—for no other reason than good public relations. That way, if an officer not assigned to the Task Force responded to a call about missing or murdered children, he would just slip on the armband and become part of *the* Task Force. At the very least, it would reassure a certain segment of the public that the Task Force was a model of omnipresence, instead of an invisible non-deterrent.

On March 13, 1981, thirteen-year-old Timothy Hill disappeared. He was the last young black child (under 17) to vanish in connection with the "children's" cases on The List.

But once again, the police refused to put Timmy Hill on The List. Just another "runaway," they said. Which was yet another non-response in the midst of a calamity that demanded absolute response. There were no charitable words to describe the colossal lack of understanding.

I sat in the conference room at Channel 11, discussing the cases again—this time over a swig of Kentucky bourbon (there is no other kind). Ron Becker came in, saying that a woman had called to report that she had seen Timmy Hill in the crowd on Channel 11's coverage of a downtown march which memorialized the victims and was led by Coretta Scott King and others. It seemed that people were always seeing Timmy Hill. Maybe it was because he was last seen wearing a red baseball cap. What people were seeing was a red cap, not Timmy Hill. Even during one of the volunteer searches, several searchers reported seeing Timmy Hill. If so, why didn't they reclaim him and take him home? The searchers were looking for *live* kids, too, I hope.

Ron Becker wanted to show the videotapes to Timothy Hill's mother, so she could determine if the caller had been right. If she were to identify Timmy Hill on the tape, the station would notify the police right away.

At Becker's insistence, Paul Crawley, David Page, cameraman Mike Zakel and I piled into one of the station's sedans emblazoned with WXIA-TV's red-white-and-blue "11 ALIVE" logo. Close on our heels was a remote truck. We drove along Gordon Street, past slain 9-year-old Anthony Carter's house, then past the street where still-missing 15-year-old Jo-Jo Bell lived. Just before the corner where slain 10-year-old Jeffrey Mathis had disappeared one year and two days before Timmy Hill, we turned right and drove the last three blocks to Timmy Hill's residence. Yes, the points for Timmy Hill and Jo-Jo Bell also fit the pattern of my map.

As we pulled to the curb across the street from the brownish-pink apartments where Timmy Hill lived, another car sped from the opposite direction and stopped nose-to-nose, headed the wrong direction in front of us. It was an unmarked Atlanta police car.

A trenchcoat-clad detective bounded out of the car and dashed across the street. We followed. He knocked and was immediately admitted. We knocked and were admitted, too. We stood there quietly while the detective questioned Timmy's family. He seemed most concerned to learn the whereabouts of one of Timmy's older sisters.

In a few minutes, the detective left, but Paul Crawley and I would run across him again in our search for Timmy Hill. One thing we learned from listening to the conversation is that Timmy Hill had relatives who lived across the street from victim Eric Middlebrooks. Along with the geographic connections, we now had a possible personal connection that told me that Timmy Hill belonged on The List—despite whatever misinformation Lee Brown might have that was keeping him from assigning the investigation of Hill's disappearance to the Task Force.

Paul explained to Annie Hill, Timmy's mother, why we were there. She accompanied Paul, David and Mike to the remote truck, which had been brought along solely to allow us to show her the videotape.

I followed, but stopped at the corner, waiting for them to finish inside the now-crowded, van-type truck. I started chatting with Timmy's 26-year-old brother, Richard Hill.

"Does Timmy know any of the victims in the children's murder cases?" I asked him.

"Oh, yeah," Richard Hill answered quickly. "He knowed Anthony Carter, the little boy that was stabbed, and he knows Jo-Jo Bell [interestingly, Richard Hill recognized Jo-Jo, who was not on The List, as a part of the problem, even though the police didn't]. Jo-Jo and Timmy are friends. He come by here to play with Timmy all the time."

"Could he know Alfred Evans?" I asked. I brought up Evans' name because only moments before, Richard Hill had told me that Timmy hung out at the West End Mall. I knew that Alfred Evans, though he had lived across town, often visited that mall, too.

"Oh, he probably did know Evans and Jefferey Mathis, too," Richard Hill volunteered. His knowledge of the victims surprised and more than interested me.

"Richard, did Timmy by any chance know Patrick Rogers?"

"No, I don't think Timmy knew Pat Man, but I did."

I couldn't believe my ears. At that moment, David and Paul alighted from the truck with Annie Hill. She had said that the video footage did not contain any picture of her son.

"David! Paul!" I hollered. "Come over here! You've got to hear this!"

I turned to Richard Hill and said: "Richard, tell them what you just told me."

"You mean about me knowing Pat Man?"

"Yeah, and the other kids your brother knows."

Richard Hill started rehashing the connections of his missing younger brother, Timmy Hill, with other victims. David Page stood, staring in wide-eyed disbelief, his mouth open.

"Richard, Richard," I pushed. "How did you know Pat Man?"

"Oh, he and I are good buddies."

"But Pat Man was only 16, Richard. Are we talking about the same guy?"

"Yeah, we talkin' about the same guy—the Pat Man Rogers what live in the Thomasville apartments and drown in the river—that Pat Man."

"That's Pat Man, all right."

"Well, I know he was a young dude...," Richard Hill went on, "but he was more like a growed-up man. Pat Man liked to run with older guys."

Yes, and he liked to run with younger guys, too, I thought to myself. Pat Man might be a perfect selection for a go-between—if that is, in fact, what we had in these cases.

"How did you meet Pat Man?" I asked.

"I met Pat Man when I was the maintenance man at the Thomasville apartments."

Bong! Bong! Bong! Bells were going off in my head. I looked at Paul and David. They smiled knowingly.

"Thank God, we've got the remote truck—what time is it?" David rattled without pausing. It was almost 10:45 p.m. "I've got to get to a phone to call the station." Mrs. Hill volunteered her phone. Paul hustled back to the apartment to arrange a live, remote broadcast from the front yard of Timmy's home.

Paul, David and I had spent the better part of the last 10 days checking out the Pat Man connections as a thread to the cases. What Richard Hill had told us considerably lengthened—and strengthened—those threads. It was becoming increasingly clear that Pat Man might hold the key. There was no question now among Paul, David and I that Timmy Hill belonged on The List.

While David talked on the phone to someone at the station, Paul and I sat on the apartment steps. We talked with Timmy Hill's young siblings and cousins.

Timmy Hill's youngest sister said that the last time she saw Timmy, a man arrived in a taxi cab. Timmy got in, she said, then the man put "mud" on Timmy's face, and they drove off. She talked lucidly about the incident and never changed a detail, no matter how many times we asked her to repeat the story.

Now David was wired up and perfecting his audio delivery and timing. Paul and I talked on with the kids. One little girl said, "Timmy knows Patrick Baltazar—he was in my class in school."

I waved frantically, trying to catch David's attention. But he was about to go on the air in only seconds. So I printed in large letters on a stray cardboard box: "HE KNOWS BALTAZAR, TOO!"

David's jaw dropped. He scribbled something quickly and mouthed a few words audibly to himself. Soon David went on the air, with Paul and I furiously scrawling notes to David on scraps of paper that served as makeshift prompters. How David kept his poise, I'll never know.

Captain Johnny Sparks, who was in charge of the Atlanta Police Missing Persons unit, said it was just a matter of time before police would find Timmy Hill alive. Timmy was still considered a "runaway," and Lee Brown persisted in refusing to put his case on The List.

"He's dead," David Page said in the WXIA-TV car on the way back to the station.

"Who's dead?" Mike Zakel asked.

"Hill is," David said matter-of-factly. "Too many connections. That little boy is gone."

David was probably right. "Why doesn't Brown see it like we do?" I wondered aloud.

"Simple," someone chimed in. "He doesn't want to see it."

"Nah," David Page disagreed, "that's not it. The difference is, we've got the map, and he's only got the Task Force."

The next morning, David went to police headquarters to interview Captain Sparks. He told Sparks what we had learned in our visit to Timmy Hill's apartment. David later would tell me that Sparks replied, "You're telling me things I know nothing about."

This statement told me even more. It said the investigation was flawed in another way. The police were not monitoring news reports on the cases. Apparently the police hadn't yet recognized that many people would tell reporters things that they wouldn't tell the police. These cases were pregnant with instances where reporters were seeking—and getting—information that the police could have used, but weren't even asking for!

Soon Sparks became angered with David and ordered him out of his office. David went downstairs and set up a remote broadcast from the front stoop of Atlanta police headquarters. On the air, David told the full story about Timmy Hill, including the part about getting kicked out of Sparks' office. Then he said, "It's a shame Sparks didn't let me finish. I only had one more question: 'Why didn't your detectives learn what we learned by talking with the Hills?'"

The detective who went to Timmy Hill's apartment when we did had the same opportunity we did. Sparks had all but said it: The police knew little, if anything, about the Timmy Hill case. Now, for the umpteenth time, we had offered to tell them things they knew nothing about. They could have known, but they wouldn't listen.

One week later, still another Atlantan was missing, and Timmy Hill and Jo-Jo Bell still were not on The List of Atlanta's missing and murdered children.

It had gotten ludicrous. It was as if stubbornness would determine the course of the investigation. It did, and the investigation continued to go nowhere. And the police would continue to place a higher priority on investigating murders that were beyond prevention than on bringing back kids who still might be alive. In my book, that is absurd.

Atlanta's mystery and misery deepened. By March of 1981, the cases of "Cinderella" and "Gypsy"—14-year-old Cynthia Montgomery and 16-year-old Angela Bacon—were on *my* list, but not on The List. But I hadn't yet had time to give them a hard look.

I met Jeff Prugh of the *Los Angeles Times* for the first time, over breakfast in a coffee shop on Atlanta's north side. As I spread my maps over the table, I pointed out the geographic and inter-personal connections among the victims, including those *not* on The List.

Jeff was intrigued. He had covered the story since it came into public light, but he was puzzled by my information.

"Who are these people?" he asked about names like Montgomery, Bacon, Harvey, *et cetera.*

I explained that they were murdered Atlantans who had not made The List. He proceeded immediately to look into the slayings of Cynthia Montgomery and Angela Bacon.

He found Eula Montgomery, Cynthia's mother, who supplied him with a wealth of information that she said the police had never bothered to ask about. He checked out the Memorial Drive address reported by a medical examiner's investigator in the death of Angela Bacon. But the address didn't exist. This was the third time that an address taken from a report of a medical examiner's investigation had turned out not to exist. One wondered what got verified and what didn't in those medical examiner's reports.

Jeff left his business card with a woman who lived in the same block as the non-existent address. She promised to check around. A few days later, Isabel Porter, Angela Bacon's grandmother, telephoned Jeff—from the correct address—several doors away.

Eula Montgomery said the police still had not come to question her, two months after her visit to the Homicide Division. She said she was unaware that a man in his 20s, who lived around the corner, had been questioned in January of 1981 in her daughter's case and then released. (The man was not Anthony "Amp" Wiley, a neighbor who would be charged and convicted in the beating death of a 34-year-old woman later in 1981.) "Somethin' ain't right," Eula said. "I've never heard nothin'."

Jeff telephoned Detective Mickey Lloyd, who declined to be interviewed. Lloyd referred him to Lieutenant B. L. Neikirk, the commander of the homicide division. When Jeff explained the nature of his call, Neikirk interrupted and said, "Oh, I know what you're tryin' to do. You're tryin' to write a story that asks why those two cases aren't on the Task Force list."

"That's right," Jeff said.

Neikirk would not explain why the two girls' cases were being ignored (when the cases of two other females—7-year-old LaTonya Wilson and 12-year-old Angel Lenair—were on The List). He referred Jeff to Morris Redding, the Task Force commander.

When Redding did not return Jeff's calls, Jeff went to Task Force headquarters. Barely inside the door, Jeff was intercepted by a police officer. Jeff explained that he was a reporter and that he was advised to see Morris Redding.

"He's not in right now," the officer said. "Do you have any information to give, or questions to ask?"

"A little of both," Jeff said.

The officer asked Jeff to sit at a nearby table, there to be interviewed by a young police recruit. As the recruit jotted the names of Cynthia Montgomery and Angela Bacon, apparently unaware of who they were, Jeff suggested that the recruit could save time by obtaining the same information from the police reports already on file at headquarters.

The recruit looked up. He tossed his head back in bewilderment. "Are reporters allowed to have police reports?" he asked.

"These are on public file," Jeff replied.

The recruit persisted in writing all the pertinent information about the two girls' cases. Jeff asked the recruit to be sure to write, too, that he had been sent there by the homicide division commander to see Morris Redding and to ask Redding to call him. The recruit politely obliged.

Later, when Jeff still had not heard from Redding, he left a message stating that the matter was "urgent." Redding never called.

Jeff's next stop was Chief of Police George Napper's office. A police officer at the reception counter scrawled the names of Cynthia and Angela on a notepad, then excused himself. Ten minutes later, the officer emerged from Napper's office and said, "The chief says this girl is on the Task Force list." He pointed to the name of Angela Bacon.

Then he referred Jeff to Sergeant H. L. Bolton of the Task Force, who refused to talk and referred Jeff to the public affairs office. There, a police spokesman contradicted what the police officer in the chief's office had told Jeff that Chief Napper had said. Now Jeff was told Angela Bacon was *not* on The List. Who was briefing Napper?

The run-around had come full circle. Jeff then arranged to see Lee Brown, the Atlanta public safety commissioner, who was in overall charge of the Task Force investigation and who had the final say about who went on The List.

"I'd like to know the status of the investigations," Jeff said, "of the deaths of Cynthia Montgomery and Angela Bacon."

Brown's face went blank. It was clear that the two girls' names meant nothing to Brown, even though it was Brown—not Jeff—who was being paid to know who is murdered in Atlanta.

Brown assured Jeff that both cases were being worked by the Homicide Division.

"How could the Bacon case be worked," Jeff asked, "when murder charges have been dropped and the police have lost the case file?"

Brown's normally stoic face radiated astonishment. "That doesn't sound reasonably logical," he said. Then, in a rush of rare candor, he added, "This is the first I've heard of it. You're telling me something I don't know."

Again, Brown explained that the two cases were "not connected" to those on The List. But then, he had been saying for months that the cases on The List were not connected, either. The tangle of illogic now seemed about as easy to figure out as Rubik's Cube.

Brown wrote the two girls' names on a scratch pad. "I'll get back to you," he said.

Several days elapsed. Jeff still had not heard from Brown. On March 15, 1981, the *Los Angeles Times* published a story by Jeff, headlined: "Atlanta Task Force Excludes Slayings of Some Black Children From Its Inquiry." The article, which discussed the deaths of Cynthia Montgomery and Angela Bacon, was the first to challenge the validity of The List. It was bigger news in California than in Atlanta, where it was non-news.

Three days later, the telephone rang in Jeff's office.

"This is Lee Brown," the caller said. Brown went on to complain that "you misrepresented to me that the file was lost."

"No, I did not." Jeff said.

Brown explained that he had sent an investigator to the Fulton County District Attorney's office and that a prosecutor there denied that the Angela Bacon file was missing.

"What is the investigator's name?" Jeff asked.

"That's not even important," Brown said.

Jeff said he would stand by his story. He telephoned the prosecutor to ask if Brown's account were true. The prosecutor sighed. "I've said enough already," he said, without further comment.

Four days after Jeff's story appeared, Georgia state Representative Tyrone Brooks (D-Atlanta), a young black civil rights activist, was among those wanting to know why Angela's and Cynthia's murders were not given the investigative priority of the Task Force. He wrote a letter to Mayor Jackson, urging him to add both cases to the investigation:

> ". . . due to these very similar and unusual connections and because we cannot afford to leave any stone unturned . . . Let us not lose any more valuable time, evidence, leads, or clues that could just possibly help us end the most horrible tragedy this city has ever faced."

Brooks had summed up the feelings I had been trying to get across to the authorities for more than nine months now. Maybe they would listen to a state representative. But Brooks said later that Jackson never answered his letter.

When Brooks inquired of the mayor's staff as to whether he would receive a response, he was told the letter had been sent to Lee Brown. In April, more than a month after Brooks had written to the mayor, Brown replied in writing with his customary refrain: the two girls' deaths had "no relationship" to those on The List.

Weeks later, Jeff and another *Times* reporter, Lee May, visited Captain Johnny Sparks of the Missing Persons unit. (Jeff had been advised by Detective Carolyn O'Neal, who declined to be interviewed, to see Sparks.) There, Jeff tried to interest Sparks in having someone send an investigator to question Eula Montgomery more thoroughly. The next day, Jeff received a telephone call from Eula.

"Detective Lloyd called," she said, her voice edged in fear and anger.

What had he told her? What did she find out?

"He told me I can't talk to the press anymore," Eula Montgomery said.

The scenario was becoming wackier. Eula Montgomery, a mother of an "unofficially" murdered child, could not talk to the press, while many mothers of "officially" murdered children were traveling across the United States, fielding questions from reporters, appearing on talk shows and raising money.

"No," Lee Brown would say, weeks later at a news conference, "we have no policy against mothers talking to the press. They don't work for us."

In the spring of 1981, Paul Crawley pressed Brown on the connections of victims not on The List. But Paul found, too, that trying to spar with Brown about these cases was like playing verbal racquetball. The wall of illogic was as impenetrable as ever.

Paul did, however, report on Channel 11 that the killings of Cynthia (Cinderella) Montgomery and Angela (Gypsy) Bacon were being ignored by the Task Force—and by the mothers on the Committee to Stop Children's Murders. The money that the committee had raised, he reported, was going only to those families of victims whose names appeared on The List. Channel 2 (WSB-TV) also ran a feature on Cynthia. Ernie Bjorkman called me for information on her case.

Soon the committee agreed to add the cases of Angela and Cynthia to its list. But, unlike the families of the two girls already on the committee's and Task Force's lists, the families of "Gypsy" and "Cinderella" received no funds—nor asked for any.

I wondered what the committee had done in the cases of Aaron Wyche and Patrick Rogers. Had the committee gone back and paid a proportional share of the contributions to those families whose children had been dead before others, but who didn't go on The List until months later? Why muddy the waters by asking? It had taken me 10 months just to get the Wyche and Rogers cases investigated by the Task Force.

Long after the conviction of Wayne Williams, I would call victim Jefferey Mathis' mother, Willie Mae, to verify the age of her daughter for a magazine article I was writing. Willie Mae would tell me that she no longer believed that her son was buried in the grave marked "Jefferey Mathis." She said that originally then-Chief George Napper had convinced her that the medical examiners were positive of their identification (which, of course, they were not). She now says it is not Jefferey buried there.

Then Willie Mae confided that she was having financial difficulties. They had cut off her power, she said, and wouldn't turn it back on because she was unable to pay her utility bills. She asked if I could help. I called Paul Crawley, who did a story on it.

In 1981, the mothers' committee received a letter from a white woman, Ruby Fornwalt, whose son, Gary Lynn Haynes, 22, had disappeared in December of 1978 and is believed to have been murdered. Mrs. Fornwalt resided on Sells Avenue in predominantly black southwest Atlanta, the same street where 13-year-old Timmy Hill lived.

"The six or seven years difference in his [Gary Lynn Haynes] age doesn't make me care any less for him than you do for your children," Ruby Fornwalt wrote in her letter to the committee.

Like most, Ruby Fornwalt didn't realize that people older than her 22-year-old son would make The List. ". . . I feel like Mrs. [Camille] Bell," she wrote, "that our *poor* children or just *poor* people doesn't [sic] [make] news and maybe someone would hear it and talk. But it was not important to the people downtown. He was just another one gone from the Southwest Atlanta area . . . I feel so sorry for each of you mothers who are going thru the same experience I have. But what can we do about it? Please let me know if there is anything I can do to help any of you. And please remember me as one of you who has lost a son."

In return, Ruby Fornwalt received an undated form letter from the Committee to Stop Children's Murders. It was signed by Venus Taylor, the committee's secretary-treasurer and mother of slain 12-year-old Angel Lenair. It expressed thanks for "your concern regarding the horrendous abduction and murder of our children." The letter also asked for a donation, stating that the committee's existence depends on "your future spirital [sic] and financial support . . ."

As late as May of 1981, the volunteer searchers—like the police, the mothers' committee and most of the press—would persist in focusing only on those murder victims who had been put on The List.

City Councilman Arthur Langford Jr.'s social-service agency, the United Youth Adult Conference (UYAC), would announce that it would commemorate the deaths of Atlanta's "murdered children."

One by one, white wooden crosses would be ceremoniously placed at the scenes where the victims on The List had turned up dead.

There would be no crosses where "Gypsy" and "Cinderella" died.

A hangout and/or workplace for several victims, Cap'n Peg's fast food stand was where police apprehended a man with victim Jimmy Ray Payne's prison ID card. A contract between Williams and one of his singing groups bore the address of Cap'n Peg's. At no time in Williams' trial was Cap'n Peg's mentioned. (John White/Chicago Sun-Times)

18

The House on Gray Street

March, 1981

Spring was only one day away, and Atlanta's murders took their first important twist since Patrick (Pat Man) Rogers turned up dead three months earlier in the Chattahoochee River.

On March 20, 1981, some residents of the Techwood Homes housing project were up in arms. Literally. They protested that the police were not protecting them. They vowed to take to the streets to protect themselves. No one had yet disappeared from Techwood Homes, but I could identify with their frustration with the system's handling of these cases. Then, too, they were led by a local activist named Chimurenga Jenga and a Communist Workers Party leader named Nelson Johnson, who showed up unannounced and without fanfare, 16 months after five of his comrades were killed in a bloody shootout with Ku Klux Klansmen and neo-Nazis in Greensboro, North Carolina.

Together the residents formed a "bat patrol"—not with "Batmobiles" and help from Batman and Robin, but with wooden Louisville Sluggers (which actually are made in Jeffersonville, Indiana) and other baseball bats made of metal and plastic. When police arrested Jenga and two other men on charges of carrying weapons in a public place (one carried a .38-caliber revolver), a jeering crowd of about 100 residents and outsiders surrounded a police car and chanted discordantly: "One, two, three, four—we ain't gonna take this junk no more!"

Meanwhile, the Guardian Angels, a controversial, red-beret-clad, vigilante group from New York's subways, also took to the streets and taught martial arts to children. Unfortunately, although the "bat patrol" and the Guardian Angels were well-intentioned, they, like the mothers of the victims, labored under the misinformation fostered by police misunderstandings of the cases that someone was kidnapping children off the streets and then killing them.

Tensions ran so high that, in at least one instance, violence flared. An auto-parts dealer from Atlanta's Mechanicsville section (where Camille Bell and her slain son, Yusuf, had lived) chased and shot at two white men he thought had coaxed a black child into their car. (Actually, they were negotiating with a streetwalker.) The police charged the man with aggravated assault.

Long before this incident, it should have been clear that no unknown "monster" was lurking in dark corners—or, for that matter, riding the streets and offering rides or other enticements to strangers. These were not random killings. Too many of the victims knew each other.

In the end, I found that each victim on The List, with the possible exception of Angel Lenair, most likely knew at least one other victim on The List—inter-personal connections that the authorities, to this day, haven't acknowledged. Some victims, like Pat Man, knew at least 17 others.

At about the same time that the "bat patrol" held a rally in Techwood Homes (which adjoins part of the Georgia Tech campus), a 34-year-old man who had been missing from Atlanta was arrested in Hartford, Connecticut.

The man's name: Larry Marshall. At least, that's what he said his name was. In fact, his name was Larry Hill, and he had a 13-year-old son named Timmy Hill. However, this Timmy Hill is not the same 13-year-old Timmy Hill who was missing in Atlanta. But did someone think that the missing Timmy Hill was Larry's son?

Larry Marshall had worked as a security guard. Among other locations, he guarded a telephone company facility near the East Lake Meadows housing project. Larry Marshall's Atlanta home was less than a block from that of victim Patrick Baltazar.

In an interview in a Fulton County Jail cell, Larry Marshall would tell an NBC reporter an intriguing story: He was at home when 13-year-old (victim) Timmy Hill, whom he had known for some time, visited and left a note to him. The note, Larry Marshall said, advised him to get out of Atlanta. He added that the note was signed "the Reverend E. C." I considered the message a warning, not a threat, to Marshall.

Marshall had been jailed in Connecticut at the request of Atlanta officials. When he had left Atlanta, he was awaiting trial for a street robbery. Larry Marshall would be the Atlanta murders' first active suspect whom the press would learn about.

Of course, there had been the usual run of suspects who had been reported on—those picked up with candy bars, police badges, *et cetera.* A man in Tennessee had been a momentary suspect when he was arrested on another charge and police found that his wallet was small, "like a child's." A man in New York kidnapped a child in a truck with Georgia license plates; it turned out that the truck had been rented in New Jersey.

Neighbors became suspects when their neighbors suspected them for whatever reason. There were psychic-conjured suspects, real suspects that the press never learned about and one suspect whom some members of the press knew but wouldn't write about—me!

There also was 17-year-old Kenny Brown, who became a suspect when a young boy accused him of male rape. And an FBI agent in Macon, Georgia, caused a furor when he was quoted as saying at a public gathering, "Some of those kids were killed by their parents." Without providing specifics, his boss, FBI Director William Webster, hinted likewise. Some victims' parents challenged the FBI to "put up or shut up." The FBI shut up.

But Larry Marshall now was a real suspect that the press knew of and could find out things about. I thought it significant that on March 20, 1981—the very day that Larry Marshall was arrested in Connecticut—the first adult to make The List disappeared in Atlanta.

His name: Eddie (Bubba) Duncan, 21. Duncan lived at and disappeared from, of all places, Techwood Homes—and on, of all days, the very day that the Techwood Homes "bat patrol" took to the streets.

After that date, no one but adults would make The List—unless you consider a 17-year-old just home from the prison system. By March 20, 1981, the child murders—as understood by the world—were over in Atlanta. The last child had disappeared on March 13.

With Bubba Duncan's disappearance, the touts were back on the line, theorizing that the killer was following the press coverage of the murders, that he would show up the "bat patrol" marching at Techwood Homes. "He's taunting the police—he wants to be caught," my friend, Mike Edwards, said. To which I retorted, "Bullshit! . . . If the killer wants to be caught, he or she is doing a helluva poor job at it."

Bubba Duncan disappeared on the day before the article that Steve Dougherty had written on my work would appear in the *Atlanta Constitution.* An editor inserted a box in which he editorialized that the disappearance of Bubba Duncan did not fit the geographic parameters depicted in the story about my map.

Had the editor ever been where Duncan was last seen alive? Well, Duncan disappeared from North Avenue. About one block from his home is a small metal sign on a telephone pole. It reads: "U.S. 278," one of the 12 major connecting streets on the map.

Bubba Duncan disappeared on the same highway that marked the finding of Terry Pue's body, the home of Curtis Walker, the place where Curtis

Walker was last seen alive, and the home of slain 14-year-old Milton Harvey. Bubba Duncan's house was very close to the home of slain 11-year-old Patrick Baltazar and even closer to a house on Gray Street. Would the media ever understand?

The timing of Marshall's arrest as a suspect is significant because he had become chummy with children, including List victims Timmy Hill and Jo-Jo Bell, and because Bubba Duncan's disappearance on the same day of the arrest would immediately signal a rapid succession of adult killings. The implication was that these adult slayings could be intended to squelch information that, with Marshall in jail, the police might now be expected to come across.

Eddie Duncan was tall (some reports say 5-foot-11), slim and industrious. He regularly worked at a small grocery on the edge of Techwood Homes and performed other odd jobs. The addition of his name to The List caused reporters, writers and on-the-air news readers to struggle with this new wrinkle to their "missing and murdered *children*" story. Most never learned to deal with it.

The police, too, were at a loss to explain Bubba Duncan's inclusion on The List, so they began to manufacture answers that sounded plausible. His mind was "child-like," they would say. The mayor of Atlanta and police officials would say that the authorities were keeping such a close watch on youngsters that the killer had turned to older victims. And the news media would report such inane statements without qualification. After almost two years of failure, what magic change in police activities had occurred in only the one week since 13-year-old Timmy Hill had disappeared? Of course, Timmy Hill wasn't yet on The List, so he didn't officially exist for reporters to raise this question about.

It sounded good, but like many declarations by public officials, it simply didn't jibe with the facts. Plenty of children were still available for the random selection by a killer or killers, if that's what was happening.

The search for Timmy Hill went on, although he was reported to be spending the night at a university dormitory. I would remember that report when an incident would occur later at a Georgia Tech dormitory, leaving a young man dead.

Some had begun to look into suspect Larry Marshall's lifestyle. Marshall had lived in a house on Rock Street, on the corner of Haynes Street, less than one block from the home of slain 11-year-old Patrick Baltazar (in the rear of the Omni). Marshall lived with a roommate, Frankie Mealing, who told me he was a homosexual, but that Marshall was not. Some men in the neighborhood explained to Paul Crawley and me that whoever takes the active role in an all-male sexual partnership is not considered—in their culture—a homosexual, while the passive partner is.

Frankie Mealing told Paul and me that Timmy Hill had come to visit Larry Marshall and himself on many occasions. Mealing's sister also was there and verified Timmy Hill's visits. They also told us that Timmy Hill and Larry Marshall hung out at "Uncle Tom's" house (Tom Terrell, no relation to 11-year-old victim Earl Lee Terrell) in the 500 block of Gray Street.

We drove the few blocks of Haynes Street until it crossed Simpson and changed names to Gray Street. In another block, we passed the tiny house of the Reverend Earl Carroll, the man in the clown suit. Could this be the same "Reverend E.C." in the note that Larry Marshall says he received from Timmy Hill?

Surely the police had been suspicious of Earl Carroll. It dated back at least as far as Willie Mae Mathis' complaints that occasioned my attendance at the Wheat Street Baptist Church. At that rally, Carroll had introduced Atlanta's police chief, George Napper, as keynote speaker. Now Carroll had filed suit against Napper and other Atlanta officials, alleging harassment. Everywhere Carroll went, plainclothes cops with walkie-talkies were two steps behind. Carroll began taking reporters with him. They photographed and videotaped the surveillances and showed them on television with the images electronically distorted.

"Uncle Tom" Terrell was a lean, weathered, 63-year-old black man. He had two houses on Gray Street. One was vacant, and youngsters used it as they liked. Larry Marshall's roommate, Frankie Mealing, insisted that he had seen at least 10 of the victims on The List go in and out of the vacant house at one time or another.

The second house was where Tom Terrell lived. It was a dreary, unkempt old cottage. The yard was littered with the artifacts of years of not throwing anything away. The house shared several steps with a house next door.

As Paul Crawley and I sat on these steps, the man who lived next door told us of Tom Terrell and his unabashed homosexuality. He also spoke of children who visited Terrell, particularly Timmy Hill. The man said that Timmy often sat on these steps, waiting for "Uncle Tom" to come home. Tom would give him money, he said, and Timmy would stay there overnight. Now the man was in tears. "Why would anybody want to hurt that little kid," he said, sobbing. "I loved that little guy."

The man took us inside his house. He introduced us to his wife and showed us pictures of his children. He said he was almost late for work, but he kept talking. Most notably, he added that Timmy Hill had spent March 12, 1981—the night before he was reported missing—next door at Uncle Tom's house.

The neighbor also pointed out a large bucket that contained a substance that he said the kids get "high" on. They stole buckets of the stuff from a company that was nearby. He said the youngsters often held it to their noses and inhaled it.

Paul and I dipped the brown sticky substance from the bucket. It smelled like acetone. It looked like mud. We looked at each other, remembering what

Timmy Hill's little sister had told us about the man she saw in the taxi cab putting "mud" on Timmy's face.

It wasn't the only time that someone would link Timmy Hill with drugs and "highs." Timmy had been angry with his older brother, Richard, who, according to a DeKalb County police report, "did in fact shave Timothy's head prior to his disappearance to punish him for stealing his reefer."

Tom Terrell's neighbor confided to us that while the Atlanta police had not been by to see him, he had told these same details to the FBI the day before, when agents had come by and "asked just about the same questions." He volunteered that he had shown the FBI the warehouse where Larry Marshall had "taken Timmy" a few weeks earlier to buy him a Coke.

Paul and I went back to Larry Marshall's house. We talked with Frankie Mealing and his sister again. They were charging us a fee that amounted to the cheapest checkbook journalism I have ever seen—one cigarette per question. They had asked Paul for money, which he refused to give them, even though they protested that "other TV people paid us for our information."

"When is the last time you saw Timmy Hill?" Paul asked Mealing's sister.

"It was the day that Larry left town," she said. "I remember because the next day the police was by, askin' about him. The officer stood right here on the corner and talked to Jo-Jo Bell, askin' him if he knew where Timmy was."

"He was talking to *who*, ma'am," I interrupted.

"To Jo-Jo Bell," she repeated innocently.

"*The* Jo-Jo Bell?" Paul asked.

"Yeah, the other little boy what [sic] is missin.'"

"You mean the police were talking to Jo-Jo about Timmy?"

"That's right."

"Did they know it was Jo-Jo?" Paul asked.

"I don't know," the woman said, "but I knowed it was him because he come around here all the time, too, and he hangs out with Timmy and them other boys at Uncle Tom's."

I looked at Paul and said, "That's incredible." Both of us knew that 15-year-old Joseph (Jo-Jo) Bell had been missing for 11 days before Timmy Hill disappeared.

"Here, you can call the policeman and ask him," Mealing's sister suggested. She went to the mantel, which shrouded the space heater that stifled my breathing. She returned with the police officer's business card. It read: "Detective N.S. Tiege." This was the same Atlanta policeman whom Paul, David Page and I had followed into Timmy Hill's apartment a few days before.

"Uncle Tom" Terrell never became a serious suspect in the Atlanta murders. He later was sentenced to prison for engaging in sexual relations with another minor who apparently had nothing to do with these cases.

Two years later, a witness would swear in an affidavit that he saw Jo-Jo Bell murdered at Tom Terrell's house. There were too many flaws in the witness' story to give it any credence. But Tom Terrell seemed to be exactly the kind of suspect the police had been looking for and the public was expecting them to find. Attention stayed glued, instead, on Larry Marshall.

Still another boy would say weeks later that he had been to Tom Terrell's house on Gray Street. A policeman would ask him if he knew any of the children whose names had been in the news. The boy said he knew both Jo-Jo Bell and Timmy Hill.

"How do you know Jo-Jo Bell?" the officer asked.

"We went to the same school, Kennedy Middle School, and at Cap'n Peg's and Tom Terrell's house," the youngster replied.

The policeman then asked him when and where he had last seen Jo-Jo Bell.

The youth answered: "Over [at] Tom's house on a Friday night because Jo-Jo Bell was wearin' a suit, baggy pants, jacket to match, tie, short sleeve white shirt. The suit was blue pin-striped. I walked in Tom's house. Tom Terrell and another man was arguing.

"I looked over and I saw Jo-Jo Bell. Jo-Jo was sittin' on the sofa. Jo-Jo was in the first bedroom when you walk in the door and he was sittin' on this couch. I asked him what was he doing over here and he didn't say nothing. He asked me to come and go with him over to a friend's house. I told him that I would be there [sic] when he got back. He got back in about 30 minutes."

The youth went on to tell of how Jo-Jo Bell said that "some dudes" tried to pick him up in a black-and-white Cadillac. His comment reminded me of another Atlanta police report I had seen. The officer apparently misinterpreted a term used in ghetto slang. He wrote on the report form that a child had been chased by a person identified as "A. Dude."

The boy who had visited Tom Terrell's house said it was the last time he had seen Jo-Jo Bell (he would tell a different story later). Now he was asked to pick out pictures of any "missing or murdered children that he may have known," as the police report put it. The youth pulled the pictures of Jo-Jo Bell, Timothy Hill and an adult, 20-year-old Larry Rogers (who would turn up dead in April of 1981).

I noted that the officers conducting the interview never asked him if he had seen either Timmy Hill or Larry Rogers at Tom Terrell's house on Gray Street. In fact, they never brought up Hill or Rogers with the youngster again.

Still another young man proved to be an enigma throughout this phase of the cases. I thought he was an ideal candidate to be a victim, but others later would contend that he was a murderer. To understand these cases fully, one might keep in mind that this dual role of victim and killer is not necessarily inconsistent with the facts. If not in this young man's case, then certainly in several others.

He and Timmy Hill were good friends, the youngster told police, adding that they often went to Uncle Tom's at 522 Gray Street. He said Terrell and another man gave Timmy Hill oral sex for $10 to $15. The last time he saw

Timmy Hill, the young man reported, "he was going to wash a lady's dog for $50." A pretty mean dog, I thought.

The young man said that he, too, participated in oral sex at the house on Gray Street and that many black males visited there. He added that Larry Marshall had taken him and Timmy Hill with him on March 9, 1981. They planned for Larry Marshall to let Timmy Hill into the Salvation Army store on Marietta Street in downtown Atlanta, where Marshall worked as a security guard. The object was to let Timmy steal, the boy said. Timmy, he said in interviews with the police, went inside and emerged crying and complaining that someone had anal sex with him. There was no more talk of stealing from the Salvation Army after that. The young man went on to say that he had known another victim, but only slightly. The victim: 9-year-old Yusuf Bell.

Tom Terrell, according to police reports, said he had met Timmy Hill in the summer of 1980. Timmy, he said, often visited and would smoke pot with him and Terrell's niece. Terrell said that on the morning of March 12, he gave Timmy 50 cents to catch a bus to school. He and Timmy boarded the same bus, Terrell said, but he got off at the Omni—and Timmy rode on.

Tom Terrell's roommate told him that Timmy had returned later in the afternoon, but Terrell said he did not see him. Terrell also told police that Timmy Hill had sex with him.

Al Starkes of CORE had talked to Timmy's little sister—the same one whom Paul and I had talked to—about the "mud."

Starkes, who says he is a child psychologist, thought there was something to her statement. Well, I'm not any kind of an "ologist," but I agree with Al Starkes. I think the little girl was telling the truth as best she could.

Still another young witness' story intrigued me a great deal. First, he lived on Kimberly Road, off which slain 14-year-old Edward Hope Smith lived. Second, he admitted having sex with "Uncle Tom" at the house on Gray Street. And finally, he said that one suspect—not Wayne Williams—had told him that Timmy Hill would be found in the Chattahoochee River and that others would be, too.

It doubly interested me when a phone number in victim-to-be Jimmy Ray Payne's pocket led to a house on Kimberly Road. The witness said that all of his own homosexual affairs, which included at least two other "clients," had been encouraged by the individual I had earlier called an ideal candidate to be a victim, but whom others would call a murderer and who obviously *was*, at 15 years old, a third-party procurer.

This fit into my theory (one of the few theories I allowed myself while preferring to deal with facts) that Atlanta, like Chicago, had a John Wayne Gacy-like situation, with four levels:

1. Young victims.
2. Older procurer/victims/killers.
3. Still older user/victims/killers.
4. *The* kingpin killer(s).

But the real answer is still out there, elusive as ever. One thing is certain: No answers to any of my questions about these police reports of some victims' sexual encounters would come out at the trial of Wayne Williams. Certainly there would be no explanation of the affairs inside the house on Gray Street. None of these people who had told police about them was called to testify by the prosecution or the defense. Why not?

After all, police had found exactly what they had been looking so hard for—a house common to more than one victim, admissions of homosexuality and drugs, as well as eyewitnesses. It is unbelievable that Wayne Williams would be convicted without the story of what happened in the house on Gray Street being told in his trial.

Frankie Mealing was Larry Marshall's roommate when they lived at 422 Rock Street. After Marshall fled to Connecticut, Mealing moved in with his sister in a house three doors away. It was there that Paul Crawley and I had traded them cigarettes for information.

When we found them, Frankie Mealing was asleep on the floor. Apparently Mealing didn't live there all the time. The statement Mealing had given to DeKalb County police described himself as 34, black and an "admitted homosexual." He also had lived with Tom Terrell on Gray Street for eight months, according to a police report.

The same report goes on to tell of Timmy Hill's final visit with "Uncle Tom" on March 12, the day before Timmy was reported missing:

"Timmy and [another juvenile—name withheld] came over to Tom's house together about 5 p.m. They were walking when they arrived at approx. 5:00-5:30 p.m. Frankie Mealing and Timothy walked to 530 Gray Street [the vacant house owned by Tom Terrell] for the purpose of having sexual relations. The house is partially burned. Tom used to live in the house. It has since been razed.

"There was a sofa in the main room where Frankie allowed Timothy to have anal sex with him. Frankie layed [sic] on his stomach while Timothy entered him anally from the rear. Before Timothy had finished, [the other juvenile] entered the house and began teasing Timothy about his method. Timothy then dismounted. [The other boy] then had anal intercourse with Frankie while Timmy watched."

Everybody remained in the house for approximately 10 minutes, whereupon Frankie Mealing walked back to the house where Tom Terrell lived. The police report goes on:

"At approx. 9 p.m., Timothy walked back over to Tom's and asked him if he could stay the night. Tim said [the other boy] was going to stay next door. Tom told Timothy that he had better catch his bus and go home. Tim said his bus had stopped running for the night. Tom allowed him to stay. Tom fixed

Tim some collard greens and possibly pig tails.

"Frankie, Tom, Curly and Timothy were sitting in the main room. Timothy was sitting on the end of the bed in front of the fireplace. Curly was laying on the same bed. The fire was still burning in the fireplace.

"Timothy slept on a sofa where Frankie normally sleeps. Frankie slept in a chair in the same room. Curly slept in his bed in the same room and Tom slept in his bed which is in the front room.

"About 4 p.m. Frankie saw Timothy standing on the sidewalk with a black female about 16 years old." Soon Timmy Hill was seen no more.

March 30, 1981: A fusillade of bullets from a would-be assassin's gun seriously wounds President Reagan, his press secretary, James Brady; a Secret Service agent and a police officer outside a hotel in Washington.

Meanwhile, in Atlanta, Captain Johnny Sparks appears in a TV interview taped earlier that day. Sparks explains that the police expect to find Timmy Hill and return him home safely in just a few days.

But a news bulletin interrupts that very newscast: A body had been found in the Chattahoochee River south of the Georgia 166 bridge, southwest of Atlanta. The pattern of my map continued to expand to the west along this route. Many speculated that the body could be that of 15-year-old Joseph (Jo-Jo) Bell, who was by then on The List. But the body was that of 13-year-old Timmy Hill, whom police had refused to add to The List, even though he'd been missing now for 17 days.

Years earlier, when I first came to Atlanta, a war had erupted over control of the homosexual entertainment industry. It was a war that was to be recalled later in the Atlanta murders as firebombings of homosexual and sexually oriented entertainment spots broke out again.

But it was the earlier years that interested me the most now. Back then, several operators and employees of nightspots catering to homosexuals were found shot to death "assassination style"—in the back of the head from close range. Was it pure coincidence that Timmy Hill's body had washed ashore on the same property where those earlier victims had been found?

Timmy Hill would be the only child victim under 16 to be found in the Chattahoochee River. This fact, and the claim of Larry Marshall that Timmy had delivered to him the note that caused him to leave town, made me wonder some more. If someone at the top of a pyramid was killing off the "adult users," might he not also kill off "messenger" Timmy Hill, too? Did the location of Pat Man's and Timmy's bodies in the Chatthoochee, where only adults would otherwise be found, lend credence to my "procurer" theory?

Timmy delivers a note. Marshall is scared out of town. Marshall is arrested. The killing of adults immediately begins. The last child killed is Timmy Hill. His body is found in the same circumstance as most of those adults. It may mean nothing, but then again . . .?

That same afternoon, when Timmy Hill's body was found, 20-year-old Larry Rogers (no relation to Pat Man) was seen alive for the last time. He was small for his age, police said. Like still-missing 21-year-old Eddie (Bubba) Duncan, Larry Rogers was "slow" and "retarded," they added. His foster father vehemently denied that Larry Rogers was retarded.

But Larry Rogers, another "child-like" *adult*, according to the police version, would be added to The List of "murdered and missing children."

And now that he was found dead, Timmy Hill finally made The List—too late. Two days later, the *Atlanta Constitution* reported that "sources close to the investigation" said the Task Force was looking into the possibility of a "homosexual link" to Timmy Hill's slaying.

To which Public Safety Commissioner Lee Brown retorted: "There's no validity to that information. It appears to be one of many rumors running around."

Rumors? The reports of homosexual activity among Timmy Hill and others in the house on Gray Street came from purported eyewitnesses who weren't afraid to tell police—and give written statements—about what they had observed. And they came from the homosexuals themselves. Both Mealing and Terrell admitted sexual relationships with Timmy Hill, according to police reports. These were not merely rumors.

Of course, others at the trial of Wayne Williams would testify under oath for the state about incidents stretched to suggest alleged homosexual activity and Williams. However, the jury never would hear any testimony from those witnesses who had told police vivid details of what went on inside the house on Gray Street (which, along with the house next door, has since been destroyed by fire). No one will ever be able to check it for fibers! Nor can they check Tom Terrell's other house on Gray Street. It has been razed.

As a consequence, the jury in the Williams case would be deprived of meaningful information, and our criminal-justice system would short-change us again. The point is, the police decide which witness' stories they want to believe and those they don't want to believe. A jury doesn't get an opportunity to sift among all the evidence—even though the jurors may *think* they do. The validity of these reports should have been left to the jury—not the public safety commissioner—to decide upon. Now, we may never know!

Months after Timmy Hill turned up dead, Andrew Young would campaign for mayor of Atlanta. He would praise Lee Brown for publicly defusing any hint of homosexual connections with Atlanta's murders.

The question is: Had Lee Brown read any of those police reports on Timmy Hill's visits to the house on Gray Street? Had Andrew Young? Since there obviously were homosexual connections, was it defusion—or a coverup? If so, for whom?

Inexplicably destroyed by fire, "Uncle Tom" Terrell's house on Gray Street was a rendezvous point for avowed homosexual men and some victims, including Timothy Hill, 13, and Joseph (Jo-Jo) Bell, 15. Statements to police about sexual activity involving victims here were known to both prosecutors and defense attorneys, but the Williams jury never heard about them. (John White/Chicago Sun-Times)

19

Color Murder Green

March, 1981

They came all gussied up in their Sunday-go-to-meetin' and big-night-on-the-town clothes: Buckhead matrons in full-length minks and gowns. Peachtree bankers in stickpins and pinstripes. A Sandy Springs lawyer in a coyote-skin jacket. *Charlie's Angels* look-alikes from the north side and ravishing regulars at Cisco's and Mr. V's Figure 8 discotheques on the south side—in party dresses slit thigh-high or cut provocatively low.

As two teen-age girls pinned green ribbons (green to symbolize "life") on the hundreds of blacks and whites who arrived in almost equal numbers, some folks sold souvenir programs for $5 and posters for $10. A cluster of reporters mingled among the crowd. A French TV crew showed up.

Soon a tall black man swept into the lobby of Atlanta's Civic Center Auditorium. He was resplendent in red robe, and conspicuous in swastika and shapka, the brimless, furry cap worn by Soviet leaders from Stalin to Andropov when they pose for those photos outside the Kremlin in the dead of winter. A reporter casually approached the robed man, but the man brushed him aside. "I don't talk to honky reporters," he said.

The occasion on this March evening in 1981 was the Frank Sinatra-Sammy Davis Jr. concert, which would raise $250,000 for the Task Force's investigation.

It all was yet another bizarre, if dichotomous, interlude in Atlanta's murders—big-name entertainment thrown into the middle of all those grisly discoveries of bodies, the weeping by victims' families and schoolmates, the motorcades to graveyards. It was as if everyone was getting an emotional "fix" to ward off the anguish that wouldn't go away.

Atlanta's suffering had inspired prayers in churches across America, a candlelight vigil attended by 10,000 persons in Harlem and donations of money to the investigation and victims' families from just about everyone from schoolchildren to prison inmates. In Atlanta, "A Concerned Citizen" put up a billboard paraphrasing Psalm 127:1: "Unless the Lord watches over the city, the watchmen stand guard in vain."

On the Civic Center stage, Mayor Jackson introduced the families of many victims, and the crowd applauded warmly. He introduced politicians and entertainers. He thanked the Coca-Cola Company for sending a $25,000 check to the investigation. He said Mayor Jane Byrne of Chicago had telephoned to say that a check for $10,000 raised among Chicagoans was in the mail. He urged everybody to support a pending Congressional bill that President Reagan soon would sign, authorizing the first increment of federal money ($1.5 million) to Atlanta's investigation.

"We have the largest, most effective operation going," Jackson told the crowd, which was largely unaware that, in truth, the investigation was dreadfully inept. "We cannot tell all we know," the mayor went on, perpetuating the myth that police silence is intended to hide knowledge, not *lack* of knowledge.

The mayor then introduced actor Burt Reynolds (a donor of $10,000), who, in turn, introduced the stars of the show. "They've put a little bread in the coffers for us," Reynolds said.

Sinatra and Davis. Legends in their time. A touch of Hollywood and Las Vegas had come to Atlanta at a time when many were in no mood for laughter and applause. When Sammy Davis Jr. sang his hit, *"The Candy Man,"* someone wondered aloud if anyone had realized that "candy man" is slang in some ghettos for dope pushers.

Frank Sinatra sang to a grateful crowd. A young girl gave him a hug—and an award from the Police Athletic League (PAL). Sparing, but eloquent, in his sentiments, Sinatra told the crowd: "I feel very deeply about this tragedy in this town . . . Justice will prevail. Honorable people will triumph over dishonorable deeds. I love you, and pray for you."

Security was tight. Thirty police officers were on duty, and dogs sniffed the auditorium for bombs. The Atlanta newspapers had received an anonymous, threatening letter: "Consider . . . while everybody's watching Sammy and Frank, who'll be watching the children?"

Reporters were confined to a concrete storage room in the bowels of the auditorium, where they could watch the concert only on closed-circuit television. It was, Steve Oney would write in *Atlanta Weekly,* "a state of affairs that symbolized the distance most of them had been from the story all along."

When the concert was over, only those who held $100 tickets were admitted to a benefit auction in the main ballroom of the Peachtree Plaza Hotel. There, they stood in a swirl of disco lights, hoisting cocktail glasses and feasting on boned capon stuffed with ground veal in a curry sauce, red snapper, Spanish red crayfish with asparagus and ginger sauce, chocolate truffles and fresh fruit.

Once again, Atlanta's tragedy donned a cloak of slick commercialism. Among the items up for auction were five hours of tax and financial planning from Price Waterhouse, a week of cooking lessons from Rich's department store, a VIP membership in the American Fitness Center, season tickets to the Atlanta Braves' home games, and a trip for two to the resort of Cancun, Mexico—compliments of Eastern Airlines. All for the investigation.

As if that weren't enough, a $100 ticket enabled you to watch Monica Kaufman, a WSB-TV news reader, auction off a flat of red raspberries, "impossible-to-get" tickets to the 1981 Atlanta Steeplechase and a "small but wonderful" Louis XV table. At times, the bidding got extravagantly high—not unexpectedly for a crowd that included such luminaries as Coretta Scott King, singer Roberta Flack and jazz singer Peabo Bryson, clad in white suit and red sash.

Clearly, this was a night for Atlanta's upper social strata to rub elbows, raise toasts and bask in glitter, far from the tears and agony of Thomasville Heights and East Lake Meadows. This was a night when well-intentioned Atlantans had paid $25 to $100 per person (some made $500 donations) for theatrical therapy and relief from the barrage of bad news.

Unlike the multiple killings in Los Angeles, New York, Chicago, San Francisco and Houston, the nightmare of Atlanta had spawned a new way to spell "relief": throw money.

Gladys Knight and the Pips recorded a musical paean to the slain victims—*"Forever Yesterday [for the Children]"*—on the CBS Records label, with sales proceeds going to a group called the Atlanta Children's Foundation.

Comic-strip creator Morrie Turner drew his *"Wee Pals"* characters for a child-safety cartoon series on public television. Atlanta schoolchildren entered a poster contest that stressed safety, but not spelling. One entry on display at Rich's department store read: "DON'T EXCEPT RIDE FROM STRANGERS."

Throughout its ordeal, Atlanta came across awkwardly self-conscious and tinged with guilt. And the money poured in. It came in cash, checks, pledges and government funds—hundreds of thousands of dollars of it.

It came in tiny amounts with notes of heartfelt sympathy from John and Jane Q. Public in cities and towns across America, in contributions of $10,000 and $25,000 from corporate giants and big-time entertainers and in grants totaling $4.2 million from the Reagan Administration.

But along with the stacks of money arriving every day at City Hall and at other busy collection points, where telephones rang off the hooks, came confusion, skepticism, criticism, cynicism and still-unanswered questions.

Even some victims' families—who said they each received checks for $255, $59 and $618 through March of 1981 to defray burial and other expenses—are not sure who paid them or what became of the large sums collected, but apparently never shared. A mother of one slain child, upon hearing how much money had been disbursed to other victims' parents, was annoyed. "I didn't get my check," she fumed, as other mothers tried to assure her that she would receive it soon.

Months later, one victim's sister and mother eagerly reminisced about the fund-raising forays across America by the Committee to Stop Children's Murders. They spoke of meetings chaired by private detective Don Laken, the "Dog Man," and his wife.

At those meetings, trips around the nation were shopped around the room:

"Cambridge! I've got Cambridge! Who wants to go to Cambridge?"

"Cambridge? Where's Cambridge?"

"Massachusetts? No way! It's too cold up there!"

The victim's mother recalled the trip to Washington, where Camille Bell spoke to a crowd from the steps of the Lincoln Memorial, where Camille's 12-year-old son, Jonathan, read Martin Luther King Jr.'s "*I Have a Dream*" speech, which King delivered on those very steps 20 years ago.

The victim's sister told of her trip to another city in 1981 as a "stand-in." Mothers were in such enormous demand for radio and TV interviews and fund-raisers that elder children were thrown into the breach. The sister said she was told: "Whatever they give you in cash is yours. Stick it in your pocket and enjoy it."

When the Committee to Stop Children's Murders temporarily refused to open its books, and when secretary-treasurer Venus Taylor (mother of slain 12-year-old Angel Lenair) was reported to have spent $900 on waistline-slimming "tummy tuck" surgery, it only poured more fuel on the fire in skeptics' eyes.

The committee was scolded by Georgia's Consumer Affairs director, Dr. Tim Ryles, for not having properly registered with the state as a charitable organization. When challenged by some reporters about the committee's zeal to raise money, Willie Mae Mathis shot back, "What's wrong with it?"

Even today, there remains little, if any, agreement on exactly how much money flowed to Atlanta, how much was earmarked for the investigation and victims' families, how carefully the money was being controlled and how it was supposed to be distributed.

The confusion and snarls of red tape apparently also prevented sums of money from reaching Atlanta. That includes about $8,000 raised by the United Auto Workers in 1981 for victims' families.

"Maynard Jackson explained to me, 'Buddy, we have a bedlam here, we got things coming from everybody and everywhere,'" Robert Battle III, then a union official and now an aide to Detroit Mayor Coleman Young, told the

Associated Press in 1983. "He [Jackson] turned me over to a fellow he put in charge, and he told me they had 10 or 12 different organizations claiming they were the lead organization and therefore they should handle the money. He said, 'Hold it and give us a couple or three days to put it together.' The couple or three days went into about two or three weeks."

But as contributions to Atlanta rolled in from around the world in 1981, some Atlantans became resentful and embarrassed. "We need to close down the sideshow," Associate Editor Bill Shipp of the *Atlanta Constitution* wrote. "We need to close down the collection booth and tell the crowds to go home and tend to their own business."

One Georgia state legislator, Representative Tyrone Brooks, stood on the steps of City Hall and told reporters: "It's an insult to offer a family money just because their child has been killed. What about all the hundreds of poor people in this city, in this state, who have lost children? Are they entitled to compensation, too, just because they've suffered a tragedy?" Brooks also refused to the attend the Frank Sinatra-Sammy Davis Jr. concert because "this is not the place for a festive mood—not with all these tragedies. I don't like it."

For that matter, neither did Kenneth Almond, the stepfather of slain 14-year-old Edward Hope (Teddy) Smith, victim No. 1 on The List. He accused fund-raisers of "using our kids to make a profit. They can take that money and shove it. All I care about is catching the person that's doing it." Almond was dubious about the investigation. "Our child was the first one to disappear," he said, "and we caught hell trying to get a cop out here."

While some out-of-state donors shared this resentment, others were piqued that not all Atlantans welcomed their generosity. "A lot of people in America are going to a lot of trouble to give," said Chester Heathington, a Chattanooga, Tennessee, fireman who organized a fund drive to culminate in a motorcade to Atlanta. "Up until all these statements," he said in 1981, "things were going great."

In public money alone, at least $9 million was expended as a consequence of Atlanta's murders (including the $5 million "Safe Summer '81" recreation program). But that figure is only approximate because there is no central accounting of the various fund-raising efforts. That also applies to monies contributed to victims' families. City Hall handled some of it; but so did nonprofit organizations such as the Southern Christian Leadership Conference, the civil rights group founded by Martin Luther King Jr. and other black ministers during the 1950s. At one point, SCLC officials divided a $60,000 increment 28 ways—for disbursal to families of the 28 murder victims on The List. Some donors ultimately were chagrined when they learned that money designated for "children's" families also went to families of adult ex-convicts on The List.

To its credit, the city of Atlanta arrested and fined some persons for fraudulent collections. Atlanta police also kept watch on the Reverend Earl

Carroll after he had become the first to raise money for a "reward fund" back in 1980—months before the Task Force was formed.

But there was no way for the city—or anyone else, for that matter—to monitor *all* fund-raising activities, which seemed to spread like wildfire across the nation, all in the name of Atlanta's "children." Many victims' mothers—notably Camille Bell, Willie Mae Mathis and Venus Taylor—traveled from New York to Los Angeles, appearing at fund-raising rallies and on TV talk shows. Vendors hawked "Save Our Children" T-shirts. By mail order, a man in a Midwestern state peddled "STOP the Atlanta Killer" bumper stickers for $1 apiece, promising that the proceeds would go to the investigation.

One Atlanta woman artist collected money for a citywide poster contest called "Operation Survival," in which schoolchildren were invited to compete for three $50 savings bonds by illustrating their "responses to the missing and murdered children." When asked to disclose the amount that was contributed, she refused. "I don't think that's important," she said testily.

From Hollywood came a country-and-Western ballad called *"Atlanta's Black Children,"* written and sung by Dave McEnery, a character actor-cowboy entertainer who calls himself "Red River Dave." McEnery, who said he would turn over proceeds to "the victims' families" (he didn't say *which* victims' families), had turned out other tunes based on newsmaking events: *"The Ballad of Patty Hearst," "Reverend Jimmy Jones," "The Ballad of Three-Mile Island," "Song of the U.S. Hostages," "The Shooting of President Reagan," "D.B. Cooper, Where Are You?"* and *"When Ol' Bing Crosby Said Goodbye."* A sampling from *"Atlanta's Black Children"*:

> *"In that great and Southern city called Atlanta,*
> *In the year of Seventy-nine in that fair land;*
> *Little children who are black start disappearing,*
> *Murdered by some evil unknown wicked hand.*
> *Chorus:*
> *"Sleep little children of Jesus, safe from the world's alarms;*
> *No one can kidnap or kill you now, you're safe in*
> *the Master's arms . . ."*

By far the biggest share of public monies came from the federal government, beginning with the $1.5 million that President Reagan authorized on March 13, 1981, for the Task Force investigation. He earmarked another $979,000 for so-called "mental-health" and "social-service" programs for Atlantans who suffered from stress and other problems attributed to the slayings.

Political overtones couldn't be ignored. Some wondered if the President had acceded to Mayor Jackson's requests for money so he could blunt criticism by many that the Reagan White House was insensitive toward blacks. For his part, the mayor was so elated, as one insider put it, that he was "walking with one foot off the floor."

In early 1981, both Jackson and Public Safety Commissioner Lee Brown had insisted that the police were running out of money and that the Task Force was costing $150,000 a month—mainly for computer and overtime costs—beyond what they said the city could afford. Jackson and Brown called them "extraordinary costs."

However, what few Atlantans knew was that these so-called "extraordinary costs" were routinely being paid from the city's general fund and that computer time, software and expertise was being donated by IBM. What's more, one city official told Jeff Prugh and Lee May of the *Los Angeles Times* that the city was not as desperate as its leaders conveyed—and that the city's general fund was capable of financing the investigation for several more months, at least until June of 1981, the month Wayne Williams would be arrested.

What *did* happen to all the money? Fannie Mae Smith, the foster mother of still-missing Darron Glass, would complain on national television in 1984 that someone (she didn't say who) at City Hall had taken unspecified sums intended for families of victims.

". . . the mail man put out four big sacks every day at City Hall," she said. "We didn't get to look at our mail. . . They took out what they wanted to take out. We didn't see it. . . .If there was any money in it, they took that. We got cards. . . that said, 'Maybe this will help you.' Whatever it was, we didn't see it."

There were all kinds of considerations for making The List—that arbitrary, stupid List—and none seemed to have anything to do with any "pattern." Among these considerations were politics and public pressure.

Timmy Hill almost never made The List. Cynthia Montgomery, Angela Bacon, Joseph Lee, Faye Yearby and others never did. But 13-year-old Curtis Walker, who lived in the Bowen Homes project, where the mayor had been booed in 1980, made The List within five hours after he disappeared. The children of members of the mothers' committee made it. They included two daughters. (No other females would make The List.) Still-missing 21-year-old Eddie (Bubba) Duncan made it quickly. People already were marching in the street where he disappeared from, so Duncan's case, like that of Curtis Walker of Bowen Homes, was assigned to The List with strong political considerations.

On a hot summer night a few years ago, 20-year-old Larry Rogers' younger brother got into a fight at a party. He was hit on the head with a 2-by-4.

A young man who lived close to Larry Rogers' house heard the call on his police monitor and beat the police to the scene. He took the young man to a hospital and notified Rogers' foster mother. Later, the foster mother would say that the young man visited her and left his business card. His name, she said, was Wayne Williams.

Later, the woman said, Wayne Williams would hide Larry Rogers' younger brother and another foster son in an apartment on Simpson Street. He later would take her, she said, in a big, black car to find them.

When Larry Rogers' body was found on April 9, 1981, it lay in an abandoned apartment near Simpson Street. Although the location was approximately the same as the hiding place, the woman was unable to say whether it is the same apartment where she found her foster sons earlier. Neither the foster mother nor Larry Rogers' younger brother would be asked to testify in Wayne Williams' trial. Wayne Williams later admitted to me that the woman's story is true. He denied knowing that the younger Rogers boy was involved. "My concern was the Gonzales kid." He told me where the apartment was and estimated that it was about a mile from where Larry Rogers' body had been found.

On March 31, 1981, the day after Larry Rogers (no relation to Pat Man) had disappeared, the police returned to the same Chattahoochee River bridge on Georgia 166, where they had been the day before.

This time, the corpse of 21-year-old Eddie (Bubba) Duncan was pulled from the river on the Douglas County side southwest of Atlanta—a few feet from where 13-year-old Timmy Hill's body had been removed from the river 24 hours earlier, on the Fulton County side.

Typically, Lee Brown was vague and rambling when questioned by reporters on April 8, 1981, about the finding of one slain adult—Bubba Duncan, 21—and about a second adult, still-missing Larry Rogers, 20.

"We know that the two young men in question are, in context of age, small in stature," Brown said at a news conference. "We know that they are black. And I guess our concern at this point is that we've lost the life of one young man who happens to be a few years older than the other cases we're carrying. And another young man is missing who happens to be a little older than the other cases that we're carrying. . .

"Age is not, and I'm repeating myself, is not a determining factor. What we do is look at the holistic circumstances surrounding the case and then make a decision. Obviously, we're concerned about *anybody* that loses a life in our city. In this instance, there are similarities in terms of characteristics that suggest we want to carry it to the Task Force. But as we investigate, we can look at *all* the cases and attempt to find commonality. If there is a common thread in all the cases, then we can, indeed, use that information in an effort to solve the case." How he'd changed his tune since Pat Man had been found.

Again, Brown's words *sounded* plausible. But most reporters merely recorded them like stenographers, without challenging or dissecting exactly what Brown was—and was *not*—saying. When Brown said "all the cases," did he mean those children and adults who had *not* been put on The List, too? And when he said "if there is a common thread," no one pressed him on the common threads that *did* exist—the geographic and personal connections among many victims.

Three predictable events occurred with the finding of Bubba Duncan's body. First, no one knew—and no one would find out—what caused Duncan's death. The cause of death was ruled "probable asphyxia" and reported as "undetermined" on a police background report on The List. Second, although the body could have been deposited almost anywhere upstream and could have been pulled from either side of the river, the wags returned to the public stage. They theorized about why they thought Duncan's body turned up on the Douglas County side. Ridiculous! Then Annie Rogers, mother of slain 16-year-old Patrick (Pat Man) Rogers, would tell us that Bubba Duncan had been a friend of Pat Man years ago.

Five days before Larry Rogers disappeared, a 23-year-old man was missing. He was an ex-convict named Michael (Mickey) McIntosh.

His house, which he had inherited, was a cottage that had been damaged considerably by fire. It sat on the corner of Glenn Street, facing the rear door of Cap'n Peg's. McIntosh did odd jobs at Cap'n Peg's and knew another young employee, 15-year-old Jo-Jo Bell, who was missing and made The List.

But Michael McIntosh would not go on The List—not yet, anyway. Unlike Bubba Duncan, who was said to be "child-like," and Larry Rogers, who was said to be "child-sized," there was no way to liken McIntosh to a child.

A man who ran an import shop on Bankhead Highway (U.S. 278), near the house of the drug dealer who was mentioned as having cavorted with 12-year-old Charles Stephens (slain back in October of 1980), told police that McIntosh came into his shop, crying and apparently having been severely beaten. McIntosh, the man said, had cuts over his nose and one eye, and his face was swollen.

It had been about March 25, 1981, the time that McIntosh was last seen alive. "The guy told me some blacks had beaten him up," the businessman said. "They gave him $12 and showed him where the MARTA bus was. I last saw him headed toward the Chattahoochee River." This witness would not be called to testify in the trial of Wayne Williams.

People other than Paul Crawley of WXIA-TV began to raise legitimate questions about The List. Now, people had to "die" to get on it. Obviously, it was fast becoming a *murdered persons* list. You could hardly make it by simply disappearing. Oh, they still maintained a non-list, which is where the murdered body of 28-year-old John Porter would be put on April 12, 1981, when he was found stabbed on a sidewalk, not far from McIntosh's house and Cap'n Peg's. Porter, like McIntosh, was a man. No one could say he was "child-like."

On one occasion in the spring of 1981, the police would put a missing young man on The List. But he didn't meet my geographic parameters. I would tell Paul Crawley that this is someone who does not belong on The List. The missing young man was said to be "retarded." "Paul," I said, "they [police] don't have the slightest idea what the pattern is in these cases." The next day, the young man was found picking peaches in eastern Georgia, hours from Atlanta.

Three days before John Porter was found dead, a routine incident led to the discovery of 20-year-old Larry Rogers' fully clad body. Someone had stolen a green Buick from the Prado shopping center at I-285 and Roswell Road, north of Atlanta. The thief left the car next to an abandoned apartment building off Simpson Street at Temple, near downtown Atlanta. The car was stripped and left only as a hulk on blocks, without wheels and tires.

After it sat there a few days, someone called the police. The officer arriving on the scene first detected a terrible odor. It didn't come from the Buick, but from the abandoned building. Inside, he found a body identified as that of Larry Rogers. The Fulton County medical examiner ruled that the cause of death was imprecise as usual—"probable asphyxia."

A young woman reporter for the Associated Press had contacted me earlier in 1981, but our meeting had been postponed by the arrival of AP reporter Peter Arnett from New York. Peter didn't think it necessary for two AP reporters to meet with me.

But now, Peter had left the AP, and Nancy Kenney called me again. She was eager to take the "tour of death." Her interest had been rekindled by an *Atlanta Constitution* story of the tour and my map.

As we drove, I told Nancy that one of the most important, but overlooked, aspects of the cases was the work by medical examiners. I told her that I feared that the authorities would catch a murderer, only for him or her to walk away free because they could not prove the *corpus delecti.*

"What do you mean?" Nancy asked.

"Well," I said, "we know that there's a great question about some of the identifications. And we know that the medical examiners don't know in what manner many of these people were killed. In order to convict someone, you have to prove there was a murder to be convicted of.

"Let's suppose you were on the jury and the defense attorney would ask the medical examiner, 'Are you sure that this is the body of Jefferey Mathis?' and the medical examiner were to say, 'No, I'm sure it isn't Darron Glass, but it could be almost any 10-year-old.'

"Now let's say that the defense attorney would continue, 'Now, Mr. Medical Examiner, how was this person that you can't identify murdered?' And the medical examiner would have to say, 'Probable asphyxia'—that is, he probably stopped breathing. Would you, Nancy, convict this man of murder?"

"Of course not," she replied.

Ironically, the grand jury would indict Wayne Williams for two "probable asphyxia" murders.

Nancy Kenney was intrigued. She wanted more explanation.

"Don't take *my* word for it," I said. "Check with someone else."

Nancy telephoned Fulton County prosecutor Lewis Slaton, who, she said, gave her about the same explanation that I did. "Slaton," she said, "told me, 'I would not choose to prosecute any of the probable-asphyxia cases'!" Which, ironically, is exactly what Slaton would do successfully in 1982 in the Wayne Williams trial!

Because of our conversation, Nancy looked very closely at the causes of death. When the Fulton County grand jury would indict Wayne Williams in July of 1981 for the murder of 21-year-old ex-convict Jimmy Ray Payne, she checked the death certificate. It reported the cause of death as "undetermined." The medical examiner did not rule the death of Jimmy Ray Payne a murder. After Nancy made an inquiry at the medical examiner's office, she said, the death certificate was changed to reflect a murder.

Nancy told me that I probably would never get credit for the discovery. If I hadn't explained the problem to her, it probably would have gone unnoticed that Wayne Williams had been indicted for killing a man who the criminal-justice system had ruled had died of undetermined causes.

In early 1981, I appeared on Cable News Network's *Freeman Reports* show for the first time. The show originated in the main studios of CNN in Atlanta. I appeared with Jack Perry. I had told the moderator, Sandi Freeman, that I would appear only on one condition—that she not imply, or expect me to imply, that I was in any way critical of the Atlanta police department's ongoing investigation.

Until then, I had never said one critical word publicly about this investigation. Abysmal as it was, I knew that criticizing it would do no good and would make no difference. (This book, of course, is highly critical, but only after Atlanta's police hierarchy decided to shut down the Task Force investigation.)

Even in Los Angeles, which has had its share of multiple murders (the "Hillside Strangler" cases, for instance) to test its very efficient police department, any solution would be based on luck. Matters in Atlanta were completely out of the hands of the police. They could not prevent these murders, and they could not solve them without luck or an informant. I knew it, but their top officials didn't. In any event, Jack Perry would supply Sandi Freeman with plenty of on-the-air poor-mouthing of the police.

Sandi opened the program by introducing Jack and me as two ex-police officers who were highly critical of the work of the Atlanta police. I was seething. Jack spoke first and blasted the police. When it came my turn, I stated for the first time on national television that many more people—including children—were being murdered in Atlanta than were being put on The List.

"How many are there?" Sandi asked.

"At least 24," I replied. The official count then was 17. I proceeded to tell the story of Cynthia Montgomery.

"Have you told the police about this?" Sandi asked.

I laughed. "Should I have to tell the police who has been murdered?" I asked.

"Have you told the mayor—and Lee Brown?" she prodded.

"Yes, I've told Lee Brown. I've told anybody who would talk to me about it, including you. It's the first thing I said to you."

Slightly flustered, Sandi Freeman began insisting that there was nothing that I could expect her to do about the discrepancies in the body count.

Yes, there was, I thought, but I didn't want an argument. She could help get the story right and inform the public of what is really happening in Atlanta. I thought, "It's *your* job, not mine."

But the news media would continue to regurgitate the party line. *Life* magazine published an article on the killings in early 1981. I counted at least 27 factual errors in it. I immediately wrote to *Life,* pointing out the errors, in March of 1981. No one responded until December of 1982. Although someone at *Life* found that I was right on each point, he didn't say so, but merely stated back to me what I had stated to *Life* in my letter.

Among other things, *Life's* response included one point that jabbed at a nerve: "Any list other than the Task Force list is pointless."

"What is this?" I asked Jeff Prugh. *"Pravda?* Or Tass?"

Twenty-eight-year-old John Porter had mostly lived with his grandmother until January or February of 1980. But he had been in and out of jail so many times over the previous 15 or so years that he didn't have an opportunity to make regular friends in the neighborhood. A few years earlier, John Porter was in the Georgia state penitentiary at Reidsville. While there, he developed mental problems and was transferred to Georgia Regional Hospital for psychiatric help. Whenever John Porter left his grandmother's house at all, he visited the neighborhood around the McDaniel-Glenn housing project and Cap'n Peg's. Sometime in early 1980, Porter's mental problems became so severe that his grandmother, Selite Allen, "threw him out of the house," she told investigating officers. The police report went on:

"Due to Porter's time in jail, he had developed severe mental problems and would wander about the house talking to himself or mumbling. [Mrs.] Allen stated that she had observed him standing in the back room of her residence talking to himself in a low mumbling tone.

"She said she felt that he had become a 'sissy.' She explained that 'sissy' meant to her that Porter either had or was engaging in sexual activities with males. She recalled overhearing one series of mumblings from John Porter which, to her, sounded as if he was giving instructions to another male who was 'sucking him.'"

The grandmother said that on two occasions she observed Porter (who would have been about 27 at the time) with the 2-or-3-year-old male child that she is rearing. The report went on:

"Porter would lay the child on the bed and pull the boy's pants down low on his hips, and then would fondle or the feel the lower abdominal area of the child."

When Selite Allen became concerned for the child's safety, she ordered John Porter from the house. Porter then moved in with his mother on Capital Avenue, near Atlanta-Fulton County Stadium.

Porter's mother said that whenever she and her son quarreled, he disgustedly took his belongings and moved next door to an empty unit in the condemned apartment building where James Charles Gates lived. (Gates was purported to be the driver of a blue station wagon that had a butcher knife stuck through the sun visor.) Porter did exactly that on the day he disappeared in the spring of 1981. At 5-foot-10, John Porter was not "child-like."

John Porter was stabbed six times. The wounds were about ⅜ of an inch wide and penetrated about 2 to 2½ inches into his body. He was found on a sidewalk, propped on the steps of what used to be a house, but now is a vacant lot, not far from Cap'n Peg's and along the route.

Pictures taken by the Atlanta police crime-scene unit show that dogs run freely in the area where Porter's body was found. Would John Porter have dog hairs on his body, as so many other victims did? Would police surmise that the killer has a fox terrier like the one that is shown in one police photo, about three feet from Porter's body?

Selite Allen, Porter's grandmother, was shown six black-and-white photographs, one of which was of Wayne Williams. She said that all the individuals in the photographs were unfamiliar to her.

John Porter *never* made The List. But the introduction of his case at the Wayne Williams trial by the prosecution would affirm what some of us had been saying all along: There were killings that should have made The List, but had not.

I had put Porter on my list when he was found dead in April of 1981, simply because his case fit the geographic pattern. The police did not put him on The List, although they later would say he had five fiber matches to tie him to Wayne Williams.

Proposed solutions became symbols of the problem. Chevron spent $58,000 for trash-bin posters. The Atlanta Braves wore green ribbons painted on their batting helmets. Yet as more money and manpower poured in, the problem got worse. (Brandi Woody)

20

"I Didn't Kill Anybody"

April, 1981

The dingy old building near the corner of Peachtree and West Peachtree streets in downtown Atlanta had been leased to house the special unit investigating Atlanta's murders. By now, on April 17, 1981, the multi-jurisdictional unit was unofficially the fifth largest police department in Georgia.

The telephone call I got three days earlier nearly knocked me out of my chair: I was being called in as a *suspect*. To me, it was like asking the canary if it had swallowed the cat.

A closed-circuit TV camera scanned the row of cars which lined the shady side of the building. As I turned the corner to the entrance, I noticed that the aluminum-framed glass door was swung *open* against the front of the building—out of sight of everybody inside. A metal-ringed paper key tag jiggled in the wind.

I couldn't believe my eyes. The key to the front door of the Special Police Task Force—Atlanta's top-secret undertaking of the century—was there for anyone to steal. I was surprised to find that no electronic, Orwellian eye stood watch over this side of the building. I thought there should be one. Two weeks later, the Task Force probably thought so, too. A television camera might have helped dissuade the rabid Marxist who stormed into the building on May Day and splattered almost everything in sight—including police officers—with red paint.

The temptation to take that key was barely resistible. Maybe I'd snatch it on the way out—that is, *if* I got out!

Task Force headquarters once had been a new-car showroom. It looked as if the last car it had showcased might have been a 1946 Studebaker. From eight feet down, it was strictly contemporary American plywood—in drab, gun-metal gray.

This was the nerve center for one of the biggest murder investigations in the annals of American crimes. A row of tables on the right and a scattering of office dividers on the left formed a corridor into the inner-sanctum of the investigation. At a break in the partitions, I arrived in a makeshift room with three desks, occupied by two women who were engaging in small talk.

"Can I help you?" one asked.

"Yes, I have an appointment with Morris Redding."

Morris Redding was the most recent and the highest-ranking of a succession of Atlanta police officers who had been appointed to direct the Task Force. He shared the job in a not-fully-explained way with a Georgia Bureau of Investigation (GBI) agent by the Dixiefied name of "Robbie" Hamrick.

A motley assortment of young people sat at the long row of tables that separated the administrative area from the rank-and-file workers. Their ill-fitting uniforms reminded me of the kind issued to Army basic trainees on their first visit to the Quartermaster. Their shirts were in varying shades of fading blue. On their shoulder patches was the word "RECRUIT."

One worker ate a cheese sandwich. Another was talking on the telephone to his girlfriend. Another kept score as he made toss after toss of wadded-up paper at a wastebasket. A female recruit pored over "nut letters," missives from psychics and people with dreams. She carefully transferred information from the letters to forms. When she finished a stack, she filed the letters in one drawer and the forms in another. I sensed that the drawers would be the final resting place for both.

The walls were covered with artists' composites. I recognized only two that had a possible bearing on the murder cases. The rest, dozens of them, had been conjured up by psychics. As I gazed at these disparate images, it was obvious that there were either more killers than victims or the psychics weren't very good. These pictures seemed to narrow the field of suspects to all the world's males who were older than 7.

I wandered unchallenged into the farthest corners of the Task Force building. In one corner stood a battery of computer terminals. A lone operator was running a program I couldn't get close enough to see.

I looked in vain for charts or maps. There weren't any, save one map of metropolitan Atlanta which bore no markings that would have related it to the murder cases. Perhaps they were using graphics terminals to reproduce whatever information they wanted from the computers. Maps particularly interested me because they formed the framework for my understanding of the cases.

This was not the dynamic engine of an investigation that one might imagine—having pictured situation boards and a room bustling with people scurrying around to make constant updates from the computer printouts.

Not even the crackling of a police radio broke the stale atmosphere of the place.

Two investigators, who were conspicuous by the revolvers, handcuffs, keys and various other paraphernalia which hung from their belts, wandered in independently. One made a phone call, and they left together. Where were these thousands of calls Mayor Jackson and Lee Brown had publicly said the Task Force was receiving each week? The battery of phones sat mute on the table.

Morris Redding appeared at the end of the hallway and motioned for me to join him. Until now, I hadn't had a moment of anxiety since walking in the door. It was only this morning that I contemplated such options as the Fifth Amendment, taking along an attorney, even strapping on a body bug to record our conversations. I don't share the naive presumption that one should co-operate fully if he has nothing to hide. I know there are a lot of innocent people in jail—perhaps even a few I myself sent.

Redding introduced me to Robbie Hamrick. The two cops were a study in contrasts. Redding, fiftyish with brown hair, is a diminutive man who wears an almost perpetual, no-nonsense scowl. Hamrick is a large man, with black-framed glasses separating his graying hair from his engaging smile. He looks like he should have a pipe dangling from the corner of his mouth and a grandchild bouncing on his knee.

They screwed up the interview from the start. I had expected, at the very least, a perfunctory Miranda warning (statement of my rights). But Redding, referring to his notes and seldom looking up, jumped right into the questioning. He made marks on his notes with his pencil as I answered, as if he were checking off from a list of questions.

At that point, I could have confessed to anything and legally they could not have used it in court. But I'm afraid that any such legal niceties are not always what they're advertised to be. First, you have to get the interrogator to admit in court that he didn't give the warning. What's one more lie, more or less, in the cause of justice?

"Would you be willing," Redding asked, "to take a polygraph test?"

His question had been somewhat oblique. I decided that my answer would be even more indirect. "If you were to ask me to," I said, "I'd have to think about it." I already knew that my answer would be "No!" I don't think polygraphs work and I trust the interpretations of their operators even less than I trust the machines themselves. Polygraphs are like political debates—one should only get involved if he has absolutely nothing to lose.

Redding was gracious with me. He conceded that the situation was embarrassing to him, presumably because we knew each other from my days with the Atlanta police department. I countered that it wasn't embarrassing to me, only surprising. I was surprised, I explained, that they had waited so long to call me in. I thought that I was a much better suspect five months earlier, when I first began predicting where victims would be missing from and where bodies would be found.

"Oh, we've been watchin' you very closely for a long time," Redding assured me. "A long time," he repeated as if to underline the statement.

I told him that I suspected that my phone had been tapped. I added that if they were following me, they were doing a better job than usual because I hadn't picked up the tail, while a lot of less-experienced subjects had been giving regular reports to the media of police efforts to keep them under surveillance.

At the time of my questioning, I was director of the Regional Police Training Academy in Rome, Georgia—a 160-mile round-trip commute from my home in Atlanta. Now, informed by Redding that his investigators had been watching me "very closely for a long time," I was astounded almost to the point of laughter by the next question:

"Do you still live in Atlanta or did you move to Rome?"

"I still live in Atlanta," I replied. I couldn't conceal the smile that the question triggered. I wondered: How close can you watch someone?

Redding asked for the license numbers of my cars. I purposely missed one number on one plate. I figured that if he had really checked me out at all, he would have my license numbers in front of him. If I missed one digit, he might correct me. He just kept writing. I was satisfied that he had questions and claims in front of him, not answers with which to check my consistency.

The questions turned more serious. What was I doing out on Suber Road after dark? Suber Road was where the FBI had discovered skeletal remains that were identified as those of 10-year-old Jefferey Mathis.

"Which time?" I asked. I had been on Suber Road numerous times. I had even landed there in a helicopter. On reflection, I could only remember being there one time after dark, so I tried to pinpoint the date for him. I found it difficult. I could pick the day of the week, but I wasn't sure which week. I gave him two dates to choose from.

"Why did you get out of your car and walk into the woods with a flashlight?"

"I didn't," I said. It dawned on me that, stupidly enough, I had never taken a flashlight to any of the scenes. "As a matter of fact," I went on, "I can't find the exact spot on Suber Road in the dark." The place was clearly marked with yellow plastic crime-scene ribbons which wind through the area and are supposed to keep out unauthorized persons, but I couldn't find them at night.

I told them that the one night I could recall being on Suber Road, I had been with a Belgian journalist—representing *Paris Match*—who was accompanied by a former inspector of the Paris police. I had taken them there in a rental car. Who could forget the gales of laughter my broken college French provoked along the way?

"Why did you go there after dark?"

I had gone there after dark because I had worked that day. The visitors had come from thousands of miles away. They wanted to observe the crime scenes. Like anyone else with a genuine interest in learning more about these cases, I offered to take them—a service I had provided for many (including Task Force officers) and would provide for many more. By the time we had arrived at Suber Road, it just happened to be dark.

Redding contended that I had no business being out there after dark. This pricked my constitutional conscience. I didn't even like the curfew imposed on Atlanta's youngsters, 14 and under. There certainly was no law against my being there. I felt I was making a positive contribution in an attempt to stop the killings. I could be there any damned time I pleased, and the police could remain as interested as they cared to be in why I was there.

The question I had been asked meant that someone—probably in a police stakeout—had said I was wandering around the woods off Suber Road at night with a flashlight. They were wrong. But when it's the police's word against a suspect's, the police almost always win—even before a jury. There is an unwarranted presumption of truthfulness and accuracy that accompanies the wearing of blue uniforms and badges.

I explained that I had been to all the scenes many times, and I told them with whom and in what vehicles. But my interrogators pressed on in the same vein:

"Do you remember being stopped by a security guard at Corporate Square?"

It was one thing for some cop with a super-duper, infra-red spy scope to *think* he saw you walking through a distant wooded area at night. But it was quite another thing for someone to say he had, indeed, challenged you face to face—and you don't remember it.

"No, hell, no," I said. "I haven't been stopped by anybody, any time." The only time I was even challenged was at the scene where Terry Pue's body was found in Rockdale County, and that was twice on the same day, by two sets of uniformed Rockdale County sheriff's deputies. On that occasion, they walked up to Mike Edwards and reporter Gail Epstein, who were with me. I had to walk from the woods across the road and volunteer my presence and my identification.

I told Morris Redding that I recalled riding through the stakeout. An unmarked white Ford was positioned so that its occupants could see any car that turned onto Sigman Road. I saw it when we drove by and I expected someone to come along and check us out.

The only other time I saw an obvious stakeout, I explained, was late one night on Redwine Road, where three bodies had been found in Fulton County, southwest of downtown Atlanta. I was accompanied by a black reporter from *Black Enterprise* and a white woman, Judy Farmer, who had toured the scenes with me previously and now was in the back seat with her husband. As soon as I drove into a turnaround by a lake, I saw two men strapping on gunbelts as they watched us from beside an old Ford van. I immediately backed out and proceeded slowly on my way. They did not follow.

"How did you know," came the next question, "the exact spot where [Patrick] Baltazar's body had been found?"

"I didn't know the exact spot when I arrived there," I replied. The first time I went to Corporate Square, Paul Crawley was with me. Paul had been broadcasting from the scene on the day the body was found. He had watched the DeKalb police bring the body up the embankment. He also remembered that a nurse had come from a specific door in the building across the parking lot and that the door was pretty well in line with the point where Patrick's body had been lying.

I had walked along the grassy knoll until I arrived at a spot about 10 feet wide. It was devoid of grass and virtually everything else. Not even a chewing-gum wrapper was there to contrast with the Georgia red clay. There even were holes where entire bushes had been uprooted as possible evidence by the DeKalb County police crime-scene unit. It looked like a mini-desert in the middle of an oasis.

"Why did you walk down the hill and into the woods?" Redding and Hamrick wanted to know.

"I didn't," I replied. "Paul Crawley did. I walked along the ridge, but never went down the hill."

Redding was called away from the office. He had to take a telephone call from the mayor, he explained. "Bullshit," I thought. I was sure that his departure had more to do with something I had—or had not—said than it did with a call from the mayor.

While Redding was out of the room, Robbie Hamrick and I talked easily—not about my involvement in the cases, but about my theories about them. I told Hamrick that there were five valid reasons to question the Fulton County medical examiner's identification of Jefferey Mathis. Hamrick seemed genuinely interested. I ticked off the five reasons for him.

In a few minutes, Redding returned. He asked Hamrick if he had any more questions. "No," Hamrick replied. "We covered it all while you were out of the room."

Redding glanced again at the notes in front of him.

"Where were you on the days of February 6th and February 19th?" he asked.

"I'm not sure," I said. I recognized those dates as having to do with the Patrick Baltazar and Curtis Walker cases.

"February 6th," I repeated quizzically. "Let's see, that's the day they found Baltazar's body, wasn't it?"

Redding thumbed rapidly through his notes. He leaned forward, staring over my head and straining to read the calendar on the wall behind me. "I don't know," he said. "There's so many of these dates."

He turned to Hamrick. "Do you know?" he asked.

Hamrick lifted his gaze to the calendar. "No," he said, a puzzled look squinching his face.

Almost as soon as the words left my mouth, I realized that February 6 was *not* the day that Patrick Baltazar was found, but rather the day he was reported missing. I didn't correct myself. My rhetorical question had been spontaneous.

Anyway, I figured it was just as well if they didn't know that I knew exactly where their questions led. What amazed me was that *they* didn't! They were asking me questions that someone had prepared for them. And they obviously didn't know the rationale behind them. There was no way they could pick up a nuance. I sensed immediately that we're in worse trouble coming up with a solution in these cases than I had thought.

My answers that I didn't know my whereabouts on February 6 and 19—plus my first reaction of not being aware of the exact significance of one of those dates—were the right answers. Most people wouldn't know where they had been and what happened on a specific date two months earlier. The fact that Redding and Hamrick didn't know—and they were in charge of the investigation—would have made it seem unusual to them that I did know. In any event, it amazed me that I knew more about it than they did.

I told Redding that if it was really important that he know what I was doing on those dates, I would try to reconstruct them and let him know. He said it was important. "Let me know at least whether you were in Rome or Atlanta on those dates," he said. "I need to know."

I realized anew that Redding's assertion that the police had been watching me "closely for a long time" was laughable. If they had been, they would have known that there was not a single day when I had been in Rome without also being in Atlanta. Of course, on some of those days, I might not have been in Rome at all.

Redding told me to gather the information and to call him or Hamrick. I told him I would if I could. I felt the hollowness of another piece of U.S. criminal-justice folklore: "You are innocent until you are proved guilty."

Hamrick then took up most of the questioning. "I thought he'd said we'd covered it all," I thought to myself.

Hamrick took a different tack. He wanted to know what efforts I had made to convey my information to the Task Force. He tried to phrase the question several ways, but it never quite came out right. I became more engrossed in trying to figure out his motivation than in framing my answer, and I told him so.

"If you'll tell me where you're coming from," I said, "I'll try to answer your questions the best I can."

Hamrick replied that this was fair, allowing that he often had the same problem himself. "It's still your problem," I thought to myself. "I don't have a problem."

He then made it clear that he was put out by the "fact," as he called it, that I had been giving my information to the news media. The implication was that I was trying to undercut the investigation. I wanted desperately to tell him that the Task Force didn't need anybody's help in screwing up. They were masters at it. But I suppressed the temptation, realizing that more people go to jail for "contempt of cop" than for any other single reason.

Still, Hamrick's innuendo infuriated me. It was clear that, in his eyes, I was the enemy. He didn't realize that I had tried every possible way, in the face of continued rejection—even disdain—to get my information recognized by the Task Force. I began reciting the efforts I had made, plus the names of those with whom I had shared my information. On September 19, 1980, I had given everything I had to Dale Kirkland, the only GBI representative on the Task Force at that time, I told him.

"Oh, yeah," Robbie Hamrick interrupted. "That was the day Mike Edwards asked him to come to a meeting, and when he got there, the place was full of reporters and TV lights."

"Bull-*shit*!" I retorted loudly. They finally got my dander up.

If Mike Edwards ever set up Dale Kirkland, I sure as hell wasn't aware of it. Mike Edwards doesn't operate that way. On the day I was talking about, only one reporter was present. Actually, Jeff Scott was a freelance writer who was writing a feature article about some victims' mothers. There was only Jeff Scott's still camera. There were no television lights. Perhaps Kirkland had come to our press conference and Hamrick was confused.

I assured Hamrick that we had previously and subsequently shared all of our information with Sergeant H. L. Bolton, who then commanded the Task Force. But no one ever bothered to tell us what happened to one iota of the information we had given. The Task Force seemed to be a large vacuum, both in ideas and in its ability to suck in information without ever sorting it or giving anything in return for it. An excellent example, I pointed out, was the result of my efforts in the identification of Alfred Evans.

What's more, I said that I had given my information to two Atlanta police officers, Mike Shannon and John Woods, who were temporarily assigned to the Task Force. The three of us had ridden the route together in the bogus taxi cab.

I pointed out that these two officers had told me that they took my information to Chief Napper, and that Napper then called in Major W. J. Taylor and shared the information with him. Major Taylor had been the fourth commander of the Task Force, which then was only five months old.

I also told Robbie Hamrick that in January of 1981, I personally gave the information to Lee Brown, whom everyone recognized as the overall commander of the Task Force (However, Brown was largely unresponsive to my ideas, as if they didn't exist.)

I added that in January of 1981, I had shared my knowledge of the cases with the FBI—then subsequently with Dick Hand, DeKalb County's public safety director.

Now I bristled as I pushed on with my impassioned response to Hamrick's question. I had told anyone who cared to listen to what I knew about the cases, as I was at this very moment willing to tell Hamrick and Redding.

"Have you personally ever called the Task Force telephone number with any information?" Hamrick asked.

"No, I had not," I said, an edge of anger still in my voice. I knew it would be an absolute waste of time. After all, if I telephoned the Task Force directly, I would have been talking to one of the *recruits*. I mean, if you know the hotel owner personally, why discuss problems with the bellhop?

How much more of an effort did I need to make? Did I have to offer to pay them to accept my information? It seemed to me that the shoe was on the other foot. Instead of Hamrick complaining about my assumed reluctance to share my information with the Task Force, he should be complaining about the Task Force's neglecting to share my information with him. The problem wasn't a case of the Task Force not having my information. It was a case of the Task Force not understanding it or caring about it, or both.

Redding and Hamrick then assaulted my relationship with the news media. They contended that members of the media would keep files on me and then turn against me. "Ha!" I thought, as my daddy used to say, "It takes one to know one..." It was the police whom I feared would keep files on me and turn on me. I had seen it done before! What turnip truck had they thought I just fell off?

They also warned me that I "could get shot" going to the scenes. Those were dangerous neighborhoods I was visiting, they said. I had spent hours policing "dangerous neighborhoods" by myself. I took what they were saying as a very thinly veiled threat. I didn't like it.

Redding then turned to my relationship with Mike Edwards and Jack Perry. I explained that Mike is my friend, that I didn't work for him, that he didn't work for me and that I often disagreed with him, as I do with nearly everyone. As for Jack Perry, I hardly knew him then. I disagreed with many of Jack's public statements and I knew that he didn't fully understand my work. In sum, I said, "I don't speak for them, and they don't speak for me."

Redding began philosophizing that Mike Edwards had made a mistake in being so critical of the police department and that he had allied himself with the "wrong" people. I wondered if Redding realized what he had just said to me. I am one of Mike Edwards' strongest allies. I thought that Redding and I must come from different worlds. In mine, you don't have to agree with people to like and respect them.

Finally, Morris Redding rose from his chair—body language that the interrogation was over. I realized that I had learned a few things, but confirmed hundreds more.

If they were seriously considering *me* as a suspect, they simply didn't understand what was happening. Their investigation had gone nowhere. Here they were, 21 months into the tragedies, and they still were not even close to a deduced solution in any of these cases. I knew what no one else could possibly know for certain: I didn't kill anybody.

Morris Redding escorted me from his office onto the street. On my way out, I suddenly thought of that jangling door key. "Damn! There went my chance to snatch that key," I thought. I would have taken great pleasure in returning the key to them anonymously.

Outside, I tried once more to strike up a meaningful conversation with Morris Redding as we stood on the sidewalk of West Peachtree Street. I really thought I could help him understand these cases, which seemed such an enigma to him.

I brought up the case of 10-year-old Aaron Wyche. I began to tell Redding, "You know, Morris, it took me seven months to get you people to put that kid's name on the Task Force list and—"

Then, before I got to the significance, he interrupted me. "I never did think," Redding said, "that kid fell off that railroad trestle."

Since I had known for months that there *wasn't* any railroad trestle to fall from and Morris Redding—the Task Force commander, of all people—had obviously not realized it yet, I knew how futile it would be to talk with him about the really complex nuances of the cases.

"So long, Morris, I'll call you," I said, waving goodbye. I had an appointment with Jeff Prugh of the *Los Angeles Times*. We were going to tour the murder sites together that afternoon.

As Jeff and I drove from site to site, I clasped the steering wheel too tightly. I was tense. Did I really have a right to be on those streets, particularly with someone from the news media—after Redding and Hamrick had just warned me against both? Of course I had that right! I came back to my senses, but I became furious at the realization that I had let myself become the slightest bit intimidated.

All weekend, I was upset. I relived my questioning at Task Force headquarters again and again, while trying to reconstruct my whereabouts on February 6 and 19—the dates they had asked me about.

"I should have said this," I thought. "Or, I should have said that. Or, should I have said something else?" What difference would it have made? Had I realized how quickly those veiled threats would become a reality, I would have been an emotional wreck.

The behind-the-scenes maneuvering to bring me before the Task Force commanders had begun earlier in April, when Redding telephoned Sheriff

Bill Hart, who was the advisory board chairman of my employer—Floyd Junior College.

The sheriff had called and advised me to contact Redding, who in turn told me that I was to be interviewed as a suspect. Redding also told me during that same telephone conversation that he had called the sheriff—rather than phoning me directly—because he did not want to endanger my job. Now that was pure balogna. It would be logical if Redding had called *me* first.

On Monday, April 20, three days after my interrogation, I succeeded in assembling the information that they had asked for—plus additional data. I decided to try it Hamrick's way. I telephoned the Task Force office and asked for Redding or Hamrick.

"I'm sorry, they are both in a meeting," the voice on the telephone said. "Could someone else help you?"

"No, but you can give them a message for me."

"Certainly, I'll be glad to take a message," the voice said.

"Tell them that Chet Dettlinger called, and that I have the information they asked for—and some other things to tell them," I said. I then gave my home phone number, my office phone number, my paging-beeper number and my wife's office number.

Nearly three years have passed since I left that message. Neither Redding nor Hamrick has contacted me again. I have made no further effort to contact Redding or to send them the information that they said was important to their investigation of the Atlanta murders.

As far as I know, they still don't know where I was on February 6 or 19, 1981. I don't think they were interested, anyway.

I got their message on May 11, 1981, in the form of bad news. My position as the police-academy director was no longer mine—it was being assumed by my boss. And my job as professor of criminal justice at Floyd County Junior College was being abolished. The reason was "an internal reorganization," I was told. I'm sure it was for much more ulterior reasons. In any event, I lost my job!

In February of 1982, I unexpectedly ran into Robbie Hamrick at the studios of WGST radio in Atlanta. By chance, and without the prior knowledge of either of us, we were to be on a talk show together. I asked Robbie Hamrick if I could come to his office and talk with him sometime.

"Sure, sure you can," Hamrick said. "But I won't talk about the Wayne Williams case. That's all over."

Maybe some day he'll change his mind. I'd still like to talk with him about it. I'm sure we could both learn something.

Thursday, April 16, 1981. Jeff Prugh received a tip that Atlanta police Captain Johnny Sparks had predicted to an *Atlanta Journal* reporter that yet another body would turn up during the weekend. Moreover, the body was predicted to be that of still-missing 15-year-old Jo-Jo Bell.

Jeff would tell me later that he was somewhat skeptical of what he had heard, but decided to keep the information to himself—and wait and see.

Sunday, April 19, 1981. Persons on horseback were riding on their property at about 3:30 p.m., on the banks of the South River in southeast DeKalb County. It was near the Rockdale County line and the place where 15-year-old Terry Pue had been found dead. But it was even closer to the abandoned farmhouse where the bullet-riddled body of Mercedes Masters, a 15-year-old white girl nicknamed "Tree Lady," had been found on Christmas Day of 1979. As mentioned, Mercedes Masters' murder has never been solved. She never made The List.

The horseback riders thought they saw a body. They were right. The body was that of 15-year-old Joseph (Jo-Jo) Bell.

To reach this secluded area of the South River, you had to walk about two miles through the woods. When the medical examiner arrived at about 4:30 p.m., he noted that the river was "quiet, deep and relatively gentle flowing," although he also observed "small rapids" within several hundred feet upstream.

In his report, the medical examiner also wrote: "There was a large open field on the Rockdale County side of the river, slightly above the point where the body was found. The body was in the river where the river takes a sharp turn south into Rockdale County. The body was floating in some debris that had become caught in the eddy currents of a cove-like area protected by fallen trees. There was considerable amount of trash, as well as stick and wood debris . . . floating in the water and around the body.

"The exposed part of the body was that of the back, and Jockey underwear with large gaping holes was visible on the body. It was necessary to approach the body by way of a small boat. A disaster bag and clean white sheet were placed in the bottom of the boat and the body was manually removed directly from the water and placed on the clean sheet which was folded over the body and the disaster bag secured . . . At the scene there was noted to be various areas of the body that were skeletonized. There were areas that had been partially eaten by aquatic and wildlife."

Because of some claims that were to be made later, it is necessary to delve further than usual into the autopsy description. A small part of the more vivid description is deleted because it is not necessary to anyone's understanding of the Jo-Jo Bell case: "The *chest* is robust. There is a large defect in the left ancillary area exposing the rib cage . . . Again no evidence of a vital reaction is noted in the tissues of the area that would be suggestive of ante-mortem injury having been present.

"The *abdomen* is somewhat distended by underlying gas . . . There is an area of apparent bruise in the right lower quadrant on the skin of the abdomen. No other injuries are noted other than those that are post-mortem in nature.

"The penis is present and shows no evidence of significant injury. The scrotal sac is present and there is no evidence of any injury."

Last things first: there would be persistent—but still unsubstantiated—claims of mutilation of victims. The Jo-Jo Bell autopsy clearly rules out sexual mutilation or castration in his case, which the same persons making these claims say is related to the others.

But more important, a group of victims' mothers supported by Wayne Williams' attorney on appeal, Lynn Whatley, would publicly proclaim in 1983 that they had an affidavit from a witness who claimed to have seen Jo-Jo Bell murdered by someone other than Wayne Williams.

After the affidavit had been offered in court and its existence made public, Lynn Whatley invited me to his office to hear the tapes which had been made by a female private detective and from which the affidavit had been drawn.

There were far too many discrepancies in the witness' statement to assign it too much importance without other corroborating evidence. First, I knew that the same witness had given a previous statement to the police, completely contradicting this one. But, most important, he said that Jo-Jo Bell had been stabbed in the stomach, chest and abdomen.

The ruling of Joseph Burton, the DeKalb County medical examiner, in the Jo-Jo Bell case is "asphyxia," but Burton also defined "asphyxia": "Asphyxia is a general term that simply means that the body, tissues and cells are deprived of sufficient oxygen to sustain life [stopped breathing]. Asphyxia can be caused by a number of mechanisms, including suffocation, strangulation, chemical poisoning causing asphyxiation such as cyanide, drowning, electrocution and certain injuries that cause one to be unable to breathe properly or for the heart or cardiovascular system to function properly."

Perhaps this will help explain why I am appalled at someone being charged with murder in a case where the medical examiner rules that the cause of death is: "*probable* asphyxia"!

Considering what we have reproduced of the Jo-Jo Bell autopsy, it is obvious that either the medical examiner or someone else is very wrong. It is also a case in which a so-called eyewitnesses' story—this time a witness for the *defense* (not a trial witness)—is seriously challenged by other non-circumstantial evidence.

This further discussion of eyewitness testimony reminds me to apply some of these tests to the eyewitnesses in the "yellow-rope" strangulation of 13-year-old Clifford Jones, a case which we discussed earlier. Did the eyewitnesses know the person they were accusing? Yes. Was the person apprehended at the scene? Yes. Were the witness' claims challenged—or supported—by other non-circumstantial evidence? Answer: the non-circumstantial evidence in the

Clifford Jones case *supported* the claims of the witnesses. The Jones eyewitnesses pass the validity test.

Monday, April 20, 1981. Jeff Prugh telephoned Captain Sparks and asked if it were true that he had predicted that Jo-Jo Bell would turn up dead over the weekend. Sparks denied that he had made the prediction. "That's heavy," he said. "I didn't say that."

Not even 24 hours after Jo-Jo Bell was found in April of 1981, Atlanta had still another "probable asphyxia" victim. This time the body of 23-year-old ex-convict Michael (Mickey) McIntosh was pulled from the Chattahoochee River.

McIntosh had ties to other victims already dead and to another yet to come. He was known around Cap'n Peg's (where Jo-Jo Bell worked). He also was known at the house on Gray Street, as well as bars frequented by homosexuals. He and Nathaniel Cater, a victim-to-be, worked out of the same manpower labor pool. He and Cater had ties with the suspect in the Jones case.

Michael McIntosh was, at 23, the oldest victim yet to be put on The List. He would be one of six List victims on whom no fiber matches were found to tie him to Wayne Williams, according to the prosecution. He also was another of those victims who had not been added to The List until too late—after he was found dead.

21

"Who the Hell is Willie Sherman?"

April, 1981

A 21-year-old ex-convict walked away from the apartment he shared with his mother and sister near the house on Gray Street. In earlier days, 11-year-old Patrick Baltazar might have been playing in the yard outside this apartment house, as he often did. But no more. Patrick was dead.

Or the ex-convict himself, Jimmy Ray Payne, might have been going off to visit another friend named Patrick, 16-year-old Patrick (Pat Man) Rogers. But Pat Man, too, now was dead.

Payne was due to meet his girlfriend at the bus stop that Wednesday afternoon, April 22, 1981, but he didn't show up. Following a pattern that applied to so many before him, Jimmy Ray Payne now was missing.

A young man named Jerome Young had pleaded guilty to robbing a coin shop in East Point, Georgia, a suburb of Atlanta. He said that he had seen Jimmy Ray Payne in yet another coin shop on East Ponce de Leon (U.S. 278) in Atlanta. This interested police because Payne had told his sister he was on his way to a coin shop in the Omni the last time she saw him.

Young told police, according to a story in the *Atlanta Constitution,* that Payne was part of "a burglary ring that would break into houses and steal precious metals for resale at jewelery and coin shops." Fulton County prosecutor Lewis Slaton said he doubted the latter part of Young's story, although Jimmy Ray Payne did have a record for burglary convictions and had served a prison sentence for a 1978 burglary conviction. I wondered why Slaton "doubted" it. What did Slaton know?

The police remained unconvinced by Jerome Young's story. I probably would have, too. But then, I remain unconvinced by most things I hear.

As far as police were concerned, the last person to see Jimmy Ray Payne alive—and talk about it—was his sister, Evelyn Payne. According to a police report, she saw him last on April 21, 1981, at approximately 11 a.m., at their home at 556 Magnolia Street. She stated that he was seeking to sell "six or seven old nickels, and one was dated 1949."

Even though this police report said one thing, Payne's girlfriend said quite another. She testified that she last saw him when he walked her to the bus on the morning of April 22, not April 21. I said to myself that Jimmy Ray Payne must have had more to sell than he told his sister about. From her description, the seven nickels could have been worth 35 cents.

On previous occasions, Jimmy Ray Payne had made several attempts to take his own life, or so the authorities said. In one incident, he tied his shirt around his neck, then to an overhead pipe and jumped off a toilet seat. The incident report went on to say that a "Dr. Roseman" had said, "The boy was merely depressed by his mother not coming to see him."

One social worker who had counseled with Jimmy Ray Payne back when Payne was 14 had written: "I found Jimmy Ray Payne, being supported by a sheet hanging from the ceiling. The sheet was under his chin and he and it [sic] was choking him. He also had a blanket over his head. I removed the noose from around his neck and laid him on the bed. He was either holding his breath or unconscious and he began to shake as if he was having a seizure. I held his tongue and got him to breathing again. . ."

She went on to write: "Dr. Roseman saw the child and Roseman stated that Jimmy Payne had previously threatened to shoot his mother. Dr. Roseman felt that Jimmy *might* [emphasis added] have a violent streak and warranted careful observation. He felt that Payne needed psychiatric evaluation because of the hostilities. Upon reviewing the first part of his file, I found that Jimmy Payne apparently was on probation and has an extensive juvenile record."

When I read this report, it raised major questions. I would recall defense attorney Al Binder trying to make a case that Jimmy Ray Payne could have committed suicide rather than having been murdered. After all, he was found in the Chattahoochee River, and the medical examiner would testify that he could not rule out "drowning" as a cause of death.

Jimmy Ray Payne was another of those "probable-asphyxia" deaths. But the probability that Payne's probable-asphyxia death was murder was not very high, in the judgment of the medical examiner. He had not ruled Payne's death a homicide.

Rather, he had ruled that the cause of death was "undetermined" when Wayne Williams was indicted on July 17, 1981, for Payne's *"murder"* and that of 27-year-old Nathaniel Cater. The grand jury might have decided differently had it known the facts about Payne's death certificate. Grand-jury proceedings are not adversary hearings, and the defendant is not represented. Only the prosecution tells it side. And, in secret.

So many sexual overtones permeated these cases that I wondered if Jimmy Ray Payne might have acquired an often fatal fetish, which usually goes overlooked as a cause of death.

This sexual vagary has to do with the enhancement of orgasm by a loss or near loss of consciousness at the point of climax. Many with this fetish design elaborate fail-safe devices, some of them resembling crosses. These devices enable someone to lose consciousness completely, and the weight of his body is supposed to trip a release mechanism, which will allow him to regain consciousness.

When no elaborate device is available, such practitioners will devise other methods, most of which (but not all) involve taking oneself to the brink of unconsciousness, but not actually passing out. Other methods involve a twist, instead of a knot, in the garrot. That way, when the person does pass out, his hand automatically releases the pressure on the twist, and the garrot falls harmlessly away. Others involve the assistance of a *second party*. Many involve a shroud for privacy and enhanced oxygen deprivation.

Sometimes the participant is too successful. The result is death. Until the late 1940s or early 1950s, such deaths usually were ruled "suicide" when, in fact, most, if not all, were "accidental." Throughout Atlanta's murder cases, I had thought about this fetish. I wondered if it might manifest itself in an inability to climax, if not causing someone else to lose consciousness. Or, perhaps we had something even more bizarre. Maybe, just maybe, some of those "probable asphyxias" weren't murder at all, but accidental deaths.

Jimmy Ray Payne's case was the first that looked to me as if the chances were as good as not that it might involve just such a fetish. It struck me when I read the social worker's report that he was "supported by," not hung by, a sheet and "he began to shake as if he was having a seizure." To anyone not familiar with this fetish, it may never occur that he might be witnessing the manifestations of a sexual orgasm. The blanket over Payne's head wasn't necessary if the object was suicide.

So blatant were the sexual overtones throughout these cases that I never could understand the prosecution's reluctance to lay them out for the jury at the Wayne Williams trial. These weren't guesses and theories; these were the admissions of people about their own sexual activities and eyewitness testimony about the sexual activities of others.

Perhaps the so-called good and bad connotations of heterosexuality and homosexuality still cloud some people's minds. And, like a group of children, we are not allowed to discuss such realities—even in court—when the matters they touch are those of life and death. We should grow up!

Indeed, many of these cases were touched by homosexuality. Not only should the police have suspected it, they had the information in their laps to prove it.

Charles E. Ohara, in his book, *"Fundamentals of Criminal Investigation,"* wrote: "As a general rule, the investigator cannot trust his unaided observation of a person to deduce that homosexuality exists, but rather must rely on eyewitness testimony and other evidence to support such a judgment. The investigator should, in fact, as in other types of investigations, make no conclusions but simply describe the facts and amass evidence . . . The discovery of one homosexual in the course of such an investigation *often leads to the uncovering of a number of others* [emphasis added]."

With regard to Jimmy Ray Payne, a prisoner in the Suffolk County Jail in Massachusetts told Boston authorities:

"I met Jimmy Ray Payne in October of 1979 and then again in March of 1980. I had met him at the Peach [sic] Street, ah, hustling area book store in Atlanta and he was hustling. At that time we got to be good friends, and so forth and formed [sic] kind of trust relationship with him. I later then was asked to take some pictures by this black heavy-set guy at the book store . . . he would pay me money for the pictures that I brought him of Jimmy and then . . . he gave me $60 for the two pictures.

"In one, Jimmy was lying on the bed nude and in another, standing up at the bathroom door of the bedroom at the hotel . . . And there was another one, a Darrin [sic]—I believe his last name is Glass—that hung around the Peach [sic] Street book store and was getting paid for sex by these older guys. . ."

The prisoner in Massachusetts went on to name names, and to detail the operations of a nationwide pornography ring, which he said was headquartered in Troy, New York.

There was no obvious interest in this inmate's claim. I can understand that. I wouldn't put much credence in his story, either. However, you can bet your last dollar that if Wayne Williams had been a "heavy-set" guy, there would have been an effort to get this testimony introduced. As it is, the jury never heard this story.

Jimmy Ray Payne's body was found in the Chattahoochee River west of Atlanta, at I-285 and Bankhead Highway (U.S. 278), at 6:30 p.m. on April 27, 1981. It was exactly the same intersection where 23-year-old Mickey McIntosh had last been reported alive. Again, the cause of death was said to be "probable asphyxia".

The body count had mounted with ever-accelerating speed. It had been a long time since the body of one victim would be found before still another had been reported missing. Only 10-year-old Darron Glass, who had disappeared in mid-September of 1980, was a missing person on The List, which now numbered 26 victims—still far short of the count on my list of possibly related cases.

Earlier on April 27, a man named Fred Wyatt was arrested at Cap'n Peg's on Georgia Avenue. He was accused of simple battery. Unexpectedly, the arresting officer's search of Wyatt yielded Jimmy Ray Payne's identification from a state prison in Alto, Georgia. Also found in Wyatt's pocket was the business card of FBI Agent Len Carroll.

Fred Wyatt described himself as a scavenger. He said he had picked up the picture and the card on Georgia Avenue in the vicinity of Atlanta-Fulton County Stadium. Later, he would say that the exact location was the trash bin at the liquor store on the corner of Georgia and Stewart avenues. Several victims on and off The List died, or turned up dead, at or very close to this intersection.

On May 2, 1981, Jeff Prugh and I, along with a *Los Angeles Times* photographer, went to the church where Jimmy Ray Payne's funeral was in progress. Like many of the funerals, it was a media circus. Throughout these cases, all the sobs, the moans, the tears, the eulogies—even poems read by bereaved schoolmates—were caught in the glare of TV strobe lights and hand-held "mini-cams."

Television's intrusion into these grief-torn settings sometimes lapsed into poor taste. At 13-year-old Curtis Walker's funeral in March, a British camera-crew director scurried between the altar and the coffin, noisily clacking a Hollywood movie-style clapboard. At the same funeral, a cameraman propped his elbows up on the coffin to capture the full effect of the mourners' anguish.

A woman emerged from the door of the small church during the funeral of Jimmy Ray Payne. Wailing uncontrollably, she swooned into the supportive arms of two men. They began to assist her as she stumbled forward on rubbery legs into the wide, busy street. A photographer dashed toward her, his camera lens only inches from her tearful face. Snapping pictures, he back-pedaled across the street, oblivious to the traffic flow.

I would see that same cameraman make like a broken-field runner again, on another street, at another time. I also would learn that he had taken photos on the stage of the Sammy Davis Jr.-Frank Sinatra benefit concert. For security reasons, only this one still photographer had been allowed on the stage, by arrangement with City Hall. Had the mourner of Jimmy Ray Payne known later who the photographer had been, she probably would have had another strong reaction. I wonder if, to this day, she knows.

Meanwhile, after the Payne funeral, Jeff Prugh, his photographer and I toured the scenes and took pictures. On the car radio, we heard commentator Paul Harvey quoting Robert Stivers, the chief Fulton County medical examiner, that the number of Atlanta's child murders was no more than normal. What Harvey didn't tell his listeners was that the medical examiner was using only the number of victims on The List (adults included) for his comparison. Remember, many other slain children were murdered during this same period, but never made The List.

At home that night, I twisted the TV dial, watching the various local coverage. Gloria Murry of Cable News Network was the first to report that Jimmy Ray Payne had been buried upside down—at the urging of a spiritualist who said it would end the deaths.

It didn't. But it just about foretold the end of The List.

On the streets, they knew 17-year-old William Barrett by his nickname, "Billy Star." Whenever anyone referred to it as his "street name," Barrett's mother became angry. She thought this had a very bad connotation.

But "Billy Star" had certainly had his problems on the street. He was now a parolee from a juvenile institution. He lived on my route—on 2nd Avenue near Memorial Drive, near East Lake Meadows in east Atlanta. It was one block from here that Kenny Brown said he heard the gunshot murder of the small boy. Barrett also lived close to the homes of Alfred Evans, Darron Glass and Angela (Gypsy) Bacon.

On May 11, 1981, Barrett's mother asked him to go across town to the McDaniel-Glenn project, near Cap'n Peg's, to pay some money she owed to a man. The two locations—his home and Cap'n Peg's—are many miles apart, but show commonalities with so many other victims. She would never see her son again. Early the next morning, William Barrett's body was found at Glenwood Road and Green Cove. From that location, only the width of Interstate 20 separates the points where Barrett's and List victim Eric Middlebrooks' bodies were found. Just two blocks away is the home of victim Lubie (Chuck) Geter.

The medical examiners said William Barrett died of strangulation, but the examiner also commented about some stab wounds.

According to one young man's story to police, "Billy Star" had not exactly stayed out of mischief since leaving the Georgia corrections system. The man said that William Barrett had broken into homes and stayed high on "grass". Barrett, he added, always carried a "pop blade" (switchblade knife) and had recently sold a "Saturday-night special" (handgun) to a friend (of Barrett). It might have been interesting to have found that gun—and checked the ballistics in the case of Edward Hope Smith, the only gunshot victim on The List.

Other police reports noted that a "hit man" was out to get William Barrett. One witness told police that he was approached by a man who offered him $3,000 to kill William Barrett. Since the would-be "hit man" he referred to was in elementary school at that time, I along with everyone else wrote that one off. Perhaps I shouldn't have.

Two witnesses said "Billy Star" made it back to the East Lake Meadows area from McDaniel-Glenn. They said they saw him get into a two-door white car with a black male who carried a purse slung from long straps over his right shoulder. The Atlanta police arrested a suspect who fit that description (which had been given by more than one witness).

But the suspect who interested me most was a man whose phone number was found in the pocket of William Barrett's trousers. One witness who would not be called to testify in the Williams trial identified the man as someone who picked up boys at the Omni and at the Five Points MARTA station, in the heart of downtown Atlanta. The suspect is white. The witness said he saw Barrett with the man in March of 1981, two months before Barrett died.

Still another witness who would never testify in the Williams trial would tell police he had visited the white man's house and had sex with him. Later, he said, the man left to pick up someone—William Barrett. The witness said he saw Barrett at the man's house one week before he disappeared. The man, he said, had given Barrett's brother a bicycle. The jury in the Wayne Williams trial would hear none of this. But the jury would hear a so-called eyewitness testify that Wayne Williams had been at the house of a cousin of William Barrett on a day unknown, at a time unknown, and with other people who were unknown.

As if this weren't enough, the witness who said he had seen Barrett at the white man's home also said he had seen 14-year-old victim Lubie (Chuck) Geter at the white man's apartment on five different occasions. Remember, other witnesses had placed Lubie Geter at another white man's house on other occasions, and that the man was convicted of child molestation.

The same witness said the white man had a police scanner in his car and other police radio equipment in his home. He also said the man had attended William Barrett's funeral. The jury in Williams' trial would hear none of this, either. But, the jury would hear so-called "eyewitnesses" for the state implicate Wayne Williams by saying he had police radio equipment in his car and that he had attended Jimmy Ray Payne's funeral.

Again, I ask why should not the jurors hear *all* of this and decide for themselves? This information was available to defense attorneys. What do we need to change in our system to guarantee the introduction of such testimony? I can think of a few simple changes, such as not forcing the defense to rely on whatever resources it can come by to locate and subpoena witnesses.

If it were my decision, the court would be responsible to use whatever resources necessary to locate and force witnesses with evidence to appear for *both* sides. Justice, not conviction, should be the business of the court. The state uses the police department and the sheriff's office to locate its witnesses. The defense uses volunteers. Under no circumstances can the defense have resources to match those available to the state.

Paul Crawley of WXIA-TV accompanied me to interview Lois Evans, mother of slain 14-year-old Alfred Evans, about "Billy Star" and other connections among List victims. That night on television, Paul reported those personal connections.

Soon the station's anchorman and news reader, John Pruitt, called him aside. "Paul," he said, "if all of that is true, then that means that these cases are not random."

"John," Paul said, "Dettlinger told us that in a staff meeting three months ago. Where have you been?"

Today, more than four years after the date arbitrarily selected by the Atlanta police for the beginning of this series of murders (those on The List), I still hear news stories about Atlanta's "28 murdered children." For example, on the first anniversary of the conviction of Wayne Williams, WSB-TV (Channel 2) in Atlanta carried a feature which gave viewers misinformation that ex-convicts Jimmy Ray Payne and Nathaniel Cater were strangled.

Amazingly, many editors and news directors across America are convinced that the story of Atlanta's murders has been covered exhaustively by the news media. The truth is, most Atlanta reporters who covered—and lived with—the story still don't know most of the story, even though they think they do.

My hero, Thomas Jefferson, missed a terribly important point when he opted for a free press (which abused him so badly), even over democracy. He should have noted that the press itself must also be *informed.* Free, but uninformed, press coverage of Atlanta's murders, as Abby Mann (who won the Academy Award for his screenplay, *"Judgment at Nuremberg"*) put it, was "mentally and morally bankrupt."

When Lois Evans (who still isn't convinced that her 14-year-old son, Alfred, lies under the grave marker inscribed with his name) told Paul Crawley and me about all those personal connections among Alfred and other victims, she said the police hadn't asked the questions that Paul and I did. It was clear the police overlooked these connections because they weren't backtracking in their investigation. Apparently their computers were not programmed to do so, either.

I vowed I wouldn't make the same mistake. I would review every document in my files to make sure that I had plugged every shred of information into my thinking.

In the meantime, I tried to persuade those who would listen—police officers, reporters and the public—not to let The List narrow their perception of Atlanta's tragedy.

The List was not purported to represent connected cases. It was not purported to represent *all* of metropolitan Atlanta's unsolved murders. Therefore, as an investigative tool, it was meaningless. Lee Brown understood this, but the press and the public did not. Brown's biggest problem came when he had to go on the witness stand and testify that the cases he had understood not to be connected were, in fact, connected.

If The List was meaningless, getting a name on it was *far from* meaningless. For example, it meant that a half-million-dollar reward fund was available to pay for information leading to the arrest and conviction of the person or persons responsible for the murder of one of its victims. Thus, no "List" status, no reward.

It meant that the family of each victim on The List was eligible to participate in the hundreds of thousands of dollars being donated by well-meaning people all over the world. Thus, no "List" status, no donations.

It meant that the $4.2 million in federal tax money that the Reagan Administration sent to Atlanta for the investigation was—and is—not used to attempt to find out who murdered all those victims (children and adults) who *didn't* make The List.

It meant that cases of victims *not* on The List were ignored by virtually all of the news media. It meant that families of victims *not* on The List weren't treated to expense-paid trips to fund-raising rallies, as were many members of families of victims on The List.

Just as nothing is logical about the placing of victims on The List, nothing is logical about when The List was started or ended. For example, no one can say with any certainty that July of 1979—when the two boys' bodies were found along Niskey Lake Road—was really the beginning of Atlanta's nightmare. Now police say one of those two victims is connected to other cases—and the other victim is not. Balderdash! If those two aren't connected, who could say that any are connected?

Throughout the investigation and right up to the arrest of Wayne Williams in June of 1981, prosecutor Lewis Slaton argued unconvincingly that the earlier cases on The List were not connected to the later ones on The List. On another occasion, Slaton said that as many as 10 killers could be responsible. The Atlanta newspapers gave Slaton's theories considerable play because he happened to be annointed with the title of "prosecutor." But, the title didn't help his predictions much.

The press described Lewis Slaton's belief that two sets were not connected as the "two-string theory"—one string of early cases, another of later cases. Unfortunately, Slaton didn't differentiate between exactly who was an "early" victim and a "later" victim—as to when each victim disappeared, when each turned up dead and when each went on The List. For instance, nearly nine months elapsed between the time that 10-year-old Aaron Wyche died and the time his name was added to The List.

In December of 1980, the Fulton County police arrested a 64-year-old man on a charge of child molestation. They publicly considered him a suspect in Atlanta's "child" murder cases. Most interestingly, they also publicly considered him a suspect in the Dewey Baugus case.

Dewey Baugus was a 9-year-old white boy whose murder fit my map's geographic parameters. He was killed close to Moreland Avenue and within blocks of at least four victims who made The List.

But Dewey Baugus died in April of 1979, and The List wouldn't be created for 15 months yet. And even then, The List would be made retroactive only to July of 1979—quite arbitrarily. Dewey Baugus also was murdered too early to fit onto either of Lewis Slaton's now incorrect "strings"—incorrect, according to Slaton himself.

Clinton Chafin, the veteran policeman who had been caught up in the mid-1970s turmoil over Mayor Jackson's attempt to fire Chief John Inman, now is chief of the Fulton County police. Earlier, as an assistant chief in the Atlanta police department, he had been the boss of Jack Perry, who in 1979 commanded Atlanta's homicide division when young Dewey Baugus died.

Chafin told me that he remains unconvinced that Jack Perry put the right man in prison for the Dewey Baugus killing. Perry, on the other hand, told me that he is convinced that he did. In any event, Chafin's Fulton County police released information that a man they held as a suspect in the Atlanta murders was also a suspect in the Dewey Baugus case, even though another man had long before been convicted and sent to prison for Baugus' murder. At least one major metropolitan police department considered it possible that The List should have started much earlier.

One afternoon in May of 1981, I reread documents I long ago had filed away.

One was the very first document issued by the Atlanta police in their "missing and murdered children" investigation back in July of 1980, when the Task Force was first formed. This document clearly reflects the lack of understanding, muddled thinking and sloppy investigating by police in one of history's most widely publicized multiple-murder cases.

Yes, I will nit-pick, but my children's lives are worth nit-picking about. How about yours? We deserve and must demand better than what appeared in the Atlanta police investigation's original document. Conventions and downtown business be damned. We need all the facts, not just those which the Chamber of Commerce might approve.

In the police document, slain 9-year-old Yusuf Bell's name is misspelled throughout as "Yusaf." The police version of where Yusuf was last seen differs from his mother's. The document states that the body was in "a advance [sic] state of decomposition." Grammatical and spelling mistakes crop up all too frequently throughout the document.

What follows is one of the three "facts" developed in the investigation of Yusuf Bell's death:

". . . there have been *speculations* [emphasis added] as to why the victim was killed. The homicide squad attempted to establish and develop [sic] leads geared to those speculations but to no avail."

Fact? Save us from such "facts" and from investigations developed around them.

The report continues with more gobbledygook:

"This investigation was assigned full time to a homicide investigator until all leads were exhausted, and / or began to diminish." Come on, which was it? Were they exhausted, or were they beginning to diminish? Or both? (Could it be both?)

In the slaying of 14-year-old Eric Middlebrooks, we are told that ". . . his body was discovered on May 10, 1980 . . ." Yet the report goes on to say that ". . . the last time she saw her son [Middlebrooks] was approximately 10:30 p.m. on May 18th . . ."

Middlebrooks left home on a bicycle. The bicycle was found a few feet from his body. Yet we are told that one of the facts developed in the investigation is: "The victim's body was discovered within reasonable walking distance of where he lived."

The Atlanta police surmised that Middlebrooks was a victim of a "sudden anger or revenge-type killing." This conclusion is based on the "fact that the victim was not sexually assaulted nor [sic] did he have any valuables to suspect robbery."

If the killing was "sudden," the killer must have worked up his need for revenge in a hurry. I wondered: Did they reach the same conclusion in all the other cases on The List, since they all meet these criteria (except possibly 12-year-old Angel Lenair)? And how do you determine that a person was not robbed because he doesn't have any valuables on his person? Wouldn't the presumption be the other way around? For example, if a person had plenty of valuables left on his person, robbery would not seem to be a motive.

In the Eric Middlebrooks case, the report lists the cause of death as "multiple puncture wounds including the head." The head is not a puncture wound. Nor were there any puncture wounds on the head. The puncture wounds were on the trunk; they were not fatal. Middlebrooks apparently died from blows to the head with a blunt instrument, which leaves just the opposite kind of wound from that described as a puncture wound.

The report mentions that Middlebrooks borrowed a key from his mother to open the house in order to get a hammer to fix his bike. Yet at least one police officer didn't seem to know anything about a hammer. Eric Middlebrooks' half-brother, an Atlanta police officer, said he was not aware of any mention of a hammer when he was asked about it 14 months after the murder. The hammer is mentioned in a police report. Were all of these reports shared with *all* police officers? If not, why not?

In the case of 9-year-old Anthony Carter, the report lists no date when the body was found and perhaps misses the time by as much as five hours. The report states that Carter was found dead in the rear of 657 Wells Street. This is not so. The rear of 657 Wells Street would be an address on Bluff Street, just as the rear of Glenn Street would be an address on Wells Street. The body was actually found across from 657 Wells Street, in the rear of buildings that front the 600 block of Glenn Street.

The report lists slain LaTonya Wilson's age as 8. She had just turned 7 when she was reported missing. It lists her address as "226 Verbena." Her address was 2261 Verbena, Apartment 7. It goes on to inform us that the child is "still missing and has never been located."

The report further tells us that a witness "allegedly reported". Well, did the witness report—or didn't she? After several more items of misinformation, the report states, "There have been no new developments [sic] in this investigation with the exception of a lead . . ."

As for the still-enigmatic case of 14-year-old Alfred Evans, the document states that he was reported missing to the Atlanta police on August 8, 1979. His mother, Lois Evans, says she reported Alfred missing to the DeKalb County police on July 26, 1979, and to the Atlanta police on July 27, 1979.

The document states that Jefferey Mathis was 11. He was 10. It states that he was reported missing on March 12, 1980. His mother says she flagged down a police car and reported him missing on the night of March 11. The officer told her to call the Missing Person squad the next day if he had not returned home. The report says the disappearance occurred about 7 p.m. The mother and two eyewitnesses say it was 7:30 p.m.

One has to realize how important this kind of information is in developing patterns in a multiple-murder situation. If you take this shoddy information at face value, you have a victim disappearing on a Tuesday when he actually disappeared on a Monday. Then you start looking for suspects who fit the pattern, and you don't consider one because he has an alibi for that Tuesday. And, wasting your time, you consider 10 more who did not have an alibi for Tuesday, but may have had one for Monday. It is from this type of slipshod work that "3½-week cycles" that never existed are born. It is from some greater dearth of intellect that they are believed and followed.

In addition, the report in the Jefferey Mathis case states that "the entire geographical area surrounding the house, for a radius of about three miles, including parks and cemeteries were [sic] searched." One wonders what parts of the *entire* area that was searched were *not* searched. If parks and cemeteries were included, what was not? Wayne Williams lived within nine-tenths of a mile of Jefferey's house. Was Wayne Williams' house and/or grounds searched then?

The police had eight murdered or missing children on their list. The mothers' committee, too, had eight murdered, missing and "accidently" killed children on their list. Accidently killed? My thoughts returned to 10-year-old Aaron Wyche, whose name I had first seen—and circled with a pencil—on the rally program at the Wheat Street Baptist Church.

Both the police and the mothers' lists contained eight names, but it quickly dawned on me that they were *not the same eight names.* In fact, only five of the names were the same on both rosters. If they were both right, then there were *at least 11* missing or murdered kids (including Aaron Wyche), not eight.

Or 12! Neither list included the second body (then still unidentified) along Niskey Lake Road.

As the case unfolded, I identified at least 17 children who could have been on that eight-name official list. Although I couldn't know it, all were dead at the time. I say "at least" because I continue to learn about other victims (some children) who were slain during the period starting with the unmagic date of July 20, 1979, but who never make The List. And The List parameters kept changing to include more and more possibilities for consideration.

By now, the best I could say about the original police staff work on these cases was that it was incorrect; but at least, it was incomplete. One might expect that the police, who keep the records, might be able to account for at least half the children who have been murdered since the date arbitrarily picked by the police themselves. Now, perhaps, we should know not to expect so much from our law-enforcement authorities.

Who were these nine murdered children whose names were *not* on the original police list of eight names?

No. 1 was 14-year-old Milton Harvey. Apparently Milton was not placed on The List originally because his body had been found outside Atlanta's jurisdiction, in the city of East Point. Milton's body had been found eight months *before* The List was compiled. The List was retroactive for 12 months. Milton was quickly added to The List.

No. 2 was 11-year-old Christopher Richardson. At the time the original list was published, Christopher was still among those missing. His name apparently escaped the original list for the same reason that Milton Harvey's did. Christopher was missing from DeKalb County, even though he disappeared less than 1½ miles from where 14-year-old Alfred Evans disappeared on the same street, Memorial Drive.

No. 3: In January of 1981, Dick Hand told me that sometime between July of 1979 and January of 1980, his DeKalb County police had found the remains of a black female child near the Columbia Mall on Memorial Drive. The child never had been identified, and the cause of death was unknown. This child never made any of the published lists, including the sieve-like FBI Uniform Crime Report. We may never know where the child lived or where she disappeared, but she was found on Memorial Drive. By 1981, I didn't need a better reason to put her on my list.

No. 4: Also, in January of 1981, I learned about Mercedes Masters. Gail Epstein of the *Atlanta Constitution* called her case to my attention. She had not thought about Mercedes until 15-year-old Terry Pue's body was found on Sigman Road in Rockdale County on January 23, 1981: She thought of Mercedes then because her body had been found just inside the DeKalb County line from Rockdale County.

Mercedes Lynne Masters was 15 and white. She lived in Sandy Springs, a well-to-do community of about 50,000 in unincorporated Fulton County, north of Atlanta. Sandy Springs did not fit the geographic pattern of my map. But, her body had been found too close to the location of another victim to be ignored. Mercedes had been shot to death and left behind an abandoned dwelling. The body was found on Christmas Day, 1979. Her killer was never caught. The location she disappeared from did turn out to be within a few blocks of U.S. 278.

No. 5: Beverly Harvey? She was 18, a new arrival in Atlanta from south Georgia, when she was found stabbed to death near Grant Park. Her home and the park are in the area just south of Memorial Drive. There is an Atlanta police precinct station in Grant Park. Beverly's murder wasn't solved. She never made The List.

What differentiated Beverly Harvey from Angel Lenair? Why did Angel make The List and Beverly not make The List? Beverly was black like everyone else on The List. She was stabbed, but so was Anthony Carter, who was to die about four months later and be put immediately on The List when it was drawn up about two weeks after his death.

Beverly Harvey was a female, but two females made the original list, including Angel Lenair, who died the same week as Beverly Harvey.

Ah, yes, at 18, Beverly Harvey was too old for The List, which later would include victims up to 28 years old. She was three years younger than the younger person Wayne Williams was convicted of killing.

No. 6: Another female turned up murdered the same week as did Lenair and Harvey. She was 16-year-old Tammy Reid. She never made The List, either. Tammy's was one case in which an arrest and conviction were obtained quickly. Atlanta police detective L. N. Hensley obtained a confession from a 23-year-old black man who knew Tammy. Tammy died at Northside and Kennedy, one block from the house on Gray Street. When I added Tammy Reid to my list in November of 1980, knowing the police said her killer was in jail, I thought it was a mistake, but one I couldn't afford not to make. Tammy Reid, like Beverly Harvey, had been stabbed to death.

The only other child on The List who was stabbed to death was 9-year-old Anthony Carter, whose body also had been found next to Northside Drive. Had these been the only three child murders, I knew that the police would suspect that there might be one killer because of *modus operandi* (M.O.).

No. 7 is a youngster I didn't know much about until June of 1981. He was 17-year-old Joseph Lee. Joseph was shot to death in July of 1980—the month that the Task Force was formed—at Desert Road and Camp Creek Parkway. Anyone familiar with the geography of these murders will recognize that this location is one intersection away from where three victims on The List were found murdered on Redwine Road. It is the exact location where Mike Edwards and I once stopped to ponder the route in late 1980. Joseph had also lived on Camp Creek Parkway, which makes the geographic connections complete.

Joseph Lee's shooting death didn't make The List, the East Point police said, because it happened during an attempted robbery. I doubt that they know that for sure, and I'm positive that police could not rule out that same motive in many of the deaths on The List. They simply don't know.

In any event, Joseph Lee is another example of being "*not* one of Atlanta's murdered children," while obviously being one of Atlanta's murdered children. The illogic is not mine, it belongs to The List. The death is no less real and the tragedy no less felt by those intimately involved.

Dr. Andrew Short, a professor who was West Georgia College's representative at the NFLPA summer camp, remembers that when the assistant director received the call about her brother, she ran screaming down a corridor. Because Lee Brown didn't put Joseph Lee's name on a list (he may not have known about Joseph Lee), the news media didn't bother to transfer the pain *en masse* to the rest of us. One thing about making The List was that your family didn't have to suffer alone.

No. 8 was 10-year-old Aaron Wyche, whom we have written of before. Aaron didn't make The List until February of 1981, more than eight months after he died in a "fall" from a railroad trestle that didn't exist.

No. 9 was Willie Sherman. Now who the hell is *Willie Sherman*? I made two big mistakes during and immediately after the Wheat Street Baptist Church rally in July of 1980. I laid down the program after taking a deep interest in the listing of "Aaron Wyche, accidental death," without going on to read the last names on the mothers' committee's list. Second, I hadn't paid attention to the introduction of the parents.

At home, I filed the program away until May of 1981, when my visit with Alfred Evans' mother prompted me to review all of my information on these cases.

Now, as I reread the program from the Conference on Children's Safety, right there—hitting me on top of the head—was this entry on the mothers' list:

"Carolyn Sherman, mother. Willie Sherman, age 10, murdered."

I blinked in disbelief. I never had heard of Willie Sherman and I prided myself on knowing more about these cases than anyone. I telephoned Jeff Prugh of the *Los Angeles Times*.

"Hey, Jeff," I began without formalities as was common in our conversations, "who the hell is Willie Sherman?"

"Willie who?" he came back, reminding me of Lee Brown's replies on two occasions when reporters had asked him about three murdered Atlanta children.

I told Jeff that I was looking at the mothers' original list and that it contained the name of a 10-year-old murder victim named Willie Sherman, a kid I'd never heard of.

"Jeez, Chet, you've got to be kidding."

"No, Jeff, I'm not. I'm sitting here looking at it in astonishment. I've got to know who Willie Sherman is."

"Gee, sure, I'll try to help."

I then called Paul Crawley of WXIA-TV and Kaleeka Rogers of WSB radio with exactly the same results. Both of these reporters had closely covered the story, and neither knew who Willie Sherman was or could even recall having heard of him. But they, too, volunteered to look.

Within an hour, the returns poured in. They were all negative. No one seemed to know who Willie Sherman was. I had called several police departments. Paul had called several more. Kaleeka had called the Fulton County medical examiner's office and someone she knew in the Bureau of Vital Statistics. Jeff had telephoned the mothers' Committee to Stop Children's Murders. There, too, Willie Sherman's name drew blanks.

Jeff's experience was particularly memorable. When he telephoned the mothers' committee, the woman who answered didn't know who Willie Sherman was.

"But his name was listed on one of your official publications," he pleaded.

"You sure it was one of ours?"

"Yes, it was the program for the meeting at the Wheat Street Baptist Church."

Jeff heard the woman's voice, removed from the phone and asking loudly, "Does anybody here know Willie Sherman?"

She came back on the line and said, "I'm sorry. Nobody here knows anything about him."

"Could you take a minute and look it up?" Jeff inquired.

"No, I'm sorry. We can't help you until after the rally."

(The Committee to Stop Children's Murders was planning a major fund-raising rally on May 25, 1981, on the steps of the Lincoln Memorial in Washington, 10 days hence.)

"But," Jeff protested, "this is about a *murdered child*!"

"We can't answer your question," the woman said.

Jeff says he can still hear the click in his ear.

If the mothers' committee had been concerned about "Willie Sherman" in July of 1980, its interest seemed to have waned by May of 1981. I never will forget Camille Bell, the committee's president, speaking on national television from the shadow of Lincoln's statue. The children, she said, were their first concern. But there had seemed to be less concern with "Willie Sherman" than there had been with preparations for the rally.

In a few days, Paul Crawley called to ask if I had read an article in a back issue of *Atlanta* magazine about the investigation of 14-year-old Eric Middlebrooks' death. I told him that I had. "In fact," I said, "it's lying here in the pile of crap on my desk."

"Look at it again," Paul recommended. "Call me back and tell me what you see."

On Page 122 of the August, 1980, issue of *Atlanta,* I found the following: "William Sherman, the owner of a liquor store in southwest Atlanta, had just left his bank carrying thousands of dollars in a briefcase . . . Sherman is now criminal homicide victim number 81."

Could this be Willie Sherman? He was hardly 10 years old. Rather, he was 56.

It crossed my mind that Willie Sherman might be a "straw man." Someone might have placed a bogus name on the mothers' list. I have no idea who might have done so, but I can think of a lot of ways to profit from it.

But, what should disturb us is that in all the inquiries made of officials, not one person in authority had the acumen or recall to say, "Wait a minute! We don't have a kid by the name of Willie Sherman murdered, but there is this 56-year-old man."

If the police and the medical examiners don't remember our names when we are murdered, what chance is there for anybody?

Are there so many murders that the people in charge of them can't keep usable records? "Yes!" according to the New York City police, who said in 1981 that they had not kept records on murders by race, sex and age for four years because of a "lack of manpower."

Are there so many murders that even computers can't give us exacting printouts? Of course not. There is only an incompetent system which is obviously incapable of setting the correct priorities.

It is a shame and a farce that two years into Atlanta's murders—and even today—we still don't know how many people have been victims of unsolved murders over any given period of time. Lee Brown was asked to furnish information on unsolved murders to the Public Safety Committee of the Atlanta City Council in 1981, but at least twice he did not do so to the committee's satisfaction. Again, how can we solve or prevent murders when we don't know who is being murdered, how many are being murdered, or even the most obvious of victim characteristics?

Outside the glare of publicity, it is likely that several of the victims who did make The List never made the FBI Uniform Crime Report (UCR). It is highly likely that 21-year-old Jimmy Ray Payne, for whose death Wayne Williams was convicted, never made the FBI report.

The reason? When Payne's death was recorded by police in April of 1981, his death was not ruled a murder. Ergo, no entry in the FBI Uniform Crime Report. Although it is impossible to say for sure because of the incredibly poor record-keeping by police, Jeff and I have not found a murder added to the UCRs (after Payne's death certificate was changed) which would match with the circumstances of Payne's death.

It is likely, too, that Alfred Evans and Aaron Wyche also did not make the UCRs. It is probable that none of the "probable asphyxia" victims would have made the UCRs had they been considered separately. In other years, these "undetermined" causes of death never would have been ruled murders.

Why, when the entire citizenry assumes that officials know the answers to these questions, have the officials not yet set up even the most basic procedures to find out? Obviously, the system is not far enough along in expertise—despite the awarding of Ph.D.s—to ask the right questions. Atlanta is not alone. This is the rule, not the exception.

And, yes, who the hell is Willie Sherman?

22

The Splash Heard 'Round the World

May, 1981

"1st Black Youth to Testify in Child Sex Trial," the *Atlanta Journal* headlined, on Thursday, May 21, 1981.

John David Wilcoxen, a 50-year-old truck driver, stood trial in Atlanta, the last of three middle-aged white men accused of running a child sex-for-hire ring involving more than 100 boys in south Atlanta. Earlier in May, 49-year-old Francis Hardy was convicted of child molestation and received a 30-year sentence. And before that, 40-year-old Lionel St. Louis pleaded guilty to sodomy and other charges. He was sentenced to 12 years in prison.

Prosecutors and police insisted all along that the cases of Wilcoxen, Hardy and St. Louis were in no way related to Atlanta's "missing and murdered children's" cases. All the boys involved, prosecutors and police said, were white.

At Wilcoxen's trial, an unidentified black youth joined a parade of white boys as state's witnesses. Several young boys testified that they had received $5 to $10 at various times from all three men for sexual favors and for posing nude in photos and films. GBI Agent Dale Kirkland, who had ridden with me on the route in September of 1980, testified that he had found about 200 photographs featuring 53 children in a motel on Stewart Avenue, near the Stewart-Lakewood Shopping Center, where Lubie Geter had disappeared. This was at variance with another police report I had read earlier, which mentioned up to 4,000 pictures.

Wilcoxen's lawyer, Catherine LeRow, argued that those state witnesses who were older than 14 were male prostitutes who sought out Wilcoxen and other men. "I contend they are just as guilty as he is," she told the jury of nine men and three women. She also said that one witness who was scheduled to testify on Wilcoxen's behalf had shot and killed himself when an attempt was made to serve him with a subpoena.

John David Wilcoxen showed no emotion when Fulton County Superior Court Judge Osgood Williams read the verdict: "Guilty" on two counts of child molestation and one count of sodomy. Wilcoxen was sentenced to 30 years in prison.

For all the courtroom drama surrounding the cases of Wilcoxen, Hardy and St. Louis, the authorities and the press treated them as sideshows. At Wilcoxen's trial, the state introduced no testimony about those reports of visits to Wilcoxen's house by two of Atlanta's murdered children—Earl Terrell and Lubie Geter. Now two juries stood deprived, by some administrative decision, of the opportunity to hear testimony that certainly was germane to the cases before them, whether it was legally relevant or not.

Meanwhile, also on May 21, Wayne Williams—six days shy of his 23rd birthday—sat down at his typewriter and prepared a $70 invoice for having taken still photographs of a client of Hotlanta Records. Williams had delivered the bill that night, he would tell me, to the recording company, located in College Park, south of Atlanta.

That's where Williams would tell me he was when, according to a prosecution witness at his trial, he was seen, instead, emerging from a downtown Atlanta theater, holding hands with a 27-year-old convicted felon named Nathaniel Cater.

Hours later, after the stroke of midnight, Wayne Williams would make another journey to another part of town—and there, his life would turn for the worse.

Neither Wayne Williams nor the police may be correct. Neither may be telling the truth. But they agree on one point:

Wayne Williams was driving south toward the James Jackson Parkway bridge, northwest of downtown Atlanta, in the predawn hours of Friday, May 22, 1981. As motorists on the bridge reach the mid-point of the Chattahoochee River below, the county changes from Cobb to Fulton for those heading south—or vice-versa for those heading north.

At about 2:50 a.m. on May 22, Atlanta police recruit Freddie Jacobs was stationed at street level on the Fulton County (or south) end of the bridge. He would say that his first inkling of any vehicle approaching the bridge was the glow created by the vehicle's headlights on the trees around his stakeout position. The trees were illuminated before he could see the beam of the headlights, Jacobs would explain, because the southbound vehicles came up a rise (which actually was nine-tenths of a mile from the bridge) before they leveled off and made a downhill approach toward the bridge.

A second Atlanta police recruit—Bob Campbell—was stationed under the bridge, across the river from Jacobs, on the Cobb County riverbank. He would testify that he knew when a car was on the bridge by the loud sounds made by vehicles crossing an expansion joint at the Cobb County (or north) end of the bridge. Two loud clanks in rapid succession were made by two-axeled vehicles at average speed.

Then, as the world soon would be told, Campbell heard a "splash"—not an unusual occurrence on the Chattahoochee River at nearly 3 a.m. during the spring. Residents who lived up to one mile away had complained for years to the Park Service about the noise made by beavers jumping into the river.

If you accept Freddie Jacobs' version, which differs importantly from Bob Campbell's, Campbell then radioed to Jacobs: "Freddie, is there a car on the bridge? I just heard a loud splash down here." Jacobs would testify that he had to lean out under the railing on the Fulton County (or south) side before he could see anything. But when he did, he said he saw a car approaching very slowly, with its lights on.

The vehicle, Jacobs would say, was a white 1970 Chevrolet Chevelle station wagon driven by Wayne Williams. Then, he said, the vehicle crossed the bridge, drove into a liquor-store parking lot off to the right at the Fulton County (or south) end of the bridge. He also said he had to duck down to keep from being seen. In a ducked-down position, he could have seen nothing on the roadway.

Behind the liquor store, Atlanta police officer Carl Holden was parked in a privately owned Ford Granada that he was using as a "chase car." According to Holden and Jacobs, the station wagon turned around in the parking lot and headed back north across the bridge.

The standing order for officers driving the chase cars was that if anything suspicious happened on the bridge, they were to seal off the bridge to prevent anyone from leaving. Neither chase car driver at this stakeout followed these instructions. Instead, Holden, the Atlanta police officer, began following Williams back across the bridge and north into Cobb County.

If you accept Bob Campbell's version given in court, he says he heard a "splash," then looked down, shining a flashlight into the river. He said he could see the point of the splash and the water rippling away from it in concentric circles. He said he looked up, then down, then up again, then down again, then up—and he saw headlights on the bridge at a point above the splash.

At the trial, Campbell would testify that he had radioed to FBI Agent Greg Gilliland about the splash. (Gilliland sat in a chase car parked on the Cobb County side and had seen and heard nothing.)

Defense attorney Al Binder would ask Campbell to come down from the witness stand and mark the location where the splash occurred on an elaborate model of the Jackson Parkway bridge—a model constructed by the FBI and said to be second only to the model of the John F. Kennedy assassination site in cost and detail. Campbell did so, marking a point in the mock-up of the river nearest the shore of Cobb County, where he had stood. He even sketched in the concentric circles.

Then, and now, the police and prosecution are stuck with a "splash." No matter what else, they have to maintain that Wayne Williams was on the bridge where and when that splash was heard. No splash, no probable cause. No probable cause, no legal stop. No legal stop, no legal arrest. No legal arrest, no case. No case, more embarrassment. The prosecution isn't about to budge from its contentions about the "splash."

Wayne Williams, for his part, is stuck with his own story that he was looking for the apartment of a young woman with whom he had a business appointment scheduled for hours later, after sunrise. He is stuck with a story about a woman who no one has been able to prove exists, a telephone number that for one reason or another isn't correct, an implausible story about his reason for being there and—if his attorney's version of his original story is correct—a lie about where he was going, to say nothing of two life sentences.

If both the police and Wayne Williams are correct, then four-tenths of a mile before Wayne Williams reached the bridge, he drove in front of—and within 10 feet—of the FBI chase car occupied by Agent Greg Gilliland.

As I sat writing for the first time about the Jackson Parkway bridge episode, I saw what I thought might be another fatal flaw to the state's case. Wayne Williams had already passed the first anniversary of his conviction by then. The problem I saw was one of venue.

First, I had just seen a network made-for-television movie, *"Murder in Coweta County."* The story, based on a book by Margaret Ann Barnes, told of a 1948 Georgia case that hinged on venue.

Now I looked at the Wayne Williams case, in which the state had been very careful to establish venue in the normal way. No one knew where the murders of Jimmy Ray Payne and Nathaniel Cater had been committed. So, the state relied on what is usually the next best evidence—where the bodies were found. Clearly, both bodies had been found in Fulton County. But if the offenses could be shown to have been committed in a county other than Fulton—and if no change of venue had been granted—then the state's conviction might be in jeopardy.

Now the Fulton County prosecutors were really stuck with the splash. The probable cause was no less important—undoubtedly more important, in the long run, than the venue question. But the state, in establishing its probable cause, relied on testimony that a splash had occurred *not* in Fulton, but in Cobb County; that the source of the splash was in Cobb County, and that the cause of the splash was the body of 27-year-old Nathaniel Cater. Then the state went on to demonstrate that Jimmy Ray Payne's body probably had entered the water at the same point. The state did so by laboriously eliminating other possibilities, showing hundreds of photographs and relying on lengthy testimony.

Could it be that if the body of Nathaniel Cater had been placed in the water in Cobb County—and it could be proved—that Fulton County had no jurisdiction to try Wayne Williams for murder? The point where the officer swore he heard the splash and saw the ripples and looked up and saw the vehicle is clearly in Cobb County, not Fulton County. The boundary line between the two counties runs down the center of the river, and the testimony of the state's witness (police officer, then-recruit, Bob Campbell) in establishing probable cause clearly places the events of the crime in Cobb County.

Meanwhile, in the wee hours of May 22, Wayne Williams was being pursued north by the Atlanta police officer toward Agent Greg Gilliland, who would testify that the first time he saw the station wagon was when it was coming north toward him, with officer Carl Holden following. Gilliland would say that he maneuvered his car between Williams' station wagon and Holden's chase car and continued to follow Williams north, with Holden bringing up the rear.

Wayne Williams then swung onto the ramp that would take him onto Interstate 285. Then, about 1½ miles from the Jackson Parkway bridge, the FBI agent used his siren and emergency lights to pull Williams to the shoulder.

Police recruit Bob Campbell would testify that he had seen the lights of a car come on at about the point where he thought the splash originated and that he had radioed to FBI Agent Gilliland about the splash.

The scenario that the prosecution was attempting to paint was this: Wayne Williams sneaked onto the bridge. His vehicle lights were turned off, and he was traveling so slowly that the station wagon didn't make the clank-clank noise when it crossed the expansion joint. Then, according to the state's theory—which would be presented as if it were fact at the trial—Williams removed Nathaniel Cater's body (Cater was bigger than Williams) through the tailgate opening of the wagon. The motor of Williams' 11-year-old vehicle would have had to be so silent it could not be heard in the still of the night. Wayne Williams would have to open and shut two doors without making a sound. He would then have to accelerate with no engine or exhaust sounds. I doubt it.

The state would re-enact just such a scene (though surely not silently) for photographers. But in one of the few objections granted to the defense,

Judge Clarence Cooper would refuse to let the mock-scene pictures be introduced into evidence.

The state's conjecture would include Williams lifting Cater's body over the bridge railing without so much as a grunt or an "oof." No marks would be left on the bridge railing or the nude body. After silently returning to his vehicle, for a reason that escapes me, he didn't bother to sneak back off the bridge. Then, though still "running silently," he turned on the vehicle's lights. But, instead of trying to escape, he turned around and drove at normal speed back across the bridge.

To support this scenario, Freddie Jacobs would testify that no headlights shined on the trees to warn him that Williams' station wagon was approaching from the north. Then Campbell would testify that he heard no noise from tires crossing the expansion joint and that he saw the lights "come on."

If Freddie Jacobs' sworn testimony that he saw no illumination on the trees is correct, then Wayne Williams must have driven up the rise (nine-tenths of a mile north of the bridge) with his station wagon's lights off.

However, Agent Gilliland was parked between the rise and the bridge, four-tenths of a mile north of the bridge, and facing the roadway closest to the southbound lane. It is almost 3 a.m. Unless Gilliland was blind, asleep or completely inattentive, how could he miss a white station wagon "sneaking" for almost a mile from the crest of a rise toward the bridge with its lights off, when the agent's sole purpose for being there was to take action if he saw suspicious persons or vehicles?

Preparing for the trial, one member of Wayne Williams' defense team went to the location below the bridge where recruit Bob Campbell says he participated in the stakeout. Another drove his car back and forth across the bridge at varying speeds. As slowly as the car would travel, the expansion joint would still make a loud clank audible to the man beneath the bridge amid the noises of the day, compared with the still of the night. Then the driver parked the car and directed his 10-year-old son to run across the expansion joint. Then, too, you could still hear the clank.

The defense then arranged for a radio newsman who is knowledgeable about sound to run a more scientific test. But Judge Clarence Cooper would rule the test inadmissible, explaining that the conditions did not exactly duplicate those of May 22, 1981. This is the same judge who would rule admissible the results of a state test of the flow of the river in which dams were opened to duplicate "as closely as possible" the conditions of May 22, 1981. But these results would also not take into account such variables as temperature, time, mock-ups instead of human remains, *et cetera.*

If Gilliland's testimony is correct, then Wayne Williams *didn't* drive south from Interstate 285 across the bridge *when* the police say he did. But perhaps Williams might have done so earlier, as Williams says he did. Gilliland's testimony tends to support Williams' version of the events.

Wayne Williams contends that he did not turn around in the liquor store parking lot at the south (or Fulton County) end of the bridge, as the police allege. Rather, Williams said he continued south toward a Starvin' Marvin gas-convenience store, at the Bolton Road intersection, six-tenths of a mile farther south, beyond the bridge (a drive of less than one minute, at the speed limit). There, he says, he stopped to use a pay telephone and pick up some cardboard boxes that his mother had asked him to get while he was out. Only then, Williams says, did he return north across the bridge again—back into Cobb County. At that same intersection is a store that has alcoholic beverages advertised in the window. Williams says this is the store he was talking about.

There are two scenarios which would make all of the testimony on both sides add up. But, of course, they are both pure conjecture on my part. Both involve a side road at the northeast corner of the bridge. In one scenario, Williams is guilty—in the other, he is innocent.

If you travel north across the bridge and into Cobb County, you see a side road on your right—immediately after the bridge railing ends. That side road takes you to Georgia Power's Plant McDonough, site of the giant smoke-stack with flickering strobe lights that had intrigued me so much when I first flew into Atlanta at night, back in the early 1970s.

After proceeding a short way down that side road, you come to a guard shack. But immediately before the guard shack is a boat ramp of paved concrete, which slopes off to your right and disappears into the water at the river's edge.

Let's assume for a moment that Wayne Williams is guilty. If so, events could have happened this way: At some point, perhaps even before the police stakeout is in place at 8 p.m. on May 21, 1981, Wayne Williams drives north on Jackson Parkway toward Cobb County. With him is 27-year-old Nathaniel Cater, whom he had met earlier at a downtown moviehouse.

They cross the bridge, then immediately turn right—onto the side road—to the boat ramp. They do not pass the guard shack, as the state's testimony would intimate they would have to. Physically, they *don't have to.* The guard shack is across the road. And we have no evidence, or even an indication, whether the guard house is occupied on this night.

Wayne Williams drives down the boat ramp to the river's edge. He and Cater do whatever they do, and Wayne Williams kills Nathaniel Cater for whatever reason (no motive was ever established by authorities—although they offered several to choose from).

Then, shortly before 3 a.m. on May 22, Williams easily rolls Cater's body into the river (the boat ramp is upstream from the bridge). Williams then starts his station wagon and returns to where the side road empties onto Jackson Parkway. There is a stop sign. He stops. Then he turns left onto the Jackson Parkway bridge, moving slowly from a dead stop.

At that moment, a huge beaver jumps into the water. There is a loud splash.

Just then, the lights from Williams' vehicle, swinging through a 90-degree arc, hit the bridge rail at the exact point where Campbell, seeing them for the first time, thinks they are turned on. This point on the bridge rail is just south of the Cobb County shoreline.

Williams' tires do not roll over the expansion joint at the normal speed. Nor do they hit the expansion joint two at a time, but rather, one at a time because of the turning radius of the vehicle. What sounds there are go unheard because Campbell is already preoccupied with the sound of the splash.

If this scenario actually happened, the only person who is lying or incorrect in his testimony is Wayne Williams. First, no lights illuminated the trees around Jacobs because the station wagon never came across the rise. Second, Williams didn't drive past Agent Gilliland, explaining why Gilliland never saw him go south across the bridge.

It all fits, but the prosecution cannot buy it because it no longer would have probable cause to arrest Williams. Remember, no splash—no probable cause.

Now, let's assume that Wayne Williams is *not* guilty. He is driving south across the bridge. In close proximity are two other vehicles also heading south. It is 10 or 15 minutes yet before the beaver will jump and make a splash. Williams proceeds to the Starvin' Marvin, and heads back north toward the bridge.

Meanwhile, another vehicle—it might even have been another white station wagon—leaves Plant McDonough. The driver of this vehicle doesn't have to be a killer. Nathaniel Cater's body may have been in the water for some time. Based on what I saw of the medical examiners' work, their guesses would have supported this contention had they not been told in advance that the splash occurred on the morning of May 22. Except for that prior knowledge, no one would argue that Cater could not have been in the water longer.

The other vehicle stops at the intersection with Jackson Parkway, then turns left onto the bridge, pulling away slowly from a dead stop. The beaver jumps. There is no illumination on the trees. Again, the expansion joint makes a noise, but not one that police on the stakeouts are used to hearing. The lights come on at the right place and at the right time.

The driver of the other vehicle crosses the bridge and starts to turn off the road into the liquor store parking lot. But the driver sees a sinister-looking car parked there in the darkness (Carl Holden's chase car). The driver thinks better of it and swerves back onto Jackson Parkway, quickly disappearing around a curve.

At that precise moment, Wayne Williams passes the entrance to the liquor store, headed back north from the Starvin' Marvin. Officer Holden, who has momentarily lost sight of the vehicle that had just come into view in the parking lot, emerges from behind the liquor store and falls in behind Williams. Freddie Jacobs hears Holden say that he is following the station wagon and assumes that it is the same vehicle he saw seconds earlier, coming south toward him across the bridge.

Now nobody is lying, and everyone can understand how a dedicated FBI agent missed Williams' station wagon coming south.

Williams explained to me in a recent conversation (without having heard these theories) that a brown Toyota he says was on the bridge when he was passed him headed south, just as he got to the bridge headed north. This point would not be clarified at his trial.

The defense would attempt to indicate that the boat ramp was a spot available for the bodies to enter the river. But the state would contend that the bridge was the only such spot. The state would maintain:

(1) That it was necessary to pass that guard shack to get there. But the state would not say the guard shack was manned and it would not indicate that it was the *side,* not the front, of the shack that you had to pass. Moreover, the state doesn't point out that the guard shack is there to challenge entry to the power-plant grounds, not the boat ramp.

(2) The state would say there was a chain stretched across the boat ramp. What the state wouldn't say was that the chain was at the water end of the ramp to prevent cars from slipping into the water, rather than at the top of the ramp to deny access to the ramp. The chain has since been moved to the top of the ramp, just as the expansion joint has been fixed to eliminate the loud noise.

Certainly tales of sleeping, drinking, horseplay, hallucinations—and even of chase cars leaving their posts to pick up and deliver beer, food *et cetera*—had been told about the stakeout teams. A member of one of those teams, former Atlanta police recruit Ken Lawson, would testify for the defense. He would say that stakeout team members slept, drank and swapped ghost stories. He said that Campbell had pitched a tent beneath the Jackson Parkway bridge. Lawson testified that the S.W.A.T. team was summoned to the Jackson Parkway bridge one dark morning when Freddie Jacobs reported seeing a "hazy white figure" in the woods.

I've been a cop long enough to assume that at least one of those people on that bridge detail was sleeping. It would be the exception if someone wasn't goofing off, rather than a surprise that someone was.

Before the fixed stakeouts waited in hiding at the bridges, small groups of cops, mostly recruits, patrolled the Chattahoochee River at night in small rubber rafts—each equipped with police radios. The cops' code name for the Chattahoochee River was "Stewart Avenue."

On one occasion, spillways in a hydroelectric dam—many miles up the river—were opened routinely by the Georgia Power Company. That sent a surge of water downstream. Water gushed through the narrows and around the bends, finally tossing and capsizing the police rafts. One officer managed to scream a "May Day" message into his radio, saying his boat had overturned on "Stewart Avenue." Apparently not linking the call for help with the code name for the Chattahoochee River, a dispatcher sent police cars and fire-department units to the *real* Stewart Avenue, miles from the Chattahoochee River, in a vain, if not laughable, search for overturned boats.

Something tells me to pay attention to the testimony of FBI Agent Greg Gilliland. I said that to Wayne Williams once during his trial—and I explained why. I think it may have given Williams problems in his cross examination by assistant prosecutor Jack Mallard. Williams said, on the stand, that he thought Gilliland was the only one telling the truth. Then Jack Mallard stung Williams with a litany of Gilliland statements that were damaging to Williams. Each time, Mallard prodded Williams with the rhetorical question: "Was he telling the truth when he said that . . .?"

Perhaps I liked Gilliland's courage under cross examination by Al Binder. The agent pointed out that the highly regarded scale model furnished by his agency was inaccurate, at least insofar as the distance it showed between his car and the north end of the bridge. It was farther in reality than it scaled on the model, he told Binder. He left the witness stand to walk to the model and demonstrate to the court how wrong the supposed scale model was. That couldn't have been a happy moment for the FBI.

It is important to understand that the splash and the body of Nathaniel Cater are not necessarily connected. This is simply a theory of the prosecutors that supports the state's version of the events of May 22. Wayne Williams can still be guilty or innocent if you don't buy the story of the splash. If Wayne Williams is as familiar with the area as both he and the prosecution contend, why would he "sneak" onto a bridge over the Chattahoochee River, using a busy highway, and go through the physically difficult (if not impossible for him) task of lifting the deadweight body of a grown man—at least 2½ inches taller than he—over a bridge railing and then dump the body into the water? Would he—or could he—do this and be the cunning killer who for months had been seen by no one? Why wouldn't he go to the boat ramp, only 100 yards away, where he could, in relative seclusion, effortlessly roll the body into the same river? On reading this, Wayne Williams called to tell me he didn't know the boat ramp was there.

No one would testify that Wayne Williams threw a body into the water. No one would testify that Wayne Williams threw anything in the water. No one would testify that Wayne Williams even stopped on the bridge. Witnesses would only intimate that he did and that his actions were the cause of the splash that was heard 'round the world.

Abby Mann, motion-picture producer and screenwriter, who attended the Wayne Williams trial, asks an ever-intriguing question: "If Wayne Williams didn't throw Nathaniel Cater's body off that bridge when the police say he did, what are odds that the real killer would be riding across that bridge at the exact moment that an accidental splash was heard?" In agreement with Mann, I'd say the odds are on the low side of slim and none. So the state will forever be stuck with the splash.

Out on Interstate 285, Agent Greg Gilliland identified himself to Wayne Williams by shouting, "FBI! FBI!" Williams, who had pulled over at the sight of the emergency lights and howl of the siren, now stepped from his station wagon. He walked to the back of the wagon to meet the agent.

Williams told me later that he knew they were stopping him "in relationship to the murders." Why else would an FBI agent stop someone in Atlanta, Georgia, in May of 1981? Remember, too, that Williams' friend, Jim Comento, already had been stopped and questioned by the Fulton County police.

According to Wayne Williams, neither the agent nor anyone else advised him of his rights before they started talking with him. In fact, in the approximately two hours that he stayed there with them along Interstate 285, he never was given a Miranda warning, Williams said.

If true, that would have been unforgivable procedure, but it wouldn't have changed the outcome of anything, since there was no confession. But it is clear that Jack Mallard relied very heavily on the things Wayne Williams told his questioners that morning—and they were questioning him without the shield of a Miranda warning, unless Williams is lying about this.

What makes me think that he might not be lying? Later, when Williams was questioned by the FBI, he willingly signed a waiver of his Miranda rights and he willingly submitted to more than one polygraph examination. Too bad no one asked about a Miranda warning at Williams' trial. But the lack of a Miranda warning would become an issue on appeal.

The agent bent down and picked up a piece of rope, or wire (the testimony was conflicting, and neither was introduced as evidence) from the shoulder of the expressway, behind Williams' vehicle. Williams said he told the agent, "Remember where you got that."

Williams and the police agree that they asked his permission to look into his station wagon, and he said he let them. A pair of shoes and several bags of clothing lay in the vehicle, according to Williams. No one looked through the bags or inventoried the contents of Williams' vehicle. A while later, a parade of police officers and agents arrived. Eventually, one of the FBI agents phoned his supervisor at home for instructions. The instructions were: "Let him go."

While he was being questioned along Interstate 285, Williams said, he saw helicopters with powerful lights searching the waters of the Chattahoochee. Nothing was found, and there was no reason to detain him further.

I sat in defense attorney Mary Welcome's office, arguing with her and Al Binder. They said Wayne Williams was driving back north across the bridge to go home. In fact, I apparently never would convince Binder because, in his closing arguments, he would say that after the incident on the bridge, Williams did not try to run away, but instead went straight home and told his parents.

Actually, Wayne Williams did *not* go straight home and didn't intend to. When Mary Welcome argued that it was closer to Williams' house from the bridge to go by way of Interstate 285 and Interstate 20, I answered, "Bullshit!"

Southbound on the Jackson Parkway—the direction Williams was traveling when he first went across the bridge—was a much faster and more direct route to his home. If Wayne Williams was in a hurry, and Interstate 285 were quicker, I argued, why drive 1½ miles past it before turning around to get back on it?

Why was Wayne Williams on that bridge at that early-morning hour? Williams has explained that he had been in Cobb County, looking for the apartment of a woman he had an appointment with after sunrise. Not a handful of people believe that story. But keep in mind that it's up to the state to prove that Wayne Williams did what it contended he did. That Wayne Williams is stuck with a story he can't seem to prove is his fault, but it doesn't constitute proof of murder. And, unfortunately for Williams, it isn't even an alibi.

Wayne Williams told me that he wasn't going home. "I was going back to the Sans Souci," he said, referring to a downtown nightclub. Then why did Binder and Mary Welcome think he was going home? Was he going home when he went south across the bridge—and then changed his mind?

Wayne Williams said he gave the agents the telephone number of the woman he hoped to meet, Cheryl Johnson, saying that he might be wrong by one digit. But the number that agents say Wayne Williams gave them had been changed to another number. Dialing the second number—one not even similar to the one given them by Williams—they reached a cosmetic company, which, not surprisingly, had no one there named Cheryl Johnson. The trail of Cheryl Johnson, if she existed, was said to lead to Tennessee, but no one located her, her address or her phone number.

The search for Cheryl Johnson was poorly conducted. No search at all would have done as well. If there were a Cheryl Johnson, Wayne Williams had said things about her that could have been checked out, but weren't. No effort was made by the defense to pinpoint with Williams the possible incorrect digit and to eliminate other numbers mathematically in an effort to locate her.

Williams said he had already made an audition appointment with Cheryl Johnson beyond the meeting at her apartment. No one checked to see if she might have tried to keep that appointment.

Certainly the FBI could have tracked her down had it wanted to—perhaps through the U.S. Census Bureau. Nothing (laws notwithstanding) can really stop an agency like the FBI or the IRS from finding out what it wants to know. Unfortunately, the justice system is geared to produce convictions, rather than the truth.

In the days immediately after the incident on the bridge, Wayne Williams and his father did a major cleanup job around their house. They carried out boxes and carted them off in the station wagon. They burned negatives and photographic prints in the outdoor grill.

Wayne Williams told me in jail that the cleanup involved making a room ready for his aunt. His father, Homer, told me, as I sat in the Williamses' living room, waiting for a plausible explanation, that he and Wayne had carried some of the boxes, those that contained books, to a dumpster near a school downtown. He told of carrying the other boxes to a dumping area off Fulton Industrial Boulevard, where the bicycle that had been used by 14-year-old victim Milton Harvey was found. Homer Williams said he had used the same area for dumping on several occasions. But when I asked him for directions, he said he only knew how to drive it. I asked him if he would lead me to it. But now, he said he probably couldn't find it.

The pictures they had burned, Homer Williams explained, were excesses from his job as a freelance photographer. They were unclaimed, extra copies, and photos that just didn't turn out right. I've never been satisfied with any part of the explanation about the cleanup, either Wayne's or Homer's. The best I can say is, it could be true.

For the moment, the bridge incident was just that, a bridge incident. Wayne Williams moved about freely. It was business as usual on the peripheries of Atlanta's murders.

Barely 48 hours later, on Sunday, May 24, 1981, another body was found—floating nude and face down—in the Chattahoochee River, not far from where 21-year-old Jimmy Ray Payne had turned up dead nearly a month before. Could this be the victim of *the* "splash"?

The medical examiner said the body was that of 27-year-old Nathaniel Cater. Cater hadn't been on The List as a missing person. No one knew Cater was missing. He had been living at the Falcon Hotel, downtown by the bus terminal, during the month since he had left his family's apartment home at 2261 Verbena Street in Dixie Hills. There, he had lived in the apartment above 7-year-old LaTonya Wilson on the night she was allegedly kidnapped from her bedroom.

The Nathaniel Cater case is one that convinced me that pathology is not a science, but a bill-of-goods sold to the public by people who make a lot of money for making guesses that other people are conditioned to accept as facts. No one with an open mind could study the so-called medical science of pathology as applied in these cases and not come away with the impression that pathology is little farther removed from exact science than is flipping a coin.

Surprise, surprise, the Fulton County medical examiner decided that Nathaniel Cater's body had been dead for just enough time for it to have been thrown in the Chattahoochee River when police say Wayne Williams did it. This is one case in which the chicken came before the egg. The defense pathologist would say the body had been dead for a much longer time. Both were value judgments without any scientific validity. If it were science, both would have agreed in the first place, or one could have been proved wrong.

Then, too, four witnesses (two of whom knew Nathaniel Cater) said that they saw him alive on May 22 or 23—*after* the bridge incident. The defense didn't bring any of these witnesses to the stand. All four were known to the court, and one, Jimmy (Tightrope) Anthony, 39, had been quoted in the *Atlanta Journal* as saying he had seen Cater on the morning of May 23, 1981. This story appeared before the bridge incident became generally known. Therefore, no contradiction was recognized, and no questions were raised by the reporters. At that point, the media knew only that Cater had been found on May 24. They didn't yet know that the police would accuse a man of throwing Cater's body in a river on the morning of May 22. I wondered, though, why the reporter who wrote that story never thought to resurrect the question when the bridge incident became public. And I wondered why the jury would hear none of this testimony.

I told Jeff Prugh about "Tightrope" Anthony. Jeff found him at the corner of Verbena Street and Shirley Place. It turned out that Jimmy (Tightrope) Anthony had lived in the same apartment house where convicted killer Amp Wiley lived (actually, Anthony's cousins' aparment), next door to Nathaniel Cater and LaTonya Wilson, and across the street from Cynthia Montgomery.

For his part, "Tightrope" Anthony is sure he saw Cater alive on Saturday morning, May 23, while entering the Healy Building, miles from the bridge. "Nate saw me and said, 'How ya doin'?'" Anthony said. "I told him I was goin' inside to pay my rent, and I asked him how he was doing. He said, 'I just got me a new job.'"

I told Durwood Myers, Al Binder's righthand man, where Jimmy (Tightrope) Anthony could be found, but Anthony never was subpoenaed.

When Jeff asked Anthony to explain the discrepancy between his story and that of the authorities as to when Nathaniel Cater was dead, he shrugged and replied: "Maybe Nate's got two lives."

One pathologist said that Nathaniel Cater could have died from heart problems. Another pointed out that Cater sold his blood—and far too often. If AIDS (acquired immune deficiency syndrome) had been a buzzword in

January of 1981, it would probably have turned up in somebody's findings. Still another pathologist said drowning could not be ruled out in the Cater case. No one knows how Nathaniel Cater died.

Nathaniel Cater's case was yet another in a panoply of questionable judgment calls by medical examiners. By mid-1981, these calls had pertained to one victim falling off a railroad trestle that wasn't there; victims whose identifications had been accomplished by dental charts that had been said earlier to bear no similarities with the teeth of those same victims; a positive identification based on a 3-to-2 vote; identification of one victim by eliminating another and then saying, in so many words, that it might have been almost any other dead 10-year-old; a death certificate changed after an indictment; the official cause of death of one victim being changed twice before it was reverted to the original "cause unknown," and conning the media and the public with the meaningless term "probable asphyxia," as if it were some specific felonious cause of death.

In 1983, I read of at least two occasions in other U.S cities, where victims of "accidental" fire deaths were found to have bullets in them when their bodies were exhumed. Medical examiners merely guess, and we need to know that. The medical examiners themselves know it, and juries should, too. People's lives and freedom depend on this knowledge that it's purely guesswork, and tilted toward the prosecution at that.

Nathaniel Cater, if it *was* really Nathaniel Cater, probably stopped breathing. Someone *could* have come up from behind him and applied a choke hold, one medical examiner would testify.

If the judge would not let the prosecution enter pictures taken by the police of how they *think* Cater's body was unloaded from the station wagon and dumped into the river, why is a medical examiner allowed to tell the jurors how he *thinks* a person died? Why is his guess admissible and the investigator's not admissible? Is it because the medical examiner is an "expert"? Then why not put a wrestler on the witness stand, as someone who might really be an expert in "choke holds"?

If it didn't happen after Wayne Williams was questioned near the Chattahoochee—as "Tightrope" Anthony says it must have been—then nobody knows *when* Nathaniel Cater disappeared, let alone when he died.

Some customers at the Silver Dollar Saloon across from the downtown Atlanta bus station (and the Falcon Hotel, where Cater was staying) said Cater was a regular, but they couldn't remember the last time he was in. A neighbor of Cater at the Falcon Hotel said he didn't remember the last time he had seen Cater, but that Cater used to sit on the front porch of the hotel and drink beer. The neighbor said he would see Cater quite often at the Cameo Lounge and the Silver Dollar Saloon. And when he did, he said, "Nathaniel was usually alone and intoxicated."

Another neighbor said that the last time he saw Nathaniel Cater was "Wednesday or Thursday of last week at approximately 11:30 a.m. to 12 noon." Since the neighbor made that statement to authorities on May 26, 1981, that would have fixed the date at May 20 or 21. He, too, said that Cater was usually drunk.

The hotel manager said that Cater was a "slick hustler who would attempt to get away with anything," although the manager added that Cater usually paid his rent on time and never tried to steal anything or cause trouble at the hotel. Cater was, the manager said, a loner who stayed drunk, who usually could be found at the Silver Dollar or the Cameo, hustling both males and females. He added that if Cater ever was with anybody, it would be John Henley.

A self-described "running partner" of Cater for at least eight years said that Cater had a bad drinking problem: "He just continued to drink straight alcohol without chasers." When asked if Cater was connected with drugs, the man answered, "No, not as I know of."

"What about smoke?" the investigating officer asked him.

"Yeah," the man replied, "but I don't consider that drugs . . ."

"Oh, yes," he added, "he used to go to the blood bank often and give blood about twice a week."

The man said he didn't know if Cater had homosexual tendencies.

"What did Nathaniel do to make money?" the investigator asked.

"Go to the blood bank or check out a job. He said he used to rob people, but I didn't believe him. He used to catch winos in the alley and take their money. The last time I left him, it was dark on Saturday . . . I hadn't seen him since." That Saturday would have been May 23. Which means that yet another witness says Nathaniel Cater was alive after Wayne Williams is supposed to have dumped Cater's dead body off a bridge.

Records at the American Plasma Corporation, a mercenary blood bank, indicate that Cater was last there on May 21, 1981, hours before the predawn May 22 bridge incident. Personnel at the blood bank refused to take his blood that day. Another commercial blood bank, the Plasma Light, produced records showing that Cater had been there May 16 and 19.

Spokesmen at one labor-pool service said that Cater and slain 23-year-old Michael McIntosh—"using the alias of Mickey Michael *Williams* [emphasis added]"—both had worked out of its offices. On March 26, 1981, Cater and McIntosh were at the labor pool at the same time, but went out on separate jobs.

The Atlanta police did an exhaustive check of all employees and patrons of the Silver Dollar, but could not find anyone who had ever seen Wayne Williams there. The same effort was undertaken at the Cameo Lounge, with the same results.

On May 29 (which would have been Nathaniel Cater's 28th birthday), police questioned a man at the "Add-a-Man" labor pool. The man told them that he knew Cater "real well," and that Cater hung around the Cameo and the Silver Dollar and accepted money from homosexuals to let them perform oral sodomy on him. The man advised that he, too, did the same thing and that Cater loitered at the bus station and the Omni for the same purpose. Cater, he told police, was involved in a burglary of the Athens restaurant—in Atlanta—during the summer of 1980. I wondered since if the police cleared the restaurant break-in.

The man at the labor pool also said he had seen John Henley (Cater's roommate) scared and crying. Henley told him, the man said, that he feared he would be killed next. The week before Cater turned up dead, Henley told him, he said, that a white man dressed in a luxurious gray three-piece suit, carrying a briefcase and accompanied by a large black man dressed in expensive sports clothes, came to the hotel room, looking for Cater "five or six different times." Henley, he said, didn't know who they were or what they wanted with Cater. (The man also told police that he had met Michael McIntosh at the same labor pool.)

One man who knew Nathaniel Cater said that Cater "hustled slum dope" outside the Cameo and the Silver Dollar. The man said that on May 21, Cater stopped him near the bus station and asked to borrow $3. "I loaned him the money," the man told police, adding that Cater said he was "going off with a white guy to make a little money." The man said he had not seen Cater since approximately 11 a.m. on May 21.

Inside the Cameo Lounge, a customer named Howard Campbell told Special Agent Barbero and Investigator J. Farmer that he had seen Cater many times—the last time on *May 23,* 1981, at approximately 2 p.m.

This again was the day *after* Williams is said to have thrown Cater's body off the bridge. The investigators repeatedly challenged Campbell's recollection of the date, but Campbell stuck to his story, insisting that it was May 23. The defense would not attempt to locate Campbell to testify at the trial of Wayne Williams.

A researcher working on a screenplay for CBS interviewed Al Binder. He told me that Binder "admitted" that he had just barely had time to study the pathology and laboratory reports in preparing for the trial. Many of the witnesses' names we have been discussing were in the "Brady" material selected by Judge Cooper and furnished to the defense attorneys for Wayne Williams—at least a month before the trial. I do recall that Mary Welcome made abstracts of the Brady material prior to the trial. I didn't come across much of this material until after Wayne Williams' conviction, and didn't get around to reading some of it until just before spring of 1983. This may shed some light on why some or all of these witnesses were not called in the defense of Wayne Williams.

On May 24, 1981, police helicopters made a routine air surveillance—from 10:30 a.m. to 3 p.m.—of the Chattahoochee River between the Jackson

Parkway bridge and Gordon Road (which included the area where Cater's body was found). Below them was the Fulton County Fire Department's scuba diving team, which found a safe, some old clothing and a Thompson-submachine gun in the river.

Al Binder was interested in that safe. He thought it might have been stolen from a place where Jimmy Ray Payne had worked. He thought, too, that this offered a plausible explanation of what Payne might have been doing in the Chattahoochee River. But Binder's inquiries were in vain. No one at the police department would give him any information about the safe.

Why was it a secret? It was a secret because, once again, our criminal-justice system is geared to convict suspects, not expose the truth. Attempts to expose the truth have heretofore been looked upon as "coddling criminals."

I don't want to coddle anybody, but I think we would all be better off if we knew that our system was designed to surface as much truth as possible, rather than to *"win"* cases. Recall for example, that the medical examiner gave two reasons for finally ruling Jimmy Ray Payne's death a murder—and neither was medical. But one of those reasons was that Jimmy Ray Payne was not known to "frequent" the Chattahoochee. Well, if there was a reason for Payne to be there on this occasion, wouldn't the medical examiner only be half as sure that he was murdered? Why should the police be allowed to deprive the jury—through the defense—of the facts of the matter? In any event, the helicopter officer's report read: "Nothing of significant value was found on this search."

Margaret Carter would say that she had seen Wayne Williams talking with Nathaniel Cater in a playground near the Cater family's apartment in Dixie Hills. Williams' German shepherd was "romping" in the area, she said, adding that her daughter, too, had seen Cater and Williams together. Mrs. Carter said this happened on May 18. But before she gave this statement, she had been interviewed on television by Paul Crawley of WXIA-TV. In that interview, Mrs. Carter had placed the date as May 25—the Monday on which Memorial Day was celebrated in 1981, and the day *after* Cater's body was found!

Both Margaret Carter and her daughter, Gwinette Carter, were shown pictures of several of Wayne Williams' shirts by a police investigator. Each positively identified the shirt that Wayne Williams wore when, they said, he sat there talking with Nate Cater. But, each picked a different shirt.

If a German shepherd was "romping" in the area, as Mrs. Carter said (it was the prosecution that decided it was Wayne Williams' dog), then it definitely wasn't the Williamses' dog, Sheba. Sheba was old and feeble and cannot even walk without staggering (the dog has since died). Probably its longest walk in years was down the aisle of the Fulton County courtroom where Binder had it brought to show how unlikely it was that this dog was "romping" in Dixie

Hills—or, for that matter, that this dog was actively engaged in anything.

Cater hadn't lived in Dixie Hills for weeks when Mrs. Carter said she saw him sitting there in front of his family's apartment, talking with Williams. Of course, Cater could have been there. Like another of the victims of this "pattern" murder case—a pattern which, according to the prosecution, included coming from a "broken home"—Nathaniel Cater was a man who was almost 28 and who had been kicked out of his "unbroken" family home.

Contrary to the public's perception of List victims, Cater—like others on The List—had a criminal record. It included two criminal trespass charges and a conviction for attempted burglary, for which he was sentenced to two years probation on a *nolo contendre* plea.

Cater's brother was expecting Nate to show up for his birthday party, but Nate hadn't shown up. The younger Cater was sure that something was "bad wrong." Cater's father always gave the children money on their birthdays. The youngster had been sure that Nate wouldn't pass up the chance for a few free bucks. But he did.

On May 27, 1981, Wayne Williams' 23rd birthday and five days after he had been questioned near the bridge and released (and three days after a body identified as that of Nathaniel Cater turned up), Public Safety Commissioner Lee Brown met behind closed doors with his top supervisory officers.

The press reported the meeting as "secret," but it couldn't have been that secret. It was simply closed. Reporters stood in a corridor outside a crowded room on the fourth floor of Atlanta police headquarters.

There, they overheard Lee Brown tell about 150 officers that the Task Force still had no significant suspects or leads that would break the Atlanta cases. "Some of you have complained that you are not getting enough information about these cases," the *Atlanta Journal's* Bill Berkeley quoted Brown as saying. "But let me suggest to you that we do not have a lot of information to give out."

Brown went on to tell the officers that we are "indeed in a crisis situation. We do not know who we are looking for, we do not know the problem we are facing—the fact that we have 29 unsolved cases. We're doing everything we possibly can to bring to closure this prolonged tragedy . . ."

The mandatory meeting had been called by Brown amid increasing reports that Atlanta police morale remained low and that cops on the streets still were told little, if anything, by the high command about what to look for in the investigation.

Was this really Lee Brown's understanding of the cases on May 27, 1981? I think it was. And I think this is a perfect example of my reasons for arguing that the case against Wayne Williams was built *after* he became a suspect—and not that Williams became a suspect because of the case that had been built against him.

Afterward, Brown refused to talk specifically about what was said in the meeting. All during the investigation, Brown was fond of boasting—with big numbers—how busy the Task Force was in trying to solve the crimes. Unwittingly, he was proving one of my favorite charges against the police establishment—i.e., they spend an awful lot of time and money efficiently being ineffective.

Beside all those thousands of tips the Task Force fed into its computers each week, he said, Task Force officers had worked "approximately 86,739 regular and overtime hours." (By mimmicking standard police misuse of the word "approximately," Brown illustrates the kind of semantical problems that turn bridges into railroad trestles and foul up murder cases beyond redemption).

Actually, non-Atlanta officers assigned to the Task Force didn't get paid any of those federal dollars for the overtime they worked. Which may account for some of the low morale. Was the city of Atlanta discriminating against non-Atlanta Task Force officers in its use of the $4.2 million sent by the federal government? Probably. Could Atlanta help it? Probably not. But that is of little solace to the officers of DeKalb, Cobb, Fulton, Rockdale, East Point, *et cetera,* who are also federal taxpayers.

For months, too, Brown insisted that the investigation that he had commanded—and which had failed completely—was a "model of cooperation" among the Task Force, the FBI and other agencies. The truth never was publicized—that the Federal Bureau of Investigation never joined the Task Force, but conducted a completely separate investigation, as did the DeKalb County police after January of 1981 and the Fulton County police for a portion of 1981.

If Atlanta's investigation really exemplified such teamwork, then why was Lee Brown telling his supervisory officers—on May 27, 1981—that the Task Force had no solid leads or suspects? Hadn't Brown yet been told that FBI agents and his own Atlanta police stakeout officers had stopped a man named Wayne Williams five mornings earlier? Didn't Brown yet know that the FBI now was surreptitiously monitoring Wayne Williams' activities from a house in Williams' neighborhood?

If this was one of the "front" stories ("I knew it all along, but it had to be business as usual to keep the lid on" kind of things), why hold a secret meeting and tell the cover story only to your own high command? He wouldn't have needed to call a meeting to leak anything.

From May 22, 1981, the Wayne Williams show became very much an FBI show—and soon, early on the night of June 3, Brown wouldn't know that Wayne Williams had been taken to FBI headquarters for questioning.

It's clear that Lee Brown's Task Force investigation had accomplished absolutely nothing in The List cases. But on May 27, 1981, didn't Brown even know that one of his own Atlanta police recruits on a stakeout (not to be confused with an investigation) had heard a "splash" heard 'round the world?

Beneath the Jackson Parkway bridge, a police recruit on stakeout duty heard a "splash" in the Cobb County waters of the Chattahoochee River. The state tried Wayne Williams not in Cobb County, but in Fulton County, saying Williams caused the "splash" by throwing the body of Nathaniel Cater, 27, off the bridge. However, no one at the trial testified that Williams stopped on the bridge or threw anything into the river. (John White/ Chicago Sun-Times)

23

Trial by Media

May, 1981

Within days of his 23rd birthday, Wayne Williams was secretly placed under surveillance by FBI agents. He apparently realized it not long after he had been released by authorities near the Chattahoochee River bridge.

Wayne Williams tells it this way: "It was a day or two after the bridge incident and I was ridin' with Comento in his EMS unit and I told him, 'Jim, the FBI had got a tail on me.' And he said, 'Well, let's see if they can follow us code 3,' and he jumped on the siren and we took off to make this injured-person call. And it was, so help me God, Chet, the one and the only time I was ever at the Silver Dollar [a lounge where Nathaniel Cater hung out]. It was the only time I'd been there, and we finished up and I was standin' out front of the Silver Dollar, talkin' to the police, waitin' for Comento, and one of them had the paper and we were reading about finding Cater's body."

"Did that affect you any?" I asked.

"Nah. Affect me? Why should it affect me? I didn't know who Cater was and I didn't connect him up with my gettin' stopped at all."

"But isn't that ironic as hell? You standing there, talking to the cops and reading about Cater's body and all?"

"It's somethin' else, but that's all hindsight. There wasn't nothin' to it then."

Williams seemed almost to enjoy playing cat-and-mouse with the authorities. He still chuckles when he talks about how one of his deft driving maneuvers caused two "shadow" cars to collide.

Meanwhile, one of Williams' acquaintances—City Councilman Arthur Langford Jr.—quietly went to California. He would become a "no show" at a dinner where he was supposed to be guest speaker. His hosts would wonder if he were "missing," and I would half-kiddingly count him as one of Atlanta's "missing persons," realizing, of course, that he was too old, at 31, to make The List, but just barely.

On June 3, 1981, not quite two weeks after he had been stopped near the bridge, Wayne Williams was in a phone booth when two FBI agents approached him. In a few minutes, he was on his way downtown to the FBI's Atlanta field office for questioning—again.

A local TV station reported that the FBI had bugged Williams' white 1970 Chevrolet station wagon. The FBI disagrees, admitting privately that it intended to put electronic eavesdropping devices in the vehicle while Williams was being interrogated downtown. The premature news report prompted the FBI to abort the plan.

Wayne Williams signed a waiver of his rights to remain silent and to have legal counsel. He took not one—but two—polygraph tests. He was questioned by FBI agents into the wee hours of June 4. Overnight, hordes of reporters and cameramen massed outside the federal building on Peachtree Street.

Early on the evening of June 3, one of my informants called and said that the FBI had picked up a 23-year-old freelance photographer named "Williams." "They're ready to charge him in 10 cases," the voice said.

I notified WXIA-TV's Paul Crawley, who in turn telephoned Public Safety Commissioner Lee Brown at home. Brown told Paul that he knew nothing about it, although Paul's call was the second that Brown said he had received. I'm convinced that Brown was left out on the "kill" deliberately. The FBI considered Williams *its* suspect, not the Task Force's suspect. (For me, the FBI's involvement in Atlanta's murder cases still raises questions about how the bureau was allowed to circumvent its legal charter and participate in a local murder investigation.)

Homer Williams telephoned Marc Pickard, a newsman for WSB-TV (Channel 2). By the time Paul Crawley called me back to report about his conversation with Lee Brown, Channel 2 was rolling with a tease for the 11 p.m. news, which was about one-half hour away. Across the nation, the three major television networks—ABC, CBS and NBC—reported during prime time that authorities had a "major suspect" in custody. One Los Angeles station, KNXT (which would send a crew to Atlanta), reported that "authorities say they have the strongest case yet."

ABC News went even further. On a special West Coast edition of *Nightline,* Atlanta correspondent Bob Sirkin said, "ABC has learned that the man may be charged with as many as 18" of the killings. Within an hour, however, viewers were told that what ABC had learned was wrong.

Wayne Williams was released again—for the second time. He was permitted to elude reporters through a remote exit of the building. At a 3 a.m. news conference, Lee Brown, in shirtsleeves and his tie loosened, wearily told reporters that the man who had been questioned for nearly 12 hours was *not* a suspect and was no longer in custody. Fielding rapid-fire questions, Brown said, "We have not, nor do we intend to, make an arrest." Brown also refused to identify the non-suspect by name. He asked the media to withhold information about him for his safety.

Now the ball was in the news media's court. With Williams released and "free to go," as Brown put it, wouldn't reporters simply let the matter drop? Hardly. This second questioning of Wayne Williams had turned into a "media event." And soon authorities would leak information about the questioning of Williams—near the bridge on May 22—which the media hadn't yet heard about.

What's more, the *New York Post* headlined "ATLANTA MONSTER SEIZED." The *Atlanta Constitution,* in its morning editions of June 4, published Wayne Williams' name and address. That, in turn, touched off a stormy debate among news executives and reporters. They quarreled about legal and ethical reasons why Williams, a non-suspect, should or should not be identified on TV and in print.

Atlanta's three national network TV stations chose not to use Williams' name in their newscasts, out of "fairness" to Williams and "sensitivity" to the community's emotions. By contrast, network reporters decided, along with their bosses, that Williams was a "public figure." When they identified Williams by name, their reports ran on the national news on those same three Atlanta stations (whose locally produced reports didn't identify him by name) and across the nation. It all was a classic case of "gray-out": a partial eclipse of the news, strangely symbolic of how news judgment worked—and didn't work—throughout Atlanta's murders.

Long after the smoke cleared, I thought back to 1980, when the Atlanta police questioned a suspect and eyewitnesses in the yellow-rope strangulation of 13-year-old Clifford Jones, but made no arrest. Unlike the questioning of Wayne Williams in 1981, the questioning of the black male suspect in the Clifford Jones case in 1980 was a closely guarded secret. Had it become a "media event" like the questioning of Williams, some Atlantans almost surely would have exerted pressure on authorities to arrest and try the man who eyewitnesses said strangled Clifford Jones.

Of course, Wayne Williams himself didn't exactly discourage media coverage of his questioning by the FBI. At about 7 a.m. on June 4, within hours of his release, he invited reporters into his parents' home for a news conference. The ground rules: no cameras, but tape recorders were permitted. Williams also handed out copies of his resume.

He denied knowing any victims or their families, but said he was considered a "prime suspect."

When asked what he thought about the slayings, Williams replied, "...You may have, to me, just a bunch of murders. I mean, some of them may be connected...I worked with kids awhile, and some of these kids [are] in places they don't have any business being at certain times of the day and night. Some of them don't have any kind of home supervision and they're just running around in the streets wild...

"That's not giving anybody a license to kill, but you're opening yourself up for all kinds of things...I just feel some of these parents just need to tighten up and get strict on these kids."

One reporter asked Williams if he thought he would hear from the authorities again.

"Uh—I may," he said.

"Did they ever call you a suspect? Did they ever use the word 'suspect'?"

"They—they did it stronger than suspect. They—they openly said, 'You killed Nathaniel Cater, and you know it, and you're lying to us.' They said that. And they said it a number of occasions. They said it on that night, uh—one of the Task Force captains on the scene pointed his finger at me and said it, and said he was tired of all the, uh—B.S. about working the long hours, working the stakeouts, and that he was ready to pull the thing to an end. They said that a number of times."

"All the way through until they released you?"

"All the way through it to the end."

(Surprisingly, no reporters at the news conference saw the significance of—or at least asked Williams about—his remark that he was accused at the scene of killing Nathaniel Cater. When Williams was questioned near the bridge on May 22, Cater had not been reported missing and no one knew that Cater was dead. The body identified as Cater's wouldn't be discovered until two days later, May 24.)

Williams would claim later that a question asked, but not picked up by the recorder, caused the discrepancy. Jeff Prugh said: "No way. There's not even a pause in his answer."

"Did you ever ask to see a lawyer?" a reporter asked.

"Uh—no, I didn't," Williams replied.

"Why?"

"Uh—because I was advised at that point that I was not making an official statement."

"Were they taping it?"

"They—no, they—they were just taking notes. I never made a statement or signed or made an affidavit on anything, for them."

"You said you signed a waiver, though?"

"Uh—just on the rights to talk with them. That's correct."

"And you never asked to see a lawyer? They never offered you one?"

"Uh—no, they didn't."

"But how about—do you have a lawyer now?"

"Yes, I do."

"Who is it?"

"Uh—he'll be in contact with you."

Williams' use of the pronoun "he" made me wonder about lawyers he might have contacted as a result of his work in the music business. It turned out that one of his lawyers would be Tony Axam, who had been called upon when City Councilman Arthur Langford Jr. was being investigated by federal authorities in 1979 and who is a partner of David Franklin, a political strategist for Maynard Jackson and Andrew Young.

(Franklin has represented and managed business affairs of such entertainers as Richard Pryor, Roberta Flack, Cicely Tyson, Gladys Knight, the Staple Singers and Peabo Bryson. In 1983, a Fulton County Superior Court judge would order Franklin to pay Richard Pryor $3.1 million in allegedly improper fees and withheld income. Tony Axam, representing Franklin, vowed to fight the judge's order in court.)

The first public awareness that Wayne Williams was represented by any lawyer came within hours after his news conference at home. The lawyer was Mary Welcome, 39, who held court with reporters, complaining that Williams had been "harassed" by the news media and that he was a "non-suspect suspect." Had Williams changed his mind about attorneys? Mary Welcome is no "he."

On June 12, 1981, Mary Welcome would go to U.S. District Court in Atlanta and seek a restraining order against 17 news organizations (some of which had not yet released Wayne Williams' name) and nine public officials, including Maynard Jackson, Lee Brown and FBI Agent-in-Charge John Glover.

Mary Welcome's petition on behalf of Wayne Williams charged that he had been the subject of a "blitzkrieg of media harassment in and around [his] home...of unrelenting, prejudicial, misleading and false nationwide publicity regarding the facts surrounding his 'arrest' which has not only caused him substantial embarrassment, humiliation and injury, but has and continues to interfere with his professional, personal and business endeavors."

Furthermore, Welcome's petition was right on target when it accused the news media of attributing information to "sources close to the investigation," "sources familiar with the investigation" and "law enforcement officers." The information, the complaint said, was "conflicting, inaccurate, erroneous and prejudicial" to Williams.

Mary Welcome is no stranger to combat in the courtroom, or to politics and social activism. The daughter of Verda Welcome, Maryland's first black woman state senator, and Dr. Henry C. Welcome, a surgeon, she was arrested and jailed, at 16, after joining a lunch-counter protest. She also worked as a legal clerk for President Lyndon B. Johnson in 1967 and 1968.

She made headlines as "Wild Mary" in the late 1970s when, as Atlanta's city solicitor, she crusaded against pornography businesses, including at least 15 bath houses and massage parlors (one was called Wild Mary's). Then she resigned in the wake of a dispute with Mayor Jackson over the 1978 police-cheating scandal. She had opposed Jackson's ouster of A. Reginald Eaves as public safety commissioner.

From there, Mary Welcome became the first black to join a law firm headed by Ed Garland, one of Atlanta's most powerful attorneys, who has represented pornography kingpin Mike Thevis.

Although she represented Thevis' former girlfriend, Patricia McClean, Welcome told an interviewer that she could not defend distributors of pornography. "I might even sabotage those cases," she said.

At the same time, she said she never could represent anyone accused of molesting a child. "I could represent a guy charged with murder easier than I could a child abuser," said Welcome, herself a single parent with a 12-year-old son, Gregory.

Even so, Welcome worked cases that had sexual overtones. She and Tony Axam defended an Atlanta police officer who was charged with robbing a woman who worked as a nude dancer and forcing her to commit sodomy during a drug raid at the strip joint where she danced. The officer was found not guilty, and Mary Welcome won her first trial as a criminal-defense attorney.

After she left Garland's firm to start her own practice, she represented three defendants in a rape case in December of 1980. She and Tony Axam and lead counsel Louis Polonsky defended three Morris Brown College football players charged with raping a coed in the athletes' dormitory. The players escaped a conviction of rape; they were convicted only of simple battery. Polonsky credited Mary Welcome with imparting to the jury a feeling of "compassion" for the three players.

Now, Mary Welcome would move up to faster company—her first murder trial.

Arthur Langford Jr. was 3,000 miles from Atlanta.

The young City Councilman and leader of UYAC's volunteer searches in Atlanta was scheduled to be the keynote speaker at a dinner Saturday night, June 6, 1981, in San Bernardino, California. The event's purpose: to raise money so six Atlanta children could spend part of their vacation in San Bernardino, as part of a program called "From Atlanta to the Pacific: A Summer for Six."

Harry L. Jacks, a San Bernardino businessman, had read about Atlanta's wave of murders. He wanted to do something nice for a few of Atlanta's youngsters. When he telephoned City Hall in Atlanta, seeking help to organize the program, he said, someone had recommended Arthur Langford Jr.

A crowd of 500 was anticipated in the San Bernardino Convention Center. Harry Jacks estimated that $6,000 would have to be raised to finance the vacations for six Atlanta children. But fewer than 75 people showed up, and the event raised only $347.

One who didn't show up was Arthur Langford Jr. At 2:25 a.m. Sunday, June 7, Jacks telephoned Atlanta police to report that Langford was missing. Jacks said he also called law-enforcement agencies in Los Angeles, 60 miles west of San Bernardino.

Finally, Jacks reached Langford by telephone on Monday, June 8—in Atlanta. Langford, he said, told him that he took a bus ride by mistake to Pasadena, near Los Angeles, and also lost his luggage. Langford was said to have left a message for Jacks at a San Bernardino hotel, explaining his predicament. The hotel had no such message, Jacks said. "I think something's a little fishy, don't you?" Jacks told the *San Bernardino Sun.*

Langford had found his way to San Bernardino on Friday, June 5, when he held a news conference at City Hall. Reporters questioned him about Wayne Williams. "I do not believe that he was involved at all," Langford said. "Many of us have known him down through the years. He is a native Atlantan, he attended school in Atlanta, and I just doubt that he is really involved at all."

In Atlanta, Langford told a reporter that he had known Williams for "four or five years," adding that Williams' "involvement in the community with youth" had been exemplary. After Williams was interrogated by authorities, he said, Williams telephoned him to assure him that he was not guilty.

Langford added that Williams had participated in some of the volunteer searches, although he said he didn't recall which ones. He had "a little movie camera" on those occasions, Langford said. But Carolyn Long Banks, an Atlanta City Councilwoman who said she joined all the searches, said she never saw Williams on any of them. "He is unusual-looking enough," she said, "that he would have stood out." (For his part, Wayne Williams denies that he engaged in any searches.)

Meanwhile, an *Atlanta Journal* reporter asked Langford where he was between Saturday, June 6, and Monday, June 9. Langford didn't answer. "What's the big deal?" he said.

Wayne Bertram Williams longed for bright lights, loud music and socko success. As a teen-ager, he operated a tiny, 50-watt radio station from his family's house, but it could be heard only within a few blocks. He advertised his station, WRAZ, on posters: "640 on the AM Dial, Where You Hear the Most Music."

Then he not only played music and performed odd jobs for other small local radio stations, he sought young black singers and musicians, who, like himself, dreamed of riding records to riches.

An only child, Williams was energetic and enterprising. He had workers circulate flyers advertising talent auditions in housing projects such as

Thomasville Heights and East Lake Meadows, and entertainment centers like the Omni.

And sometimes Williams traveled more than 100 miles to Columbus Georgia, a town that was terrified during 1977 and 1978 when seven elderly white women were strangled. Those cases still are unsolved. Records show that Williams once joined an Atlanta TV station's crew that went to Columbus to report on the slayings. Williams says he didn't actually go himself, but sent a "crew" to cover a funeral for a local station.

Homer and Faye Williams worked hard to pay for their son's expensive hobby in electronics, only to be forced into bankruptcy court in 1976. Nevertheless, Wayne Williams remained riveted to his pursuit of the American Dream—and to his unabashed zeal for self-promotion.

His five-page, typewritten resume—which he distributed to the reporters at his June 4 news conference—portrayed him as in "good" health, 5-foot-7½ and 160 pounds, an honor student at Frederick Douglass High School in Atlanta, interested in "various sports, reading, flying, photography, astronomy, music and semi-pro auto racing," a rifle marksman and "heavily involved with various media." The resume added that he attended Georgia State University in Atlanta, but it did not mention that he dropped out after the 1977-78 academic year.

Williams also fancied himself as a promoter of soul groups like the Jackson Five, but he sometimes was said to have tried to drum up interest in youngsters who could not sing well or make saleable music. On one occasion, he traveled to Los Angeles with a young performer he introduced as a strong prospect to an independent record producer. But apparently no deal materialized, and the producer said he did not recall the youth's name.

In December of 1980, Williams attained a measure of popularity at the Oasis Ballroom on Bankhead Highway (U.S. 278) when he helped a youth group raise funds for recreational and vacation activities. He staged a talent show, screened the performers and played records on a sophisticated sound system. "He did an excellent job," Corine Brown, who directed the city's 9th District Youth Council, said. "He was very big with the kids. He directed the whole thing. The children seemed crazy about him."

Williams also succeeded in winning over local and network television news executives during the late 1970s when he sold video footage of car wrecks, fires and other fast-breaking events to the highest bidder. As a cameraman, he was quick, but not polished, some editors said. Even so, his professional reputation was enhanced in April of 1977, when he was among the first to arrive at the wreckage of a Southern Airways plane crash near New Hope, Georgia, about 20 miles west of Atlanta.

Described as a "scanner freak" who monitored police-radio frequencies, Williams photographed news events in Atlanta and Columbus, and sold the film to Atlanta stations. "He knew the back roads and the shortcuts, and he got to places before the police did," said Jim Rutledge, a Cable News Network executive who had purchased footage from Williams as assignment editor at WSB-TV (Channel 2).

Hal Lamar, a broadcast journalist for National Public Radio and various Atlanta radio stations, remembers covering a story about a prison break and trying to determine the fastest route to the scene. Suddenly Williams drove up, he said, and shouted, "Follow me!"

Lamar did just that, speeding behind Williams' car, swerving through traffic and reaching the scene in a blink.

When Williams used to hang around the news department at one station, Lamar said, "He seemed to be a fickle kid. But he was smart, a genius. For a minute—I kid you not—I didn't think he was in high school; I thought he was a midget. He had old mannerisms."

The odyssey of Wayne Williams shifted every now and then to Columbus, a medium-sized, southwest Georgia city near the Army's Ft. Benning infantry training base and across the Chattahoochee River from Phenix City, Alabama, the once-notorious "Sin City of the South."

Columbus long was the hometown of Homer and Faye Williams before Wayne was born, and is where an uncle of Wayne resides. It was in Columbus that Wayne Williams once purchased automated radio equipment that Charlie Parish, who then owned station WCLS, no longer wanted. Parish's surname is misspelled and listed among "professional refrences [sic]" on Williams' resume.

Jeff Prugh, who once had reported on the Columbus stranglings for the *Los Angeles Times,* and I drove to Columbus one weekend.

Newspaper stories quoting police pronouncements during those killings in 1977 and 1978 are strikingly similar to news reports quoting Atlanta's baffled authorities. One report that particularly roused our interest again in the Columbus story stated that an unidentified voice warned that yet another victim would be strangled. The voice, the report stated, had broken in on a police-radio frequency.

Paul Crawley and I would return to Columbus to check out the item about the voice on the police radio. The police sergeant in charge of communications remembered that incident. He told us how he had specially marked the tape recordings of those voice communications. He said he would be happy to let us hear them.

While the sergeant was away looking for the tapes, Paul said he wanted to make a courtesy call on the chief of police. I told him that was a mistake. "Let's dub the tape and get the hell out of here," I suggested.

But Paul went off to see the chief. The upshot was that the chief suddenly decided that the tape "couldn't be located." We were also told that neither the Task Force in Atlanta nor the FBI had yet made any inquiries.

However, a few days later, as we prepared a story on our Columbus visit, we were informed that the Task Force had told Paul's boss, then-news director Ron Becker, that all possibilities of connections between Wayne Williams and the Columbus stranglings had been ruled out. I wonder where they got the idea to check it out?

Meanwhile, Jeff and I looked up Charlie Parish to talk about Wayne Williams.

Parish, a genteel, fiftyish fellow, recalled that Williams had visited him several times before deciding to buy the radio equipment for an undisclosed price in 1976 or 1977. Williams also asked for a job and wrote a programming proposal for station WCLS, which then played popular music, Parish said. He added that he told Williams he had no job openings. "He would have made an A-1 newsman and an A-1 program consultant," Parish said. Williams says it was more like 1975 when all of this took place. Based on the date of the Williamses' bankruptcy (1976), Wayne Williams is probably correct.

Now, with Williams' name emblazoned in headlines around the world, Parish told us that he had been deluged with questions about Williams from reporters.

Where were the police? Parish shrugged. "You fellas," he said, "are the first to come down here from Atlanta. I haven't heard from the police—or the FBI."

Finally, I asked Parish and his wife, Ramona, who had joined us in the front room of their home: "Were you living here at the time of the Columbus stranglings?"

"Yes," Parish said. "We lived a few miles away—up near the [Wynnton] section where the women were being strangled."

He motioned out the window toward a nearby house. "Another victim lived right over there," he said. "They found her after we moved here."

Ramona Parish shuddered. "It was," she said, "like the killer was following our every move."

Jeff and I soon thanked the Parishes and left. We drove to the Wynnton section, looking up addresses of some of the strangled elderly women. We would discover a geographic coincidence. Within one block of where we made a U-turn in one Wynnton neighborhood was the home of Wayne Williams' uncle, where the Williamses' 1970 Chevrolet station wagon had been on blocks until the Williamses obtained it in October of 1980!

As Wayne Williams rapidly became a public figure, Atlanta became rife with published and verbal reports of Williams' purported activities. One Atlantan reported seeing Williams with Nathaniel Cater at the Silver Dollar Saloon. Williams also was said to have visited the Marquiett Club, a bar frequented by homosexuals on Martin Luther King Jr. Drive.

Some reports stated that Wayne Williams had been picked out of a physical lineup as having worked at an adult bookstore. This information never would be introduced at Williams' trial. Instead, the jury would hear conflicting testimony about whether Williams had been a customer at still another adult store.

At about this same time, it was reported that a foreign television crew had found a plastic bag containing a police uniform in the Chattahoochee River. The clothing had been taken from a suburban police officer's home, where a gun also had been reported stolen. When Wayne Williams was reported to have told police that he threw trash into the river (a report that was never substantiated), some Atlantans wondered if the trash—not a body—had caused the splash heard 'round the world.

Still another published report stated that Wayne Williams used to take his Gemini recording group (named after the astrological sign of Williams, who was born on May 27, 1958) to the Apogee Recording Studio on Simpson Street. The posh studio—complete with grand pianos, Jacuzzi whirlpool and sauna—had been owned by Mike Thevis, 52, who had turned the 25-cent peep show, among other things, into an estimated $100-million pornographic enterprise. With Thevis in federal prison, the Internal Revenue Service auctioned away the studio in June of 1981 for $370,000. The new owner said he had been threatened by an anonymous male telephone caller before the auction. The caller, he said, told him: "You bid, you die."

At both the studio formerly owned by Thevis and another studio where Wayne Williams reportedly had worked, vandalism occurred after Williams was implicated in the Atlanta murders. Expensive equipment was smashed, and recordings were destroyed. Some investigators asked a valid question: Were the voices of any of Atlanta's young murder victims on those recordings that had been destroyed? Or was there something else of interest? One recording studio owner claimed that it was the police who had broken in.

Barely days after Wayne Williams' second interrogation by the FBI, the glare of worldwide publicity now had far surpassed the attention Williams received as a precocious youngster 10 years earlier. That's when Felicia Jeter, a television reporter currently on CBS News' *Nightwatch* program, had interviewed Williams and reported on an Atlanta newscast about his homemade radio station.

"I watched that kid grow up," said Jeter, who also grew up in Atlanta. "He was bright and abrasive, but sweet."

In 1980, when Felicia Jeter spoke to an Atlanta convention of news-media women, she said Wayne Williams and his father greeted her afterward. Wayne Williams, she said, took her picture. She said she asked him what he was doing with his career.

He replied: "Oh, getting into the media."

The news media, too, found itself on trial. Some of its practitioners came to call the Atlanta cases a "laboratory." Reporters had trouble getting information from the police; and when they did get it, they had to perform their usual balancing act—the public's right to know against the chance that disclosure of some stray fact might undermine the investigation.

But the Atlanta cases should have taught reporters one thing: the police really knew very little, if anything, for reporters to seek out. The truth was, the police didn't know the names of all the victims. They refused to investigate some cases. They tried to arrest Patrick (Pat Man) Rogers, months after he turned up dead. And of all those computer files, not one contained the name of Wayne Williams. There is old advice that would be good advice for the media to follow in dealing with officialdom: Consider your source—what you don't know that they don't know may be the death of all of us.

By hiding behind veils of secrecy and walls of "no comments" and "off the records," police all too often blow smoke where there's no fire. They project the impression that they know a lot more than they're saying. For police to adopt this false air of omniscient knowledge is wrong, just as it's wrong for reporters to accept at face value—and report without qualification—what police say, just because it happens to be "official." Official is to true as might is to right. Again, the media's credo seemed to be: never mind that The List is inaccurate, incomplete and illogical. At least, it's official.

Inundated by information surrounding the Atlanta story, but starved for hard facts by all those rigid "no comments," too many reporters rushed into print or on camera with anything they did get from the police, even if it wasn't true, valid or relevant.

Some reporters went to Lee Brown's weekly media "rap" sessions during the height of the killings. When they came away knowing no more than when they went, some good-naturedly nicknamed him "No Rap" Brown.

Other reporters worked sources inside the Atlanta police department. One police recruit at Task Force headquarters said recruits who answered the phones were instructed to relay calls from certain reporters to a particular Task Force detective for off-the-record comments—the kind that Washington bureaucrats give to reporters as "deep background" and not for attribution. These comments often find their way into print—unchallenged, uncorroborated and attributed merely to "sources close to the investigation."

Yet even if reporters got little hard information from authorities, some learned valuable lessons from the Atlanta story. They learned to question themselves more closely about the impact of their news judgment on readers and viewers. Their eyes were opened once again to the realities of life in American black society. They dug deeper for facts simply because they were forced to and, as a result, turned up vital information that police didn't. Some even began questioning the illogic of some police thinking and reported what the police were *not* doing.

For many reporters, the Atlanta story was a marathon of long hours, crash deadlines and surprise developments; of tracking rumors, cultivating sources and fighting overwork and burnout. ABC News' Bob Sirkin said he waged a losing battle with fatigue. WSB-TV's Hank Phillippi and WXIA-TV's Paul Crawley said they experienced nightmares about the cases. Jeff Prugh of the *Los Angeles Times* telephoned me one morning, dejected that his editor had told him during a visit to Atlanta that he had become "obsessed" with the cases and that the murders were no longer a national story. The editor was probably right about the obsession, but he was wrong about the story's significance.

Forty-eight hours later, another body turned up in the Chattahoochee River. It was identified as the body of Nathaniel Cater.

The so-called sightings of a green station wagon always intrigued me. Throughout the cases, news reporters were aware that various cars surfaced as suspect cars. The most prominent were blue cars and green cars. Also, several station wagons turned up prominently in police reports.

Wayne Williams drove a *white* station wagon. That, of course, doesn't mean that he could not somehow obtain a green station wagon from time to time. But it is relatively certain that he didn't own one, that he never owned one and that none of his family or immediate acquaintances did, either.

But, so conditioned were the media and the public to reports of a green station wagon that when Waync Williams' white 1970 Chevrolet station wagon would be towed to the state crime lab for processing, an Atlanta television station would send a crew there.

The crew would find a green station wagon and build a whole segment of a newscast around it, only to discover the day after the newscast that the vehicle in the report was, in fact, a state police station wagon assigned to the crime lab.

One thing Wayne Williams told the world at his June 4 news conference was that the FBI had told him that his polygraph answers were deceptive.

Which was nothing new in Atlanta's murders. A father of one victim who would be linked to Williams by fibers also "flunked" the polygraph. (I have no faith in these stress-measuring devices and their operators' ability to interpret their results.) Other witnesses would flunk or pass the polygraph without it apparently having any effect on whether they would testify as witnesses at Williams' trial.

On the morning of Williams' news conference, WSB-TV (Channel 2) reporter Marc Pickard—whom Homer Williams had telephoned the night before—visited the Williamses' house. Pickard was said to have known Wayne Williams when the latter worked as a freelance video cameraman.

The story is told by Williams that he and Pickard sat down and made a tape recording and that Williams gave the tape to Pickard to keep—in case Williams needed it. "It would clear me," Williams said.

(However, before and during the trial of Wayne Williams, his lawyers tried unsuccessfully to retrieve the tape from Channel 2. Each time attorney Alvin Binder would ask for the tape, the station's answer was the same: "No.")

Meanwhile, as soon as word leaked out that the young man who lived with his parents at 1817 Penelope Road was considered a "suspect" in Atlanta's murders, a police and media stakeout began outside the house on Wednesday evening, June 3.

Soon after Wayne Williams' news conference early Thursday morning, the stakeout became another mass-media event, if not a comic opera. But there was nothing comic about it to the young man who Lee Brown now said was *not* a suspect. Wayne Williams' parents weren't amused, either.

During the stakeout, Williams got into his station wagon and led officers on a wild chase to another part of town. He led them to Lee Brown's and Maynard Jackson's houses. This time the police were not amused. On another occasion, Homer Williams was reported to have gone to the Charlie Brown Airport in southwest Fulton County to inquire about chartering a plane to South America. Wayne Williams said the plane story was a joke. If so, I thought it was a good one.

I had told Paul Crawley that if the police weren't considering Williams a suspect, they certainly wouldn't be camped out at his front door, wearing Izod shirts, jeans and pistols. "But since they say he *isn't* a suspect, I know how I would bring it to a head," I told Paul. "If I were Wayne, I'd go to Hartsfield [International Airport], buy a ticket on the first plane to California and get on it." It would have been fun to watch.

The clatch of reporters grew. Penelope Road was dotted with garishly painted vans with logos like "Action News," "Newscene," "Newswatch" and "11 Alive." Then came the more subdued vehicles of ABC, CBS, NBC and CNN. Arriving, too, were reporters from the Associated Press and United Press International, radio crews, national newspaper correspondents, freelancers, hangers-on, *ad infinitum*—in a motley collection of station wagons, rental cars and taxi cabs. Keeping watch over this gathering were assorted plainclothes policemen, some lolling on the hoods of their unmarked patrol cars.

As photographers and video cameramen jostled for position, pushing and shoving matches flared into hard-boiled arguments. Tempers blew, and punches flew. Then the pastor of the nearby True Light Baptist Church, where most of the vehicles were parked, called the police to have the squatters removed.

The police succeeded in having all the vehicles removed from the church parking lot. But they weren't as successful when it came to moving media *people.* One policeman loudly ordered a cameraman to leave. The cameraman refused.

The policeman shouted, "Oh, you'll move all right, or I'll—"

"You'll what?" the cameraman shot back. "You'll arrest me? Go ahead! Arrest me! I'm not moving."

The cop backed off.

The nearest public telephone was about a block away, at the West Lake MARTA station. Paul Crawley and I would take advantage of that phone.

As we sat in Channel 11's air-conditioned van, a message came over the two-way radio, confirming that Wayne Williams had contacted an attorney. The message was not in code, but the dialogue was purposely cryptic.

"Is it the good-looking woman that the man called, according to our friend?" Paul asked.

"Yes," the radio voice replied.

The woman was Mary Welcome. The man was Wayne Williams. The friend was a Channel 11 informant in the offices shared by Mary Welcome.

We went to the phone at the MARTA station. Our call confirmed the radio conversation. We also learned that Mary Welcome did not receive Williams' call until after he had finished his news conference, early on Thursday morning, June 4. This would be an issue with Mary Welcome later.

Paul jotted down a telephone number that someone at the television station had given him, and we returned to Channel 11's van.

Soon a ragged-looking Chevrolet arrived and caused quite a stir. Inside was an official-looking person, carrying a piece of paper. Was this a sheriff with a warrant for Wayne Williams? No. It was a man from Western Union. He faced a forest of microphones and let the reporters peek at the paper.

"Will I be on the 6 o'clock news?" he asked as he drove off.

"Yeah, sure, sure," the disappointed photographers yelled.

The telegram was from a member of the news media—a resourceful, but abortive, attempt to establish communications with the Williamses, who were inside the house.

At a prearranged time, Paul and I walked back to the MARTA station. Paul dialed the number he had been given by someone at Channel 11. The phone rang, and Wayne Williams answered. Paul held the phone so I could listen in on their conversation. Williams agreed to give Paul an interview, if Paul would enter the house alone. Again, a time was decided upon. We returned to the van.

One by one, some reporters approached the house, trying in vain to peer into the front windows. Others boldy knocked, but no one answered.

Now Homer Williams emerged from the house, two cameras slung around his neck. He yelled at the hordes to stay off his property. A shouting match then turned into a shooting battle that would rival an aerial-combat "dogfight." But this battle consisted not of guns and bullets, but cameras and film. Homer Williams and the cameramen rapidly snapped pictures of each other. Click, click, click. Snap, crackle, pop.

The photographer who had emerged from the house was the man I had seen at Jimmy Ray Payne's funeral. It was the man on the stage of the Sammy Davis Jr.-Frank Sinatra concert. It was Homer Williams, father of Wayne Williams. Much later, Wayne Williams would call me from the jail. His father, he said, denies that he took pictures at the Payne funeral. If not, it was his identical twin. Then Paul Crawley would recall—as I do—that Homer Williams told Paul and me earlier that he had taken pictures at the Payne funeral.

At the appointed time, Paul Crawley sauntered across the street, trying to look as inconspicuous as possible. He nonchalantly mounted the steps of the small concrete stoop of 1817 Penelope Road. The front door opened. Paul disappeared inside, much to the surprise and chagrin of those who watched.

Later, when Paul departed the house, he was rushed by his colleagues. Now the news media interviewed the news media, desperate for a glimpse of what was going on inside the house. Paul was uncommunicative.

Back in the van, Paul told me that Wayne Williams said he would soon take some action to "take care of the situation." What did that mean?

As 6 p.m. approached on June 4, all the local TV crews set up to do their remotes from the scene on Penelope Road. Now most viewers were treated to yet another view of the small, unpretentious, brick house of Homer and Faye Williams. But Paul knew something the other reporters didn't know. After every other crew disassembled its cameras and other gear, Paul's Channel 11 crew kept grinding away.

Suddenly the front door of the house opened. Right into the lens of Channel 11's camera walked Wayne Williams. He waved, then climbed into a vehicle with three other men. They drove away. By pre-agreement, the stakeout fell into parade position behind the non-suspect, whom everybody watched around the clock. Channel 11's helicopter, forewarned by Crawley, followed on high.

NBC's national newscast picked up Channel 11's pictures of Williams, and soon they were shown all over the nation. But by agreement, the local stations didn't identify by name or show the non-suspect, whom everyone knew, by now, was Wayne Bertram Williams. So, by 11 p.m., even on Paul's station, the pictures of Williams were shown with a small disc clumsily superimposed over Williams' face, although they'd been shown live at 6 p.m.

Now came the disparity between local and network policy. As Atlanta's stations continued to avoid showing Williams' face or disclosing his name and address, the three major networks did all of the above. So, the 6 p.m. local news referred to Williams not by name, but as the "man" or "suspect." But, at 7 p.m., when these same local stations switched to the network news, viewers saw him referred to as "Wayne Williams." Then, at 11 p.m., the local stations again called him the "man" or "suspect."

Wayne Williams' mission to "take care of the situation" was exactly that. He had not left home, as most assumed, to surrender. Instead, he went to see his lawyer—and his parents visited their lawyer—to have a petition drawn up, seeking an injunction that would prohibit the media circus in front of the Williamses' home.

Ironically, it was the very circus in which Wayne Williams himself already had played ringmaster—by calling a news conference and handing out copies of his resume.

The scenario inside the house at 1817 Penelope Road on the evening of June 4 took on the air of both an inquisition and a pep talk.

While plainclothes cops and members of the news media were encamped outside, two Georgia state legislators—Representatives Hosea Williams (D-Atlanta) and Tyrone Brooks (D-Atlanta)—were inside, questioning Wayne Williams far into the night.

Neither legislator was a stranger to Wayne Williams, who, like convicted killer John Wayne Gacy of Chicago, knows an extraordinary number of politicians and public officials, to say nothing of members of the media. Hosea Williams said that Wayne used to be engineer for his Sunday broadcasts on radio station WIGO. Brooks said he had been interviewed by Wayne on Southern Christian Leadership Conference and civil rights activities, back when Wayne operated his own radio station.

Brooks said he had received a telephone call from Wayne Williams on June 4 and that Wayne had invited him to the house. Along the way, Brooks said he picked up Hosea Williams, and they arrived in the middle of the police and media stakeout.

'I said, 'Wayne, do you know anything about who's doing these killings?' and he said, 'No,'" Brooks said. "Then I asked him, 'Wayne, do you have *any* information on these killings?' He said 'No.' I then said, 'Wayne, tell me the truth—are you involved or guilty in any of them?' And he said to me, 'Tyrone, absolutely not. If I was, you'd be one of the first persons I'd tell.'"

Brooks said he then told Wayne Williams: "If I ever find out that you're guilty, I'll go to the authorities."

For his part, Hosea Williams said he told Wayne: "If you are guilty, give yourself up and I'll arrange for your family to receive every nickel of the $500,000 reward money." He added that he told Wayne that he had tentatively arranged for Atlanta lawyer Ed Garland (counsel for pornographer Mike Thevis) to represent Wayne—at no charge. "I told him that Ed Garland is one of the very best lawyers in the Southeast," Hosea Williams said. "I also said that if Wayne would give himself up, we would see that his story would be told in the national news."

Through it all, Hosea Williams said, Wayne watched the news on two TV sets and listened to radio news through a head set—all at the same time—while "running around like a chicken with his head cut off." To me, that seemed normal behavior for someone implicated, as Wayne Williams now was, in one of the biggest multiple-murder mysteries in American history.

Brooks remembers a slightly different verison of events that night in the Williamses' house. He said that Hosea Williams had promised that he would try to obtain defense lawyers Howard Moore (counsel for 1970s activist Angela Davis) or William Kunstler (counsel for the Chicago Seven anti-war defendants).

He recalls, too, that when he and Hosea Williams asked Wayne about who would represent him, Wayne told them only that Mary Welcome was under "consideration." "The next day," Brooks said, "we learned that Wayne had settled on Mary Welcome. He hadn't told us ahead of time, so we just dropped the idea of trying to find him a lawyer."

Still another version of these events on June 4 was shared by Homer and Faye Williams one day in 1983 when they visited my home.

As Homer Williams recalls it, "Hosea said to Wayne, 'If you take the rap for these killings, I'll have $4 million tomorrow. I just got back from Washington, and I know people there who can make the money available. I'll have a cashier's check for $4 million in 24 hours, so why don't you take the rap?"

It was Hosea Williams' intention, Homer Williams said, to "control" the money and to give a substantial—but unspecified—portion to Wayne Williams and his parents. But Wayne Williams wasn't buying his proposal, his father said.

Finally, Wayne left the family room where he and his parents, Hosea Williams and Tyrone Brooks had talked. He went into his bedroom. "See if you can't talk Wayne into going along with this idea," Hosea Williams was quoted by Homer Williams as telling him.

Soon Homer Williams went alone into Wayne's room, where he said he told Wayne: "Son, do you understand what Hosea is saying?"

To which Wayne Williams, according to his father, replied: "Yeah, Daddy, I understand. But I'm not selling my soul for a *billion* dollars!"

Later in an interview at the jail, Wayne told me that his father's version of the conversation with Hosea Williams was not accurate.

The police and media merry-go-around whirled outside Wayne Williams' house for the better part of 17 days. Lee Brown continued to insist that there were no suspects. Amazingly, he said it with a straight face.

The stakeout people got tired. Tempers got shorter. Reporters rented turf from neighbors to protect their own vantage points from other media squatters. Simple matters like going to the toilet, buying drinks or fetching food became logistical nightmares.

News executives at Channel 11 discussed whether Paul Crawley and his crew should fold up and leave. But leaks from DeKalb County police headquarters indicated that if Fulton County didn't move to arrest Wayne Williams, then DeKalb County would. I think DeKalb County would have moved, except that a spokesman for the governor "requested" that DeKalb officials refrain from moving against Williams.

For federal, state and local law-enforcement officials, these were times of hard negotiations and head-banging and not-so-friendly persuasion. The FBI, whose charter allows the bureau to investigate murder cases only if they are assassinations of the President or members of Congress, was pushing for an arrest of Wayne Williams as a result of its investigation of the Atlanta murders.

State and local officials wouldn't budge. They didn't like the FBI's handling of the bridge incident. Nor were they happy about the prospects for a successful prosecution. Fulton County District Attorney Lewis Slaton had said publicly that he was reluctant to prosecute Wayne Williams unless he were convinced that the case would stand up through the appellate process. And Slaton also had told Associated Press reporter Nancy Kenney that he would not choose to prosecute any of the "probable asphyxia" cases.

It was clear, too, that the political heat was turned up more than ever—and that the pressure was applied from as high up as the White House. No one needed to remind Atlanta's officials that Vice President George Bush had come to the city in 1981 as President Reagan's special envoy, pledging federal help, if necessary, to bring Atlanta's nightmare to an end. No one needed to remind anyone that the Reagan Administration had thrown as much as $4.2 million at Atlanta's problem—and that the federal government had better have something to show for all its benevolence.

This, then, was the backdrop for a secret meeting of federal state and local officials at the Georgia Governor's Mansion in Atlanta late Friday night, June 19, 1981. Published reports of what went on behind those closed doors left the impression that FBI Special Agent-in-Charge John Glover and Acting U.S. Attorney Dorothy Kirkley pressed for an immediate prosecution, pointing out that Wayne Williams might elude his surveillance and slip out of town. There also was talk that the governor might appoint a special prosecutor if Slaton didn't move against Williams, but it was only talk. Other participants in the seven-hour meeting: Georgia Governor George Busbee, GBI Commander Phil Peters, Georgia Attorney General Arthur Bolton, and Lewis Slaton, among others.

This kind of pressure—coupled with reports that Busbee was unhappy with the police and media carnival lingering outside Williams' house—apparently did most to bring the issue to a head.

Finally, on Sunday afternoon, June 21, Wayne Williams was arrested and charged with the murder of 27-year-old Nathaniel Cater. At a crowded news conference at the Fulton County Jail, where Williams was incarcerated without bail, Lee Brown refused to say why Williams was being arrested now, instead of back on June 4. He also would not say whether Williams was a suspect in any other killings.

"How do you feel, Commissioner?" one reporter asked Brown. "It's been a long haul!"

Brown, stoic and laconic as usual, replied: "We are going to continue our efforts even at this point. We've made an arrest in one case." Apparently Brown was still not convinced that The List cases were connected.

The arrest of Wayne Williams shifted the spotlight away from reports that City Councilwoman Mary Davis, chairperson of the council's Public Safety Committee, had asked Brown for an accounting of all unsolved homicides in Atlanta.

When Brown finally furnished a list of female victims of unsolved homicides, it provided the basis for a *Los Angeles Times* story in which Jeff Prugh reported that at least 38 girls and women had been slain in Atlanta, dating back to late 1978. Which meant that Atlanta was ignoring a bigger problem than the one that had created the so-called "children's" Task Force and the worldwide media hype. Which was obvious as early as November of 1980.

What's more, at least two of those victims were teen-agers whose deaths never were investigated by the Task Force: Angela Bacon and Cynthia Montgomery.

At Wayne Williams' preliminary hearing, Georgia state crime lab analyst Larry Peterson testified that he found "no significant microscopic differences" between fibers removed from Nathaniel Cater's head hair and carpet fibers taken from Williams' bedroom.

After three hours of testimony, Fulton County Magistrate Albert L. Thompson made a predictable ruling—that the state had presented sufficient evidence to warrant a grand jury hearing. Williams was ordered held in the Fulton County Jail without bond.

At the rear of the packed courtroom, City Councilman Arthur Langford Jr. rose slowly and exited with the crowd, shaking his head. He whispered to a reporter that the state's evidence against Wayne Williams was "awfully light. I thought they had something."

Meanwhile, hardly anybody noticed that the oft-delayed trial of 17-year-old Kenny Brown—the "earwitness" to murder—had begun 10 miles away, in DeKalb County Superior Court, in suburban Decatur.

But Kenny Brown's account of how he had "heard" a young boy shot to death after having been dragged into the woods along Memorial Drive in 1980 was not the issue here. Kenny Brown had been indicted earlier in 1981 on charges of kidnapping and aggravated sodomy against 14-year-old Tracy

Jordan, a black male. He had awaited his trial while out on bond, rekindling old friendships, including a romance with his teen-age girlfriend.

Still unable to hire a private lawyer, Kenny Brown was represented by a white public defender, Alden Snead. An all-white jury was impaneled before Judge Keegan Federal, also white. The prosecuting attorney was Thomas Nave, who, like Kenny Brown, is black.

When the Georgia state crime lab report was introduced, Kenny Brown's lawyer said he had not been given the report until that very day. The report was exculpatory for Kenny Brown. It stated that no seminal fluid was detected during an examination of Tracy Jordan or found on Jordan's clothing.

The judge scolded the prosecutors for not releasing the report until that same day. He also asked Atlanta police officer R.A. Brown why he had not made the report available when it was ready—back in January of 1981.

R.A. Brown shrugged. "I've been working on the Task Force," he said.

Thus, on June 24, 1981—one day after Wayne Williams was bound over to a grand jury in Atlanta—Kenny Brown was found guilty of aggravated sodomy, but was acquitted of the kidnapping charge.

Kenny's girlfriend was two months pregnant. She was in the courtroom at Kenny's trial, but she never was called to testify.

Kenny Brown listened stoically as the jury rendered its "guilty" verdict on the sodomy charge. But it devastated him more than anybody knew.

Three days later, on June 27, 1981, Kenny Brown tried to kill himself. He was found hanging in his cell in the DeKalb County Jail, a bedsheet fastened in "hangman's noose" fashion around his neck. He was rushed to the criminal ward at Grady Memorial Hospital, where he stayed one week before he was returned to jail to await his sentencing.

Kenny Brown's depression lingered. On the telephone, he told Jeff Prugh that he still wanted to kill himself if he had to remain in jail. He also contended that most—but not all—of the tape recordings of his interrogation by the Atlanta police had been doctored with someone else's voice.

On July 16, 1981, Kenny Brown sat on the witness stand at his own sentencing hearing. He told the court that he had been given a tranquilizing drug, Thorazine, for "some bad nerves." He still exhibited suicidal tendencies.

"...I worry, and I cry every night, you know, sit down, you know—my heart just been broke all the time, you know," Kenny Brown told the court, "and if I—if I, you know—if I get sent to prison, it will [be] just like killing me.

"I can't stand it. Everybody done been up there to talk to me. They tell me to hold on. If I can get sent to prison, I am going to kill myself.

"That's all I've got to say. I'm going to kill myself because I can't take it. I know I can't take it."

Moments later, Thomas Nave, the prosecutor, asked Kenny Brown: "You have been to Augusta [to a juvenile detention facility] for doing something to young boys before, haven't you?"

"No, sir. I ain't—I ain't done nothing to no young boys."

"You say you have never done anything to any young boys beside this one?"

"I ain't done any. They got me charged with it."

The prosecutor asked for the maximum sentence of 20 years in prison.

Alden Snead, the public defender, asked the judge for a lesser sentence. He argued that Kenny Brown had been cleared of the kidnapping charge. He also questioned whether the other charge should have been simply sodomy, not aggravated sodomy. Snead added that Kenny Brown had come from a motherless and fatherless home—and that his lifestyle in Atlanta's black ghetto was not all that unusual.

Finally, Judge Federal asked Kenny Brown to stand. He stated that he was about to sentence him to slightly less than the maximum and that the "protection of society" must be a priority in his decision.

"...the court at this time sentences you," Judge Federal said, "to serve 18 years in the state penitentiary."

Kenny Brown was escorted by two sheriff's deputies out a side door of the courtroom. Suddenly Kenny Brown squirmed loose and exploded into a kicking, fist-swinging rage. He kicked a corridor ash can so hard that it was nearly bent into a "V." "I'm not gonna do no goddamn time!" he screamed. A paper cup half-filled with Coca-Cola had rested atop the ash can, but when Kenny Brown booted the can, the impact sent droplets of the soft drink splattering all over Kenny's aunt.

"I'm sorry, Aunt Mary!" Kenny Brown cried out, as his aunt and other spectators watched in horror. It took the deputies almost three minutes to wrestle Kenny Brown, a spindly youngster, into submission and place him in handcuffs.

The Kenny Brown story never made banner headlines or the 11 o'clock news. You could not even find it back among the truss ads. What never had surfaced publicly, either—back in October of 1980—was that when the Atlanta police sent those helicopters whirring over Kenny Brown's neighborhood, they thought that maybe they had cornered the Atlanta child killer.

Yet even as the story now unraveled far from the TV lights and packs of reporters, it embraced nearly all the elements of the Atlanta murders: sex, poverty, race, anguish, heartbreak, the criminal-justice system and intrigue. It also happened in the shadow of where so many victims lived, were last seen alive and turned up dead. It focused on Kenny Brown, who said he knew a child who had played in his neighborhood and made The List—still-missing 10-year-old Darron Glass.

All but forgotten in the legal quest to determine Kenny Brown's guilt or innocence in the male-rape case was his "earwitness" story back in August of 1980.

Did Kenny Brown really see—or at least hear—a murder along Memorial Drive? Could he have been involved some way himself?

Kenny Brown's story interested me for other reasons. When Dreenna Andreu contacted me about Kenny Brown, she had heard me say on television that the corner of 2nd Avenue and Memorial Drive—Kenny's and Dreenna's old neighborhood—was significant to the cases.

That was early in 1981. Fourteen-year-old Lubie Geter, who lived on Dahlgren Street just off Memorial Drive, had been last seen at the Stewart-Lakewood Shopping Center, which is less than a mile from where Dreenna worked when she was followed home. Lubie Geter had been purchasing the materials he peddled in the shopping center from a man who drove a small green car. Could it have been a green Chevy Nova that Kenny Brown said he saw?

On July 17, 1981, one day after Kenny Brown was sentenced to 18 years in prison, Wayne Williams was indicted by the Fulton County grand jury. And—surprise! Wayne Williams was indicted not just for the murder of 27-year-old Nathaniel Cater, but also in the case of 21-year-old Jimmy Ray Payne, whose death had *not* been ruled murder by the medical examiner.

For its part, the news media remained on trial. Now it had to do its delicate tightrope act between the First Amendment and the Sixth Amendment. Reporters had to judge how much information to reveal about Wayne Williams because the public had a right to know. But then, Wayne Williams also had a citizen's right to privacy, just as he would have the right to a fair trial.

24

"The Enemy Is Us"

It was not until October 8, 1981—three days *after* Wayne Williams originally was supposed to stand trial—that I was first contacted by the defense team representing Williams. His trial for the murders of Nathaniel Cater, 27, and Jimmy Ray Payne, 21, would be pushed back by a succession of delays and courthouse jockeying to late December.

It would be a celebrated trial, but to those of us who had plunged headlong into the mystery for more than a year, the trial would be anticlimactic.

The Atlanta "monster" the *New York Post* had referred to was perceived as a daring, shadowy phantom who had skillfully eluded a massive manhunt by local and state police, the FBI and thousands of volunteers. For almost two years, children ranging in age from 7 to 16 had been disappearing and turning up dead in vacant lots, on road shoulders, in motel rooms, in abandoned buildings, in woodlands, on busy streets and in or near rivers (including two in the Chattahoochee River). But, on March 20, 1981, all of that changed. Except for one 17-year-old ex-convict, the rest of Atlanta's officially listed "child murder victims" would be 20 or older.

As far as the public knew, no one had seen anything. The victims on The List were male and female. They had died in almost every imaginable way—and many in unimaginable ways, so devious that we never learned how. The List recognized only one commonality: they all were black.

That the trial had been postponed came as a surprise to no one. Exactly when Wayne Williams would go on trial was simply another pawn move in a chess game in which neither defense nor prosecution was ready to commit its major strategy.

I chuckled when a representative of Williams' attorney, Mary Welcome, asked me to meet him in his office—Room 1313. Was that ever an omen! Once inside Ken McCleod's office, I was introduced to Durwood Myers, chief investigator for the defense. Our paths had crossed years before in New Orleans, when Myers conducted a seminar for my erstwhile employer, the U.S. Justice Department.

I had known for some time that the prosecution's case was in disarray. Plagued by an ineffective investigation and a gross misunderstanding of what was happening in Atlanta, the state suddenly had a fluke suspect dropped in its lap.

Under these circumstances, a delay couldn't hurt the prosecution. From what I could gather from snatches of behind-the-scenes conversations, Tony Axam, another of Williams' attorneys, must have sensed that the prosecution wasn't ready. He seemed eager to try a bold gambit: get on with the trial and bluff through it, counting on the prosecution to lose rather than the defense to win. Too bad for Wayne Williams that Axam wasn't around to try it. It probably would have worked.

But if the prosecution was in disarray, the defense was in shambles. Each side was its own worst enemy. The atmosphere on the defense team was strictly prime time Perry Mason. The game plan was to identify another killer, and walk Wayne Williams out the door. Meanwhile, witnesses were not being interviewed and files were not being created. Information about victims and events was incomplete and inaccurate. Wayne Williams had not been asked for a single alibi in the 28 murder cases (the addition of 28-year-old victim John Porter was not yet known by the defense) he might be charged with. To compound the defense's problems, it didn't know whether it was defending Williams against two or 28 charges. As it turned out, it would be 12 of 29 (including the addition of Porter's case). Fair trial?

The prosecution had provided the defense with computerized lists of "prospective witnesses," without any explanation as to which of the cases they might be testifying about. By this time, these lists contained more than 1,400 names, and the defense had no idea which of these witnesses would be called by the prosecution.

"The first thing you should do," I suggested in my first meeting with the defense investigators, "is try to find 'Tightrope' Anthony."

The faces in the room went blank. "Who?" someone asked.

Before I could fully explain why Jimmy (Tightrope) Anthony was so important to the defense case, the telephone rang. Durwood Myers answered it, and then had to exhort whoever was on the other end to calm down. Soon he bolted out the door. He was off to see Wayne Williams at the Fulton County Jail, to put out a fire that was causing the defense team's in-fighting to boil over.

Mary Welcome and Tony Axam, Williams' principal attorneys, seemed to be quarreling as if there were no other adversary. Wayne Williams was tugging on the reins again, but Tony was geeing and Mary was hawing. The battle between the attorneys was about to spill out of their paneled offices onto the front pages of the *Atlanta Constitution* and the *Atlanta Journal.*

Apparently with Wayne Williams' blessing—the kiss of death to all of his attorneys, whom he kept so stirred up that they could seldom function well—Tony Axam was about to fire Mary Welcome. But after Durwood Myers' visit to the jail, Welcome top-handed the dispute by firing Axam. A few days later, a compromise was reached—at least for public consumption. But it wasn't long before Axam was out for good. Or was he?

At least, this is how it looked from Mary Welcome's office. In fairness to Axam, I know Williams was sorry that he ever let him go. I also know that by the time Williams' appeal rolled around, he wanted Axam back. He should have thought of that a lot earlier. Wayne Williams is no favorite of the attorneys who have tried to work for him.

Just before Axam departed, Durwood Myers asked if I would help the defense team. He offered a grandiose title and the grand total of 25 cents compensation.

My misgivings about taking on the job had nothing to do with remuneration. I didn't want to work for the investigator. I preferred to work for the attorney of record. Further, I was concerned about the literary rights and the proprietary rights to the treasure trove of information I had gathered. Finally, I was extremely concerned that my objectivity would be forever compromised. I wanted it clearly understood that I could not take the position that Wayne Williams was innocent. I didn't know whether he was guilty, and I still don't. For that matter, I haven't gotten my quarter, either.

I didn't hear from the defense again until three weeks later. This time, a new attorney was on board. He was Alvin Binder, Esquire—gentleman lawyer from Mississippi. Binder brimmed with competence, a quality theretofore in short supply in the entire panoply of Atlanta murders. My pulse quickened at the possibility of working with him.

Alvin Binder is 54 and white. Outwardly, he is the very embodiment of Southern gentryhood, with a courtly manner and a rich baritone drawl. But then, the composite Southern gentleman would not be Jewish, which Binder is. Nor would he have gone to battle against the Ku Klux Klan, which Binder did.

You would expect Al Binder to remind Mary Welcome of her ladyhood whenever her profanity got explicit. But you had to know that he was capable of spewing a string of expletives of his own—not often, but with such obvious feeling. Al Binder can cuss you out with his eyes. His mind is lightning quick, but his arrival in the case was way too late.

Mary Welcome is an engaging, slender woman who, at first glance, looks scholarly and matronly with her horn-rimmed glasses and touseled hair. Well, she *is* scholarly, but up close, her dark-brown complexion is smooth and her narrow features are soft, radiating a much more youthful countenance than her 41 years. There is nothing matronly about this attractive woman.

The Mary Welcome who, as city solicitor, had made those extravagantly publicized raids on massage parlors and bath houses, exuded a more self-assured presence than the Mary Welcome who, behind the scenes in the Wayne Williams defense, broke down and sobbed in the heat of arguments with Al Binder. But then, Binder's verbal thunder—and the menacing gaze from behind his eyeglasses—would make even the strongest witness shudder on the stand.

Al Binder walked with a slight stoop. Perhaps it was his diabetes or his troublesome heart that made him appear fragile despite his rigid frame and rugged bearing. He had been recommended to the defense team by Durwood Myers. There was something unsettling, yet indefinable—something out of synch about Binder's relationship with Myers, an ex-cop from Jackson, Mississippi, who lived in an absolutely gorgeous home in suburban Atlanta and maintained another in Mississippi. In any event, it was Alvin Binder who breathed the first hint of life into the defense of Wayne Williams.

Massed around Binder was what he rightly called a "rag-tag army" of lawyers, would-be lawyers, investigators, hangers-on and "go-fers." To be sure, none of them was being paid anything, except for the legal staffers who were drawing their regular salaries.

Whatever trickled into the so-called "defense fund," primarily from an *Us* magazine article on Wayne Williams (arranged by Mary Welcome, to the absolute pique of Fulton County Sheriff Leroy Stynchcombe), didn't filter to the defense-team underlings. The money couldn't have stretched very far into the ranks, anyway. I know it didn't come down to me and I doubt it got as far as a feisty, hard-working and likeable fellow named Luis (Angel) Ortiz, who shocked Mary by handing her a bill for services rendered: $20,000 plus.

If Mary Welcome got any money from the case, she put on an Academy Award-winning act. During the trial, her telephone was shut off for non-payment. Not long thereafter, she was sued by her landlord for non-payment of her office rent, and she missed paying her bar dues. I don't know if Mary Welcome ever will be able to assess accurately the total cost of her attempts to defend Wayne Williams. I know it cost her dearly, and I know in my heart she didn't deserve the cost.

For his part, Binder paid the expenses of expert witnesses out of his own pocket. Some vital witnesses declined to come to Atlanta because there was not enough money available to pay them. I've never fully understood the reasons for not attempting to get Wayne Williams declared a pauper, but I'm relatively sure that whatever they were, they backfired to nobody's benefit. To accomplish what had to be done in the defense of Wayne Williams would have quickly made a very, very rich man a pauper.

I took two trips for the defense. They cost me $150. I told Binder they cost me only $50. He gave me $75 because he knew I was lying, but not by how much.

I felt for Binder because he pushed buttons and nothing would happen. Obviously frustrated, he would push the same buttons again and again, hoping that the defense team's assorted monumental missions somehow would be accomplished. Unfortunately for both Binder and Wayne Williams, too many tasks identified and delegated by Binder were left undone.

Among the volunteers, the most incongruous was Camille Bell, mother of slain 9-year-old Yusuf Bell and president of the Committee to Stop Children's Murders. She said she was convinced that Williams didn't kill her son. She was accompanied by the colorful, hefty Philadelphian, Don Laken, the "Dog Man."

Under Binder's stewardship, files began to take form, witnesses were interviewed and expert witnesses were contacted. By trial day, the information that we had gathered filled four file drawers—all of it neatly indexed and cross-referenced. Four drawers may seem like a vast repository—that is, until you contrast them with the rows of file cabinets and the hundreds of thousands of dollars worth of computer storage at the fingertips of the prosecution. Remember, facing this "rag-tag army" in the Fulton County Courthouse were the resources of the City of Atlanta, nine other metropolitan jurisdictions, the State of Georgia and the government of the United States of America.

Presiding over the proceedings would be Clarence Cooper, then 39, a black Fulton County Superior Court judge who had worked for the chief prosecutor, Lewis Slaton, in the District Attorney's office for more than a decade. Published reports stated that Cooper had been randomly selected to try the case by a computer while he was out of town (sure!).

It was Judge Cooper who personally selected the "Brady" information that the state, by law, must make available to the defense in advance of trial. The "Brady" is material such as police reports and laboratory examinations, gathered by the prosecution, which tends to be exculpatory (supports the innocence of the accused). Since the Brady material was not delivered until after the original trial date, it is fair to assume that the court was not ready to try the case, even if the state and defense were (which they were not). Or, more likely, the game of "criminal justice" was being played to the hilt again, and information was being withheld from the defense as long as legally possible, as part of the strategy of "winning" the case.

The Brady was turned over to the defense primarily in 29 black, metal-fastened folders, none more than one inch thick. Each binder was titled with the name of a victim.

Just before turning over the Brady, Judge Cooper had imposed a

Judge Clarence Cooper (left), who presided over Wayne Williams' trial, meets socially with his boss of 11 years, District Attorney Lewis Slaton, who prosecuted Williams. (W.A. Bridges/ Atlanta Constitution)

stringent "gag order" on everyone connected with the case. The Brady was a particularly sensitive area. I got my first look at the Brady files only moments before *Atlanta Constitution* reporters Ken Willis and Gail Epstein did—in clear violation of Judge Cooper's gag order. They had come smilingly into Mary Welcome's office and began casually perusing Judge Cooper's top-secret Brady documents.

Al Binder asked the two reporters to leave. They didn't. When he asked them again and again—and they still didn't leave—he *told* them to leave, and they did. Violations of Judge Cooper's gag order were common. The gag order was of questionable constitutionality, inasmuch as it prohibited anybody connected with the case from saying anything at all about it to anybody else. But the order went unchallenged and, for the most part, unheeded.

As the trial dragged on, violations of the order became a torrent. For reporters, one of the busiest sources of information was, of all places, the offices of Judge Cooper. A pre-trial Christmas party given by the attorneys in the offices shared by Mary Welcome also attracted reporters Willis and Epstein, who, as uninvited guests, hung on Mary's almost every word, hoping, perhaps, that something might slip in a moment of champagned conviviality.

The gag order not only was a nagging annoyance to Binder, but it also caused him personal embarrassment. When two out-of-town defense "experts" shot from the lip in back-home press interviews, Judge Cooper cited Binder—not the "experts"—for contempt of court. It was a bum rap. I had been present when Binder strongly admonished Dr. Daniel P. Stowens, a pathologist who was to testify for the defense, not to discuss the case with anyone. But, Stowens returned to California and made like Snuffy Smith's wife at the "gossip fence."

Another defense witness, Dr. Brad Bayless, a psychologist, went home to Arizona and expounded publicly on his knowledge of the cases. Judge Cooper was furious. Al Binder and Mary Welcome were cited for contempt. Binder considered it a very serious ethical and professional matter. But on several occasions later, he arrived to find Welcome closeted with the press, whereupon Binder became furious.

During the trial, I turned down several lucrative media consulting offers because of the "gag rule." Working with the defense of Wayne Williams paid *nothing*. Soon I began getting calls from friends in the media, some of whom I had declined consulting stipends from. Now they were asking me to "verify" information "slipped" to them by the defense.

"What's their motivation in planting this stuff, Chet?" a national network bureau chief called and asked.

"Who planted it?" I asked.

"Myers," he said.

Now it was my turn to be furious. I asked Myers and Binder to join me for lunch and I told them just exactly what I thought of the situation. Judge Cooper also cited Homer and Faye Williams for contempt for their telephoned on-the-air comment to a local radio talk show about their son's case. In the end, all contempt citations were set aside, with no penalties meted out.

Late one evening in December of 1981, Mary Welcome telephoned me. She wanted to discuss what she said was a "bombshell." The rest of the Brady material—specifically, the laboratory reports—had arrived. On the surface, she said, they looked devastating to Wayne Williams. She asked me to meet her in her office the next morning and take a look.

I had dealt earlier with the infamous green rug fibers in a way that had impressed her. I hardly know one end of a microscope from the other, but I do know that non-expert conclusions often are reached by so-called experts.

Mary cautioned me that she had agreed with Binder not to discuss the lab reports with anyone beyond the group that already knew. That group included Myers, Gail Anderson (Mary's assistant) and Clifton Bailey, an attorney. She also said I should let her explain to Binder before I ever let him know I had seen the reports. The next morning, she locked me in her office with the sheaf of lab reports—and instructions not to open the door for anyone.

A half hour hadn't elapsed when the lock on the door turned at the urging of a key held by Mary's legal assistant. In a moment, she was talking on the telephone to Dr. Brad Bayless in Arizona, telling him what I had been told not even to tell Binder that I had seen. This was the same Brad Bayless who had been partially responsible for the earlier contempt citations. But this matter was far more crucial to the defense than any gag order. For the moment, it looked as if there might be no way to deal successfully with the weight of this newly revealed state's evidence.

The next person through Mary's office door was Al Binder himself. He asked what I was working on. His question put me in an awkward position, and I didn't like it. I asked Al if he had talked with Mary yet, and he said, "No. What difference does that make?" I asked Al, as a favor, to talk with Mary because I felt uncomfortable talking about my immediate project.

Soon Binder called a meeting of Welcome, Myers, himself and me. What followed was a terribly unpleasant confrontation—gnashing of teeth and an unleashing of pent-up sentiments. Epithets spewed. Fingers wagged. Tears flowed. Hard feelings criss-crossed the room like laser beams in *"Star Wars."* I brought up the telephone conversation to Bayless in my presence a few hours earlier.

Al then lit into Mary, with both eyes blazing. "God-damn it! If I can't trust you," he roared, "who in the hell can I trust? We made an agreement and you violated that agreement and I'm tired of this going behind my back!"

"Well," she said, "I told Chet because..."

"I don't give a god-damn why you told him!" Al screamed. "You agreed with me that you wouldn't tell anybody!"

Al looked at me and then turned to Mary again. "This man may be able to get us off the hook on one or two or three kids on fibers!" he yelled. "But he isn't Houdini! He can't get us off on 23!"

From there, the professional rapport between Al Binder and Mary Welcome went into a tailspin, if not a crash landing. There were whispered snipes, and rival camps formed. Each faction didn't trust the others. As a consequence, each conversation seemed to contain a loyalty test. I no longer knew whether a project was aimed at gathering facts for the trial, or determining the politics of the infighters. I'm afraid I, too, failed many of those tests.

Eventually, it led to a scene straight out of a CIA novel. Mary Welcome decided that I was a double agent, working with the defense by day and huddling with FBI agents and prosecutors at night. She also saw me as a confirmed member of the "Binder camp."

For some time, I was cut off from the defense attorneys.It didn't cost me a thing. It was more like a promotion. Now I didn't have to work not to get paid. From what I read, the cost during that interim was paid by Wayne Williams.

I wasn't at the trial to help with the cross-examination of the state's fiber experts. The reason was Mary Welcome's apparent paranoia. During the trial, I often wrote notes to Binder—notes which she would decide were not important enough to pass along. She was wrong. It severely cut into my effectiveness, and I'm sure I irritated her more than a little, dealing directly with Binder.

State Representative Mildred Glover had invited me to a party at her house. I had known Mildred and her husband, Bill Hopkins, since long before the trial and long before I had met Mary Welcome. I had been a guest in their home on other occasions.

I wasn't feeling well and had other work to do, but I didn't want to appear ungrateful to Mildred, whom I often disagree with, but like a great deal. I showed up in my work clothes. Everyone else was dressed to the hilt. I spoke briefly with a doctor I had met in the defense room at the trial. Then I helped the kitchen crew and left.

Later, Wayne Williams told me that Mary Welcome thought I had attended the party because I was "a spy for the prosecution." My sides still ache from my laughter. In any event, Mary Welcome convinced Al Binder to remove me from the defense table. I was given some "important" assignment that I recognized immediately as make-work to get me out of Mary Welcome's hair. I calmly ignored the assignment, delighted to have time to take care of other neglected chores of my own. But Binder soon would ask me to come back.

As we began the monumental task of pre-trial planning, an inner sanctum

Wayne Williams' lawyers, Al Binder and Mary Welcome, often battled each other as if there were no other adversary. On appeal, attorney Lynn Whatley would claim that they provided Williams with an inadequate defense. (Bill Mahan/Atlanta Constitution)

emerged. The participants in the major decision-making were Binder, Welcome, Cliff Bailey, Durwood Myers and I, with considerable help from Gail Anderson. Unmistakably, the chief executive officer was Al Binder.

One issue that had to be addressed immediately was the press conference that Wayne Williams had called in his home on the morning of June 4, 1981.

The first problem raised by Williams' press conference was the inadmissibility of lie-detector tests which had been administered to Williams at the FBI office. Normally, the results would not have been admissible without the agreement of both the prosecution and the defense. But, in this instance, Williams had publicly acknowledged at his press conference that he twice had taken a polygraph test and that the FBI told him that his answers were deceptive. Translation: he flunked.

An important collateral issue was whether Williams was represented by an attorney when he held the press conference. He had told the reporters that he was represented by counsel, whom he identified only as "he." Mary Welcome told Al Binder that she had been retained by Williams before the press conference. As much as I thought that Mary should know when she was retained, I also thought she was wrong—based on what Paul Crawley and I had learned about Mary not yet having received Williams' first telephone message until *after* the press conference.

The next sticky problem with Wayne Williams' press conference was one that I raised. It concerned one of Williams' remarks that had been brought to my attention by Jeff Prugh:

> "They openly said, 'You killed Nathaniel Cater, and you know it, and you're lying to us.' They said that. And they said it a number of occasions. They said it on that night, uh—one of the Task Force captains on the scene pointed his finger at me and said it, and said he was tired of all the uh—B.S. about working the long hours, working the stakeouts, and that he was ready to pull the thing to an end. They said that a number of times."

Jeff and fellow *Los Angeles Times* reporter Lee May had discussed the remark on the tape with Mary Welcome in July, weeks after Williams' arrest. She dismissed it as unimportant. I thought it necessary to raise the question again. I waited until Mary, Al and I were together—with no one else present. The opportunity came one morning in Mary's office.

I told Al the tape of the press conference revealed that Williams had said that the police had accused him at the scene of killing Nathaniel Cater.

What was vitally important about that statement was that *no one at the scene, including the police, should have known that Nathaniel Cater was dead.* That is, unless he were the killer. Cater, a drifter, had not been reported missing, and it would not be until two days after Wayne Williams was stopped near "the scene" that a body identified as Nathaniel Cater would be discovered downstream in the Chattahoochee River.

Mary Welcome insisted that Wayne Williams never really said what I said was on the tape. Al Binder agreed with her. He explained that he had listened to the tape very carefully and that Williams had not said what I thought he said. But I knew differently.

Mary said that Williams had been talking on the tape about his interrogation at FBI headquarters on June 3 and 4, not about his questioning near the Chattahoochee River bridge on the morning of May 22. I told Mary that I agreed with her. "That's what Wayne meant," I said, "but I'll be damned if that was what he *said.*"

"All right, Mr. Detective," Binder said to me, "I'm going to teach you a lesson." He sent for the audio tape of Williams' news conference. He placed it on the multi-purpose machine in Mary's office, and we began to listen. (While we had waited for the tape to be brought into the office, I telephoned Jeff. I knew he could tell me exactly at what point in the tape Williams' curious statement came.)

I waited patiently for the cues on the tape and said, "Here it comes!" Binder bent his ear closer to the machine. His face brightened. He heard it. Suddenly he jumped up, hurried to the machine and began replaying that sequence.

Mary clung tenaciously to her own interpretation of what Wayne Williams had said on the tape. I tried in vain to tell her that it could just as easily be interpreted the other way.

"Damn it, Mary! You are interested in this case, aren't you?" Al Binder snapped. "Listen! Listen to the man! I heard it. You heard it. We all heard it. Wayne was saying that they accused him *at the scene* of killing Nathaniel Cater. I apologize, Chet."

Al Binder slumped wearily into his chair.

When Al Binder first saw those laboratory reports, he seriously doubted Wayne Williams' innocence. Long before I finished analyzing them, Al and I had a long talk. For Al, it was an examination of conscience. It was the reason for one of several trips he made to the jail to confront Wayne Williams.

What was this "bombshell" of state's evidence? First, the combination of fibers was far more vast than the defense had known. Second, there were more different fibers. Finally, there were various combinations of fibers found on far more victims than the defense knew about.

It all was enough to flatten Binder, but Mary said it wasn't the end of the world and that we had, after all, succeeded in poking holes in the prosecution's rug-fiber contentions.

The prosecution furnished the defense a numerical breakdown pertaining to the fiber evidence:

—Twenty-two victims had fibers which connected them to Wayne Williams.
—Five victims, they said, did *not* have fibers to connect them to Williams.
—One person was still missing.

This added to 28—the number of names on The List officially compiled by authorities.

I noticed, however, that victim Patrick (Pat Man) Rogers was *not* on the prosecution's list of those who had matching fibers. And he wasn't on the list of those who did *not* have matching fibers, either.

Patrick wasn't among those who still were missing, so where was the laboratory report on the evidence in the Patrick Rogers case? Pat Man had been overlooked again! I pointed this out to Binder and Cliff Bailey. "Something's wrong with these lab reports," I said. "The information on Patrick Rogers is missing."

The defense still was trying to plod through the blizzard of names of state's witnesses, trying in vain to priortize them. At one point, Binder asked if I could relate the witnesses' names to specific cases, simply by applying the geography of their addresses to the geography of the cases. I did with some success. But, for the most part, we didn't know who they were, what they would testify to, or even if they would testify. A lot of valuable time was wasted talking with people who, if they were to be witnesses and knew it, still denied any such knowledge.

Even when the witnesses who were listed as police officers were sought out, the Atlanta police offered no cooperation. On one occasion, a key police witness could not be located by the defense. Sources in the office of the chief of police told the defense, "We can't find him."

How to deal with witnesses is a part of the game of criminal justice—and another unfair part at that. The defense was preoccupied with the problem—and was forced to tie up resources—in a way that Patton's paper army tied down the Germans at the Pas de Calais.

It was at this juncture that Al Binder decided that I should sit at the defense table during the trial. "You are the only person," he said, "who knows enough about these cases to tell me what to ask on cross examination."

During the trial, we didn't know who the next witness presented by the state would be—or what he or she would be testifying about. As each witness' name was called and we saw that witness for the first time as he or she entered the courtroom, one of us at the table would whisper to Binder who it was, what case might be related and, if possible, the thrust of what he or she might say.

Al Binder brought Dr. Daniel Stowens into the conference room. Stowens reputedly was an expert on the pathology of children's deaths. Binder's own perceptions had been clouded by the publicity attendant to The List. He thought he was coming to Atlanta to defend an accused "child murderer." Unfortunately, Stowens would testify about two *adults.*

Stowens shocked me by stating that Nathaniel Cater's body had been in the water for at least two weeks. He also said that Jimmy Ray Payne had been in the water for at least seven days. Although we didn't know exactly when Cater disappeared, we knew it had been less than two weeks before his body was found. We also knew that Jimmy Ray Payne had been missing for less than seven days.

I was still under the impression that the defense might introduce witnesses who would swear Cater was alive *after* the morning of May 22, 1981. In my naivete, I wondered if it then were wise to have a pathologist testify that Cater had been dead for two weeks when his body was found.

I argued with Stowens that unless Cater and Payne had been misidentified (a possibility in these cases, as witnessed by other identifications), then he could not be correct. Stowens then began backing off, revising downward his estimates of how long the two bodies had been in the water.

I was really disturbed. Like police who still think it is possible to prevent "crime" by patrolling, I still thought a pathologist could tell how long someone has been dead. Not so. I told Binder that we needed stronger medical testimony. I figured if Stowens knew he was correct in his estimates, he would have not given in so easily.

During November and December 1981, we gathered early and worked late. Sundays were blue jeans, sandwiches, gallons of coffee and stacks of legal pads. A nurse was on call for Binder whenever his diabetes flared up.

All too often, Binder was called away to Judge Cooper's chambers for a hearing, or to extinguish another brush fire ignited by Wayne Williams. Binder's presence with the brain trust of the defense team was vital for Williams' trial preparation. When he left, it was like turning off the engine of a car while moving. We coasted for a minute or two, but soon ground to a halt.

Where would the state begin its case? To be sure, the state was supposed to prove *corpus delecti* (that a murder had, indeed, been committed) in the Nathaniel Cater and Jimmy Ray Payne cases before it could introduce any other cases to attempt to show a "pattern" of killings.

Al Binder and I sat down to begin drafting his opening remarks to the jury. Before we wrote the first sentence, Binder was called away again. He instructed Mary Welcome and me to finish writing on two specific points. Soon, Mary, too, was called to something else.

I wrote as best I could.

Again, a button was pushed and nothing happened. "Oh, Mr. Binder, " I said aloud to myself. "The enemy is us!"

25

Anything but the Whole Truth, So Help Me

"A mixed jury will have to decide whether a bright young product of the black middle class could have systematically murdered children of his own race."

—Atlanta Weekly
September 20, 1981

The Sunday magazine of the *Atlanta Journal-Constitution* got it right on one count: the jury was mixed racially and by the sexes, but the magazine had merely predicted so. The jurors weren't chosen until three months later.

The magazine was wrong on another count, and thus helped reinforce the false perception that Wayne Williams soon would stand trial for murdering children. The fact is, Williams would be tried on charges of killing two adults, one of them four years *older* than Williams.

On Christmas Eve of 1981, Homer Williams visited my house to deliver a letter which Wayne had written in his cell at the Fulton County Jail.

Santa Claus would arrive just three days before Wayne Williams would go on trial in a case that had drawn reporters and camera crews from around the world—and even was reported in Moscow.

But that had happened during the height of the killings. Demonstrators had marched in Atlanta, with members of the Revolutionary Communist Party carrying a banner that read "STOP RACIST KILLINGS." Civil rights leaders such as the Reverend Joseph Lowery of the Southern Christian Leadership Conference had aroused fears that the killer or killers probably were white. The world was swayed to conjure up stereotypical visions of robed and hooded Ku Klux Klansmen snatching and killing black children in—where else?—the American South.

Now the man on trial happened to be black. The rest of the world was no longer interested. The story didn't fit preconceived notions that what happened in Atlanta surely must be a sequel to *"Birth of a Nation,"* or a paean to the Old South.

Of the hundreds of foreign correspondents to scamper around Atlanta, searching for and expecting the worst, only two bothered to apply for credentials to attend the trial. Only one picked up his credentials. None stayed to cover the entire trial, which would be merely a vignette in the Atlanta story. The lone demonstrator at the Fulton County Courthouse during the trial was a black man who stood outside, wrapped in an old-style, olive-drab, wool Army overcoat, carrying a sign urging Williams to fire Al Binder and "hire a brother." Someone did, however, visit Mary Welcome's office, hawking "Free Wayne Williams" buttons.

A few miles away from the courthouse, no Christmas tree or boughs of holly could hide the devastation left by two police searches, which had turned Homer and Faye Williams' modest house on Penelope Road into a shambles. Huge chunks of carpet had been ripped up. The draperies had patches cut from them in helter-skelter fashion. The Williamses have had their attorney draw up a lawsuit in an attempt to collect damages from the city, but that suit is as yet unfiled.

Now Homer Williams had stretched his tall, paunchy frame across the lounge in my den. On an earlier day, it had been my map that sprawled there. We talked about Gallileo, Pope John XXIII, Machiavelli, John and Robert Kennedy, Lyndon Johnson, Thomas Jefferson and Martin Luther King Jr. We shared our mutual interests as educators. We talked about building a Rube Goldberg digital thermometer.

"Wait till Wayne gets out," Homer Williams said. "He's smarter about things like that than I am."

"*If* Wayne gets out," I thought. But I cautiously buried the words deep beneath my collarbone.

I now felt rather odd, trying to explain to my holiday guests that the man who had just departed is the father of Atlanta's accused "child" killer. "*Child*" killer? Bullshit! Wayne Williams might well be a child killer, but he was charged with killing a 21-year-old parolee from a Georgia prison and a 27-year-old convicted felon who cavorted with drifters and derelicts, and robbed winos.

These victims hardly were children. Yet some members of the news media weren't bothered by semantics. WSB-TV, Atlanta's ABC-affiliated television station, persisted in identifying Wayne Williams as "the man accused of killing two of 28 black children killed over a two-year period," without recognizing that five of the 28 were adults.

Nationally, the *New York Times* helped kindle a second false perception—that Atlanta's killings had stopped. The *Times* reported on December 27, 1981, that a law-enforcement official familiar with Atlanta police activities—and who requested anonymity—said that the city had "not had any unsolved cases of murdered juveniles since Mr. Williams was arrested."

The truth was that the city of Atlanta accounted for only half the murders on The List. The truth was that there had not been an unsolved murder of a *juvenile* since three months before Wayne Williams was arrested. But after?

The truth was that there were at least seven unsolved murders (including two juveniles) who fit the age, race and sex parameters of The List between the time Williams was jailed and the *Times* published this unenlightening report.

The newspaper also quoted Jan Douglass, executive director of Atlanta's Community Relations Commission, as saying, "What is on everyone's mind is that when Wayne Williams was arrested, the killings stopped. Everyone was enormously relieved that the killings stopped . . ."

The *Times* went on to report in the same article that both Nathaniel Cater and Jimmy Ray Payne "fit a pattern of being small in stature . . ." What the *Times* did *not* report in this article was that Nathaniel Cater, being, at 27, the oldest victim on The List and almost five years older than Williams at the time of the "splash," also was one of the *tallest*. Cater, at 5-foot-10, was 2½ inches taller than the man accused of killing him, Wayne Williams.

Had the *Times* and other news organizations—and, for that matter, the unnamed police source and interviewee Jan Douglass—checked, they could have found the facts. The unsolved murders were—and still are—listed in the FBI Uniform Crime Reports for Atlanta. Yet in January of 1984, Fulton County Medical Examiner Robert Stivers told CBS: "I can say—with the evidence that we have and the cases that we've seen—that it did stop."

What stopped? *What* evidence in *which* cases? Stivers' perception of the parameters of The List remains as blurred as it was when Paul Harvey quoted him three years ago. Unquestionably, murders fitting the parameters of The List still are being committed.

Again, the news media's coverage—and the public's view of Atlanta's problems—had been narrowed by The List and by uninformed "official" pronouncements.

Clarence Cooper insisted on starting the trial during the biggest annual holiday week. The gavel fell on December 28, 1981. The first order of business was *voire dire*, the selection of a jury.

There were the usual pre-trial motions, including one for change of venue. Lynn Whatley would later contend, on appeal, that the court never ruled on the motion, but proceeded with jury selection. But Whatley would contradict himself by arguing that Al Binder was incompetent for trading the change-of-venue motion for a "broader *voire dire*." Lynn Whatley tried to explain to me why, legally, this was not a contradiction, but I told him that out here in the real world, away from Latin and legalese, it sounded like a contradiction to me.

Those parts of the jury selection that I witnessed were no different than all the others I had seen over the years. There were candidates who wanted no part of the jury and used the flimsiest excuses imaginable. And there were those who itched to get on that jury. One woman, for instance, insisted that she had heard no publicity about the cases. She said she didn't take the paper, didn't own a TV and although she had a radio, she only occasionally listened to music on it and never heard the news. She didn't make the jury, although she tried hard.

There also were those who knew when to interject a prejudice, real or by design, to make sure they were not selected. And then there was an "ex-Detroit cop." "A ringer," someone on the defense team would say when it was learned that his police experience was a short stint with a suburban police department. But there were two people on the defense—Al Binder and Wayne Williams—who wanted that juror on the panel, although he was an ex-cop and white to boot. There were the obviously wrong guesses of psychologists about who would best serve the defense.

The Fulton County Courthouse is a venerable, gray building with steps that show the wear of millions of feet. Once inside the second set of doors, spectators and jurors found the Wayne Williams trial a warm escape from a winter that would bring Atlanta a freak storm dubbed "Snowjam '82."

The lobby was crowded with media types, those with the more boring, but freer, job of guarding the front doors for "pix" and quotes from principals and personalities. They, at least, could sip coffee, munch on vending-machine snacks, run to the potty as nature required, or even smoke a cigarette. But once inside Courtroom 404, you stayed—unless the judge let you out or threw you out.

Security was conspicuous, but more irritating than thorough. Outside, two sharpshooters watched from adjoining rooftops. Inside the courtroom, two members of the Wayne Williams defense team wore concealed weapons, acting as bodyguards. Only one of the bank of three elevators was allowed to stop at the fourth floor. Once out the door, you were greeted by a line of spectators waiting for each session.

The ropes of draped velvet that queued the masses seemed appropriate for the theatrical setting of this trial. A corps of uniformed deputy sheriffs watched spectators pass through a metal detector, a la 20th Century

American airport. Some were spared the ignominy of the search: the principal attorneys, for instance. On the other hand, some of their staffs were searched, while others were exempt.

Originally, the defense team met in a single room, but soon it was given access to an adjoining room. There was no phone. There were no restroom facilities and, for that matter, no facilities that you didn't have to go through "Check-point Charlie" to get to, and again to get back. A water fountain was in the hall, and there would have been an available restroom, but it was kept locked. A deputy who never was there had the only key.

The only available phone, without your being searched before using it, was in the *Atlanta Journal* and *Constitution* press room—not exactly the place to hold a conversation and observe the judge's gag order. The defense finally paid to have one phone line installed.

Off the hallway, across from the elevators, was the closest thing to heaven on the fourth floor—the makeshift media room. Actually, it was two rooms. One was a large room, where each of the various news outlets had installed a typewriter and a telephone. The room had vending machines and even lounge chairs. In the adjoining room, closed-circuit television had been set up to accommodate the overflow of reporters. Seating for the press in the courtroom was limited.

The tariff for using the closed-circuit TV room was as high as $550. When Paul Crawley walked in one day, he didn't think he would be called to task for not having a pass with him, since his station, WXIA-TV, had purchased several. In addition, the station had furnished the closed-circuit equipment. Paul was ordered to purchase another pass or leave the room. The station bought another pass. Then Paul went straight to the chambers of Judge Cooper and demanded that the police officers who watched closed-circuit TV in the room show their passes or be booted out. They had to leave.

The closed-circuit TV room had served as sort of a command post for the prosecution. When something was said that needed checking, a policeman watching the television in the press room would see that the necessary work got under way immediately.

Television had been one of the major sideshows preceding the trial. The news media and no one else fought the judge's gag rule, but the media went to court to attempt to force the judge to allow live television of the proceedings. They lost. Then, on appeal, the judge agreed to let the closed-circuit cameras in, but still no live coverage outside that room.

The courtroom itself is large enough to accommodate only 60 spectators, who sat in wooden pews. The judge's bench was raised—to lend more stature to those who serve as gods of the criminal-justice system. As I had once told my students, "The law isn't always just, it's just always the law—and that is what the judge says it is when he says it."

The jury sat to the right and just forward of the judge, with the witness stand and the door to the judge's chambers in between. Everyone else had to be seated before the jury and the defendant were escorted into the room—and everyone else remained seated until the escort back out of the room was completed. A wooden railing divided the room roughly in half. It was like a theater. The spectators all sat behind the railing, while the actors performed on the stage beyond. Between the railing and the bench were two long tables—one for the defense and one for the prosecution. The prosecution sat closest to the jury.

Whenever the judge ordered the courtroom emptied, which was always for lunch and usually for two or three other occasions, the spectators had to go to the end of the line, in which others waited, to get back in. Families of the victims on The List had to take their chances on getting in—just like any other spectator. But in the back corner of the press section each day were three familiar faces. One belonged to state Representative Mildred Glover.

The only person arrested by the inside security was nabbed on a marijuana charge. The police would have an opportunity to arrest another pot smoker later, but wouldn't. Once, the judge had to threaten to have Nathaniel Cater's father removed from the courtroom. Alonzo Cater argued from his seat that his son's age was erroneously stated as 28 in the opening statements. Reminded from the bench that order must be maintained, Alonzo Cater settled down and remained. No reason for a murder victim's father to confuse the issue with facts. Maybe we need just a little less decorum and a hell of a lot more facts in our courtrooms.

During the weeks immediately preceding the Wayne Williams trial—one of America's most celebrated ever—21-year-old Anthony (Amp) Wiley was sentenced to life in a DeKalb County murder case. The public was up in arms because the jury had been hung by one man from giving Wiley the death sentence.

DeKalb Superior Court Judge Clarence Peeler took the exceptional step of ordering that the juror who hung the death sentence be publicly identified—thus subjecting the juror to harassment and threats on his own life. The judge castigated the man in open court.

Amp Wiley had murdered a white woman. He was black. He lived next door to two victims on The List and one who was not. And he dated the same girl as did another victim on The List.

But in Fulton County court, not even a whimper was heard—nor did anybody argue either way—when the prosecution didn't ask for the death penalty for Wayne Williams. There was no public outcry against him and no half-cocked, knee-jerk protestations of persecution, rather than prosecution, as there are in almost every other nationally publicized trial of a black. I wondered why. I still do.

Ten days before the jury selection began in December of 1981, a front-page story in the *Atlanta Constitution* was headlined: "Atlanta Police

Looking Into Similarities in Stabbing Deaths of 4 Black Women." One of those women killed that very week was 32-year-old Juanita St. George, who had been at one time a baby-sitter for List victim Yusuf Bell.

One of the other three victims named was 22-year-old Faye Yearby, found murdered at Pickfair Avenue and Pickfair Way a year earlier. Another case was that of 37-year-old Catherine Lois Clark, who had been found in almost the same spot where 16-year-old Angela (Gypsy) Bacon was murdered, but a month earlier. The fourth was 18-year-old Beverly Harvey. We didn't have Wayne Williams in the courtroom yet, and they were already beginning to repeat the mistakes that led to his being there. Were we going to have yet another list? And was Cynthia Montgomery not a murdered female, either?

On the day the Williams jury selection began, a headline in the *Atlanta Constitution* read: "Skeleton of Missing Girl is Found Wired to Trees." She was a south Georgia girl, not one from Atlanta. She was white, not black. She had disappeared from home on June 28, 1981. She didn't make anybody's list because no one needed a scorecard to count dead bodies in the victim's tiny hometown of Richland, Georgia.

Meanwhile, the judge was denying a defense motion that it be furnished records on other unsolved murders in Atlanta.

As the selection of the jury neared, an *Atlanta Journal* article nicely summed up the problems facing the prosecution: "The Fulton District Attorney and three of his assistants will spend the coming weeks attempting to prove . . . [that Williams is the killer] . . . [They] will not have the advantages of eyewitnesses to the killing [sic], or a readily identifiable murder weapon, or an obvious motive . . . They must rely heavily on . . . a multicolored collection of tiny fibers and dog hair."

The sun rose on day No. 1 of *State of Georgia versus Wayne B. Williams.* Wayne Williams had selected an attorney (Mary Welcome) who had never defended a murder suspect. The state had selected a judge who had never presided over a murder trial. And D. A. Lewis Slaton hadn't prosecuted a major murder case since 1975, when he won the conviction of Marcus Wayne Chenault in the shooting death of Martin Luther King Jr.'s mother. One might have expected a more experienced cast.

Almost 900 prospective jurors were available to be whittled down to a panel of 12, plus two alternates. The front row of the press box strained forward as the first of these prospects were led into the room, 46 in all. Most of those straining for a better view were sketch artists whose talents were required because the judge followed the anachronistic practice of not allowing cameras in the courtroom.

To these 46, the defense read a boring list of prospective prosecution witnesses whose number had been shaved from more than 1,400 to a "mere" 554. By my calculations, they would have to do this 18 more times. The first day was history.

As folks filed out from the first day of jury selection, they were greeted by this *Atlanta Journal* headline: "Richland Offering Reward for Arrest of Weirdo Killer." Problems were growing in Stewart County. Someone had suddenly remembered that Tayna Nix was the second girl to die there with her hands bound to a tree. Would a $5,000 reward "shake the trees?" I doubted it. Hadn't I seen all this before? And wouldn't I see it again? Yes, again and again.

Of the 46 (or was it 47?) potential jurors called the first day, 11 were still around after the first round. The *Atlanta Constitution* reported "46;" the *Atlanta Journal* "47." Which proved that somebody couldn't count prospective jurors any better than most, including authorities, could count victims.

Binder and Slaton argued hotly over the qualifications and disqualifications, but by Wednesday, December 30, 1981, the panel had been honed to 24—16 whites and eight blacks. They were two dozen happy people when the judge told them to take the New Year's holiday off. When they came back, there would be still other prospective jurors to look at.

On January 5, the jury was finally selected. It consisted of nine women and three men. The racial breakdown: eight blacks and four whites (one man is white). The same confusion over body counts and prospective jurors carried over to the reporting of jury selection. The *Atlanta Constitution* reported that prosecutor Lewis Slaton struck 13 prospects, of whom 12 are black. The *Atlanta Journal* noted that "of the 13 prospective jurors struck by the prosecution, all but two were black." The two newspapers managed to agree on the number of prospective jurors, black and white, struck by the defense.

The jury would travel each day from its hotel near the airport, about a 10-mile ride in a school bus to the courthouse in downtown Atlanta. It wasn't clear why closer accommodations weren't chosen. The jurors would occupy private rooms with the televisions and telephones disconnected. In a separate room, a TV and phone were available, but a deputy sheriff stood by with a remote-control device to intercept any news of the trial. For this discomfort, the jurors were paid the whopping sum of $15 a day.

There was an incident in the jury lunch room, where someone had left on the table a drawing of a generic-looking character with the word "GUILTY" over his head. One male member of the jury joined the bailiff in an occasional nap while court was in session, their chins sometimes falling off their fists and jarring them awake with sheepish looks on their faces.

That night, on January 5, former U.N. Ambassador Andrew Young would be inaugurated as Atlanta's mayor. During the festivities, outgoing Mayor Maynard Jackson would reminisce about helping A. Reginald Eaves join a fraternity at Atlanta's Morehouse College. Just as Jackson later helped Eaves into—and out of—the fraternity of police executives, I thought. For his part, Reginald Eaves was still saying that Maynard Jackson dumped on him.

Both sides gave opening arguments on January 5. Al Binder said something that sidestepped the issue: "The theory of our case is you don't get a killer from a boy that was raised the way this one was."

I was terribly disappointed that he had taken this tack. Obviously, Binder was playing on the jurors' emotions with talk about altar boys, Cub Scouts and Lionel trains for Christmas. He got to the heart of the matter, though, when he stated that "the medical examiner has said he would have ruled Jimmy Ray Payne's death an accidental drowning if the previous series of killings had not occurred."

Now it was Lewis Slaton's turn. At 61, Slaton comes across as your prototypical, no-nonsense, hard-bitten veteran of courtroom skirmishes. He has chiseled features, receding black hair and a gravelly drawl of his native Coweta County, Georgia. As District Attorney since 1965, Slaton is perhaps the most visible of metropolitan Atlanta's last old-guard white politicians, a survivor amid the storms that have swept a tidal wave of blacks into public office. Whether Slaton would have survived if elected from the city of Atlanta, rather than from Fulton County at large, is another question.

But, without opposition, Slaton has been re-elected four times to four-year terms and remains very much a behind-the-scenes, manipulative force in Atlanta's power structure. Some say he has survived by riding political waves, rather than making them. "He could be a flaming liberal if he's in a place where they are in power," attorney Al Horn told *Atlanta Weekly* in 1980, "or he would be an ass of a conservative in a place where conservatives are in power."

Now, Lewis Slaton talked about a "jig-saw puzzle," promising that the jurors would see the whole picture at trial's end.

He was absolutely right. In my opinion, a lot of the pieces were forced in where they really didn't fit—and the picture was distorted. But the prosecution did as fine a job as possible to orchestrate its pitifully small amount of hard evidence into a crescendo at just the right time.

Slaton then spoke bologna about some of the prosecution witnesses being "worried and reluctant . . . they know the defense may try and twist around what they say . . . making them look like they're not too smart." Wouldn't Slaton and every other lawyer out to *win* do exactly the same thing?

But some of the witnesses didn't need much help in not looking very smart. And no one in the media questioned Slaton's ability to *"know"* that something *"may"* happen. I know that Iceland may attack the Soviet Union anytime, but I'm not too worried that it will.

The opening statements were, for the most part, theatrics. They could have better been spent explaining this very complicated case. But, in the

"Game of Criminal Justice," everything must be kept a secret from the other side so it won't have an opportunity to counter effectively. The question is, if a revelation can be countered effectively, why shouldn't it be? This game is played too much for the egos of the opposing attorneys and too little for "justice"!

The nonsense that Al Binder talked about while referring to Wayne Williams' upbringing was underlined the next morning in a report and newspaper headline about still another brutal murder in Atlanta: "Bus Suspect's Past Gave No Hint of Violence." So much for the Boy Scouts. And what if the bus suspect's past had given some hints of violence? Psychiatrists can't predict what a person may or may not do. How could Al Binder?

John Blamphin, a spokesman for the American Psychiatric Association, told the Associated Press in relation to the shooting of President Reagan, *et al,* by John Hinckley: "Studies show that even when doctors are dealing with patients who have already committed violence, they cannot predict accurately which ones will do it again. In fact, their predictions are *wrong two times out of three* [emphasis added]."

I can't believe he admitted that. It means that your chances of predicting human violence are *better* (50-50) by flipping a coin than they are by seeking psychiatric opinion (1 in 3). Based on Blamphin's statement, I might want to enlist a psychiatrist's opinion and assume the opposite, which, according to Blamphin, offers the greatest probability of success (2 out of 3).

Thank goodness there was no psychiatric testimony to further muddy the waters in the Williams trial. Since the prosecution always has one psychiatrist to say one thing and the defense has one to say just the opposite, why have any at all?

Al Binder and I had guessed where the state might start its case. We figured it would be to establish *corpus delicti*—proving that a murder had been committed. First, the state put Jesse Arnold on the stand, and he testified that he saw a body floating in the Chattahoochee River. The body was *north* of the Interstate 285 bridge.

This testimony was extremely important because the state had an elaborate technical report prepared by the U.S. Army Corps of Engineers. That report originally contended that a body found where Jimmy Ray Payne's body had been found would have entered the water between the Interstate 285 bridge and the Bankhead Highway (U.S. 278) bridge. This, of course, would have been south of Interstate 285 and consequently downstream from the Jackson Parkway bridge, where the splash was heard.

When the prosecution saw what the Army report would do to its case in the Jimmy Ray Payne death, it went to the Corps of Engineers with the Arnold information and urged a change in the report. Once again, pseudoscience was foisted off as science. Just as medical examiners had cloaked their guesswork in the guise of science, so, too, did this engineer agree to alter the report.

The defense knew about this change in the report because the other co-author, a National Weather Service hydrologist, refused to take part in the alteration. He volunteered the information to the defense that the report was being tampered with.

Next, Mark Stanley Arnold testified that he, too, saw the body while fishing and followed it to the point where it hung up in the flotsom.

Jim Haldeman from the GBI then took the stand to show pictures of the scene. He also introduced evidence—the red shorts worn by Payne when his body was found. Under different circumstances, the state would have chosen to call these shorts "swimming trunks."

During cross-examination of Haldeman, Binder scored points for the defense. First, knowing that the lab had reported finding no rope fibers on Payne's body, Binder got Haldeman to say that the body was heavy and that it took three or four men to pull it from the water with a rope. Shouldn't there have been rope fibers found on Payne's body? And wasn't the state contending that the body had been lifted and thrown into the river by a small man, acting alone?

Jimmy Ray Payne's mother, Ruby Jones, took the stand next, and I passed Binder a note reminding him of allegations that she had been mistaken about her son's height and weight. Some even alleged that she had erred deliberately on Payne's size, simply to get his name on The List, which still was widely perceived as exclusively a list of children.

Ruby Jones testified that her son was several inches shorter and several pounds lighter than what was reported in the autopsy of Jimmy Ray Payne. Mothers and pathologists had problems throughout these cases agreeing on identification characteristics of victims.

Was it Jimmy Ray Payne? Most probably. Yet, only if the state's identification technicians were wrong could defense pathologist Daniel Stowens, have been right about how many days he thought Payne's body was in the river.

Catherine Turner, Payne's girlfriend, evoked a titter from the spectators when she testified to the color of Payne's red shorts, which she said he wore on the last day she saw him alive. This was Disney stuff for most of the crowd, who had come to the trial expecting a Harold Robbins sex story.

Neither spectators nor jurors were to hear any lurid details, except in veiled references and testimony about the fondling of a genital here and there. On cross-examination, Catherine Turner told Binder that she had known Jimmy Ray Payne for six years, but had never heard of, or seen, Wayne Williams.

After an Atlanta police identification technician testified that he had identified Jimmy Ray Payne from fingerprints, Saleh Zaki, an associate medical examiner for Fulton County, told Binder that in the identification of a cause of death, "It depends on your objectives and opinion." Please remember that a medical examiner said that; I didn't. "Can I exclude drowning?" Zaki said, when asked about Jimmy Ray Payne's death. "The answer is 'no,' I cannot."

In my opinion, the state lost any chance of proving *corpus delecti* in the Payne case when Zaki made that statement, and *corpus delecti*—like it or not—is an absolute prerequisite for a murder conviction.

Zaki denied that the cause of death in the Payne case had ever really been changed. First, Binder confronted him with death certificate No. 1, which stated the cause of Payne's death was: "undetermined." Next, Binder whipped out death certificate No. 2, dated *after Williams was indicted for Payne's murder*. This one said the cause of death was "homicide." The medical examiner explained that he checked the wrong box.

I wondered, could he be speaking figuratively? I was looking at copies of the death certificates, and there is no box to check. Instead, the word "undetermined" was typed in the appropriate block on one certificate and "homicide" was typed in the appropriate block on the other. If Zaki had made any mistake at all, he had dictated the wrong word. There is a hell of a difference between checking the wrong box and dictating the wrong word.

Zaki explained that the appearance of five other young black "murder victims" in the South and Chattahoochee rivers since March of 1980 (again, Pat Man was ignored) and what he called the "fact" that Payne didn't frequent the Chattahoochee River led him to conclude that Payne's death was not an accident.

This is scientific medical work? Had they wanted to call the death an accident, they would have used the same "fact" and said his unfamiliarity with the area contributed to the accident. Remember that the medical examiner's "objective" in this case is to provide a "murder" to prosecute.

Next to the stand came Atlanta Public Safety Commissioner Lee Brown. Whatever advantage Binder had won by his successful attacks on Zaki's "medical" testimony, he probably lost in his disastrous cross examination of Lee Brown.

Brown was as poor a witness on the facts as any cross-examiner could have hoped for. His testimony could—and should—have been torn to shreds. He demonstrated on the stand that he knew little about the investigation he had commanded for the previous 18 months and even less about the cases which were the subject of that investigation.

But Binder, pushing an almost meaningless point about unmanned police booths in downtown Atlanta, took a cheap shot at Brown, who obviously and with sufficient reason didn't understand Binder's question. After several attempts to elicit an answer to the question, Binder glowered at Brown and said, "You can understand English, can't you?"

Brown stared at Binder coldly. The room hushed. Brown finally spoke: "I have for a number of years—yes, sir."

Assistant prosecutor Jack Mallard was assistant in name only. Actually, he was the fuel that made the prosecution run and, for the most part, he was the engine itself. It was Jack Mallard who successfully prosecuted Wayne Williams. His performance was improved by Slaton on only a few occasions when Slaton, with a cool head, tugged at Mallard's coattail to curtail his enthusiasm of the moment.

With the case of victim Nathaniel Cater, the state had only probable cause—a splash—and a weak one at that. The addition of Jimmy Ray Payne had given the state a geographic pattern (the Chattahoochee River), three fiber matches between the two victims and an extension of fiber matches from Payne which would reach other victims (who would not have had fiber matches with Cater). The state had little else going for it. The *corpus delicti* (the ability to prove that the crime had been committed and the ability to link the suspect to the crime) was virtually nonexistent.

Obviously, the state thought so little of its case against Wayne Williams in the Payne and Cater deaths that it prepared to draw on evidence from other available "pattern" cases. Remember, everyone was conditioned to assume that this was a 29-victim case, even though the state had sought indictments in only two murders.

But Binder thought the law was clear that "pattern" evidence could not be introduced unless the *corpus delicti* had been proved. Just when Jack Mallard drifted into pattern testimony with his direct examination of Lee Brown, Binder immediately approached the bench. The judge motioned for Mallard to join himself and Binder at the bench. The following conversation took place, out of the hearing of the jury:

"He's deliberately and diabolically using the word pattern; and he knows *corpus delicti* is not in here," Binder whispered emphatically to Judge Cooper.

Whereupon Judge Cooper said, "Okay, I think you asked him, you know, what the purpose of the Task Force was."

"Judge," Mallard argued, "I'm leading up to the next area of my inquiry."

The judge asked Mallard, "What's the question going to be?"

Mallard: "Was there any significant change in the pattern of the killings about the first of March, 1981?"

Binder waded in, obviously irritated: "*Pattern* is not admissible, your honor! At this stage of the trial, he hasn't shown a homicidal death—"

Mallard shot back, "I stated to the court, we'll connect it up."

Binder: "He can't do that. He's got to show homicidal death and causal connection to the defendant before pattern is admissible. We haven't had our argument on that—"

"You don't have to show it first," Mallard began to argue in earnest.

"And he's using the word 'pattern' diabolically to prejudice the jury," Binder continued. "Your honor, can we go in and argue law on this or what? You haven't ruled that 'pattern' is admissible."

Mallard, sensing that he might be in trouble, offered: "I can rephrase the question, Judge."

"See if you can do that," Judge Cooper said, skirting one of the main issues of the trial.

"Pattern" was seeping in, and there would be little use to argue the law later. By then, it would be a *fait accompli*—a fatal one for the defense.

The actors returned to the stage. "Let me rephrase the question again, Commissioner," Mallard said, addressing Lee Brown. "Did anything happen on or about February 11, 1981, with regard to confidential evidence that had been previously found in the investigation?"

Any law student who needs a shining example of a leading question (supposedly not allowable in a court of law) needs to look no farther than the preceding question. Amazingly, it wasn't objected to by the defense!

Lee Brown answered, almost as if on cue: "Yes sir. On the—on that date, February 11, 1981, a front-page article in the *Atlanta Constitution* indicating or reporting that fiber evidence was found in the cases that we were investigating through the Task Force." (Actually, the article stated—for the first time—that fibers had been found on *two* victims, but it didn't say which victims.)

"Did that surprise you when you read it?" Mallard asked.

"Yes, sir, it most certainly did," Brown replied, "because in any investigation, certain information such as evidence should not be made public."

In response to further questions, Brown testified that the source of the story had been the Georgia State Crime Lab.

Mallard pressed on: "And was he quoting someone from the state crime lab as releasing this evidence about body fibers?"

"Your honor," Binder interrupted, "that's pure hearsay. Objection!"

"I'm going to sustain the objection," Judge Cooper said.

Mallard to Brown: "Did you read the article yourself?"

"Yes, sir," Brown answered.

Mallard went on to produce a copy of that issue of the *Atlanta Constitution* and note that it was entered in evidence. In a few moments, he continued, "Now after the publication of that news article on February 11, 1981, tell us when the first body hit the Chattahoochee River after that."

"This would be in the first part of March, about the 5th or 6th of March, 1981," Brown answered incorrectly. "I'm sorry, that would be in the South River," Brown went on, correcting himself. "It would be the 30th of March in the Chattahoochee River."

This time, Brown correctly answered the question that was put to him, but the jury was being misled, purposely or otherwise.

"All right, and did you then—," Mallard continued, "I believe you said earlier there were three in the south end of the Chattahoochee River."

Mallard believed incorrectly. Brown had testified to no such thing.

"South" end of the Chattahoochee? If Mallard meant the southwest corner of Fulton County (the southernmost point where a body had been found), and not the Florida Panhandle, where the south end of the Chattahoochee is, there had been two—not three—bodies found there. Three had been found far upstream, near U.S. 278. And Pat Man Rogers, whose slaying still was being ignored, was found farther north—(very importantly) even north of the Jackson Parkway bridge.

To his own dismay, Mallard even with leading questions soon had Brown tangled up and unable to explain where the Chattahoochee and South rivers are. Brown obviously didn't know the route of either river through metropolitan Atlanta, and his testimony demonstrated again the Atlanta police's ignorance of the geography of these cases.

Brown compounded the problem by answering "Yes, sir" to Mallard's question about Brown having said earlier that "three" bodies were found at the "south" end of the Chattahoochee River. Actually, Brown was wrong on two counts—and even contradicted himself in the process.

By saying "Yes, sir," Brown was in error because he never had said anything whatsoever about three bodies being found at the south end of the Chattahoochee. And, Brown's same reply of "Yes, sir" meant that three bodies turned up in the south end of the Chattahoochee (actually, *two* bodies—not three—had turned up in the location Brown was talking about. They were the bodies of Timmy Hill and Bubba Duncan).

That, in turn, set up Mallard's followup question about those "three" bodies in the river's south end: "All after this article was published on February 11, 1981, about body fibers?"

"Yes, sir," Brown replied again.

"Now prior to the article, Commissioner," Mallard went on, "were the bodies generally found with clothing?"

See how "pattern" glided in? If Mallard wasn't talking about "pattern" cases, then he would have had to be talking about Cater or Payne—obviously, Cater and Payne had not been found prior to February 11.

Adding to the injustice, these "three" cases that were being testified about now (in the "south" end of the Chattahoochee) were not even among the 10 "pattern" cases that the court, to this day, understands itself to have permitted into the trial. By asking Brown that leading question about bodies found in the south end of the river, Mallard was, in his own way, introducing "pattern," or other cases beyond those of Cater and Payne, the only two cases that Wayne Williams was standing trial for.

But soon the prosecution itself would become entangled in its own web of illogic. Those 10 so-called "pattern" cases that the prosecution would succeed in getting Judge Cooper to allow into the trial against Williams really amounted to no pattern at all.

Certainly none of these 10 cases selected by the prosecution bore any resemblance to the Cater and Payne cases in at least one important respect: Unlike Cater and Payne, who had turned up dead in the Chattahoochee River, not a single victim among those 10 "pattern" cases had been found in the Chattahoochee. And only *one* of those 10 victims, Joseph (Jo-Jo) Bell, turned up in *any* river (the South River).

"Pattern"? What pattern?

Furthermore, not all the bodies found (that Mallard now was asking Brown about) before February 11 were included among those 10 "pattern" cases. So, evidence clearly was coming into the Cater and Payne cases that was of questionable admissibility.

Responding to Mallard's question about clothing prior to February 11, Brown again answered incorrectly: "Yes, sir, prior to the article, the bodies were found with clothing."

Besides erring in his answers to some of Mallard's questions, Brown suffered two other problems with his testimony: (1) The basis of his theory about the change in the pattern is illogical. The condition of the bodies when they were *found* had no relevance to the timing of the article about the fibers. Bodies found after that date had been murdered before that date. Patrick Baltazar is a case in point. So, if Brown's theory seemed to be supported by the facts, it was accidental; (2) Brown may have been a victim of his own List in not recognizing the pitfall that Pat Man Rogers' case offered to his theory. Although Pat Man was found dead in a river long before the article that is the basis for Brown's theory (Pat Man was found on December 7, 1980), Pat Man was not recognized on The List until more than two weeks *after* the article.

To put Brown's testimony in proper perspective with the facts, one need look only to the week preceding the critical February 11 date and to the week following: On February 6, the body of Lubie Geter was found semi-nude, a condition that Brown said did not begin until after February 11. On February 13, the body of Patrick Baltazar was found fully clothed. But Brown had said, after February 11, "we then started finding bodies . . . nude or semi-nude."

Also on February 13, the skeletal remains of a victim identified as Jefferey Mathis were found. No clothing was found. Which fit Brown's newly changed "pattern"—found nude after February 11. But Mathis had been missing and presumed dead for 11 months when the skeleton identified as his was found "nude." Absolutely nothing fit Brown's so-called pattern! Psychic Dorothy Allison had done better.

"After the article," Mallard led on, "were the bodies recovered from the river nude or semi-nude or fully clothed?"

"After the article appeared in the paper," Brown replied in follow-the-leader fashion, "we then started finding the bodies in the river either nude or semi-nude [whatever semi-nude means]."

This time Brown was correct, but it was a damnable half-truth. He didn't say—nor was he asked to say—that they also continued to find List victims *not in the river* and *fully clothed*—victims Brown would say that Wayne Williams murdered.

Many observers had been struck by the apparent insult that Binder had dealt to Brown, but they overlooked the real issue about the English language, which was the illogic and misinformation woven into Brown's eloquent answers. He wasn't testifying to the facts, so you have to give him the benefit of the doubt and assume he didn't know them. That is the nicest thing that can be said about it.

Here, then, is a quick recap of the facts concerning Lee Brown's testimony about this so-called change in the pattern to rivers and to nude or semi-nude:

Before the article appeared on February 11, 1981, there had been 18 List victims found. One was *in a river.* One was within a foot or two of a river after apparently having been thrown or pushed off a bridge. Five were either nude or semi-nude.

Of the 10 List victims (plus John Porter, added at the trial) found after February 11, seven were found in rivers and *four were not.* Seven were found nude or partially clothed, and four were found fully clothed.

Thus, there was *no change* which can be related to the February 11, 1981, newspaper article. There were river victims before *and* after that date. There were nude or partially nude victims before *and* after that date. There were fully clothed victims before *and* after that date. There were non-river victims before *and* after that date. Lee Brown's so-called pattern change was another police farce.

Soon the state would clearly introduce 10 "pattern" cases against Wayne Williams (all except that of 28-year-old John Porter had made The List):

1. Patrick Baltazar
2. William Barrett
3. Joseph (Jo-Jo) Bell
4. Alfred Evans
5. Lubie Geter
6. Eric Middlebrooks
7. John Porter
8. Terry Pue
9. Larry Rogers
10. Charles Stephens

Now what was Brown's changed-pattern testimony all about? Logic would suggest that the "pattern" cases the state had selected would be victims who went into rivers, either nude or semi-nude, right? See for yourself:

Incredibly, of these 10 so-called "pattern" victims, *only two were nude or semi-nude* and *only one went into a river.* Jo-Jo Bell was found in the South River, not the Chattahoochee River, where the two victims that the "pattern" was supposed to match—Cater and Payne—had been found. Four of the 10 disappeared and turned up dead after February 11.

If, as Lee Brown testified, the pattern changed to nude or semi-nude victims in rivers, where is the pattern in the state's hand-picked "pattern" cases?

The mistakes in Brown's trial testimony were perpetuated by the news media—and thus never were corrected for the public's benefit and understanding of Atlanta's murders. Even distinguished reporters such as Murray Kempton of *Newsday* and Art Harris of the *Washington Post*, reviewing their courtroom notes, subsequently reported in error that bodies first turned up in rivers as late as March of 1981. (Kempton's report was reprinted without correction after the trial in *Atlanta Weekly*, the magazine of the Sunday *Atlanta Journal-Constitution.*)

Like so many others, notably the prosecution and police, both reporters apparently had forgotten—or, because of The List, didn't know—about Patrick Rogers. Perhaps reporters for out-of-town newspapers (even those who live in Atlanta) can be forgiven. At least, Lee Brown should have remembered Pat Man. He had taken enough heat from some reporters and critics of the investigation for refusing to assign Pat Man's case to The List until nearly four months after he disappeared.

There is a valuable lesson for the news media here: Getting the story from officialdom—and even quoting a public official's courtroom testimony and other statements correctly—is no guarantee that a reporter is telling the story of what actually happened.

I handed a note to Al Binder (and later wrote him a detailed letter) about the discrepancies in Lee Brown's testimony, as they pertained to Pat Man. But it wasn't until weeks later, only about one hour before his closing arguments began, that Binder would recall them and ask me to explain them to him again. Too late, perhaps, for Wayne Williams.

Lynn Whatley, Williams' attorney on appeal, gave me the following list which he says assistant prosecutor Joe Drolet spelled out as *the* "pattern" in the Williams case:

1. Black male.
2. No evidence of forced abduction.
3. Broken home.
4. No apparent motive for disappearance.
5. Poor family situation.
6. No vehicle.
7. Defendant claims no contact.
8. Body disposed of in an unusual manner.
9. Street hustlers.
10. Body found near expressway ramp or major artery.
11. Transported before (or after) they were killed.
12. Asphyxia by strangulation.
13. No valuables.
14. Missing clothing.
15. Similar fibers.

Do these characteristics add up to *the* "pattern," much less any pattern, against Wayne Williams? Let's look at them, one by one, as follows:

—**1. All black males?**—Well, maybe. But remember that two females had made The List and others could have. At least one of them can easily be connected to Nathaniel Cater. There is no reason—absolutely no excuse—for saying that the death of 7-year-old LaTonya Wilson, who lived downstairs from Cater, cannot be related to the others, if the death of Nathaniel Cater can. And if Nathaniel Cater can't be related, then the state has no case against Wayne Williams.

—**2. No evidence of forced abduction**—This is true—again, only if you ignore LaTonya Wilson, Jo-Jo Bell, Earl Terrell, Timmy Hill and the events at Pickfair Avenue and Pickfair Way, *et cetera.* I don't think they were forcibly abducted, either; but there *was evidence* that they were.

It depends on which evidence you choose to believe. In LaTonya's case, a witness says she witnessed a kidnapping. Lee Gooch, who knew several of the victims, said, "It's a kidnapping deal." Patrick Baltazar telephoned the Task Force and said the killer was pursuing him. Earl Terrell's family got a call that he was being held for ransom. A co-worker says Jo-Jo Bell called him for help. Timmy Hill's sister said she saw a man put "mud" over Timmy's face and take him away in a taxi.

These claims may not be authentic, but they are evidence. Why are any of these witnesses less believable than one who testified that he saw Wayne Williams with Payne as the witness was being driven 50 miles per hour down a street? One reason may be that no one bothered to call them to testify.

Moreover, if the state's contention is right, it hardly constitutes a pattern. First, the statement is fallacious. Insofar as there is no evidence that a victim was forcibly abducted, there is an equal lack of evidence that they were *not* forcibly abducted. What we really have is *no sure knowledge* of the circumstances of the disappearances. To say they *were not* forcibly abducted (any or all) because there is no evidence that they *were* forcibly abducted is the fallacy of *non-sequitur.*

Secondly, I would contend that in almost all murders, there is no evidence of forcible abduction. The complement of the state's claim is that all murder cases where there is no sign of forcible abduction were committed by Wayne Williams.

—**3. Broken home**—Nathaniel Cater didn't come from a broken home, having lived with his family—mother, father and siblings—until he was almost 28 years old. There is really no indication that Jimmy Ray Payne ever had a home to be broken. But let's suppose his situation qualifies as a "broken home." If the pattern of "10" cases is supposed to match the two cases in which Wayne Williams was convicted, you can forget "broken homes" because one-out-of-two (50%) is a random happening—*not a pattern.*

Even so, are we supposed to believe that Wayne Williams ran background checks on his alleged victims? In the state's case, there is something for everybody—hardly a "pattern," if you follow the evidence closely. There was the Williams who cultivated his victims for months, even years. Then there was the Williams who skulked around the Omni, waiting to get his hands on a hapless victim. It is ludicrous to think that Williams selected victims on the basis of whether they came from a broken home. A pattern shared by the victims has no relationship to the killer unless it put them in contact with the killer. Coming from a broken home does not necessarily put anyone in contact with Wayne Williams.

—**4. No apparent motive for disappearance**—Of all the people who disappeared without an apparent motive, only those whose names appear on a pre-selected List are included in the state's pattern. If all those victims whose disappearances were without apparent motive did fit this "pattern," then most of the missing persons in the world would fit the "pattern" of Atlanta's murders.

—**5. Poor family situation**—Are we talking about economics? Or is this another synonym for a broken home if one of the combatants would move out? Or, is this a situation which might be *better* if it were a broken home? What does "poor family situation" mean? "Poor" cannot be defined. It is a relative term based solely on subjective judgment. You can't measure "poor," so it cannot be a part of a pattern because you can never be sure that it is there.

—**6. No vehicle**—This is incorrect. Now we are back to the visions of the "random killer." These victims are susceptible to him because he offers them a ride and "they have no vehicles."

Bunk! Eric Middlebrooks was found within two or three feet of the bicycle he was riding, and the bicycle Milton Harvey was riding was found abandoned. Did they mean "motor vehicle"?

Not surprisingly, most of the victims on The List didn't own cars. Twenty-two of the 29 (including John Porter) murder victims were not yet old enough to drive in the state of Georgia. Therefore every victim under 16 years old fits the state's pattern, and many over 16 do, too. But these victims had access to cars. Lubie Geter was taken in his brother's car to the point where he disappeared.

Wayne Williams didn't own a car, either. Therefore, according to the state, Williams fits the "pattern" of the victims.

—**7. Defendant claims no contact**—Wayne Williams also claims no contact with any other murder victim. Therefore, if one follows the logic of the state's "pattern," *all* murder victims fit the pattern. Of course, we know better than that.

—**8. Body disposed of in an unusual manner**—The last time I looked, "unusual" was an antonym for pattern. "Usual" means that a similarity or "pattern" exists. If these bodies were disposed of in an unusual manner, what, then, is the *usual* manner for disposing of a body? They were laid on their backs, assistant prosecutor Joseph Drolet would say. So?

Try a test with a child or small person. Pick the person up and hold him in your arms. Is he lying across your arms on his back or his stomach? Now lay him down. Is he on his back or stomach? He's on his back because people don't bend the other way. It is absolutely usual for someone to be laid on his back.

Moreover, since victims were found on land, in water, indoors and outdoors, that leaves only in the air and underground. There was no attempt to cremate, dismember, use acids or any number of other gruesome methods of disposal which might be considered unusual. There were almost as many ways of disposal as there were methods of killing, which indicates that the only "pattern" here is that *there is no pattern to the disposals.*

Approximately 25% of The List victims went into water. Both, or 100% of the victims Williams is accused of killing, went into water. Yet the "pattern" picked by the state, as the "pattern" that Cater and Payne fit, included only one, or 10%.

—**9. Street hustlers**—Patrick Baltazar, Jo-Jo Bell, Bubba Duncan and possibly others had jobs. Lubie Geter made as much as $20 on some days, selling car deodorizers. Which are street hustlers and which are not? In my neighborhood, it isn't called hustling; it's called enterprising.

Of the total number of young black males murdered in America (which is by far the largest recognizable group of murder victims), how many were *not* street hustlers—if those on The List are? I would guess that most of them are, since young black males also make up the largest recognizable group of the unemployed.

Again, "street hustler" is one of those terms thrown out for those who think that Wayne Williams was an opportunistic random killer. Street hustling puts kids in a dangerous position, if a random killer is out there looking for victims.

—**10. Body found near expressway ramp or major artery**—What happened to rivers? Indeed, there was—and perhaps still is—a geographic pattern to these cases. But being found near an expressway ramp or a major artery wasn't it. Of 29 victims, only four were found close to an expressway. William Barrett and Terry Pue were found relatively close to one (about a half mile away), as was Eric Middlebrooks. But Middlebrooks was with the bicycle he was riding. Otherwise, in a city like Atlanta, it is almost impossible not to be found "near" a major artery.

In four cases where victims turned up dead near expressways, down to a matter of yards, they still were as far away as miles from the nearest exit.

—**11. Transported before (or after) they were killed**—How could the state possibly know this? No one knows and no one has ever testified (except express theories) where or when any of these victims died. We know only where the remains were finally found, but we don't even know that they were always there after their deaths.

One witness would say she saw Wayne Williams transporting 20-year-old victim Larry Rogers, and her insinuation was that Rogers was dead. The defense would not call still another witness who says he saw someone other than Wayne Williams transporting the dead body of 12-year-old Charles Stephens. But there is even better evidence that 14-year-old Eric Middlebrooks was not transported.

—**12. Asphyxia by strangulation**—Wrong again. Only six of the 29 victims (those on The List, plus Porter) were said to have been "strangled," and there are real doubts about some of these. The prosecution says from time to time that one of these "strangulation victims" was stabbed, when it suits its purposes better. For example, when it talks about blood stains in Williams' station wagon matching the blood type of William Barrett, it talks of Barrett being stabbed. Otherwise, he is a "strangulation victim."

Only four of the 10 victims selected by the state as "pattern" cases might have been strangled, if you agree with the autopsies. We already have discussed the wide variety of methods of death in these cases. There's no "pattern" here, either.

—**13. No valuables**—Does this mean that the motive was robbery? In the case of Eric Middlebrooks, there was some pocket change lying nearby. I don't know whether the state is trying to say that the victims didn't have valuables to steal, thus ruling out robbery, or vice versa.

—**14. Missing clothing**—Insofar as the state means "nude or semi-nude," we have already disposed of this notion. But, if the state means the rumors that each of the victims was missing some item of clothing, then—if substantiated—this could be one item of the state's 15 "pattern" criteria that could constitute a real pattern.

The problem is, the state never attempted to substantiate it. Nothing was introduced at the trial concerning it. As attorney Lynn Whatley told me, "Man, they didn't bring any evidence into court to even try to prove their pattern. There was no testimony about broken homes or the economic conditions of the victims' families. It's just like they pulled this stuff out of the air." They did.

—**15. Similar fibers**—Now that we know the other 14 criteria are invalid, based on the evidence submitted, it remains to be seen whether the fiber connections are valid, let alone true.

I was astonished to hear Lee Brown testify to *any* pattern. Was this the same Lee Brown who had steadfastly insisted during the investigation that there was *no pattern*? Wasn't it also Lee Brown who had called a meeting of media executives back in November of 1980, urging them to help him dispel the rumors that there was a pattern to these cases?

Was prosecutor Lewis Slaton the same Lewis Slaton who had contended, when The List totaled 20 victims, that there was no connection between an early group of killings and the later group of killings? The "two-string" theory, the local newspapers called it. Was this the same Lewis Slaton who said there might be as many as "10 killers"? He was, of course, basing this assertion on the differences among the cases. Obviously, this 15-point "pattern" was meaningless to Slaton then—just as it still seems meaningless to me now.

For me, it was indeed strange to sit there at the defense table, hearing the state suddenly say what I had pleaded with the authorities to understand for 1½ years—that there *was* a pattern to the murders. Too bad, I thought, that they still didn't know what that pattern was—that it encompassed myriad personal and geographic connections among the victims.

I had found exactly what the state needed—a plausible pattern. I would have been delighted to take the prosecution and the jury, too, on the grand tour of death. It would have helped them understand the cases.

Even Wayne Williams agreed that it was good for him that I wasn't sitting at the prosecution table. Binder and Whatley were glad, too. In fact, Binder asked me to write a paper, pointing out the things that might tend to convict Wayne Williams. Neither the prosecution nor the defense would make available to the jurors any information or testimony concerning the much stronger pattern of geographic and personal connections among the victims. What a shame for the jury and the public.

I always thought that both Lee Brown and Lewis Slaton, true to law-enforcement tradition, were hung up in the *modus-operandi* myth. Slaton had said as much with his "two-string" theory. If they were wrong, I suspected that they would hide behind the "police business" screen and say that they knew otherwise all along, but couldn't say so for fear of jeopardizing the investigation. Nonsense! They were guessing about the cases then, and Brown's testimony about the "changing pattern" shows he was still guessing, and poorly.

But now, here was Lee Brown in the Wayne Williams trial in 1982, saying the pattern that he said didn't exist in 1980 and 1981 had changed. He had also said earlier that none of the cases not on The List was connected to those on The List, which he also said were not connected to each other. Now, Brown was telling the jury about the *changes* in the "pattern."

It was shocking that Lee Brown knew so little about the cases—and even more astounding that the prosecutors obviously shared Brown's lack of knowledge of the cases and even put him on the witness stand to show to the world his lack of knowledge of them.

The implication by the state, of course, was that the killer was reading the newspapers and he saw this February 11, 1981, story about fibers, which presumably caused him to begin throwing victims, nude or *semi-nude*, into rivers to keep police from finding these fibers.

Horse hockey! This would have made the killer a very selective reader since he chose to ignore a follow-up article that said even though the bodies were now being found in rivers, the state crime lab was still able to find the fibers!

They still don't know what the pattern is. As late as May 16, 1983, in the prosecution's brief and testimony before the Georgia Supreme Court, the state still struggled to get a handle on the pattern in these cases. At least one Supreme Court judge made it no secret that he couldn't find the state's "pattern," in the brief or testimony.

The police said the pattern changed to throwing bodies into rivers. But the prosecution selected only one river case to include in its 10 "pattern" cases. You just can't have a "pattern" of one. The remainder of the state's pattern is, in reality, a fabricated non-pattern.

If the state's 10 "pattern" cases match the two cases Williams is charged with (they are supposed to match, in order to be admissible), I can't find the similarities other than "black males." There is no real doubt in my mind that Cater and Payne were murdered or that their deaths were connected to other deaths. But this connection certainly wasn't in the dreamed-up way that the prosecution contended, to wit:

—The average age of victims Cater and Payne in the charged cases was 24. The average age in the "pattern" cases was 16.

—The cause of death in the charged cases was unknown (called "asphyxia"). Of the 10 "pattern" cases, only three were unknown (called "asphyxia"). One victim was bludgeoned, one was supposedly suffocated, four were strangled and one was stabbed. Suffocation and strangulation are specific forms of asphyxia, thus "known" causes of death.

—Both victims in the charged cases (Cater and Payne) were found in the Chattahoochee River. No victim in the 10 "pattern" cases was found in the Chattahoochee River, although one, Joseph (Jo-Jo) Bell, was found in the South River. The other nine were found on dry land.

—Two victims in the 10 "pattern" cases did not have the green trilobal carpet fibers, but four of the non-"pattern" victims (those not selected by the state) did. All 10 victims in the "pattern" cases had the light-violet acetate fiber, but so did eight of the non-"pattern" victims.

—One of the "pattern" victims (Alfred Evans) was found within 100 yards of—and on the same day as—his murdered friend (Edward Hope Smith), who is a non-"pattern" victim. In fact, the authorities still say Wayne Williams didn't kill Edward Hope Smith.

The state's 10 "pattern" cases were introduced against Wayne Williams *not* because they fit a pattern, but because they enabled the state to introduce certain evidence into the trial, just as others were left out to keep certain evidence out of the trial.

The state needed the cases of Eric Middlebrooks, William Barrett and John Porter because there were no other "blood" deaths, except those of Pat Man, whom the state overlooked, and Smith, whom the state did not want to associate with Williams.

The state needed Patrick Baltazar because of its obsession with the Omni. It needed the cases of Jo-Jo Bell, Lubie Geter, Terry Pue, Larry Rogers and William Barrett because these cases provided the so-called "eyewitnesses" (none saw Wayne Williams do anything to anybody).

Moreover, the state needed Alfred Evans' case because it tied the Plymouth formerly owned by Wayne Williams to one segment of its fiber evidence. This, in turn, provided the provocative "blue light, siren and police radio" testimony (for random-killing theory buffs).

Why the state picked Charles Stephens as one of its 10 "pattern" cases, I don't know. Even in hindsight, it doesn't seem to have been a wise choice, since Stephens was one of those victims who *could not* have gotten fibers the way the state's fiber experts said he would have had to have gotten them.

Drolet, the assistant prosecutor, then stated that the later victims were older because of the dusk-to-dawn curfew instituted by the city of Atlanta. This showed Drolet's lack of understanding of the cases. But perhaps his remark seemed plausible to him. We've already discussed the illogic of any such contention.

Additionally, Drolet said that proving many of Williams' statements false is "evidence of consciousness of guilt." If that's true about false statements, then many people including prosecutors, defense attorneys and witnesses, share in the consciousness of guilt because they all made a lot of false statements—unwittingly, perhaps, but surely false. Many false statements were made in the trial of Wayne Williams. It was anything but the whole truth, so help me!

This long, foregoing discussion of "pattern" is important. For without "pattern," the state could not have introduced the mountain of evidence from its 10 "pattern" cases that virtually buried the jury in quantity, but not quality, of evidence. I am of the opinion that the state so far had failed to show a pattern, just as it never proved *corpus delicti.*

So it came down to this: the only viable "pattern" the state could have was in its so-called "similar fibers." Would they hold up?

Next, the prosecution called Benjamin Kittle from the Army Corps of Engineers. Kittle gave a very technical and detailed report which added up to the body of Jimmy Ray Payne (not Nathaniel Cater) coming from the bridge where the "splash" (supposedly Cater's body) was heard. He denied that there was any problem with the report's co-author about changes Kittle had made in it after it was first submitted.

The study was purported to be a hydrological study. Binder got Kittle, an engineer, to admit that he was not a professional hydrologist, but that the co-author is. In the report, Kittle had said that the validity of the findings would depend on the experience of the investigator.

Then Binder asked him about his experience at projecting the path a body would travel through a specific body of water—which is what this study purported to do. Binder asked how many times he had done such a projection.

Kittle's answer: "Once, this time."

Major Watson W. Holley of the Atlanta police department had been in charge of coordinating the bridge stakeouts. But, he could not say whether the Jackson Parkway bridge was under surveillance during the time that Jimmy Ray Payne was missing. He did say that no one was under the bridge until April 26, 1981, the day before Payne's body was found.

A large, finely detailed Corps of Engineers map of Atlanta was placed on an easel. Holley stood before it in full uniform. His foot in a cast, he tucked it up behind his right calf while his weight rested on a yellowed crutch.

Assistant prosecutor Jack Mallard asked Holley to point to U.S. 278, Bankhead Highway, on the map. Holley couldn't find it. Mallard tried hard to lead him. Holley still couldn't find Bankhead Highway. Binder finally objected to Mallard's efforts to coach his witness, arguing that Holley was an Atlanta police officer and should be able to find a clearly marked federal highway, and one where Holley had positioned stakeout teams.

Holley finally made a stab and selected Georgia Highway 166.

"Farther up, farther up," Mallard coached.

"Your honor!" Binder exhorted.

Mallard gave up. Major Holley never did find U.S. 278 on the map. It was embarrassing.

As the second day of testimony progressed, the jury got its first look at the sophisticated (but inaccurate) "scale" model of the bridge scene which had been constructed by the FBI. The model was 12 feet long.

More dismal commentary on the criminal-justice process greeted me on the morning of the third day of testimony. The January 8, 1982, *Atlanta Constitution* story read, in part:

"Despite a confession and eyewitness testimony, an Atlanta man accused of stabbing the bartender of Mary Mac's restaurant last year has been found innocent by a Fulton County Superior Court jury."

Wayne Williams should have been so lucky as to have drawn that jury—and it could have just as easily happened. Lawyers would like to have you think that they are skilled in jury selection. Mary Welcome brought a psychologist, Brad Bayless, to Atlanta to advise her on jury selection. He joined the defense at the table during *voire dire*. Phooey! There's a hell of a lot of luck in the criminal-justice game, and most of it pertains to whomever sits in that jury box.

Police recruit Bob Campbell testified that he knew the splash was a body because he was on a high school swimming team and had experience as a lifeguard. He said this made him familiar with the sounds of bodies hitting the water.

At the trial, Al Binder and I would share the same thought at the same moment. As I framed the question in my mind, it spilled from Binder's lips. He asked Campbell, the erstwhile swimmer and lifeguard: "Did you jump into the water and try to save that person?"

Campbell's answer: "No." Binder would point out that the officer didn't know whether this object that the officer thought was a body was dead or alive when it hit the water. Binder also pointed out that it was a policeman's duty to save lives. The officer agreed, but went on to say that he didn't know what was in that water, that it was dark and that he wasn't about to jump in to find out. Binder would say that the people of Atlanta must be proud to have such brave officers working for them.

The slur apparently went over Campbell's head, and he agreed with Binder, as if Binder's sarcastic crack had been a compliment.

One additional detail Campbell added to the events of May 22, 1981, at the Jackson Parkway bridge was that an Atlanta police sergeant came to the bridge that morning and chucked a concrete block into the water. He was trying to duplicate the sound of the splash that Campbell had heard earlier that morning.

The splash from the single concrete block was not "big" enough, Campbell said he told the sergeant. So, a double concrete block was obtained from blocks that were conveniently stacked at the nearby liquor store. The double block was tossed in the water from the bridge. That wasn't loud enough, either. (A standard concrete block weighs 27½ pounds.)

Now they hurled three blocks. That was it. That sounded like the splash. If three concrete blocks sounded like the splash Campbell heard, how can he tell the difference between a splash by three concrete blocks and a splash by a 140-pound body? He couldn't, of course—his lifeguard training and swim-team membership notwithstanding.

Former police recruit Ken Lawson, who also worked on the bridge details, contends that the block test did not take place that same morning (May 22). He says that Campbell was subsequently called out of recruit school and taken to the bridge to do the block test.

The timing didn't bother me. What bothered me was that the defense was letting in the absolutely unscientific results of this test without objection. Then Campbell was allowed to give hearsay evidence about a test conducted by the police weeks after the Wayne Williams incident that determined the expansion plate in the bridge would not make the clanking noise when a car went across it at less than 10 miles per hour. Again, the defense didn't object.

Interestingly, the defense later would produce an accoustics "expert" who would have testified differently. But he never got a chance. The prosecution objected and Judge Cooper would bar the testimony on the grounds that the testers could not duplicate the *exact* conditions of the morning of May 22, 1981. But "concrete-block" bodies are acceptable?

(The defense would eventually come up with an accoustical engineer and sneak in the comment that if a police recruit said he did not hear Wayne Williams' car roll onto the Jackson Parkway bridge, the recruit was either asleep or wasn't listening.)

When Atlanta police recruit Freddie Jacobs took the stand to testify about the "splash," defense attorney Mary Welcome took over the cross examination. Binder had recovered pretty well from his *faux pas* in asking Lee Brown if he understood English.

Now Binder was the relentless cross-examiner that everyone expected him to be. There was a definite feeling that Binder was on a roll and he had momentum with him.

Even so, Mary Welcome had questioned Jacobs before—during the preliminary hearings. She should know his weak points.

But now, she was embarrassingly inept.

In answer to a Mary Welcome question, Jacobs said, "It was November, the last time I was here in the courthouse."

"And this is December," Welcome rejoined. Her point was that a meeting involving Jacobs at the courthouse had been quite recent.

"This is January," Jacobs said, correcting her. Laughter rippled across the courtroom. Mary Welcome was flustered.

"Of course, Officer Campbell," Welcome said.

"I'm Jacobs," he corrected her again.

It didn't get much better for Welcome with this witness. He kept answering the questions she asked, but she wasn't asking the right questions, although she tried time and again.

Al Binder's face reddened. "She turned a two-bit witness into a superstar," he whispered in disgust. A spectator leaving the courtroom at the next recess said, "If I was Wayne Williams, I'd fire her on the spot. That was pitiful, man." The spectator's companion shook her head in agreement.

The defense lost momentum when Binder stopped cross-examining, even briefly. And Mary Welcome had dug a hole. That momentum was never regained. After watching Binder outwit doctors, engineers and cops at their own game, I had thought that he might be invincible, if only he softened the contentious manner he had exhibited while questioning Lee Brown. But Binder never came back as rapier clean as he had been before Mary Welcome's bumbling cross-examination of Freddie Jacobs.

FBI Agent Greg Gilliland testified that Wayne Williams asked him, when Williams was first stopped: Had the agent seen the two Purolator trucks or station wagons that were on the bridge at the same time that Williams was?

Jack Mallard then asked Gilliland, "Did you see any other vehicle on the bridge?"

"There was only one vehicle," Gilliland responded.

"So what," I thought. Had it been forgotten that Gilliland also had said he never saw Wayne Williams' vehicle until it came north on the bridge, with police officer Carl Holden following?

Wayne Williams was talking about seeing these other vehicles when he first crossed the bridge going south. So while Gilliland's testimony was correct, it really didn't dispute Williams' testimony, even though it was left for the jury to suppose that Gilliland had.

Purolator's regional manager would testify that no vehicles belonging to the company were in the area of the bridge between 2 and 4 a.m. on May 22. Williams later told me that he wasn't sure they were Purolator trucks, just that their markings resembled Purolator markings. He said they most closely resembled "El Caminos with camper tops." I was able to demonstrate later that only one El Camino might have been involved.

Officer Carl Holden, who drove the unmarked chase car, testified that Wayne Williams did not make a telephone call or gather boxes before exiting the liquor store parking lot, as Mallard said Williams had told Agent Gilliland when he was first stopped.

Williams says that is not what he had told Agent Gilliland. Rather, he says, he told Gilliland and the others who stopped him that he had gone on to the next intersection and turned around at the Starvin' Marvin food store after gathering boxes and trying to make a phone call there.

If Williams did what stakeout officer Carl Holden said he did, then he made a right turn into the liquor store parking lot and turned around before making another left turn and heading back north across the Jackson Parkway bridge.

Were those empty boxes in Williams' vehicle? Amazingly, no one asked. And would Williams have said he gathered the boxes if they were not in his vehicle? Of course, boxes could have been in the station wagon all along. But were they there at all? "Yes," Wayne Williams told me. "The boxes filled the wagon. If I didn't pick them up when I said, then there wasn't room enough in there for no body like they said."

If Agent Greg Gilliland had seen Wayne Williams' station wagon come south across that bridge within moments before the supposed turn-around, I would have concluded long ago that Wayne Williams was probably lying. But Gilliland didn't see him come south.

If either Carl Holden or Freddie Jacobs made one mistake or one assumption, then what happened on that bridge that morning is still up for grabs. Except for where Wayne Williams turned around, there is no real difference between what Wayne Williams says happened and what the police say happened. The only differences that remain are in what the police theorize happened—not in what they said they saw.

The state would imply that the murder scenes were at Wayne Williams' house. Its testimony of the bridge incident raises a question about the contention that the murders happened at Williams' house. If so, then Wayne Williams was carrying the body the wrong way—toward his house—before, the state says, he dumped the body off—if he did. Jack Mallard would make the point about direction toward Williams' home later, without realizing it to be a two-edged sword.

Monday, January 12, 1982, was the coldest day of the 20th Century in Atlanta. The temperature plunged to 5 degrees below zero. I fumbled, trying to get my all-but-frostbitten fingers to manuever eight quarters into the little slot that would allow me to park within two blocks of the Fulton County Courthouse. I pulled my jacket tight against the scathing wind and ran (well, trotted) to the courthouse.

There, an FBI agent, William McGrath, testified that he went to the Williamses' home later the morning of May 22. The stories of Wayne Williams' parents and of the FBI differ sharply about what happened while Agent McGrath was there. Homer and Faye Williams, for instance, insist that they gave Agent McGrath the piece of paper on which the phone number of Cheryl Johnson was written. The FBI says it received no such paper.

Prosecution witnesses said they didn't see Williams at the Sans Souci nightclub—another stop in Williams' account of his activities of the night and morning of May 21 and May 22, 1981, respectively.

McGrath said that after the incident on the bridge, he returned to the FBI office and tried to telephone the number that Williams had given him for Cheryl Johnson. Williams had told McGrath that he tried the number from a phone booth.

A voice answered, Williams said, with a curt "She ain't here," and hung up. When McGrath dialed the number that he swore Williams gave him, he got a recording telling him the number had been changed. Dialing the new number, McGrath reached an employee of Merle Norman Cosmetics. McGrath would later admit that Williams had told him he could be wrong, by one digit (which is a bunch of possibilities in a 7-digit number—about 5,000).

The phone number the FBI said Williams gave it is not the same number that Williams says he gave the FBI.

Agent McGrath also testified that a handwritten message shown to him by Williams indicated that the Cheryl Johnson he was trying to find lived on Benson Poole Road, in an apartment designated partially by the letter "F."

Although I had never accepted either version of what happened on that morning of May 22, the fact that Williams had a handwritten note to furnish to the FBI leads me to think that Williams' information may be incorrect, but truthful.

Can you imagine someone preparing a handwritten note in advance as an alibi, then giving it to the FBI, knowing that it will be checked out and found false? And, what kind of filing system would Williams have had to have in his car to produce a note documenting what he was doing at any given location wherever he might be stopped? I was beginning to accept that Wayne Williams must have been the most stupid "cunning" criminal of all time. He baffles the "experts" for almost two years and then, when they catch him, he virtually hands them their case by giving them all of this phony information that he knows is going to check out as false. He takes a lie detector and flunks, then takes another and flunks, then holds a news conference and tells the world he flunked. He waives his constitutional rights and requests a meeting with the prosecutor to tell him his story. I don't think Williams is bright enough to play that good a game of "he thinks, I think, he thinks, I think."

Several apartment managers (but obviously not all) from the general area where Williams said Cheryl Johnson lived were brought in by the prosecution to testify that there was no apartment with a designation of "F"—and no Cheryl Johnson—in their complexes. Under cross-examination, they also admitted that they had no idea who might be residing with any tenant at any given time.

Williams also had told the officers that morning near the bridge that he had been to the Sans Souci to retrieve his tape recorder. Gino Jordon, operator of the nightclub, testified that it was Friday, May 22—not

Thursday night, May 21—when Williams came to get his recorder. Perhaps he went back. Williams said he wasn't successful in seeing Jordon on May 21. There's no conflict in Jordon's and Williams' stories.

The *Atlanta Constitution*'s Gail Epstein and Ken Willis betrayed a lack of understanding of the trial process by reporting: ". . . no witnesses were presented who could say they saw Williams at the nightclub on Thursday night and therefore back up his alibi."

No one can say that this reporting isn't true, but certainly it misleads the reader. Did Epstein and Willis expect the *state* to call witnesses to back up Williams' alibi? Certainly they should understand that the defense is not at liberty to call witnesses during the prosecution's presentation of its case. Shouldn't they?

Now the state moved to the case it said the splash was all about—the death of 27-year-old Nathaniel Cater. A man named Alan Maddox told of seeing Cater's body, floating as if at anchor, snared on a tree.

Fulton County Medical Examiner Robert Stivers testified that a "choke hold" *probably* administered from behind was *likely* used to strangle Cater. Pure guesswork again. The doctor has no idea how Cater was really killed. He doesn't even know for sure that Cater was strangled. Too many people don't hear—or they brush aside the significance of—words like "probably" and "likely." The sheer conjecture of the medical examiner comes across like "scientific medical fact."

Harking back to the Payne case, Stivers, who is Saleh Zaki's boss, was asked about changing autopsy reports. Dr. Stivers said it wasn't unusual to amend a death certificate, as was done in the Jimmy Ray Payne case. He said they often learn things later that cause them to change their findings.

But the question and the answer didn't address the issue. Zaki had testified that he did *not* change his findings in the Payne case. Instead, in answer to a prosecutor's question, he said he issued a second death certificate to correct an error he made in the first.

Stivers' answer did nothing to resolve the sinister implications of the second death certificate. It might not be unusual to amend a death certificate, *as was done* in the Payne case. But it was unusual as hell to amend a death certificate *for the reason* it was done in the Payne case. The question and answer seemed carefully worded to fool somebody.

Stivers went on to say that "methods of determining an exact time of death are often unreliable." This was an effort to head off defense claims that Cater had been dead longer than the two days dictated by the state's case. Here, the prosecution attacked medical examiners' ability to fix the exact time of death because that fixing was important to the defense's case. Had the prosecution needed the exact time of death to prove Wayne Williams' guilt, it would have been the defense arguing that the time could not be accurately fixed. The *game* of criminal justice goes on.

In *"Weekend with the Rabbi,"* Harry Kemelman likens the criminal-justice game to football. I think it is rather more like baseball. There are opposing teams. The judge is the umpire and the jury spectators. The defendant is the ball being knocked and tossed about. The umpire stands by and lets either team violate the rules—the onus is on the other team to catch them in the act. Occasionally, the umpire will call a "balk," while the jury sits in the stands and wonders what the arguments at the bench are all about.

Next, Margaret Carter would come to the stand to give her previously discussed testimony about Williams talking with Cater in front of Cater's Dixie Hills apartment, while Williams' dog romped in the area.

The next prosecution witness said that Wayne Williams paid him to distribute flyers inside the Omni. The flyers advertised for musicians for Williams' talent-promotion business, a point that Williams doesn't deny. I wasn't in court that day. I wish I had been. I would have advised Binder to ask the witness about handing out flyers in Thomasville Heights, where Pat Man and Aaron Wyche lived. But the question would go unasked. It was the prosecution which needed the answer.

Then a witness was brought to testify that he once saw Wayne Williams eating a sandwich and drinking a beer at the Omni. The "random-killer" theme was being dredged up again. The witness later admitted that the person he saw could very well have been someone other than Williams.

Frank Wright, an attendant from a gas station about one-half mile from the Jackson Parkway bridge, was called by the prosecution to say that he had sold gas to Williams twice in May of 1981.

The defense should have thanked the prosecution. The attendant worked at the Starvin' Marvin where Williams said he had gone on the morning of May 22 to use the phone and gather boxes. The witness' testimony merely reaffirmed what Williams had said all along—that it wasn't unusual for him to be in that neighborhood and that he drove by other places with phones because he was familiar with the Starvin' Marvin and chose to go there.

Meanwhile, Lyle Nichols, the desk clerk of the Falcon Hotel, provided the first hint as to when Nathaniel Cater was last seen alive before the bridge incident. Four persons had said Cater was alive after the bridge incident, but none was called to testify. Lyle Nichols told the jury he last saw Cater alive at 3 p.m. on May 21, the afternoon before Williams crossed the bridge.

However, the *Atlanta Journal* reported that Nichols testified he last saw Cater alive at about 3 p.m. on *May 22*. The newspaper should have headlined this report instead of burying it in an article on Page 2, Section C. If the *Journal* report was correct, it would have meant that the state's witness had testified to Williams' *innocence,* since Williams had been accused of throwing Cater's body from the bridge almost 12 hours earlier—shortly before 3 *a.m.* on May 22.

January's curse brought Atlanta to a standstill. The winds whipped the rain into a driving storm, and it wasn't long before the rain turned to snow and Atlanta was snarled in "Snowjam '82." Businesses shut down. Schools closed.

That wasn't news in Atlanta, which reacts to snow as if it were an enemy attack. The news was that it really snowed hard this time—and snowed and snowed and snowed. The court recessed at 3 p.m. and stayed recessed for several days.

I had time to ponder the state's testimony that Wayne Williams had lied to FBI agents when he said that some clothes in his station wagon were those he used to play basketball in. They included a pair of long pants. I wish I knew if these pants would have fit Wayne Williams or Nathaniel Cater. They could not have fit both. But no one had bothered to find out if they would have fit Williams.

There were more clothes in Williams' vehicle—two bags full—and I've wondered for almost two years now: Whatever happened to them? According to Williams' mother, the bags of clothes which had been in the station wagon during the events of May 22 had been transferred to her back porch. There they sat, unmolested, during the police searches of the Williamses' home and yard.

Later, a private detective, Sam Walker, working for Mary Welcome, would come across the bags.

"What's in here?" he asked.

When he learned that the bags had been in the station wagon when Williams was stopped near the bridge, he took the bags of clothes to Mary Welcome's office. There, they were stuffed into a drawer.

I mentioned the clothes several times to Al Binder and to Mary Welcome. I suggested that the defense's fiber analyst should take a look at them—and we might look at them, too. To my knowledge, the bags never were opened by the defense. They certainly were not introduced in court. Nor were the contents gone over thoroughly by any fiber analyst. Faye Williams later said she got one bag back.

Since Mary Welcome left that office in a rent dispute, the important bag of clothes probably has long since been consigned to a dump by some cleanup person. Calls to attorney Cliff Bailey of the defense team to ask about their whereabouts have gone unanswered. What was in the bag?

Richard Ernest of the state crime lab described the search of Wayne Williams' station wagon. It was conducted, he said, in the FBI garage overnight on June 3 and 4, 1981, while Williams was being questioned upstairs. The search, Ernest said, took 8½ hours and yielded various fibers, hairs and some suspected blood stains on a seat.

The chief prosecutor, Lewis Slaton, attempted to introduce a recording he had made of an interview he had conducted with Williams at the Fulton County Jail, in the presence of Mary Welcome. Robert McMichael, an investigator from Slaton's office, began the testimony by saying that all questions had been submitted for Williams' and Welcome's approval before they were recorded.

Al Binder rose to object to the admission of the tape. After a prolonged recess, the judge announced that he would require that certain segments of the recording be deleted.

"In view of your honor's ruling," Slaton said, speaking of the order to delete portions, Slaton withdrew McMichael as a witness.

That was a strange twist. The interview with Slaton had been held at the request of Williams himself, who thought that he could convince Slaton of his innocence. Now Williams' attorney, Binder, was objecting to the introduction of a tape that had been pre-approved by Williams' attorney, Welcome.

What was the big secret? It sounded as if it might be dynamite, but it really wasn't much. The recording simply bared several arguments between Wayne Williams and Mary Welcome. The verbal clashes were not uncommon, but Binder thought that the jury might be prejudiced by knowing about them. Apparently Slaton thought so, too—because if the jury wasn't to hear the attorney-client bickering, Slaton wasn't interested in making the jurors privy to the rest of the tape.

Next, the state introduced another recording. This time it was the tape of the press conference that Wayne Williams held in his living room on the morning of June 4, 1981, hours after his overnight interrogation by the FBI. The part about being accused *at the scene* of killing Cater zoomed over everyone's head.

Meanwhile, the *Atlanta Journal* reported that Williams' statement that he knew none of the 28 murder victims on The List, or still-missing 10-year-old Darron Glass, was in conflict with the testimony of Margaret Carter, who said she saw Williams and Cater talking together on a park bench.

I couldn't agree with the *Journal*'s assessment. Even if it was Williams and Cater she saw talking together, it proved nothing. People often talk with people they don't know while sitting on a park bench or in thousands of other circumstances, for that matter.

But the *Atlanta Journal* had particular problems throughout the trial in figuring out what was—or was not—in conflict in the testimony. For example, the newspaper took no issue when it reported that Cater had been seen alive 12 hours after the bridge incident. It didn't see any conflict there, but then it saw them where none existed.

The *Atlanta Constitution* also dwelled on "discrepancies" in Williams' statements. Here are the "damning" inaccuracies:

—The FBI says that on May 22, Williams told agents he took a call from Cheryl Johnson on May 20 and his mother took another call the next day. However, on June 3, the FBI says Williams said he took the call on May 21.

—On May 22, Agent McGrath says, Williams told him he was going to interview Cheryl Johnson at 6:30 a.m. But, on June 3, Williams said the interview with her had been scheduled for 7 a.m. on May 22.

—On May 22, McGrath says, Williams told him there were two trucks or station wagons crossing the bridge at the same time he was. But, on June 3, McGrath says, Williams "changed his story" to a brown Toyota and two El Caminos.

—On May 22, McGrath says, Williams told him he left home during the late evening of May 21. At the June 4 news conference, Williams said he had left his home about 1 a.m. on May 22.

—On May 22, McGrath says, Williams told him he stopped in a liquor store parking lot to call Cheryl Johnson and then he headed back across the bridge. On June 3, according to McGrath, Williams said he stopped at the liquor store to check the woman's number.

If you're looking for lies, you may have a bunch of them. But there is nothing to indicate even the first one. The inconsistencies are in detail, not in concept. Differences in detail are often a result of a difference in perception between the speaker and the listener. Discrepancies in detail may or may not be consequential. And nothing is consequential that is not mutually exclusive.

Wayne Williams could not take the *first* phone call from Cheryl Johnson on both May 21 and May 22. But he could have taken a call on both days. If you carefully read what the *Atlanta Constitution* reported, you will find nothing that is mutually exclusive. But what if there were? Would it be consequential? No, because the issue is whether—in one of those calls—he obtained her address and whether—in one of those calls—he made an appointment with her on May 22.

You can't have a single appointment with someone at two different times on the same day. But is that consequential? No, not if there is still time to arrive for the earlier of the two. It might, however, have been consequential had both times already passed. The time of Williams' appointment in the future had no bearing on what he was doing in the past.

Since an El Camino is a truck, there is nothing mutually exclusive about Williams' statements about the traffic that was on the bridge when he crossed. He mentioned a third vehicle the second time he was questioned. However, that is not a discrepancy. Williams later explained that he saw two vehicles when he went south across the bridge (which is what the police asked him about the first time)—and one vehicle when he returned north.

The time Williams left home would be consequential only if it served to provide him with an alibi. It did not. He had ample time to kill Nathaniel Cater and take him to the bridge before the splash—whether he left home at 1 a.m. or late the evening before.

Williams' statements that he stopped at the liquor store to call Cheryl Johnson and that he stopped there to look for her telephone number are not mutually exclusive. The difference here is probably attributable to perceptions—i.e., what Williams said and meant *versus* what McGrath heard and understood.

Perhaps the overriding question here is: Was any of this necessary to determine whether or not Wayne Williams killed Nathaniel Cater? The answer is "no," despite the time, money and energy spent trying to ferret it all out.

Contrary to the impression given by much of the media, the meeting with Cheryl Johnson is *not Wayne Williams' alibi.* Wayne Williams offered no alibi. He wasn't asked for one. Rather, he was asked to explain what he was doing at the bridge when the police observed him there.

So much for glaring inconsistencies.

But at his news conference, Williams had said many things that never were made clear in court. To understand them, you had to study the resume he handed out, as well as other important documents he distributed on that occasion.

Williams mentioned that a Task Force captain had pointed his finger at him *at the scene* and said, "You killed Nathaniel Cater . . ." Now that was a discrepancy worth reporting.

If Wayne Williams didn't lie in his resume, at least he embellished the truth. He chronicled rapid advancements to the top of his *one-man* radio operation. One-shot assignments became long-term positions of responsibility. He flew in fast military jets and drove NASCAR racers, according to his resume.

But another document Williams furnished at that news conference was never mentioned at the trial—more indication that the facts of these cases and the jury were like two ships passing in the night. This document was, to me, the most damning inconsistency of all. When asked to explain his many contacts with young children, Williams produced a contract for his singing group, "Gemini."

The prosecution would try later to make something of the name "Gemini," the fact that Wayne Williams' birthsign is Gemini and the fact that the astrological sign Gemini—the twins—is often associated with split personalities.

Normally, if a *defendant* mentioned astrological signs having any bearing on his case, it would win him an all-expense paid trip to the psychiatrist. It's much like the *inconsistency* of being asked to raise your right hand and *swear before God,* to tell "the truth, the whole truth and nothing but the truth." But if you ever mention God again during the trial in connection with the real world, people might want to have you committed.

As it was, the prosecution ignored the real issue about Gemini. The contract could have been used by the prosecution to link Williams with at least seven victims on The List and several more who never made it. The contract bore the address of Cap'n Peg's.

These were the kinds of inconsistencies I would have liked to have seen explained in court and reported in the press. But the jury and most of the world knew nothing about Wayne Williams' self-announced connection with Cap'n Peg's, with all that it implied. When I asked Wayne Williams about Cap'n Peg's, he denied ever having been there.

The state was ready to launch into the intricate web of its fiber case. To lay the background, it brought on Herbert T. Pratt of E.I. Dupont de Nemours & Company. Pratt's lecture of the court looked for all the world like a training seminar, complete with overhead projectors, slides and blackboard chit-chat.

Gene Baggett took the stand, representing a major carpet manufacturer, the West Point-Pepperell Company of Dalton, Georgia. He testified that his company sold 1,555 square yards of "Luxaire" carpeting to residential customers in 10 Southeastern states from January to June of 1971. From these figures, the state had reached the unsubstantiated conclusion that only 86 rooms of "Luxaire" could have been sold in 10 Southeastern states during the "first half of the first year" it was on the market.

In an earlier interview, Baggett told me that "Luxaire" was not the only carpet manufactured by West Point-Pepperell that contained the unusual trilobal fibers in question in the Williams case.

This was hole No. 2 in the state's "86 rooms" argument: He said the trilobal fibers of interest to me were used in other models of carpet that were of differing weights from Luxaire, which had been identified as the carpet in Wayne Williams' house.

Hole No. 1 was the state's assertion that estimates were based on *residential* sales. Commercial sales, including apartments, made up another sizeable market. And what happened to the fibers that were used after the "first half of the [first] year['s]" production?

Other carpet also came in the same green color and with the same fibers that were found in Williams' house. Further, Baggett said, the records on the sales of these carpets were incomplete. Hole No. 3.

He added that he had no idea of how much of these carpets had been sold, although he furnished printouts showing that the fiber was in much more abundance than the state was representing.

Baggett also said that unknown quantities of the fibers had been sold to a manufacturer of automobile floormats and that he had no idea of what quantities had been redistributed, or in what colors. Hole No. 4.

I wrote a report on my interview and presented it to Al Binder along with fiber samples, carpet samples, sales printouts and duplications of the laboratory tests performed on the fibers for the FBI by Bell Laboratories in Dalton.

When I heard the state's "86 rooms" claim, I knew immediately that it was presenting another fallacy, wittingly or unwittingly. It was saying that the carpet in Williams' house was rare, but implying that the *fiber* was rare. Obviously, the fiber was *not* nearly as rare as Williams' type of carpet, meaning—to Williams' benefit—that there were *many* places to get the fiber, other than his carpet or carpets like it.

Binder sent along what I had given him to a fiber analyst in California. Twice, the analyst said he had not received the material. A third package was sent. But the analyst never showed up to testify. It was widely conjectured that his testimony might harm Williams' case. What I heard from inside the Williams defense team was that he hadn't come to Atlanta because he hadn't been paid.

In a press conference televised live from the Fulton County Jail, Williams told his version. He said that Durwood Myers (Al Binder's righthand man) had come to the jail to inform him that there was no money to bring the experts in. Williams said Myers told him that the money would be made available if Williams would name Myers as his literary agent over the next 20 years. Then, Williams said, he told Myers what he could do with that offer.

Fiber experts proved difficult to come by. Not the least of the reasons for this was that the state had held a symposium on the fiber evidence prior to the trial, thus co-opting most of the knowledgeable people who might have provided consulting assistance to the defense.

The defense never did mount a qualified rebuttal to the mountains of state fiber evidence. The state's case was certainly attackable, but little was accomplished by the defense. In my estimation, it was much more a case of a weak defense than a strong prosecution.

During the trial, I tried painstakingly to convince whomever would listen—especially Homer and Faye Williams—that the defense team's concern over the carpet in their home was unnecesary. The only thing that could possibly be accomplished was to show that the carpet was not as rare as the state said it was. I thought that my findings in Dalton gave enough ammunition to the defense attorneys to cross-examine Baggett and establish this fact without the dispute about when the Williamses' carpets were installed.

I rue the day that I suggested to Homer Williams that if he wanted to find out when he installed the carpeting, he should go to the morgue clipping files at the *Atlanta Constitution* or the public library and look for a copy of the advertisement that he said had prompted him to buy the carpet.

Homer Williams knew that the ad had run about Christmas time, so it narrowed the search for the ad considerably. I am convinced that he got the wrong ad. He came back, waving the ad that he said had convinced him to buy the carpet. It had appeared right around Christmas, just as he thought. But Christmas of 1968. According to the spokesmen at West Point-Pepperell, "Luxaire" like that which the Williamses had installed wasn't manufactured until 1971.

This became a *cause celebre* for the prosecution and an albatross for the defense. In either case, by the state's contention or the Williamses' contention, the carpet was in the Williamses' home years before the first victim on The List died—and this was all that was important. I could get excited about proving the carpet was not there when one of the victims said to have the strange trilobal fiber had died.

The ensuing testimony of Homer and Faye Williams destroyed their credibility on points which were more important to Wayne Williams than when his rug was installed. The advertisement made the Williamses rationalize a lot of things.

Homer Williams brought pictures to court. They were dated by the developer prior to 1971. Homer said they were pictures of the green rug he installed after Christmas of 1969. The problem was, the carpets looked *brown.* Oh, that was because of the filters on the camera. From a professional photographer—the jury wouldn't buy that, and I wouldn't, either. Wayne Williams told me later: "I tried to tell him [Homer] not to use those damned pictures. They *were* of the brown rug."

Then Faye Williams showed records from the loan she said was taken in 1969 to pay for the carpet. But officials of the loan company said the loan was for an air conditioner.

The defense sleuths found Wayne Gano, the carpet installer. He took the stand, recognized his signature and confirmed that he had witnessed the 1971 installation contract between the Williamses and the Southern Prudential Company. Gano's testimony was a surprise, to the defense. When it had interviewed Gano, he had said that the signature was not his.

Still, the Williamses, Faye and Homer, insisted that the carpet had been put down in 1969. They remembered Sheba, their German shepherd, was a puppy in 1969, and while the carpet installer was at lunch, Sheba—the puppy—chewed up an edge of the carpet. Does anybody have an aspirin?

The *Atlanta Journal* and *Constitution* tore into the Williamses' carpet testimony with all guns blazing in an exhibition of what they could do. It was a performance I wish I could say was the rule rather than the exception. Inane as the whole issue was (of when the carpet was installed), we probably got more truth on this issue than any other in the trial, thanks to the local newspapers.

The newspapers published photos of two carpet ads side-by-side—the one from December 7, 1968, which Homer said he and Faye responded to, and one from December 4, 1971. Both ads headlined three rooms of carpet for $149.

The reporters had checked deed records and found that on December 7, 1971, the Williamses signed a loan agreement with the Southern Prudential Company in the amount of $1,738.80, including interest. Southern Prudential was the firm that placed the December 4, 1971, advertisement.

When the salesman come to the house, Homer Williams testified, the Williamses signed up to buy a much more expensive style.

With Faye Williams taking the stand, the defense got snagged even worse on the question of when the green carpet was purchased.

She testified that she had bought an air-conditioning system in August of 1971. It cost $1,700, she said, explaining that the family "couldn't have scraped up the money" to make payments on both an air-conditioner and a houseful of carpeting in 1971.

Could the Southern Prudential loan be related to the air-conditioner purchase? Not likely. Courthouse records show that the Williamses had more than one outstanding loan in 1971. Faye Williams borrowed an undisclosed amount from the Community Loan and Investment Company on November 11, 1971. She swore that her 1968 carpet purchase was financed by the North American Acceptance Corporation and that her monthly payments were $56.83. Foiled again! Records at the courthouse show that the Southern Prudential loan was later taken over by the North American Acceptance Corporation, with payments of $54.83.

So taken were some members of the defense team with an unworthy and unwinnable fight that they were still pursuing it more than a year after Wayne Williams was convicted. In April of 1983, I appeared on a television show in Philadelphia. The Williamses, Homer and Faye, were there along with Wayne's attorney, Lynn Whatley, and the "Dog Man," Don Laken. Laken told me, "I can prove that carpet document was a forgery."

"Who forged it and how can you prove it?" I asked.

He said he didn't quite have it tied down yet. Or perhaps he just didn't want to discuss it with me.

Herbert Pratt, the DuPont technician who had lectured us before, was now back on the stand. He testified that he had never before seen a fiber like the trilobal carpet fiber brought to him by the FBI. He said he traced the fiber to Wellman, Incorporated, a fiber manufacturer in Johnson, South Carolina. He never would have made the connection had it not been for the observations of a female colleague.

Wellman's technical services director, Henry Poston, testified that from 1967 to 1974 his company manufactured a trilobal fiber which was "completely different" from anything else in the world of fibers.

Binder got Poston to admit under cross-examination that the fiber was not patented and could have been duplicated by anyone without his knowledge. But more important, Poston said that 9,000 pounds were sold to West Point-Pepperell in 1970 and 1971.

Documents which became a part of the court record indicated that the sales to West Point-Pepperell of the unique trilobal fiber, dubbed 181B by

Wellman, were much greater than testified to at the trial. According to the documents 870,898 pounds had been sold to West Point-Pepperell.

Since this trilobal fiber is only one small part of the blend which went into the manufacture of any given product, it was a small percentage of the total fiber blend in the Williamses' carpet. For instance, the rugs in those "86 rooms" must be terribly heavy, indeed, to account for so much of Wellman's production.

Significantly, too, according to the documents, Wellman made 15.5 million pounds of that "181B" trilobal fiber. These 15.5 million pounds were sold to 10 companies—all located in Georgia. The rarity of this increasingly less rare fiber should be determined by the 15.5 million pounds produced. But the state continued to base its case on how rare the carpet installed in the Williamses' house is.

(Using the state's own mathematics—but not its numbers—the 15.5 million pounds of "181B" is enough to carpet 92,688 rooms—while there might be only enough of the Luxaire to do only 86 rooms. We talk of a criminal-justice system that deals with matters "beyond a reasonable doubt." But here is the system dealing in probabilities based on the wrong set of facts.)

Pratt himself cast two more doubts on the state's fiber evidence, testifying under a relentless cross-examination from Binder. "Color dyes in fiber can lose their original chemical properties if they are exposed to the elements," he said.

His response to Binder's next question was: "It is possible a manufacturer might not maintain his machinery well enough, and the shapes of the fibers can be altered by worn instruments." I detect some reasonable doubt about the state's fiber case. How about you?

When Al Binder questioned Herbert Pratt about the transfer of fibers, Pratt replied that it would be "improbable"—but not "impossible"—for fibers to transfer through *limited* personal contact. The *Atlanta Constitution* opined that Binder was trying to show that the police officers were leaving fibers from the officers' environment on the bodies.

Not quite. The point of the question was to see if police officers and others might be picking up fibers from one victim and transferring them to another—thus contaminating the fibers before they were placed on slides (which the laboratory people relied on to safeguard the integrity of their evidence). Beyond a reasonable doubt?

Keep in mind that what was found on the victims were microscopic fibers. Of the various types found, one was a trilobal fiber. To see the trilobal design, one must look at it in cross section—as if you were looking at the end of a hair.

Trilobal fibers are not all rare. But this particular kind of trilobal fiber—181B—is an unusual variety. Its unusual nature results from trying to develop a trilobal fiber which would not violate a DuPont patent on trilobal fibers.

Imagine a cake-decorating nozzle. Forcing the icing through the nozzle creates a strand of material that has the same cross-section shape as the opening in the nozzle. This is the same principle used in manufacturing synthetic fibers. The trilobal design is obtained by using a nozzle with a trilobal opening.

Now imagine an equilateral triangle—like a "YIELD" sign. Now push the sides in at the middle so they resemble parentheses. Each side of the triangle is now concave. You have a trilobal shape. Now flatten one of the points of that shape, and you have the shape of the Wellman 181B fiber.

Wellman 181B fibers make up a small part of the blend used to make many products. One of those products is carpets. And one of the varieties of carpet made with 181B is Luxaire. Luxaire carpet is what is installed in the Williamses' home.

What were found on some of the victims were individual filaments of 181B (among other fibers). Some victims among those said to have the trilobal fibers on them had only one. The state's fiber experts would say that the trilobal fibers found on the victims were similar to fibers found in the Williamses' carpet.

Only 86 rooms of such carpet in the entire Southeast? Nonsense! Where are the other almost 15 million pounds of 181B? Some of it could be on the victims, and you need to understand that.

The FBI's fiber expert, Harold Deadman, said that fiber evidence is "merely circumstantial. No two things in the world are exactly the same."

Binder produced an FBI manual. He had Deadman read aloud from it. In part, it stated that fibers were only circumstantial evidence and that other supportive evidence was necessary for conviction. The author of that statement was Harold Deadman.

Gene Baggett of West Point-Pepperell then took the stand to amend his previous testimony. He raised the figure of 86 rooms in the Southeast to 860. Baggett said he had found additional information during the overnight recess.

The FBI's Harold Deadman returned to the stand with more numbers that were pure conjecture, not scientific fact. Again, life and freedom would swing in the balance of someone's "educated" guesses. If, as some predict, the Williams case will become a landmark case for fiber evidence, then I fear that others will become victims of similar flimsy arguments.

Deadman alluded to a study reputed to be research showing that 82% of fibers that have been transferred will be lost within a four-hour period and "within 32 hours, only 3% of the transferred fibers will remain." He stated that if a garment were washed, it is likely all of the transferred fibers would be lost in the washing machine.

I would like to suggest another "research" or "study" to Deadman. It's called "doing the laundry." Let him do some laundry, even with a good fabric softener, and then tell us how easy it is to wash fibers off clothes in a washing machine. Or, is the machine taking fibers from one set of clothes and depositing them on another—something that might happen at, say, a laundromat? Certainly something is happening, because freshly washed clothes often have fibers from other fabrics adhering to them.

The problem with the study that Deadman talked about occurs when you apply it not to Williams' environment, where it seemed to work to perfection, but instead to the *victims'* environment, where it didn't seem to work at all.

Fourteen-year-old Eric Middlebrooks, whose case was one of the 10 "pattern" cases introduced against Williams, was found less than 12 hours after he disappeared. If transferred fibers disappear at the rates claimed by Deadman, then Eric must have been covered with fibers when he was left by his killer.

And if this "study" is accurate, I wonder what the probabilities were of finding "matching fibers" on the skeletal remains of 11-year-old Christopher Richardson or on his clothing. Richardson had been missing for 5,136 hours, give or take a day, between June of 1980 and January of 1981. Yet authorities say they found not one—but two—varieties of fibers (in multiple numbers) on his remains.

If this were a simple arithmetic progression that Deadman proposes, then during the first 32 hours, a victim would give up 97% of the fibers that had been transferred to him or her. Then, after those 32 hours, all fibers would have been gone in only 33.003 hours.

Even if it were a more complicated, descending geometric progression (like the half-life cycle of a radioactive substance), the chances of finding *one* fiber after more than 5,000 hours would be virtually non-existent. The chances of finding two different varieties would be infinitesimal—even less than the chances of finding the eight so-called "Williams" fibers in another environment.

The "Deadman deadline" of 33 hours was clearly designed to blunt defense questions as to why no fibers from the victims were found on Williams or in his environment. It was not expected that it would be applied in reverse, as we have just done. It seems that fiber determinations, like determinations of cause of death as we were told by Dr. Saleh Zaki, associate medical examiner for Fulton County, "depend on your objectives . . ."

Deadman conceded that every time a person touched the bodies of Nathaniel Cater or Jimmy Ray Payne at the crime scene or in the morgue, he could have transferred a fiber (or more than one) to their bodies. I wished that Binder had asked about taking fibers, as well as leaving them, and had asked Deadman to verify that the same transfer that was possible with victims was also possible with the evidence that lay in the lab.

Then Deadman, couching his words, said it was possible to expect to find fibers from the victims on their assailant. Would anyone realize that it is "possible to expect" *anything*? But it is not likely that we will expect some things, such as Martian landings.

The correct answer is, yes, you would expect to find fibers from the victims on their assailant. Actually, finding fibers from the victims on their assailant is as likely as water in a creek. A creek dries up sometimes, but not often.

If one couldn't expect to find the victims' fibers on the assailant, then one couldn't expect to find the assailant's fibers on the victims. The transfer principle is exactly the same.

So here we had the state implying that it is more likely to find the assailant fibers on the victims than vice versa, and more likely that fibers would disappear from the assailant's environment than from the victims' environment.

Larry Peterson, the chief fiber analyst at the Georgia State Crime Lab, took the stand. He said what everyone was waiting to hear—that "fibers found on the bodies of Jimmy Ray Payne and Nathaniel Cater appear to be the same types of fibers found on eight different objects in Wayne Williams' home and automobile."

Peterson's recap of the numbers of fiber matches exceeded the figures that had been furnished the defense under the "Brady" ruling. Al Binder objected, but his testimony was allowed to continue, even though it seemingly was in violation of "Brady."

"In my opinion," Peterson said, "it is highly unlikely that any other environment other than that of Mr. Williams' home and car could account for the combination."

So this is where the "scientific" premises of these cases start, with an *opinion* that something is *highly unlikely*. If Peterson had known, he would have said he knew. If it was the only possible environment, he would have said that, too. What Peterson's statement really means is, "Yes, it could have come from another environment, but I don't think it did." Beyond a reasonable doubt?

While Peterson was on the witness stand, no one asked him about possible contamination. But in a private interview, Peterson would deny that contamination could have taken place. When asked how he knew fibers had not been transferred to the Cater and Payne bodies, he said, "Because that stuff had been mounted [sealed on glass slides] months before." Actually, in the case of Nathaniel Cater, it could have been mounted only days before.

Peterson, assuming that the fibers on the victims had come from Williams' environment, also assumed that contaminating fibers would have had to originate in Williams' environment. What prevents the fibers found on Cater's body from having come from Payne's body via the lab fixtures? Or via an investigating officer; or from vehicles used to transfer victims or evidence, or from Peterson himself, who had been to many of the scenes and presumably later handled some of the evidence from each case?

Again, the *Atlanta Constitution* reporters misinterpreted the testimony when they wrote: "Defense attorney Alvin Binder painted the state's fiber evidence as a one-way street, implying that the state's experts set out to find incriminating evidence against Williams without looking for exonerating evidence."

Binder was not implying what the *Constitution* reporters said he did. Instead, Binder was talking about the state's failure to find incriminating fibers from the victims in Wayne Williams' environment, although the state did look. That the state did not look for exculpatory evidence in the fibers is not open to question. It discarded tens of thousands of fibers found on the victims without further analysis, solely on the basis that these fibers did not match the fibers they were looking for—the ones they found in Williams' environment.

Binder got Peterson to concede that he had found no traces of Cater or Payne in the home or car of Wayne Williams during the two searches (a statement Peterson would later modify). But Gordon Miller, a Fulton County assistant district attorney, pointed out that Cater was nude and Payne clad only in undershorts when they were found dead, and there was nothing to use for comparison.

This made me chuckle inwardly because it would mean that Cater and Payne would have had to have disposed of their own clothes before they came into contact with Williams.

Had I been at the defense table that day, I would have urged Binder to ask on re-cross why Peterson hadn't found any reverse transfers from 17-year-old William Barrett. The state would put Barrett in Williams' car by blood type—if you believed its evidence. But Barrett's fully clothed body was found between the discoveries of Payne and Cater. For Barrett, the state would have had to have thought up another plausible-sounding answer. "Nude" wouldn't work. And I wonder what happened to that bag of clothes left in Mary Welcome's offices.

And since both Cater and Payne had matching fibers in their hair, there were also hairs to look for. The state certainly did have samples of the victims' head and body hairs to use for comparison. But, the state found none!

Peterson has explained since the trial that Williams' station wagon apparently had been vacuumed before it was searched. Hair, he said, is vacuumed up much easier than fibers. Fibers, he continued, tend to get entwined in the fabric much easier than hair does. You don't normally see hair that clings to your shirt, he said, adding that it's going to be removed more easily.

I wanted to suggest that Peterson join Deadman in the wash-day experiment. I have a German shepherd and I wear knit clothes. Sometimes you can't pull the dog's hairs off my knit shirts after they have been washed and dried.

Also, if the station wagon had been vacuumed, was there any chance that the sweepings still existed? As a matter of fact, there was a damned good chance. Peterson, again talking after the trial, said, "In fact, we had vacuums in the house [which] to this day [about a year after Williams' conviction] have not been examined. It would be impossible to [examine] . . . hundreds of thousands of hairs . . ."

When asked how he knew the vehicle was vacummed, Peterson said, "I'm speculating."

Unfortunately, as with most of the "expert" testimony in this trial, Peterson often speculated. Otherwise he would not have sprinkled his testimony with "in my opinions," "highly likelys" and "could haves." I wouldn't want to go to jail on speculation. Would you?

A fiber found in the sheet in which Jimmy Ray Payne's body was transported by ambulance was said to be similar to a blue fiber found in Williams' home. But no one could say where the sheet came from. Was it also similar to the blue rugs of an ambulance? Or the blue uniform of a policeman, or the blue serge suit of a detective, or the blue slacks or shirt of a technician? Probably not. But we may never know because no one was looking to find out. Did the sheet put the fiber on the body? Or did the body put the fiber on the sheet?

Peterson said that 12 dog hairs in the Payne case could have come from the Williamses' dog, Sheba. Yes, and they *could* have come from my German shepherd, Kaiser, too, or almost any other German shepherd, malamute or husky. But Peterson didn't say that. The whole truth?

The state already had suggested that green fibers found on Cater came from Williams' carpet and that light violet fibers found on Cater came from Williams' bedspread.

Now, at the trial, Peterson stated that Williams' 1970 Chevrolet station wagon had "particularly unusual characteristics." According to Peterson, a (one) blue-gray fiber was "somewhat rotten" and frayed, similar to a (one) fiber found on Payne's body. A single fiber from the vehicle carpet was burned in a "fashion similar" to *one* found on Cater's body, he added.

Which raises other questions: How does one burn just two fibers in a carpet? And in how many ways can a fiber be burned?

In his post-trial interview, Peterson raised still other arguments that I had to question. He theorized why there were Williams fibers on victims, but no victim fibers on Williams. People who move around, he said, lose fibers more rapidly than bodies that lay motionless.

That sounds plausible, but it's invalid. The bodies had lain in rain, sleet, snow, wind, or whatever elements were present while the victims were missing. For many of the victims, that would include all the elements, yet these victims still had fibers.

Then, too, we had the river victims. Deadman said fibers would come off in a washing machine. Yet victims were found in rivers where water sometimes surged strongly enough to capsize rafts, and the fibers stayed on those victims.

Besides the hairs taken out of the vacuuming of Williams' car, Peterson suggested that the victims' fibers were removed. If the victims' fibers were removed, why weren't Williams' fibers removed? Some fibers found on victims who had been long dead were said to match fibers found during the search of Williams' station wagon.

Next, Peterson talked about areas of search. For example, the carpet fibers could have come from, say, 1,000 square feet of carpet.

But where do you start looking for the victims' fibers? Well, I would say in the vaccum cleaner bag that was used to collect the carpet sweepings during the authorities' search for evidence.

How about a fiber that is partially burned—a fiber that the state says came from a toilet-seat cover? That seat cover measures, say, 2 square feet, with maybe a one-half square-inch cigarette burn on it. Where would you start looking for a fiber from the victim who had that partially burned fiber on him? So much for areas of search.

Binder stressed to the jury that of the mountains of fibers discussed, there had been 90 fiber matches. His point was, the weight of the evidence isn't thousands of fibers discussed 10 times each, making them sound like ten-thousands of fibers, but rather a more understandable 90 fiber matches. Some of those matches involved only one single microscopic fiber found on a victim. And one match involved not simply one fiber on a victim, but also only one fiber found in Williams' station wagon. The origin of this one-to-one fiber was never discovered.

Peterson conceded that his opinion about the fiber matches was *subjective.* Subjective is an antonym of scientific. Yet the news media insists on calling the fibers "scientific evidence." Peterson testified, "There is no scientific means of saying that a particular fiber came from a particular source."

When asked about the commonality of the fibers, Peterson said that for the most part he didn't know. But he did say that "only 620 of 2.3 million vehicles" in the seven-county Atlanta metropolitan area had black carpeting similar to that in the Williams station wagon.

Had Peterson forgotten that the Williamses' station wagon was not one of those 620 vehicles, since it still was registered in Muscogee County (Columbus), more than 100 miles away? So much for what Peterson says he *does* know about the commonality of the fibers.

Peterson conceded that the color of the fibers taken from Jimmy Ray Payne and Nathaniel Cater differed from the color of the fibers taken from Williams' environment. But he said those on the two bodies had faded, "apparently" because they had been washed by the river.

He told of placing fibers from Williams' environment in a sample of Chattahoochee River water. The immersed fibers were then placed in sunlight for three days (Cater had not, according to the state, been in the water for more than two days, and not in the sunlight for much of that time). Most of the fibers, Peterson said, became faded and bleached by varying degrees and became more like those on the bodies. However, he conceded that he never was able to make exact matchups.

"Except for color differences," he said, "microscopic examination showed the fibers recovered from objects in the Williamses' home and car were basically the same as those on the bodies in the kind of material they contained—diameter, length and internal cross-sectional shapes." "Except for color . . ." Beyond a reasonable doubt?

Harold Deadman testified that it would be "virtually impossible" for the multiple-fiber matchups to occur unless the two victims, Cater and Payne, had some contact with those two environments. But what about that third environment—the crime lab? And what about victims Charles Stephens, Clifford Jones and Earl Lee Terrell? Would the same be true for them? Would it be "virtually impossible" for these three victims to have the multiple-fiber matchups the state said they had, without coming in contact with Williams' home or car?

Deadman went on to say that the fibers found on a body "usually" reflect the environment that the victim was in—either shortly before or shortly after his death. Tell that to Scotland Yard, which claims to be able to tell everywhere people have been, simply by examining the residue in their pockets.

Deadman said that because the matching fibers were found on the undershorts of Jimmy Ray Payne and the head hair and pubic hair of Nathaniel Cater, it would indicate that the fiber transfer took place while the victims were undressed.

Was Jimmy Ray Payne wearing a hat? I don't think that anybody but the state ever contended that the killer(s) undressed the victims after they were killed. And that was back when the state was trying to tell us the victims were being undressed so that no fibers could be found.

Both Deadman and Brown couldn't be correct. Thus, the state's fiber case was now contradicting its "pattern" case.

In addition, Deadman said he had calculated the chances of randomly finding the Williamses' type of carpeting in Atlanta were no better than 1 in 8,000. Here we were, back to the illogic of determining the chances of running across an apple, based on an estimate of the number of apple pies baked. And at that, it still gave 64 possibilities for metropolitan Atlanta. Beyond a reasonable doubt?

On cross-examination of Peterson, Binder asked if he ever found anything of Jimmy Ray Payne's in the searches of Williams' house or vehicle.

"I found a red cotton fiber with the same characteristics as Mr. Payne's [red] undershorts in the Williams car," Peterson said. His surprising answer stunned Binder. It was one of those landmines that the prosecution seemingly had left there for Binder to step on.

Out of the courtroom and long after the trial, Peterson would tell an interviewer: "I looked through the vacuumings [those taken by police technicians] to see if I could match some things back to the victims. But again, it was a much tougher thing to do. The time had already been so long. I did find a cotton fiber, a red cotton fiber, in the sweepings of the car that matched Payne's shorts. And if I recall, that came out in the facts.

"I didn't say anything about that in the direct [examination]. Binder asked me . . . where the other half of the transfer [was] . . . , and he more or less stumbled into it . . . I told him flatly that I didn't put great significance upon [sic] it until he [Binder] started bringing it out . . ."

But all through the trial, the prosecution seemed to have put itself into little boxes. As it answered one problem, it created others. If you listened to individual pieces of testimony, it sounded fine. But, if you kept the entire case in perspective, the prosecution's fiber case was snagged and tangled and coming apart.

For example, Peterson insinuated that the victims all wore cotton fibers such as blue-jean fibers. Such fibers are so common that no identification could be made of them, even if they were found in the Williams environment. No, most of the victims were *not* wearing blue jeans. At least 21 of the 28 List victims, plus Porter (29), did not have on blue jeans.

Actually, the victims would have picked up fibers from their own environments and transferred those fibers to the Williams environment. Fibers from those environments could have been catalogued and searched for—but they were not—in the sweepings of Williams' car and home. Although the state played it straight by not introducing the Payne fiber, it had to be overjoyed when Binder asked the question and received Peterson's surprising answer.

Peterson testified that the blanket which provided many of the fiber comparisons when the Williamses' house was searched on June 3 could not be found when the house was searched again on June 21.

I wondered about this for a long time. Then one day in 1983, as I sat in the Williamses' front room, I remembered to ask about the missing blanket. Faye Williams got up and went to the linen closet.

"Here's that blanket," she said, producing a yellow blanket (more gold than yellow) that was heavily stained with the black fingerprint powder that polluted everything in Wayne Williams' room. Swatches had been cut from the blanket.

She said that when the police searched the first time, the blanket was lying on a hassock in Wayne Williams' room, Before they came back, she said, it had been picked up by a relative, folded and placed on the floor of the linen closet where, Faye Williams says, it remained until she heard Peterson's testimony that it could not be found.

Faye Williams says she took the blanket to the courthouse the following day and gave it to Al Binder. The missing blanket had bothered me for some time. I thought that the fact that it was left unchallenged was one of the more incriminating things to happen during the trial. Certainly most people who heard the testimony left the trial thinking that something had been done to that blanket between the two searches. I don't know why the defense didn't introduce it to refute Peterson's testimony.

Somewhere in all this fiber jumble, it occurred to me that if victims could come in contact with the Williamses' environment and come away with all these fiber matches, why couldn't a killer come in contact with that environment in the same way and leave the fibers on the victims? That is basically what the state insinuated that Wayne Williams did.

But did it have to be Wayne Williams? The answer, of course, is a resounding "no!" Even if you buy the state's entire fiber case, you haven't eliminated Faye or Homer Williams. All you've said is that these victims were in the Williamses' environment, not just Wayne Williams' environment.

The flood gates were about to open and engulf Wayne Williams in a tidal wave of fibers. Remember, we still had 10 "pattern" cases to be introduced. But before the deluge, let's recall some operative words that were oft-heard in Williams' trial to this point. *Every* so-called scientific fiber match was discussed in one or more of the following terms:

possibility	probability	improbable
not impossible	unusual	circumstantial
similar to	could have orginated	appear to be
might have come from	apparently	highly unlikely
opinion	subjective judgment	particularly unusual
similar fashion	suggests	no scientific means to say
similar type		

Would you want to go to prison on so-called scientific evidence that offers not one iota of scientific proof—and even admits there is no scientific proof? Is the opinion that something "appears to be" proof that it is? Beyond a reasonable doubt?

The state of Georgia contended that the general circumstances surrounding each of the 10 cases it intended to introduce as "pattern" were similar to the circumstances in the deaths of 27-year-old Nathaniel Cater and 21-year-old Jimmy Ray Payne, the only two victims Wayne Williams was charged with killing.

If the state's fiber case was a feeble giant, then its version of the "pattern" of the killings was the invisible dwarf. It is so poorly conceived as to be ludicrous.

Assistant prosecutor Joe Drolet (pronounced "Dro-LAY") said the "pattern" was "so obvious it caught the attention of virtually the entire Western world." As was typical of the state's approach to this case, Drolet had ignored yet another element—this time the Eastern world, which also had sent reporters and camera crews to Atlanta during the height of the murders. Yes, the pattern was obvious, but there was at least one part of the "Western world" that had not seized upon it: the Atlanta police Task Force and the Fulton County prosecutor's office.

The court recessed for the weekend, and Judge Cooper promised a ruling on Monday whether to allow the "pattern" evidence, although as we know, Lee Brown and Jack Mallard already had told the jury about "pattern" and facts from other cases—beyond the official "pattern" cases.

On Monday, to no one's surprise, the judge allowed the "pattern" into the trial. Remember, the jury was supposed to use the evidence from these other 10 cases *only* to decide if Wayne Williams killed Nathaniel Cater and Jimmy Ray Payne. The jurors were to use the evidence only to determine "pattern, bent of mind and identity" of the killer. The judge wrote an order containing this fact as part of a warning to be read to the jury *before* the introduction of each "pattern" case. This was by pre-agreement among all parties. But Cooper promptly disobeyed his own order. His cautions to the jury were not given in the manner that the judge agreed that they would be. That raised the ire of Binder, who protested, but to no avail.

Generally, evidence of other criminal acts by a defendant is inadmissible, since it tends to place the defendant's character into evidence. However, exceptions to this rule have emerged over the years. Now, there are occasions in which evidence of other crimes committed by a defendant can be admitted ostensibly for limited purposes.

But I don't think you can limit a person's conclusions once the thought has been planted with him. That's why mind controllers and book burners try to destroy ideas before others whom they don't wish to think for themselves can hear or see them.

Judge Cooper's decision in favor of the state against Wayne Williams was based on the Georgia Supreme Court's ruling in *State of Georgia vs. Johnson* in September of 1980 (in a case which Lewis Slaton also prosecuted):

> "Before evidence of independent crimes is admissible, two conditions must be satisfied. First, there must be evidence that the defendant was in fact the perpetrator of the independent crime. Second, there must be sufficient similarity or connection between the independent crimes and the offense charged, that proof of the former tends to prove the latter.
>
> "Once the testimony of the accused as the perpetrator of the offense separate and distinct from the one for which he is on trial has been proven [sic], testimony concerning the independent crime may be admitted for the purpose of showing identity, motive, plan, scheme, bent of mind and course of condition."

Fulton County Chief Medical Examiner Robert Stivers testified that a total of five persons were asphyxiated in Fulton County during the five years from 1975 through 1979. That statement cannot be correct. Perhaps he meant murders; perhaps he meant to say murders that he knew of, but his statement cannot stand as is.

Fire deaths, drowning deaths, electrocutions, some poisonings and many forms of natural deaths are asphyxial. The low number of asphyxial deaths which are ruled homicide is attributed to the practices of the police and medical examiner, not to the choices of method by the murderers. Unknown deaths are, as a matter of practice, not ruled homicidal. The death-certificate form itself is a certain giveaway on which "undetermined" and "homicide" are listed as excluding choices. In my opinion, they should not be. Just because you don't know how a person died doesn't mean it is not a homicide. (This, of course, does not lift the burden of proving a homicidal death before convicting somebody of murder.)

Most of the cases in the Atlanta murders would not have been listed as homicides had they happened as isolated incidents. Those that were called "probable asphyxia" would, in the years before 1979, have been listed as "unknown" or "undetermined" and would not have been considered homicides.

Meanwhile, Al Binder dropped a "bomb" by subpoenaing the Georgia governor, George Busbee, and others who participated in a secret meeting at the Governor's Mansion on June 19, 1981. Out of that meeting came a decision to arrest Williams if he continued to lead the police and the press on high-speed chases (they'd arrest you or me for speeding, without an order from the governor and the FBI) or if he tried to leave Georgia.

Busbee, Slaton and the others immediately resisted testifying. They petitioned to quash the subpoenas, and Judge Cooper went along, defusing Binder's bomb. The whole truth?

Lubie Geter's uncle and a girlfriend who said she had a date with Lubie to go to the Omni testified about the circumstances surrounding Lubie's disappearance, back in January of 1981.

An FBI agent testified that he found a blue T-shirt—identified by Lubie's mother, Assie Geter, as belonging to her son—about 300 yards from where the body was recovered. The agent also testified that shoes were found near the shirt and that pants believed to be Geter's were discovered about three-quarters of a mile from the body.

On Monday, January 25, Binder nailed Robert Stivers, the Fulton County medical examiner, to a cross of Stivers' own making. Binder quoted from a March 13, 1981, article in the American Medical Association's publication, in which Stivers wrote that there was *no apparent pattern* among the Atlanta "child" slaying cases.

Now the police (Lee Brown), the prosecution (Lewis Slaton) and the medical examiner's office (Stivers), by their own "expert" opinions, had gone on record before the arrest of Wayne Williams to say that there was no pattern. But now they were in court, trying to convince the world of exactly the opposite.

Under orchestration from assistant prosecutor Jack Mallard, Stivers testified that in the previous six months, his staff counted only one asphyxiation death in which the body was not found in a river or near a road.

"Hey, wait a minute," I thought. That asphyxiation death had better have occurred in the previous 25 days because I already accounted for all of the asphyxial deaths in 1981 that Stivers had previously testified made up the total for 1981. All in Stivers' previous testimony are on The List and all are on roads or in rivers. So, if Stivers counted an asphyxial death that wasn't in water or near a road in the previous six months, then his previous testimony of the total number of asphyxial deaths in 1981 was incorrect. All of which shows that both before and after Wayne Williams went to jail in June of 1981, the authorities had trouble counting asphyxial deaths.

But if this trial were to prove anything, it would be that consistency is no jewel when it comes to putting people in the penitentiary.

Saleh Zaki, a Fulton County associate medical examiner, took the stand again and testifed that 14-year-old Alfred Evans had died an asphyxial death. I passed a note to Al Binder, pointing out that the medical examiner's original determination in the Evans case had been "cause of death unknown." Binder asked Zaki about his having changed the cause of death in the Evans case.

Zaki denied that the cause of death in the Evans case had ever been changed. But Zaki was contradicted a short time later by his boss, Stivers, who testified that there had been only one asphyxial death in all of 1979.

I passed another note to Binder. It read: "Yusuf Bell 1, Alfred Evans 2." Both had been found dead in 1979. In reply to this challenge, Stivers said that Evans' death never had been considered an asphyxial death, even though Zaki, who performed the Evans autopsy, said it had. Nothing but the truth?

Each officer in charge of the death scenes of Lubie Geter, Alfred Evans and Charles Stephens was called to the stand. Their testimony, plus that of the medical examiners, merely reaffirmed that no one yet knows how Geter, Stephens or Evans died.

Oh, in the Stephens case, the court was told that he might have been suffocated. By what? It might even have been a plastic bag. I hoped that the jury knew that the second half of a "might have been" statement always is "and it might not have been."

We all agreed that these three youngsters were murdered, but the medical examiners' guesses were tailored to fit the case against Wayne Williams.

Since the investigation had not led anyone near Wayne Williams, then the case had to be built after he dropped into their laps. In a sense, this is a "legal frame," wherein you decide who's guilty and build your case around that suspect. It's done all the time.

Wayne Williams' fried chicken dinner had long since gotten cold. It had been at least 45 minutes since the brown-and-tan-clad deputy sheriff had pushed open the door to the holding cell behind Judge Clarence Cooper's courtroom. The deputy had brought Williams his lunch.

Wayne Bertram Williams comes across as an enigmatic, if not complicated, young man—smart, but not brilliant; well-spoken, but under-educated.

He often isn't easily understood because when he's not embellishing or exaggerating the truth, he's obfuscating it. But in either case, he has a knack of using his mild voice to project sincerity. He can look you right in the eye and give you straight answers; or, if he wants to fend off questions for any reason, he will look away and almost always ask *you* a question that *he* thinks is important.

Now he sat there on January 27, midway through his trial, engrossed in the myriad geographic and inter-personal connections I had discovered among many victims—both on *and* off The List.

"Oh, no," Wayne Williams groaned slowly. He lowered his head onto the interlaced fingers of his hands, which formed an arrow on the tabletop, pointing to me on the other side.

"I've got to be the most unlucky son-of-a-bitch in the world," he said, peering through ⅜-inch-thick glasses, which make his eyes and cheekbones appear too small for his features. "If I had known half this shit you're tellin' me now a year ago, I sure as hell would have changed where I went."

I tilted my head and let that one sink in for a long time.

Williams became intrigued with the implictions of the map I had drawn for him on his notepad. He asked what I thought the map meant. I told him that all I could say it meant was that a definite connection existed among many, if not all, the victims and that they lived, disappeared and turned up dead on or near only 12 major connecting streets.

"What does it say about the killer or killers?" Williams asked.

" I really don't know," I said, "but I have some theories that I don't like to talk about because I simply don't like to conjecture."

He was interested in my theories. I told him about the night in November of 1980, when two Atlanta police Task Force officers (who soon were reassigned) and I had driven by the house of two yet-to-be victims, following the map to the home, vanishing point and death scene of another.

"Guess what else we passed on that short ride," I said.

"What's that?" Williams asked.

"Your house, buddy."

"You've got to be kiddin'!" A quizzical smile tugged at the left corner of his upper lip.

I nudged the point a little further. I showed him that 7-year-old LaTonya Wilson, 27-year-old Nathaniel Cater and 14-year-old Cynthia Montgomery had lived in Dixie Hills, a few blocks from Williams. I explained to him that LaTonya had disappeared from there and her body was found not far away. Williams' eyes were riveted to each point I added to the makeshift map.

"Who," I asked, "owned a radio tower in Dixie Hills?"

"Oh, shit!" was Williams' only reply.

"Wayne," I asked, "are you a homosexual?"

"No, hell, no," he said. His answer was calm and matter-of-fact.

(After his conviction, Wayne Williams would call Atlanta police to the Fulton County Jail to investigate a homosexual ring involving a guard and a man who has been a suspect in several of the cases attributed to Williams.)

I didn't ask Williams the question that might seem obvious from an interviewer's standpoint, to wit: "Did you kill .....?" My approach was different because I already knew that Williams had said, "The only thing I've killed is a roach in my cell." To ask him the question would be tantamount to calling him a liar. And, in any event, I hardly expected him to break down suddenly and confess.

I asked Williams if he knew anyone who knew any of the victims. I already knew that he had denied—at his press conference before his arrest in June—knowing any victims. Williams' answer surprised me. He said that Carla Bailey, whom he knew quite well, was related to 14-year-old Lubie (Chuck) Geter through Lubie's uncle—the same uncle who had just testified for the state!

Williams asked me about the answers to some questions he had asked in his December 24 letter. I told him that I had given the letter to Mary Welcome and that Durwood Myers, the defense investigator, had taken care of it. Williams repeatedly stressed the importance of finding the answers to his questions.

Frankly, I couldn't see their relevance. The things he wanted to know tended to prove that he was what he said he was, and that he was where he said he was on certain dates. The problem was, I couldn't see how any of that mattered at this point. None of his questions—or their answers—proved that he wasn't what the prosecutors said he was or where they said he was on certain dates.

I explained to Williams that he needed to prove where he was when at least one of the victims died. That was obvious, but it apparently had eluded Williams. I recited to him the names of victims who had been missing for less than 24 hours when they were found dead. These victims would be the easiest to account for. Since the prosecution now had linked Williams to 22 of the cases through similar fibers, an iron-clad alibi for one should alibi the others, or at least destroy the state's fiber case.

The deputy sheriff poked his head through the doorway. "Just a few minutes, Wayne," he said, "if you got to go or something before the jury comes back in." Williams grimaced at the white Styrofoam box that sat unopened on the table beside him. As I left, Wayne Williams was gnawing on a cold chicken leg.

A young boy who the court said it would not identify by agreement among counsel was, instead, called by his name at least three times during his testimony against Wayne Williams. This was the boy who said Williams had taken him to Pickfair Avenue and Pickfair Way and fondled the boy's genitals.

"Jeezus Christ," Wayne Williams muttered, pulling the fingers of his right hand hard across his brow while pushing on his temple with his right thumb. "Jeezus Christ," he repeated. Then he turned to me and said, "I ain't never killed anybody, but I'd like to wring that little son-of-a-bitch's neck right now!"

"God damn, Wayne," I whispered. "I wouldn't say that too loud around here."

But I could see that Wayne Williams was stung by those words from the witness stand. His reaction was that of someone who has a distaste for homosexuality.

Soon Gail Epstein would remind me that this witness had told a different story to the police when the incident occurred in August of 1980. She would write a story about the inconsistency, which would appear the next morning in the *Atlanta Constitution.* Later, she would ask me why Binder didn't bring it up on cross-examination.

All during the investigation, I had referred to this witness as the "X kid," for his own protection. I, too, remembered the other version that this same boy had told more than a year before. Nothing but the truth! But which time?

The first time the boy told the story about this alleged incident at Pickfair Avenue and Pickfair Way, he said it was a blue car and that there were two black males. He also said he was taken to a dirt road. Pickfair Avenue and Pickfair Way is a paved intersection.

The first time the boy told police about seeing Lubie Geter in the white Oldsmobile, he stated, then reiterated, that he knew one of the two persons in the car—Lubie Geter. He said he had *never* seen the other man. Then the young boy would swear in court that the culprit in both instances was Wayne Williams.

Question: Why didn't he recognize Williams when he first saw him with Lubie Geter in January of 1981, when he swore it was Williams who assaulted him in August of 1980? According to his story, he was sitting close enough to Wayne Williams for Williams to "fondle" his genitals.

For two years, Wayne Williams had supposedly killed people, and nobody had seen anything. Now, with Williams in custody, hordes of witnesses came forward to say that they had seen him with one victim or another. I think most really thought that they had seen him. But I wondered why they hadn't come forward when it might have saved someone's life.

People looked for Jo-Jo Bell for weeks and no one came forth with the information that anyone had seen him with anyone, let alone with someone these people knew. But now, at the trial, people were saying they saw Jo-Jo Bell with Wayne Williams, they'd know Jo-Jo Bell anywhere, and that Williams was even passing around notes that said he could be the killer. Where were these witnesses when Jo-Jo Bell needed them?

I'm sure that some witnesses saw dollar signs. A half-million-dollar reward can be pretty tempting, particularly if somebody else has already accused the guy. I don't think any of those witnesses ever saw Wayne Williams with any of those victims. I'm still not saying Williams is innocent; I just don't have that much faith in eyewitnesses.

The X kid became a font of information on the stand. He seemed to be in the right place at the right time for just about any hole in the state's case that the state wanted to plug while he was on the stand. He testified that he had seen Wayne Williams with Lubie Geter on Stewart Avenue, near where Geter disappeared. He said he'd seen Williams at Terry Pue's funeral, too.

One man might have refuted all or part of the X kid's testimony. He was Brandon Southern, director of the Challenge School, where the X kid was a student with Terry Pue. Brandon Southern was an old friend of Jefferey Mathis' family and knew several more of the victims or members of their families. Beside Mathis and Pue, Southern was associated with McIntosh, Geter, Gooch, Larry Rogers' younger brother, the X kid and Homer Williams.

During the trial, I tried to find Brandon Southern, but learned that he mysteriously had recently lost his job after 10 years there. I was told he was "in hiding." But I obtained the phone number of where he was staying. When I dialed it, I found out that Southern was there at that moment. I gave the information to Durwood Myer, Al Binder's chief investigator. But Brandon Southern was never called to testify.

Now a woman swore that she had seen Wayne Williams with Lubie Geter at the Kroger supermarket on Stewart Avenue. She said they were in a white Oldsmobile. Tough guess, wrong day, wrong car, wrong location. On top of that, she picked out a picture that looked more like Willie Stargell, the ex-Pittsburgh Pirates slugger, than Wayne Williams. Then she selected another photo of convicted murderer Amp Wiley. But the second selection was not made known to the jury.

I thought back to the X kid and what he said about Pickfair Avenue and Pickfair Way and I remembered that 22-year-old Faye Yearby was found murdered there. I doubt that the prosecution even knew that, since she hadn't made The List. Had the state known about Faye Yearby, it might also have thought about Charles Stephens, who lived right there, and Lubie Geter and Earl Terrell, who disappeared from so close by.

But the state didn't know and it missed a beautiful opportunity to make yet another geographic connection between Wayne Williams and the geographic focal points of this case. First, the state missed the connection of Williams to Thomasville Heights—part of the Pat Man connections. Then it missed the entire saga of Cap'n Peg's. Now the significance of Pickfair Avenue and Pickfair Way zoomed over the prosecution's head like a U-2 spy plane. The prosecution had slept through the whole movie and now it was writing the review.

If the state knew the facts of the cases, would it put two witnesses on the stand to say that Wayne Williams was in different places, with different victims, in different cars, at virtually the same time?

It interested me, too, that the witness who put Williams with Geter in the white Oldsmobile on the wrong day had selected the picture of a convicted murderer who was an acquaintance of the X kid.

Faye Yearby's death, though dissimilar, might fit the X kid's friend and convicted murderer's crime—the slaying of a young woman—closer than it would the Atlanta murders that the prosecution was concerned with. But that wouldn't alter the fact that Faye Yearby's death had strong ties with the cases on The List, too. There were, of course, the M.O. (*modus operandi*) links to the Angel Lenair case and the geographic links to Stephens, Terrell and Geter.

But, the convicted murderer also had personal connections with List victims LaTonya Wilson, Nathaniel Cater and Jimmy Ray Payne, as well as non-List victim Cynthia Montgomery, to say nothing of the X kid. Moreover, when he was first charged with murder, he was out on bond for the alleged rape of his next-door neighbor.

All of this demanded close scrutiny, but there would be none because neither the police nor the prosecution knew the significance of one otherwise obscure intersection to the cases that confounded them.

On cross-examination, Al Binder asked the X kid about his criminal record, which the X kid started admitting to before the prosecution objected. Binder then asked if he was sure about his identification of Williams. The X kid pointed at Williams and said that Williams had offered him a job washing cars and then engaged him in general conversation, asking about brothers and sisters and whether he played a musical instrument (close, but not close enough: Williams was primarily interested in singing talent).

The X kid then said Williams asked him if he had any money. Then Williams stuck his hand in the X kid's pocket, the youngster testified. "He wasn't really feeling of my pocket, he was feeling of my sexual organ," he said.

The youngster wasn't asked why he thought that Williams had gone through the difficult, if not impossible, task of putting his hand in the pocket of someone who was sitting next to him, when there was a much easier way. But then, Williams was said to do things the hard way. After all, hadn't he lifted the body of a man over a bridge railing and dumped him in the water when he could have driven 100 or so extra yards and rolled the body in the river?

"Why did the X kid live?" I wondered. Here he was, an eyewitness who had come forth with a description of "the killer" in August of 1980. He had said he had seen Williams not just once, but on three occasions. Yet this insidious murder suspect seated beside me at the defense table had chose to let him live. Nothing but the truth, so help me?

The question of conjugal visits for the jurors provided a refreshing sidelight to the trial. Judge Cooper had an agreement with the defense, waiving defense presence when the judge conversed with the jury for the express and limited purpose of informing the jury that he would relax his rule that sequestered the jurors. He said he would allow conjugal visits for married jurors.

Thereafter, the judge told the jurors that he had held prior conversations with one or more of the jurors, off the record (a violation of the defendant's rights). The judge indicated that unmarried jurors might have visits with girlfriends, best friends or "whoever."

The judge told the jurors that there is a law against fornication, but he assured them that no one will supervise "what you do."

Later, however, the judge withdrew his permission for the non-married conjugal visits, in keeping with his original agreement with the defense. When asked if this was because of a complaint from the defense, he told the concerned jurors that perhaps the defense lawyer might have assumed everyone was married. Of course, this hardly could make certain jurors happy with the defense. The possible prejudical effect on the jury because of this incident became a matter of the defense's overall appeal brief.

On the witness stand, a Rockdale County law-enforcement officer swore that Wayne Williams had tried to go through the police lines at the death scene of 15-year-old Terry Pue. I've manned many a police line, and six months afterward (Pue died in January of 1981 and the officer recognized Williams after his arrest six months later), I couldn't identify any stranger who approached me on that line, someone I hadn't seen before or since. Had someone who was 9 feet tall approached, I might be able to pick him out, but not a pudgy black guy with an Afro.

The officer also stated that Williams had given him a business card at the scene with the name "Wayne Williams" on it and that the officer had passed the card along to someone he couldn't recall. But, no one could produce the card. Whoever ended up with it no doubt threw it away. I would have. What did the police need with the card of a photographer? I also wouldn't remember the name on a card I had looked at briefly six months ago. That's why people give you cards—so you can keep them to remember their names later.

Later, the defense would produce a witness who would say that he—not Wayne Williams—was the man who gave his card to the police that day. The witness was a black man and a photographer. So much for another "eyewitness," this time a so-called "trained observer." So much for training to observe, too.

One nattily dressed young woman testified about the day she had seen Wayne Williams with 15-year-old Terry Pue. She would be certain of her testimony. The prosecutor then asked her when this sighting took place.

"April of 1981," she answered.

The prosecutor pressed on, oblivious of the facts. Before Al Binder cross examined her, I passed him a note. It read:

"Pue had been dead then for three months."

Binder looked at me and smiled. The implication of the witness' testimony had eluded Binder, too.

On cross-examination, Binder asked the witness if she was as sure about her identification of Wayne Williams as she was about when it was she saw him with Terry Pue. She was, she assured Binder.

"Then if I told you that Terry Pue had been dead for three months when you say you saw him with Wayne," Binder asked, "would you say you were wrong?"

She agreed she would be wrong if this were the case.

"It *is* the case," Binder said.

The woman would leave the stand, still a model of composure. The state would then unblushingly bring another in the parade of witnesses who had "seen" Wayne Williams with someone.

Next came witnesses in the discovery of the body of 11-year-old Patrick Baltazar. The *Atlanta Constitution* reported that the "prosecution continued to draw a connection with the Omni complex by suggesting that Baltazar frequented the place, just as many other victims had done."

Did the *Constitution* writer realize that Baltazar couldn't help but frequent the Omni since he lived in a house next door to it? And who were these "many other victims" who had frequented the Omni, according to the *Constitution* article? Jimmy Ray Payne's sister said Payne went to a coin shop in the Omni "once." Lubie Geter's girlfriend said she had met him at the Omni, and had a date to return there with him—a date Geter would never keep. Terry Pue was said to go there on occasion.

Other victims may well have been to the Omni. If they had been, I didn't hear about it. But everyone in my family has been to the Omni; most Atlantans have been to the Omni. Victims of these cases also frequented Atlanta-Fulton County Stadium, Grant Field and Grant Park, among other entertainment centers. Finding a pattern of kids at the Omni is about as surprising as finding soldiers at Fort Knox. But Cap'n Pegs? That's something else.

When the prosecution suggested that Baltazar was found close to an expressway, I pushed a note to Binder, urging that he point out how much closer Baltazar's body was to where he worked part time than he was to the Omni, which the prosecution suggested the expressway led straight to. The finding of Baltazar's body on Buford Highway (the body was closer to Buford Highway than to Interstate 85) was not an anomaly; it was very close to Baltazar's job. Because Baltazar might have lived for as long as 72 hours after he was last seen "headed for the Omni," it was more likely that he was headed for his job than for the Omni when he was killed.

Dr. Joseph Burton, medical examiner for DeKalb County, testified that Baltazar was strangled by someone "probably" standing behind him. Here we go again. The "pattern" tightens. Now Burton's guess fits with Stivers' guess. But Burton's is a strangled, "probably" from behind, and Stivers' guess about Nathaniel Cater is only a "possibly" strangled from behind. But the strangulation pattern quickly falls apart again because Baltazar definitely was strangled with a rope, while Cater, if he was stangled at all, definitely was not strangled with a rope.

Next, Kent Hindsman came to the stand. He has known Wayne Williams for years. When he said he saw Wayne Williams on a certain date, at a certain time and in a certain car, I thought he was wrong about the car. He could have been wrong about the date and/or the time, but you can bet he was right that it was Williams.

The date and time he said he was with Williams have since been established from logs and documents of the recording studio where the meeting took place. That means you can pretty well disregard the other prosecution witness who said Williams was far across town in a white Oldsmobile with Lubie Geter, at about this same time.

Now, Kent Hindsman was not alibiing Wayne Williams. He was a state witness who said that 15-year-old Jo-Jo Bell, a victim on The List and one of the state's 10 "pattern" cases, was with Williams and him that day.

However, Hindsman didn't know Jo-Jo Bell. Hindsman might have known, though, that Wayne Williams had business dealings with a young black named Joseph (Jo-Jo) Bell, but I doubt if he knew it was not The List victim, Jo-Jo Bell.

Carla Bailey, an associate of Williams, and Williams himself both say they were with Kent Hindsman that day. They admit that a young black boy was with them, too, but both say it was neither of the Joseph Bells. The defense, through the efforts of Camille Bell (mother of victim Yusuf Bell, but no kin to either of the Joseph Bells), was able to locate the second Jo-Jo Bell and produce him in court.

Hindsman, however, picked out a picture of victim Jo-Jo Bell and swore that it was The List victim he was talking about. But Hindsman kept insisting that the station wagon he rode in with Williams, Carla Bailey and "Jo-Jo Bell" was blue, not white.

In unusual testimony, Hindsman said that while he was at the studio with Wayne Williams, he was handed a note, which he implied that Williams wrote. Hindsman said the note read: "I could be a president. I could be a mayor, or I could even be a killer."

Williams, for his part, doesn't deny the existence of the note. Instead, he said it was written by a youngster as part of the application process for joining the Gemini singing group. Carla Bailey testified that the word "killer" was not in the note, which she said she handed to Hindsman. The note was not produced in evidence.

Hindsman testified that he and Williams had spoken of the murders and that Williams had said they ought to keep their "damned asses" at home. I had heard a lot of policemen, black and white, say the same thing almost two decades ago when black kids were being shot in street riots and on looting sprees.

Williams has confirmed that he basically felt that way about Atlanta's youngsters. He told me that the "kids" had no business out there running the streets (note how Williams also speaks of the Atlanta murders as "kid" murders), but he also said, "That don't give nobody the license to kill." But Williams denied from the stand that he said that to Hindsman.

Wayne Williams talked to me at length about Kent Hindsman. He still considers him somewhat of a friend, their relationship built on a music-business rapport. If Williams is what Hindsman says he is, Hindman doesn't need any enemies. On the other hand, if Williams is not a killer, then with friends like Hindsman, he doesn't need any enemies, either.

Perhaps more than any other single reason, faulty eyewitness testimony has sent innocent people to jail. My own rule-of-thumb: never trust an eyewitness who doesn't know the person he or she is testifying about—unless the suspect is apprehended at the scene.

An eyewitness who knows the person is more believable. For example, I would believe your testimony more readily if you swore that it was *your* friend whom you saw, rather than *my* friend. For this reason, I tend to believe Kent Hindsman's testimony that he saw Wayne Williams, whom he knows.

But I'm not so sure that he saw Jo-Jo Bell, whom Hindsman doesn't know, even though he had no problem identifying Jo-Jo Bell's picture.

Meanwhile, during a recess, a guy who looked like a nightclub bouncer entered the defense room, saying, "I just thought you ought to know . . ." He proceeded to tell of having sat in a waiting room where he said he heard prosecution witnesses being coached in their testimony.

The state's next witness, 21-year-old Eugene Laster, testified that he saw Jo-Jo Bell get into Williams' car, but he couldn't remember when. The Hindsman testimony would have put Williams with Bell, but that would have been two months before Bell disappeared.

Laster said he knew Bell because he played basketball with him. He would also say that he knew Williams because he had met him at his (Laster's) grandmother's house. Laster met my first criterion for an "eyewitness": he apparently knew both people he was talking about. But when did he see this? What was he an eyewitness to?

Eugene Laster's 15-year-old younger brother, John, would testify next. He told the jury that he had talked to Jo-Jo Bell about Wayne Williams and that Jo-Jo Bell had Williams' telephone number. The younger Laster said Williams had once told him that he knew Jo-Jo Bell. But which Jo-Jo Bell?

The latter statement could be explained away. If Bell had Williams' phone number, it would come as no great surprise since Williams was paying people to distribute flyers with his phone number on them. But how would he put Williams' name with that number? Williams' name was not on the flyer. But under any circumstances, if he had Williams' number, it couldn't be sloughed off.

The important part was: Did victim Jo-Jo Bell know Wayne Williams personally?

If Jo-Jo Bell did know Williams, it could well be the most damning testimony of the trial. It had become a trial in which knowing a victim became synonomous with guilt of murder. It was a trial in which even if the state's fiber evidence held up, it would put victims in the environment of the *three* Williamses. But it wouldn't prove that anyone touched, let alone killed, anybody. Now the "eyewitnesses" could prove only one other thing if they were right—that Wayne Williams lied when he said in his news conference that he didn't know any of the victims.

Al Binder pounced on Eugene Laster on cross-examination. He wanted to know about the three detectives Binder contended had been "coaching" Laster on his testimony before he took the stand. But Laster said that the detectives "just refreshed my memory of what I seen when they first came to my house." Apparently, he meant what he told the detectives, when they first came to his house, about what he had seen earlier of Jo-Jo Bell and Wayne Williams.

Tilbert Bynham, 35, nicknamed "Cool Breeze," told the jury that he had taken a few "herbs" before taking the witness stand for the state against Wayne Williams.

Jack Mallard committed what to me was a fatal error. He asked Bynham about a lie-detector test he had *passed.* What Mallard did was a big no-no—one that the Georgia Supreme Court would castigate him for. The witness was then allowed to proceed over Binder's objection.

"Cool Breeze" testified that 20-year-old Larry Rogers (no kin to Pat Man), one of the state's 10 "pattern" victims, had bought a marijuana cigarette from him for $1 and then went away in a car with Wayne Williams. It looked like a "fast car," he said. The date "Cool Breeze" gave for seeing Williams and Rogers together was several days before Larry Rogers disappeared in March of 1981.

Next on the stand, Nellie Trammell—grandmotherly looking, God-fearing and church-going—testified that she saw victim Larry Rogers slumped in the front seat of a faded green station wagon driven by Wayne Williams on March 30, 1981. Larry Rogers was not seen alive after that day. But it wasn't until three days later that he was reported missing.

Nellie Trammell also said that she had seen Williams 10 days earlier and that he was taking pictures of the confrontation between the police and the "bat patrol" in Techwood Homes. This, of course, would have been the day 21-year-old Eddie (Bubba) Duncan, who lived in Techwood Homes, disappeared. She testified that she saw Duncan on that same day and told Duncan, "It's too bad someone's killing all these children." She also said she saw Williams at Duncan's funeral.

Judge Cooper later instructed the jury to disregard any mention of Bubba Duncan during the testimony because Duncan's slaying was not among the state's 10 "pattern" cases. Which was interesting enough, since Duncan, like Payne and Cater, was a victim who died of "probable asphyxia" and was found in the Chattahoochee River "pattern" criteria that none of the 10 so-called "pattern" cases met. And most importantly, Duncan was one of those unnamed bodies in the "south end" of the Chattahoochee River that Judge Cooper permitted Lee Brown to testify about—over the objection of Al Binder.

This also showed that Cooper didn't understand the so-called "pattern." When the state introduced testimony about a body (which, in reality, was Duncan's, but was not named), Cooper permitted testimony about it, thinking that the Chattahoochee River victims being discussed were part of "the pattern." But when Duncan was testifed about by name, Cooper would not allow the testimony into the record because Duncan wasn't one of the admissible 10 "pattern" cases.

Nellie Trammell's testimony upset Binder, not because she got the Duncan story into the trial. Instead, he knew that the kindly looking grandmother and church goer would be as hard to attack as apple pie. Binder was convinced that her testimony had been very damaging to Wayne Williams. "I don't know how we'll ever recover from that," Binder said, slumping into his chair.

So taken was Binder himself with Nellie Trammell's testimony that he went to Wayne Williams' holding cell to "confront Wayne" about the Trammell testimony. There, Williams would tell Binder to his face that what Nellie Trammell said was not true.

Meanwhile, Jim Kitchens, a Mississippi lawyer friend of Binder and a former prosecutor, joined the defense team. He and Binder just happened to meet on a plane, Kitchens said, and Binder invited him to Atlanta to watch the proceedings.

Maybe so, but Binder had placed a call to Kitchens and I don't think the invitation was just to watch. Binder needed help, and he called on someone he knew and trusted. He thought that the cross-examination of Nellie Trammell was an excellent place to deploy Jim Kitchens. Binder didn't want to come across as a "heavy" with the likes of Nellie Trammell on the stand.

Under cross-examination, Nellie Trammell told Kitchens that she had seen Wayne Williams before—because her church "is across from" Williams' house. She added that she had picked out a picture of Wayne Williams from a photo lineup presented to her in April of 1981, by one of the prosecutors. When asked, "Which prosecutor?" she pointed to and identified Jack Mallard. Well, the star witness who worried Al Binder so much had feet of clay. I knew it right away, but it wouldn't be until that night when I could put all of Nellie Trammell's testimony in proper perspective.

I pointed out to Binder that Nellie Trammell couldn't have picked a picture of Wayne Williams from a lineup in April of 1981 because Williams didn't even become a suspect until the last week of May of 1981. No police photo lineup had included a picture of Wayne Williams in April of 1981.

That night, Paul Crawley of WXIA-TV telephoned and said he had called the pastor at the True Light Baptist Church across from the Williamses' house. Paul and I had met and spoken with the pastor during the police-media stakeout prior to Williams' arrest. Now the pastor told Paul that he didn't know Nellie Trammell and she was not a member of his church, as she had stated from the witness stand.

Paul also told me that he had talked to the man who had directed Nellie Trammell to the prosecutors and that the first time she talked with them was in December of 1981, not in April of 1981, as she had testified.

That bothered me a lot. If that were so, then Jack Mallard, the assistant prosecutor, must have known that she was wrong in her testimony. I didn't understand why, as an officer of the court, he wasn't obligated to correct the misinformation for the court at the time that it was given by Nellie Trammell.

I figured that Mallard had to know whether he met Nellie Trammell in April or December of 1981 and whether he had then, if ever, shown her a picture of Wayne Williams. I took his non-disagreement with her testimony as support for what she said. Wouldn't the jury, too?

I asked Binder, "Why not call Mallard to the stand and ask him about the incident?"

Binder's interpretation was that under Georgia law, he wouldn't want to do that since it would leave the state open to ask Mallard questions on cross-examination and, through his answers, introduce into evidence things the state could not otherwise get in the record. It was yet another gambit in the criminal-justice game. "The whole truth"?

Then "Serpico," ex-Atlanta police recruit Ken Lawson, came forward to tell Binder that Nellie Trammell had spent a lot of time around the Task Force headquarters. They considered her a "psychic," Lawson said. The defense wouldn't bother to check her story of seeing Williams at both Larry Rogers' and Bubba Duncan's funerals. Wayne Williams told me later he wasn't at any of the funerals "period," although his father had attended some, taking pictures for the *Atlanta Daily World.*

DeKalb County Medical Examiner Joseph Burton testified that the pattern of stab wounds in the body of 17-year-old William Barrett "suggested" (still more verbage to cover these "scientific" medical findings) "a type of ritual associated with the body."

I listened in dumbfounded disbelief. Now the state was serving up the occult to those who chose to accept the "more supernatural" of the *potpourri* of motives offered by the prosecution.

Whoever heard of a ritual being performed "once"? If Barrett was "ritually" marked, then it only served to separate him from the state's "pattern" since neither Cater nor Payne, nor any of the other nine "pattern" cases; nor, for that matter, any of the victims on The List had been "ritually" marked, as Burton suggests Barrett was.

Burton also said that Barrett's stab wounds were made after Barrett was killed, he said, by strangulation. How can a dead body bleed? In fact, the medical evidence is that there was no external bleeding. Where, then, did the blood come from that left stains from Barrett in Williams' station wagon?

Now the stab wounds were said to "resemble" those suffered by 28-year-old John Porter and 14-year-old Eric Middlebrooks. I don't know how, except that they were puncture wounds. But so is a bullet hole.

The wounds on Middlebrooks had been described as superficial and V-shaped. Porter was stabbed deeply, and six times, while Barrett's wounds were "ritualistic" markings. To me, the evidence once again seemed convenient and tailored to specific objectives, even objectives that are mutually exclusive.

Reporters Hyde Post and David Hilder of the *Atlanta Journal* summed up the state's so-called "eyewitnesses" (eyewitness to what?): "The quality of witnesses used to link Williams with the 10 other cases," they reported, "has run the gamut from a well-spoken graduate of Clark College who knew the defendant and a victim [which he most certainly did not] and who placed them together, to a fast-service restaurant employee who, on cross-examination, said she saw victim Terry Pue with Williams in April 1981, three months after Pue was buried."

Notice the *Journal* took the perspective that the testimony was to link Williams with the 10 other cases. Of course, this was the purpose of the testimony; but the fact is, the jury was now deciding whether Williams was the murderer of these 10 victims. Even Cater and Payne were quickly all but forgotten and they should not have been. The jury should have been asking itself with every piece of evidence introduced, "What does that have to do with proving that Wayne Williams killed Nathaniel Cater or Jimmy Ray Payne?"

Remember the law on which the admission of the "pattern" testimony was based:

> ". . . Once the testimony of the accused as the perpetrator of the offense separate and distinct from the one for which he is on trial has been proven [sic], testimony concerning the independent crime may be submitted. . ."

But no one had proved Wayne Williams killed any of the 10 "pattern" victims, or anybody.

Now testimony was brought in an attempt to place Williams with 17-year-old victim William Barrett. "An aunt and cousin of Barrett testified that Williams had come to their home with Barrett in late 1980, several months before he was killed," the *Atlanta Journal* reported.

Actually, Mary Harris said she wasn't sure whom Wayne Williams had come to her house with, and "several months" had to be more than six months because Barrett didn't die until mid-May of 1981. Wayne Williams would surprise me after the trial by telling me that he thought he might well have been at Mary Harris' house, although he couldn't remember what the occasion might have been, either.

Then the state brought a witness to show that the Williamses owned or rented eight vehicles during the series of slayings. The problem is, other than the station wagon Wayne Williams was stopped in, none fit the vehicle descriptions given by the state's "eyewitnesses" or the fiber evidence.

Meanwhile, Al Binder cross-examined medical examiner Burton on the William Barrett case. Binder asked if the knife injuries to Barrett could have been inflicted by one person while another held him and strangled him. Binder had asked a "could it be?" question that had it been asked by the prosecution would have been answered with an enthusiastic "yes."

But since it was asked by the defense, "yes" came out this way: "Your theory of two killers for Barrett is not necessarily correct. But that's a possibility." He was right, of course, so why did we have this testimony? Everything was still a "possibility," it seemed.

Binder could have said the same thing about Burton's theories and those of Stivers, Zaki and Feegel. But all these theories came in as medical evidence.

Former Atlanta Police Bureau homicide detective R.H. Buffington testified that he recovered a "tuft" of red, woolen-looking fiber, from one of Eric Middlebrooks' tennis shoes after the youngster's body was found.

Then GBI Agent Dale Kirkland testified that samples of red carpet were retrieved from a "1979 Ford LTD owned by the Williamses from May 15, 1979, until December 4, 1980."

Kirkland also missed "the whole truth" about that 1979 Ford. His testimony didn't explain why Middlebrooks, who was last seen leaving home on a bicycle, was found only a few feet from that bicycle if he had been riding in Williams' burgundy 1979 Ford LTD. But the state would say Middlebrooks had fibers from both the floor rug and the trunk.

Of course, Middlebrooks could have gone riding with Wayne Williams or, for that matter, a lot of other people. But the killer returned the victim to the exact point where he picked him up—unless he went to the trouble to haul the bicycle around, too.

Eric Middlebrooks was *bludgeoned* to death. Head wounds are notoriously bloody. Although the state ostensibly found blood from William Barrett, who was stabbed after he was strangled to death, it found no blood from Middlebrooks in Williams' car. Instead, it found Middlebrooks lying in a pool of blood.

In the less than 12 hours between Eric Middlebrooks' disappearance and when he turned up dead in May of 1980, Wayne Williams says he was with the mother of James Comento, a white friend. Williams wouldn't tell me that until long after the trial. He said he hadn't been asked for an alibi until I asked him. He also said he didn't know the disappearance and finding dates of any of the victims until I sent them to him two months after his conviction.

When he told me of this alibi, I was less than overwhelmed. Not that he might not be telling the truth, but I knew what the immediate reaction would be among the police and prosecutors. It was, after all, suspicion about Comento (who was driving the vehicle registered to Williams' news-gathering service) that first led the police to talk to Williams.

The first month of the trial ended with Fulton County Sheriff Leroy Stynchcombe increasing his estimate of the cost of the trial. He revised it from his late December estimate of "approximately" $117,216 to as high as $1 million. Something seems amiss in the sheriff's budget department, which reflects the level of accuracy usually found in "official" estimates.

February dawned with the state's fiber experts back on the stand again. The FBI's Harold Deadman said fibers from the body of 12-year-old Charles Stephens matched those in Wayne Williams' bedspread, his bedroom carpet (carpet which, by the way, extends through most of the Williamses' house, but it sounds more sinister to say the fibers came from Williams' bedroom than from the family dining room); carpet squares from the office area of the Williamses' house, the 1979 Ford LTD's trunk liner and other fibers found in the 1970 Chevrolet station wagon that Williams had driven. No mention was made of the blanket thrown over Stephens' body by an East Point policeman. Which, the FBI said, "contaminated" the fiber evidence.

In sum, Deadman testified that the fiber transfers "came about through contact either with items from the home of Wayne Williams or the automobile of Wayne Williams."

When I had first studied the state's fiber evidence in December of 1981, I found what I thought was a fatal flaw in the state's case. Then I heard Deadman testify that fibers from the Williams vehicles found on victims came about by contact between the victims and those vehicles.

But when I heard Deadman say that if it could be proved that the victims did not come in contact with those environments, then his findings would be virtually "meaningless," I *knew* I had found that fatal flaw, to wit:

In his pre-trial letter dated December 7, 1981, Deadman wrote to assistant prosecutor Gordon Miller:

> ". . . The trunk liner [trunk carpet] present in the trunk of a 1979 Ford sedan, item #233C [item 233C identifies the 1979 Ford LTD once owned by the Williams family], is a felted material composed primarily of numerous different types of man-made fibers, all of which have a black substance adhering to the fiber's surface . . . [and] were recovered from . . . the following victims: Eric Middlebrooks, Aaron Wyche, Anthony Carter, *Earl Terrell, Clifford Jones,* and *Charles Stephens* [emphasis added].
>
> "Some of these undyed fibers from the above mentioned victims exhibit the same microscopic characteristics and the same optical properties as fibers present in *the* [emphasis added] 1979 Ford trunk liner and could have originated from

> this trunk liner. Other fibers from these victims, while not matching a specific fiber type in the trunk liner, are consistent with having originated from material like *the* [emphasis added] 1979 Ford trunk liner. . ."

First, one must understand that these are as strong as any statement ever made about the comparison of any fibers. When the jury was told the fibers matched, it was this kind of language that supported those matches.

Now, track the following chronology:

—July 30, 1980. At 9 a.m., the Williamses' 1979 Ford sedan (identified above as item 233C) is left at Hub Ford in Atlanta for repairs. The Williamses rent a Ford compact.

—July 30, 1980. At 3:30 p.m., Earl Lee Terrell disappears after being banished from the South Bend Park swimming pool (his remains would be found six months later).

—August 7, 1980. The Williamses return the rental car and retrieve their 1979 Ford sedan from Hub Ford.

—August 8, 1980. The Williamses' 1979 Ford will not start. Hub Ford dispatches a wrecker and tows it back to its garage for further repairs. The Williamses rent a second time—either a Pinto or a Fairmont.

—August 20, 1980. At approximately 1 p.m., Clifford Jones disappears (his body would be found, wrapped in plastic, beside a dumpster near the laundromat at the Hollywood Plaza Shopping Center at 2 o'clock the next morning).

(Meanwhile, the Williamses are notified that repairs to the 1979 Ford would cost more than $1,300. They contact an attorney, who informs Hub Ford and the Ford Motor Credit Corporation that the Williamses no longer want the car and will not pay for it. The Williamses never again have access to the car, which would not be formally repossessed until December of 1980.)

—October 9, 1980. At approximately 8 p.m., Charles Stephens disappears (his body would be found at a trailer park in suburban East Point, Georgia, at about 7 o'clock the next morning).

—October 21, 1980. The Williamses obtain a white 1970 Chevrolet station wagon in Columbus, Georgia. In the rear of the station wagon is a white throw rug (fibers from which, the state would say, were found on Charles Stephens, even though he already had been buried for about one week *before* the Williamses obtained the vehicle). The Williamses return the second car they had rented from Hub Ford.

According to these facts—and by his own definition—Deadman's findings of fiber matches among victims Earl Lee Terrell, Clifford Jones and Charles Stephens are meaningless. These victims could *not* have come in contact with the red 1979 Ford—item 233C!

If these fiber matches are meaningless, what does this say about the validity of *all* of the fiber evidence? In my view, the foregoing chronology renders the state's fiber evidence against Wayne Williams worthless.

I had spotted this gaping hole in the state's fiber case in one of the matrices I had made of fibers and victims on the very first day I had seen the evidence. The state argued that an "undyed man-made fiber with a black substance adhering to it," which matched those from the trunk liner of a 1979 Ford LTD owned by the Williamses, had been found on several victims. Among those victims were Earl Terrell, Clifford Jones and Charles Stephens. But I asked myself: How could this be? Look at the chronology again, if you must, but ask yourself the same question.

Apparently Investigator M.F. Jones had relied on registration (ownership) records to determine that the Williamses' 1979 Ford was in their possession until December of 1980, as Dale Kirkland testified. Either that, or he assumed that the repossession by Ford Motor Credit corresponded with when the vehicle left the Williamses' possession. But, in either case, he was wrong, and the state went blissfully along, building a case against Wayne Williams that was a house of cards. But, to some, it looked like the Rock of Gibraltar.

Again, one of the plausible pieces of the state's jig-saw puzzle didn't fit when checked against the whole mosaic.

Deadman also mentioned that a "slapjack" had been found in the ceiling of Wayne Williams' home during a search. Then John Feegel, a Fulton County associate medical examiner, testified that Eric Middlebrooks died from blows from a blunt instrument, which, he said, "could have been caused by blows from a slapjack."

There's that word again: "could." Sure, they *could* have been caused by a "slapjack." But no one had ever mentioned a slapjack causing the wounds until more than a year after Middlebrooks died—not until a slapjack was found in Wayne Williams' house. Until then, it always had been something like a board that was presumed to cause the blows on Middlebrooks. It could have been a lacrosse stick or a canoe paddle, too. There were no blood stains or other evidentiary material on the slapjack.

Even though the state made 15-year-old Jo-Jo Bell one of its 10 "pattern" cases, Deadman refused to connect Bell with the "pattern," explaining that he could find only two matching fibers with Williams' environment. Deadman linked the other nine "pattern" victims to Williams because, he said, four matching fibers were found on each victim. But later, the count for Alfred Evans would be lowered to 3.

Now we had to deal with a new set of arbitrary, pulled-out-of-the-air numbers. And whatever happened to the combination of "*eight*" fibers which made it "unlikely" that any other environment could account for the combination? All the victims did *not* have the so-called unusual trilobal fiber. Now, mark well that only one victim had the combination of eight; some had only a single fiber and not the trilobal one at that.

Again, the state's case was buttressed with yet another arbitrary judgment call. Keep in mind that Bell was the *only* one of the 10 "pattern" victims who was found in a river. Lee Brown had testified that the "pattern" after

February 11, 1981, was that bodies started turning up in rivers. Cater and Payne, the victims whose cases the "pattern" was supposed to relate to, had both turned up in the Chattahoochee River. Now, Deadman says Jo-Jo Bell, the only one of 10 "pattern" cases to turn up in a river (the South River), cannot be connected to the "pattern." What pattern?

Meanwhile, in another courtroom, Linda Wyche, the mother of victim Aaron Wyche, was being cleared in the stabbing death of her common-law husband. Hardly anybody noticed.

Now another fiber "expert," Barry Gaudette, scientific adviser to the Royal Canadian Mounted Police, took the stand to corroborate what was, to me, dubious testimony because of the cars and the "Deadman deadline" (fibers disappearing in a fraction more than 33 hours). Gaudette testified that "it is nearly certain" that there was some form of association between the victims and the environment of Wayne Williams.

Then Gaudette, using ultra-violet and specially dyed material, performed a demonstration of fiber transfer. The deputy sheriffs guarding Wayne Williams moved close to him, and then the courtroom lights were turned off. Assistant prosecutor Gordon Miller lay on the floor, resting his head on the treated carpet square. With the lights still off, an ultra-violet light was shined on Miller's hair, highlighting the colorful fibers.

Could the jury see them? "Yes, oh yes," came the reply. Al Binder, none too happy with the demonstration, missed a chance to demand that the state now also demonstrate the transfer of fibers from Miller to the carpet square. Thus, the jury didn't get an opportunity to see the "whole truth."

"Let the record reflect that the district attorney just laid down on his back and rubbed his head on the carpet," Binder said, and walked away.

Binder said that the defense would show that the 1978 Plymouth once owned by the Williamses did not have a trunk liner in it when they owned it. Hyde Post of the *Atlanta Journal* noted, "If true, the assertion by Binder would cast serious doubt on the validity of a purported match between fibers found on the body of one victim and the trunk liner, and it could also cast shadows on the reliability of the other fiber links." I was glad to read this report, but I couldn't understand how the reporters had completely missed the same issue involving the 1979 Ford LTD and three other victims.

Actually, I don't think Binder could prove that "the 1978 Plymouth didn't have a trunk liner," although Wayne and Homer Williams both insisted that it didn't. The problem for me was that the Williamses owned five Plymouths, from 1975 through 1978.

But the state, too, had problems with the 1978 Plymouth. The description it gave for the fiber that matches the trunk liner from the 1978 Plymouth is, word for word, the same description it used for the fibers from the 1979 Ford, down to and including the notation of "with a black substance adhering thereto."

I never did think that the state had a fiber from a 1978 Plymouth. I think it had a list that showed that Williams owned a Plymouth in July of 1979.

Did the state know that the Williamses owned the Ford at the same time? I'm not sure the state did because one of the main features of the prosecution's appeal brief was a graphic display of how the character of the fibers changed as the Williamses changed cars. There was no validity to this claim.

It works perfectly for the state because it has no trouble ignoring the facts that the Williamses did have the Ford in July of 1979, but didn't have it in August, September and October of 1980.

I looked in vain for a comparison between the "undyed manmade fibers with a black substance adhering thereto," which purportedly matched fibers from the trunk of Wayne Williams' Plymouth, and the "undyed manmade fibers with a black substance adhering thereto," which purportedly matched fibers from the trunk of Wayne Williams' 1979 Ford. I never saw one comparison. But the state would have had to have made one, right? It was "anything but the whole truth!"

Next, state crime lab analysts came to the stand to say that five blood stains had been found in the Williamses' 1970 Chevrolet station wagon. Three of those, they said, matched with two blood types from two victims. The other two stains could not be typed. Two of the stains were blood Type A—William Barrett's type. One was Type B—John Porter's type. Then the types were further matched by enzymes.

The analysts disagreed on whether the age of a blood stain could be scientifically determined. This was extremely important. One analyst said that the blood stains were less than eight weeks old because of a certain enzyme that still was present—an enzyme that was in both Porter's and Barrett's blood. And, both Porter and Barrett had died within the eight weeks before the blood stains were examined.

The other analyst said it wasn't possible to determine how old a blood stain was. If she was right, then the allegations that the blood stains came from Barrett and Porter were weakened considerably.

Williams' blood type was "O". But no one checked the blood types of Wayne Williams' mother or father, and no one checked the blood types of the Barnhart family (Wayne's aunt, uncle and cousins), who actually owned the station wagon in which the blood stains were found.

At this point, Larry Peterson of the state crime lab conceded to Binder that fibers similar to those found on the bodies of some victims had been found on the clothing of missing children who later were located alive.

But Peterson said the matching fibers among these children did not match fibers from Wayne Williams' home, so he "disregarded their matching fibers from the slaying victims." Peterson also conceded that "thousands of fibers" found on the victims' bodies were similarly disregarded.

"As far as you know, some of those fibers you disregarded could be the fibers of a killer?" Binder asked.

"I don't know," Peterson replied.

Could they have matched fibers from the house on Gray Street? Did anybody bother to find out? If so, no one told the jury. But then, the jury didn't even know there was a house on Gray Street, as you now do.

Binder, meanwhile, caused somewhat of a stir during the trial by calling Williams "boy." Some reporters asked Mary Welcome, who is black, if the remark weren't racist. How could the 23-year-old Williams be called a "boy"?

Her answer was on target. "It happens the same way a 30-year-old man is called a missing or murdered child," she said.

Indeed, many were offended, saying that Wayne Williams was insulted by the word "boy," which many consider a racial epithet. But few of these same concerned people, if anybody, would care about Wayne Williams' "feelings" about being sentenced to life on testimony that merely suggests he "could" have been a killer.

Andrew Hayes told the court that Wayne Williams had offered him $20 for sex. He swore that he met Williams two or three years earlier in the game room of the West End Mall and that Timmy Hill was there, too.

Hayes also testified that he went to martial-arts movies with Williams and drove around with him in a Buick Skylark equipped with a police radio. He couldn't remember when all of this happened. He said he was confused about the car's color. The Williams family did at one time own a Buick Skylark, but it was for only three months in 1974. Wayne Williams was 16 then. Timmy Hill was 6.

The state then attempted to introduce charred photographs found in the barbecue grill at the Williamses' house. Even though the state admitted that it didn't know what had been on the photographs, it suggested that sometime between the May 22, 1981, bridge incident and the June 3, 1981, search, Wayne Williams destroyed evidence that would link him to the deaths of Nathaniel Cater and Jimmy Ray Payne, among others.

During a pre-trial hearing, Task Force commander Morris Redding had testified that Atlanta police detective Sidney Dorsey saw books on fingerprinting and on forensic and scientific identification techniques in Williams' house during the June 3 search. But, Redding said, the books could not be found on a later search.

One witness called by the prosecution should have been called by the defense. He was a youngster who said that Wayne Williams, who had recruited him to join a singing group, had admonished him about smoking pot, and had come to his house and introduced him to other people in the music business. Both the boy and the prosecutor implied that these activities were sinister. Recruiting young musicians, however, was exactly what Wayne Williams said he did for a living.

Another boy told the court how Wayne Williams had met him and the boy's parents, had paid the family's way to Atlanta, had again sent him round-trip bus fare from home in South Carolina to Atlanta, and had taken him to a recording studio.

When he wanted to go home, the boy said, Homer and Faye Williams arranged an earlier return by bus and took him to the station.

Did Wayne Williams touch him? "No," the boy said.

Did he suggest anything that might be out of line? "No."

Then what did Wayne Williams do that called for this prosecution testimony? One day, Williams drove the boy across *a* bridge! The youngster said he himself could even find the bridge again.

The boy said he met Willie Hunter, who, he said, asked him about sex and that while he was at Williams' home, he met someone named "Nathaniel."

He said Williams never made a recording of him. Williams said later that he didn't record the youngster because the boy "froze up" in front of the microphone.

Then came the testimony about the repossession of the Williamses' blue Plymouth. In it was a two-way radio, a scanner (capable of receiving police calls), a blue light and a yellow flashing light. The radio was licensed and broken. The vehicle carried a license for an emergency flasher. The scanner is legal and can be owned by anyone. The blue light is illegal, if used.

Wayne Williams said he used the car in the news-gathering business. In 1983, WSB-TV (Channel 2) aired a news segment on Williams' friend, Jim Comento, in which Comento drove his own private car, light flashing and siren blaring, to the scene of an injured person whom Comento had heard about on a police radio.

It was Comento who used to drive the Williamses' Plymouth on the same kind of missions. What had been painted as sinister and damaging circumstances by the media during the trial of Wayne Williams suddenly became the basis for a feature segment about a Good Samaritan. Now the driver was Mr. Clean and Dr. Kildare rolled into one, not Dr. Jekyll.

Here the state wants us to believe that these radios and lights are instruments of the devil, allowing a man to prey on street children who think he is a policeman. Then the state conjures up images of this killer who sits around in parks and talks to victims, weeks before he kills them. Then the state portrays this killer as someone who cultivates his victims for years before he kills them.

All of this seemed carefully calculated as "evidence" only to satisfy how the victims were enticed into a car—the standard perception. But there was no need to lure these victims into vehicles. In context, police radios, blue lights, *et cetera,* do not fit the big picture, except that they come across as individual jig-saw pieces, not yet snapped into the mosaic. Surely these pieces should help complete the picture. They don't!

Denise Marlin, an employee of an ambulance company, said she knew Wayne Williams as a news photographer at accident scenes. The assistant prosecutor, Jack Mallard, asked her whether Williams ever used language "derogatory of his own race."

"Yes, sir," she responded. "He used to call his own race 'niggers.'" Gasp! This means that Wayne Williams had done what many other blacks have done. Comedian Richard Pryor, who made a fortune out of calling other blacks "niggers," recently said he is stopping the practice and urged others to stop as well. So we're not talking about anything that is in any way unusual.

The motive for all these killings, the prosecutors suggested, was that Wayne Williams, a young black, hated young blacks. But he had, according to these prosecutors, killed someone older than he.

Now a state witness said he had seen Wayne Williams walking out of the downtown Rialto Theater, "holding hands" with Nathaniel Cater. I had heard this story months earlier, but at that time the storyteller purportedly was the witness' cellmate, who mysteriously died before the trial.

Meanwhile, in the same testimony, it was said that Williams had walked "close" behind a transvestite. Does any of this prove murder? Hardly. About all it proves is that a take-your-pick variety appealing to alleged biases or prejudices can be thrown at the jurors by one witness' testimony.

The state presented a singer, Joe Graham, who testified that he went to Wayne Williams' home to pose for promotional photographs and that Williams had him take off his coat and tie to provide a "sexier pose." End of this witness' incriminating testimony.

The defense introduced in evidence the posters of Graham, which had been made from photographs by Williams. It was, after all, Wayne Williams' business. He never concealed the fact that he did promotional work for musicians.

The next witness, Billy Pitman, a 22-year-old singer, testified that Williams had signed him to a contract, taken publicity pictures of him and invited him to several music showcases. But, Pitman said, nothing had ever come of it. From this, Pitman deduced that Williams "was not what he said he was, or who he said he was, at least to me." End of another piece of outrageous testimony that was supposed to prove Wayne Williams a murderer.

Then came an 80-year-old witness, A.B. Dean, who was hard of hearing. When asked if he had a hearing defect, his answer was "Huh?"

Dean testified that he saw Wayne Williams standing next to a taxi cab (the driver was inside), talking to Jimmy Ray Payne on Bankhead Highway (U.S. 278), about a mile from the Chattahoochee River. Williams' white 1970 Chevrolet station wagon, he said, was parked across the street. He said this occurred on April 22, the day Payne was said to have disappeared.

Although no one except his murderer(s) could know when Jimmy Ray Payne had died, his indictment said that he was murdered on—not on or about—April 22, 1981. Did this mean that Wayne Williams would have to account for his own whereabouts on the one day to alibi the Payne charge? I think not. But, conversely, I do think the indictment is faulty.

Dean further testified that he saw all of this while his nephew drove rapidly along Bankhead Highway. He said he already had cautioned his nephew to slow down—and the muffler blew off their car. They stopped about 500 feet from Williams and Payne, Dean said, and he watched them from across the street.

Then, Dean testified, Jimmy Ray Payne's picture appeared in the newspaper. Dean said he took the picture to a sheriff and told him he had seen Payne. Then, Dean said, when Williams' picture appeared in the paper, Dean went to another sheriff and said he had seen Williams with Payne.

Oddly, although Dean said he recognized Wayne Williams from a speeding car, he did have trouble recognizing someone while standing still in the courtroom, from less than 30 feet away. Dean testified that defense investigator Durwood Myers (who was standing in the rear of the courtroom) wore the same type of clothes in court that he wore when he visited Dean at his home on January 5, 1982. Myers, tall, well-dressed and distinctive looking, said he never had been to Dean's house. Instead, two other investigators had. The taller investigator of the two was 4 inches shorter and 40 pounds lighter than Durwood Myers.

So much for eyewitnesses who can't hear or apparently see very well.

The prosecution now brought another ambulance employee, Bobby Toland. Under oath, Toland stated that Williams once asked Toland if he ever had considered "how many niggers you could eliminate by killing one black male child." Remember, please, that Wayne Williams was on trial for killing a man who was four years older than Williams himself is—and that the state was suggesting that the reasons for that killing were "homosexual."

Now the trial took a turn for the worse for Wayne Williams. Shyron Blakely, who testified that she was a former business associate, stated that Williams had told her during the previous summer that he would "confess" if he feared getting "hurt" by the authorities.

She said that after Williams became a suspect, she asked him on the telephone: "If they get enough evidence, will you confess before you get hurt?" She said Williams answered, "Yes." Williams also told her, she said, that "he could knock out black street kids in a few minutes by putting his hand on their necks."

This was the most devastating testimony against Wayne Williams in the entire trial. And with this salvo, the state rested its case.

Al Binder immediately moved for a directed verdict of not guilty, and the judge immediately refused. Now it was the defense's turn.

Ken Lawson, a tall, drawling, free-spirited cop, had received citations of merit for his work with suburban Atlanta police departments before joining the Atlanta Police Bureau as a recruit. Unlike some other Atlanta police recruits, Lawson didn't hesitate to dive into water to save someone's life—in Lawson's case, the life of a small child. And for this, Lawson was cited for bravery.

But in June of 1981, Lawson resigned under a cloud of domestic problems, poor grades at the academy and missing four days of training.

Even so, Lawson had occupied a front-row seat with other recruits at Task Force headquarters and on the river stakeouts. He had come forward with information that he believed should be known. Thus, he acquired the nickname "Serpico," after the ex-New York cop, Frank Serpico, whose expose of police corruption had inspired a book and movie of the same name.

Testifying for the defense at the Wayne Williams trial, Lawson said that recruit Freddie Jacobs had spoken of seeing "ghosts" on the riverbank. He said that recruit Bob Campbell told him that Campbell and Jacobs were asleep on the same side of the Jackson Parkway bridge on the morning that Williams was stopped. Lawson also told me that some officers had consumed alcoholic beverages while on the stakeouts and that their wives brought beer to them and they all shared in the liquid refreshment together.

Meanwhile, both the pastor and the chairman of the board of the True Light Baptist Church—across the street from Wayne Williams' house—testified that they never had seen prosecution witness Nellie Trammell at their worship services and that she was not a member of the church. They conceded, however, that she could have visited the church without their knowledge.

Next, Daniel Stowens, a pathologist from New York, by way of Louisville, was called by the defense. Stowens was experienced with children's deaths and had been associated with the Children's Hospital while I lived in Louisville.

But Stowens testified about two deaths that were *not* children's cases. He stated that 27-year-old Nathaniel Cater appeared to have been dead for at least a week when the body was found on May 24, 1981. This was a much shorter time than what he first had suggested to me before the trial. But it still was a time span which was completely refuted by the evidence in the case—if the body was that of Nathaniel Cater.

Stowens disagreed with the findings of murder in the Cater and Jimmy Ray Payne cases and in at least three of the state's 10 "pattern" cases. I couldn't care less. They all (including Stowens) were guessing. If there were anything scientific about it, you would expect a precise sameness in their testimony. Science is supposed to produce replication, not confusion.

Cater and Payne might have died from any number of causes, including leukemia or pneumonia, Stowens testified. He was "shocked and incensed,"

Stowens added, that murder charges had been brought in the deaths of Cater and Payne, in which he found no evidence of foul play.

Then Stowens said, interestingly, that Fulton County Medical Examiner Robert Stivers, who performed the Cater autopsy, had said with reference to the state's plans to prosecute the Cater case, "They aren't going to use that case, are they?" During cross-examination, assistant prosecutor Jack Mallard pointed out that the medical examiner's remarks were made in December of 1981 and that Williams had been indicted more than four months earlier. But did Stivers know that? Stowens' testimony didn't add up very well.

Mallard made Stowens look particularly shaky when Stowens had to admit that a reference about Nathaniel Cater's eyes was not in the autopsy report, contrary to what Stowens had testified to earlier. It was from this reference that Stowens had estimated how long Cater had been in the water.

Mallard also attacked (as I would have) Stowens' contention that homosexual slayings are particularly violent. I don't know that homosexuals tend to do more of anything than heterosexuals do, except have sex with persons of their own sex.

Moreover, Mallard jumped on Stowens' description of knife wounds on slain 17-year-old William Barrett as "teasing." Stowens insisted that the wounds were not the kind one sees in a "sexual rage." Just what is a "sexual rage"?

Stowens went on to admit that he had granted press interviews in violation of the judge's gag order. While Stowens testified, some reporters watching in the closed-circuit TV room laughed and scoffed at him. Many made no secret that they were convinced that Wayne Williams was guilty, even though this was only the first day of testimony for the defense.

What bothered me most about the reporters' scoffing is that they hadn't scoffed at the same kind of speculative testimony served up by the medical examiners against Wayne Williams.

At this point in the trial, Judge Cooper refused to allow the defense to introduce audio tapes of a van driving across the bridge. Thus, the jury didn't hear them. But for the record, the van—even traveling at an extremely slow speed—made considerable noise when it crossed the expansion joint.

The person who had conducted the test was Mike Bucki, a freelance reporter. In an unusual twist, Bucki lost his job reporting on the trial for Associated Press Radio as a result of his having designed the sound test for the defense. The AP said it wanted to avoid even the appearance of a conflict of interest.

Another former police recruit, Donald Wright, who had since joined the

Navy, took the stand to support Ken Lawson's contention about prosecution witness Nellie Trammell. However, Wright picked out a photo of a "Mrs. Tribble," who, the state admitted, had spent time around the Task Force because her son worked there as a police officer. Remember, these "eyewitnesses" for the defense are no different than the same so-called "trained observers" who are "eyewitnesses" for the state. In other words, police officers have no corner on accuracy when it comes to identifications. They're as inaccurate as anyone.

Lois Evans, meanwhile, challenged the identification of the remains which the state had contended were those of her 14-year-old son, Alfred Evans. She based her contention on the fact that the body had no pierced ear, that Alfred Evans' dental bridge wouldn't fit the mouth and that Alfred never wore a belt. The body wore a belt when it was found.

Again, was the body that of Alfred Evans' friend, 14-year-old Edward Hope Smith? Does Alfred Evans lie in Edward Hope Smith's grave? Does anyone know for sure? I haven't heard from anybody who does.

WXIA-TV's Tracey Lyons said in her live report from the courthouse that she didn't see anything significant in Lois Evans' testimony questioning the identification of Alfred Evans. The *Atlanta Journal*'s Hyde Post and David Hilder reported that "prosecutors contend the body is Evans', but its identity is not crucial to their case..."

If it is not crucial in a murder trial that the medical examiner might have misidentified the victim, then Stalin is the father of our country and the Pope's daddy was a cantor. There already was a question about the identification of Nathaniel Cater. If Evans, then, had been misidentified, then how can we be sure that Cater is Cater?

We faced a situation wherein Wayne Williams was being told: We don't know how you killed. We don't know where you killed. We don't know when you killed. We're not even sure whom you killed, but you're guilty as hell. It's not supposed to happen that way. No, sir—not in the U.S.A.

Actually, Williams wasn't being told that, but his attorney, Al Binder, was. In a post-trial interview of Al Binder conducted by a third party, Binder said that prosecutor Lewis Slaton told him that it was the first time he ever won a case when he didn't have the slightest ideas about when, where, why or how the victim was killed.

At the trial, Binder then called on the hydrologist who had performed the tests for the state. David Dingle testified that prosecutors had pressured his erstwhile colleague, Benjamin Kittle, to change a report on how a body would float down the river—which, Dingle said, caused him to come forward and notify the defense. "I was very upset," Dingle said. "I didn't think things were being dealt with squarely."

Earlier, Kittle had testified for the state that Nathaniel Cater's and Jimmy Ray Payne's bodies most likely had been put into the river at the Jackson Parkway bridge. Kittle said he amended the initial report, which was co-authored by Dingle, to eliminate the Interstate 285 bridge and two other locations after being notified by prosecutors that two eyewitnesses reportedly saw victim Jimmy Ray Payne's body in the river *upstream* from those locations. Remember, no one saw Nathaniel Cater's body upstream from where the report would have said his body entered the water, too.

Dingle says that Kittle told him he had been under pressure from Assistant D.A. Gordon Miller to change the report. Dingle said that he didn't believe that the eyewitness accounts were basis enough to change the conclusions of a "scientific" report. I couldn't agree more.

Dingle detailed the six times he conducted experiments for the defense in late 1981 and early 1982. Dingle and investigators working for the defense used mannequins to study the rates at which a body might be expected to drag along a river bottom or float once it had surfaced. One mannequin, dubbed "Horace" by Mary Welcome, was 4-foot-10 and weighed 115 pounds. Another, nicknamed "Ferdinand," was programmed to float. Oranges also were used in float tests because they float in ways similar to a human body. Or so Dingle contends.

Dingle said it was "highly unlikely" (more so-called definitive expert testimony laced with "likelys," "unlikelys" and "could be's") that the body of Nathaniel Cater could have been dumped into the Chattahoochee at the location (Jackson Parkway bridge) that the prosecutors contend.

"Horace," Dingle said, sank immediately when it was dropped into the river. He said the weighted dummy floated no more than 20 feet downstream and did not move farther downstream once it came to rest on the river bottom. Was Dingle trying to tell us that Cater would have floated 20 feet? He said "not more than 20 feet," as if that were a short distance.

If Cater was the cause of the splash that police recruit Bob Campbell says he heard, and if he floated 20 feet, then Campbell would have had to have seen Cater's body rather than concentric circles in the water, wouldn't he? But when Dingle said that the weighted dummy moved no farther downstream, that, in my opinion, rendered the whole experiment meaningless. Real bodies *do* move!

"Ferdinand," Dingle testified, always floated on the side nearest the right (north or west) bank of the river—the Cobb County side—and did not drift over to the left, or Fulton County side, as it floated downstream. Cater's body (which the police said splashed on the Cobb County side) was found on the Fulton County side, as was Payne's. Out of 100 oranges tested, not one drifted to the left bank, Dingle said.

On cross-examination, Dingle testified that more than half the oranges floated as far downstream as Cater's body was found from the bridge. But this admission that the state wanted to draw out of Dingle was hardly to its benefit. You had to forget, first, that if more than half did, then the rest didn't. Which meant that the great orange float was meaningless insofar as demonstrating how far even oranges would drift downstream from the Jackson Parkway bridge.

Then, too, if the state was taking solace in bringing out that some of the oranges indicated how far Cater's body would have floated from the bridge, it was giving the test credence it didn't deserve. Thus, it added to the defense's equally fragile claim that since all of the oranges stayed on the Cobb County side of the river, so, too, would Cater's body.

Dingle also admitted that the river levels varied when he performed his tests and that he had limited knowledge of the effects of decomposition on a floating body. Unfortunately, no one at the trial had that kind of knowledge. The prosecution objected to the admission of the results of Dingle's tests, and Judge Cooper delayed a ruling on the motion.

Then Mike Gurley, a scuba diver for the Fulton County fire department rescue team, was called by the defense. He testified that he had told prosecutors after Nathaniel Cater's body surfaced that "the distance traveled was out of the bounds of likelihood" for two days worth of travel from the Jackson Parkway bridge.

Gurley, who stated that he has recovered the bodies of nearly 50 drowning victims, testified further that he and four other members of the rescue team were called on May 23, 1981, to the bridge, where the "splash" was heard the morning before, to check for anything unusual.

The divers, Gurley said, searched "35 to 40 feet" downstream, as they normally would—not the 1¼ miles Carter's body is said to have traveled. He estimated the distance that a body would have traveled in that water during a two-day period not at 1¼ miles, but at 200 feet maximum, which would be correct if Cater's body entered the water at the I-285 bridge.

Under cross-examination, Gurley admitted that his knowledge of body movement was limited to drowning victims, not to victims who were already dead, as the state argued Cater was.

The state's contention that Cater was dead when his body entered the water (on the Cobb County side) would only add ammunition to my argument that Fulton County did not have venue to try Wayne Williams—an argument that Al Binder wouldn't return my call to hear and one that Lynn Whatley, Williams' attorney on appeal, told me that he didn't agree with.

The defense also called an Atlanta police helicopter pilot, Robert Ingram, who testified that an aerial search of the river down to 2 feet over the water on May 23 showed no signs of a body.

It dawned on me that nature and the killer(s) had provided us with the best possible study of how the bodies of Cater and Payne might have moved in the Chattahoochee River. We didn't need oranges or dummies. We had the bodies of Cater and Payne. The state commissioned a test by a hydrologist and an engineer. The results were that a body found where Cater's and Payne's had been would have entered the river near the I-285 bridge, not the Jackson Parkway bridge.

The state produced a witness who says he saw Payne's body floating in waters upstream from the I-285 bridge. The state asked that the report be changed. The hydrologist refused. The engineer agreed. The report was changed to say that Payne's body had entered the water upstream at the Jackson Parkway bridge. No one ever saw Cater upstream from I-285. The state's report doesn't say that Cater's body came from the Jackson Parkway bridge. But the testimony about the splash concerns Cater, not Payne. The state's quick shuffle from Payne to Cater at the Jackson Parkway bridge fooled a lot of people.

The state's witnesses testified that Cater's body had been in the water no more than 2 days. Payne's body, they said, had been in the river for 5 days. Cater's body was hung up on debris. Payne's body was floating freely. Why did it take 5 days for Payne's body to float as far as Cater's had floated in only 2? This would have to be the case if Cater's body entered the river at the Jackson Parkway bridge.

The most likely reason is that Nathaniel Cater's body didn't enter the water at the Jackson Parkway bridge but near the I-285 bridge, where the state's study, the hydrologist, the diver and nature say it did. Whatever Campbell heard splash into the Chattahoochee River on the morning of May 22, 1981, odds are it wasn't the body of Nathaniel Cater.

Binder already had called Gerald Hightower, a technician with the Park Service, who testified that the Chattahoochee River area's beavers, which grew to 55 pounds, make "fairly large splashes" with their tails.

Then Binder called Keith Andrews, owner of Atlanta Studios, who testified that Wayne Williams used the studio's facilities on January 3, 1981, between 4:30 p.m. and 8:30 p.m. If Williams was indeed at Atlanta Studios during those four hours, it raises questions about the state's testimony that placed Wayne Williams on Stewart Avenue with victim Lubie Geter at about that same time. Of course, another state witness had already created that doubt.

Paul Crawley of WXIA-TV was called by the defense to testify about his televised interview with Margaret Carter, who had testified for the state that she saw Williams with Nathaniel Cater in a small park on the Friday before Cater's body was found. Crawley testified that when he interviewed Margaret Carter on August 27, 1981, she said she saw Williams and Cater not on Friday, May 22, but instead on Monday, May 25, the day *after* Cater's body was found.

Then Dr. Charles S. Chisolm testified that Wayne Williams is legally blind without his eyeglasses. The defense intended to use this information to refute the testimony of Ruth Warren, who had said she saw Lubie Geter with Williams. But Williams, she said, was not wearing glasses.

Judge Cooper, meanwhile, ruled that the defense's motion to have the jury taken to the Jackson Parkway bridge would be honored. But the judge also dealt the defense a blow. He blocked an attempt by Binder to have 15-year-old Jo-Jo Bell's older half-brother, Edward Mays, take the stand to refute the testimony of Eugene Laster that he had seen Jo-Jo get into Williams' car. The judge ruled that the defense had not laid the proper "groundwork" in its cross-examination of Laster.

"The whole truth"? What Edward Mays wanted to tell the jury was that he had talked with Laster when Mays was looking for Jo-Jo Bell on the day of Jo-Jo's disappearance, and at that time, Laster told him he didn't know whom Bell went with or what kind of car he got into.

Outside the courtroom, some victims' mothers who were spectators at the trial already had made up their minds.

"Just look at him. He looks like he did it. I know he did it," Helen Pue mother of slain 15-year-old Terry Pue, told Bob Dart of the *Atlanta Constitution*, referring to Wayne Williams.

Then Helen Pue added a refrain to a chorus that I would hear well into the future—even to this day—and never would understand the logic behind it: "I don't know if he killed all of them, but I believe he killed my boy. I sure do." Keep in mind that it was the state's fiber case that said, in effect, "all or nothing at all." If Williams didn't kill them all, then the state made no case that he was guilty of killing any. And if the splash wasn't Cater's body . . . ?

Camille Bell, slain 9-year-old Yusuf Bell's mother, said, "Wayne's just one of those people who doesn't look right to other people. That doesn't mean he killed anybody." I would remember that Camille Bell once asked, "Do you know who Wayne Williams looks like? He looks like me." Later, she would take issue with Williams' conviction—and with the worldwide perception that the murders stopped. "It had to stop," she said, "and, to make it stop, they scapegoated somebody, put him in jail, and called an end to it."

Then Willie Mae Mathis stood outside the courtroom and declared that Wayne Williams killed her 10-year-old son, Jefferey. Her daughter, she explained, had seen Williams ride by the house in a blue car on the night Jefferey had disappeared in March of 1980.

Well, there was a story that *had* changed. When Willie Mae Mathis told me that story in 1980, she thought it was the Reverend Earl Carroll who drove by her house. It wasn't the night that Jefferey disappeared, but days later. And her complaint wasn't that her daughter, Valerie, had seen someone in a blue car, but rather than someone in a blue car had tried to pick up Valerie.

Willie Mae Mathis at first agreed with the medical examiners that the skeletal remains were those of her son. But later, she changed her mind and said on television that she didn't believe Jefferey's remains were in Jefferey's grave. She told me after the broadcast in which she announced her change of heart that Police Chief George Napper had sat at her kitchen table and told her that the medical examiners had positively identified the remains as Jefferey's.

Of course, they didn't and still haven't done any such thing. They merely claimed to have ruled out the remains being those of another 10-year-old, Darron Glass.

Now, Willie Mae Mathis has changed her mind *again*. Her position, at this writing: "I don't even know who killed my son. You said Wayne Williams did it, but you won't bring him to trial . . . to prove his innocence or guilt."

(Jefferey Mathis is one of only five List victims whose deaths have *not* been attributed by the state to Wayne Williams. Which illustrates the lack of understanding about these cases even by parents of the victims.)

Now it was the defense's turn to address the trial's sexual overtones raised by the state.

Binder called Howard Peoples, who said that Wayne Williams had helped him in the music business. He said Williams had never made a homosexual advance to him in the three years that he had known him.

Actually, this testimony reflects the same fuzzy thinking by the defense that existed with the prosecution. The implication here is that Wayne Williams is not a homosexual. The prosecution had, of course, used the same kind of non-sequitur allegations to suggest that Williams is, as if homosexuals are some sort of hunters in constant search for prey. I am heterosexual, but I swear that there are females I have known for three years whom I have never made a heterosexual advance toward.

Carla Bailey, a close friend of Williams, testified that Williams had dated her sister, didn't make racial slurs and was generous. What possible difference could all that make? I suggest that there are murderers and non-murderers who share these traits. On cross-examination, Carla Bailey admitted that she originally had told police that Wayne Williams never had dated anyone.

Carla Bailey is another person whom Wayne Williams relies heavily upon. But Carla, like other Williams friends, doesn't always act that friendly to him. Lynn Whatley told me that he had statements from Carla Bailey that "I won't even let you see."

Another companion of Williams, Willie Hunter, who is about the same age as Williams and also worked in the entertainment business, testified that the business was one of "hype." "I think I'm the greatest television producer in the world today," Hunter said, "...but you might think I'm nothing."

Meanwhile, Al Binder found a new pathologist—one who certainly had dealt with violent deaths—and a lot of them. Dr. Maurice Rogev, chief of the medical-legal bureau of the Israeli Army, testified that he—like Daniel Stowens—found no evidence that Nathaniel Cater or Jimmy Payne was murdered.

Again, the point was driven home: No evidence showed that either victim

Wayne Williams would be convicted of murdering *was* murdered. To my own mind, there is little doubt that they were—but there has to be that reasonable doubt, without proof to the contrary.

Rogev said that Jimmy Ray Payne might have drowned, and Payne well might have. Keep in mind that drowning is an asphyxial death and that even the medical examiner—who had not ruled Payne's death a murder, changing the death certificate *after* Williams was indicted—testified that he could not rule out drowning as the cause of Jimmy Ray Payne's death.

Rogev said Nathaniel Cater had been dead for at least five days when his body was found. If you looked at the pictures of Cater's corpse, it would be hard to disagree with him. It would have taken four to five days for a body to surface at 67 degrees (the temperature during the period in question varied from 63 to 77), according to Rogev. And he said that drowning had not been properly ruled out by the local medical examiners. Was it Cater?

Gwen Hardin, a 30-year-old woman, testified that Wayne Williams had participated in a sexual relationship with her. Is that supposed to mean that Williams is not a homosexual? It doesn't say that to me. Instead, it says only that he at least could be bisexual.

Who knows and who cares? Homosexuality is not—and cannot be—a motive for murder. Jealously, anger or any of the more traditional motives of a heterosexual murderer will apply. If homosexuality were a motive, why weren't any of the homosexuals who are known to have had sexual relationships with some of Atlanta's victims on trial? There were homosexual connections galore which did not involve Wayne Williams.

Nathaniel Cater's friend and roommate, John Henley, took the stand to say that Cater wasn't holding hands with anybody (any male) because Cater wasn't homosexual. Which would prove nothing. Henley testified that he last saw Cater alive on May 19, 1981.

Not surprisingly, this would jibe with the estimate by Rogev, who, like the medical examiners, knew how long the body could have been out and still support his side of the case. Under these circumstances, Cater's body could have floated as far from the Jackson Parkway as it was found (1¼ miles). But it would have had to have been placed in the water on May 19, three days before the "splash."

And if Cater wasn't at home, or at his parents' home, where was he? An innocent person might have come forward to say Cater stayed with him from May 19 through May 22—but none did.

Wayne Williams did not transport a body that had been dead for three days in his station wagon to the bridge. Had he done so, the odor would have been obvious to police and FBI agents, even after the body was removed. Henley said that after he learned of Cater's death, he left Atlanta and went to Iowa. Henley said he had been told that he would be "next." "Told by whom?" I wondered.

Then Cater's 18-year-old brother, Anthony, testified that he had talked to

Nathaniel on May 18, 1981, and that "Nate" had said he would be at the house for Anthony's birthday celebration on May 20. Anthony Cater said, "Dad always gave us money on birthdays, and Nathaniel would not have missed the opportunity to collect." But Nathaniel Cater didn't show, Anthony said.

If trials are supposed to be fact-finding missions for jurors, the Wayne Williams trial again fell short on February 13, 1982.

When the 12 jurors visited the Jackson Parkway bridge on that cold, gray, damp Saturday morning, it was more a "media" event than one tailored to the jurors' curiosity. Reporters and photographers swarmed to the scene in cars and vans—despite Judge Cooper's order to stay away. They were restrained by police roadblocks. A reporter in a helicopter flew in very close and drew a rebuke from the judge.

For the jurors, it hardly was a re-creation of events of that morning of May 22, 1981. First, they arrived by school bus in daylight from the Fulton County side—not the Cobb County side, as Wayne Williams had, in the dark. And second, even though they walked along the bridge (some gazed over the railing at the river), they wandered only to the river's edge on the Cobb County side.

No juror proceeded the several hundred yards up the incline of Jackson Parkway, where Cobb County police had mounted roadblocks. If any juror had gone that far from the river, he would have seen two locations: (1) where FBI Agent Greg Gilliland had waited during the pre-dawn hours of May 22 in a stakeout car, and (2) the side road to Georgia Power's Plant McDonough and the boat ramp that provided easy access to the river.

But then, the jurors might not have recognized these two points. Throughout their visit to the bridge—which lasted less than one hour—the jurors were not permitted to ask questions or hear testimony. Judge Cooper's orders.

"The whole truth"?

Carla Bailey returned to the stand on Monday morning, February 15, 1982. She told of the night that Wayne Williams had given Kent Hindsman a ride from the studio. She said they rode in Williams' white station wagon and that the young passenger was not Jo-Jo Bell, as prosecution witness Hindsman had testified, but instead was a young singer named David Stephens (no relation to victim Charles Stephens).

No one asked Carla Bailey, but according to data later put together by Williams, she could have testified as to Williams' whereabouts when Eric Middlebrooks disappeared. She also help establish where Williams was when Jefferey Mathis disappeared, which might be of some solace to Mrs. Mathis.

Israel Green, president of the Techwood Homes residents' association, testified that he had not seen Wayne Williams at the press conference announcing the "bat patrol." Nellie Trammell had testified for the state that Wayne Williams was there. This testimony referred to 21-year-old victim Bubba Duncan.

Did Binder have to call a witness to refute testimony that the judge already had disallowed because of Binder's own objection? Binder would not call other witnesses who could have refuted other important testimony that the judge *did* allow into the record.

When Mary Welcome repeatedly objected to Jack Mallard's questions on cross-examination, Judge Cooper repeatedly overruled her. Finally, the judge said, "Have a seat, Ms. Welcome."

Then Israel Green refused to answer any more questions, saying he was exercising his Fifth Amendment rights. But when Mary Welcome started to question Green on re-direct, the judge stopped her, saying that the witness had refused to answer any more questions. It's very unusual to have the opportunity to take the Fifth Amendment whenever one chooses. Usually, you must answer all or none of the questions asked. What a tool to defeat cross-examination!

Jimmy Ray Payne's sister then took the stand to say she had never seen Wayne Williams with her brother and that she does not know him.

Meanwhile, Wayne Williams complained of sickness. He said he had vomited earlier while at the jail. Judge Cooper ordered him taken to Grady Memorial Hospital, where he was diagnosed as having a mild stomach virus. Doctors prescribed medicine for Williams, who was taken back to jail.

Before the interruption, Al Binder had called three young members of the Gemini group to the courtroom. The three—Jimmy Howard, Stewart Flemister and Broderick Burns, along with their mothers—testified that Williams had worked with the families in selecting the youngsters for the group and that he never made homosexual advances to the youngsters.

A young woman named Faith Swift testified that Williams liked to "flirt" with women. She said that Williams had come by on Labor Day of 1981 to pick her up in his 1970 white Chevrolet station wagon. Jack Mallard alertly seized on this in cross-examination. Williams was in jail then, Mallard pointed out, and on Labor Day in 1980 he didn't have the white 1970 Chevrolet station wagon.

I wonder why Mallard hadn't pointed out the same discrepancy about fibers and the station wagon to his own fiber experts—or why he hadn't also pointed out to Nellie Trammell that she was off by a few months when she testified that Mallard had shown her pictures of Williams *before* Williams became a suspect. "The whole truth"?

Meanwhile, Mary Welcome and Judge Cooper engaged in verbal combat again. After the mother of Gemini member Jimmy Howard testified that she did not worry about her son being with Williams, Welcome asked her what she thought of the murder charges against Wayne Williams. Jack Mallard objected, and the judge sustained the objection.

Welcome tried four times to ask the same question. Each time Mallard objected; and each time the judge sustained. I wondered why our system allowed the "non-medical" opinions of medical examiners, but barred the opinions of others about anything. I would prefer not to hear anyone's *opinion* in a court of law. What people know, rather than think, might lead us closer to "the whole truth."

On other occasions, Mary Welcome engaged in private verbal battles with Wayne Williams, even on the floor of the courtroom while the trial was in session. On one occasion, Williams insisted that she ask a particular question. She rightly refused.

Williams retorted, "If you don't want to ask the damn question, you can leave now."

She did leave and wasn't back until the next day, her feathers somewhat less ruffled. But almost everyone in the courtroom had missed a most dramatic moment with Williams firing Welcome in mid-trial.

On Tuesday, February 16, Judge Cooper informed Binder that he had quashed the defense's subpoenas against all of the public officials who had met at the Governor's Mansion—along with those for some who hadn't—two nights before Williams' arrest. In his ruling, Cooper said, "Testimony concerning the alleged motive of a prosecutor is irrelevant and therefore inadmissible." Should the prosecutor have "motives" beyond his oath of office for prosecuting accused criminals? If so, shouldn't we know?

The defense brought the *other* Joseph (Jo-Jo) Bell to the stand. He testified that he met Williams in 1980 when Williams came to his school to interview him about a singing group. He said they met about four times that year, but he hadn't seen Williams since.

But this Jo-Jo Bell probably did Williams more harm than good. In a trial conducted to influence emotions, beliefs and prejudices—not only racial, but moral, sexual and religious—it didn't help Williams when the soft-spoken youth said that Williams had asked him a lot of personal questions. Most prospective employers do; they call them "job interviews." He said that Williams had hypnotized him and that he (the witness) was somewhat excited.

More lapses by defense witnesses made parts of the defense's case look no less confused than parts of the prosecution's. Gemini member Jimmy Howard testified that as the "leader of the group," he knew Gemini member Broderick Burns. But when Mary Welcome asked Burns about Howard, Burns said he didn't know him. Does anybody know the truth?

Meanwhile, in another courtroom across town in DeKalb County, a woman was found guilty and sentenced to 10 years in prison for plotting to kill her husband. Her husband was Judson Ray, who was assigned to the "Atlanta child murders" by his employer, the FBI. (The bureau's files referred to these cases as "ATKID," as in "ABSCAM.") She had been accused of hiring three men to murder him.

Agent Ray was shot, but he didn't die. To be sure, this incident wasn't exactly among the FBI's proudest moments of 1981.

Now the defense called deposed Atlanta Public Safety Commissioner A. Reginald Eaves, who testified that he had arranged for Wayne Williams to take pictures for the Atlanta Fire Bureau. He said he did it after Homer Williams twice sought his help in getting his son, Wayne, a job. But Lee P. Brown, who replaced Eaves, had said that no record of Wayne Williams being on the payroll existed. It wouldn't surprise me that the city of Atlanta could not find a record.

Mike Williams (no kin to Wayne), who was listed in Williams' resume and who was a broadcast technician for Atlanta station WAGA (Channel 5), testified that he taught Williams to take pictures at fire scenes. He added that he had suggested that Williams take pictures during the early-morning hours when stations maintained only skeleton crews. Mike Williams said that both he and Wayne Williams filled out employment applications for the Atlanta public safety department, but they never received a reply.

During the trial, the prosecution would contend that Wayne Williams had applied for a job taking photographs at the morgue. Williams told me that he had seen a civil service notice announcing several openings. He said he didn't apply for a specific job.

The Atlanta police sketch artist was called by the defense. She testified that none of the more than 50 suspect composites she drew for the Task Force before Wayne Williams was arrested looked like Williams. One composite drawn after Williams' arrest, she said, did look like Williams, which could mean little since Williams' countenance was available wholesale on TV and in the newspapers. To me, it meant even less than a little. The drawing she was talking about was the one that looked to me like ex-ballplayer Willie Stargell.

Douglas Candis, an announcer on a nationally syndicated radio program called "Coast-to-Coast Soul," said he knew Wayne Williams for 10 years. He said that he had an agreement to help Williams and to back Williams' "Metro News Productions." When Williams' interest turned to music, Candis said, he thought Williams was trying to mold an Atlanta enterprise based on Barry Gordy's phenomenally successful Motown Records, the richest black-owned company in America.

Jim Comento testified that Wayne Williams had introduced him to a number of public officials and members of the press. Williams, Comento said, had tried to help him get official approval for his volunteer paramedic activities.

Interestingly, Comento raised the eyebrows of the police long before Wayne Williams would. In fact, the Fulton County police had talked to Williams as early as January of 1981 about Comento. Comento is the man who used "the other Plymouth" of Wayne Williams.

Comento insisted that Williams owned permits to operate emergency lights and sirens on his car. But Jack Mallard said that the police could find no record of a permit ever being issued for the siren, among other things they couldn't find—like U.S. Highway 278, I thought.

Then one of the strongest witnesses for the defense was called. Terry Lamar McMullin, an Atlanta freelance photographer, volunteered that he—not Williams—was the man who went to the crime scene where 15-year-old Terry Pue was found in Rockdale County. He said he gave his business card to the police at the scene. Could the "trained observers" have missed another one? Of course they could have. In my opinion, it is not possible to train someone to observe.

Keith Knox, who once worked for Wayne Williams' homemade radio station, testified that he was with Wayne Williams from 2 p.m. to 7 p.m. on March 30, 1981. This testimony, I presume, was designed to try to come close to alibiing Nellie Trammell's claim of having seen Williams with 20-year-old Larry Rogers at about noon that day.

But, as it turned out, Keith Knox was as good a prosecution witness as Nellie Trammell seemed to be at first. The problem was that Knox was supposed to be a defense witness. On cross-examination, Knox said that Willie Hunter, Williams' business associate, struck him as being effeminate. Knox said he never knew Wayne Williams to date girls or even talk about them. He said Williams told him he knew karate.

Knox went on to tell of being at Wayne Williams' house in late May of 1981, shortly after the bridge incident. Williams, he said, was cleaning out a storage room and loading items into boxes.

An Atlanta radio announcer, Doug Steele, said that Homer Williams took great interest in his son. Steele said he once asked Homer why he spent so much money on Wayne Williams' radio station (this free-spending had placed Homer and Faye Williams into bankruptcy in 1976). Homer Williams, Steele said, told him that he would do anything to keep Wayne off the street.

Then the defense presented some of Wayne Williams' schoolteachers. Their testimony reflected that they apparently knew less about Williams since they last saw him than the medical examiners had said they knew about the cause of death in the Jimmy Ray Payne case.

Both sides had tried this overkill of character witnesses. Al Binder, finally and mercifully, stipulated that the rest of the scheduled character witnesses would say nice things about Wayne Williams.

The defense then called Nesha Nanji, who attacked businesswoman and prosecution witness Shyron Blakely's reputation. She suggested that Blakely was developing a young talent without giving Wayne Williams credit for the discovery. Shyron Blakely had given the devastating testimony about Williams telling her that he would "confess" if authorities got too close to him.

Another witness said that she had served 15-year-old victim Terry Pue hot chocolate in January of 1981, less than seven hours before he turned up dead, and that Pue was with another man, not Wayne Williams. However, under cross-examination, she said she had confused the date and it was 31 hours before Pue was found dead. This seemed similar to a state's witness who put Pue with Williams about three months *after* Pue's death.

But, in this instance, if the woman had actually seen Pue (which I always think is questionable at best with stranger identifications), at least it had been while Pue was *missing,* whether it was seven or 31 hours before Pue was found dead.

Darlene Cann, a Clark College (Atlanta) student who was recruited by Wayne Williams to sing, testified that Williams disliked homosexuals and that he insisted that his music recruits be of "the highest moral character." She said Williams particularly questioned whether one young man was gay. If so, she said, "he didn't want to mess with him." This testimony was given to show ostensibly why Williams and/or his associates asked personal questions of the aspiring singers.

Josephine Derrico, whose son was connected with Williams through the Gemini group, testified that Williams had instructed her son to act "manly." The defense was obviously trying to show that Wayne Williams is not gay, inasmuch as the prosecution had implied that he was.

But this strategy seemed to me to be of little importance since, among the other "possible motives" in the prosecution's grab bag, was a scenario in which Williams killed homosexuals because he "hated" them. The defense was tilting with windmills and losing as often as not.

Meanwhile, Corine Brown, the director of the 9th District Youth Council, testified that Wayne Williams helped her produce shows that would entertain children and raise money for programs that would keep them off the streets during the summer of 1981.

Suppose, then, that the state is right, and that Wayne Williams is a killer. It shows once again the futility of the system's archaic thinking when it comes to dealing with problems such as child safety.

Programs like Corine Brown's—and those of Atlanta's federally funded, $5-million "Safe Summer '81"—were never necessary. They could only possibly have helped if the killings had been random kidnappings, which this strategy—like curfews and other "safety tips"—is designed to combat. It probably wouldn't do that. Had Williams been the killer, some of Corine Brown's programs provided a place where he could meet with potential victims.

Al Binder next called his fiber "expert," Randall Bresee, who was working on a laser-identification method for fibers. He criticized the state's testing procedures. But he admitted that he had spent only five hours looking at the various slides. He said he "wouldn't jump to a conclusion like that" (referring to the state's fiber matches, based only on microscopic and optical qualities).

In challenging Bresee's credentials (which is part of the needlessly silly game lawyers play at trials) assistant prosecutor Gordon Miller became even more snide and insulting with Bresee than Al Binder had gotten with Lee Brown. Noting that Bresee had received his Ph.D. from a school of home economics, Miller wisecracked, "I'm not going to ask you any questions about baking pies right now."

Most of Bresee's testimony, to me, was meaningless. I had no more reason to accept his opinions and guesses than I did those of Peterson or Deadman, who testified for the prosecution. The most interesting thing Bresee had to say could not have mattered. He stated that "the river seems to be full of fibers." He explained that he had bought a pillowcase, attached it to a stick, then submerged it in the Chattahoochee River. When the pillowcase was removed from the water, 500 or so assorted fibers stuck to it. He testified that there had been *no comparision* and no contention that any of the fibers match with those in evidence.

Had Binder told Bresee that two out of every three victims who had fibers had not been found in the Chattahoochee River? With that in mind, Bresee's experiment proved nothing.

Homer Williams, Wayne's 68-year-old father, took the stand, with defense counsel Jim Kitchens asking the questions. Referring to the bankruptcy caused by overinvestment in Wayne Williams' radio station, Kitchens asked: "When that happened, did you consider your son a failure in life at that point?"

"No, I didn't," Homer Williams answered. He then told of an opportunity to secure a backer for the station. But when the backer demanded control for his investment, Homer and Faye Williams elected, instead to bankrupt and close the station.

Homer Williams testified that Wayne had come along late, when Homer was 45. He said he spent quite a bit of time with Wayne, sometimes hunting and fishing together. Homer said he had bought Wayne a shotgun, but Homer was quick to interject, "Wayne lost interest because he didn't kill very much." I wondered: Did he mean "wasn't able to" or "chose not to"?

Wayne Williams never had been away from home longer than one night, his father testified, except for the trip he took to California. Homer Williams said he taught physics and general science and left science books around the house. He said his son appeared to read those books. But then he swore that Wayne never showed a particular aptitude for chemistry.

This part of Homer Williams' testimony, of course, was intended to cover the possible uses of chemicals in overcoming victims. Oh, how attorneys do make sure that certain things are said in testimony.

Jim Kitchens then asked Homer Williams about chloroform, a colorless, volatile liquid used mostly in medicine as an anesthetic and a solvent.

"No," Homer answered, almost as if on cue, "I wouldn't let chloroform in my house."

Kitchens also got Homer to explain that Wayne had switched bedrooms in the house several times—once because a leaky roof had forced Wayne out of one room in 1981, and once for his mother's convience after she underwent a radical mastectomy.

When Kitchens asked Homer whether any rooms in the house were "off limits" to him or his wife, Homer jumped on the question: "No, sir, not in my house!"

Homer Williams also swore that Wayne never had access to any rental cars that Homer rented from Hub Ford. This rings partially true, only because Wayne Williams—unlike the picture the defense would paint of him—was not 100% kind toward or appreciative of his parents. Al Binder told me that Wayne once had a furious argument with his father because his father would not let him use a rental car. But Homer Williams denied this from the witness stand.

Homer testified that he drove the white 1970 Chevrolet station wagon most of the time, but that Wayne drove it, too. Asked if he had ever smelled anything "foul" in the vehicle, he answered that he had not.

The back room, which used to contain Wayne Williams' radio station, Homer testified, was recarpeted with green carpeting on May 25, 1981—the day after Nathaniel Cater's body was found.

What a coincidence that would have to be. Instead, I chose not to accept it. A state's witness had testified earlier that fibers found on Cater and two other victims were matched by fibers collected from the same room during the police search of June 3, 1981.

Turning to events surrounding the May 22, 1981, bridge incident involving his son, Homer Williams testified that on May 21, he was using the family's only vehicle, the white 1970 Chevrolet station wagon, until about 11:30 p.m. He said he went to a Kiwanis Club meeting and then photographed a Garden Club meeting for the *Atlanta Daily World*. When he returned home, he testified, Wayne was in bed.

This, of course, is the same time that the state's witness swore he saw Wayne Williams "holding hands" with Nathaniel Cater while they left the Rialto Theater in downtown Atlanta. And it is the same time when Wayne Williams would tell me after the trial that he was at Hotlanta Studios. Williams also would tell me that he was in bed when his father came home and that he got up and left the house about midnight. "Nothing but the truth"?

I later learned it wasn't the truth at all. In 1984, I would sit in a holding cell with Lynn Whatley and Wayne Williams. Williams discussed his alibis. He mentioned Hotlanta.

"Wayne, I've got real problems with that," I said.

"What's that, Chet?"

"Well, it flies in the face of what you and your daddy both testified to at your trial."

Williams turned to Whatley and said: "Well, you know I couldn't raise my right hand and swear to God that I told the whole truth about that and you know why."

The cell filled with silence. I would wait for an explanation. For the moment, I was astounded.

I got my chance days later when Williams telephoned me from the jail.

"What did you mean when you said you couldn't raise your right hand and swear you told the whole truth and that Whatley knew why?"

There was a long pause. Then Williams replied:

"Daddy just can't stand to be wrong about anything. I just can't convince my daddy he's wrong. But you got to remember that it was hard to get all these dates together. I didn't mean to tell no lies."

Homer Williams' logs would not support his own testimony that he had taken photographs at the Kiwanis Club and Garden Club meetings on the evening of May 21. When pressed by assistant prosecutor Jack Mallard, Homer said, "If it's not here [meaning in the log], it must have been cancelled." But the entry wasn't scratched out—it hadn't been made. So where did Homer go?

Homer Williams testified that Wayne returned home about 4:30 or 5 a.m. and told his parents that he had been stopped and questioned by the FBI for two or three hours. Then Homer told the court of the FBI agents keeping the slip of paper inscribed with Cheryl Johnson's phone number.

As for the slapjack, Homer Williams said it never was in the ceiling (where police searchers said they had found it), but in a closet, where he had put it in 1962, when he took it away from a student. Were the searchers wrong about where they found that slapjack? I doubt it.

Homer Williams also said his son didn't know karate. Kitchens then asked if his son was an athlete.

"No, you can look at him and tell that," Homer answered, evoking a chuckle from Wayne Williams.

When asked if Wayne ever exhibited any homosexual tendencies, Homer replied, "I can say, without a doubt, no."

Beside denying the story about his fight with Wayne over the rental car, Homer Williams denied the prosecution's contention that Wayne had assaulted Homer over Homer's refusal to write a check and that, in the heat of the argument, Homer grabbed a shotgun and "threatened to shoot Wayne."

Jack Mallard contended that a piece of rug removed from Wayne Williams' room was soaked through to the pad with blood. Homer Williams denied the blood was there; but under redirect examination, he explained that he and Wayne had killed a rat there and that the blood could have come from the rat. The explanation for the "blood that wasn't there" didn't impress me and wouldn't have, even if Homer had admitted it existed before he tried to explain it away. "Nothing but the truth"?

The prosecution, meanwhile, indicated that both the Williameses' red 1979 Ford LTD and white 1970 Chevrolet station wagon had been averaging about 4,000 miles a month (which is unusually high). When asked about the Ford's mileage, Homer Williams said that he had noticed that himself, but blamed it on a faulty odometer. He gave no explanation for the mileage on the Chevy.

So what! The state was conjuring up visions of the random killer prowling the streets in search of prey. And, for his part, Homer was making excuses for something that didn't need excusing. Neither side was very convincing.

What's more, Homer Williams testified that he burned photographs in the outside barbecue grill "two or three times a week."

From where I sat, Wayne Williams' daddy was not an award-winning witness.

It was February 20, 1982, the trial's only Saturday morning courtroom session. Mary Welcome was questioning a defense witness named Tom Jones, who was expected to supply testimony about persons playing basketball in shirts bearing the logo of Schlitz beer. An FBI agent had stated that Wayne Williams had told him that he played on such a team.

But, on the stand, Tom Jones—when asked by Welcome if he had ever seen anyone with a Schlitz jersey playing basketball—said, "No!" That wasn't supposed to be the answer, and from that point on, Mary Welcome's examination of this witness went downhill.

The court recessed for lunch, and Mary Welcome never returned that day. Cooper advised the spectators that someone who had played a key role in the trial had become ill. He did not say it was Mary Welcome. Nor did he describe the nature of the illness, which has yet to be made public.

The defense then tried to introduce a month-by-month account of Wayne Williams' life, starting with him sitting on Santa Claus' lap. But Jack Mallard quickly objected, and the judge mercifully sustained the objection. The defense needed to give an account for just one particular full day of Wayne Williams' life, I thought—one on which a victim disappeared, died and was found. There were seven possibilities, but the defense didn't find any, It really wasn't looking.

Faye Williams had never heard the names of "Nathaniel Cater" or "Jimmy Ray Payne" spoken in her house before Wayne was indicted, she said. Maybe not, but Wayne Williams had spoken Nathaniel Cater's name during the press conference in the Williamses' front room on June 4, 1981, more than one month before he was indicted. If the defense was coaching the elder Williamses in their testimony, it wasn't doing a very good job.

A number of local and national political figures had been heard on her son's radio station, Faye Williams said, and had campaigned "from my utility room." Among them were former Atlanta Mayor Sam Massell, then-Congressional candidate Andrew Young, NAACP Executive Director Benjamin Hooks and civil rights activist Tyrone Brooks (before Brooks became a Georgia state legislator).

I didn't see how this testimony could help the defense. I thought it had at least two flaws:

1. The complete absence of any support from any of these prominent people for Williams said to me that they weren't willing to bet on his innocence. Thus, it seemed to me to be almost negative testimony.

2. This testimony reminded me so much of Chicago's John Wayne Gacy, who was convicted of killing one or more of a group of at least 33 boys and young men he was accused of killing. Gacy had had his picture taken with First Lady Rosalynn Carter, among others.

I thought the celebrity name-dropping was a foolish parallel to draw or even invite someone else to draw, particularly when no amount of visits by public figures would have proved anything about Wayne Williams' innocence.

Mary Welcome attempted to call a witness to testify about another suspect in one of the slayings. But Judge Cooper ruled that the testimony would not be relevant.

If it was the testimony that I thought it was going to be, it might well have been the most relevant information that could have been introduced in the trial.

Had the jurors heard this testimony concerning those eyewitnesses and the black male suspect who never was arrested in the "yellow rope" strangulation of 13-year-old Clifford Jones in 1980, and realized that Jones was among those victims with "matching" fibers, it would have made their decision to convict Wayne Williams much more agonizing. Not relevant? "Nothing but the whole truth"?

On Monday, February 22, 1982, Wayne Williams took the stand. "I haven't killed nobody," he said in response to Al Binder's questions. "I haven't thought about it, and don't plan on thinking about even doing it to nobody."

BINDER:	"Have you ever taken your hands and put them around anybody's neck and choked them to death?"
WILLIAMS:	"Never."
BINDER:	"Have you ever taken a knife in your hands and put that knife in someone else's body?"

WILLIAMS: "No."

Now Binder's baritone drawl crescendoed. His words were loud, crisp and direct.

BINDER: "Have you ever taken a rope and put that rope around someone's neck and squeezed it until they were dead?"

WILLIAMS: "No, sir."

Wayne Williams already had told Binder on the stand that he was scared and had talked about his childhood and his parents. Then, after recounting the failure of his radio station, Williams denied knowing anything about karate. He then talked at length about his music business.

Now the defense interrupted Williams' testimony to bring the Williamses' dog, Sheba, into the courtroom. Slaton objected. Binder glared at him and said, "Mr. Slaton, give me just *one* thing." The defense wished to exhibit Sheba's lethargic nature, a condition brought on by sickness and old age, in contrast to the "frisky" dog that one witness said she saw with Williams and Nathaniel Cater.

From there, Wayne Williams told the jury that he had had an argument with Bobby Toland, the ambulance driver who had testified for the state that Williams had called young blacks "niggers." He explained that Toland had stopped his ambulance on an interstate highway and told a drunken, indigent patient, "You either pay or you get out and walk." Williams testified that he formally complained to the agency that issues ambulance licenses. He told the court that Toland knew it was he who made the complaint.

At one point, Binder asked Williams, "Do you hold any grudges against Mr. Slaton or the prosecution staff?"

"You want me to tell the truth?" Williams answered.

"I want you to tell the truth."

"Well, I talked with Mr. Slaton out at the jail one time, and I don't have any malice against him or any of them because I'm saying I understand it wasn't their decision that they got this mess. I don't have any grudge against him, but then again, I wouldn't invite him home for dinner."

When Binder brought up the subject of homosexuality, Williams replied, "There ain't no way. I'm no homosexual, uhn-uhn, no." When asked about the youngster who had said that Williams fondled him, Williams shot back, "He's a barefaced liar!"

Williams admitted that the reference to NASCAR was put in his resume for "hype." He already had revealed his limited knowledge of auto racing by calling competition on oval tracks "slot car racing."

Among several goals in his life, Williams said, one was to make the music business a success. He added: "I've got the need to do some kind of social work or community work. I don't know how you phrase it, but just to promote people and help people."

Williams said he hadn't seen the slapjack since 1965 or 1966. He remembered the scene with the rat. Binder said, "You called for help—"

"That's an understatement," Williams interrupted. "I got out of that room." He went on to say that he wouldn't go near the rat and that his father was mostly responsible for killing the rat.

Now Wayne Williams talked about the red (sometimes called burgundy) 1979 Ford LTD and how he watched it being towed away on August 8, 1980.

"Regarding Master Charles Stephens and his demise in October of 1980," Binder asked, "you didn't have the use of that burgundy car in October of 1980, did you?"

"That's right," Williams replied.

"And, if fibers from that car were found on Master Stephens, do you know how they got there?" Binder continued.

"If there were any fibers on it," Williams replied, "I assume they [the authorities] put them there."

As for events on the early morning of May 22, 1981, near the bridge, Williams said that he was going "20, 25, maybe 30, 35" miles per hour when he crossed the Jackson Parkway bridge. "I don't know," Williams said, "but it wasn't no 3, 4 or 15 miles an hour, I know that." He said he never stopped on the bridge.

Williams reiterated that three vehicles—a brown Toyota and two El Camino-like vehicles—crossed the bridge when he did. He denied that he turned around in the parking lot of the liquor store next to the bridge on the Fulton County side. He also testified: "I did not throw anything off of that bridge." He added that he wasn't sure if he could lift 140 pounds. "I don't know," he said. "I've never tried."

Williams denied that he agreed to go to FBI headquarters for questioning on June 3, 1981. "No way," he said. "They physically put me in the car." He said that he was prevented from calling a lawyer and that FBI Agent William McGrath snatched the phone out of his hand.

When he returned home early the next morning, June 4, he said, the crowd outside his house shocked him. He said he wasn't sure that the large group of reporters and cameramen waiting in front of the house wasn't a lynch mob. He then gave the press conference, he testified, to tell his side of the story, since his name and address already had appeared that very morning in the *Atlanta Constitution.*

Also during his testimony, Williams denied the stories of every so-called "eyewitness" presented by the state. Of Nathaniel Cater and Jimmy Ray Payne, he said: "I don't know them. I've never seen them before in my life."

Williams said that the only law-enforcement officer who told the truth was FBI Agent Greg Gilliland, the first to question him. This interested me because I had sensed often that only Gilliland knew what he was talking about when discussing the incident on the bridge. And I had told Williams that.

In addition, Williams said that he was shown a Task Force ID on the morning of May 22. That, he went on, is why he said to the FBI agent, "It's about those boys, isn't it?"

That remark near the bridge was one of the most innocent statements I heard Williams make. Surely, even if the media, the police, the prosecution, the defense and no one else in the world understood these cases, at least a murderer who was 22 years old would know that Nathaniel Cater, at 27, was an *adult,* not a boy.

Wayne Williams' last words on direct examination were: "It's just that I know I haven't done anything wrong, that's all."

Jack Mallard, slender and mid-fortyish, with a flat Georgia drawl, is one of those relentless prosecutors who figuratively goes for the jugular. Maybe that's why his colleagues call him "Blood." One had said, "He's pulling the hammer back, and eventually it's going to fall."

Even as I sat at the defense table beside Wayne Williams, I shared a personal empathy with Jack Mallard. His wife was ill with cancer. My daddy was dying of cancer, back in my old Kentucky home.

Early in the trial, Jack Mallard and I happened to leave the Fulton County Courthouse at the same time. He turned to me and said, good-naturedly: "I'd sure like to see what you've got in those files." I didn't have the heart to tell him that he did know what was in the files. Almost all the information in the defense files had been extrapolated from the "Brady" material, which had been furnished the defense by the prosecution.

Mallard took issue with Wayne Williams' testimony that he had been shown a Task Force ID near the bridge. Officers there, Mallard said, were not assigned to the Task Force and didn't have Task Force IDs. But Williams insisted that Atlanta police stakeout officer Carl Holden had shown him a red Task Force ID.

Then Williams denied knowing anything about the yellow blanket that was seen by FBI agents during the first search of the Williamses' home, but was missed on the second search. If Faye Williams had delivered this blanket to Binder, why wasn't it produced at his point?

Now Mallard revved up his cross-examination. He harked back to the testimony of three prosecution witnesses who said that they had seen scratches on Williams' face and arms, and that Williams had told them different stories about how he got them.

"Isn't it true," Mallard asked, "that while you were choking them to death, with the last breath they were scratching your arms and face?"

"No," Williams replied.

"Did you experience any panic...during that time that you were killing these victims?"

Now Wayne Williams, who for the better part of two days had remained unflappable on the witness stand, began to lose his composure. "Sir," he told Mallard, "I'm about as guilty as you are."

Then Williams challenged Mallard, in front of the jury, to find any scratches on him. I would ask Williams after the trial about those scratches while we talked in the jail. I wouldn't like his explanation, which attributed the scratches to his having moved file cabinets. However, in court, Williams had told a different story—that the scratches were scars from hot grease. Perhaps we were talking about different markings.

Jack Mallard had launched his cross-examination by referring to the Gemini group and to Wayne Williams' astrological sign (Gemini) symbolizing a split personality. Utter nonsense! Then Mallard took his Gemini questions to their logical end and mentioned "Jekyll and Hyde." Binder objected, but Judge Cooper overruled the objection. What does astrology have to do with proving murder?

As for his resume reference to NASCAR, Williams admitted that it was strictly self-promotional. But he insisted that he did ride in an F-4 jet. He refused to identify the pilot by name; he said only that the pilot is a black captain, explaining that he didn't want to get the pilot in trouble. So Wayne Williams flew in an F-4 jet and isn't a NASCAR driver. So what!

At first, Williams was mildly contentious. For example, when Mallard alluded to Williams flying F-4s, Williams retorted, "I didn't say I flew F-4s. I said I flew *in* an F-4."

Then Mallard dredged up Williams' references to taking up karate and elicited the same denials. In general, Mallard tore apart Williams' resume, which is something that Wayne Williams himself should have done years ago.

From there, Mallard ticked off every other discrepancy he could find in Williams' pre-trial statements. Williams had said that he was working on a record album produced by Wade Marcus of Los Angeles. Mallard asked him, "Would it surprise you to know that Wade Marcus has failed to corroborate your statement...?"

Williams answered, "It wouldn't surprise me, no."

Williams had told the police that Cheryl Johnson (the purported mysterious phone caller) seemed to be in her late 20s or 30s. He also had said that that she had called in reply to one of his flyers. Then Mallard quoted from Williams' pamphlet: "If you're between the ages of 11 and 21, call for an interview."

Mallard pointed out that although Williams said she could have been in her 30s and his pamphlet said he sought persons under 21, Williams contended that he still wanted to talk to her. It would have been quite simple, Mallard said, to ask her how old she was when Williams talked to her on the phone and made the interview appointment.

Soon Jack Mallard had Wayne Williams all tangled up in his Cheryl Johnson story. He had Williams trying to explain why he had set up an audition with her for Saturday, May 23, but also was trying to interview her to see if she would be auditioned. And I wondered: Did she show up for the audition? She might have. No one asked.

Then Mallard turned some of Williams' own words against him—particularly remarks about FBI Agent Gilliland telling the truth. Mallard brought up several things that Gilliland said Williams said—and that Williams denied saying. Williams said that those disagreements were "minor points."

Mallard asked Williams how much money he had invested in Gemini. Williams replied, "Fifteen thousand." Then Mallard referred to a statement made by Williams at his bond hearing: "We have got about $80,000 of personal money sunk in it..." Williams asked to see the document and began "qualifying" it.

Now Mallard tried to take Williams through the Cheryl Johnson story again. "And you went to the Sans Souci," Mallard said. "What time did you arrive?"

"1:30, 1:45, it was before 2," Williams answered.

"So you were not in the area—and decided to stop off and find the Cobb County address?" Mallard came back.

"No, no."

"So it was a special trip?"

"No, it was a pre-planned trip."

I knew where Mallard was taking Williams, who now followed like a dog at heel. Williams had said in his tape-recorded news conference on June 4, 1981, that he "just happened to be in the area" and decided to try to find Cheryl Johnson's address. Mallard then reminded Williams of his trial testimony on direct examination. "And I believe you said earlier," Mallard said, "...as to why you crossed the bridge, to get to the other side of the bridge to get home."

Now Williams changed the answer he had given on the stand just hours before. "Well, actually, the reason I was going that way," he said, "was I wanted to make a last phone call to try to find this girl before I went home, but that is essentially right."

"Why did you pass 25 telephones between Benson Poole Road and the river?" Mallard asked.

"The only phone I knew about was at the Starvin' Marvin station," Williams replied. Williams could well have been right. I used to smoke heavily and I know that I have passed 100 places that sold cigarettes while I looked for a place that was familiar or convenient to make the purchase.

Mallard pushed on: "And if you were crossing the river, the bridge to get home, why did you eventually turn around and go back to [Interstate] 285,"

"Because 285 is a quick way to get home," Williams replied.

"Come now, Mr. Williams," Mallard retorted. "At 3 o'clock in the morning...you were within a few miles of home when you were at Starvin' Marvin's, if you were at Starvin' Marvin's."

Mallard had landed a telling blow, but the blow was struck with a two-edged sword that had wounded the state's case as well. Did Mallard realize that he inadvertently had pointed out that Wayne Williams was originally headed in the wrong direction to be dumping off a body that the state claimed Williams had killed at home?

For his part, Williams again was arguing the same story that I had told Binder about months before. This story of Wayne Williams just didn't seem to wash.

Finally, Williams broke off the argument by saying: "Mr. Mallard, I'm on trial for my life, and I wouldn't be sitting up here lying about something like that."

"You wouldn't?" Mallard struck back. "Can you think of any better reason to lie, Mr. Williams?"

Jack Mallard clearly was winning this battle. I thought to myself that Mallard must be "hell on wheels" when he has a case to argue. Amid all those "probabilities" and "could be's" in the Wayne Williams trial, Mallard was damned close to turning a lot of what Williams would call "hearsay mess" into a successful conviction.

Mallard talked to Wayne Williams about going back to the Sans Souci after being stopped and questioned about the murders.

To which Williams said: "Well, I wasn't questioned about the murders. To be honest with you, I just thought that at the time they thought I was a suspect or something and they just did that. They told me that they had stopped other people and questioned other people the same way. And as one officer said, it wasn't no big deal because he was sleepy and wanted to go home, so I didn't think nothing of it."

When asked by Mallard if he was concerned, Williams said, "It was upsetting to me, but then I didn't know the ramifications of what they were talking about. If I'd have known the ramifications then, my first stop would have been to a lawyer's house, if I knew what I know now."

"Well," Mallard said, "they emphatically accused you of throwing a body in the water, didn't they?"

"One person did," Williams replied. "Mr. Spence."

My friend, Jeff Prugh, was right about the tape-recording of Wayne Williams' press conference on June 4, 1981. Mary Welcome was wrong. Wayne Williams was, indeed, referring to the bridge scene. Now, was it really a Freudian slip when Williams had said at his news conference on June 4: "...they openly said, 'You killed Nathaniel Cater, and you know it, and you're lying to us.' They said that. And they said it a number of occasions. They said it on that night, uh—one of the Task Force captains on the scene [Julian Spence] pointed his finger at me and said it..."?

At that point, Mallard moved to another of the state's theories—that the Atlanta killings represented a battle of wits between Wayne Williams and the police, to wit: "Didn't you consider this a challenge, really, as your mother put it, you love a challenge?"

Mallard then brought up Williams' assertion that when police put him under surveillance, he knew it "within an hour or two."

"You were proud of that, weren't you?" Mallard said, his voice rising.

"No, I wasn't proud," Williams shot back. "It makes *you* all look stupid, not me...If anything, it makes me sick that my tax dollars are being spent like that."

"Didn't you feel you were outdoing the police?"

"No. It's not my fault they did a sorry job."

Every time Williams had had a chance to talk with someone about the case, Mallard asserted he had done so—"even to the extent of sending word for the D.A. to come out there to the jail to see you."

Williams responded that he would talk to anyone, explaining that he had nothing to hide.

Now Mallard sprang a quote at Williams from the June 4 news conference: "...and I was out in the area anyway making some pickups. I had to go to a local nightclub...so I was in the area and I just decided to see if I could try and find the address..."

With Mallard, you just wait for the other shoe to drop. Now everything in this cross-examination was dropping on Wayne Williams' head. If only any of it were "relevant" to murder.

Then Mallard turned to a highly effective, but fallacious, tactic. He suggested that Wayne Williams had said that all the witnesses who had testified against him had lied. Thus, the jury had the choice of believing that all of these people conspired against Williams or that only he was telling the truth.

Actually, Williams never contended that all the witnessees lied. There is even an important semantical nuance in the word "lying." Some lies had been told in the trial by both sides. But, for the most part, there were rationalizations, poor perceptions, misidentifications, theories that were perceived as "truths" after they had been expressed often enough.

One assertion by Mallard would concern me as to its authenticity, even to this day. Mallard had stated that bubble-gum wrappers had been found in Williams' garbage and that bubble gum had been found in some of the victims.

I never saw any mention of bubble gum in the autopsies. Thousands of bubble-gum wrappers turned up in the garbage of Atlantans that week. But now, bubble-gum wrappers belatedly became "evidence."

Many things came back to haunt Wayne Williams. There was the June 4 press conference, his resume and his multiple explanations for otherwise simple facts.

But now came another. With Mary Welcome's help, Williams had granted an interview to *Us* magazine, months before the trial. On the stand, Williams insisted that he and his father had never had any serious arguments. He denied that he ever got completely drunk.

Suddenly Mallard whipped out a copy of the *Us* magazine article, in which Williams was quoted as saying, "My father and I had disagreements...I don't drink, but one weekend I got plenty wasted, plenty drunk, and my relationship with my father got much worse."

Mary Welcome would remember that testimony, too, for after the article was used against Williams, he accused Welcome of forcing him to give the jailhouse interview to *Us* magazine. Williams told the court: "Ms. Welcome said we needed to raise some money...It was on her instructions that I did it. I didn't want to."

Now Wayne Williams was on the stand for the third day. Some say he "broke" under the withering cross-examination by Jack Mallard. When the change in Williams' demeanor appeared, Mallard winked at his cohorts at the prosecution table. (But Williams now says that he was told by his attorneys to be more aggressive.) On the stand, he called Mallard a "fool" and a "drop shot." He described two FBI agents as "two of the main goons."

During one exchange, Mallard asked Williams if he recalled that Atlanta police recruit Freddie Jacobs had testified that Williams had proceeded slowly across the bridge from a parked position.

"That was something he added after you got him in front of these folks here," Williams retorted. "He didn't say that in any other hearing."

"Let me ask you," Mallard said, "were you concerned about the evidence being found on the bodies?"

"Sir," Williams replied, "I haven't killed nobody, so I wouldn't be concerned about it. And all you are trying to do is keep driving home, driving home a point that you were trying to make me out, to say that, well, Wayne Williams killed somebody. You haven't got no proof that I did anything. All you're trying to do is come up with some suppositions."

Williams commented on the chase to Public Safety Commissioner Lee Brown's house, where he stopped and blew the horn. Williams' explanation: "You were trying to put your little two bits of mess together and I got tired of it."

His temper rising in concert with his voice, Williams shouted, "Why don't you answer some of *my* questions?" Soon he snapped: "You want the real Wayne Williams, you've got him right here!"

Jack Mallard smiled. Wayne Williams had demonstrated the Gemini "split personality" myth better than the prosecution ever could have.

"All you got is a bunch of hearsay mess...," Williams went on. "Nobody saw me throw anything off that bridge. Nobody saw me kill anybody."

Indeed, no testimony ever was introduced stating *where* or *when* any of the victims died. No eyewitnesses to killings were presented (even though some persons had told police they had seen murders committed by persons *other* than Wayne Williams).

When Wayne Williams finished testifying, Al Binder said softly, "Wayne, you can come back here and sit down now." Williams returned to his seat at the defense table. He held his head in his hands and wept.

State of Georgia vs. *Wayne B. Williams* was all over, except for a handful of rebuttal witnesses, the lawyers' closing arguments, the jury's deliberation and the verdict. The defense rested.

Al Binder called Faye Williams back to the stand, primarily to refute some very damaging testimony given by prosecution rebuttal witnesses. She denied that her son and husband had ever fought in public.

Earlier, Henry Ingram, who worked at a downtown Atlanta parking lot, said Williams' parents drove into the lot about 5 p.m. one day in 1981. Two younger men, he said, approached the car, and one "snatched open" the driver's side door, pulling Homer Williams from the car. The two then scuffled in the parking lot, he said. After he saw Wayne Williams' picture on television, Ingram said he recognized the younger man as Wayne Williams.

Ingram said he chased away the two younger men. As Homer Williams left, he said, he explained that the young man in the scuffle was his son and that he was angry over his (Homer's) refusal to rent a car for one of Wayne's friends. Then Wayne returned with his companion, Ingram said, and stopped his father's car and shouted, "Don't come home tonight!"

Binder, meanwhile, suggested that the argument really was over Homer Williams' refusal to go to the hospital for tests. Ingram said he couldn't deny that since he didn't hear the actual argument.

Wayne Williams' mother again refuted Sheldon Kemp's claims of Wayne choking Homer, and Homer threatening Wayne with a shotgun. Binder said that Sheldon Kemp "tried to shake down" Williams' parents for a motorbike.

The calling of other rebuttal witnesses provided a mysterious spinoff of the Wayne Williams trial. The state wanted to recall Nellie Trammell as a rebuttal witness, but she could not be found.

As Wayne Williams was led toward the courtroom for a day of final arguments, he waved to photographers outside, with two fingers on one hand forming a "V" to symbolize victory. Also in the courtroom for this climactic session on Friday, February 26, were Public Safety Commissioner

Lee Brown, Police Chief George Napper and Task Force commander Morris Redding.

Leading off for the prosecution, Jack Mallard branded Wayne Wiliams a "mad-dog killer" and a "pathological liar" with a "Jekyll-and-Hyde" personality who lived in a "dream world" and killed "over and over without any apparent motive."

"On the first day, he was a calm, cool, deliberate witness," Mallard said. "What happened on the second day, he was a completely opposite person. He showed the other side of him. He showed contempt for everyone. He showed a raging explosion inside him..."

Conceding that the state's case was "circumstantial," Mallard insisted that the jury of eight blacks and four whites had an "overabundance of circumstances, of facts, all pointing with certainty to this man on trial." Mallard said, too, that the law does not require the state to prove Wayne Williams' guilt "to a mathematical or absolute certainty," but that the state must prove guilt only beyond "a doubt founded upon reason."

"If you wait until we prove to a mathematical certainty anyone's guilt," he said, "we would never convict anyone."

For her part, Mary Welcome caused a furor among her fellow defense lawyers when she used up much more than her allotted portion of the two hours allowed each side for closing arguments. She made a sentimental appeal to the jurors, saying: "Wayne is young, gifted and black. Mr. Mallard says he was a dreamer. Well, Martin Luther King Jr. was a dreamer."

She concluded her sometimes wayward, disjointed argument by placing a small plastic thimble on the railing of the jury box. "I leave this with you," she told the jurors. "A thimble full of evidence. Which is not enough for a conviction."

Al Binder used a small bridge display built by his wife and supported by what he called the "pillars" of the state's case. As he attacked each point made by the prosecution, Binder knocked out a pillar. When the last one fell, the bridge did, too, leaving the words "Reasonable Doubt."

At one point, Binder grabbed Wayne Williams and towed him in front of the jury. "This pudgy, fat, little boy," Binder said, wasn't strong enough to dispose of two victims' bodies, as the prosecutors contended.

Then, Binder added: "Black men of Mr. [Nathaniel] Cater's and Mr. [Jimmy Ray] Payne's ages are still being murdered in this community."

Using information that I had supplied to him, Binder then pointed out that Lee Brown's testimony about "pattern" changes and the time when victims started turning up in rivers was wrong. The finding of 16-year-old Patrick (Pat Man) Rogers in the Chattahoochee River, Binder emphasized, predated Brown's claimed "first" river victim (13-year-old Curtis Walker) by three months, almost to the day.

Suddenly the prosecutors wore question marks all over their faces. They frantically whispered among themselves and passed scraps of paper with handwritten notes to each other.

Later, assistant prosecutor Gordon Miller departed from his prepared arguments to finesse the state through its Pat Man dilemma. "There's not one shred of evidence in this case," Miller told the jury, "and we have never contended that the defendant killed Patrick Rogers. Larry Rogers, yes, but not Patrick Rogers." (Larry Rogers, no kin to Pat Man, happened to be one of the state's 10 "pattern" victims; Pat Man was not.)

Binder had also stung the state with the revelation that Wayne Williams and his parents did not have access to the family's red 1979 Ford LTD when 12-year-old "pattern" victim Charles Stephens died in 1980 (Stephens' body was said by the state to be among three that had fibers from the trunk of that very car.)

Now Gordon Miller tried to rescue the state from this second dilemma. This time, in final arguments, Miller said nothing about the fibers coming specifically from the Williamses' red 1979 Ford LTD, which is what the state had introduced into evidence, based on FBI fiber expert Harold Deadman's report (which identified the car as "item #233C").

Miller misstated the state's own evidence by saying that the state had claimed the fibers could have come from *any* Ford. "We have never contended in this case," Miller said, "that the fiber from the trunk liner on Charles Stephens had to have come from a 1969-79 Ford LTD. What we contended was that it was consistent with having come from a Ford product." (If so, that would make millions of drivers of Ford products potential suspects.)

There was no chance for Al Binder to rebut Miller's argument and straighten out the state's misstatement. You have seen the pertinent part of the December 7, 1981, letter from Deadman to Miller. What do you think?

Now it was chief prosecutor Lewis Slaton's turn. In his raspy, sandpaper voice, Slaton delivered a rambling, incohesive argument, speckled with incomplete sentences, an apology for a lapse of memory at one point and yet another misstatement of fact about the Williamses' cars. "From July 30, 1980, as I have said, through October 21, 1980," he said, "they [the Williamses] had a Fairmont of some kind every day except one day. That matches up with our fibers." Yes, the state felt wounded by the hole in its fiber case.

Many of those days, it was a Pinto, not a Fairmont, that the Williamses had. Also, it was nice of Slaton, as far as the defense was concerned, to confirm that the Williamses didn't have the 1970 Chevrolet station wagon until October 21, since Charles Stephens, according to the state's fiber evidence, also had a fiber from that station wagon when he died on October 9 or 10.

Meanwhile, I knew that my discovery about the fibers and the 1979 Ford was recongized by the state as extremely damaging to its case. Apparently the jurors didn't see it that way, if they saw it at all.

Slaton also raised a point that no one ever established as fact—precisely *where* victims died—that is, if you ignore the laundromat where 13-year-old Clifford Jones, a non-"pattern" victim, was strangled with a yellow rope by a black male suspect who was *not* Wayne Williams, according to eyewitnesses.

"The bodies," Slaton told the jury, "were dumped someplace other than where they were killed."

Where were they killed? Slaton didn't say. Nor did anyone else during this nine-week trial. They left the jury to believe the killing occurred in Wayne Williams' bedroom.

Slaton served up yet another misstatement when he said, "...the older people [victims] were all small. [Nathaniel] Cater, I think, is the largest one in the bunch. [At 5-10, he was 2½ inches *taller* than Williams and I have seen victim Bubba Duncan's height reported at 5-foot-11]. They're all small people."

Finally, Lewis Slaton—who eight months earlier had stated that he wasn't sure if there was enough evidence to arrest Wayne Williams—buttressed the false notion that the killing stopped when Williams went to jail.

"You will have to be responsible for putting Wayne Williams back in the community." Slaton told the jurors. "It won't be us. It will have to be you.

"Doing away with inferiors, Attila the Hun, Adolf Hitler, Idi Amin from Uganda, and Wayne Bertram Williams, master race, doing away with inferiors, 'doing away with one black male child, I've got statistics on how many that will do away with.'"

Now there was no opportunity, by the rules of the court, to remind the jury that Wayne Williams was not on trial for killing any children. Slaton, wrapping up his closing argument, looked earnestly at the nine women and three men on the jury and said:

"Ladies and gentlemen, all of us, the defense, the prosecution, the court, appreciate you. I know all of you, I'm going to see you, and we're going to talk about this case, and we're both going to say we met our responsibility. Thank you."

The case went to the jury late Friday afternoon, February 26, a day of sleet and ice in Atlanta. The jury would recess that evening, returning the next morning to work all day into Saturday evening.

I had come into this courtroom nine weeks earlier, hoping to find out if Wayne Williams was guilty or not guilty. Nothing had happened to enlighten me one iota. This was a trial in which the state introduced *weight* of evidence, not *quality* of evidence.

I thought of the masses of information that the jury *didn't* hear. The jurors heard not one word about the house on Gray Street, Cap'n Peg's and the Pat

Man connections. I was disappointed that the testimony didn't convince me one way or the other.

In our system of justice, a defendant is innocent until *proved* guilty beyond a reasonable doubt. Had I been a juror, hearing only the testimony that was allowed into the Wayne Williams trial, I would have been consumed by doubt—and the fact that there was no proof. I could have voted only "not guilty."

Deja Vu

26

The Beat Goes On

The left corner of Wayne Williams' lower lip quivers involuntarily. Stifling sobs that fill his throat, he slowly moves his bowed head from side to side, reflecting disbelief as the voice of prosecutor Lewis Slaton intones the verdicts: "As to count number one, the murder of Jimmy Ray Payne, we the jury find the defendant guilty as charged. As to count two, the murder of Nathaniel Cater," Slaton continues, ". . . Guilty!"

A tear glistens, runs, pauses and drips to the floor from his cheekbone, but Wayne Williams stands quietly, his hands folded in front of him below his waist. The game is over and, incredibly, from his point of view, Wayne Williams has lost. Is this the *"Twilight Zone"?* The "Keystone Cops," enjoying the last laugh, have cornered Wayne Williams, and the picador has set the final lance. It's no longer a laughing, taunting, childish joust. Wayne Williams wakes up to find that the game has been serious all along.

Close behind Williams and slightly to his left stands his father, Homer Williams, an arm draped across Wayne's slumping shoulders. The elder Williams raises the arm and, with clenched fist, punctuates a verbal attack on the prosecution for "railroading" his son.

Now the judge, Clarence Cooper, says, "Life!"—and then the judge says, "Life!" again. Wayne Williams has continued to protest that he is innocent, but he is led from the courtroom to continue his stay at the Fulton County Jail. It will be years, if ever, before he sees the inside of a real penitentiary. There are those who feel he will never survive in the pen, and those who feel he won't survive on the street. They contend that the guilty verdict was, in its own way, a death sentence—one the prosecution didn't request, but one that presumably will be carried out some way, some day, by somebody.

In January of 1984, two and one half years after Wayne Williams first

Moments after the jury finds Wayne Williams guilty, his father, Homer, unleashes a scathing verbal attack on District Attorney Lewis Slaton, accusing him, among other things, of "railroading" his son. (Bill Lignante / ABC News)

Most of the media insists on calling Wayne Williams "child" killer, though he never was convicted of killing any children. He is escorted to jail to begin serving life sentences for the killings of two adults by sheriff's captain Charles A. Smith, who was later convicted of trafficking in narcotics and went to jail, too. (Jerome McClendon/ Atlanta Constitution)

walked into the Fulton County Jail an accused murderer, I sat with him, Lynn Whatley and Chief Jailer E. L. Brownlee while Whatley and Brownlee discussed Williams' future in the prison system.

"Who do I have to see to make sure Wayne gets to stay here in the jail?" Whatley asked.

"That'd be up to Judge Cooper," Brownlee replied. "But, I'll tell you one thing: the state's chompin' at the bit to get their hands on Wayne. I don't know why, but they are."

Brownlee went on to say that Williams would probably end up staying at Jackson (state prison).

Later, I talked to Williams.

"Where do you want to go, Wayne?" I asked.

"I know I don't want to go to Alto. I'd rather go to Reidsville [the prison with the hardest reputation in Georgia]."

"What's the matter, too many whites at Alto?"

"Un-uhn, Chet, too many young guys. You know, wantin' to make a name for themselves."

"Do you fear for your life?"

"No, nah, I put my trust in God. That's all anybody can do. I've already been threatened."

Sheriff Stynchcombe had told the press that he had received many threats on Williams' life. But Lynn Whatley denied that he knew of any threats.

"There was a guy out here," Williams continued. "His name was Terry. He tried to get me once and he stabbed another guy tryin' to get to me. We had a fire out here right after that happened, and they were leadin' us out of here and they tried to handcuff me and this guy, Terry, together. There was no way I was goin' to let that happen, so I fought 'em."

"Who'd you fight, Wayne?"

"The deputies—the guards."

Williams went on to tell me that he thought he could spot trouble coming, but that he did not want to be locked up tight (maximum security) because he was afraid "somebody would come by and throw in a Molotov cocktail."

He added: "My problem will be: Can I get them [the authorities] to do anything about it if I do spot trouble?"

After the trial, a deputy sheriff escorted Williams from the courtroom, pushing at his elbow. The sheriff would walk this way again. Months later in 1982, the deputy would be the prodded instead of the prodder. Convicted of trafficing in drugs, Fulton County Sheriff's Captain Charles A. Smith would hear the door slam shut between himself and freedom, just as Wayne Williams is about to.

The verdict genuinely surprised me, too. I'm not one step closer to being convinced of Wayne Williams' guilt or innocence. Certainly nothing was introduced at the trial that would have persuaded me one way or the other.

But 12 of Wayne Williams' "peers" have made up their minds. In their unanimous opinion, Wayne Williams murdered both 21-year-old Jimmy Ray Payne and 27-year-old Nathaniel Cater. These jurors obviously had been swayed by Lewis Slaton's closing argument that the killings had stopped, that if the jurors set Wayne Williams free and someone else were killed, it would be the jurors' cross to bear—not the prosecution's.

Indeed, it would be easier for the jurors to live with an innocent man's incarceration on their consciences than somebody else's blood on their hands. I wonder what the verdict would have been had the death penalty been applicable. Then whose blood would be on whose hands?

To many in the news media, the guilty verdict had been rendered against Atlanta's "child" killer—despite the fact that "children" were not mentioned by judge or jury.

A younger Chet Dettlinger would have found the verdict of a jury sacred. He would have assumed that justice had been served. But, the Boy Scouts, infallibility and naive perceptions of authorities as the "good guys" are long behind me, along with Catholics going to hell for eating meat on Friday.

Somewhere I have discovered that right does not follow from consensus. The verdict doesn't mean that Wayne Williams really is guilty, as I would have assumed at a less thoughtful period in my life. Likewise, a verdict of not guilty would have been no better assurance of his innocence.

What the jury verdict does mean is that we all are free to wash our hands of this gruesome situation, content with the rationalization that the ends of justice had been met. Now the Chamber of Commerce could get about the really important business of attracting those lucrative conventions back to Atlanta. Surely dollars had been lost to Chicago, where John Wayne Gacy killed at least 33, and to New York, where 33 homicides might constitute a quiet week. Local newspaper columnists now can write such tripe as "Atlanta is found not guilty." After all, the murders stopped when Wayne Williams went to jail. Well, they did, didn't they?

Jeff Prugh and I had, for some time, looked at other homicides that occurred after Wayne Williams went to jail. We found that in the city of Atlanta alone, according to the Atlanta police-FBI Uniform Crime Report tabulations, seven blacks who fit the admittedly broad parameters of The List had been murdered by person or persons unknown during the six months of 1981 while Wayne Williams languished in jail.

It is important to understand the significance of the words "in the city of Atlanta alone" because barely 50% of the murders on The List fell within the jurisdiction of the city of Atlanta. Fifteen out of 28 were Atlanta cases. The other 13 were scattered among DeKalb, Fulton, Cobb, Rockdale and Douglas counties, as well as the city of East Point.

Therefore, in the city of Atlanta, during the first six months of Williams' incarceration, there were seven unsolved murders that could have gone on a list, compared to the 15 that did go on The List in the 23 months prior to Williams' jailing. Before Williams' arrest, the city of Atlanta—not the other jurisdictions—added a victim to The List every 46½ days. In the first six months after Williams went to jail, the city of Atlanta was not putting victims on The List at the rate of one every 26 days.

The truth had to be that the authorities and the news media simply had stopped counting. It was The List—not the murders—that stopped when Wayne Williams went to jail.

Among the post-Williams-arrest murders we found—and there were many more than the seven that did fit the parameters of The List—was that of a 16-year-old boy whose body was found in the street within a block of Wayne Williams' house. This murder occurred during the first month that Williams was in jail. Like most of the post-Williams-arrest victims, he died of a gunshot wound. But so, too, had 14-year-old Edward Hope Smith, victim No. 1 on The List.

Barely after Williams' trial, police and prosecutors would say, in effect, that Edward Hope Smith was not killed by Wayne Williams (Smith's case was among a handful on The List *not* closed). Their reason, they said, was that no fibers were found on Smith's body. However, this contention did not take into account the fact that Smith's body was found along Niskey Lake Road within yards of the body identified as that of The List victim No. 2—14-year-old Alfred Evans. Smith and Evans had been found at the same time and apparently had been killed at about the same time. The police, by closing Alfred Evans' case, contend that Wayne Williams killed Evans. Fiber evidence in Evans' case had been introduced at the trial as part of the prosecution's "pattern."

Investigators found no fibers on 23-year-old victim Michael McIntosh. But police and prosecutors added McIntosh to the group of 22 cases "cleared by arrest" and attributed to Wayne Williams. The reason they gave was that McIntosh was found in the Chattahoochee River, where five other victims had been found.

It is charitable to call the authorities' logic in the Smith and McIntosh cases inconsistent. Could it be that they wanted to rule out Smith's death because it was the only gunshot case on The List? Certainly they would use the absence of gunshot victims attributed to Williams to rule out connections among cases which occurred after Williams went to jail.

By closing those other 22 cases, then, they would contend that Wayne Williams had killed by strangulation with a rope, by strangulation with his bare hands, by suffocation, by bludgeoning (they suggested he used a slapjack), by stabbing and by other unknown or undetected means. Yet the shootings, they would say, could have "no possible connection," even though every other parameter and pipe dream of their own List fit the shooting victims like a glove. Again, their reasoning is conveniently illogical.

Another of those seven victims slain in 1981 after Williams went to jail was a 21-year-old man named Stanley Murray. He was the same age as Jimmy Ray Payne, for whose murder Williams would be convicted. Stanley Murray had been found shot to death near the streetcorner where 13-year-old Curtis Walker, who made The List, had last been reported alive. But again, Lee Brown and Lewis Slaton insisted after the Williams trial that these victims slain after Williams had gone to jail had no connection whatsoever to those who made The List before Williams was jailed.

Five days after the trial, a young black woman answered Jeff Prugh's knock at 946 Wilkes Circle, Apartment 497. "Excuse me, ma'am," Jeff said, "I'm inquiring about Stanley Murray. Did you know him?"

"Yes," she said. "He was my brother."

Jeff has a way of being solicitous with his eyes. With a sympathetic look, he continued: "I understand Curtis Walker lived in this same building, too. Is there a chance that Stanley might have known Curtis?"

"Yes," she said. Then, pausing again, she added, "Curtis lived here in this apartment with Stanley and me. Curtis was my son."

Jeff was stunned. He later would speak of the heartbreak and confusion in the eyes of Catherine Leach at that moment.

Here, then, was an example of a blood-kin connection between someone on The List and someone murdered after Williams went to jail. Two of three geographic points for Curtis Walker and his Uncle Stanley had been the same. Jeff and I would tell some members of the news media about the kinship between Stanley Murray and Curtis Walker. But it would go unreported by the media, and probably unrealized by police and the prosecution, because nobody was asking. No one was adding names to The List anymore. No one was reporting the Atlanta story anymore.

If the police and prosecution ever learned that Stanley Murray and Curtis Walker were connected, it wasn't from Catherine Leach. She said the police never had talked with her about her brother's death. She was even surprised that the murder of her son was among those additional cases that had been cleared and charged to Williams. "Nobody ever discussed it with me," she said.

In September of 1981, a 10-year-old girl was found strangled on Memorial Drive, near the Krystal hamburger shop where 15-year-old Terry Pue had last been reported alive, back in January of 1981. But when the girl turned up dead, Williams (who now is accused of killing Terry Pue) had been in jail for three months. The girl wasn't put on any list and, in fact, the story of her death did not make the front section of the *Atlanta Constitution*.

A man was arrested and charged with the girl's murder. He has written to me several times from his cell in the DeKalb County Jail. One thing I learned is that he never had been considered a suspect in any of the slayings on The List, even those so closely associated with Memorial Drive. After all, the murders stopped when Wayne Williams went to jail, right?

In March of 1983, a 13-year-old Atlanta girl named Lucretia Bell (no kin to either slain 9-year-old Yusuf Bell or 15-year-old Joseph [Jo-Jo] Bell, who both made The List) was found strangled in her bed. The story was not reported by either of Atlanta's two major daily newspapers. The girl's death is unexplained. Her father said that the "police don't think she was strangled, but the medical examiner says she was." He spoke of bruises on his daughter's neck.

Lucretia Bell joins Cynthia Montgomery, Angela Bacon, Joseph Lee, Beverly Harvey and other teen-agers who were murdered, but didn't make The List of Atlanta's "murdered and/or missing children and [later] young adults."

Kenneth Johnson, 17, was another of those post-Williams-arrest victims who police say had no possible connection with those on The List. Well, he lived across the street from Cap'n Peg's, as did 23-year-old victim Michael McIntosh, who made The List. He worked part-time at Cap'n Peg's, as did 15-year-old Joseph (Jo-Jo) Bell, who made The List. His body was found near the house of 11-year-old victim Patrick Baltazar, who made The List. He was another gunshot victim. His case is unsolved and, in what seems to be typical of murder investigations in Atlanta, a relative says the police never have seriously looked into the death of Kenneth Johnson in November of 1981.

Wayne Williams spent the Thanksgiving holiday of 1981 securely locked in the Fulton County Jail. Meanwhile, a Georgia Tech student—returning to school in Atlanta from a turkey dinner at home—discovered the dead body of his roommate, 18-year-old Kevin Alexander, crushed between a bed and a wall. The dormitory room had been ransacked, but only valuables of the victim were missing.

Not long before this incident, two other Tech students were accosted. A gunman had tried to force them to commit a homosexual act. When they refused, they were shot and left for dead, but both survived. Wayne Williams was in jail, but eight months earlier—when Eddie (Bubba) Duncan disappeared from Techwood Homes, the housing project that abuts the Georgia Tech campus on its south side—the 21-year-old Duncan was added to The List of murdered "children."

A funeral director in Kevin Alexander's hometown of Dallas would tell Kevin's mother that Kevin had suffered injuries to his neck. This would not jibe with what Mrs. Alexander was being told by Fulton County medical examiners, who had ruled Kevin's death "accidental." Mrs. Alexander tried in vain to obtain an autopsy report of her son's death.

In frustration, she hired the Dallas law firm of Burleson, Pate and Gibson (the same firm that represented Jack Ruby and secured the exhumation of the body of Lee Harvey Oswald, the accused assassin of President John F. Kennedy). In May of 1982, six months after Kevin Alexander's death, an attorney in the Dallas firm met me in Atlanta. We went to the Fulton

County medical examiner's office on Coca-Cola Street in Atlanta. We were told that no copy of the autopsy was available because it had "not yet been transcribed."

We were told to return the following day. When we did, we were handed a photocopy of the freshly typewritten autopsy. We asked for copies of the medical examiner's notes, some of which the attorney had perused the previous day when he was handed the file. We were told that the medical examiner "often keeps his notes in his head." The receptionist explained that the examiner uses a recorder that is actuated by a foot-pedal and that he doesn't take notes *per se*. Sometimes, she said, he will mark on a chart the location of certain wounds and other marks.

Soon I talked with the ramrod-straight commander of the Georgia Tech campus police. He had the crew haircut and single-minded dedication of a Marine drill instructor. Two wasted weeks of red tape and run-arounds later, I finally caught up with the Georgia Tech police officer who investigated the death of Kevin Alexander and the shootings of the other two Tech students. He explained that the police thought the death was related to the theft of Kevin's valuables. But the Kevin Alexander case was dropped when the medical examiner said that the death was an "accident" due to an overdose of tripelennamine, a non-narcotic decongestant that had been prescribed for—and used by Kevin Alexander—for years before his death.

An examination of the Georgia Tech police file was not very informative. The campus police asked if I could furnish them with a copy of the autopsy, which they, too, had been unable to obtain. Looking over the material I gave them, I noticed that the chart made by the medical examiner indicated that the body was that of "Calvin"—not Kevin—Alexander, and it listed his age as "29," not 18. Obviously, typical amounts of care—or non-care—had been taken in preparing these documents, which someday might be used to try to convict some as yet unknown person of a crime.

For the moment, I couldn't help but recall the litany of similar performances by medical examiners during the murders that made The List—i.e., misidentified bodies, causes of death questionably attributed, death certificates changed after the fact. Now I was watching a re-run—or a sequel.

Since the trial of Wayne Williams, I have appeared on numerous radio and television talk shows across the nation. No matter where I go—Atlanta, New York or Oakland—the reaction is always the same: the news media people ask where the media was during the height of the killings, and listeners and viewers express shock at what they didn't know about the Atlanta murders.

Disillusionment has set in, too. A radio talk-show host in Texas said that if he had known that some victims were ex-convicts in their 20s, he never would have sent a $25 donation to City Hall in Atlanta for the "children" of Atlanta.

By late summer of 1982, Georgia state Representative Mildred Glover (D-Atlanta) assisted some victims' mothers in drafting a petition, which they took to a meeting in Washington with William French Smith, then Attorney General of the United States. In the petition, they asked that the cases of their offspring's murders be brought to trial.

They, too, wanted their day in court—a free person's right that you would think should override the administrative needs of the local District Attorney. Wayne Williams had been accused of killing their sons, and they wanted him tried for the murders. After all, isn't that the ideal we're all taught to believe in?

The real world, however, knew that William French Smith was not about to open this Pandora's box that his own FBI had been so instrumental—with much difficulty—in trying to force a lid on. But the mothers went to Washington, had their say and were summarily forgotten.

Even so, they didn't let the mystery die. In December of 1982, the parents of 12 murder victims—and the foster mother of still-missing 10-year-old Darron Glass—filed suit in federal court, demanding that Wayne Williams be tried in their children's cases or that the investigations be reopened.

On the first anniversary of Wayne Williams' conviction, prosecutor Lewis Slaton was asked in 1983 by an *Atlanta Journal-Constitution* reporter if any action was contemplated in the 22 cases Williams had been accused of, but never tried for. Slaton answered that he would not waste Fulton County's money since another conviction could only lead to another life sentence for Williams.

What if Wayne Williams were found *not* guilty in one of those other cases? One must presume that this option is still open in America's criminal-justice system. Of course, the state could not easily live with an acquittal in a case that was linked to one of its convictions by fiber evidence. The whole case against Wayne Williams rests on the fiber connections. There is no logical way for Williams to be guilty of one of these murders and innocent of another, according to the state's case.

To avoid this pitfall, the state will not investigate to find another—or a different—murderer. The state also cannot afford to try Wayne Williams on one of the other charges and risk a "not guilty" verdict.

In the parents' lawsuit, many contentions are made—not the least of which argues that a coverup existed in the investigation. The suit contends that three funeral directors told parents who are plaintiffs that the condition of four bodies—those of Patrick (Pat Man) Rogers, Lubie Geter, Patrick Baltazar and Curtis Walker—was "often quite different from the conditon as reported by Defendant Stivers [Fulton County Medical Examiner Robert Stivers]."

One problem with this contention is that the bodies of Rogers, Baltazar and Walker were found outside of Fulton County and thus were not within Stivers' jurisdiction. Another problem: the funeral directors—Alfonso Dawson (who owned a Chevrolet dealership I once worked for), W.C. Meadows (who was assigned to the police Task Force under one hat and handled victims' burials under another) and Paul Jacobs—denied having told anyone of such differences.

The implication in the lawsuit was that some victims had been sexually mutilated. The three funeral directors said, in interviews, that they had no knowledge of mutilations. All three said they weren't aware that their names had appeared in the lawsuit, although Meadows said he had heard only rumors to that effect.

What's more, the Atlanta newspapers—while reporting that the parents had filed the lawsuit—did *not* report that the suit also had accused Meadows of a "conflict" in his dual role as Task Force police officer and funeral director. In fact, Meadows' unusual double life during the height of Atlanta's murders was known by some members of the news media, but not reported.

For his part, Meadows said that his funeral home provided transportation for the body of 13-year-old Curtis Walker and buried 14-year-old Lubie Geter. When asked to comment on the complaint that his double role as cop and mortician represented a "conflict," Meadows declined—on grounds that Wayne Williams' two convictions were under appeal.

On March 1, 1982, not even 48 hours after the trial, Public Safety Commissioner Lee Brown called a news conference at Task Force headquarters.

There, the top brass of the investigation, along with Lewis Slaton and his prosecutorial staff, joined Brown *en masse*. They happily posed together for pictures that someone said looked like those of a college reunion.

The news media was there in force, too, and one Atlanta television reporter approached Task Force commander Morris Redding and smilingly offered a handshake. "Great job," the reporter complimented Redding.

Lee Brown thanked Redding and Slaton, along with other law-enforcement officials, for their "support," as well as the people who "kept the faith with us."

Brown announced that the Atlanta police were shutting down the Task Force and closing 21 more cases (including that of 28-year-old non-List victim John Porter), along with those of Nathaniel Cater and Jimmy Ray Payne. Grand total: 23.

(These 23 also included the yellow-rope strangulation of 13-year-old

Even after Wayne Williams was arrested, Atlanta Public Safety Commissioner Lee Brown (right) persisted in denying that the cases were connected. But when he closed the Task Force, he said Williams killed 23 people. Brown then moved to Houston as chief of police and was succeeded by Atlanta Chief of Police George Napper (left), whom Brown earlier had taken off the cases. (W.A. Bridges/ Atlanta Constitution)

Clifford Jones—the case with five eyewitnesses who said the suspect was *not* Wayne Williams.)

That left these seven open (unsolved) cases: Edward Hope Smith . . . Milton Harvey . . . Angel Lenair . . . LaTonya Wilson . . . Jefferey Mathis . . . Patrick (Pat Man) Rogers . . . and still-missing Darron Glass.

Now the questions shot at Brown like machine-gun fire.

"Commissioner," one reporter asked, "do you believe Wayne Williams committed 23 murders?"

"Yes, we do," Brown replied.

Then Brown was asked by Jeff Prugh why he and other officials said Atlanta's killings stopped, when the Atlanta police statistics intended for inclusion in the FBI Uniform Crime Report showed seven Atlanta unsolved-murder victims who fit the authorities' own parameters for The List, since Williams went to jail.

Brown dodged and weaved. "We have looked at all the cases that we have," he said, "and the cases that we felt, based upon the evidence that we have that were related to the cases carried by the Task Force. We have none that's open at this time."

Now other reporters bored in on Brown.

"How did these asphyxial deaths occur?" someone asked. "How did these people die?"

"I don't think it's appropriate at this time," Brown shot back, "to respond to that question."

"Commissioner, do you know *where* the killings took place?"

"OK," Brown said, rising from his chair. "I think one of the things we wanted to do at this particular meeting—and not get into any more detail than we've already gotten into—is to advise you of what our decision was [to shut down the Task Force and close 21 more cases]. That we've done, and we've responded to your questions. Thank you."

Just like that, the news conference was over. But the murder mystery wasn't. Many reporters followed Brown and other officials outside like ravenous pack dogs, spewing questions and getting no more answers. Brown couldn't answer that last question—about *where* the killings occurred—because apparently no one except the killer or killers knew.

Two days later, under some community pressure, Brown called another news conference and announced that the Task Force wasn't being shut down, after all. Actually, he said, the regular Atlanta police Homicide Division would move into the Task Force building, and Atlanta would thus have a Homicide Task Force, investigating all homicides.

Two nights after Wayne Williams was convicted, ABC News' *Nightline* program served up a smorgasbord of good and poor journalism.

Bob Sirkin, an Atlanta correspondent who long had covered the story for the network, reported responsibly that Atlanta's officials were ignoring more unsolved murders that didn't make The List than the 28 that did.

Sirkin's report included an interview with Eula Montgomery, non-List victim Cynthia Montgomery's mother, who said: "I want them to find out who did this to her. I want them to find that out like they do the other kids."

From there, the program turned into a mixture of vitriol (Lee Brown charged that ABC "has made a religion out of attempting to create some theory of conspiracy") and sloppiness. Moderator Ted Koppel mistakenly thought "28 cases involve strangulation." *Atlanta Constitution* columnist Lewis Grizzard, even though he had been closer than Koppel to the scene, also was in error when he commented: "The truth is, a jury that included eight blacks ruled that a black man, with his own sick motive, strangled black children."

The truth *is,* Nathaniel Cater and Jimmy Ray Payne were *men,* not children. And no one knows how Cater and Payne died.

On that same *Nightline* program, Al Binder recited names of some of those seven victims who were found dead within six months after Williams went to jail.

That triggered a retort the next day from Atlanta's newly inaugurated mayor, Andrew Young, who castigated Binder for retrying the case in the media. Young suggested that Binder should have brought out this information in court.

Did Andrew Young forget? Binder had, indeed, tried to introduce evidence of other unsolved Atlanta murders stretching back 10 years (which would have included the latter half of 1981, while Williams was in custody). But Binder's pretrial motion was rebuffed by Judge Cooper, and the city of Atlanta had petitioned to keep records of all those additional unsolved murders out of court.

Andrew Young later commented on Wayne Williams in an interview by Allan Sonnenschein in the February, 1983, issue of *Penthouse* magazine.

INTERVIEWER: "Are you completely satisfied that Wayne Williams was the killer of all those black children?"

YOUNG: "The evidence indicates that he was. It really was a massive amount of evidence. The jury, after listening to the evidence for over nine weeks, took only a couple of hours to decide he was guilty."

This points out that Andrew Young's perspective of Atlanta's murders was not much better than that of the interviewer. Both view the case as one of children's murders. Young apparently doesn't realize—or doesn't state—that Williams was not convicted of killing any children, but rather two *adults.* The mass of evidence is in no way related to guilt or innocence. The jury actually deliberated for several hours on one day and the better part of the second day.

INTERVIEWER: "Investigators in different parts of the country claim that other black children have been murdered since Wayne Williams has been in custody. Do you know anything about this?"

YOUNG: "I've heard people say that . . ."

Well, it *wasn't* different parts of the country. It was right here in Atlanta. I'm one of those "investigators." I never have said "other black children." For the last time, it is other people the same age as those on The List (some of whom were children), which is *not* a list of children who continue to be murdered. When the mayor of Atlanta and interviewers for national publications learn this one basic fact, perhaps we can all begin to critique these cases intelligently.

When Lee Brown prepared to leave the city shortly after the Wayne Williams trial to become Houston's new chief of police, a "fact-finding team" of Houston police officers visited Atlanta.

They were not overjoyed with the prospect of Brown's arrival in Houston. They have kept Brown embroiled in controversy ever since. The statistics haven't been kind to Brown, either. Houston is bucking a national trend of falling crime rates by posting sizeable increases in violent crimes.

Lee Brown also was greeted in Houston by another of those coincidences from the Atlanta murder cases. Before the arrest of Wayne Williams in 1981, Charles Watson, a 23-year-old street hustler and ninth-grade dropout from Atlanta, was serving time for a robbery conviction in a Georgia prison. However, records show that the inmate was using his teen-age brother's name—"Vincent Watson." "He had his brother's driver's license with him and I guess nobody checked things out," a Cobb County, Georgia, detective said.

From his cell, Watson convinced the authorities that he had information about Atlanta's killings and could help find the killer. Watson had written letters to the police and several prominent black leaders, contending that he knew two of the victims and possibly the person who had killed them. One detective said Watson had described himself, in his letters, as a homosexual who knew some child molesters.

The authorities, believing that his name was Vincent Watson, obtained a temporary release for Watson from prison, but not until after he had undergone several polygraph tests, was put under hypnosis and convinced officers that he was telling the truth.

In May of 1981, Watson went to work as an undercover informant for the Task Force, with Lee Brown ultimately approving the decision to allow him to participate in the investigation.

Watson rode with plainclothes officers who took him to the vicinity of several bars, including homosexual hangouts. The officers would stay in their unmarked car, and Watson would go inside a bar to await a contact. One night in June of 1981, Watson went into the Marquiett Club on Martin Luther King Jr. Drive and didn't come back.

We later learned that Watson mostly sneaked out the back door and visited his *girlfriend* at her apartment late at night—before reversing his field and rejoining the police through the front door. Atlanta authorities had a felony escape warrant on Watson. Some detectives thought he had been abducted from the bar and killed.

Months later, Watson's girlfriend would tell reporter Jonathan Dahl of the *Houston Chronicle,* Watson—"Chuckie," she called him—followed her to her new residence in Houston. There, Watson was arrested in September of 1981 for driving without a license and for two other minor traffic violations. He told authorities his real name—Charles Watson—and spent one night in jail before paying a $150 fine.

Charles Watson fell through the cracks of our criminal-justice system. Nobody in Atlanta knew he had gone through Houston's courts. The escape warrant had been issued in Watson's real name, but authorities in Houston apparently never bothered to run a check on him.

On April 5, 1982, Charles Watson was found by his girlfriend lying in a pool of blood on the floor of her apartment. Another woman friend of Watson told police that three men broke into the apartment and beat him. A gun also went off, the bullet wounding Watson in the back of his head. He lapsed into unconsciousness.

Authorities in Georgia said they doubted that Watson's shooting had anything to do with Atlanta's murders. Lee Brown, when contacted by the *Chronicle* reporter, refused comment.

About four months after the Wayne Williams trial, my telephone rang late one night.

"Hello, Chet," the caller said. "This is Wayne."

Startled at first, I put the voice and the name together and realized that the caller was Wayne Williams.

"Wayne! Where are you?" was all I could think to say.

"Now where do you think I am?" he replied, chuckling.

Of course. Wayne Williams was in the Fulton County Jail. In our conversation, I told him that I had written him a letter shortly after the trial.

He complained that he never got the letter. He said he would have my name put on his visitation list so I could talk with him in person at the jail.

Mary Welcome no longer was part of the defense team. Wayne Williams had made it clear, not long after the trial, that her services were no longer required. She ran for the post of Fulton County solicitor and lost. The most exciting part of the campaign was the challenge to her eligibility to run because she had not paid her bar-association dues on time.

Lynn Whatley telephoned and said that he had replaced Mary Welcome on the defense team. He added that he had arranged for me to see Wayne Williams the next day. I told Lynn that I would be there, and he said he would meet me. Lynn Whatley helped me a lot from that point on.

The walk to the visitors' entrance at the Fulton County Jail in Atlanta is lined by a high chain-link fence, topped off with concertina wire that looks so sharp that it hurts your skin even to look at it. Along the perimeter are a few wooden guard stands, but none is manned when I arrive.

Once you're inside the unguarded front door, a line forms at the window of a glass-enclosed area that houses several deputy sheriffs. As the line inches closer to the window, a black man stands with a stereo radio on his shoulder. Suddenly he turns up the volume from irritating to intolerable.

A white deputy behind the glass speaks into a microphone and asks the man to turn off the radio. I don't think the man heard him. The white deputy glares at him, and now a black deputy steps to the microphone. He explains to the man that the music is disruptive and orders him to turn the radio off. The man ignores him.

The black deputy then tells the man that the music "might sound good to you out there, but coming over this loudspeaker, it don't sound good in here." Still no reaction from the man.

"Wait a minute!" the black deputy yells. "I'm comin' out there to get you so you can come in here and listen to it. But if I get there before you turn it off, you ain't getting back out!"

This time the man hears him. He turns off the radio.

At the window, identification cards are passed back and forth by a sliding drawer. A note on the face of the drawer explains how money is to be deposited for prisoners.

The guard slides a pink "pass" to me through the drawer and tells me by speaker to take it to the guard on the "male" wing. Now I'm standing at a glass door that is covered by heavy wire mesh. I pass through the metal detector, and a buzzer sounds. The door is electrically unlocked, allowing me inside. A long tunnel, shaped like a quonset hut, takes me deep into the bowels of the Fulton Councy Jail. At the other end of the tunnel, you turn left to the female wing, right to the male wing.

Another sign directs me to push a button. When I do, another door is unlocked. It's a bulky, steel door made entirely of bars and crossbars. It's also enormously heavy. When I push it a bit too hard, a huge steel plate welded to the opening smashes against the wall.

Now I'm looking at another glassed-in area. It's fairly large, about 15 feet in diameter, and houses one guard. Outside, a sign reads "Take Passes to Guard at Door." An arrow points the way to the door, which is not immediately visible. The door is not connected to the guard house, but to a block of cells on the right.

Beyond this barred door, several "runarounds"—or trustys—smoke cigarettes and watch the TV that is perched precariously on the edge of the guard's desk. Soon the guard looks up and approaches the door to take my pass.

The thought strikes me that the case of Wayne Williams must be one of the hottest of hot potatoes ever to hit the black and liberal power structures. I realized that in the year since Wayne Williams had first been ushered through the door I stood in front of, no one from the NAACP, the Southern Poverty Law Center or, for that matter, the ACLU had stood there, waiting to talk with Wayne Williams. There would be no organized campaign to "Free the Atlanta 1."

Without comment, the guard disappears through a doorway to my right. In a few minutes, he returns, leading Wayne Williams to a row of meeting rooms. The guard tells me to go into the first room and wait. The heavy, barred door on my side of the meeting room stands ajar, and I step inside. Protruding from the side wall is a pedestal that supports a single round, hard-metal bench seat. In front of me is a wire-mesh partition with an opening at about elbow height. The bottom of the opening is a shelf that sticks out about 6 inches on both sides of the partition.

In a moment, the guard unlocks the door on the other side and ushers Wayne Williams in. He closes the door behind Williams, and we are left in relative privacy—free to talk about anything and to pass anything through that opening in the wire-mesh partition.

Our talk runs from alibis (which Williams still hadn't come up with) to conspiracy theories, to the status of his attorneys. We also socialize. Williams explains how the "black market" inside the jail works—how everything from money to dope is easily smuggled to the prisoners. He says he is well-treated. I get the impression that Wayne Williams feels somewhat like a celebrity and, unbelievably, may almost be enjoying his big-fish-in-a-small-pond role.

Wayne Williams has his own conspiracy theory about his arrest and conviction. He says it involves two other murder cases. In one of those cases, Wayne Williams was an eyewitness for the prosecution. Later, Williams claims he witnessed some police officers burglarizing a tavern. He says he took pictures of the incident. According to Williams, he turned the pictures over to then-Chief George Napper, who in turn gave them to a police sergeant for further investigation. This sergeant had served as an investigator in the trial in which Williams had testified. Later, this officer would be murdered near the tavern where Williams claims to have taken the pictures.

I don't know about any conspiracy, but I found it extremely interesting that Wayne Williams had been a witness for the prosecution in someone else's murder trial.

Williams asks my opinion of Al Binder, and I tell him I think Binder is the only thing he has going for him. He also asked about Lynn Whatley and, interestingly, about Tony Axam, the attorney whom he and/or Mary Welcome had removed from the case before the trial. All I could say about Whatley at this point was that I liked him. We had not yet worked together.

It would be another of Wayne Williams' power plays with his attorneys—during another visit I would have with him—that would cost me my friendship with Al Binder, a loss that I probably always will regret.

On that occasion, Williams asked me to leak the information to the press that he was firing Al Binder. He said that the sheriff was holding up his letter to that effect, refusing to let it out. I told him that I would see what I could do. Binder was very sick in a Mississippi hospital.

I telephoned one of my friends in the media at the national level, and he said to check with his employer's local outlet. This I did, only to find out that the local outlet already had the story from sources in Judge Cooper's office.

The next day, Durwood Myers telephoned me and asked how the story got out. I told him that I was partially responsible. Myers said I had stabbed Binder in the back. Binder apparently had worked out something else with the judge. I wish I had tried to call Binder in the hospital and let him know what was going on. I wouldn't have hurt him for the world.

I'm not rationalizing when I say he's better off away from the case, but I would be rationalizing if I took any solace in the fact that the information was leaked, anyway.

I think Wayne Williams made a big mistake in letting Al Binder go, and I told him so. On the other hand, I don't think it's up to the criminal-justice system to decide when and under what circumstances a convict changes lawyers, regardless of my personal feelings for that particular attorney.

While Binder does not answer my calls or letters, he has—at least on one occasion—recommended me professionally, indicating that he is far from a petty man. Perhaps someday the relationship will mend. I hope so.

Inside the Fulton County Jail, Wayne Williams leaves some scrawled information with me. The information seems to lead nowhere in particular. I leave, promising to return.

I had sent a manuscript to *Penthouse*. Someone from the magazine telephoned and said the article was compelling, but "too speculative" for the magazine. I knew I couldn't convince them that there was not one speculative word in that manuscript.

I winced later when I read the uninformed and inaccurate interview of Mayor Young by Allan Sonnenschein in *Penthouse*. Once again, the badge of office had put the imprimatur on misinformation, which then was published in a major magazine.

Penthouse doesn't have a reputation for avoiding controversy. But now, it had decided not to touch the facts with a 10-foot pole. Instead, it published the unquestionably speculative comments of Andrew Young on the "motive" for Wayne Williams killing all these "children."

The magazine said it would be interested in a "Q-and-A" with Wayne Williams. The idea didn't overly excite me because I knew the story that needed to be told. Once more, I found the media looking for the story they wanted to tell, not what they needed to know. Oh, well, it was their magazine.

Reluctantly, I prepared the Q-and-A with Williams. I already knew what his answers would be and would have been surprised only by a sudden confession. I conducted a Q-and-A interview with Williams in one of the visitors' cubicles at the jail. He asked to keep the questions, and I gave him a copy.

From that point on, Wayne Williams and his family gave me the royal run-around. I was told to contact agents who never called back and people who denied knowing anything about Williams' progress, if any, in writing the answers to the questions.

In the end, Faye Williams would tell me that Al Binder had sat in the kitchen of her house and read the copy of my questions. She would say: "When he came to the question, 'Wayne, how did Al Binder get involved in all of this?' he [Binder] tore it up in a thousand pieces."

I still had my copy, but now I didn't try to publish it because I didn't want to interfere with the first round of Williams' appeal, which had yet to be heard by Judge Cooper. But all that happened before Al Binder left the scene. Now, I think it's important that the true story, as I see it, be told whenever and however I can.

There were more meetings with Wayne Williams. And more phone calls. Perhaps the most memorable was the phone call of New Year's Eve, 1982. Williams' voice was slurred. He proceeded to tell me that he was "high on jailhouse hooch."

"What in the hell is jailhouse hooch?" I inquired.

Williams explained that the inmates hoarded grapes, grape jelly and raisins. They put them on the window sills in the sun to ferment. From all of this, they concoct an alcoholic drink they call "jailhouse hooch," which they bring out on special occasions like New Year's Eve. Actually, Williams' "high" was probably more psychological than anything else. I would have bet that Williams could pass a breath-analyzer test, even if he couldn't walk a straight line.

On another occasion, Williams would talk with me when suddenly a disturbance would occur at his end of the phone. A voice would come on the line: "Hello, Lynn? [Lynn Whatley, Williams' only attorney at the time] This is Deputy . . ."

"What?" I responded with complete surprise.

"Just wanted to make sure it was you," the voice said, and the phone was handed back to Williams.

"You're pretty quick," Williams said with a whistle of relief.

"Maybe somebody else is just a tad slow," I said.

Lynn Whatley telephoned and asked if I would help him prepare Wayne Williams' request for a new trial. I obliged. But Whatley was so inaccessible that it wasn't until virtually the eve of the appeal when we finally got to talk about it. He asked me to dictate the "pattern" arguments and a portion of the fiber arguments, which covered discrepancies in the dates when the vehicles were available to Wayne Williams. He also asked for my review of the Brady material, which I furnished him.

On the day after Judge Cooper's perfunctory denial of the request for a new trial, Lynn Whatley telephoned to say how well he thought his arguments had gone. The "pattern stuff," he said, had gone over real well. He said he had decided not to use the venue argument I had suggested (the "splash" in Cobb County, but the trial in Fulton County). He also admitted that he had forgotten to use several of the fiber arguments I had authored and that he thought were pretty good. Some of this information was later to be built into the defense brief for the Georgia Supreme Court—portions of which I also helped prepare.

I read the briefs which were presented to the Georgia Supreme Court in 1983 by both the defense and the prosecution. Incredibly, both sides' arguments were studded with errors of fact. But the defense brief was a pleasant surprise to me. Whatley had done a good job under the circumstances. His brief put the prosecution's brief to shame. Williams' lawyer on appeal, in fact, was deprived of copies of vital Brady information which Al Binder and Mary Welcome at one time had. Attempts to obtain it were fruitless. According to Whatley, even when the court was asked for copies of these missing exculpatory materials, the court refused.

The state, for its part, repeated the denial it made in closing arguments that it had ever contended that fibers identified as undyed man-made fibers with an adhering black substance—found on the body of Charles Stephens, among other victims—came from the trunk of the red 1979 Ford LTD owned by the Williamses.

What about the hordes of victims who didn't make The List? Were they, too, checked for fibers?

In 1983, we asked Larry Peterson, the state crime lab's fiber analyst, who had testified at the Wayne Williams trial. Peterson declined to answer, saying that he would have to check with the "powers that be" to see if "that kind of information can be given out."

Reminded that someone at the state crime lab had told the *Atlanta Constitution* for its February 11, 1981, article that fibers had been found on some victims, Peterson replied: "Not me [laugh]. There was some information attributed to Dr. [Larry] Howard [crime lab director], I know. Of course, I wasn't present when any of that happened. He may have let information out. I really don't know."

Then, his curiosity apparently roused, Peterson asked: "What names are we talking about?"

We then gave Peterson the names of 25 victims (ages 14 to 27) who turned up dead in 1980 and 1981—the height of The List killings—but who did not make The List. These names included Cynthia Montgomery, Angela (Gypsy) Bacon, Beverly Harvey, Joseph Lee, Kenneth Johnson, Faye Yearby and Stanley Murray, the 21-year-old uncle of List victim Curtis Walker.

Finally, Peterson paused. "Quite a list there, huh?" he said.

He promised to check to see if he could answer our question of whether any of those bodies had been checked by the state crime lab for fibers. A few days later, Peterson called back. He said he was told that no information could be released about having checked for fibers because "those are open cases."

Therein lies a problem. In February of 1981, those victims on whom someone at the state crime lab said fibers had been found—were open cases, too.

Seth Cohen, a report for a suburban paper, *the Gwinnett Daily News,* called Larry Howard, who said the crime lab has worked on some 1,000 bodies since Williams' arrest and have checked for fiber evidence in all the cases. He said there are 15 fibers associated with the Williams case and not *one* of these fibers has been found on *any* of the bodies the crime lab has checked.

Howard said his people go to the murder scenes sometimes, but usually other agencies ask for the crime lab's help. Sometimes bodies are brought in for autopsies, and sometimes the police just send the clothes and other evidence from the scene. When checking clothes, the crime lab looks for foreign fibers, he said.

The discrepancies in the reported number of fibers—from 9 to 25—can be explained by how they are classified: from different color and composition to suspected source.

Barely after reporter Paul Crawley of WXIA-TV found that the fiber evidence in Patrick (Pat Man) Rogers' case had lain in an unopened box marked "[Victim] Unknown," the state moved quickly in the wake of the

Wayne Williams trial to cover its blunder.

It announced that it would investigate possible "fiber links" between Wayne Williams and Patrick Rogers. Finally, in June of 1982, Cobb County authorities officially closed Patrick's case—and made it homicide No. 24 charged to Williams.

Ha! *Now* they tell us! This was the same criminal-justice system in which a prosecutor had just stated during final arguments that Williams did *not* kill Patrick Rogers. This was the same system that had ignored Pat Man's disappearance and murder in 1980 for four months—despite repeated pleas to investigate his case.

By ignoring Pat Man at the beginning, the authorities also had ignored the visit to Pat Man's neighborhood by Wayne Williams (or, Williams says, someone he paid to distribute handbills) in late 1980, at about the time Pat Man disappeared. Thereafter, at least 14 more victims died—13 making The List. They can't have it *both* ways!

Wayne Williams wrote a letter to Annie Rogers in July of 1982, denying he killed her son and echoing what I had been telling Williams and anyone else who would listen—that Pat Man's case is the key to understanding Atlanta's nightmare.

I also arranged for Williams to telephone Annie Rogers from the jail one day in August of 1982. Both sides say their chat was remarkably cordial, especially for one between a convicted killer and the mother of a child whose death is now officially blamed on the convicted killer.

Annie Rogers is an earthy, resilient woman of 43, not easily conned, not willing to settle for saccharine answers. She fights her battles with the same free-wheeling abandon that Pat Man surely must have inherited from her before he karate-chopped all those make-believe villains into submission and then lost his own ultimate fight for survival, at only 16.

What Annie Rogers lacks in, say, the eloquence or the intellect of a Camille Bell, she makes up with true grit—an unrelenting determination to find out how and why Pat Man died. Or, at the very least, how the investigation broke down and why the system failed her.

A few days after Annie Rogers and several other victims' mothers had visited Washington, there to voice their nagging skepticism to U.S. Attorney General William French Smith, the telephone rang at Annie Rogers' apartment in Thomasville Heights.

The caller was Wayne Williams. "He talked real nice," Annie Rogers said of Williams. "He told me he didn't know Pat Man, but he said he knew a friend of Pat Man's at Grady High. . ." Annie Rogers later said she told Williams that all she wants is "justice done," and "I don't want to see the wrong man in jail."

"I told him, 'There ain't no damned way in the world you could have killed 20-some people,'" she said. "He said there was a lot that his defense could have brought out at the trial that could have cleared him, but they didn't. He said he's just now finding out about it . . ."

Annie Rogers said she told Wayne Williams that she cannot accept the formal closing of Pat Man's case, without a trial. "I told him," she went on, "'If Cobb County says you killed Pat Man, then Cobb County should have enough proof to bring you to trial and try *you* for Pat Man.'

"He said, 'Right,' and he said he was trying to be cool . . . He said he didn't give a damn about who knows we're communicating with each other, and I said I didn't, either, because I just want to know things."

Wayne Williams was tried solely for the murders of two adults. The only way that 10 additional cases and an attendant mountain of fiber evidence could legally be introduced was if they supported a "pattern" of killing.

Would Judge Cooper have allowed them to be introduced had he known that Public Safety Commissioner Lee Brown's "pattern" testimony was wrong when he swore that the first river victim was found after February 11, 1981 (and therefore overlooked Pat Man Rogers, who had turned up dead in the Chattahoochee River two months *before*)?

Had the jury been allowed to hear eyewitnesses who claimed to have seen victims murdered by persons other than Williams, would the jurors have given as much credence to the state's eyewitnesses—who saw *no one* killed?

Had the jurors understood that it was impossible for three of the victims to have been in the vehicles where prosecution witnesses said they came in contact with the Williams fibers, would the jurors have so readily accepted the deluge of fiber evidence?

Had it been revealed that a 21-year-old uncle of one of The List victims was murdered while Williams was in jail waiting trial—a case that remains unsolved—would the world have been swayed by the false perception that the murders stopped when Williams was placed behind bars?

Should Wayne Williams have been convicted? Or, more important, is the wrong person in jail?

Wayne Bertram Williams awaits his next round of appeals. As this is written, the Georgia Supreme Court justices in December of 1983 have affirmed Williams' conviction in an 81-page opinion that spotlights the importance of knowing the rules, rather than being right or wrong.

To those of us who as kids read *"Superman"* and *"Wonder Woman"* and wouldn't dare let the American flag touch the ground, but never finished law school, the decision seems a far cry from "freedom, justice and the American way." The men who wear robes botched the case. They brought us no closer to the truth than those who wear badges did in investigating it.

The Court wrote that it must examine the evidence "in the light most favorable to the jury's decision." As a result, testimony of a witness who claims she saw Williams with Terry Pue becomes evidence that Williams murdered Pue. Astoundingly, the Court goes so far to cast the jury's decision in a favorable light that it ignores the same witness admitting under cross-examination that her so-called sighting took place more than three months *after* Terry Pue was buried!

The Court's decision is flawed by misinformation. Impossibility is given the weight of fact. There is no attention to detail. Two-lane roads suddenly become four-lane highways. The ages of victims are, in some cases, listed incorrectly.

Apparently the mistake-laden briefs of the opposing attorneys—not the trial transcript—were relied upon by the Court. Is this the "record" the Court says it must confine itself to? District Attorney Slaton has been quoted as saying that it is obvious the Supreme Court read every word of the transcript. Is it?

Page by page, the Court cuts down Wayne Williams' objections. The decision is a litany of Williams' attorneys' faults. Through 79 pages, the Court lays the blame for various predicaments at the feet of Williams' lawyers for not making timely or clever use of the rules. But, on Page 80, the Court refuses to "address the issue" raised by Williams that he was inadequately represented by counsel. When prosecutorial error is found, the Court dismisses it as harmless.

It is as if the Court were admitting that the State had put one over on Williams and, if only his attorneys had been sharp enough to let the judge know that they noticed, the Supreme Court would have granted him a new trial. But, tough turkey, the attorneys messed up, so Williams can rot in jail. It's only justice, right?

The Court wrote that the state's experts "opined that these [fiber] matches established an inference that Williams had been in contact with the victims before their deaths." The only valid inference (not necessarily a true one) that I can draw concerning Williams, the fibers and the victims is that the victims could have come in contact with the Williamses' environment. Insofar as fibers are concerned, anything that might be true of Wayne Williams must also be true of Homer and Faye Williams.

Furthermore, there is *no* logical way to infer that victims were dead or alive when they might have come in contact with the Williamses' environment. I base my inferences on the state's testimony, as the Court says it does. I do not agree with some of that testimony, however.

There are recurrent instances of *"Catch 22."* wherein Williams' pleas are disallowed based on his failure to do something that the trial court wouldn't let him do. At one point, the Court notes that there is no evidence in the record to support a claim by Williams. Yet, Williams had also appealed the court's refusal to admit that very evidence. The Supreme Court denies both appeals.

There are instances in which the Court attributes testimony to one witness, even though it came from another. The document has Payne telling his mother he was on his way to the Omni. Instead, it was Payne's sister who testified that he had told her he was going to a coin shop in the Omni.

"Probable asphyxia" became asphyxia in the decision of the Georgia Supreme Court. Likewise, cause of death: asphyxia—which encompasses non-homicidal causes such as accidental drowning—became killed by asphyxia, a clear reference to homicide.

The Court, without comment, published the following statements of "medical evidence" of Williams' guilt, virtually back-to-back:

> "Dr. John Feegel, a Fulton County medical examiner, testified that the cause of death was probably asphyxia, with the form of asphyxia probably being strangulation. He found *no injuries in the neck area* [emphasis added]." This was Feegel's reasoning in the Alfred Evans case.
>
> "Dr. Feegel examined the body [of Charles Stephens]... And, because of the *lack of injuries around the neck* he concluded that the form of asphyxia was suffocation [the emphasis was added]."

If a lack of neck injuries indicates suffocation in what is now called asphyxia in this case (until now, Stephens had been a victim of *probable* asphyxia), why doesn't it also indicate suffocation rather than strangulation in the "probable asphyxia" death of Alfred Evans?

In addressing the splash, the Court takes notice of a vehicle observed "starting up" — one it later says was "apparently stopped" on the bridge. In fact, no one testified that the vehicle Williams was driving stopped on the bridge. How can a vehicle that was never seen stopped on the bridge be seen to "start up" on the bridge?

The Court says that "Cater's body was nude and therefore the only area capable of holding fiber evidence was [sic] his pubic and head hair regions." This is patently absurd. No one testified that the *mustachioed* Cater was otherwise devoid of body and facial hair. Were Cater's underarms shaven? Had he no other hair on his body? I've met men who were bald and had hair on their arms, legs, face, chest and more. Who could deny that fibers otherwise adhere in crevices or orifices of the body? We all know that they do. Ever hear of belly-button lint? How would the Court choose to explain the findings of fibers on remains that were skeletal?

Throughout its opinion, the Court speaks about "A fiber [that] . . . exhibited the same microscopic and optical properties as . . . [those] present in [Williams'] bedroom [carpet]..." The carpet found in Williams' bedroom can be found throughout the Williamses' house.

In the case of 14-year-old Eric Middlebrooks, the Court recounts the medical evidence of two cuts on the right side of Middlebrooks' head that had caused "significant external bleeding." But the Court also accepts fiber evidence that Middlebrooks was transported in both the trunk and cab of the Williamses' 1979 Ford. Why, then, was Middlebrooks found lying in a large puddle of blood within a few feet of the bicycle he had been riding? Why was there not one drop of blood (stains) matching Middlebrooks' blood type found in either the trunk or the cab of the '79 Ford?

The same type of inexplicable hole in the state's fiber case against Williams with respect to victims Jones, Stephens and Terrell led Assistant D.A. Gordon Miller to contend in closing arguments at the trial that the state had never said that fibers found on Charles Stephens came from the '79 Ford, as it most certainly had. Miller said this while trying to escape the dilemma caused by the state's *faux pas* of not realizing that the 1979 Ford was out of the control of — and not available to — the Williamses over the entire period of Stephens' disappearance, death and finding.

But the Supreme Court, in tying Williams to Stephens, repeated the evidence that Miller denied the state had presented! I asked Lynn Whatley how the state could claim one thing to convict Williams and claim the opposite to defeat Williams' appeal. How could this be fair? Whatley said that an attorney's statements in closing arguments do not have to be accurate because he is relying on his recollection.

In the case of 14-year-old Lubie Geter, the Court gives credence to testimony placing Geter with Williams on January 2, 1981, and never returning home. In fact, Geter slept at home on the night of January 2 and disappeared on the afternoon of January 3.

The decision says that Kent Hindsman testified that he was with Wayne Williams and victim Jo-Jo Bell on December 15, (1980) in a white station wagon (the actual wording is "one week after December 8"). Hindsman actually said that it was January 3, (1981) in a blue station wagon.

This makes a tremendous difference since it was virtually the same time on January 2 (the date would have to have been January 3) that other state witnesses said Williams was with Geter in a white Oldsmobile.

The Court would rely on the testimony that Williams was with Geter on January 2 as evidence that Williams murdered Geter. It would also rely on the Hindsman testimony as evidence that Williams killed Jo-Jo Bell (who did not disappear until the following March).

Would a reasonable person actually believe beyond a reasonable doubt that Williams was in two cars with different victims at virtually the same time in locations that are about 15 miles apart? Perhaps he would, particularly if he thought the incidents were 19 days apart.

The Court accepts the testimony of a 15-year-old boy that in August of 1980, Williams drove him around town and fondled his genitals (in a white Oldsmobile). At the time of the incident, the boy reported to police that his assailants were two black men in a blue car.

The same witness says he saw Williams with Geter on January 2. But earlier, he had given police a statement in which he said that he didn't know the man who was in the car with Geter.

The Court accepts the testimony of Nellie Trammell that Williams had the body of Larry Rogers in a *green* station wagon. She describes an incident that physically is not possible to have happened. To back up this evidence, the Court cites the fibers found on Rogers that could have come from the *white* station wagon.

In keeping with the "best light" rule, the Court accepts the testimony of a state serologist that bloodstains in the Williamses' vehicle had been there less than eight weeks — a determination that is critical to the contention that the stains had been left by the bleeding bodies of William Barrett and John Porter. The Court overlooks the contradiction by another state serologist, who testified that it is impossible to tell how long blood stains have been in place.

Now, unbelievably, the Court asks us to accept the medical examiner's report as evidence of Barrett's murder. Inexplicably, it contains the information that William Barrett *did not bleed externally*. But the Court uses the state's claim that some of the blood stains in the Williamses' vehicle came from Barrett as evidence that Wayne Williams murdered Barrett. Impossible.

In its profiles of the various victims, the Court lists the following under "habits": Unemployed. No car. No driver's license. When last seen, on the way to the Omni. Worked out of a labor pool occasionally. Did odd jobs. Last seen at a mall. Was slightly retarded. Recently released from Ga (sic) Regional Hospital.

All of these are obviously difficult habits to break, but it was a *habit* attributed to 11-year-old victim Patrick Baltazar that intrigued me most. According to the Court, Baltazar had the habit of "frequently being on the streets in the area between Foundry Street and the Omni." This was Patrick Baltazar's front yard. He lived on the corner of Foundry Street and Haynes Street, only one street away from the Omni.

The Court's document lists Cater's age as 28. He was 27. Larry Rogers is said to be 18. He was 20. Barrett, who the Court says was 16, was actually 17.

The Court lists a fiber association consisting of *three fibers* as evidence that Williams murdered 14-year-old Alfred Evans. This, however, ignores the testimony of the state's fiber "expert," Harold Deadman, that he could not link Jo-Jo Bell to the Williamses' environment because there were *less than four* fiber matches. The Court later links Bell to Williams with *two fiber matches.*

The Court records that Eric Middlebrooks was "raised in foster homes" (plural). This the Court accepts as evidence linking Middlebrooks to other victims in a so-called pattern of victims from "broken homes." Eric was 14 when he died in 1980. The Court then goes on to write that Middlebrooks had lived with his present foster father since 1965—a period of more than 15 years.

The Supreme Court makes the same mistake as the trial court in accepting

Lee Brown's confused and inaccurate testimony about "the pattern." Brown introduced evidence about victims who definitely *were not* among those allowed to be admitted by the trial court judge. The Supreme Court says that Brown "did not state the number of pattern deaths to which he referred." Then the Court adds, "As we have already determined, evidence of 10 independent or 'pattern' crimes was properly admitted over a period of several days at trial."

The inference is that the unenumerated cases that Brown testified about cannot be differentiated from the 10 admissible cases. This reasoning is wrong. Brown testified about the finding of three bodies, two of whom could only have been Bubba Duncan and Timmy Hill (neither was a part of the admissible pattern). The third body never existed.

In answer to a leading question from Jack Mallard, Brown testified about "three bodies found in the south end of the Chattahoochee River." Two bodies, those of Duncan and Hill, were found near the southern boundary of Fulton County in the Chattahoochee River. All others found in the Chattahoochee—Cater, Payne, Patrick Rogers and McIntosh—were found in that portion of the river adjacent to the northwestern quadrant of the city of Atlanta. *Not one of the 10 admissible pattern cases was found in the Chattahoochee River.* It was not possible for Brown to have been testifying about a case that the judge had ruled admissible.

Brown's testimony about the finding of the unnamed (in testimony) body of 21-year-old Bubba Duncan was admitted by Judge Cooper over Al Binder's objection. But later, when Nellie Trammell testified that she saw Williams at Bubba Duncan's funeral, Judge Cooper sustained Binder's objection and ordered the testimony stricken on the grounds that Duncan was *not* one of the allowable 10 pattern cases.

The Court goes on to opine that no harm was done anyway since very early in the process — *voir dire* (jury selection) — The List of "murdered and missing children [sic]" had been read to *one jury panel.* "Because the attention of the jurors was directed . . . at that early stage of the trial we find no error," the Court wrote.

But, there is absolutely no indication that any member of that "one panel" was a member of the jury which convicted Wayne Williams on this obviously non-admissible evidence. It remains to be demonstrated that any member of the final panel was subjected to this information during *voire dire.*

The Court returns to the rareness of the carpet fiber. It points out that this same type of fiber was found on "many of the victims." What it fails to note is that it was *not* found on some of the so-called "pattern" victims, but was found on other murder victims who the state did not claim were a part of "the pattern."

Williams claims that the prosecution failed to correct false testimony by a state witness. The Court says that "after careful review, we conclude that [this] allegation has [no] merit."

I was sitting there in the courtroom when Nellie Trammell (pointing a finger at him) said that it was prosecutor Mallard who had shown her a picture of Williams in April of 1981. The very important implication here is that this is the *only* witness who claims to have identified Williams *before* his likeness became commonplace in the media, after his FBI interrogation on June 3 and 4, 1981.

Jack Mallard had never heard of Wayne Williams in connection with these murders in April of 1981. I doubt seriously if Mallard had ever seen Nellie Trammell before December of 1981. Yet he heard her answer, just as I did. And he realized that she was identifying him when she was asked by Jim Kitchens (a member of Williams' defense team) on cross-examination to point out the prosecutor who showed her Williams' photograph in April of 1981.

Williams claims he was denied certain exculpatory evidence that was due him under the Brady rule. The Court says the defendant had the burden of showing both the materiality and favorable nature of the evidence sought.

As this is written, one local police agency is pursuing a suspect in two of the murder cases which have been closed and charged against Wayne Williams. One is a "pattern case." Police say they have considered this same suspect since the murders occurred. This time he is wanted on 10 charges of child molestation. Shown this man's picture and a composite of a suspect in the Patrick Baltazar case, a deputy sheriff said, "That's the same guy." I agree. This information was not furnished to Williams under Brady — the names of other suspects were furnished.

Williams learned of this suspect when he was interviewed about it by police, long after his conviction. Is current pursuit of a supsect in a "pattern case" not material or favorable to Williams' case?

There is also the question of logic when applied to what material (investigative files and lab reports) was given to Williams under Brady. From the material he received, it is obvious that there is a lot of material that he didn't get. When the judge gives Williams one or two license numbers turned in by witnesses and says this is exculpatory and subject to Brady, and you know that hundreds of similar sightings had been made and reported to police, isn't this *prima facie* evidence that the state was arbitrary in its selection of the exculpatory information it chose to give to Williams?

The Court says that the stakeout of the Jackson Parkway bridge was established on the evening of May 22. Wayne Williams had been stopped on the *morning* of May 22.

The Court's description of the bridge scene on the morning of May 22 has recruit Jacobs on the wrong side of the bridge. He was at the southeast end as implied, but on the *southwest* corner—not the southeast corner—as stated.

The Court does not comment on the fact that the state's testimony about the bridge incident clearly places the location of the crime in Cobb County, not in Fulton County, where Williams was tried.

The Court admits that Wayne Williams may have been under arrest on the morning of May 22. My rule-of-thumb about when an arrest takes place is what police would do if the detainee decided to leave. It is clear that Williams was held until instructions could be obtained from higher command (instructions which were to let him go). Williams was questioned for almost two hours. You bet he was under arrest!

Yet Williams was never given the required Miranda warning concerning his rights. The Court does not dispute this fact. Many things Williams said under those circumstances were used against him in a court of law. It takes little more than a *Perry Mason* fan to recognize that Williams' rights were violated.

The Court says that Williams didn't adequately raise this issue or invoke a ruling by the trial judge concerning the admissibility of his statements under Miranda, either during or before the trial. "Having failed to object to the admissibility of the contested evidence at trial, appellant cannot now raise the issue for the first time on appeal," the Court says.

If it were Williams' attorneys who were facing two life sentences, I could see the relevance of their not objecting at the right time. It is Wayne Williams who seems to be irrelevant to the Court. No inadequate counsel?

The Court refused to consider the legality of a search warrant. The rule in Georgia, it says, is: "In the context of an application for a search warrant, the veracity of information received from government officials and the reliability of those officials may be assumed." Ha! And "Mother Goose ain't no nursery rhyme." ABC's *Good Morning America* recently quoted FBI Director William Webster as saying America's criminal-justice system is "rancid with corruption."

The decision by the Court says it was right for the lower court to deprive Williams of records of disappearances and murders of persons between the ages of 6 and 28 from January of 1981 to January of 1982. It says the information sought "did not bear upon Williams' guilt or innocence of the offenses charged in the indictment . . ."

How could the Court possibly know that? The erroneous conclusion fostered and publicized by the state that "the killings stopped" when Wayne Williams went to jail is a major reason for Williams' conviction and the widely held belief of his guilt. I agree with the Court. They *are* irrelevant, so why let the prosecutor speak of the "end" of the murders in closing arguments? This is irrelevant, too.

The Court says that a meeting held at the Governor's Mansion, during which the sole subject was the arrest and prosecution of Wayne Bertram Williams, is irrelevant to the case of none other than Wayne Bertram Williams.

I have a friend who happens to be black. When we first met — I as a cop and he as a "militant" in the street riots of 1967 — Gene Robinson told me about his own version of saying the Pledge of Allegiance. I think it applies here:

> "I pledge allegiance to the flag of the United States of America. And to the republic for which it stands. One nation, [sic] indivisible, with liberty and justice for *Y'all!*"

The next stop for Williams will be the U.S. District Court, with final recourse to the United States Supreme Court. Considering that a life sentence in Georgia translates to a minimum of seven years and allowing for the time that Williams already has served, Williams theoretically could be more than half-finished with one sentence before the last legal mechanisms of his trial are over.

For Wayne Williams, the beat goes on. Recently, I was a guest on a radio talk show in Texas. One caller wanted to know how I could support Wayne Williams.

I tried to explain to her that I took a neutral position on Wayne Williams.

"How can you?" she asked. "After all, the murders stopped when Wayne Williams went to jail."

I wondered who went to jail when the police and press recorded the last slaying they attributed to Jack the Ripper. Whoever it was, he wasn't charged in any of those killings.

Like so many serial murders, they stop—perhaps to be picked up somewhere else—and then the police and the press will begin counting all over: 1 . . . 2 . . . 3 . . . 4 . . . 5 . . . 6 . . . 7 . . .

And then we will grumble again about all the breakdowns in a criminal-justice system that never worked in the first place and still cannot be fixed.

Years ago, when I worked in Washington, I wrote a report on the prevention of crimes for my employer, the U.S. Justice Department. My boss, a high-ranking Justice Department official, understood the report and recommended that my ideas in it be adopted.

Subsequently, he summoned me to his office to impart bad news. The bureaucracy, he said, had aborted my report.

Together we stood there, surrounded by walls mounted with personally autographed photos of Presidents of the United States, and we looked out over a majestic panorama highlighted by the Washington Monument and the Lincoln Memorial.

Shaking his head, my boss didn't need to say anything more. His face clearly was etched with frustration and dismay over America's criminal-justice system. But he couldn't resist being candid. He turned to me and said, solemnly: "If the people knew what we were *really* doing to them, they'd bomb us—and we deserve it."

For me, too, the beat goes on.

LEWIS SLATON still is prosecutor in Fulton County, Georgia, and is trying to get the lawsuit filed by some victims' parents set aside.

GORDON MILLER was rewarded for his work in arguing the prosecution's fiber case with an appointment to head the Atlanta regional office of the President's Anti-Drug Strike Force.

JACK MALLARD is now prosecuting in Cobb County, Georgia.

LEE BROWN was appointed to the $75,000-a-year post of chief of police in Houston, the hometown of Vice President Bush, who had visited Atlanta as President Reagan's special emissary during the height of the killings.

GEORGE NAPPER was promoted to the $55,000-a-year post of Atlanta Public Safety Commissioner.

MORRIS REDDING was promoted to Atlanta Chief of Police.

ALVIN BINDER is in private law practice in Jackson, Mississippi.

MARY WELCOME no longer is in private law practice in Atlanta. Friends say she moved to Baltimore.

THE PASTOR and DEACON who disputed prosecution witness Nellie Trammell's testimony that she belonged to their church have both since died.

THE WITNESS who testified that Wayne Williams called members of his own race by derogatory names was killed in a motorcycle accident.

DEPUTY SHERIFF CHARLES A. SMITH, who guarded Wayne Williams at the trial, and received one 10-year sentence and two 15-year sentences on the narcotics conviction, served only six months in jail. He was released in August of 1983 on a $100,000 appeal bond.

CAMILLE BELL works for the Girl Scouts in Tallahassee, Florida.

DON LAKEN, the "Dog Man," is back home in Philadelphia, content with the fact that a suspect he developed early in the cases may yet play a role in Atlanta's mystery.

ARTHUR LANGFORD JR. was defeated in a try for a seat in the Georgia state legislature. He is pastor of Atlanta's Rush Memorial Congregational Church. His United Youth Adult Conference was disbanded. The reason, said someone at the church where UYAC was headquartered: "lack of funding." (UYAC's name was resurrected in 1983 in other searches.)

A. REGINALD EAVES was elected Fulton County Commissioner—an office he still holds—after having resigned under fire as Atlanta Public Safety Commissioner.

GAIL EPSTEIN reports for the *Atlanta Constitution.*

PAUL CRAWLEY was promoted to WXIA-TV's chief investigative reporter.

DAVID PAGE is an investigative reporter in Chicago.

MIKE EDWARDS is a director of loss prevention for Richway stores in Atlanta.

KENNETH LAWSON ("Serpico") is a maintenance man for an Atlanta hotel that figured prominently in the cases.

EUNICE JONES, mother of slain 13-year-old Clifford Jones, returned home to Cleveland. She married an uncle of slain 12-year-old Charles Stephens.

THE SUSPECT in Clifford Jones' strangulation murder is out of prison after serving time on another charge.

BRANDON SOUTHERN is coaching boys' athletic teams.

TOM TERRELL is out of prison. His house on Gray Street was destroyed by fire.

LEE GOOCH, the missing Atlanta teen-ager whom I found alive in 1981 in a Florida jail, is in a Georgia child-adolescent hospital, undergoing treatment for drugs.

KENNY BROWN, "earwitness" to the alleged gunshot murder of a child on Memorial Drive, is in a Georgia prison industrial institute in Alto, serving 18 years.

THOMAS NAVE, the DeKalb County assistant district attorney who prosecuted Kenny Brown on male rape charges, was convicted himself in 1983 for violating his oath of office in an unrelated bribery case. He was disbarred and received a five-year sentence that was probated to six months in the DeKalb County Jail. But he served only two weeks, having been released on an appeal bond. The foreman of the jury that convicted Nave was recently arrested for bank robbery. The beat goes on and on and on . . .

WILLIE PAUL RICE, uncle of Patrick (Pat Man) Rogers, was shot in an unsolved, assassination-style murder in 1982, not long after he was freed from his prison sentence on drug charges. Rice was slain near the residence of Jimmy Ray Payne.

WAYNE WILLIAMS has been transferred to the Georgia Diagnostic and Classification Center in Jackson, where he awaits the first round of the federal appeals process. He is serving his third year of two consecutive life sentences.

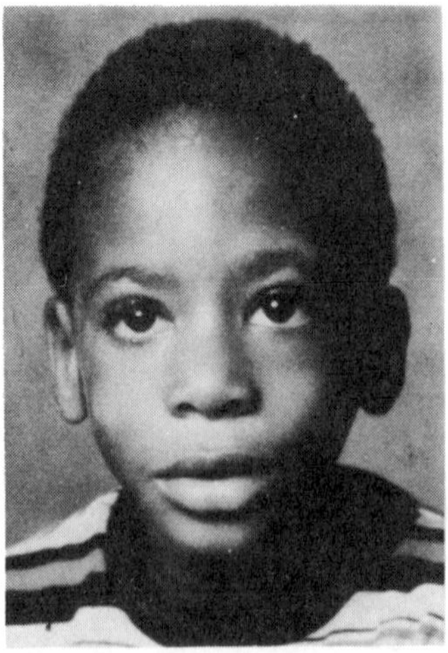

DARRON GLASS, where are you? Is anybody looking?

"The police and news people came and went,
In all our hearts was no content;
No one could rest until we knew
Whatever, whatever had happened to you."

—From a eulogy to 11-year-old Patrick Baltazar,
by his fifth-grade classmates
at Bethune School in Atlanta.

In Appreciation

Roz Abrams
Ernie Allen
Tom Allen
Gail Anderson
Dreenna Andreu
Ben Ansley
Dick Arena
Susan P. Arena
Peter Arnett
John Arrowsmith
Bill Attaway
Clifton Bailey
Dr. Tom Barber
Malcolm Barbour
Ron Becker
Camille Bell
Alvin Binder
Ernie Bjorkman
Ed Blackwelder
Jean Blake
Norman Bloom
Julian Bond
Terena Bowen
Cathy Bradford
Dennis Britton
Jack Bryant
Tyrone Brooks
Peter Broyles
Tony Brown
Ann Buckner
Jack Buckner
Stan Burroway
Ed Bush
Lorene Cary
Helen Casey
Doody Clark
Gail Clark
Richard Clarke
Sirlena Cobb
Seth Cohen
Joe Coleman
Barney Conway
Rita Conway
Tony Cooper
Bob Coxe
Fred Crawford (deceased)
Lisa Nicolos Crawley
Paul Crawley
Chris Curle
Lisa Cuttito
Jonathan Dahl
Alan Dale
Tony DeHara
Anna Dettlinger (deceased)
Chester Dettlinger Sr. (deceased)
Chester (Chip) Dettlinger III
Danny Dettlinger
George Dettlinger
Jerry Dettlinger
Jill Dettlinger
Joe Dettlinger (deceased)
Lewis Dettlinger (deceased)
Kim Dettlinger
Laura Dettlinger
Margaret Dettlinger (deceased)
Mary Dettlinger
Tracy Dettlinger
Joe Dolman
Steve Dougherty
Mike Edwards
Ken Englade
Sara Englade
Bill Epps
Gail Epstein
Jim Fabris
Don Farmer
Judy Farmer
Mike Farmer
John Fleming
Mark Foley
Fran Fossett
John Paul Francis
Sandi Freeman
Helen Friese
Bob Gailor
Gary Garrison
Dick Gentry
Dale Getman
Mindy Glazier
Gail Giorgio
Matt Glasgow
Mildred Glover
Bob Godlewski
Tom Goff IV
Dick Gregory
John Grenough
Jerry Gunn
Edwin Guthman
Mike Hamilburg
Dick Hand
Elizabeth Ellis Harmon
Clara Hart
Don Hatcher
Jim Hogan
Bob Hoover
Bill Hopkins
Nancy Horwin
Noel Horwin
Tom Houck
Diane Hunter
Columbus J. Hyde
Mary Hylbak
Roy Innis
Sharon Jimenez
Anthony Johnson
Mary Perkins Jones
Sharyn Kane
Dennis Kauff
Jim Kay
Richard Keeton
Nancy Kenney
Rosanne Keynan
William G. Kiefer Sr.
John Kinser
Jean Phillips Knick
Rabbi Robert L. Kravitz
Ed Laborowitz
Charles Lachman
Carl Lavin
Ken Lawson
Craig Lesser
Boyd Lewis
John Lewis
Richard Warren Lewis
Diana Kay Little
Eric Anthony Little
Robert Little
Trudy Lomker
Oscar Long (deceased)
Tracey Lyons
Ken Maddigan
Abby Mann
Willie Mae Mathis
Kathleen Mattingly
Bill Mattingly

In Appreciation

Billy Mattingly
Carolyn Mattingly
Donna Mattingly
Eugene Mattingly
Larry Mattingly
Becky May
Frank May
Lee May
Bob McCullough
Ed McCune
Ken McLeod
Scott Memel
Kirsten Mendler
Dave Mitchell
Les Moise
Eula Montgomery
Brenda Mooney
Laura Morris
Gloria Murry
Hardy Nagai
Joe O'Brien
Sondra O'Neal
Patrick O'Neill
Steve Oney
Jim Osteen
Charles L. Owen
Nell Owen
David Page
Mike Page
Linda Palmer
Blake Parkman
Tennyson Paul
Judy Pensoneau
Taylor Pensoneau
Matt Perkins

Jack Perry
Maury Povich
Harold Prugh
Janice Prugh
Jocelyn Prugh
Lisa Prugh
Vince Prugh
John Rabun
Patricia Reeves
Ed Reuben
Nancy Reuben
Richard Reuben
Joan Richards
Eugene Robinson
Annie Rogers
Stevie Rogers
Bill Rose
Howard Rosenberg
James Rowe
Sheila Rushlo
Wes Sarginson
Ken Sasso
Lawrence Schiller
Keena Schrivner
Tom Schroder
Maxine Schnall
Jeff Scott
Edward Sears
Cynthia Sellers
David Sendler
Janice Sevrnson
Jimmy Shade (deceased)
Mike Shannon
Norman Shavin

Thomas Sheehan
Neil Shister
Courtney Siceloff
Elizabeth Siceloff
Bob Sirkin
Sam Skinner
Donna Spatz
Al Starkes
Hal Suit
Bill Taylor
John Terenzio
Dorothy Townsend
Walter Unger
Judy Updike
Larry Updike
Raymond Vito
Donna Wagner
Donnie Wagner
Becky Ward
Don Watkins
Mary Welcome
Ila Westerkamp
Roy Whang
Lynn Whatley
Fitzgerald Whitney
Dick Williams
Fred Williams
Hosea Williams
Mary Florence Wilson
Mike Wilson
John Woods
Madonna Worldly
Deane Wylie
Mike Zakel

And to those families—especially the mothers—of victims on *and* off The List, for graciously allowing us into their homes and answering our questions, at a time when it couldn't have been easy for them.

The Authors

CHET DETTLINGER rose from a Louisville street cop to Assistant to the Atlanta Chief of Police and Assistant to the Atlanta Public Safety Commissioner.

Along the way, he was Acting Deputy Director of the Kentucky Crime Commission. More recently, he was a U.S. Justice Department consultant in Washington, director of a Georgia Regional Police Training Academy and professor of criminal justice at Floyd (Georgia) Junior College. He holds a bachelor of arts degree in political science and an associate in arts degree in social science from the University of Louisville.

Dettlinger investigated Atlanta's murders voluntarily. He ran the gamut from being called in by the Atlanta police as a suspect to being invited by the FBI to brief educators on the cases as a paid expert.

JEFF PRUGH is an Atlanta writer who was the Southeastern correspondent for the *Los Angeles Times* and an ABC News consultant. Previously, he was an award-winning *Times* sports writer, based in Los Angeles.

His work also has appeared in *TV Guide, Time, Sports Illustrated* and *Pro!,* as well as *"Best Sports Stories."* He began his career at 18 on the *Glendale* (Calif.) *News-Press* and was president of the University of Missouri School of Journalism's class of 1962.

He also is author of *"The Herschel Walker Story"* and is co-author with Dwight Chapin of *"The Wizard of Westwood,"* a biography of former UCLA basketball coach John Wooden.

Did Not Make THE LIST

Johnny Johnson, 27

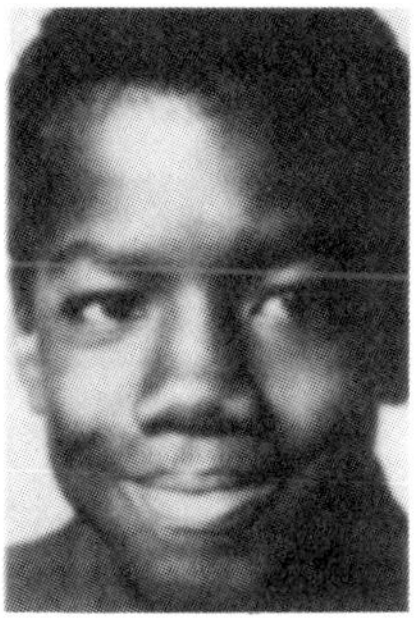

Charles Stephens, 12

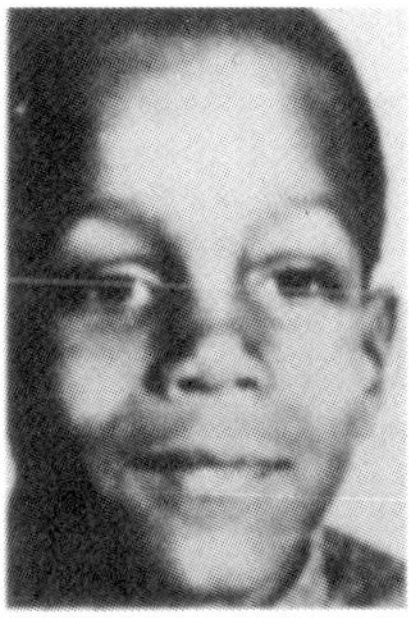

Aaron Jackson, 9

Did Not Make THE LIST

Clyde Hamilton, 25

Patrick Rogers, 16

Did Not Make THE LIST

Melvin Spencer, 24

Did Not Make THE LIST

Terry Jones, 23

Did Not Make THE LIST

Edward Scales, 26

Did Not Make THE LIST

Eldred Cheves, 23

Lubie Geter, 14

Did Not Make THE LIST

Mary Ector, 25

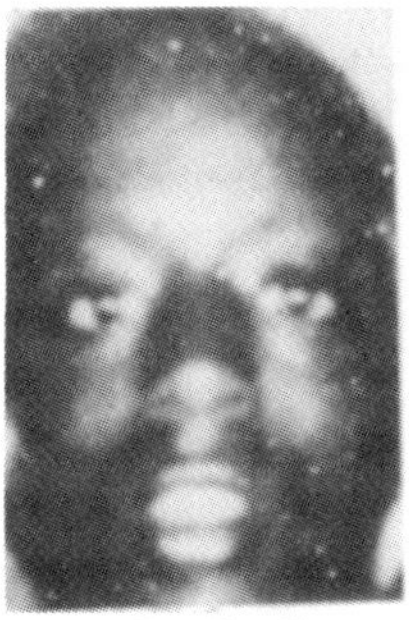

Terry Pue, 15

Patrick Baltazar, 11

Did Not Make THE LIST

Faye Yearby, 22

Curtis Walker, 13

Did Not Make THE LIST

Bronzelle Pettaway, 21

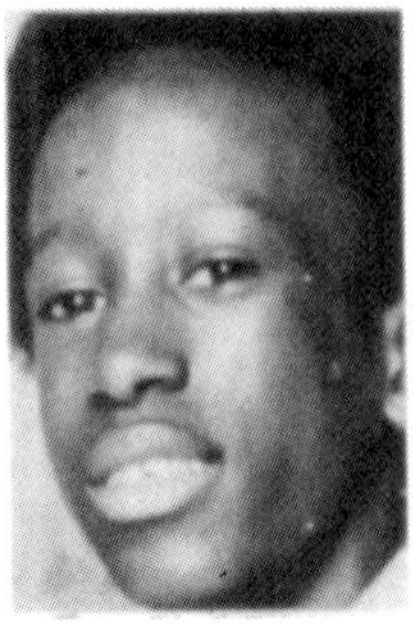

Joseph Bell, 15

Did Not Make THE LIST

Terrell Black, 24

Did Not Make THE LIST

Effie Hall, 24

Timothy Hill, 13

Did Not Make THE LIST

Jo Carron Lane, 24

Eddie Duncan, 21

Did Not Make THE LIST

Candy Lane, 26

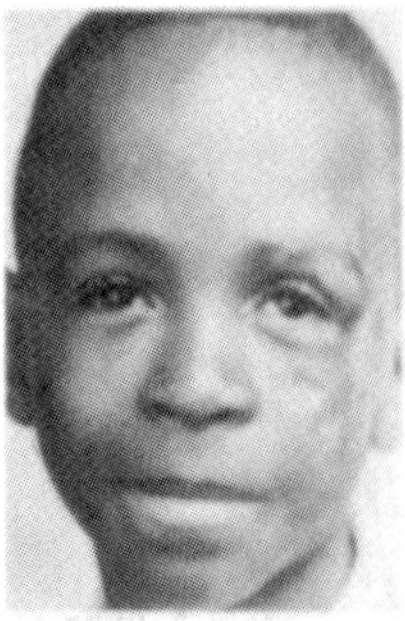

Larry Rogers, 20

Michael McIntosh, 23

John Porter, 28
(added by prosecution)

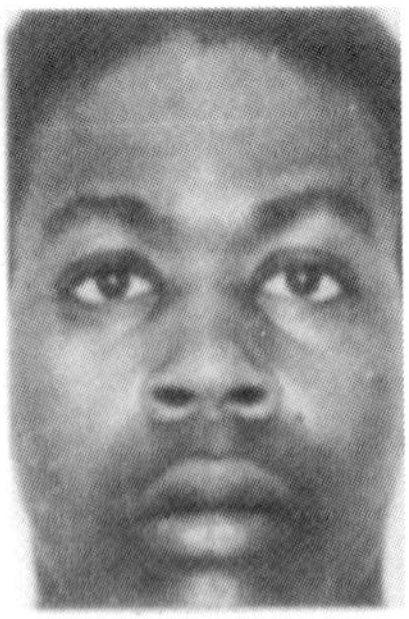

Jimmy Ray Payne, 21

William Barrett, 17

Nathaniel Cater, 27

Did Not Make THE LIST

Clarence Davis, 16

Did Not Make THE LIST

Stanley Murray, 21

Did Not Make THE LIST

Lucretia Bell, 13